INTRODUCTION TO
BUSINESS ENTERPRISE

LYMAN A. KEITH

Professor of Management, Northeastern University

CARLO E. GUBELLINI

Professor of Business Administration, Northeastern University

FOURTH EDITION

INTRODUCTION TO BUSINESS ENTERPRISE

McGRAW-HILL BOOK COMPANY

New York   St. Louis   San Francisco   Auckland   Düsseldorf
Johannesburg   Kuala Lumpur   London   Mexico   Montreal   New Delhi
Panama   Paris   São Paulo   Singapore   Sydney   Tokyo   Toronto

INTRODUCTION TO BUSINESS ENTERPRISE

1 2 3 4 5 6 7 8 9 0 KPKP 7 9 8 7 6 5

Library of Congress Cataloging in Publication Data

Keith, Lyman A
    Introduction to business enterprise.

    Bibliography: p.
    1. Business. I. Gubellini, Carlo E., joint author. II. Title.
HF5351.K383 1975   658   74-13605
ISBN 0-07-033485-4

This book was set in Craw Clarendon Book by York Graphic Services, Inc. The
editors were Thomas H. Kothman and Claudia A. Hepburn; the designer
was Betty Binns; the production supervisor was Thomas J. LoPinto.
New drawings were done by Vantage Art, Inc.
Kingsport Press, Inc., was printer and binder.

CONTENTS

PREFACE

The purpose of *Introduction to Business Enterprise* is to provide the college student with a general background to the elements and characteristics of business. By surveying the structure of business, its principal activities, and its typical problems, the text gives students a broad understanding of the nature of the business world and a preliminary idea of the various areas of business specialization.

Our business system and our economic system are unique among the nations of the world. Nowhere is there as great a degree of dependence on private enterprise to provide for the needs of society as in the United States. In the beginning, our business system consisted in the main of small units operating in small geographic areas. Business in this framework was simple and its operations easily understood. Business today is vastly more complex because of the increasing wants and needs of some 215 million Americans, plus millions of people in other lands.

The aim of this text is to develop a realistic picture of how business enterprise fits into society—what it does and how it operates. But any introductory overview of business is bound to be superficial if it tries to be all-inclusive. Therefore, we have tried to give a balanced and more selectively focused view—to depict business not as countless facts and figures in sketchy outline, but as the interaction of basic functions in enterprises of many sorts that supply the needs of our dynamic society. Well aware that we cannot hope to satisfy everyone with our selection of topics, we think nevertheless that the book's approach and organization do provide a meaningful and informative picture of business enterprise.

Part 1 is a general orientation to business and the environment within which it operates. This group of chapters sketches the reasons why business enterprise is what it is, how various environmental forces impact on business enterprise, and the nature of business responsibility to the society that sustains it. Thus Part 1 provides a basic framework for the subsequent investigations of business functions and practices. The problems of running a business firm and the reasons why business operates as it does are more easily understood when the student has first had an overall view of the business setting.

Part 2 discusses the several vehicles needed to carry out the basic business functions. Every business has owners, but the owners' relation to and involvement with the firm depend on the legal form of ownership. The key to business success lies in the firm's organization and management. Organization provides the means for achieving business goals and management is the activating force that gets things done. Part 2 explores a variety of approaches to ownership, organization, and management of an enterprise. The role of each business function is determined by the way a firm is organized and managed.

Part 3 deals with the basic business functions of marketing, production, staffing, and finance. First, each function is described in detail; then our concern is with how businessmen carry out these functions. Methods of sales planning and control, purchasing, inventory control, production planning, personnel administration, and the finance function with its attendant problems are discussed.

Part 4 takes up selected topics that further define the scope of business activity. The role of credit in the conduct of business affairs, the role of quantitative analysis in making business decisions, the handling of risks, the making of forecasts, and the role of the computer as a source of information are included here. The section concludes with a discussion of international business.

This, in brief, is the way the book is organized. It is necessarily a simplified approach to the primary functions and relevant procedures of business enterprise as seen in the larger business setting. The focus is on neither big nor small business. Rather, the concern is with the fundamental questions of what, why, who, and how—a viewpoint that centers on the elements common to all business operations. And since these are questions that management faces daily, the approach can be characterized as being managerial in its treatment of the core material.

We have attempted a variety of means to make the book—and the student's introduction to business—as inviting as possible. Short headnotes place each chapter in relation to those that precede and follow it, and a few preliminary, broadly phrased questions focus on the material to be covered in each chapter as a unit of understanding. In our writing we have aimed at a plain prose style that reads easily and, we hope, interestingly. We have worked for a natural flow and continuity in the development of topics and have tried to avoid a rigidly schematic outline. The questions at the end of the chapters are of two types: some review the chapter content, and others call for discussion to develop their implications and extend the student's interest. The Appendix deals with a number of job and career considerations. It relates organization and management concepts to jobs; it provides a basis for answering career questions; it identifies some of the problems of self-employment; and it indicates in general terms what a person must do to be successful in business. The Suggestions for Further Reading will indicate to students where they can follow up topics that have caught their interest. This is followed by a Glossary of common business terms with which all business students should be familiar.

The *Study Guide* serves the student as a supplement to the text. It provides additional focus on the purpose, organization, and salient features of each chapter; systematic vocabulary building in business terms and concepts; and a variety of self-testing questions, problems, and short cases for analysis and discussion.

The topics presented here to indicate the nature and elements of business are meant to provide a firm substantive basis for the beginning student in business administration and a balanced, integrated picture for the student who takes only one course in this area.

Lyman A. Keith
Carlo E. Gubellini

INTRODUCTION
Most readers of this text are preparing for a career that will in some way involve business enterprise. Regardless of the reader's immediate educational goal, whether it be engineering, the arts, or business, the odds are that future employment will be in some phase of business. It is important, therefore, to understand the role that we, society, have cut out for business enterprise as one of our major institutions.

The work that every person performs is related directly or indirectly to the satisfaction of society's needs. This is where it all begins—the needs of society. In every corner of the globe, wherever people live, there is the need for goods and services. The needs may be minimal, as on a South Sea island, or they may be extensive, as we experience in our society.

When the needs of a society are simple—food, clothing, and shelter—the mechanism needed to provide for them is simple. The individual or the family, in cooperation with nature, may have the capacity to adequately fulfill need requirements. When the needs of a society are more complex, more complex institutions are required to satisfy them. It becomes much more difficult to establish what is needed and who should have the responsibility for fulfilling the need. The following is one way to illustrate this situation. Obviously the list of needs and institutions is not complete, merely descriptive. Also, this listing of needs does not identify the seriousness or importance of each need. Education is not nearly as important to the South Sea islander as it is to a person in the United States.

Needs	must be satisfied by	Institutions
Security		Family
Safety		Church
Spiritual		Local government
Education		State government
Transportation		Federal government
Communication		Business enterprise
Health care		Not-for-profit enterprise
Environmental protection		

This illustration should raise a number of questions in the reader's mind:

Who decides what this list of needs will contain? Will any limitations be placed on our list of needs?

What is the relative importance of each need? That is, how much of our resources will be allocated to each need? In the final analysis, the amount of resources we are willing to commit to a particular need is the best way to show how important the need really is.

Which institution(s) should have the responsibility for fulfilling each need?

We know from our own experience that our list of needs is almost endless and that as soon as existing needs are satisfied, new needs, real or imaginary, loom on the horizon. In an affluent society such as ours it is easy for people to rationalize that they need something new or something else—another car, another TV, or a housekeeper. Certain needs are obvious, but in many instances we are convinced by business advertising and promotion that we must have this or that. And, of course, we must keep up with the Joneses. Ours is a very permissive society in this respect although we may see some changes in the future as shortages of certain materials develop. Any group, or any individual, has the right to try to convince others of the need for goods and services as long as the law is obeyed. This is the reason why we have such a proliferation of goods and services in our society.

Society decides directly or indirectly, through action or inaction, the amount of resources that will be applied to the satisfaction of given needs. This is of great importance to the reader. If society is willing to spend huge sums in an area of activity—reaching the moon, for example—the job and perhaps career opportunities in that area will also be great. We have seen this phenomenon in the area of education. For years people associated with educational institutions received low pay and few benefits. Along came *Sputnik* and society decided to spend a large portion of the tax dollar for education—and those involved shared the benefit. No matter what the need, if society is unwilling to allocate resources to it, it will go unsatisfied.

In some instances, society dictates which institutions must be responsible for satisfying a given need. It has not always been so but today the responsibility for primary and secondary education rests with various levels of government. But even here, each level of government feels that a greater degree of responsibility should fall on the other levels of government. It is not nearly as clear who should provide health care and who should pay for it. One reason so little is being done in the broad area of environmental protection is that there is no institution in existence that can and will tackle the problem. There are countless needs in our society, and in the world, that go unsatisfied because there is no institution to which they can be assigned.

Thus in every society there exists the questions: What goods and services will be made available to members of society? Who will be responsible for their creation and distribution? What must members of society do to obtain the goods and services that they want? The "best" answers to these questions will vary from society to society and with the passage of time.

THE SOCIAL SYSTEM

Society has the responsibility of deciding the answers to the questions mentioned above. More specifically, society must decide the types of institutions that will be involved in the creation and distribution of goods and services and the role that each institution will be permitted to play. In general, the number and variety of institutions that will exist in any society depends on the degree of freedom extended to its members.

A social system such as that of the United States, Canada, Britain, or Australia, for example, can be viewed as the sum of its institutions. These institutions include, as indicated earlier, the family; the churches; the government, with all its subdivisions; business; not-for-profit enterprise; and others. These institutions are common to most societies and each obtains its support directly or indirectly from society.

APPROACHES TO SATISFYING A SOCIETY'S NEEDS

Over the years a variety of approaches to satisfying the needs of a society have been developed and applied throughout the world. These range from a situation of complete individual responsibility—the head of an Eskimo family—to very complex patterns of multiple responsibility. Every country in the world uses a somewhat different approach to meeting society's needs but one of three patterns seems to prevail. Because none of these ideologies exists in a pure state, the following discussion is aimed at describing rather than defining the differences in approach.

1 The communist approach such as in China, Russia, or Cuba Here, the state, or a central government, assumes total responsibility for the creation and distribution of all goods and services. All decisions as to what will be produced, when, where, how, and in what quantity are made by a central authority, the state. The state also dictates where and how the goods are to be obtained and often limits the amount that one is permitted to consume. In a very real sense, the state, under communism, decides in advance what the needs of society will be.

As a consequence, the choice of goods and services that members of society may have is limited and beyond control of individual members of society. Under communism, the state sets the price at which all goods and services will be sold. This too restricts consumers' freedom of choice. In theory, this approach to meeting the needs of a society is very efficient because it eliminates a number of variables present in other systems. In practice, the results of the communist approach are, by our standards, disappointing.

2 The socialist approach There are varying degrees of communism and there are varying degrees of socialism. The distinction between communism, socialism, and, as we shall see, capitalism may depend more on philosophy than on fact. In a socialist society, the basic industries are owned and controlled by the state. But what constitutes a basic industry will vary from society to society and over time. Sugar is a basic industry in Cuba but not in the United States. Typically, in a socialist society, transportation, communication, steel, energy production, and the like are owned and controlled by the state, and "lesser" industries such as retailing are left to private enterprise. Although there is greater freedom of choice for the people of a socialistic society, as compared to that in a communist society, the dependence on the state to provide basic requirements is a significant limiting factor.

3 The capitalist approach Capitalism is a system wherein the bulk of goods and services needed by a society are created and distributed by private enterprise in search of profits. In Great Britain, Japan, West Germany, and other nontotalitarian societies, there are varying degrees of capitalism. Our society practices capitalism to a greater degree than any other major society; that is, more of the goods and services we want are produced by private enterprise than those produced in any other major society. This, American capitalism, will be explored in detail in Chapter 1.

The limited restrictions imposed on members of our society as individuals and as businessmen are largely responsible for the volume and variety of things we may have. Thus in the United States especially but in other capitalist nations also, the consumer of goods can make a significant impact on what goods and services will be produced and how they will be distributed. We as American consumers have a high degree of freedom to buy whatever we choose and wherever we choose. Therefore, the burden is on the individual producer to learn what goods the consumer wishes to buy, and to produce them at a price that the consumer can and will pay. Out of this interplay of individual wants and efforts to fulfill them, we have developed a complex and interrelated network of institutions that we call our business system.

THE BASIC SUPPLIERS OF OUR SOCIETY'S NEEDS

It has been established that the needs of a society are provided for by a number of institutions. Most of the goods and services that we have are provided by three distinct types of institutions: government;

business, which plays the major role; and not-for-profit enterprise. Therefore, there are only three types of institutions that can provide you with employment.

Government

Certain needs of society can be effectively provided for only by some level of government. These would include protection against invasion, protection of members of society from other members of society, building and maintaining roads, and the like. But there is considerable disagreement among members of our society as to what additional goods and services governments should be expected or permitted to provide. Should governments produce and sell electric power, own and operate railroads, and be in the business of insurance? There is no clear agreement as to the appropriate answer to these questions.

Governments are not noted for their efficiency of operation; they cannot operate like business institutions because they are political institutions. Also, governments tend to be less responsive to the wishes of their "customers" than business enterprise. This is due in part to the fact that government employees generally are to a large degree immune from disciplinary actions if their performance on the job is poor and unsatisfactory. This is also due to the fact that those in positions of power like to use this power. At one time in the United States, schools were largely private institutions and parents sent their children to the school that provided the type of program and exposure they wanted their children to have. (Under this approach to education many children received no education at all.) Today, we as individual citizens have virtually no control over the education our children will receive, or the cost thereof, because of the dominance of various government agencies.

It is very easy to permit governments to do more and more for us and there is virtually no limit as to the number of services we would like to have someone else perform for us. However, once government becomes involved in an activity, it becomes extremely difficult if not impossible to dislodge it—even if the level of service performed is poor or overly costly. However, we should expect that the government's role as a provider of goods and services will not decrease in the years ahead. An answer to this dilemma is better government at all levels.

Business

Most of us have some understanding of the role that business plays in our society because most of us have had some involvement with business organizations as employees, investors, customers, and so on. The nature of a person's involvement with business is quite apt to influence the definition he develops of business. To some people business is General Motors or Sears, Roebuck and Company. To others business is manufacturing or retailing. And it may be viewed as finance, accounting, personnel, market research, and the like. Each approach tells us something about business or a business but none depicts the entire realm of business enterprise.

Business in the United States can be described as the sum of all the activities involved in the creation and distribution of goods and services for private (personal) profit. (Note that this definition of business would not apply in Cuba, Russia, or China, for example, because private or personal profit is frowned upon in these societies.) In this context, the operation of a YMCA or a municipality is not considered business in the true sense. For an activity to be considered business there must exist both the opportunity for private profit and the risk of loss. Business is an economic institution; it must make a profit if it is to survive. It can make a profit only if it fulfills a need of society. Thus, in theory at least, every business in America is a necessary activity.

Business is described above as the sum of a number of activities. To be more specific, the activities involved include manufacturing, sales, finance, purchasing, and the like. A particular business is most apt to be directly involved with only a fraction of the total process—from raw material to consumer. No one firm completely depicts business in its entirety—not even General Motors.

Because business is so many things, it creates countless career opportunities covering a tremendous range of abilities. Some firms must employ only the most able people to achieve business success. Others can achieve their goals through the utilization of fairly mediocre talent. A firm that is concerned with fixing a communication station in outer space or with developing a guidance system to get a man to the moon and back must have a core of sophisticated thinkers on its staff. A firm engaged in the distribution of candy through vending machines can be very successful while utilizing people with modest amounts of talent.

Business can be a fascinating area of study and a fascinating career, and we can now see two reasons for it. Business involves a tremendous amount of differing activity and needs people who have differing backgrounds and abilities.

Not-for-profit enterprise

Not-for-profit enterprise enters the picture to fill certain needs of society not provided by the two basic institutions—government and business.

Not-for-profit corporations are created under state law, as are business corporations. Most states have enacted legislation which enables the creation of such corporations. Simply stated, these laws provide a convenient means for holding property in organizations which have no stockholders (owners) and which will not distribute earnings to its members. These organizations vary in character from those which compete directly with business, such as Blue Cross-Blue Shield, to those which are basically concerned with the spending of investment income, such as the Ford Foundation. Therefore, the difference between pure business enterprise and not-for-profit enterprise will depend on the similarity or dissimilarity of purpose.

We should rid our thinking of the common notion that not-for-profit enterprise is, at one extreme, money-losing enterprise or, at the other extreme, a legal means for members of an organization to profit at the expense of society. Students often ask the question: "How can the college bookstore be called not-for-profit when published figures show it earned $50,000 last year?" It is not a question of income and expense relationships but rather a question of what happens to any surplus. The not-for-profit institution must by law keep all surplus in the organization; there can be no distribution to its members.

Creating the not-for-profit enterprise Not-for-profit organizations come into being when a group of individuals joins together to achieve a common objective. This can also be true of business enterprise but there are three significant differences. First, the founders who invest their money in these organizations do so with no expectation of financial gain. Second, the founders are usually people who have been successful in their careers and who are forming these institutions because of a desire to serve. Finally, the founders do not associate with the organization for the purpose of making a living. The purpose of the not-for-profit institution is, as stated before, to fill voids in society's needs that are not being met by business or government.

What are the differences? If you are employed by a not-for-profit institution you should expect it to differ from employment in business. Not-for-profit enterprise is apt to differ from business in the following ways.

1 There is considerable evidence that the managers of business must satisfy the owners of business. A relatively high turnover of company presidents is most often accompanied by a poor record of earnings. The not-for-profit institution does not have, as we have seen, any owners. Who, then, must the managers of not-for-profit enterprise satisfy? In general these managers must satisfy that segment of society that the organization was created to serve—a group that often can be identified only in general terms. Obviously the same pressures cannot be brought to bear on the management of such institutions. There may be greater freedom for these managers to manage as they please.

2 As a result it is difficult to establish hard-and-fast standards of performance. It is difficult in many instances to ascertain whether specific managers are doing a good job or a poor job. If an institution is organized to perform an "impossible" task, as is so often the case, progress or success is hard to define.

3 An outgrowth of the above is that a shelter is created for the poor or ineffective manager, and the better manager becomes frustrated because of the difficulty in identifying his worth. Thus a fertile breeding ground for inefficiency and waste develops.

4 Much of the above stems from the fact that the profit motive is missing and other incentives must take its place. Some incentive is necessary to give vitality and a strong forward thrust to an institution. But the prime incentive here is the desire to serve, and as noble as this may be, the incentive to serve a particular cause, such as CARE, for example, does not motivate nearly as many people as the profit motive. Remember, we are a very materialistic society. Such organizations may substitute "desire to serve" for competence when hiring because of the limited number of people having a compatible motivation. In the long run, employees of such organizations often lose sight of the service objective and view their jobs merely as employment.

There are not-for-profit organizations that operate as efficiently and as effectively as any business, but they tend to be in the minority. If a not-for-profit organization must compete with business enterprise, odds are that it will engage in sound management practices. If competition is lacking for any organization, it tends to be less "businesslike" in its operation.

SUMMARY

Every person in a society makes his livelihood by working to satisfy the needs of members of that society. In some societies what constitutes need is dictated by a central authority, as in Cuba and Russia. In Cuba, the great mass of people do not need automobiles. Mr. Castro has said so. But every family needs a radio and for the same reason. When needs are dictated, the variety of job opportunities is restricted. This prevents people from engaging in the type of work they want and often forces them into lines of work where they have little or no interest. Unless new needs are prescribed, there will be few new opportunities.

In our society, we the people decide what our needs will be. No matter how frivolous or wasteful our desires, if we think we need it, we buy it. Government does not have the capacity to provide us with what we need because it is inherently slow moving and is not responsive to individual members of society. Rather, we rely on business and have designed a system for business which permits private profit. This in turn creates efficiency and provides the impetus for new and better things.

Need is a nebulous thing and as a result need does not necessarily begin with society. More likely, a person will have an idea that he or she thinks will be profitable because society will develop a need for it. We got along fine for centuries without the ball-point pen, but now we need it. Tomorrow someone will develop something new and better and we will be convinced we need it no matter how full our larders may be. Business is a must in our society; only business has the capacity to satisfy our needs.

ONE BUSINESS AND THE EXTERNAL ENVIRONMENT

Wed. Dec. 13

Chapters 1-5

T & F   Multipl Choose

Because of our frequent and varied contacts with business organizations it is easy to assume that we understand what they are all about and to overlook many aspects of business and its operation. We tend to see business as manufacturing plants, retail stores, insurance companies, banks, and the like. To be sure, these are business firms, but looking at business like this, as a series of entities, tells us little about one of society's major institutions.

Business is just one of the several approaches societies around the globe utilize to provide their members with the goods and services that they desire—to satisfy their needs. Business, then, is a need satisfier, and if the needs of a society are few in number there will be relatively less business than if their needs are many or even unlimited. In nineteenth-century rural America the needs of society were few in number and there was little business activity compared with today. Most Americans today have a level of needs that is constantly escalating, and business must expand in an attempt to satisfy these needs.

Our purpose is to examine the American system of business to see why it developed as it did and to understand its basic characteristics. In certain respects American business operates in much the same fashion as business enterprise elsewhere in the world. We could feel right at home in a Japanese supermarket, if we understood the language, or in a Canadian department store or in a restaurant in the Bahamas. However, in many respects American business is different and in the pages that follow we will systematically examine the basic features and content of our business system to learn just what business is and how it is carried on.

Part 1 of the text deals with the total framework within which business operates. Here we describe what business is, the laws, the institutions, and the basic attitudes which affect it. We need to know the various types of enterprise that make up business and their importance as contributors to our national income and as employers of society's members. Through knowing all this we will better understand why business grows and some of the problems that growth creates. We will see the changing role of government in the conduct of business and the responsibilities that business people must assume.

Most of us will work in business, and the rewards that a person receives from a business career depend on his or her total environment. Part 1 defines this environment in detail.

The purpose of this chapter "Business" is a word we use to describe a wide variety of activity. We use the word so frequently and in such a matter-of-fact way that we seldom think in terms of what business is supposed to do and how it operates. When people say that they are going into business for themselves, we tend to visualize this as a store or a shop; we neglect the fact that business is people—people as customers, as employees, as members of the public, as representatives of the government, and as owners and managers of business. The main object of business is to satisfy the needs and desires of people, and business activity is carried on by people. / In this chapter we shall explore the reasoning behind the American system of business and identify some of the relationships that appear in American business. / Questions raised in this chapter include:

1 Why is the American system of business designed as it is?

2 What is the profit motive and how does it affect the operation of American business?

3 What does free enterprise mean and how does it affect American business?

4 How is "competition" defined and what is its importance?

5 What are the main obstacles that stand in the path of business today?

BACKGROUND OF AMERI-CAN BUSINESS

That our society is a society with a fantastic array of needs that must be satisfied has been established. Our society is also an industrial society in which there is a tremendous amount of interdependence between people and businesses. The days have long passed in this country when individuals were able to provide for their every need. Picture a metropolis such as New York City with its millions of people and many more millions of needs and you will see how true this is. What force is present to assure that these needs, or the great bulk of these needs, will be satisfied? Will there be enough doctors, fuel oil dealers, grocery stores, plumbers, policemen, and the like?

Until recently, in terms of history, there have been but two ways of assuring that the needs of a society will be served—that the thousands of intertwined tasks of society will get done. The first approach involves tradition, wherein the son follows the father in his line of work. This phenomenon takes place today as we well know but perhaps for different purposes. At one point in time man was bound by a principle of religion to follow the path of his father and would commit a most horrible sacrilege if he chose another. This practice ensured a continuous supply of doctors, educators, grocers, machinists, and the like. The caste system in India is an application of this concept.

The second approach involves the use of a central authority that designates what each individual will contribute to society. To a certain extent this approach is applied today in such societies as China, Russia, and Cuba. In China, for example, a worker has little certainty as to what his or her job will be at any time in the future. If the central authority deems that society needs the bookkeeper to work with the peasants in the field, that is what he or she will do.

But neither of these approaches was acceptable to our society and for several reasons. First, at the time our society industrialized, we had not built the same traditions as existed in Europe; many of our workers were first-generation Americans. Second, the way our industrial system developed required new skills that could not be handed down from parent to child. Finally, the concept of yielding to a central authority was contrary to our system of values. We needed a better approach.

ADAM SMITH AND THE "INVISIBLE HAND"

The brilliant Scotch economist-philosopher Adam Smith had a significant impact on the structure of American business and the role that business plays in our society. According to Smith, the laws of the market will ensure that the necessary tasks get done if the laws are permitted to work.

Smith advocated a doctrine of laissez faire wherein the government—the central authority—would not interfere with business enterprise. Government would serve as an umpire but would not impose unnecessary restrictions on business.

Given this freedom, people would be driven by their own self-interest to channel themselves to whatever work society was willing to pay for. If a person could profit by satisfying a particular need, he would do so; if not, he would try something else. Since all people are similarly motivated by self-interest, competition would result providing the necessary balance in satisfying society's needs. If too many people decided to make shoes, for example, there would be more shoes produced than society needed. This would cause the price of shoes to decline as individual shoemakers tried to get rid of their inventories. Thus shoemaking would be less profitable or unprofitable and people would leave this line of endeavor. If the price of shoes was excessively high, additional shoemakers would be attracted to shoemaking and would increase the supply of shoes. This would cause the price of shoes to drop to the "proper" level. Thus there develops a point of equilibrium where at a given price suppliers are willing to supply a given quantity and buyers are willing to buy this quantity. This is the "invisible hand" that Smith envisioned that would regulate the supply of goods and services that society needs. In summary, Smith believed that the only conditions needed to assure that the needs of society were properly provided are:

*1 Laissez faire—where the government follows a hands-off policy in its relations with business

*2 Self-interest—wherein each individual seeks to maximize his personal gain as he satisfies society's needs

3 Competition—where the forces of supply and demand will properly regulate the quantity of goods and services that will be produced and the price they can command in the marketplace

Things have changed a great deal since Smith published his ideas in *The Wealth of Nations* (1776) yet his ideas have been important to the molding of our philosophy and the American capitalistic system. Nor are Smith's ideas dead. Business people today maintain that if government gets out of the business of price controls, the supply of goods and services will be maintained and prices will seek their proper level.

THE AMERICAN PHILOSOPHY

Philosophy combines the beliefs, concepts, and attitudes of an individual or group and is aimed toward establishing what is "true" or "right" in the mind of the individual or group. Philosophy is extremely important to a study of business because it guides and limits the thought processes of those who must make decisions; it establishes the parameters within which business decisions must fall. Philosophy defines for each of us what is right or wrong, good or bad, acceptable or unacceptable, or what is possible or impossible. The following illustration shows why philosophy is important.

Paul Parker, a man in his late thirties, had just completed his doctorate at the Harvard Business School and had accepted a position at a large local university. The provisions of the contract he signed stipulated, among other things, that he would be paid $15,000 for the period September 1 through June 30 of the following year in twenty equal payments. It further stipulated that he would report for work on September 6. On August 20 his wife called stating that Paul had just been operated on for a serious illness but if he recovered on schedule would be able to start teaching on October 15. On September 10, the payroll office called and asked if they should include Paul in the September 15 payroll. How would you, the department chairman, respond? What is the right thing to do?

There are many societies today that utilize a capitalistic or free enterprise system to meet the bulk of society's needs. Some measure of capitalism exists in most nontotalitarian states. American capitalism is different from other forms of capitalism because our system of values is different. In short, our philosophy is not the same. In all societies there is the desire for a better and happier way of life for people but we feel that the "right" way to this end must incorporate the following characteristics.

Materialism

We are a very materialistic society; perhaps more so than any other society on earth. Whether this is caused by some innate desire for more or simply by our capacity to produce more is unimportant—we have developed the notion that the quality of life can be enhanced through materialism. In other words, we have created a need for material possessions and therefore allocate tremendous resources in this direction. There are some signs today that our emphasis on materialism is changing or should change but it is doubtful that any significant change in attitude will come about as long as the resources for producing more are still available. There are at least two cogent reasons for this observation:

Through materialism the physical tasks of life can be made easier, time can be saved, and an opportunity to keep ahead of the Joneses is provided.

Materialism creates millions of jobs and unemployment is something we like to keep at a minimum. America's 500 largest industrial-manufacturing businesses employ some fifteen million workers. The impact on employment of producing half as many automobiles as we produce today would be staggering.

Change

Not only do we want more possessions, we demand something different, something better, as time goes on. Radio is good entertainment, black-and-white TV is better entertainment, but color TV is even better. Thus we move from a less-than-$100 investment in entertainment to over $600. And our desire for change is not limited to physical possessions. We demand change in the way we use our leisure time, in the type of work we do, and in the things we see and listen to.

Change is costly not only in the terms mentioned above but also in the area of job displacement and in the use of resources. Change, however, may create new and more challenging jobs. Very often it is difficult to justify the costs of change in relation to their benefits. In 1974 the Chrysler Corporation spent some $450 million to change their line of automobiles, and other car manufacturers followed suit. Again, there are some signs that we no longer want to bear the cost of change for the sake of change, but unless society as a whole diminishes its thirst for new and better things, the pace will continue.

Growth

Large-scale institutions, business and otherwise, have advantages over small-scale institutions and on balance, we believe that they outweigh any disadvantages. There are no laws in our society that regulate the sheer size of a business. There are laws that regulate how business will operate but they could apply also to smaller businesses.

The basic reason for large-scale enterprise should now be apparent. Small-scale enterprise just does not have the capacity to satisfy our thirst for material possessions and our desire for new and better things. Large-scale enterprise is generally more efficient and effective than small-scale enterprise. As a rule, large-scale enterprise is more complicated, requires higher levels of human competence, and provides greater rewards for those involved. This we feel is good.

Efficiency

"Efficiency" can be described in many ways but generally it refers to the relationship between inputs and outputs—accomplishing more with less. Perhaps because of our Puritan values we feel that if a job can be done with less labor or less machinery, so much the better. Efficiency increases productivity which in turn enables us to buy more for less, and this is consistent with other aspects of our philosophy.

Perhaps at this point we can begin to see more clearly the significance of philosophy. We admire materialism, change, growth, and efficiency so much that we are at least partially blind when it comes to looking at the cost—the consequences—of having such a set of values. So obsessed are we with efficiency we fail to see what it does to us. More efficiency means that fewer workers will be needed to get a job done and efficiency generally calls for more menial jobs.

Pier 4 is one of Boston's finest eating places. It grosses $8 to $10 million annually while serving some 17,000 customers per week. A *Wall Street Journal*[1] article describes Pier 4 with such comments as:

It isn't a restaurant, its a production line . . . a classic text-book example of how to run a fine, large-service operation in contrast to an overblown fish house . . . each dish is prepared to virtual perfection.

Mr. Athanas [the owner] says the reason is "overpower of equipment and personnel"—more ovens and dishwashing machines than he needs except at peak periods, and highly specialized tasks for everyone. Some busboys, for instance, only pour water, others only set tables, while in the kitchen meals are put together as if on an assembly line. There is a tempo here when it's busy. You could put music to it and it would be like watching a ballet.

It is interesting to note that the head chef makes over $25,000 per year and employees on the cleaning crew make well over $200 per week.

Paradoxically, although we desire efficiency in the production of things, we are anything but efficient in the way we use them. Nor are we always efficient in the way we use human resources. The material quality of life can be improved through efficiency but its impact on other aspects of life may not be as positive.

The nature of rewards

In a communist society, according to Karl Marx, the distribution of income should be from each according to his ability, and to each according to his need. Our philosophy reflects more a "to-each-according-to-his-ability" approach. We believe that a person's contribution should be the basis for reward, and if one person produces more than another, his reward will be higher. Since there are tremendous variations in human abilities, there are tremendous variations in people's income. Some business executives in our society are paid in excess of $750,000 annually while many people are forced to work at the minimum wage level. Consequently, we accept the idea that there will be those who will live in luxury and those who will live in poverty.

Freedom of choice

Despite the many restrictions imposed on us as members of a very complex society, we enjoy greater freedom to govern our lives than

[1] *The Wall Street Journal*, Aug. 23, 1973, p. 1.

most peoples of the world. This is perhaps the most important characteristic of our philosophy because without freedom of choice, the
other characteristics would have far less meaning.

Because the characteristics mentioned above are so much a part of
our thinking, we may conclude that they represent the prevailing
attitude throughout the world. To the contrary, some societies prefer
to shun material possessions, to live by the status quo, and to make
the goal of commercial activity the providing of as many jobs as
possible for members of society. The extent to which we apply these
characteristics makes us different from most societies and, in some
instances, the target of their criticism.

AMERICAN CAPITALISM

The American system for conducting business is commonly referred
to as *capitalism*. A capitalist system is one in which the production
and distribution of goods and services are not organized and planned
by some central authority, but left to the private individuals who
engage in these activities for profit. Of course, there is no perfect
capitalist system in which all goods and services are supplied by
private business. We have a government postal service and municipal
water supply systems, for example. But what makes the United States
different is that the vast majority of the goods and services supplied
to the public are produced by private enterprise.

Americans are said to have the best climate for conducting private
business of any country on earth, and a comparison of the problems
of business here and elsewhere seems to support this opinion. The
reason can probably be traced to three basic factors in the American
way of life, three fundamental beliefs that most Americans share. The
first factor is the institution of private property which guarantees that
whatever property a person owns is his to use as he sees fit and
without the interference of others. The institution of private property
therefore encourages the accumulation of surplus property which
ultimately becomes the capital needed in developing business enterprise.

The second factor is freedom and security of contract. This is essential to modern business operation. We are free to contract with
others as we see fit, as long as we stay within the law, and we are
certain that no law will be passed that will impair the obligation of
contract.

The third belief is free enterprise, or the right you and I have to
make and sell whatever we want (as long as the product is not prohibited by law) without interference from others. If a person wants
to open a machine shop rather than a shoe store as a means of using
his capital and abilities, he is quite free to do so. As a result, an
individual may pursue that particular endeavor which will best utilize his talents and bring the greatest possible reward to himself and
society.

		Competition
		Individualism
Private property		The price system
Freedom of contact	▶ The profit motive ▶	Specialization, the interdependence of business, and elaborate industrial plants
Free enterprise		The risk element
... the three essential factors underlying the American business system	... the impetus to economic activity	... basic conditioning features of the economic system that has developed

FIGURE 1-1 American capitalism

Basic features of capitalism

The American system of free private capitalism depends on a government policy of allowing business in most cases to regulate its own affairs. This policy permits and encourages free enterprise, in fact makes it possible. But it is the profit motive that provides the real impetus to economic activity in a capitalistic system, and the operation of the profit motive is conditioned by the basic features of the economic system itself (see Figure 1-1).

The profit motive

The major heading given to the profit motive in the physical setup of this section signifies in part its importance. The profit motive, the drive for personal material gain, is a distinctive and dominating attribute of American business. It is not that we in this country have a monopoly on the profit concept, but profit may have a lesser significance and a different meaning in other societies.

Profit Most readers of this text have some idea of what profit means; it indicates a gain of some sort. We may profit from our experiences, we may profit more from one type of employment than another, and so on. To the accountant, who measures the business person's profit, profit is the excess of income over the expenses of the firm for a stated period of time. Income is the return to the firm for goods sold or services rendered. Expenses are the costs involved in creating and selling goods and services. To the owners of business, profit is the increase in their equity in the firm—the additional amount that they now own as compared to their ownership at the start of the accounting period.

Profit has other meanings For another view of profit let us look to the Russian definition. Profit has been a part of the U.S.S.R. philosophy at least since the days of Stalin, but there it is an expression of the actual efficiency of its production system. It relates inputs to outputs. If a given amount of labor, materials, and facilities produced 1,000 units last year, and the same inputs produced 1,100 units this year, there was a profit of 100 units or 10 percent. Actually it is little more than an index of industrial efficiency. Our view, and this is very important, is that business profit cannot result until goods are sold at a price that is greater than cost. The consequence of the Russian-type approach is that profit cannot be used to measure the effectiveness of the business system accurately because it may allow the production of goods for which there is no demand.

Profit and American business   In the previous paragraphs we have described profit and stated that it is an essential part of American business. Moreover, in the United States profit is generally considered a good thing. Virtually all groups associated with business, from scientists to sales people, generally agree that making a profit is an important function of any business. We tend to question the profit motive only when big business which enjoys a partial monopoly charges prices that are too high in relation to the value of their product or service. The attitude toward profit in most foreign countries is not as positive as it is in this country.

At this point let us explore in more specific language the reasons why profit is so important in American business. Behind each reason lies the undeniable fact that Americans are very materialistic and self-centered; they can satisfy many of their needs and desires through acquisition of material objects. Profit, directly or indirectly, provides the means for satisfying this bent.

1 Profit provides the means for measuring performance   Profit means different things to different people, and the theories of income and expense determination applied in business may vary substantially. However, within a firm, and perhaps within an industry, a set of standards for profit measurement can be used as a common denominator for measuring performance.

Profit is the end result of a number of events that transpire in the business establishment. Taken separately, these events might indicate that profitable operation is or is not taking place. However, business should not be viewed as a series of isolated events. Credit losses may be the lowest in history; sales volume may have increased by leaps and bounds; and costs of production may be the lowest in the industry. These are generally good signs, but no one such sign alone can guarantee that the overall operation will achieve its profit goal.

It is common practice in American business to establish profit goals for managers who in turn are evaluated and rewarded in terms of how the profit earned through their efforts compares with the goal. This approach forces a product manager, for example, to establish sales targets, production targets, cost targets, and the like that should generate the required profit. Profit standards, therefore, provide a degree of assurance to upper management that the performance of subordinate managers will be satisfactory.

2 Profit is a means for control Implicit in the previous discussion is the idea that profit standards are a means for controlling the performance of members of a business firm. The health of a firm's earnings over a period of time is used by stockholders to control the plans and policies of the board of directors. Similarly, the board uses profit to control the actions of the president, and so on down the line.

The profit-center concept There are several ways to exercise control over the members of an organization. One way, for example, would be to employ a large number of individuals who could critically and continuously observe the performance of managers at all levels of the organization. Such an approach could be very effective, but it would be very costly and cumbersome and would be quite apt to create animosity between superior and subordinate levels of organization.[2] Another approach is to establish profit objectives for individuals, provide the resources necessary to reach these objectives, and then leave the responsible manager to his own devices in deciding the "fine points" of his operation. In many respects, such managers operate as independent businessmen. (Note: These means for control cannot be applied in many not-for-profit firms.)

The purpose of profit centers is to focus managers' attention on the basic objective of profit and away from the too common practice of emphasizing single ingredients of profit. Advertising, for example, is a single ingredient of profit. However, the best Madison Avenue advertising plan imaginable is of no value unless it can carry its weight in the generation of profit.

A profit center is created by drawing an imaginary line around some definable segment of a business and treating it largely as a separate business whose manager is responsible for reaching a profit goal. The Chevrolet division of General Motors and the Lincoln-Mercury division of Ford are profit centers, but the segment of business to be treated as a profit center does not need to be as large as these. Every Chevrolet assembly plant is a profit center that buys component parts from other GM divisions and from outside suppliers, adds value through assembly operations, and in turn "sells" the assembled parts (cars) to Chevrolet's marketing group. The marketing group too is a profit center that buys cars from the assembly plant; adds value through advertising, promotion, and distribution; and helps to sell them through Chevrolet dealers.

For years, department stores have established individual departments as profit centers, and the concept is penetrating deeper and deeper into industrial firms. General Electric applies this concept in certain of its maintenance divisions, and a number of companies have established their purchasing departments as profit centers.

Why emphasize profit centers? One may wonder how a relatively small group of people can effectively manage the far-flung and diverse

[2]It is quite generally accepted that a most important feature of a good management job is the amount of independence or freedom from supervision that it allows.

activities that comprise industrial giants such as Ford, General Motors, Sears, and others. There is a danger in attributing this to a single factor, but the profit-center concept is, at least, a major facilitating device. Profit centers permit a small number of managers to effectively manage large business operations. Since profit, not production or sales necessarily, is a basic business objective, it seems quite logical that it should be used as the criterion for successful performance.

3 Profit is an incentive for people to work more effectively In many respects the welfare of all employees of a business rests on the profitability of the firm's operations. High wages and benefits and a high standard of living can be maintained only if a firm earns adequate profit. Note that employees of publicly supported transportation systems, for example, obtain these benefits irrespective of the firm's revenue or the level of service provided. Employees of these organizations are often criticized for poor performance and poor attitude. If this is true, the blame can be placed on the fact that there is no reward for better performance and no penalty for poor performance.

The extent to which profit can serve as an incentive for employees is illustrated in the extreme by the experience of the Lincoln Electric Company of Cleveland, Ohio. This firm, the world's largest producer of electric arc welding equipment, has operated a profit sharing plan in which all employees participate for more than 40 years. In recent years the average share of profit received in cash by Lincoln employees has been between $7,000 and $8,000 per year. Some workers receive much more than this, others much less; it depends on each individual's contribution to profit. Thus Lincoln employees on an average earn about double the wages of their counterparts in other firms in the Cleveland area. What is Lincoln's magic? There is none. Employees know that they can receive big wages only if profit is earned, and as a result they dedicate themselves to more profitable operations.

The earnings of a large number of business executives are frequently tied to the firm's profitability. It is not uncommon for executives to receive "extra compensation" equal to or greater than their basic salary if profit goals are reached or exceeded.

4 Profit is the means for growth and continued existence No business firm can exist for long unless it earns a profit. Profit is necessary for new plants, equipment, and so on. Also, the willingness of individuals to invest in a business is governed largely by the firm's profit history or profit potential.

It should be apparent to the reader at this point that the profit motive is an important feature of American business and that it is perhaps the most significant distinction between our philosophy of business and the philosophy in other countries.

The challenge to profit The viewpoint of profit presented above is not shared by all people. Labor leaders are critical of firms that earn high profits. It is often their contention that anything above a "normal" profit should be shared by the workers in the form of increased wages and benefits. The federal government too has taken a critical view of the profits earned in certain industries (even though it receives about one-half of this profit in income taxes) and has imposed restrictive measures. In recent years virtually every price increase announced by steel companies and automobile makers has been decried so vehemently by the White House that the increases were rolled back to more acceptable levels. This, of course, affects profits.

Another threat to profits comes from business management itself. Time was when the owners and managers of business were one and the same. At a later date the financier with his appointed managers dominated the scene. In recent years, especially the past two decades, the relation of owner to manager has changed drastically. Today, the ownership of most large business is spread over thousands of stockholders who are in no position to be involved with the management of the firm. A new breed of manager—the professional manager—has taken over in many businesses, and his attitude toward profit seems to differ from that of earlier managers. The new manager seems to show greater concern for the corporation and for himself than for the owners, as shown in the following:

As a result of the separation of ownership and control in the large corporation the managerial function has been vested in professional managers whose motivation and point of view tend to differ in important respects from that of the owner-managers. These new managers are selected because of their qualifications as administrators and their acceptability to various groups affected by the corporation; they are interested in professional achievement as well as personal remuneration; they identify themselves closely with the corporation and view it as having an indefinitely long life; they think in terms of the long-range welfare and interests of the corporation as such; they regard the corporation as something more than a mere creature of the stockholder.[3]

In the years since this observation the trend has continued and with greater strength. The consequence is that the professional manager may decide to forego profit today in order to build a more solid base for the future; to reinvest profits rather than distribute them; to take a course of action that will build the corporate image at the expense of profit; or perhaps to take a course of action that will increase his market value at the expense of the firm and its owners. Not that all this is bad or even undesirable, but it does make us realize that the profit motive of the future may not necessarily be the same as the profit motive of the past.

[3] Howard Bowen, *Social Responsibilities of Businessmen*, Harper & Brothers, New York, 1953. p. 104.

Competition

This second feature of capitalism is perhaps the most basic element of the entire American economic system. We must be careful here to make a distinction between the simpler form of competition, the rivalry between two or more organizations or individuals who produce the same kind of goods or services, and the more complex type of competition resulting from the fact that the customer has a limited number of dollars to spend—that is, the competition for a greater share of the consumer's spending.

When two firms manufacture automobiles in roughly the same price range, the competition between them is easily understood. But there is also a sense in which all business organizations compete for the consumer's dollars. Therefore, though it may appear that such enterprises as the telephone company or the power and light company have no competition, we find on closer examination that there is a considerable element of competitiveness in their policies after all. The telephone company, for example, would like to place two telephones in homes that now have only one, or to replace dial telephones with more expensive electronic sets. To do so would increase the phone company's revenue and profits. Since other businesses are also seeking to attract consumer spending with their products, the telephone company must offer special services in order to compete for this kind of spending.

The competitive element in our society extends beyond the operation of business. Workers must compete for positions; the person who seeks a better income and status by outdoing fellow workers is also competing. For there is a limited number of better jobs available, just as there is a limited number of consumer dollars to be attracted by business competition. Since a free enterprise system cannot guarantee either jobs or profits, the competitive element plays a significant part in determining individual success.

Individualism

A third major feature of American capitalism is its emphasis upon the individual. Perhaps the principal reason is that the individual is the source of buying power in our society; each person is free to spend his earnings as he sees fit. The individual's freedom to spend has very important consequences for business. For one thing, it means that the capital used to build American business must, in the last analysis, come from the individual. If the money is spent for goods or services, business gains through profit earned from the sale. If the individual saves at a local bank, business benefits from these savings since they can be borrowed from the bank to finance a new business or to expand an older business. In this sense, the health of the entire economy depends fundamentally on the freely chosen actions of the individuals.

Specialization

The goods and services we consume can be created via a variety of processes. A suit, for example, can be made in its entirety by a single tailor. This process demands that one person possess a variety of skills ranging from cutting to the right size to sewing and finishing. It would take many years for a person to learn all the skills required in suit making. A suit made by an expert tailor could be of superb quality and it could command a very high price.

An alternate process might be to break down the entire job into a number of specialized tasks where one person would do nothing but cutting, another person would make button holes, and another would sew on the buttons. This is specialization and it should be obvious that the time it requires to develop an accomplished button-hole maker is far less than the time it takes to develop an accomplished tailor. This process might use the same skills as the previous process but each worker would have to master only one skill. If suit making required five distinct skills, five individuals with these skills could produce many more suits in a given time than five accomplished tailors. The result of specialization is more efficient and less costly production. Even if a person has the skills necessary to make a suit he would have to rely on someone to supply the material, another the thread, and another the buttons. This too is specialization.

Specialization is needed for another reason. The products produced by American industry are often so complicated that it is impossible for any one person to master all the skills their production demands. No one person possesses all the skills necessary to design, construct, and orbit a skylab in space. Specialization allows us to have the benefits that more complicated products can bring—a Continental Mark IV instead of a Model T.

Interdependence of business

The need for specialization and its advantages have produced a situation in which every business in America is dependent in some measure on other businesses for materials or services. No business has yet been able to operate without assistance and cooperation from others. Even the General Motors Corporation, the largest single manufacturer in the United States, depends on thousands of smaller businesses for many things. The United States Steel Corporation spends about 40 cents of each sales-revenue dollar for products and services bought from other companies. The interdependence between general and specialized enterprises makes possible large-scale production that is fast, economical, and efficient.

Large-scale industries

The United States is a nation where large-scale industry flourishes, and most of our basic industries are large scale. In 1972, 140 indus-

TABLE 1-1   The top ten industrial firms: domestic and foreign

| | Domestic | | | Foreign | |
Company	Sales*	Assets*	Company	Sales*	Assets*
General Motors	$30,435,231	$18,273,382	Royal Dutch Shell	$14,060,307	$20,066,802
Exxon	20,309,753	21,558,257	Unilever	8,864,440	4,680,734
Ford Motor	20,194,400	11,634,000	Philips Electric	6,207,009	6,857,254
General Electric	10,239,500	7,401,800	British Petroleum	5,711,555	8,161,414
Chrysler	9,759,129	5,497,331	Nippon Steel	5,364,332	8,622,916
IBM	9,532,593	10,792,402	Volkswagen	5,016,949	3,493,583
Mobil Oil	9,166,332	9,216,713	Simens	4,712,910	4,263,094
Texaco	8,692,991	12,032,174	Hitachi	4,353,643	6,272,115
ITT	8,556,826	8,617,897	Imperial Chemical	4,236,275	5,487,041
Western Electric	6,551,183	4,309,899	Toyota	4,187,549	3,065,952

* 000 omitted

Source: *Fortune*, May 1973 and September 1973.

trial organizations had sales of over $1 billion and the smallest of *Fortune* magazine's 500 largest industrial organizations had sales in excess of $200 million. Automobile, steel, and petroleum firms are very large; ten of the fifteen largest industrial organizations in the United States are part of these three industries. The term "large" has little meaning unless it is compared with something. Table 1-1 compares the ten largest United States industrials with the ten largest foreign industrial firms. Three of these foreign firms are based in Japan, three in the Netherlands, and two each in Germany and Britain. The figures in this illustration tell us that big business in foreign countries is much smaller than in the United States.

However, we need to remember that there are over five million business firms in the United States that are operated by owner-managers, and these are generally quite small. In some industries only the giant corporation can afford the necessary facilities for production; in other areas, the large, elaborate plants may be less efficient than smaller ones.

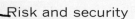

Risk and security

The American economic system is geared to the search for profits to be earned from business enterprise. The possibility of profit carries with it the risk of loss; there is no guarantee that a profit will be made. Profits are the major goal of American business; they provide the return on the owner's investment; they accumulate funds for business growth; they provide the reserves that can be used to weather financial storms. The possibility of profit is the principal incentive to enter into business; this possibility must always be weighed against the possibility of losses—the element of risk. In general, the greater the possibility of loss, the greater should be the possibility of large profits. Conversely, when the risk element is slight, the possibility of large profits is usually small. The element of risk in business therefore plays an important part in the overall pattern of business activity in the United States.

How much security?   One of the basic questions that any economic system must face is how far risks ought to be eliminated, and security guaranteed, in financial matters. In general, Americans believe that financial security ought not to be guaranteed, that the element of risk ought to remain as a hurdle to be surmounted by individual initiative and effort. In these terms, the proper role of government is conceived to be the protection of opportunities, not the guarantee of security. In other countries, a greater measure of security for investors is required—the risk is lessened—but it remains to be seen whether the security is worth the price that must be paid for it.

Whenever security is guaranteed, some measure of freedom of action by the individual must be forfeited. To take an extreme example, we can forfeit all our personal freedoms and go to jail, thereby gaining complete financial security. An obligation always has two sides; if you are obligated to the government, then the government is obligated to you as well. When a government guarantees financial security, it must demand the obligations or restrictions on freedom that are needed if it is to carry out that guarantee. These obligations can only fall on the members of the society.

Of course, there are different levels of security and different ways of obtaining security. A business can secure its position by offering a desirable product to the public. An individual can secure his future by producing better work than his competitors. This type of security is not as certain as government-guaranteed security, but it provides the best opportunity for individual development and involves the least sacrifice of individual human freedom.

PEOPLE IN BUSINESS

The business person, as well as the student of business, cannot over-look the immense significance of the human element in commercial activity. Businesses are, after all, groups of people who seek to earn a profit by providing goods and services for other people. The goods and services that business provides must be accepted by the con-sumer. The funds used to begin and operate a business are provided by people. At every stage in business activity we must deal with human beings—with employers and employees, with investors and customers, with owners and managers. A sound understanding of business must, therefore, be based on a clear knowledge of the differ-ent roles that people play in the business world.

The consumer

In a free economic system such as we have in the United States, the object of all business activity is the satisfaction of individual wants or desires. Activity that does not satisfy these wants will not yield a profit for the business and must be considered as waste. The business person's initial challenge is to find out what the consumer wants and needs. The basic necessities for human existence are few and simple and easily determined: enough food to keep the body functioning, enough clothing to keep the body warm, shelter from the elements, and some crude tools and utensils to aid in securing these basic requirements.

Americans, however, have become accustomed to the luxury of plenty and are not so easily satisfied as the consumers in many other societies. Americans are constantly driven by the desire for more—more in terms of the niceties of life. We want better homes, better clothing, and a host of other things. Paradoxically, we Americans are seldom satisfied even after acquiring the things we want.

Business and consumer wants Because people continually demand more and better things from business, new businesses are founded and older ones expanded to meet the growing needs of consumers. When there is a desire for more things, a profit can be earned by supplying them. Human desires are thus the suppliers' incentives. On the other hand, the person in business can never be certain of the types of goods or services the consumer will desire in the future, for the buying public is often fickle and capricious in its tastes. There is always the possibility—the risk—that the goods and services that a particular business supplies to the public will be rejected; such rejection will lead to losses rather than profits for the business person.

Through market research, business people attempt to anticipate changes in buying taste and to make their future plans by predicting changes in demand for goods and services. Business people also attempt to influence the attitude of the buyer toward their products by advertising, with the aim of creating a demand for particular goods or services. But they are not always successful; and each year some businesses fail, not because they are inefficient or produce a poor product, but because the public simply stops buying their product.

The worker

A second major group whose desires the business person must take into consideration is the people employed by business for wages or salaries—the working force. The employee provides the business person with labor and skills for a stipulated wage or salary. The primary concern of the worker, though not his or her only one, is to achieve gradual increments in the amount received for the services rendered. The business person must develop a loyal and efficient work team in order to produce goods and services efficiently and compete with other businesses offering the same goods and services to the public.

The business person is often placed under great pressure by the conflicting desires of worker and consumer. The consumer wants the maximum amount of goods and services for each dollar spent; the worker wants a maximum return for each hour worked. Consumers want prices to drop; yet a drop in prices reduces the amount available to the business person to pay expenses—including wages and salaries—and still earn a profit. Somehow the desires of both these groups must be satisfied, and the businessman must exercise keen judgment if he is to strike a balance that maintains consumer demand for his product and at the same time fosters worker loyalty to the firm.

The owners of business

The people who own their business, as well as those who save their money and invest in business, do so because they expect the business to earn a profit and thus to increase their savings. Most of our larger business organizations are owned by very large numbers of stockholders. The General Electric Company has $\frac{1}{2}$ million stockholders, General Motors Corporation has over 1 million stockholders, and American Telephone has over $2\frac{1}{2}$ million stockholders. Each of these stockholders invests money in the business in the hope of a return on the money invested. Its stockholders will very likely seek out a business that can provide such a return and will invest their money there. A stockholder cannot force the corporation to repay his investment, but stockholder dissatisfaction can impair attempts to obtain additional financing.

The management

Most large businesses are operated by professional managers who may or may not own part of the business. It is the task of management to operate the business at a profit and to provide each of the three major interest groups—consumer, worker, owner—with a fair return. The consumer must be given a good product for his money; the worker must have a fair wage for his labor and skills; the owner must receive a fair return on his investment. Management must reconcile these divergent interests as successfully as possible.

The business manager The businessman responsible for the operation of a business may own and operate it himself (as owner-manager), or he may be employed by the owners to operate it in their behalf (as professional manager). In either case he will face the same basic problems, but his basic goals may vary. If the owner-manager's business has a bad year, he too has a bad year because his pay is what the business earns. The professional manager is, most often, in a position where his earnings are not immediately affected by the ups and downs in business prosperity.

The managers of our large corporations as a rule do not own the firm they manage nor do they have ownership as a goal. As a result the management function is vested in people whose goals and aspirations are quite unlike those of an owner-manager. These professional managers are more apt to be specially trained administrators whose prime concern is a rewarding career in business. Consequently they plan and act in such fashion that the long-range interests of the firm are protected. To the professional manager the corporation is an institution whose purposes and responsibilities transcend the stockholder group.

The owner-manager People enter business as owner-managers for a wide variety of reasons, and understanding their motives will help us to understand why they operate their businesses as they do. Some of the goals people hope to achieve as owner-managers are:

1 To be independent and not constantly thinking of a boss looking over one's shoulder. This may be an ill-advised reason to be an entrepreneur because the ultimate "boss," the customer, is ever-present.

2 To be completely responsible for one's own development. How well a person does in business is frequently determined by one's superior. If the superior has no ambition to go places, it is quite likely that the subordinate will find it difficult to gain recognition. If the owner-manager fails, he at least knows that it is his fault.

3 To maximize earnings. For example, Barbara Shannon sold bottles for a glass manufacturer. She was paid a salary, but the salary schedule did not provide for rewarding her exceptional sales record. Consequently, she went out on her own as a manufacturer's representative and was able to enjoy the full benefit of her abilities.

4 To achieve status. There is a status associated with owner-managership which results from the first three reasons. Since the owner-manager is "top-dog" in his business he garners some of the prestige associated with the title of company president. He is the person with the answers and the authority.

5 To maintain a family institution or tradition.

Of course, there is always the ultimate goal of business—profit—behind each of these motives, but we can expect that the business person who desires independence, or who wishes to maintain family tradition, will take quite a different view of profit from that of the business person who seeks maximum earnings, or who wants to exploit his or her own invention. Accordingly, the relations among consumer, worker, and owner-manager will vary according to the reason for which the business is carried on.

The professional manager There are many differences between the professional manager and the owner-manager. When a person works for others, he must attempt to achieve goals that others establish. He is responsible to others for his actions; his performance is judged by those who employ him. He often becomes a specialist in one particular aspect of business rather than being generally responsible for the entire operation. Usually he is only one of a number of persons charged with responsibility for reaching the company's goals. In effect, a professional manager is a single cog in the gear that moves business along its chosen path.

People choose to become professional managers rather than owner-managers for a number of reasons. Obviously, the inability to raise the capital necessary to establish a personal business can be one reason. Among others are the following:

1 The desire to be free from the responsibility of making all the business decisions; the wish to share responsibility with others

2 The wish to be free from the risk of financial loss

3 A preference for a specific job with fixed hours

4 Willingness to forego the benefits of owner-managership for the status and security to be obtained from association with a well-known organization

SUCCESS IN BUSINESS

Because people enter business for different reasons and in different ways, their goals are different, and there is therefore no single way in which success can be defined for all business people. The owner-manager has goals or objectives that are largely of his own making, and success to him depends on whether he alone is satisfied. One individual may be content with a level of achievement that does not satisfy another. A small business yielding a profit of $8,500 per year may be satisfactory for one individual, for instance, while another may feel that this is not an adequate return for the risks and responsibilities he or she must undertake. The owner's conception of success is of great importance to the student of business because it will have a direct effect on the manner in which the business being studied is operated.

A professional manager, on the other hand, must adopt someone else's goals. His success will be measured in terms of his ability to achieve these goals, as well as in terms of the personal satisfaction and remuneration he derives from his work.

BUSINESS GOALS

Every business has some goal, some level of achievement that the business attempts to reach. Since a business is by definition motivated primarily by the search for profits, these goals are usually expressed in terms of sales volume, profit per dollar of sales, degree of market penetration, and so on. Generally, a firm tends to raise its goals and seek further growth and more profitable operation, though this is not always the case. The goals that business sets for itself are of great significance to everyone, whether he or she is an employee, a consumer, an owner, or just a member of the general public. The widespread achievement of business goals in the national economy brings prosperity and an expanding economic system, and this affects everyone in the society. For the businessman himself, achieving his goals means maximizing the firm's potential; a failure to do so can be catastrophic. The attainment of business goals is therefore a fundamental responsibility of all business people.

Of course, there can be no guarantee that a given business will reach the goals set for it. There are usually various obstacles to be overcome, both inside and outside the business. Inside the firm, there may be limits on the time available for a particular job, on the funds or personnel available, or on the physical capacities of equipment, which may hinder progress toward the chosen objectives. Often these obstacles can be overcome by skill and imagination in planning. The successful business person is constantly searching for new and better means of conducting business.

Even when a business operates efficiently, however, there may remain further external obstacles to success. Some are due to the competitive nature of our economy. As one business seeks to achieve sales goals, say, through advertising, another competing business attempts to nullify the effects of the advertising through a different promotion scheme. The nature and extent of competition from other firms must be continually appraised so as to minimize its effect on the achievement of one firm's business goals. Another obstacle to success may arise from the extent to which businesses depend on one another; no business firm, however large, is completely self-sufficient. Businesses often fail to perform as promised. The business person must exercise great care in the selection of sources of supply if the goals set are to be reached.

THE HUMAN ELEMENT AGAIN

Business, then, is concerned primarily with people. Business depends on people as customers, as employees, as investors, and as managers. People in turn depend on business to provide them with the goods and services they need and want. Business pursues profit as a basic goal, though the attitude that business takes toward profit depends on a number of other factors. The consumer's drive to satisfy his or her wants and needs and the business person's drive for profits create a very complex set of relationships between producer and consumer, employer and employee, owner and management, business and society—relationships that are dynamic and changing, and quite beyond anyone's ability to specify completely. But it would be folly to ignore the complexity of these relationships, and a careful study of them will lead us to a better appreciation of the role that business plays in modern society.

SOME MODIFYING OBSERVATIONS

When Adam Smith expressed his views about how the needs of a society should be satisfied, he visualized business as being composed of a large number of small, owner-managed firms operating in local, well-defined markets. We now know that American business is something quite different. To be sure we have millions of small businesses which operate in circumstances much like those that Smith visualized. But we also have a relatively small number of huge firms that operate to a large degree free from market pressures. The 500 largest industrial corporations in 1972 accounted for 65 percent of all sales in this category and 75 percent of the profits and employment. Perhaps a million or more firms accounted for the balance.

By allowing so many of our institutions—business, labor unions, education, medicine—to grow to mammoth proportions we have to a great extent lost control over them. In many instances business, for example, dictates to us the employee, investor, or customer what jobs we will perform, the return we will receive on our investment, what we will buy, and what prices we will pay. Look at it this way. What are the odds that General Motors will produce cars next year that have the wrong style—a style that will not appeal to the consumer? Since General Motors makes more than half the cars produced in America, it automatically dictates what the prevailing style will be.

As we look back at the features of American capitalism, we should bear in mind that they apply in varying degrees. Not all businesses have the same attitude toward maximizing profit, not all businesses face the same degree of competition, not all businesses are dependent to the same degree on other business, and so on. The features of American capitalism discussed above do, however, identify some basic characteristics of business as a whole.

THE CHALLENGE TO BUSINESS

Society's attitude toward business is anything but constant. This is due to the fact that society expects different things from business as time passes and if business does not respond, attitudes change. From the industrial revolution to about 1930, business was considered a good institution by society. It achieved society's goals of rapid material progress and a generally increased standard of living. Yet by today's standards business acted irresponsibly during those years what with the exploitation of child and female labor, the operation of sweatshops, and the outright refusal to accept the notion that business owed workers anything beyond the day's pay. During this period, the end justified the means.

During the 1930s business was viewed as the culprit which caused the Great Depression and consequently it was slapped down with countless rules and regulations. Business again became a good institution during the 1940s and 1950s because of its capacity to turn out the materials of war and adjust to a peacetime economy.

Today, there is a widespread feeling among Americans that our social order is somewhat out of balance—our definition of a good society has changed. It makes less and less sense to have great affluence and at the same time a deteriorating environment with poverty, dying cities, and a lack of equal opportunity.

More broadly, the sluggishness of social progress is engendering rising criticism of all major institutions—government, schools, organized labor, the military, the church, as well as business. In this context, the large business corporation is undergoing the most searching public scrutiny since the 1930's about its role in American society. There is widespread complaint that corporations have become cavalier about consumer interests, have been largely indifferent to social deterioration around them and are dangerous polluters of the environment.[4]

Ultimately the wishes of society will prevail. We should expect in the future that businesses' search for profit will be conditioned more by society. In essence, society is saying to business: "We will allow you to operate and make profit only if you pay proper attention to the needs of society."

Why the change in attitude?

The basic features of American capitalism which are responsible for our great abundance are directly or indirectly responsible for a host of circumstances we now call problems. For every individual there is a hierarchy of needs that he seeks to satisfy. These needs range from physical needs—food, shelter, and clothing—which occupy the lowest rung, to the safety need, the security need, the social need, the egoistic need, and finally the need of self-actualization. This latter need is the desire on the part of a person to become everything he or she is capable of becoming.

If members of a society are occupied with the first order of needs— they are yet to be satisfied—there is no opportunity to consider second- or third-level needs for example. Safety, security, and the like have no significance to a person who is struggling to satisfy physical needs. But our system has made it possible for most Americans to satisfy several levels of need. And as one level is satisfied, we seek a higher level of need satisfaction. Now we are in a position where the current order of need is a better society more concerned for human values and the environment. Thus, we can now make new demands on business. This is the challenge to business—to achieve acceptable business goals but not at the expense of society.

SUMMARY

Probably the outstanding advantage of the American system, as compared with either socialism or communism, is the extent to which the individual retains the freedom of choice. Freedom is never absolute, even in the United States, but the boundaries on freedom are much more tightly drawn in other countries. The benefits that have accrued to the American people from the operation of our economic system are very substantial. Among the more important of these benefits, certainly, are:

1 The very high standard of living it has provided

2 The personal freedom of choice of occupation and location that it guarantees

[4] *Social Responsibilities of Business Corporations.* A report by the Committee for Economic Development, June 1971, p. 14.

3 The wide range of choice in occupation and the range of goods and services that it makes possible

4 The freedom to manage one's own personal affairs, to earn and spend according to individual preferences

5 The right to ownership and possession of property, and its free use within the limits imposed equally on all members of society

Speaking generally, the United States has produced a system in which it is possible for individuals to develop their abilities and to forge a more prosperous and enjoyable life through their own efforts. In the world as it presently stands, this is a rare condition, and it ought to be highly valued by all thoughtful persons.

QUESTIONS

1 According to Adam Smith, what conditions are necessary for a society to be assured that the goods and services it needs will be available? How does Smith's approach differ from earlier approaches?

2 Why is philosophy so important to you as a member of a business organization? As a customer?

3 Discuss the possibility of our becoming a less materialistic society.

4 Compare the American view of profit with the Russian view. Why do we feel that the Russian view is inferior?

5 What is a profit center? Why emphasize profit centers?

6 What is the source of the greatest challenge to profit in our society today?

7 Does specialization increase or decrease the interdependence of business? Explain.

8 Explain the meaning and advantages of specialization.

9 Why do some people choose to become professional managers rather than owner-managers?

10 Why can there be no single criterion for success in business?

11 Discuss the role of profit in the American system of business.

12 Are Adam Smith's economic concepts valid today? Explain.

13 Society's attitude toward business is anything but consistent. Explain and illustrate why this statement is true.

14 There exists some negative attitude today toward the way American business acts and operates. What are the major causes for these attitudes?

15 Respond to the Paul Parker incident on page 7.

The purpose of this chapter The development and operation of any business enterprise are determined in large measure by the environment in which the business is located. This is an axiom basic to the study of business. In this chapter we will take a closer look at the major institutions—social, legal, political, economic, and technological—which determine what is legal and acceptable business practice in America. From this we will be able to see more clearly the impact of these institutions on business. In addition, the growing internationalization of business activities is briefly considered in terms of its influence on the planning and conduct of an enterprise. The environment of business in the United States must now be viewed as an international environment. / Questions raised in this chapter include:

1 What are the various groups which constitute the "voices" in the social environment?

2 How does the law provide the ground rules of business?

3 Are all areas of business subject to specific government regulation?

4 What factors help shape the economic environment in which American business is operating today?

5 Why is the state of the production system a vital environmental consideration?

THE ENVIRONMENT OF BUSINESS

Business has been defined as the sum of the activity involved in the creation and distribution of goods and services for private profit. But business is a social activity that must take place within the framework that society has established. Activity that is legitimate business in one society, or state, or country, or city may not be in another. In Massachusetts, for example, the sale of alcoholic beverages is not legal in a number of municipalities, and pari-mutuel racing must be approved by voters on a county basis before it is legalized. The type of business activity that takes place within a particular community, state, or nation is largely determined by the attitudes, beliefs, and needs of the particular locality. Sometimes, conversely, the activities of businessmen help to shape and direct life within the community. Business makes demands on society, and society makes demands on business. The sum of these interrelationships between business and the community comprises the business environment. The environment varies greatly from one country to the next; it may be favorable to business growth, or it may be hostile. The following aspects of any given society are important in this respect.

1 The social structure

2 The legal and political framework in which business must operate

3 The economic system found in the society

4 Technological progress

THE SOCIAL STRUCTURE

A social structure may be viewed as the attitudes that prevail in a society toward its many institutions—business, for example. The legal framework, the economic system, and the state of technological development are each important considerations, but the ultimate design and consequently the impact of each of these factors depends on the attitudes of society.

The social environment

These attitudes depend in large measure on whether business has been responsive to the needs of society. This has been especially true of the United States since the Great Depression of the 1930s; the increase in governmental controls and the changed attitude toward the social responsibilities of business have had a far-reaching effect on business practices. Perhaps the best way to grasp the meaning of the changes is to review briefly the major alterations in the social environment beginning with the late nineteenth century.

Late nineteenth century The Industrial Revolution which preceded the Civil War set the stage for significant change and development in the American business scene. The expansion of markets following hostilities, new supplies of cheap labor via immigration, the trend to modernization of production facilities, and the development of new sources of power to replace manual and water power all combined with other factors to foster growth and change in American business. The form of business ownership changed from single proprietorship and partnership to corporation and later to trust and holding companies. Monopolistic tendencies developed in many industries, and around the turn of the century approximately 200 large corporations were organized to merge or consolidate two or more large companies. Among these were Eastman Kodak, U.S. Steel, and International Harvester.

In several industries the concentration of power and control grew to such an extent that widespread public resentment followed. The first significant attempt by American society to regulate and control business activities dates to the latter part of the nineteenth century. The social ills, such as child labor, sweatshops, and other neglect of human needs, that had accompanied rapid industrialization and urbanization combined with the growth of very large business combinations drew an increasing volume of protest. Public agitation finally produced the Sherman Antitrust Act of 1890 and the Interstate Commerce Act of 1887, both aimed at curbing power of big business. The indifference of the businessman to public attitudes, which found expression in William H. Vanderbilt's famous epithet, "The public be damned," gradually gave way to a more genuine concern for public opinion and to a growing effort to influence it favorably. Finally, in 1911, during the administration of President Taft, the first effective enforcement of the Sherman Act was carried out and resulted in a dissolution of the American Tobacco and Standard Oil trusts.

Early twentieth century During the early part of the twentieth century, business in America struggled to work out a solution to the problems raised by its own rapid growth, the change in governmental attitudes toward business, and the changing social scene. This period saw the development of the scientific management movement fathered by F. W. Taylor. In the beginning, scientific management was concerned with maximizing efficiency of production only, which led to a growing "depersonalization" of employer-employee relationships that soon created even greater problems. The concept of the individual worker as a person, a member of the community, and a creative being was submerged under a wave of "scientific" efficiency that lasted at least until the Great Depression of the 1930s.

The New Deal The so-called "New Deal" administration of Franklin D. Roosevelt probably produced more change in the American social environment than any like period in our previous history. The Depression that began in 1929 had created a situation in which social experiment was welcomed and government interference in the economic system was demanded in the interest of the citizenry. As a result of the clamor for controls, important legislation was enacted in the fields of social and old-age insurance, child labor, and collective bargaining, together with an impressive collection of laws regulating the conduct of business. The old concept of the totally independent businessman concerned solely with his profits regardless of the interests of the community—if such a concept had ever really existed— passed away and was replaced by more realistic attitudes.

The new social environment The nineteenth-century attitude toward business was based on the concept of personal leadership in business affairs, on small-scale operation, and on skilled workers. The early twentieth century brought with it the concept of professional managerial services in very large-scale operations involving a high degree of mechanization and an impersonal relation between business and the labor force. After 1929, business recognized the necessity of giving due consideration to the personal needs of the workers, to the relation between the business and the community, and to the wider questions raised by the needs of the whole society. The answers that business now gives to these questions are the outcome of pressures exerted by various groups, the more important of which are the labor union, the consumer, the stockholder owner, the management, and the general public.

Labor influence The growth of organized labor in America moved at a spectacular rate after the passage of the National Recovery Act of 1933 and the Wagner Act of 1935. The rise of organized labor was at first resisted bitterly by businessmen. When the federal government, however, stood clearly on the side of labor organizations and in effect forced business to recognize the union as a bargaining unit, businessmen began to change their attitude. Since that time, labor and management have worked in the direction of a modus vivendi or working agreement that would permit them to coexist and to derive mutual benefit from the association. In some industries, success in this endeavor has been great, though the relationship is far from settled in its final form.

Consumer and general public   Business now must take cognizance of the general public, both as a vital force in our society and as the body of consumers that commerce must serve. Business takes great care to examine the effect of its policies on both the individual consumer and the general public. In fact, we find that large business organizations often sponsor extensive educational and informational programs designed to acquaint the general public with their problems and policies, even though the merchandise produced by the organization is not sold in retail shops. Hostile public reactions to business practices can lead to increased governmental control, for in a democracy, the *vox populi,* the voice of the people, must be heard above all other voices. It may take time, but eventually the people will be heard. Since each increase in governmental control results in a concurrent decrease in freedom of enterprise for the business person, the need for serious attention to public relations can hardly be doubted.

By and large, the giant industrial firms have taken the lead in showing concern for public attitudes, and this is hardly surprising. The small firm cannot always afford such a luxury. Further, its activities seldom generate widespread concern among the general public. The large firm, however, which has far more at stake, has a greater potential influence on public opinion, and its activities create widespread interest. Its closer relationship to the public will continue and will grow ever more complex, for the very large firm assumes the continuity of its own life; it cannot pull up stakes and start again if it makes a serious error. The only insurance open to it is careful attention to public opinion and a constant effort to maintain public opinion that is favorable.

Business people are gradually coming to the realization that technological advances are always followed by social changes, some of which are not desirable. To alleviate the undesirable effects of these changes, the technological strides must be matched step by step with plans to deal effectively with the social change which follows. If business fails to foresee social changes and to act in a responsible manner, there is no doubt that the voice of the people will be raised in a clear mandate to the government that it take appropriate action. Already in several areas on which technology has a social impact, such as unemployment, leisure time, environmental pollution, urban blight, and transportation, some business leaders are making more than a token move to mitigate the negative social effects. At the same time, consumer groups, upset with product deficiencies, have found political support for their cause. On this front, also, the business people are becoming increasingly concerned and fearful that the strength of the consumer movement may result in additional legislation in the field of consumer protection. This fear may stimulate negligent business people to develop a better attitude about consumer satisfaction and to improve their performance.

The stockholder   In the nineteenth century, the corporation was held to operate solely for the benefit of the stockholders. The early corporation, small in size, with few stockholders and personalized control, could continue to exist with this philosophy. The modern industrial giant, however, with its hundreds of thousands or even millions of stockholders, must abide by general policies that will meet with the approval of a wide variety of groups and persons. Of course, business still continues the search for profits, but the search is conditional and not absolute. That is, there are things that business cannot do in order to maximize its profits even though such actions are not illegal, because of the harmful effect on public opinion. This is perhaps one of the most significant changes in the conduct of American business in recent years.

Professional management The change from owner management to professional management that took place in large-scale industry after World War I has also had a great influence on business policy. The professional manager, although he takes pride in his ability to produce profits for the firm and though he cannot retain his position unless he does produce profits, nevertheless takes a wider view of the role of business in American society than did his predecessor. An important part of management's task, in the modern view, is to reconcile the goals of business with the needs and desires of society.

The business manager of today is a "symbol" of his business; he presents to the general public the epitome of his firm, its stockholders, and its policies. Likewise, he takes upon himself the pressures that are exerted on the firm by various outside groups. Realizing this, the modern corporation has deliberately followed a policy of choosing its managers to fit the environmental situation in which business now functions. Thus the social environment tends to determine the selection of a manager and the nature of his policies after selection.

Impact of education

One of the more significant aspects of our social environment is education. The impact of education on business and society is both immediate and significant. The challenge to business described in the previous chapter is due in part to the fact that there is a relationship between the educational level attained by members of a society and the demands that they will make on society's institutions. We need look no further than the experience of minority groups in America to verify this. Because of better education, individuals are in a position to contribute more to the successful conduct of business, and therefore they more strongly demand that business provide both opportunity and benefits for the individual and society. Today, there is a rebellion of sorts among workers who perform the routine and often dull jobs which characterize many assembly lines. This approach to manufacturing received a stamp of approval at a time when educational attainment was far below the present level. Such jobs may have been ideal for the pre-World War II labor force, but for many workers they are far from ideal today. There is much pressure on business today to improve the quality of jobs it offers. Education, therefore, works unceasingly to increase both our desires and the means for satisfying them. The resources that we, society, are willing to allocate to education are of vital importance to the development of business and other institutions.

There is a very close relationship between education and the extent to which a society can promote material progress. Despite an abundance of natural resources, an ignorant society will usually live in poverty. On the other hand, even without abundant natural resources, an educated society can generate affluence. Japan offers proof of this. Rapid material progress depends on industrialization. Industrialization depends on technology and technology depends on education. No society has yet attained a high degree of industrialization by itself when more than 10 percent of its people failed to meet the minimum tests for literacy. Fair levels of prosperity can be maintained in certain areas with a low literacy level. But such areas—a Caribbean island, for example—are more apt to have a personal-service orientation than an industrial orientation. They must depend on other societies for their material possessions, and they are extremely vulnerable to relatively minor economic reverses. A sudden drop on the New York Stock Exchange could result in bankruptcy for resort-area hotels. The lack of education is the most serious limitation on the development of any society.

THE LEGAL FRAMEWORK

A _law_ is simply a rule of conduct that society will enforce for the common good of the individuals or groups residing in the society. The breaking of a law is therefore subject to social penalties. Laws enumerate the human actions that society prohibits and punishes and the actions that are not to be controlled. In another sense law determines the rights and the social obligations of each member of society. Today we think of laws as acts of Congress or of some other body, but this is a new conception. In the Middle Ages laws were generally not "made" but were for the most part the customs of a particular people, handed down from one generation to the next. We still have both kinds of laws in our legal system; laws which are made or enacted are called _statutes,_ and laws that have been handed down through the courts for generations are part of what is called the _common law._ Much of the common law has been altered by statute law.

Public and private law

All laws of the United States fall into two other broad categories, depending on the type of activity they regulate: law that regulates the relationship between government and individuals is called _public law;_ law that controls relations among individuals is called _private law._

Public Law

Each of these major subdivisions contains both statute law and common law provisions. There are three main classes of public laws:

1 Constitutional law deals with the powers of federal or state governments. It is designed to prevent governments from denying us constitutional guarantees.

2 Administrative law regulates officials, boards, and other commissions.

3 Criminal law forbids and punishes conduct that is detrimental to the welfare of the state. Murders and kidnapping, for example, are covered by criminal law.

Private law, which is concerned only with individuals, deals with such matters as:

1 Contractual relations (law of contracts)

2 Behavior of persons acting as agents for others (law of agency)

3 Ownership (law of real and personal property)

4 Business obligations (law of business associations)

When public laws are violated, it is considered a crime against society. When private law is violated, only those directly involved are affected. In general, the practicing business person is primarily concerned with the content of the private law of this society; though as a citizen he or she is naturally concerned with all the laws that govern social behavior. Table 2-1 summarizes this brief discussion of the structure of the law.

Laws relating to business

In a brief space we can only indicate some of the broad areas of business activity that are regulated by law; the specific content of these laws is, properly speaking, the subject matter for a course in business law.

Perhaps the most common business arrangement that is legally

TABLE 2-1 The structure of law

Common law Statute law	
Public law regulating relations between government and individuals:	Private law regulating relations among individuals:
Constitutional law	Law of contracts
Administrative law	Law of agency
Criminal law	Law of real and personal property, including sales and negotiable instruments
	Law of business association

Common law, arising out of precedents established in court cases, forms the basis of private law as it affects business. Statute law is created by legislatures.

controlled is the contract—an agreement between two or more people in relation to any legitimate business activity. Contracts need not be written to be valid, and most everyday contracts are not written. A contract is made each time a sale is made or services are engaged; when a car is left at a garage for servicing, for example, there need not be a written document, and yet, a contract is made that is recognized and controlled by law. Similarly, the extension of credit to a customer, the cashing of a check, or the making of a promissory note all produce a legal relationship.

When a partnership or a corporation is formed, it must meet the conditions that are established by law for these forms of business association. And it can continue only so long as it adheres to the laws governing its conduct. Business may exercise only those powers and rights which the law specifies or sanctions. For example, every state prohibits the practice of law by corporations, but most states will not permit any group but a corporation to enter the banking or insurance business. In general, the law determines the rights of business firms in relation to the public, to other businesses, and to the government. American law does not attempt to direct business activity very closely; it establishes the broad framework in which business activity is carried on.

The federal system

Because the United States has a federal political structure, legal jurisdiction—the right to control and regulate behavior—is divided between the federal government and the various state governments. Certain activities, such as interstate commerce, are subject to federal control; others, such as business conducted wholly within a state, or intrastate commerce, are under the jurisdiction of the state government. Where both the state and federal government have jurisdiction, federal law is supreme. But the Constitution specifically divides legal jurisdiction between the states and federal government, and this division cannot be altered without a constitutional amendment.

Federal jurisdiction Under the terms of the Constitution, certain areas are definitely allocated to the control of the federal government. The more important of these areas are:

Transportation, communication, various public utilities

Mining

Agriculture, forestry, fishing

Banking, insurance, finance

Food, drugs, cosmetics

Other types of business activity are relatively free of federal regulation, as for example:

Other manufacturing

Wholesale and retail trade

Real estate

Business and repair services

Personal services

Amusements

Construction

Professional and related services

The above listings should not be interpreted to mean that state governments do not regulate banking, fishing, drugs, and the like; there can be dual regulation. Nor should we assume that this listing indicates all areas of business that are regulated. Virtually every business in the United States is subject to some measure of indirect control by the federal government. For example, it is hard to find any business that by virtue of its supply sources does not have some relation to federally regulated interstate commerce.

Courts and administrative agencies

Just as there are different types of laws, there are different types of courts. A civil session of court hears actions between two or more private citizens, as in a breach of contract case. The court decides the outcome and issues a judgment in favor of one of the parties. In such cases the aggrieved party must take the initiative and bring action against the other party or there will be no court case. In criminal courts, society brings an action against the accused. In a murder case, for example, the district attorney may present society's case. The penalties in criminal cases can be fines, which are paid to the government, and imprisonment. This is quite unlike civil cases. The following discussion relates to the federal judicial process.

When it appears that a law has been violated, it is first necessary to make certain that a violation has occurred, then to mete out punishment to the offender. This is the function of our courts, and of the various administrative agencies, such as the FTC, that have the power to hold hearings and issue orders to the parties subject to their jurisdiction. Of course, the authority of courts varies according to their status, but in general all courts perform the same function: they determine the facts regarding a particular case and render a decision. Some courts deal only with particular types of cases and hence are able to conduct accurate hearings more quickly. All courts, except the Supreme Court of the United States, have jurisdiction in a limited geographical area.

The federal court system

The federal government and the various states have separate court systems, each administering the law of the agency that authorized them. The general pattern of our court system is a pyramid made up of three levels or tiers. There are many courts in the bottom tier, a

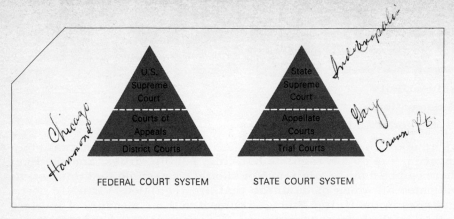

FIGURE 2-1 The pyramid of courts

few at the intermediate level, and one Supreme Court at the top, as shown in Figure 2-1. In the federal court system, the lowest rank is made up of district courts, the middle-rank courts are called courts of appeals, and the highest is the Supreme Court.

The district courts are the starting point for most cases that involve federal laws. These courts have jurisdiction over all cases that involve the Constitution, federal laws, or treaties. Some of the questions considered in the district court include bankruptcy, violation of federal banking laws, maritime cases, and some of the problems that arise between citizens of different states.

Each court of appeals has a geographic area made up of several states as its jurisdictional limit. When a case is decided in a federal district court in a way that does not satisfy one of the litigants, he can appeal, in most cases, to the court of appeals. The higher court will review the record of the case and determine whether or not the lower court conducted it properly. Usually, the court of appeals will not retry a case; however, if it upholds the appeal, it returns the case to the lower court and orders it to conduct a new trial.

The Supreme Court of the United States is the highest court in the land, and there is no appeal beyond its verdict. It will hear only a few cases, usually involving basic constitutional questions or disputes between lower courts. The Supreme Court seldom tries a case; ordinarily it reviews cases tried in lower courts and either approves the decision or returns the case to the lower court with orders for a retrial. The principles asserted by the Supreme Court in its opinions are followed by all lower federal courts and, in matters involving the interpretation of the Constitution, by the state courts as well.

Federal administrative agencies

The federal government has established a large number of agencies and commissions with authority to investigate and adjudicate within their area of competence. Among the many significant federal agencies are the Federal Trade Commission, the Securities and Exchange Commission, the Interstate Commerce Commission, the Federal Communications Commission, the Federal Aviation Agency, the Federal Reserve Board, and the National Labor Relations Board. The chief argument in favor of these agencies is that they are more flexible and informal than the regular courts and hence are able to conduct hearings, to issue orders against malpractice, and to assess penalties—or to appeal to the regular courts for penalties in extreme cases. Through the use of agencies, the case load on the court system is greatly reduced.

State courts and regulatory agencies

The organization of state court systems varies from state to state, but in general the state systems follow the pattern of trial courts, appellate courts, and one supreme court for each state. The courts have different titles and different kinds of jurisdiction from their federal counterparts in many cases, but the general principle of organization is the same.

A state also has the power to regulate through its use of the police power; it can legislate to protect public health, safety, and morality. As in the federal system, many state administrative boards and agencies have been created for special purposes.

THE ECONOMIC SYSTEM

The third prime factor that shapes the operation of business enterprise in the United States is the general pattern of economic development in which business functions—the economic system. The way that goods and services are produced and distributed by other businesses has significant effect on the policies that any business must follow. In general, as we have seen, the American economic system is founded on the principle of free individual choice by the consumer. The question of what will be produced and how, what will be bought and sold, depends on the decisions the individual consumer makes when he spends his income. There is little central direction of the operation of the economic system.

Of course, with millions of people involved in production, distribution, and consumption of goods and services, the nation's economic life becomes very complex. The fact that large numbers of people are involved, however, tends to produce overall patterns of activity that can be determined by the businessman and used in planning his own future operations. Each of the patterns discernible in this welter of transactions has a considerable influence on the conduct of business in this country. Some of the more significant factors are considered below, especially competition, prices, and technological progress (see also Figure 2-2).

Social factors:

The general public-as individual consumers and through the influence of public opinion

Labor-the increasing significance of employees and their organizations

Stockholders-the growth, spread, and variety of individual
and group investment

Management-professional managers and their wider view of the role of business
in American society

Influences on the
operation and
development of
business
activity

Economic factors:

Competition

The factors of production and their cost

Technological progress

Prices and real wages

Legal factors:

Private law as it
affects business:

    Contracts

    Agency

    Property, sales, negotiable instruments

    Business association

Legislation bringing greater government
regulation of business:

    Trade practices

    Wages and hours

    Labor practices

    Antitrust laws

    Stock and financial operations

FIGURE 2-2 The business environment

Competition

Before reading this section on competition and its impact on business and society, the reader should review the comments on competition in the previous chapter on page 16.

The economic environment in the United States is fundamentally competitive, though there are varying degrees of competition in the different industries. Before the degree of competition can be evaluated properly, we need some criteria that will enable us to decide the extent to which a particular industry or firm can be considered competitive. We can produce a set of criteria by defining the two extremes of perfect competition and perfect monopoly; we can then compare current conditions with these definitions and determine the relation between them. Pure, or perfect, competition, as it is usually defined, has the following characteristics:

1 A very large number of producers making the same goods and serving very large numbers of consumers

2 A well-informed buying public and well-informed producers

3 The absence of collusion or special arrangements among either buyers or sellers

4 Self-interest as the dominant motive for both buyer and seller

5 No differentiation between products; that is, all beer, bread, automobile tires, and the like must be exactly the same

At the other extreme, perfect monopoly would have the following characteristics:

1 A single seller and many consumers

2 Complete control of the market supply and price by the single seller

3 The seller motivated solely by his own profit margin

Competition today   The American economic scene, as has been pointed out, fulfills neither the conditions of pure competition nor those of perfect monopoly. For many products there are large numbers of producers and consumers; for others there are only a few producers and many consumers. There are only a few producers of automobiles, for example. But do we automatically agree that more auto producers are needed? In fact, an increase in the number of these producers would not necessarily, as some people believe, result in increased competition and lower prices, for additional producers of automobiles might well lead to an increase in the price of machinery, materials, and labor skills used to manufacture them, and thus actually increase the price of automobiles. Further, the very large amount of capital needed for automobile manufacture might serve a better purpose if it were used to manufacture other items.

The point here is that competition is a relative term, and its significance depends on the specific situation under discussion. Few people would be concerned if only one company in the United States produced yachts over 100 feet long; but if one company controlled all the bakeries in the country, there would be cause for concern. Even when manufacturers and their suppliers seek an advantage by combining their resources, this does not necessarily cause harm; it may prove efficient and therefore useful. Federal and state government agencies maintain a close watch over this type of association to prevent any harm to the public interest.

In any case, we cannot take it for granted that a monopoly is invariably harmful. There are various monopolies in our economic system that are sanctioned by law. Sometimes it is more efficient, or safer, to place the responsibility for the supplying of power or public transportation within a city on one particular company. Such monopolies are closely controlled by government agencies.

A further point closely related to this discussion is the question that frequently arises in connection with the size of business enterprise. Business firms are often called "monopolies" when they appear to grow too rapidly or become too large. In fact, this whole problem area has been investigated by several government groups, which have come up with no satisfactory solution. The simple condition of being large certainly does not constitute monopoly status, nor does it necessarily mean that a firm engages in poor business or labor practices. In fact, just the opposite is the case. The idea that great size means monopoly is a carry-over from the days when people rather naïvely believed that being small was "good" and being large was necessarily "bad." There is no reason to take this position for granted, and certainly no good evidence to support it.

Some criteria for competitiveness It seems desirable, when discussing the state of competition in an economic system, to avoid the indiscriminate application of terms like "pure competition" or "monopoly" to businesses or groups of businesses. A much better approach to the problem is to lay down criteria for measuring the state of competition in a given area and then to use these criteria in evaluating the position of a particular firm or groups of firms. Some of the measurements that might usefully be made for this purpose are:

1 The adequacy of the number of buyers and sellers.

2 A freedom and intelligence of choice on the part of both buyers and sellers. Buyers need to know the value they are receiving for the money spent.

3 The extent to which others are free to enter a business.

4 The efficiency with which resources are being used.

5 The benefit derived by the community under existing conditions.

Using these standards, it is possible to make a reasonable assessment of the extent of competitiveness in a given area of the economy and to decide whether or not it is adequate. Realistically, an adequate number of producers of automobiles is small; an adequate number of retail stores is fairly large. In the same way, a limit on the freedom of entry into specific businesses may produce optimum use of resources and thus contribute substantially to the well-being of the community. Such a situation would be very satisfactory, even though the amount of competition in the area might be severely limited.

The effects of competition Probably the most important single effect of competition is the change it induces. In a competitive system, forces are constantly at work to undermine the success of a particular product or business method, or even of particular worker skills, that can be marketed at a profit. Machines, methods, and tools considered the peak of efficiency only a few years ago are now on the verge of obsolescence because of new systems. Thousands of workers find that hard-earned skills can now be replaced by machinery that performs human tasks with superhuman efficiency. In the short run, this may cause hardship in particular cases; in the long run, it is the price we must pay for economic progress.

Another significant effect of competition is the production of new materials or products that make older products obsolete. We can see this effect very readily in the cork industry. For generations cork was used for bottle stoppers, fishing floats, bottle-cap seals, and other products in very large amounts. Today, cork is being nudged toward oblivion by a fast-growing brigade of man-made substitutes and new products which have replaced cork in many of its uses. The Armstrong Cork Company, which once dealt entirely in cork products, has reduced its sales in cork materials to a very small percentage of its gross sales. This fact illustrates two points: first, the extent to which a particular material can be replaced by other better materials, and second, that a well-managed company can keep abreast of changes by altering its own activities.

Other changes in goods and services come about as a result of the efforts that business people make to attract more buyers for their products. Product design and specifications change constantly as the public taste changes. Introducing such modifications is actually a very risky process, for too much change can produce customer resistance, while too little change can turn the consumer to another product. One of the most perplexing problems the business person must face is that of determining the extent to which he must change his product to attract the buying public.

The gains from competition Although competition makes American business more risky than it might be under noncompetitive conditions, it also produces benefits, particularly for the consumer. First of all, competition tends to produce better merchandise. Successful business operation depends on the ability to compete; the ability to compete depends largely on the quality of the product. As a result there is a steady trend toward product improvement in nearly every business. Automobiles, television sets, banking facilities, transportation systems, etc., have improved markedly over the years. Competition thus produces both a wider variety of goods and goods of better quality within each variety.

A second major benefit to the consumer resulting from competition is lower prices. The demand for most products is greatly increased when prices are lowered. Business people therefore strive constantly to bring prices down, usually by increasing efficiency and reducing costs. This has the effect of eliminating the inefficient business—those which cannot compete successfully. But the chief result is a better product at a lower price. For example, the first ball-point pen sold for approximately $10; it gave the older fountain pen little or no competition. But as more firms began producing ball-point pens, the product improved rapidly and the price fell very low indeed. Today's 10-cent ball-point is of better quality than many $10 ball-points of years ago.

THE STATE OF THE PRODUCTION SYSTEM

A second feature of the economic environment in which business operates is what may be termed loosely the state of the production system. Production means the creation of goods and services; it involves the organization of business facilities for that purpose. The amount of production that comes out of an economic system depends first on the availability of the factors of production (men, materials, equipment) and second on the efficiency with which these factors are used. By examining these conditions we develop a very useful index to the level of efficiency, or state of production, of an economic system.

The factors of production

The production of goods and services requires the use of materials, labor, and production facilities or capital; these three elements are known as the factors of production. Each factor contributes to the final form of the goods or service produced; each factor represents a cost of production.

The business person must attempt to weigh the relative cost of each factor of production when deciding what to produce and how much to produce. Much depends on the balance and effectiveness of the production process. High cost factors need not necessarily lead to high production costs. An expensive machine that turns out a large volume of material may cost less per unit of production than would a cheaper machine that produces less. Likewise, the cost of machines will depend on the cost of labor; if labor costs are high, the businessman may prefer to use machines that he would not use if labor costs were lower. In general, the businessman attempts to calculate the cost of each production factor, weigh the costs one against the other, and decide which mixture of the three factors will produce most efficiently and cheaply.

The cost factor invariably influences the businessman more than any other single consideration involved in his decisions. The small business with limited funds must produce, sell, and collect payment in a fairly short period of time. Needless to say, the selling price must at least cover all production costs if the business is to continue. The larger firm with a secure financial position may be able to consider the long-run implications of the cost-price relationship; that is, it may be willing to operate at a loss for a short term in the hope of long-run gains. But both large and small businesses must, in the end, reach a workable balance between costs and prices if they are to continue operation.

Prices

In business activity, a price can be placed on nearly every item or process involved. As consumers, we are all familiar with retail prices of goods. But we can also consider wages as the price of labor that the employer must pay. We can view interest earned on savings as the price paid for borrowing those savings. The landlord collects moneys which are the price of using his facilities for a given period of time. Price is a basic conception in our economic environment; the relationship between all prices in fact determines what each individual will be able to purchase as his share of the available goods and services.

Factors influencing prices If a single business firm or group of firms could control the price received for its goods, its profits would be greatly increased. Since business seeks profits, it would seem likely that all business people would try to control both the prices they pay and the prices they receive for their goods. To some degree they are able to do so. But the factors that actually determine the prices of goods and services are far more complex than the desires of a single firm or group of firms.

The extent to which a business can influence prices depends largely on its size and the amount of competition it encounters. A small firm operating alone in a competitive environment has little influence over price; much the same thing is true of a large firm that has substantial competition. Only in a very large organization or organized group of firms, operating without competition, does price control become a serious possibility. That is one reason why the government attempts to restrict monopolies in our economic system.

The two other factors that affect the price we pay are the activities of the government and trade union influence. Government can control prices in many ways. First, it can control the prices of goods and services directly as it does with prices charged by public utilities or public transportation companies. Government policy may also affect overall prices somewhat less directly; federal agricultural policies, for example, alter the price structure for farm products. Since the government controls the extension of credit—through the Federal Reserve System—this too can be used to influence the price structure of every phase of the economy. Nor should we forget the wage-price guidelines that the federal government suggests in labor-management negotiations, and the outright negating of price increases that has happened in the steel, automobile, and tobacco industries. Finally, government expenditures have a great effect on prices. Government stockpiling of strategic material, for example, can force the price of these items up if they are in short supply. Conversely, if the government sells materials from its stockpile, thereby adding to the supply of materials on the market, it can force the market price down. Even the threat of purchase or sale by the government may influence the market price of materials.

The prices that business people must pay for labor are greatly influenced by the actions of the labor unions. In most large industries wage rates are negotiated between the union and the employer, and these rates have risen steadily under union pressure. Since the higher cost of wages can be expected to be passed on to the consumer in the form of price increases, the effect of wage increases is felt by every individual of the buying public. Of course, the consumer has some effect on prices, at least in the sense that when prices reach a given level he will refuse to buy any more goods, but his influence is much less significant than the influence of the business person, the government, and the labor union.

Price stability   The movement of prices within the economy is of great importance to everyone. It makes a great deal of difference to the consumer whether prices are falling, rising, or holding steady. In a period when prices are rising, the amount that $1 will buy decreases; we say that the dollar is "worth less." Anyone who has debts outstanding will prefer to repay them with this "cheaper" dollar, for each dollar repaid will buy less than the dollar borrowed originally. Rising prices, then, are most favorable to the debtor.

For the same reason, a period of falling prices favors the creditor, since he will be repaid in dollars that will buy more than the dollars he originally lent. For the business person, the ideal situation would be to pay falling prices for the materials he uses and receive rising prices for his products. But that happy situation seldom, if ever, arises.

In general, the most favorable price level is one that is stable, or perhaps rising very slightly. In view of the dynamic nature of the economic system, price stability is seldom achieved for any length of time. Each group that can influence prices seeks to do so to its own advantage, and the result is almost always an endless fluctuation in price levels.

Real income   Obviously, the price of goods determines the real value of our personal income. Rising prices make a given income worth less in terms of what it will buy. This relation between prices and income is measured in terms of real income—the amount of goods a dollar will buy at a given time. If prices remain low and income increases, then real income increases. The relation between price changes and income changes determines the purchasing power of the dollar.

Technological progress

The application of scientific principles to industrial problems is known as technology; the improvement in machines, methods, materials, managements, etc., that results from this is called technological progress. In the past century, this progress has become one of the most important forces in the business world; it has played a vital role in the development of the American economy. The making of technological advances depends on a solid foundation of population expansion, resources, educational facilities, and encouragement of the inventiveness of the individual. It is not an accident that the United States, where individual initiative and enterprise are encouraged perhaps more than anywhere else on earth, is also the center of world technological advancement. A note of caution is in order at this point. We know, for example, that there are advocates for zero population growth and that a significant reduction in America's birth rate is a reality. We know, too, that the existing supply of natural resources is gradually running out. This means that sustained technological progress must rely more heavily on factors other than population expansion and natural resources.

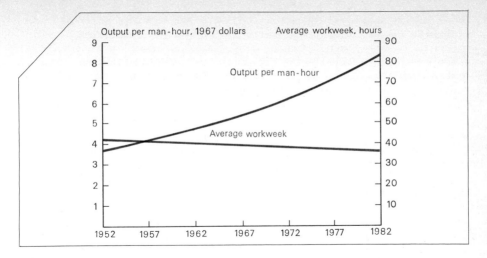

FIGURE 2-3 Benefits of technology

As productivity, the output of goods and services per man-hour, increases, the average hours worked per week decline.
Source: McGraw-Hill Publications Economics Department.

Benefits of technology For most people the prime benefit of technological progress is the vast increase in goods and services it makes available to society. Technology multiplies the output of a single worker. It leads to vastly increased efficiency of production. It acts to reduce real prices and results in a higher standard of living. It reduces the amount of prolonged and dangerous manual labor involved in business activity. At the General Motors plant that produces the Vega automobile countless jobs requiring manual labor on the conventional assembly line are now performed by intricate machines. The time may not be far off when most assembly operations will be done by machine. Indirectly, technology has led to a reduction in working hours (see Figure 2-3), to higher wages, and to much more leisure time for workers. We need only compare the United States of today with the United States of 50 years ago to realize the enormous changes due to technological progress.

Problems of technological progress Although technological progress is beneficial to society as a whole, it does produce its own characteristic problems. The gigantic production unit offers the business person a means to achieve reduced costs, increased output, and a better competitive position in the market. But it requires at the same time a very large investment in capital goods, increasing the risks involved in obsolescence. Further, the reduction of prices brought about by technological advances produces a new price-competition situation among the producers in a particular market that can seriously alter the balance of one or more segments of the economy. Finally, technological change has altered the relationship between worker and employer, producing human relations problems of considerable magnitude, particularly in large-scale industries.

Effects of technological advance Perhaps the most striking effect of technological progress is the completely new products, and the new markets, that it produces. When we stop to think of the products on sale today that have resulted from technological advance—particularly in industries such as electronics and plastics—we begin to see the implications of technology for human society. People today are buying goods that did not exist only a few short years ago; many of these new products replaced existing items, but others are completely new. The condition is more striking in terms of consumer goods, but the businessman too, finds the list of products he can use for his business purposes growing longer each year through technological advance. It would be foolish to try to list some of these "new" products because by the time you read this, they would be considered old.

A second characteristic of the modern American economic system that is at least indirectly due to technological change is the growing integration of production facilities. Large-scale production demands immense supplies of raw materials flowing at a steady rate and a mass market to absorb volume production. This has forced many companies to establish backward-integration subsidiaries that can supply their raw materials, or forward-integration subsidiaries that can market the output of the production system. The effect of integration is an assured source of supply or an assured outlet for goods, either of which can give the firm a competitive advantage.

Capital investment and technology Technological advance cannot be separated from the rapid growth of capital equipment in American industry. New inventions and discoveries are quite useless if the funds are not available to put them to work. In America today there is more than $20,000 invested in plant and facilities for every person employed in manufacturing. The ratio of equipment cost to worker has been increasing steadily.

As shown in Figure 2-4, an expanded and modernized plant and equipment increase manufacturing capacity, thereby providing a source of further capital for still greater expansion. Technological improvement, though costly, may generate more output and higher income and thus pave the way for greater savings and still greater investments. The effect is like that of a snowball rolling down a hillside: once the ball starts rolling, it increases in size very rapidly.

THE INTERNATIONAL BUSINESS ENVIRONMENT

Discussions about the environment in which business now operates and speculation about its future environment are commonplace. It is well understood that the businessman's actions are influenced by his environment and, conversely, that his actions help shape this environment. However, the environmental framework within which these

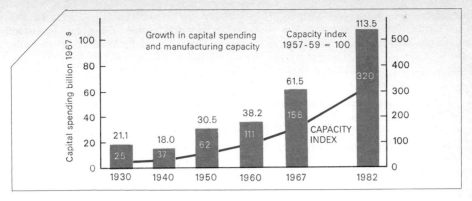

FIGURE 2–4 Capital spending and manufacturing capacity

Capital expenditures by business expansion and modernization of plant and equipment generate more output and higher income.
Source: McGraw-Hill Publications Economics Department.

interactions take place has taken on a new dimension. It is becoming more and more evident that the international aspect of the business environment and the need for all business people to relate their particular operations to this broader dimension will be of prime concern to the business manager of the future.

The day of the multinational corporation is already here. That American business people will look more and more to foreign sources for the raw materials and component parts needed for production and to foreign markets as outlets for their goods is a foregone conclusion. It is clear that the task that will confront the managers of tomorrow will require an understanding of different peoples and their cultures, philosophies, and politics. Today's typical American firm will probably develop a new face in the form of international characteristics which will enable it to take full advantage of foreign opportunities. The expectation is that in the coming decades the most rapidly expanding markets for both buyers and sellers will be found abroad.

The implications of this increasing internationalizing of business activities will be felt in several areas. Chief among them are the areas of new government regulation, changes in the nature of competition, and problems involved in training the business managers who will operate in foreign countries. With respect to government regulation, the questions of tariffs and subsidies, import and export quota systems, and other devices originally intended to minimize the unwanted effects of foreign competition will have to be reexamined. The very nature of competition as we understand it, based on the concept of free enterprise, will no doubt undergo changes to include new approaches to pricing, profits, production, and distribution. Many of our economic concepts are applied differently or not at all in most foreign countries. The manager of the internationally oriented enterprise will likewise need to change—more so if he is actually located in a foreign

country. He will probably have preparation in international economics and business operations, a concern for business on a global basis,
greater consciousness of social responsibility, and a more active role
in government relations; and he must possess an ability to keep up
with and utilize technological developments as they occur both at
home and abroad.

There is no doubt that our attitudes toward the external environment of business are changing. We are accustomed to measuring the
achievement of the business firm solely in terms of the profits which
it earns. The changing environment will certainly bring other considerations into the evaluation of business performance.

SUMMARY

The current business environment is hardly comparable to that of the
nineteenth century, and presumably our current business environment will be considered outdated in a few decades. The principal
change up to this point has been a gradual modification of the profit
conception, which, although it remains as the fundamental incentive
for economic activity, has been altered and limited substantially by
the influence of the business environment. The ever-widening
framework of legislation, the increased significance of the employee
and his organization, the growing influence of public opinion, and
the effects of business activity on the whole society have brought new
dimensions into business. These features have made business more
complex and specialized. Large-scale industry in particular has so
altered its fundamental conceptions that it is very unlikely that a
businessman of the nineteenth century could operate successfully in
today's environment. Likewise, it is unlikely that today's typical
businessman would have the capacity to successfully operate an
enterprise in tomorrow's environment, with its demands for a breadth
of knowledge and activity which is unappreciated by the businessman
whose sole concern has been local or national business activity. The
need for business people trained in international matters is already
apparent. An attitude of business statesmanship will have to be
brought to bear on matters of policy and decision which arise in
connection with business carried on in a global environment.

BUSINESS ITEMS

Supreme Court: Too much business hurts business

Increasingly, the U.S. Supreme Court is accused of declining to hear
cases that involve substantial questions of law in the business

community. One cause of this seems to be the ever-increasing backlog of cases submitted to the High Court for review. During the past two decades, the Supreme Court's case load has risen 300 percent, and in the face of this steadily increasing workload, the court is accepting an ever-decreasing proportion of appeals, leaving unsettled a great number of legal issues important to business. Because the High Court has been too busy to settle controversies, Federal Appeals Courts in different geographic areas have rendered contradictory decisions on identical matters of law.

Some suggestions have been made to streamline the process of handling cases. One proposal is that Congress establish a seven-judge National Court of Appeals to screen cases now being appealed to the Supreme Court and to cull out the vast bulk not worthy of review. Another proposal which would have a more direct impact on business is the creation of a national panel of judges who would hear a variety of specialized cases now heard on appeal in the eleven Circuit Courts of Appeals. Precedence for such a specialized court already exists in the U.S. Court of Customs and Patent Appeals which is assumed to have such expertise in the matters brought to its attention that the Supreme Court virtually never chooses to review its decisions.

As a start in establishing specialized courts, it has been suggested that tax and labor cases be handled in this manner. This would certainly be a start in the process of clearing the backlog of cases as well as applying the concept of specialization to federal court organization.

Businesses depend on each other

The motoring public and the automobile manufacturers were not the only segments of the population to be faced with new problems or opportunities as a result of the energy crisis in the United States and in particular the gasoline shortage.

The prime source of income for many companies has been from equipment sales to gasoline stations. As the gas supply became scarce, business with the stations all but dried up.

The 1960s were the highest point for the construction of new gas stations. By 1972 the number of new stations per year had declined from a high of 6,500 to 2,500. In 1973, only 950 stations were built. How many were shut down is another aspect of the problem.

In any event, those companies which sold gas pumps, auto lifts, and automatic car washers all faced severe business declines. Some of these declines appeared overnight, as in the case of car-wash equipment. The oil companies suddenly developed the attitude that they no longer needed to offer a free car wash to stimulate gasoline sales.

About the only major gas station equipment suppliers who were not bleeding from their wounds were the makers of gas storage tanks. Their loss of sales to gas stations was more than made up for by their sales to private customers and business firms.

Some business people want more laws

It is not often that business expresses interest in the enactment of more legislation but a recent survey showed that in some areas there is a strong indication that business people would welcome specific legislation. When the question "What single law would you like to see Congress enact?" was asked, American executives gave top priority to reforming labor laws, which they feel are badly out of balance in favor of the unions. The second most popular choice was legislation to set tight controls on federal spending. Many other suggestions for legislation dealt with specific problems in specific industries, ranging from minimum wage impact to a realistic welfare bill which would provide jobs instead of handouts.

A relatively small group of the business people surveyed declared that the country already had too many laws and that Congress should be thinking of getting rid of some.

QUESTIONS

1 What are some of the basic features which make up a business environment?

2 What is law? What are the sources of law in the United States?

3 With which area of law is the business person most concerned? Why?

4 Distinguish between civil law and criminal law. How do the penalties differ between them?

5 Explain the relationships between the state and federal governments in the control and regulation of business.

6 Identify and briefly describe the importance of the following (check library sources if necessary): (*a*) FTC, (*b*) NLRB, (*c*) SEC, (*d*) Sherman Antitrust Act.

7 Describe the basic structure of a court system and indicate how this basic structure is exemplified in the federal court system and in the court system of the state where you now live.

8 Why must competition be considered a relative rather than an absolute term? Is there any way in which competition can be measured? Explain.

9 What is technology? What is technological progress? How, if at all, is productivity related to technological progress?

10 Under what circumstances could a business person have a free hand in establishing prices? Is this idea of freedom in setting prices in any way consistent with the concept of competition? If so, how?

11 Is it realistic to conclude that small business is as much taken up with the idea of its social responsibility as is big business? Why?

12 What, if any, evidence exists to indicate that management is worthy of being labeled a profession?

13 What new dimensions dictate the framework of business environment once the scope of activity becomes international or global in character? Why should this new environment have influence, if any, on the qualifications required for successful business management?

14 What factors must be overcome if we are to sustain technological progress?

The purpose of this chapter   Because business has been such a dependable provider of goods and services, we often view it as matter-of-fact, and we seldom bother to consider what goes on behind the scenes. A commonplace occurrence such as the filling of an automobile gasoline tank really involves a business organization of staggering complexity. There must be close cooperation among a number of industries—mining, transportation, refining, retailing, etc.—to move crude petroleum from the ground into the automobile as gasoline. Each operation produces business problems of a different nature from the others, and each industry contributes in its own way to the overall activity of the economy. In this chapter we shall examine the major sectors of the economy, learn some of their problems, and observe the manner in which they work together to keep goods and services flowing throughout the country. / Questions raised in this chapter include:

1 What does industry produce?

2 What are the current trends in industry as regards production and employment?

3 How do changes in industry affect employment?

4 What are the implications of specialization, mass production, and automation?

5 What are the service industries and what is their importance?

THE SCOPE OF BUSINESS

The basic purpose of American business is to produce goods and to provide services to be sold at a profit. If successful in doing this, the owners get the profits which are necessary to make ownership worthwhile and to provide the basis for business growth, and the customers get their satisfaction from using the products of business. What products and services does business provide? We have only to look down the aisles of a large retail store or thumb through the yellow pages to get a partial view of the great variety and immense volume of goods which are available. In addition to this evidence of the complexity of output, there is also the tremendous volume of products and services which business produces for the use of other business firms. We do not ordinarily have any reason to think about these products, but if we are to take a close look at the scope of business, we cannot overlook any of its dimensions. Just as the environment of business is subject to change, so too is the scope of business subject to change. It widens every year as new businesses are established and old businesses expand their operations.

Obviously no one could effectively study the great mass of facts about American business without first organizing them into meaningful patterns. That is, we need a way to classify businesses and group them together that will make possible a useful comparison of one with the other. There are various ways of approaching this problem. We may divide businesses according to size, or number of employees, or type of goods produced, or volume of goods produced. From another point of view businesses can be classified according to the type of equipment they require or the type of organization they employ. Each of these approaches to the study of business provides us with different kinds of information, and some are more useful than others when we attempt to describe a particular business.

BASIC BUSINESS FUNCTIONS

The basic ingredients of any business are materials, men, and machines—the factors of production. But the proportion of each factor required for a particular business depends on the product or service and how it is produced. An automobile factory needs large amounts

55

of machinery; a taxi driver needs only a single machine. The exact needs of any business organization are determined by the purpose of the business. We can begin our analysis, then, by defining the major purposes of American business—the basic functions they perform. Every business performs at least one of four major tasks:

1 Providing the raw materials from which goods are fashioned.

2 Converting raw materials into finished products.

3 Marketing—or distribution—which involves getting products into the hands of the consumer. The consumer may be you or it may be another business.

4 Providing services, including not only personal services but also those that are necessary in business activity, such as banking, advertising, insurance, communications, and research.

The tasks mentioned above define the four major categories of business enterprise. Some businesses encompass more than one of these categories while others are limited to one. But in each case, the need for men, materials, and machinery is different and can only be determined by observing the actual work performed by the business.

CLASSIFYING BUSINESS

There is no single classification that will tell us all we should know about the different types of businesses operating in this country. But our purpose in discussing the scope of business is to add a number of dimensions to the reader's understanding of business so as to make future topics more meaningful. Because the object of all business activity is the satisfaction of human wants, one useful breakdown of business is by the type of customer served by the firm and the general type of goods that it handles.

Type of customer

There are businesses whose only customers are other business firms. Freight carriers and production-machinery manufacturers fall into this category. Then there are businesses which produce goods to be purchased by you and me, the ultimate consumers. These two kinds of customers, however, may be purchasers of the same goods. Both buy the same makes of automobiles and use the same telephone service, and the electric drill used in the home workshop may be identical to the drill used in a Westinghouse maintenance shop. Nor will a business necessarily limit its market to a single type of customer. Steel mills and wholesalers generally do have such a limitation, but for other businesses, including Westinghouse, General Motors, and General Electric, it is advantageous to have both types of customers. However, when a firm caters to both types of customers, it is wise to realize that the firm is actually engaged in two types of business that are quite different. The marketing strategy that could lead to a high level of response by the ultimate consumer might be completely inadequate to reach business customers. The prime reason for this is that although "need" and "best buy" are purchasing criteria for each type of customer, the meaning that each attaches to these criteria is quite different. Business customers can be, and generally are, much more objective. Business buyers are trained to be objective; to match purchases to the specific needs of the firm; to ascertain that maximum value will result from expenditures. Business purchases often must stand the test of yielding a predetermined return on investment.

Business buyers do not always use these criteria for purchasing nor are all consumers wasteful when they buy. The record shows, however, that the great bulk of consumers interchange the terms "want" and "need" and do not know enough about the marketplace to ascertain that they have made the best buy. In the business-goods market, far greater emphasis is placed on function than appeal, for in theory at least, the purpose of every purchase is to facilitate, directly or indirectly, the production of goods and services. In fairness, we need to remember that the same people who make purchases for business also walk up and down the aisles of the supermarket.

Types of goods

We can also distinguish between businesses by the types of goods they handle. Some firms are involved primarily with goods classified as durable in nature—that is, they have a relatively long life expectancy—such as machines, appliances, and many forms of clothing. Other firms handle goods that are consumed in a relatively short period, such as food, cigarettes, and paper products, called nondurable goods. This classification is not clear-cut because there is no specific line of demarcation between long and short life. A pair of shoes may last one person 6 years and another only a month. However, this classification is useful because it helps to delineate the general problems that must be faced.

General Motors, General Electric, and Ford, and in fact most of our largest industrial organizations except petroleum, are concerned mainly with durable goods. General Foods and National Dairy are primarily concerned with nondurable goods because their products are consumed in a short period of time.

This distinction is quite useful because each type of good presents a different array of problems. The customer who buys bread on Monday will quite likely buy bread again on Tuesday or Wednesday. She may not buy the same brand again, and she may buy from a different retailer, but the fact remains that she is a bread customer and some bakery will make a sale. Businesses in the nondurable-goods field have frequent opportunities to serve their customers. Chrysler, on the other hand, knows that after a customer has made a purchase it will be a long time before that customer is back in the market for another car.

The demand for some goods can be deferred for extended periods of time. Many people normally buy a new car every 2 or 3 years as a matter of choice, not necessity. Such customers may change their minds and postpone buying a new car until it is 5 years old. Consequently, durable-goods producers not only have to convince people to buy their brand but they must convince people that they need a new car, refrigerator, and so forth. We see this every day in the attempts by business to make us believe that the durable goods we own should be replaced.

Every business is deeply concerned about consumer acceptance of its products, for without acceptance the products will not sell in sufficient volume to yield a profit. As a rule, obtaining consumer acceptance is more difficult in the durable-goods field, often because large amounts of money are involved in each purchase. Penetrating the market for home appliances, automobiles, and the like is nearly an insurmountable task for new businesses. Kaiser failed in his attempt to enter the automobile market in the 1950s and Raytheon, noted for excellence in electronics, failed in its bid to enter the television and appliance field. For many nondurables, including food and clothing items, brand recognition is virtually nonexistent. Thus it is often much easier to enter a business involving nondurable goods.

Other business classifications

Once these fundamental classifications have been made, it is possible to undertake a more detailed examination of the operation of business within each classification. In each industry group we can look at the total number of employees, the number of firms involved, the volume of business of the different industries, the dollar amount of each payroll, the state of technology, the amount of capital investment, the value of the industry's products, and so on. Each of these measurements can be made quite accurately, and each tells us something significant about the industry being studied.

INDUSTRY CHARACTERISTICS

We are now in a position to begin a more detailed consideration of the characteristics of various American industries. How many people do they employ? How much income do they create? To what extent have they become specialized? Are they engaged in mass production? To what extent do they make use of automation?

The answers to these and similar questions provide us with very significant information about the state of American business. We cannot, of course, expect to make a complete survey of the whole

TABLE 3-1 Employment by industry division: 1960, 1964, 1969, and 1971 (in millions of persons)

Industry division	1960	1964	1969	1971	Percentage of change 1960–1971
Mining	0.7	0.6	0.6	0.6	−14
Contract construction	3.0	3.1	3.1	3.3	+10
Manufacturing	16.4	17.3	20.0	18.6	+14
Wholesale and retail trade	11.6	12.2	14.2	15.2	+31
Finance, insurance, and real estate	2.5	2.9	3.5	3.8	+56
Transportation and public utilities	3.9	4.0	4.4	4.5	+15
Services	6.7	8.5	10.7	11.9	+78
Total (nonagricultural)	44.8	47.6	56.5	70.7	+58
Government	8.4	9.5	12.8	12.9	+53
Agriculture	5.7	5.0	3.8	3.3	−42

Source: *Statistical Abstracts.*

economic system in an introductory text, but we can consider some of the fundamental characteristics of industry.

Employment in industry

Table 3-1 shows the number of employees in nonagricultural establishments from 1960 to 1971 and also the percentage growth in employment in each industry during those years. It is interesting to observe the amount of information a simple table of this sort can supply.

As might be expected, the manufacturing division employs a greater number of workers than any other single industry division. This figure is somewhat misleading because prior to the 1950s, manufacturing employed more workers than all other divisions combined. The wholesale and retail trade group employs the next largest number of workers. But we can also see from the information in Table 3-1 that the number of manufacturing workers has not grown nearly so rapidly as several other groups. Manufacturing employment increased about 14 percent from 1960 to 1971, whereas wholesale and retail trade employment grew by 31 percent, and the finance, insurance, and real estate group of the services group grew in total employment by about 56 percent. Of course, government employment, which includes federal, state, and local governments, increased by 53 percent during the same period. Why have some divisions grown so much while others have actually lost ground in terms of numbers of employees? Why is it that mining and manufacturing show small or negative employment trends?

We suspect that the role which machinery and automation play in effecting change in industry is involved in the answer to these questions. In addition, we expect that increased efficiency in the use of manpower may help account for some changes, and increased demand for personal services may account for others. In any event there is no single factor which will account for employment changes. Nor is a change in employment itself any indication of the importance of the area in which change takes place. Manufacturing will always be an important industry regardless of the number of people it employs.

For a more specific insight into employment changes, detailed statistics are available from government sources which spell out the employment data for the various industries included in the durable and nondurable goods categories. These data will allow you to determine whether an increase in durable-goods industry employment is a reflection of expansion in machinery, electrical equipment, motor vehicles and equipment, or any of the several other industries which are in the durable category.

Some factors to consider

No single factor can explain all the changes that have occurred in the American labor force in recent years, but there are certain important characteristics and trends that do help to explain the available facts. For example, there has been a substantial increase in the number of employees who are not directly engaged in the production of goods and services. This is true, generally, for all industries whether they are engaged in manufacturing, construction, wholesale and retail trade, or some other field. The extent of this trend in the manufacturing industry is shown in Figure 3-1.

What types of jobs do these nonproduction workers fill in industry? In general, they occupy supervisory or staff positions. Their function, in many cases, is to provide the businessman with the information necessary to conduct his affairs. Others are involved with processing

	Production workers (millions of workers)	Nonproduction workers (millions of workers)
1958	12.0	3.8
1960	12.4	4.4
1962	12.2	4.6
1964	12.8	5.5
1966	14.2	5.2
1968	14.5	5.4
1970	14.0	5.3
1971	13.5	5.1

FIGURE 3-1 Production and nonproduction workers in manufacturing

For a number of years nonproduction workers increased faster than production workers in manufacturing. Now there is a gradual decline which has not reduced productivity at all.
Source: *Statistical Abstracts.*

	1960	1965	1969	1970
Footwear	98	101	97	97
Hosiery	59	80	108	117
Bottled soft drinks	75	94	117	125
Gas and electric utilities	64	89	115	119
Agriculture	70	89	112	123
Manufacturing	81	99	106	108

FIGURE 3–2 Productivity trends by industries. Output per man hour, 1967 = 100

The main reason footwear is a depressed industry is that there has been no productivity gain in 10 years.
Source: *Statistical Abstracts.*

paper work or may handle production planning, research, location and design of facilities, pricing, personnel, public relations, data processing, or other functions which contribute indirectly to the production of goods.

Productivity

A second major change which has taken place in recent years, and which has had significant effect on the composition of the American work force, has been the enormous increase in productivity—in the quantity of goods that are produced for each hour of labor applied to raw materials.[1] This has been due chiefly to the increased use of machinery, to the use of scientific production methods that are more efficient, and to the enormous advances made in technology. Increased productivity enables industry to produce more goods while using less labor, and at the same time it has made labor less arduous and tiring for the worker. The implications of this trend—shorter workweek, higher real wages, higher standard of living, a lighter work burden—need to be examined very carefully (see Figure 3-2).

The number of business firms

Table 3-2 shows the number of firms doing business in the United States. Such statistics are not completely accurate because there may be no record that certain unincorporated businesses exist. However, from 1959 to 1969 the number of businesses increased from about 9.9 million to 12 million, or by 20 percent. The greatest rate of growth was in the broad category called services, which recorded an increase of 129 percent. The increase of the number of firms in each category does not tell the entire growth story because of the merging of one or more establishments into a single business and the trend toward

[1]In 1972, General Motors' sales increased $2 billion over 1971. The average number of employees was 13,000 less in 1972.

TABLE 3-2 Number of firms in operation: 1959, 1962, 1966, and 1969 (in thousands)

Industry division	1959	1962	1966	1969
Mining	60	64	71	84
Contract construction	779	836	858	903
Manufacturing	391	407	405	405
Wholesaling	429	492	461	473
Retailing	2,023	1,981	2,011	2,191
Transportation, communication, and public utilities	345	354	371	367
Finance, insurance, and real estate	951	1,061	1,248	1,258
Services	1,250	2,450	2,645	2,868
Other	3,663	3,600	3,326	3,472
Total	9,891	11,245	11,396	12,021

Source: *Statistical Abstracts.*

larger-scale operations by individual firms. We need to consider also that these are net figures and do not reflect the thousands of firms that go out of business each year.

Business survival

For anyone interested in beginning a new business, the question of survival is very important. Is it true, for example, that in business as in marriage, the first few years are the hardest? How many years does it take to get established in a particular business? Some of these questions can be answered in part by looking at Table 3-3, which shows the percentages of businesses in different categories that survive to a given age. According to the figures in the table, the first few years are definitely the hardest in all businesses, and within five

TABLE 3-3 Percentage of failures occurring at specified age of business (based on 1968 experience)

	Type of business					
Business age in years	Manu-facturing	Whole-sale	Retail	Construc-tion	Service	All concerns
Up to 3 years	27.6	23.4	38.3	20.4	28.7	30.8
Up to 5 years	49.6	46.1	61.3	43.4	54.5	53.9
Up to 10 years	68.2	70.7	82.4	72.9	80.4	77.2
Number of business failures	1,513	981	4,366	1,670	1,106	9,636

Source: Dun & Bradstreet, Inc.

TABLE 3-4   Why businesses fail

Underlying causes	Manufacturing, percent	Retailing, percent
Neglect	2.3	2.9
Fraud	1.9	1.4
Inexperience, incompetence:	93.6	91.5
Inadequate sales	50.7	51.2
Receivables difficulties	15.3	6.3
Inventory difficulties	6.4	9.5
Excessive fixed assets	7.1	3.9
Competitive weakness	15.8	23.3
Disaster	1.3	1.1
Reason unknown	0.9	3.1
Total	100.0	100.0

Because some failures are attributed to a number of causes, the total of the individual cause under "Inexperience, incompetence" will exceed the total given for that heading.

Source: Dun & Bradstreet, Inc.

years nearly 50 percent or more of the firms in each of the various categories fall by the wayside. The highest mortality, or conversely, the lowest survival rate, is in retail trade. This is perhaps the quickest and easiest business to enter because it does not always require a large supply of capital goods. The best opportunities for long business life seem to lie in manufacturing. Table 3-4 specifies some of the common obstacles to business longevity that business people in the various categories of firms must overcome.

There is a common belief that most businesses fail simply because they do not have enough money to continue. This is understandable because few firms in a strong financial position fall by the wayside and all firms that run out of cash do. Table 3-4 begins to put the finger on the basic cause of business failure—inexperience and incompetence. Too many businesses are ill-conceived and poorly operated. Financial problems generally result from too slow a flow of cash; that is, cash gets tied up in inventories, and the like. This in turn often results from a lack of marketing initiative and drive: the failure to get customers. The following illustrates these thoughts:

The author was approached by a young man and woman who wanted to go into business. They had read in a magazine that "big money" could be made in plastic engraving. Almost all organizations, large and small, business and otherwise, use all sorts of signs and desk plates that are plastic engravings. "Every organization is a potential customer." Furthermore, a 20-cent piece of plastic could be made into a name plate that sells for $3.95 in less than 20 minutes. And as the ad states, it would take only a matter of weeks for the $1,400 machine to pay for itself. After that, most of every sales dollar would be profit. Does this sound like a good deal? Against the author's advice, the young man and woman purchased the machine and their business was an instant flop. Why? They had absolutely no idea as to how customers are located and sold. With enough customers, any business can be successful; without them a business will fail.

Concentration in industry

The extent to which industrial production is concentrated in the hands of a few large firms is a matter that has been under careful scrutiny by the government for many years. The government keeps watch primarily for signs of monopolistic practices. There is no doubt that a tendency to concentration exists, though the degree of concentration is hard to demonstrate exactly. Figure 3-3 indicates the extent of concentration in several manufacturing industries where the degree of concentration is very high.

Even among the giant corporations of American industry the facts of their size and financial importance indicate tendencies toward concentration. In 1972, for example, the 500 largest corporations had sales of $558 billion and net profits of $27.8 billion. The ten largest firms had sales of $121.8 billion and net profits of $8.8 billion (about 31 percent of the total). These ten firms also accounted for 23.4 percent of the sales receipts of the combined 500 firms.

Percentage of industry shipments by four largest companies

Industry	Percent
Locomotives and parts	97
Flat glass	94
Steam engines and turbines	93
Electric lamps	92
Cathode ray picture tubes	91
Chewing gum	90
Cereal preparations	86
Cigarettes	80
Household laundry equipment	78
Typewriters	76

FIGURE 3–3 Concentration in selected manufacturing industries, 1969

Source: National Industrial Conference Board.

TABLE 3-5　National income by industrial origin
(in billions of dollars)

	1960	1965	1968	1971
Agriculture, forestry & fisheries	16.9	21.0	22.5	25.4
Mining and construction	26.5	35.2	42.8	51.8
Manufacturing	125.8	172.6	215.6	226.7
Transportation	18.2	23.2	28.0	32.2
Communication	8.2	11.2	14.3	17.4
Electric, gas, and sanitary service	8.9	11.4	14.0	15.8
Wholesale and retail trade	64.4	84.3	105.5	131.6
Finance, insurance, and real estate	45.9	61.9	77.3	94.5
Services	44.4	64.1	83.3	111.6
Government	52.9	75.2	104.5	137.5
Total	412.1	560.1	707.6	844.5

Source: *Statistical Abstracts*

Creation of income by industry

One of the best indexes of the value of an industry to society is the amount of national income created by firms in the industry. The *national income* is simply the aggregate earnings of every individual and every firm in the United States. This amount has no relation to the number of firms in an industrial sector, for a few large firms producing great volumes of goods may well contribute more to the national income than thousands of smaller firms. As a rule, manufacturing is by far the greatest contributor to the American national income; Table 3-5 shows that it accounts for about 30 percent of the total in most years.

From 1960 to 1971, manufacturing and trade (wholesale and retail) and contract construction increased their contribution to the national income by roughly 90 percent. The areas of finance, insurance, and real estate increased by more than 100 percent. Governments, the services, and communication increased their contribution by more than 150 percent.

CURRENT TRENDS IN INDUSTRY

In which direction are industries moving? Predictions of this sort are difficult to make, but it is possible to discern certain trends in the industrial system that seem significant for the future. In particular, the growth of specialization, the development of mass production, and the trend toward automation all seem likely to continue. These trends, and their consequences, are of great interest to students of business since they are likely to indicate the nature of the business environment in which today's students will someday find themselves.

Specialization

More and more, American industry is committed to the principle of specialization. A worker becomes a specialist in a specific production job; machines are specialized to perform a few functions very efficiently; whole factories are devoted to the production of single items. Specialization has the great advantage of producing high-quality, low-cost goods in large quantities.

The pressure for specialization has resulted chiefly from the desire of the business person to achieve the maximum production and the maximum efficiency. By standardizing products it is possible to standardize work procedures, machine functions, and material requirements, and to achieve great efficiency in production. A complex product is broken down into its separate parts, and for each part specialized production facilities are set up. Each is produced in the most efficient way, and subsequently all the various parts will be combined into complete units. This is the way in which automobiles are produced on the assembly line.

Specialization affects organization Specialization requires a completely different attitude toward the organization of production facilities than is needed in a nonspecialized system. A specialized production system is organized in a manner similar to a squad of ball players. Each member of the squad is trained to do his job as well as possible. The coach is then responsible for putting the squad together so that it operates as an effective team and plays a winning game. Each man on the squad is not expected to play every team position. If each member of the team does his job well, we expect victory. In industry, complex jobs are broken down into simpler tasks (division of labor). Simpler tasks can be performed more consistently and efficiently than complex tasks. Workers can be trained to do the single, simple task more easily and quickly than the complex job. Ideally, each person in the production process would have a single task to perform.

The tendency to assign persons to a single task is not restricted to the production-manufacturing aspect of business. Most companies divide their nonproduction work into departments—sales, finance, advertising, accounting, etc.—and train workers in the type of work carried out by their particular department. In large organizations, the work of major departments is again broken down into specialized tasks. The advertising department, for example, may have a section devoted to radio, another that deals with television, a third concerned with outdoor advertising, and a fourth that concentrates on newspapers. In general, both human beings and machines are being used for increasingly narrower purposes. The trend toward specialization has no effect on the machines, of course, but its effect on the worker, who may be forced to perform a single simple operation many thousands of times each day, often presents serious problems.

Mass production

Mass production is the term we use for a production system that manufactures very large quantities of a standard product. Light bulbs, for example, are mass-produced; in fact, all the light bulbs made in the United States are produced by fewer than a dozen machines. The principle of mass production is to make each unit of output like every other unit; the product must be standardized. If there has to be variation in the units produced, some, and possibly much, of the advantage of mass production can be lost.

A mass-produced water glass costs only pennies; a hand-blown, hand-engraved water glass may cost several dollars. There may be some small difference in the cost of materials used in these two products, but the significant difference is in the time and skill required for manufacture. Mass production, then, has its greatest effect on the cost of manufacturing, and its chief aim is to make the most efficient use of manpower and machinery.

Although large-scale industry is common in the United States, mass production is not nearly so widespread as is sometimes assumed. Industries such as shipbuilding and the manufacture of railroad equipment are certainly large scale, employing many men and using vast amounts of equipment, but they are not mass-production industries. In many instances the construction and airplane industries do not practice mass-production techniques. True mass-production systems are those engaged in turning out a large volume of an identical product, such as in the manufacture of cigarettes and automobiles.

The basis of mass production Before mass production is either possible or profitable, at least three preliminary conditions must be satisfied. First of all, there must be a very large market for the product, since mass production depends on maintaining a large output. A second condition that must be met is an advanced state of technology. Modern mass production depends on machines able to operate efficiently at very high speeds. Obviously, if the technology of the industry has not yet produced the necessary equipment, mass production is impossible. At the time of this writing, radial tires are produced by very costly, labor-oriented methods because we have not as yet developed the technology necessary to make them as efficiently as other types of tires. As a result, most radial tires are imported; they are very costly; and they are in limited supply.

Finally, mass production demands sound and very skilled organization and management. This is especially true in the areas of planning and coordinating. A typical automobile has as many as ten thousand parts and without any of these parts a car could not be completed. A prime problem is to assure that the right part is at the right place and at the right time. Since these component parts come from thousands of suppliers located here and abroad, it is easy to visualize the magnitude of the planning and control problem.

Automation

There is some confusion in the public mind between the concepts of mass production and automation. The industries that use mass production techniques are not necessarily automated, and conversely, it is possible to make use of automation without mass producing. Automation is a term used to describe a production system employing a minimum of human labor and a maximum of continuous self-regulating machinery. Usually, automation involves the following elements:

Automatic machinery

Integrated material-handling and processing equipment

Automatic control systems

Electronic computers and data processing equipment

In a fully automated factory, the phrase "untouched by human hands" would probably be true of the product. The materials would flow automatically into the production line and along to the next stage without outside direction; the production line would automatically control the quality and quantity of its output, and would stop if a malfunction occurred; and the finished product would be found, ready for market, at the end of the production line.

The concept of laborsaving machinery is not new, certainly, but the extent to which it is now possible to replace workers with modern equipment is much beyond anything seen in American factories as little as two decades ago. A tremendous output of goods can now be produced with only a handful of skilled workers to maintain and monitor the automatic equipment. Machines can be controlled by punched card or electronic systems. Data processing equipment can maintain inventories, make out invoices, and keep records at astounding speed, relieving the company of the need to keep whole batteries of clerks. In general, automation means the introduction of this concept of automatic machine-controlled production into a particular firm or industry.

Automation and management The concept of automation, even to this day, is accepted as a technical concept when in truth it is a management concept. The glamour of the computer and the automated process, with their high degree of technical sophistication, wooed and won over the business people into the mistake of believing that a machine could solve business problems. The attention which has been paid to the machine has in great part been misplaced, for the more significant concern should be with the managerial implications inherent in the utilization of the technology of automation. Computers are wonderful but experience shows that hundreds of millions of dollars have been wasted by firms that were not ready for a computer or who did not know how to utilize it properly. This concept should not be overlooked. The machine or technology is but one component of this system. Other components are people, organization, methods, and integrated system design, which has an overall impact. The reliance on technically oriented people to do the job called for in integrating these components is a misplaced assignment. The task is a managerial task. Automation is a critical area which calls for the greatest degree of managerial competency and involvement.

Automation and employment In recent years more publicity has been given to automation as a factor in unemployment than to any other of the several causes. There is no doubt that specific jobs can and will be eliminated by machinery, but it is not totally clear which jobs are lost to automation and which are lost because management is forced to retool in order to stay alive in the competitive market. Since 1950, a date which some mark as the beginning of the automation era, over 10 million job opportunities have been created, and since World War II the United States economy has experienced a growth which has doubled the gross national product (GNP) in real terms. The number of unemployed has risen during this same period, though much less than the gain in the size of the labor force. How much has automation contributed to this unemployment? This is a good question and despite the fact that much has been said in answer to it, nobody has yet been able to count the total number of jobs lost or gained because of automation.

In most cases, automation has produced new jobs that partly replace those eliminated, and it is generally true that its introduction has not resulted in serious dismissals in any one industry. An example of how automation has contributed both new products and new jobs is duPont's Teflon. When discovered 35 years ago, the family chemicals from which Teflon is descended were curious and marvelous specimens but relatively useless. After millions of dollars and many years invested in research, duPont learned how to manufacture and fabricate a useful product from these chemicals in large quantities and at reasonable prices. More than 1,000 new jobs have been created at duPont as a result, and many hundreds of additional jobs have been either created or sustained in other businesses which use the new chemical product. Technology was of prime importance in the development of this new chemical product, and the processes that were ultimately developed would have been impossible without a considerable use of automation.

On the other hand, automation will have certain long-range effects on the work force that cannot be ignored. For one thing it will make determination of the individual worker's contribution to production very difficult and will probably require a change in the basis for determining wages in systems where formerly the individual worker's output could be readily measured. With so much work being done automatically, experts believe that the concept of teamwork (people and machines) may replace that of individual work as the basis for wage payment.

The transition to automation Automation need not be considered an ogre, or a threat to the working person. Actually, the introduction of automation is often compared with the introduction of machinery at the beginning of the industrial revolution in the last century. The transition was quite painful for some workers, but the long-term effects were worthwhile.

Already automation has produced visible changes in manpower requirements in the factories and offices. There is little need for unskilled labor in manufacturing, but the demand for highly trained supervisory staff and mechanics and maintenance specialists is rising in proportion to the number of machine operators and assemblers. The record-keeping function of business calls less and less for people who can add and subtract and more and more for those who know how to program computers and operate data processing equipment. Production and office workers will almost certainly require more formal education than is now needed, particularly in technical matters. The college-trained foreman and supervisor should appear in large numbers as the supervisory tasks become increasingly complex.

American labor leaders, who are extremely conscious of the problem, have suggested a number of steps that might be taken to make the transition period less harsh. Specifically, they have suggested that the introduction of new machinery be controlled and that the worker affected be retained at the same salary level, but on a shorter working week, during the transition. The argument asserts that the additional profits from automation will justify the shorter workweek, and the cultural effects of the shorter workweek (if the worker uses his free time in cultural pursuits) will prove beneficial to the entire society in the long run.

To minimize the negative effects of automation, many employers have transferred workers to other jobs and made adjustments in their recruiting program to meet the changed labor requirements. Retraining programs have been started to assist the worker in developing new skills. Efforts to help displaced employees find new jobs, pensioning, and liberal separation pay are other devices which have been used by business to minimize or eliminate the effects of transition to automation.

Automation and tomorrow Despite the problems which may be inherent in automation, its progress must continue. The industrial countries of the world are fostering technological improvements as fast as their resources permit. In this day of increasing worldwide competition, the United States will be increasingly hard pressed to maintain technological leadership. Despite its upsetting consequences, such as eliminating some jobs and rendering certain skills obsolete, automation is contributing to the nation's well-being. New products emerge; new employment opportunities result; a rising standard of living; and the generation of strong expansion forces in our economy are some of the benefits to be reaped from the technological advance which our generation calls automation.

Greater opportunities will exist in some areas of employment than in others in the years ahead. Partly because of automation and mechanization, agriculture and mining will offer decreasing opportunities for employment. There will be both gains and losses in employment in manufacturing and transportation industries, depending on the individual firm and how successfully it responds to the problems of technology, competition, costs, and other factors. Great opportunities for future employment exist in some areas, including education, selling, construction, service industries, office workers, and recreation and travel.

The service industries

A segment of our economy that is growing in importance with each passing year includes those industries which are classed as services. They do not, like the basic industries, produce goods; but this does not mean they are nonproductive. They perform services and are paid for them. We can see how important these services have become in our lives by examining the following partial list of service industries:

Retail trade

Insurance and real estate

Banking and finance

Travel and transportation

Entertainment and recreation services

Hotels and lodging places

Laundries, cleaning establishments, etc.

Legal, engineering, and other professional services

Government

Wholesale trade

Medical and health services

Domestic services

Education (private)

Business services

Automobile repair services

Hair styling and beauty shops

Welfare, religious, and membership organizations

As you look at this list you may say to yourself that there is nothing new here; these services have been performed for generations. What is new is the magnitude of the service industry. More people are spending more money for services than ever before and there is a reason for it. A fast-growing goods-producing industry is a prerequisite to a large service industry. Without agriculture and manufacturing industries, there would be no base to support the service industry. We can do without many services if we have to, but we cannot exist without goods. Specialization, mass production, and automation are in part responsible for our huge service industry.

Employment in the service industries The various service industries form a substantial sector of business activity in the United States today. They employ more than 28 million persons which is about 40 percent of the total work force. About 40 percent of all personal spending in the United States goes for services of various sorts, and the percentage is increasing.

One of the reasons why the services employ such a large part of the work force is that mechanization and scientific work techniques have not yet spread extensively through the service industries, though this is beginning to occur in some areas. The service industries do not deal in tangibles, and their output is hard to measure.

Size and volume of service businesses Most of the firms that supply services to the public and to business are small, both in terms of employees and in volume of business. These small establishments, usually operated by owner-managers, are for the most part not incorporated. Much of the labor in service industries is supplied by the owners. Compared to the average manufacturing establishment, an average service firm will have about one-tenth as many employees, and a much smaller sales volume.

Figure 3-4 shows the relative importance of incorporated and unincorporated forms of business in service-industry categories. It is interesting to note that, in total, the unincorporated forms enjoy a relatively greater proportion of the net profits than do the incorporated forms.

The size and complexity of the service-industry group are a very useful index to the state of development of an economic system. In the United States, nearly one-half of the entire labor force is engaged in the production of services; few other societies in the world could possibly afford to use so many of their workers in this manner. The ability to do this is, of course, a result of the very high level of productivity in those sectors of industry which produce goods. If the productivity were lower, more manpower would be required for the production of goods and less would remain for the provision of services. Another point of interest is the extent to which services are provided to the individual consumer, rather than to other businesses. The high proportion of personal services offered the American public is yet another indication of the standard of living enjoyed by the people.

	Incorporated		Unincorporated	
	Number (000)	Profit (billions)	Number (000)	Profit (billions)
Wholesale	173	$4.9	300	$2.4
Retail	354	6.0	1,837	7.5
Finance, insurance, and real estate	432	13.3	826	3.0
Service	264	1.6	2,604	20.7

FIGURE 3-4 Service industries—predominant legal form and net profit (1969)

Source: *Statistical Abstracts.*

Professional services One of the most interesting developments to take place on the American employment scene has been the expansion of the category of jobs known as professions. Not long ago, the professions could be defined quite easily as those jobs that required long, formal educational training: doctors, lawyers, college teachers, clergymen, etc., belonged to the professions. Today, there are many other tasks that require long periods of formal training and thereby lay claim to the title of profession. This has been especially true in finance, management, research, engineering, and similar areas.

The growing complexity of American industry, the trend toward greater specialization in people and machines, and the expansion of skills needed by large-scale industry have all tended to further the development of professionalism in industry. The growth of professional management as an alternative to owner-management has undoubtedly fostered a new attitude toward the various positions in industry and their classification. Finally, the current emphasis on technological advance, carrying with it an added emphasis on research requiring long and intensive training, has also had its effect. The trend has not, as we might think, been in the direction of fewer people who are more highly skilled than ever before, but in the direction of more people who are highly skilled and professionally competent. Perhaps the greatest need of industry in the near future will be some means of ensuring an adequate supply of these high-quality employees.

The "professionalization" of the upper skill levels of the industrial work force has not been an isolated phenomenon. It has been accompanied by a steady increase in the skill requirements of positions at the lower or operating echelons of industry.

The effects of this change, which has been called a "brainpower revolution," will be felt for many years to come. The employment market of the future will place a high premium on education, on additional professional training, and on other experience that can be assumed to upgrade the caliber of the employee. The growth areas in employment—those which can be expected to expand rapidly and continuously—are obviously the job categories in the higher range of skills.

Growth of service industries The growth potential of the service industries depends on a great many factors that cannot be entirely controlled. Services, and personal services in particular, compete with services that can be provided within the home if necessary: if need be, laundry can be done at home, and many other personal services can be dispensed with if the need arises. The state of this sector of the economy, then, depends in large measure on the general state of the economic system, and this is apt to suffer more quickly than other sectors when economic activity slows down. Piano lessons will always take second place to necessary food for the family, for example; in the event of economic privation, we can reasonably expect this service to be set aside. The same is true of many other services, and thus their possibilities for future growth or expansion may be limited.

SUMMARY

The problem of finding a framework for studying the complex and interrelated structure of American business is a serious one, and no one approach to the subject seems a final solution. Business can be categorized according to its goods, its markets, its employees, its profits, or its contribution to the national economy. It can also be investigated through the study of characteristics such as specialization or productivity. Each of these approaches offers us some useful insights into the nature of business and the scope of business activities.

By dividing business into sectors and attempting to assess the significance of each sector for the total economy, we are led to the study of employment patterns, specialization, and productivity. The role of employment in the system is vital, for employment is directly related to living conditions of the population that business is expected to serve. Specialization and the drive for ever-increasing efficiency and productivity have led modern business increasingly in the direction of automatic equipment, self-regulating and self-operating— toward automation.

Finally, the significance of the worker—his training and experience, particularly in technical matters—impresses itself on the observer. The future of the worker in industry will depend largely on how well he is prepared and what contribution he can make to the productive process. The day of the unskilled worker in industry is passing rapidly, for industry is finding that it can produce a machine that will perform the same operations as unskilled labor and do so more efficiently, more effectively, and at lower cost.

*BUSINESS ITEM

Minicomputers run production for Polaroid

Automation in the factory may occur for reasons of savings or increased productivity. Polaroid's decision to automate the production of film for its SX-70 camera occurred because of the extremely finicky product. The film must be coated precisely with nine different layers of chemicals. The only way that the company could be certain that the plant would continuously turn out film made exactly to formula was to put the process under computer control. Human involvement in the process would allow for too many variables to ensure the required product uniformity.

Polaroid did not step into computer control without caution, for alongside the digital minicomputers which ran the production line it installed proven analog controls which depend on human operators to turn valves or push buttons. This provided a back-up system in the event of failure of the automated system. The back-up system will be gradually phased out of existence as it is no longer required.

The minicomputer control of production not only ensures Polaroid of standard quality of product but also gives the plant a flexibility that allows the production process to be changed in as little as a day's time. This is possible because all that is required is reprogramming of the computer. Analog control would require rebuilding parts of the system every time a process change was made.

QUESTIONS

1 Explain with examples how the basic functions of a business determine its requirements for factors of production. Provide examples for each of the four functions listed in the text.

2 List the major industry groups or sectors. Underline those which are considered basic and explain why they are basic.

3 The goods produced by industry fall into different categories. What are these categories, and what bearing does each have on the nature of business operations? (Consider the word "operations" in a very broad sense.)

4 What changes have occurred in the composition of the American labor force during recent years? Why have these changes taken place? What changes can be anticipated for the next decade? Explain the causes that may lead to future changes.

5 Increased productivity and increased production may under certain conditions mean the same thing. When is this so? Is mechanization necessary for improved productivity?

6 Is there any relationship between the type of business venture and its prospects for survival?

7 What are the basic reasons for failures among small businesses?

8 Prove by example that there are truly at least three preliminary conditions which must be satisfied before mass production is possible or profitable.

9 Is automation the equivalent of, a replacement for, or an addition to the modern mass production system? How new is automation?

10 What changes in the nature of working forces are expected in the next decade as a result of the direct and indirect influences of automation?

11 How may we identify a service industry? What is the role of service industries in the American economy in respect to (a) employment and (b) volume of business?

12 What are some of the factors which influence the growth of the various types of service industries?

13 How are specialization and the growth of professionalism related?

14 Point out the reasons why the failure rate of retail businesses is so high.

15 "A high level of activity in the service industries depends on a high level of activity in the goods-producing industries." Do you agree? Explain why or why not.

The purpose of this chapter Business and government are involved in a complex network of relationships, and each contributes substantially to the welfare of the other. From the government's viewpoint, the government function is to control and assist business in the best interests of the people; from the business person's point of view, government is a source of restrictions but also a source of aid and assistance. / This chapter points out some of the significant provisions for governmental control of, and assistance to, business in the United States, at the national, state, and local level. The aim of the chapter is to demonstrate the extremely close relation between everyday business operations and governmental rules and regulations, and to show the manner in which these restrictions condition business policy. It will also show that regulation, in some cases, may be a deterrent to effective business operations. / Questions raised in this chapter include:

1 Why is it necessary for government to exercise control over business?

2 What are some of the forms government restrictions take?

3 How involved are regulatory agencies in the conduct and growth of a business?

4 Why should government help business, and what sort of assistance does it provide?

5 What are the areas of federal, state, and local control?

GOVERNMENT CONTROL AND ASSISTANCE

In an economic system based on individual ownership and freedom of enterprise, the direction of business activity lies chiefly in private hands. Since early in our history, Americans have believed that government should lay down general rules governing economic behavior, but take no direct part in business affairs. Many economic activities have proved to have such a great social significance, however, that the government has been forced to control them quite closely. It now seems quite reasonable, for example, that government should regulate public utilities, health, education, and other matters which affect everyone in our society. The amount of government regulation varies from industry to industry depending upon the importance of the industry to the general public and the political persuasions of the party in power. But the principle of government regulation of business seems to be here to stay.

HOW MUCH CONTROL?

The general principle on which government acts when it sets limits on business operations is that it has a duty to protect the health and welfare of the population. Businesses which have little effect on society—the corner shoe store, the watch repair shop—are not seriously affected by government regulation. Other industries, which have the capacity to affect large numbers of persons—drug manufacture, food processing, utilities, and the like—are subject to close control.

According to American business tradition, government should interfere as little as possible with business operations, and this tradition is still respected in principle. The businessman is given most of the responsibility for conducting his business in a manner that will not damage the interests of others. Governmental regulation of business is usually applied only in those areas where the businessman has failed to live up to his responsibilities and the public welfare has suffered as a result.

77

THE ROLE OF GOVERNMENT IN BUSINESS

The proper role of government in economic matters is a question that can be discussed but cannot be solved with finality, for it is a matter of value judgment, of right and wrong, and not of fact. There are people who feel that government should have little or no influence on business decisions; others believe that government ought to take an even more active part in economic matters than it now does.

In recent years, there has been a trend in the direction of more and more governmental regulation of economic affairs, but there is no real agreement on the desirability of this trend. We cannot answer the question by observing neighboring countries, for the extent of governmental control differs from one country to the next. In the Soviet Union, all economic activity is government controlled; in Great Britain, a substantial amount of control over economic affairs is exerted by government; in the United States, controls are lighter than in most other countries. Which situation is best? That is for the reader to decide. But all students of business should know how much control the United States government exerts over economic matters and how its controls are enforced.

Why government seeks to regulate business

The underlying purposes of the control over business by federal, state, and local governments are generally:

1 Maintaining free competition

2 Protecting public health and safety; protecting the public against fraud

3 Ensuring adequate service at reasonable rates by businesses deemed essential to the public welfare

4 Producing revenue

To achieve these aims, government collects taxes from business, forbids particular kinds of business activity, and sets standards of quality and performance that businesses must meet when they sell their products or services.

Government does not merely control the businessman's activity, but also provides assistance to him. A wide variety of services is available to business through government agencies. The government provides vital statistical information that is extremely useful to businessmen. It also helps business by supplying financial assistance, technical information, assistance in procuring labor, and aid in selecting plant sites, to mention only a few examples.

Methods of control

Government may control business simply by making rules that business people must follow and by providing for strict enforcement of these rules. The government may also undertake to own and operate certain types of enterprises, such as the postal system, through a government agency. The principal methods of governmental control are by statute, charter and franchise, administrative agency, and government ownership.

Statute Government enacts laws which either prohibit or demand particular kinds of activity. For example, a law may prevent the employment of female labor in textile mills before 6 A.M. or after 11 P.M. Another law may force the operator of a dairy to make regular tests of the bacteria content of his milk, or to pasteurize all milk sold to the public.

Charter and franchise Government can control some types of economic activity by requiring the owner to obtain a charter or franchise before entering business. Bus lines, for example, are usually operated under a franchise granted by state or local government. To obtain the franchise, and to retain it, the owner must meet certain standards of operation and may have to agree to provide a certain amount of service to the area at approved rates.

Administrative agency Governments often create specialized agencies to control particular types of economic activity. Airline operation, interstate commerce, and broadcasting are supervised by federal agencies. The agency may set standards of operations, grant licenses to operate, and supervise operations in a general way, depending on the authority granted by the government.

Government ownership Many municipalities actually own and operate some of their own vital facilities such as transportation and water-supply systems. In some states liquor may be purchased only through state-operated stores. Even the federal government owns and operates a few enterprises, including the Tennessee Valley Authority, the Panama Canal Company, the Virgin Islands Corporation, the Federal Crop Insurance Corporation, the Federal Deposit Insurance Corporation, and the St. Lawrence Seaway Development Corporation. Table 4-1 indicates the areas in which federal, state, and local governments often own and operate enterprises.

FEDERAL GOVERNMENT CONTROL OF BUSINESS

In the early stages of American history, a philosophy of weak government and no interference with business prevailed. Not until the end of the nineteenth century did the federal government attempt to regulate the operation of business. Because we live in a federal system, the central government has only limited powers, for it must function within the limits laid down by the Constitution and its amendments.

Table 4-1   Areas of government ownership and operation

	Federal	State	Local
Postal service	X		
Insurance	X	X	
Resource development	X	X	X
Loan funds	X		
Electric plants	X		X
Water supply systems		X	X
Transit systems	X	X	X
Housing authorities		X	X

   Government control of business has been carried out primarily under the provision of the Constitution that allows the federal government to regulate interstate commerce. Business activity that takes place within a single state comes mainly under the control of the state concerned, and not of the federal government. However, the courts have construed this federal power of regulation very broadly, and it is difficult to find a major business which is not in some way affected by interstate commerce and therefore subject to federal regulation.

The pattern of federal regulation of business

Perhaps the most important single factor in the federal government's policy toward business is the effort it makes to prevent the growth of monopoly and to preserve maximum competition. In actuality, business operates in the area between perfect competition and monopoly, and there is a tendency on the part of business to move in the direction of monopoly, or away from free competition. Any action by business which seeks to restrain trade or reduce competition is illegal, and the federal government exercises a considerable measure of control over the business community in an effort to maintain competition. In this respect, the areas in which the federal government is particularly interested and active are:

Trade practices

Wages and hours

Labor relations

The formation of trusts and monopolies

Stock and financial operations

Regulation of trade practices   Federal regulation of trade practices is carried out by the Federal Trade Commission (FTC), which has as its principal aim the protection of the general public. Although the Commission can punish, it usually depends on the use of "cease and desist" orders to business when malpractice is found. Some of the practices that the FTC is authorized to regulate are:

1 Unfair methods of competition

2 Special contracts (known as tying contracts) that exclude others and tend to foster monopoly while reducing competition

3 Interlocking directorates—those on which the same few men reappear and through which they exercise control of a number of large corporations

4 Price discrimination

5 False and misleading advertising

6 False or inadequate labeling of products

The procedures used by the FTC for the investigation of complaints against business have been widely copied by other regulatory agencies.

Regulation of wages and hours Although there is no commission to enforce wage and hour regulations, Congress has enacted several statutes dealing with the subject, particularly the Fair Labor Standards Act of 1938, as amended, and the Public Contracts Act of 1935. These are "reform laws," legislation designed to protect the worker by specifying a minimum hourly wage, a maximum work week, the terms on which overtime must be paid, and the minimum age for workers.

Regulation of labor practices The basic law regulating labor practices is the National Labor Relations Act (Wagner Act) of 1935. This organized a National Labor Relations Board (NLRB) to protect workers against unfair practices by employers. Although the act applied only to industry engaged in interstate commerce, it has been duplicated by many states and applied to intrastate commerce as well. The Wagner Act was revised in 1947 by the Taft-Hartley Act, which attempted to rebalance the relation between employer and employee by placing limits on unfair practices by labor unions. In 1959, the Labor-Management Reporting and Disclosure Act (Landrum-Griffin Act) was passed; its main purpose was to provide further regulation of the internal activity of labor unions.

Antitrust laws The first law passed by Congress to regulate the formation of monopolies was the Sherman Antitrust Act, enacted in 1890 and still our basic legislation in this area. The Sherman Antitrust Act forbade any combination in restraint of trade or any attempt to form a monopoly. Since 1890, a number of laws have been passed with the aim of strengthening this policy. The Clayton Antitrust Act of 1914 specifically forbade price discrimination, interlocking directorates, and exclusive agreements. The Federal Trade Commission Act of 1914, which produced the FTC, continued this basic policy. But even at the present time, though there is agreement in principle, the exact definition of what constitutes a restraint of trade and the question of what policy in the matter the government ought to follow in the future are far from settled.

Stock and financial operations Following the stock market crash in 1929, the federal government tried to control the activities that contributed to the catastrophe. The two basic laws regulating stock dealings are the Securities Act of 1933 and the Securities Exchange Act of 1934. These laws are administered by the Securities and Exchange Commission, which is similar in authority to the FTC. The laws specify the kinds of information that can be given the public about stocks and bonds and control the conditions under which stocks are sold to the public. They also regulate the activities of the various stock exchanges.

The Federal Reserve System—control of monetary policy

Every business is to some extent affected by the federal government's monetary policy. The federal government controls the supply of money available through the Federal Reserve System, and this is an important means of controlling business activity. The Federal Reserve Board may alter the interest rate charged by member banks and may change the reserve requirements of individual banks, thus directly affecting lending policy and bank investment.

If a bank has loaned money to the limit allowed by law, it may take promissory notes to a Federal Reserve Bank and borrow additional funds against their face value. This is called rediscounting. If the Federal Reserve Bank charges 9 percent interest on its loans, and the bank can obtain only 9 percent on its loans from the general public, there is nothing to be gained from rediscounting. If the rediscount rate is lowered, however, the local bank may profit by rediscounting, and this will usually increase the supply of money available. The use of the power of the Federal Reserve System to regulate the volume of bank credit is an important means of controlling economic conditions.

FEDERAL CONTROL AGENCIES

In addition to the Federal Reserve System, the federal government has created a large number of agencies which oversee, control, or regulate some aspect of business operation. Virtually every business in the country is subject, or potentially subject, to one or more of them. Some of these agencies can investigate only; others have law-enforcement powers and considerable authority. The more important of these agencies deal with trade, commerce, communications, and stock market transactions.

Regulatory agencies—hearing examiners

Of the approximately sixty federal agencies with rule-making and adjudicative powers affecting private rights, twenty-two employ about 600 hearing or trial examiners who hear cases and make preliminary decisions for the agencies they represent. These examiners are drawing increasing attention because of their involvements with bigger cases and because of the tendency of some of them to speak their minds freely. The examiner's job is similar to that of a trial judge. He presides over courtlike hearings and makes rulings that are subject to review by the agency's governing body. In most cases, the examiner's decision becomes the final verdict. Statistics for 1964–1966 supplied by four agencies which employ 80 percent of all federal hearing examiners indicate that the agencies overturned (in whole or in part) only a small percentage of the decisions: 6 percent at the CAB, 20 percent at the ICC, 20 percent at the NLRB, and 4 percent at the Social Security Administration.

Securities and Exchange Commission

The sale of securities—stocks, bonds, and the like—is regulated by the Securities and Exchange Commission (SEC), which was created by Congress in 1934. The two basic laws governing this business activity are the Securities Act of 1933 and the Securities and Exchange Act of 1934. The Securities Act protects the investor by requiring accurate published information about traded securities. Securities traded in national securities exchanges must be registered with the Securities and Exchange Commission together with information that can be used to judge their worth. The Securities and Exchange Act regulates the operation of stock markets and securities exchanges. Both these acts aim to ensure fair dealing and prevent improper sales of stock. The Federal Reserve Board has the power to fix the margin of credit in stock purchases (the down payment on stocks) and to prevent excessive use of credit facilities in financial speculation.

Federal Trade Commission

The Federal Trade Commission (FTC) engages in four basic types of activities:

1 It regulates and controls monopolistic practices that are forbidden by the antitrust laws.

2 It regulates unfair methods of competition and unfair or deceptive trade practices.

3 It investigates business activity.

4 It promotes the self-regulation of business by holding trade-practice conferences.

Its duties include both investigation and law enforcement, depending on the particular situation it is examining.

The FTC can investigate business practices on its own initiative or at the request of the Attorney General. When corporations have been ordered to cease particular operations by a court, the FTC often investigates to make certain that the order is being carried out. It may also investigate foreign trade, alleged violations of the antitrust acts, and the operation of any business engaged in commerce except banks and common carriers, which are subject to control by other commissions.

The act that created the FTC made several methods of competition unlawful, and gave the FTC power to prevent them. Among the more important of these unfair practices are false or misleading advertising, misbranding of fabrics or other commodities, selling used goods as new material, making false or disparaging statements about competing goods, and bribing buyers in order to secure business.

Interlocking directorates Recently, for the first time in more than a decade, the federal government, through its Justice Department, cracked down on corporate directors sitting on the boards of competing companies. This action was an extension of the enforcement of Section 8 of the Clayton Act which prohibits direct competitors from having common directors. The extension of the section made it applicable to companies engaged in partial competition. Chief targets were the interlocking directorates of several major oil companies, automotive manufacturers, machinery makers, and retailers. The attitude of the Justice Department in this case was not based on clear indication of major competition in a particular product but on the contention that all the companies sell common products to motor vehicle owners and are competitors in that sense even though this competition involves only a minor part of the companies' total business. This new test for identifying competition may be the basis for future government action against directors of conglomerates.

Efforts to identify directorate interlocks by examination of rosters of corporate directors have recently been much improved because of the availability of computer services which process and analyze the membership of corporate boards. It is quite possible that the antitrust laws may be extended to include corporate officers as well as directors within the scope of their interlocking restrictions.

Federal Communications Commission

The Federal Communications Commission (FCC) was established in 1934 to regulate all common carriers of messages sent by wire or wireless. Where wires are used, the FCC establishes the locality that will be serviced, and lines cannot be extended or removed without FCC permission. Rates for services are reviewed by the FCC to make certain they are reasonable and that no discrimination or preference is shown particular classes of customers. The FCC can also require companies to extend services across their geographical area into the areas of other companies, making possible transcontinental telephone and wire services.

The FCC requires any individual or group wishing to engage in wireless broadcasting to have a license, which is granted by the FCC in the public interest after suitable hearings. The FCC allocates television channels and radio frequencies, controls the sale of facilities, supervises radio and television network operations, and can revoke a license if the laws regulating the industry are violated.

Interstate Commerce Commission

The Interstate Commerce Commission (ICC) is the oldest federal regulatory commission, since it was established in 1887 by the Interstate Commerce Act. The original act gave the ICC control over railroads only, but its authority was extended to express-car and sleeping-car companies in 1906, and to motor transportation between states in 1935. Today, the ICC controls all railway travel, inland and coastal water transportation, motor carriers, and shipping agents.

The ICC has considerable regulatory power. It can authorize the offer of railroad securities for sale, can establish rules and regulations governing passenger service, and can direct railway service in whatever way best serves the public interest. It also controls the rates that railroads can charge for their services.

In the case of motor carriers, the ICC requires certificates of "public convenience and necessity" before business operations begin, establishes employee qualifications for motor carriers, controls working conditions, regulates the equipment used in interstate commerce, reviews rates to ensure that they are reasonable and not discriminatory, and controls mergers and consolidation of motor carrier firms.

Other control agencies

Many other agencies and commissions exercise a variety of controls over the business community. Among these agencies are the Federal Power Commission (FPC), which makes rules and regulations applicable to the electric power and gas industries. The Civil Aeronautics Board (CAB) grants authorizations to carriers to engage in interstate and foreign air transportation, issues permits to foreign air carriers, has jurisdiction over tariffs and the rates and fares charged the public, regulates mergers, and has jurisdiction over unfair competitive practices of air carriers and ticket agents. The NLRB, a five-person board appointed by the President with the consent of the Senate, is charged with effectuating the policies of the National Labor Relations Act. The Board is directed to prevent certain specified unfair labor practices by employers or labor organizations or the agents of either.

A great variety of issues are brought before the several control agencies. Typical issues on the dockets of regulatory agencies early in 1970 are:

Civil Aeronautics Board:

   Applications by airlines for new routes

   Mergers between airline companies

   Investigations to relieve congestion at major airports

Federal Communications Commission:

   Authorization of pay television

   Hearings on regulation of fair rate of return for utilities

   Establishment of private communications channels

   Decision on permitting telephone subscribers to attach nonbell devices to phones

   Hearings on rigged television quiz shows and license renewal

Federal Power Commission:

   Decision on a power project bitterly fought by conservationists

   Price at which natural gas can be imported from Canada

Federal Trade Commission:

   Investigation of home improvement frauds

   Regulation of standards for nonfood packages

   Mergers in violation of the Clayton Act

Interstate Commerce Commission:

   Mergers of transportation companies

   Rail and truck rate increases

   Decision on allowing carriers to diversify; truckers seek authority to go into air freight

Securities and Exchange Commission:

   Limits on front-end-load charges by mutual funds

   Effectiveness of federal laws relating to investor information

   Brokers' commissions

FEDERAL AGENCIES TO ASSIST BUSINESS

A number of federal agencies have been established to help the business person by providing information, technical assistance, statistical data, or other forms of business aid. Some of the more important of these federal agencies are considered below.

Small Business Administration

The Small Business Administration (SBA) was created in 1953 to provide federal help to the small business concern by giving advice, financial aid, and technical and managerial assistance. The Small Business Act states:

It is the declared policy of the Congress that the Government should aid, counsel, assist, and protect in so far as possible the interests of small business concerns in order to preserve free competitive enterprise, to insure that a fair proportion of the total purchases and contracts for supplies and services for the government be placed with small-business enterprise, and to maintain and strengthen the overall economy of the Nation.

The SBA, which has regional offices throughout the country, provides a variety of assistance for small business, particularly:

Product research and development

Marketing techniques

Technical production assistance

Financial assistance

Management and technical publications

Assistance in obtaining government contracts

U.S. Department of Commerce

The U.S. Department of Commerce is a cabinet office concerned in a general way with the promotion of foreign and domestic commerce, the manufacturing and shipping industries, and the transportation facilities of the United States. The Department is really a service agency made up of several divisions. Some of the important divisions are the Office of Business Economics, the Bureau of the Census, the Patent Office, the National Bureau of Standards, and the Register of Copyrights.

Office of Business Economics

This office is a prime source of statistical information about the American economy. It prepares estimates of national income, gross national product, individual income, and distribution of income, to mention only a few. The information provided by the office is a vital element in any business forecasting system, particularly as forecasting concerns the structure of industry, the growth of sectors of industry, or the status of current production.

Patent Office

The Patent Office administers federal patent laws. To encourage new invention, inventors are allowed by law to keep exclusive control of devices they have patented for a period of 17 years. The Patent Office also registers trademarks of products traded in interstate and foreign commerce. The owner of a trademark may use it as he sees fit, and the courts will protect him against use of his trademark by anyone else. By international agreement, patents and trademarks registered with the Patent Office are granted similar protection in a number of foreign countries.

National Bureau of Standards

The National Bureau of Standards is a technical agency that deals with the units of weight and measurement used in the United States. The Constitution gives Congress the power to fix the standard of weights and measures, and Congress has legalized both the English system of inches and ounces and the metric system of grams and meters. The standard measures of these systems are preserved by the Bureau of Standards, which also offers a calibration and testing service that is widely used by industry.

Bureau of the Census

The Constitution states that a census must be taken every 10 years, and this is the chief responsibility of the Bureau of the Census. In addition to the raw population data that it collects, the Bureau interprets and analyzes a great deal of data relevant to commerce and industry, natural resources, foreign trade and shipping, and labor-force activities. Data taken from the census are used by business and government in many different ways. Information about population, income, production, and distribution is highly significant in the preparation of production plans and marketing programs, for example.

Other forms of federal assistance

Other assistance provided by the federal government takes different forms. The tariffs which are imposed on imports are of assistance to business since they provide protection for domestic industries. The subsidizing of the United States mail system keeps down the costs of this service to its users. The Atomic Energy Commission (AEC) carries on a program of research, manufacturing, and promotional activities designed to encourage private participation in the development, use, and control of atomic energy. The Department of Agriculture provides inspection, grading, and marketing services; seeks to eradicate and control plant and animal diseases and pests; and makes loans to farmers, farmer cooperatives, and commercial concerns for the purpose of financing electric and telephone facilities in rural areas. Assistance to the business person is in many forms and from many sources.

Some weaknesses in governmental control and ownership

To believe that governmental control and ownership is without its own problems would be less than realistic. One has merely to look into the cases of AT&T (American Telephone and Telegraph) and the United States Postal Service to find current situations which point out the types of problems involved in this area of government activity.

AT&T has survived more than 90 years of political and financial problems, but today, this giant employer of 900,000 people (including its subsidiaries) faces new problems as it enters the decade of the seventies. Direct competition has always been discouraged or prohibited by the government's regulatory policy and by AT&T's dominance of its industry. This cloak of protection may have been instrumental in bringing about some of the problems which appear today. State regulatory commissions have objected to the closed door negotiations between the FCC and the company. There has long been the feeling that during the years the company has been the recipient of regulatory decisions made for its convenience and profit. Competitive thrusts made by adversaries have recently dented, if not pierced, this protective cloak. The right to connect competitive devices to the telephone network and the current contest over the offering of private line services in competition with existing interstate line services are illustrative. In addition, the company has had increasing difficulties in providing both the quality and quantity of services that have been customary in the past. All these problems are appearing at a time when the demand for telephone or communications services is rapidly increasing.

Another illustration is in the area of government ownership and operation, the United States Postal Service. This federal operation is subsidized and despite postal rate increases has been unable to eliminate a deficit which currently is at the level of about $1 billion per year. There are some private enterprises which are challenging the federal postal system. Among them is IPSA, a private postal system, which handles third-class mail at lower cost to the sender than is available from the United States Postal Service. This private system is already operating in dozens of cities and has applied for franchises in 2,000 additional cities and towns. It is making money, expanding, and providing service for its users that is more dependable than the service of the federal system. Another private enterprise competing with the federal system is United Parcel Service (UPS), which operates its interstate service in virtually all the states and is also growing because many business firms prefer it for its reliability and predictability of service. Many other private firms are making headway in the areas of mail and delivery services, are making profits, are satisfying customers, and are charging lower prices than the United States postal system.

Both these illustrations, AT&T and postal service, raise at least one valid question: Does a regulatory agency or a government department have the capacity to effectively regulate or control business operations which have grown to such a size that the organization performing the services is having difficulty in controlling its own development?

THE STATES AND BUSINESS

A substantial measure of governmental control over business falls to the governments of the respective states. In the nineteenth century, many kinds of labor legislation and other regulations of business were the domain of the state rather than of the federal government. Even today many types of business activity are subject to state control rather than federal regulation.

Corporate charters

Each state has its own policy for chartering corporations, and policies vary considerably from one state to another. The general purpose of charter laws is to protect the public interest by restricting the freedom to form corporations and regulating the conditions under which corporate enterprise is carried on. Most states define and limit the purposes for which corporations may be formed, the amount of capital required for incorporation, the period of residence required for incorporation, and the number of reports to state agencies that must be submitted by corporations.

When a corporation chartered in one state wants to engage in local business within another state, it must accept the jurisdiction of the new state, where it is considered a "foreign" corporation. Each state has its own regulations applicable to such "foreign" corporations. However, a corporation engaged solely in interstate commerce may enter any other state at will without interference with its affairs.

Antitrust laws

Although the federal government has accepted primary responsibility for the control of monopoly and similar restraints on trade, some of the states have also passed legislation dealing with these matters. States may legislate on the same questions as the federal government so long as the state laws do not conflict with federal legislation. Some antitrust laws are far more detailed and stringent than the existing federal laws on the subject.

Fair-trade laws

"Fair trading" occurs when a manufacturer establishes minimum resale prices for his goods, and enters into agreements with wholesalers and retailers to maintain these prices. Fair trading was once regarded with disfavor, but some states have begun to permit fair trading in branded goods sold through retail outlets. The law generally provides that a contract covering fair-trade prices is binding upon all sellers when notice is properly given. Goods may be sold below the fair-trade price levels only if they are damaged, or if they are being sold under court order in cases of bankruptcy, etc.

Unfair-practices acts

In addition to fair-trade laws, some states have set limits on the sale of any goods at prices below cost. The law refers to such sales as unfair practices, and the legislative intention is to force wholesalers and retailers to sell at no less than invoice cost or replacement cost, whichever is lower, or at invoice cost of doing business.

Unfair-practices laws were meant to provide a basic price for un-branded goods, or goods not covered by resale-price laws. Enforcement of the law has proved very difficult in most cases since the cost of doing business varies immensely from one company to the next, and it is not easy to prove that particular sales are below cost to the dealer.

Legality of fair-trade laws

State courts have tended to take an unfavorable view of state fair-trade laws, and the constitutionality of such laws is still in question. Under federal antitrust legislation, resale-price maintenance is illegal in the absence of specific state legislation. Even where state laws exist, the wisdom of fair-trade laws depends upon at least three considerations:

1 The fixing of resale prices may provide a protective umbrella for inefficient firms, permitting them to survive even though they are badly managed.

2 Fair-trade laws fix profits by contract, and retailers therefore cannot compete on the basis of selling price. They are diverted to nonprice bases of competition such as sales promotion or customer services. Or they may choose to compete by offering lines of products which are not covered by resale-price agreements. Efforts such as these may lead to higher distribution costs.

3 There is a real question whether monopoly would necessarily arise if resale-price agreements were not in effect.

Regulation of food, drugs, and cosmetics

Pure food and drug laws have existed since early in the twentieth century. Since protection of the public health is their purpose, these laws have been accepted by business without much argument about the need for regulation. The federal government has enacted such legislation to govern interstate commerce. Pure food and drug laws, among other things, prohibit the sale of diseased or adulterated products, establish standards of purity for drugs, and specify that medicines containing dangerous drugs should be plainly marked.

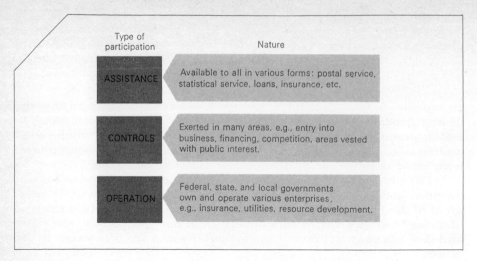

Type of participation	Nature
ASSISTANCE	Available to all in various forms: postal service, statistical service, loans, insurance, etc.
CONTROLS	Exerted in many areas, e.g., entry into business, financing, competition, areas vested with public interest.
OPERATION	Federal, state, and local governments own and operate various enterprises, e.g., insurance, utilities, resource development.

FIGURE 4–1   Government participation in business activity

Government participation in business activity is most extensive in the assistance it provides to business, and least extensive in the number of enterprises it actually owns and operates in competition with private business.

Such legislation has not been completely effective, although the federal government and state and local governments have worked to enforce it. Each year many new products enter the market, and they are often sold to a large number of consumers before their contents can be checked carefully to determine whether or not the law has been violated. Because of the complex nature of drug-product manufacture, the law is not always clear in its application, and evasion is possible through various legal loopholes.

State regulation of industries affecting the public interest

Certain businesses such as banks, insurance companies, utility companies, and common carriers are very closely regulated by all levels of government because of the extent to which the public interest is affected by their activities. Special governmental control over policies, accounting methods, rate schedules, equipment, reports, and other matters is exercised in each of these industries. (See Figure 4-1.)

Banking   Every state supervises banking carefully. A bank must be chartered to do business, and the requirements for chartering may be quite severe. The minimum amount of capital stock to be sold, the purposes for which bank loans may be made, and the amount of funds that the bank may invest are all controlled. Audits of a bank's accounts are conducted regularly by auditors appointed or approved by the government. The intention, naturally, is to provide the greatest possible measure of security for depositors.

Insurance   Insurance companies, like banks, are subject to very stringent governmental regulation. Insurance agents and brokers must be licensed. Insurance companies must be incorporated; their funds, rates, policies, and accounting methods are scrutinized regularly. Again the intention is to protect the individual, in this case one who has invested in an insurance policy with the company.

Public utilities   Most states have public-service or public-utility commissions to control public utilities—telephone, telegraph, electricity, water, gas, or transportation companies—within their borders. The federal government has an extensive regulatory program for such enterprises. Public utilities are among the most tightly controlled of all business operations, partly because they affect the general welfare directly, and partly because such firms are often given special privileges, like the right to use public property or the status of a legal monopoly.

The amount of control exercised over public utilities varies from one state to another, but every state places some restriction on:

1 The rate charged for goods or services
2 The areas in which services are offered
3 The quality and quantity of service provided
4 The financial and accounting structure of the firm
5 Discriminatory practices in selling or buying
6 Entry into business
7 Abandonment of service

Other forms of state regulation

A complete list of all business operations controlled in some measure by state government would occupy a great deal of space. But some of the more significant state regulations on business activity concern fraud, interest rates, licensing, building, and zoning.

Fraud   Most states have fairly severe laws intended to prevent fraud. Such laws may be directed at advertising, sales contracts, or the sale of securities. Laws covering the latter category are referred to as "blue-sky" laws since the value of the fraudulent securities is often about the same as the monetary value of the blue sky above.

Interest rates   To protect the borrower from exorbitant interest rates, most states have established a legal rate of interest. A maximum legal interest rate may also be established.

A distinction is sometimes made between interest rates on small loans and interest rates on mortgages or similar long-term loans. Small loans are usually allowed a higher maximum interest rate because of the higher risk involved in transaction.

Interest charges over the lawful maximum are declared to be usury, and the penalty may be loss of principal and/or interest to the lender or, in extreme cases, a term in prison.

Entry into profession or trade Entry into the professions, such as medicine, architecture, law, engineering, and dentistry, is carefully regulated by law. A period of formal educational training, perhaps an apprenticeship period, and a qualifying examination are usually required. In addition, required standards for professional conduct may be included in the provisions of the law. Many of the trades, such as plumbing, real estate, and electrical work, are also controlled by law, and licenses must be obtained before the trade can be practiced. The following news item from *The Wall Street Journal* makes this point clearly.

GOTTA LICENSE? A growing number of jobs require you to have one. Occupational licensing by Federal, state and local bodies increases sharply. The Labor Department estimates that 550 occupations are licensed by at least one governmental jurisdiction, double the number 25 years ago. Recent additions to the list: Pest-control experts, nuclear materials handlers and fundraisers. Licensing often results from public outcries against unqualified or dishonest practitioners.

But Labor Department officials worry that the licensing power is sometimes used to keep qualified workers out of certain occupations. In one small community a licensing board dominated by plumbing contractors rejected seven of eight applicants for a license required to set up a plumbing business. Despite its large Spanish-speaking population New York City gives its licensing exams only in English.

Prostitutes, rainmakers, tattoo artists, beekeepers and lightning-rod dealers are among today's licensed practitioners.

Building and zoning laws Few businesses can escape the impact of building and zoning laws. Such laws, generally established at the municipal level, regulate the kinds of buildings that may be constructed as well as the kinds of business activity permitted in various sectors of the municipality. Some towns prefer to remain residential, and will not permit any business activity within their limits except retail trade and service industries. Others open their doors to industry and provide substantial facilities for new industrial plants. In view of recent trends in the great urban centers, it seems probable that the regulation of this aspect of business will increase substantially in the future.

SUMMARY

During this century, the theory of minimum government regulation of business has been modified, even discarded in certain areas. During times of economic depression or national emergency, the need for public control of commerce has been widely accepted, and the result has been a vast expansion of government regulation.

The primary aim of regulation is to maintain the general health and welfare of the whole community. Business activity is usually curbed only when it is clearly apparent that business policies are not in the public interest. A broad pattern of federal, state, and local legislation has been enacted to achieve these social goals and a proliferation of agencies and commissions has appeared, to carry out, enforce, and administer the law.

In addition to policing or curbing business, government assists the businessman by providing him with information, financial assistance, technical assistance, statistical data, protection of patent rights, and other services that can be used in business planning and organization.

With increased size and complexity of business organizations and operations, many regulatory agencies have found themselves in a position of being too limited in terms of operating budgets and staff to effectively perform their regulatory function. The sheer burden of volume of situations requiring the attention of the various agencies has gotten out of hand in many respects. The time lag experienced in settling many cases and the lack of consistency in interpretations of rules and regulations as well as in the adoption of reasonable standards by which parties involved can anticipate future action are some of the weaknesses which are evident in the operation of governmental regulation of business.

BUSINESS ITEMS

Government bureau spurs product development

The National Bureau of Standards is conducting a unique experiment to try to spur the pace of technological innovations. As part of the Experimental Technology Incentives Program (ETIP), production specifications will be released periodically for use by the General Services Administration (GSA) as bidding standards for its equipment purchases. It is hoped that the GSA's $2.6 billion annual purchasing clout will stimulate manufacturers to introduce innovations in keeping with the specifications.

In the first series of ETIP specifications, based on National Bureau of Standards data, the government looked for improvement in the energy-efficiency ratio for air conditioners and for reduction in the decibel level of power mowers. These specifications are not to be forced on manufacturers, but those who can provide equipment according to specifications stand to gain GSA contracts.

The FTC rethinks its job

The Federal Trade Commission's antitrust arm—the Bureau of Competition—is setting up a "think tank" to chart ways that antitrust prosecutions can have more impact on the economy. This special task force of lawyers will not work on specific cases, but instead will study such questions as whether mergers in service industries should be judged on the same basis as mergers in manufacturing, and how antitrust laws affect international trade.

Antitrust hits the professions

For 20 years or so, the idea of challenging lawyers' minimum fees schedules has been considered a legitimate target for the antitrusters in the Justice Department. During the 1960s, the government moved against restrictive practices in the funeral industry and also began to take a dim view of the restrictions placed on retail drug price advertising. Increasingly, during the past 5 years, the spotlight has been focused on professional codes of ethics that inhibit price competition and cause the consumer bills to soar.

Twenty-five years ago, only 30 percent of the dollars spent by consumers went for services. Today, more than 40 percent is spent for services. Among the service professions sharing these dollars are lawyers, doctors, accountants, engineers, architects, and real estate men who, under the cloak of a code of ethics, may be encouraging a system of protection from price competition. Any price fixing or other anticompetitive device in the service area has direct and adverse impacts in the consumer's pocketbook.

A code of ethics is generally not legally enforceable, but if a professional were to cut his fee in an effort to solicit business or in some other manner violate the code of his profession, he would be subject to sanctions by the membership of his own group which in some cases could cripple or destroy his ability to work.

The Justice Department has had notable success in its prosecutions against professionals. Many groups have agreed to changes in their operating procedures and have shown increased willingness to forego their rate schedules. On the other hand, the National Society of Professional Engineers, which is fighting the Antitrust Division in court, argues that "antitrust laws were never intended to cover professional activities." This society also claims that its ban on members competing for jobs on a price basis is in the interests of ensuring high standards.

QUESTIONS

1 The general principle underlying government control of business is that of protecting the health and welfare of the population. Explain how government interference with business monopolies adheres to this principle. Explain how government sanction of local monopolies adheres to this principle.

2 What general purposes underlie government control of business?

3 What methods for controlling business are available to government? What are the means whereby each method affects control?

4 How may the operations of the Federal Reserve System control economic conditions?

5 Identify and explain the roles of each of the following: (*a*) SEC, (*b*) FTC, (*c*) FCC, (*d*) ICC.

6 What is a "small" businessman (refer to Chapter 3)? How does the SBA seek to help the small business person?

7 What is the role of the hearing examiner, and how significant is his role in the regulatory process?

8 What is the difference between local and interstate business?

9 What are "interlocking directorates," and why should the Justice Department crack down on them? How do computers help in this crackdown?

10 What are the purposes behind the enactment of state fair-trade laws and unfair-practices acts?

11 The states impose regulations on businesses affecting the public interest. Do not all businesses affect the public interest? Explain.

12 What are "blue sky" laws?

13 In what instances do state regulations fall directly on the individual? In what instances do they affect the individual indirectly?

The purpose of this chapter   The importance of business in the American way of life is self-evident. The United States has a favorable legal and political climate for business enterprise, though many believe it is not so favorable as it might be. In this chapter, we shall deal with the difficult question of how the businessman ought to approach his own obligations to the system that makes his activity possible. We are concerned not only with the strictly legal responsibilities placed on business by government but also with the basic principles of business ethics—the self-imposed obligations which the businessman accepts as right for him to fulfill. Although no discussion of this sort can provide answers to such moral questions, it is essential that every business student be aware of the nature and scope of these questions and of some of the answers that have been given in practice. / Questions raised in this chapter include:

1 How have the responsibilities of business people changed over the years?

2 Why is it so difficult to obtain agreement as to the social responsibilities of business?

3 In the network of business relationships, what determines legal obligations, publicly accepted standards of business responsibility, business ethics, and sound managerial policy?

4 What are the obligations of the business person to engage in political activity?

5 / SOCIAL RESPONSIBILITIES OF BUSINESS PEOPLE

People live in societies because they must; the human being today is part and parcel of the social organization and is utterly dependent on it. Human society, which makes possible the division of labor and specialization, also makes possible the production and distribution of goods and services. Business can exist only within an organized society, for when people are totally-self-sufficient the concept of business has no place in their lives.

The organization of society, then, makes it possible for people to engage in business activity. In return, those in business must make a contribution to the society that sustains their environment. That is, business people have an obligation to the society in which they live and a responsibility to the others who live in society with them. Like the farmer who must put back into the ground the minerals he takes out in crops, the business person must put something back into society if society is to remain a fertile ground for business endeavor. This, in general, is the concept of business responsibility.

THE NATURE OF BUSINESS RESPONSIBILITY

Although it might be possible to obtain unanimous agreement on this concept—that business people owe society a measure of responsibility—it is extremely difficult to define it precisely. Responsibility implies an obligation or debt. In the case of business, to whom is the obligation due? Certainly business has obligations to the government and to its customers. Does it also owe a debt to the general public? Is there an obligation to future generations to preserve and maintain the institutions which make business possible? Here we must move beyond strict legal obligations into the realm of morals and values. The business responsibilities of which we speak are not legal debts; they are self-imposed obligations which business people must accept if they are to preserve the structure which makes possible their own way of life.

Let us assume that we are willing to accept the thesis that business people have a responsibility to society. The next and far more difficult step is to translate this into specific action. If we were able to specify for every business firm the actions it should take to be considered a responsible citizen, the situation could be easily resolved. But such is not the case. In the first place there is no general agreement as to the extent of business responsibility. Many people will argue that business is business and anything that suggests social responsibility is out of bounds. A noted economist and adviser to Presidents contends that "few trends could so thoroughly undermine the very foundations of our free society as the acceptance by corporate officials of a social responsibility other than to make as much money for their stockholders as possible."[1] Henry Ford II, chairman of the board at the Ford Motor Company, has a different view of social responsibility.

Like governments and universities and other institutions, business is much better at some tasks than at others. Business is especially good at all the tasks that are necessary for economic growth and development. To the extent that the problems of society can be solved by providing more and better jobs, higher incomes for more people and a larger supply of goods and services, the problems can best be solved by relying heavily on business.

On the other hand business has no special competence in solving many other urgent problems. . . . In short, our society will be served best if each of its specialized institutions concentrates on doing what it does best, and refuses either to waste its time or to meddle in tasks it is poorly qualified to handle.[2]

There probably are as many different views on the proper extent of businesses' social responsibility as there are people looking at the question.

The problem of social responsibility is further complicated by our inability to ascertain in many instances whether a given action by business characterizes responsible or irresponsible action. So often when business does something it will have a positive effect on one segment of society and a negative effect on another. Trying to resolve such situations is not easy. To illustrate: In a particular community there is a paper processing plant that is the community's largest taxpayer and major employer. The local economy is dependent on the plant. Each day the plant draws thousands of gallons of water from the adjacent river for use in the production process and discharges it after use back into the river. The color of the river downstream changes frequently from white to green to red and so on depending on the color of paper being processed. The river, which flows through many towns and another state, is highly polluted. Suppose that you and I, society, issued a mandate to the plant to clean up the water or close down. The plant responds that the cost to clean up the water would be so high that it could no longer compete and would have to close anyway. Would such a mandate be a responsible action? Are you and I in a position to judge?

[1]Milton Friedman, *Capitalism and Freedom,* The University of Chicago Press, Chicago, 1962, p. 133.
[2]From remarks delivered before the Yale Political Union at Yale University, Apr. 7, 1969.

Whether a given action shows responsibility or not is often determined by one's system of values. We generally accept the notion that lower costs, lower taxes, less government, and greater efficiency are signs of increased responsibility—each is good and the reverse is bad. We need to examine these values because we can become so obsessed with "low cost" that we are willing to ignore the true cost. We are too willing to accept polluted rivers because in so doing we can keep the cost of paper at a lower level.

In the name of efficiency we often act in a questionable manner. When an automobile manufacturer takes a completely unskilled person and trains him to put two wheels on the left side of every car that passes by, is the employer acting in a responsible manner? The wages and benefits for the worker add up to more than $7 per hour but the worker may have nothing to look forward to until retirement, if he makes it, except two wheels on every car 400 to 500 times a day. These two illustrations point out that your view and my view of responsible actions may not coincide. The entire concept of social responsibility must be viewed in this light.

THE BUSINESS PERSON AND RESPONSIBILITIES

Fortunately, business people themselves have in recent years begun to accept many more responsibilities than ever before in our history. In part this has been due to governmental action which has forced obligations upon the business person in the public interest. Business people who operate banks, public utilities, insurance companies, and the like are carefully regulated by government agencies and are required to reveal to the public the true costs and benefits of dealing with them. In very wide areas business leaders have agreed to mold their policies in accordance with "publicly accepted standards." Of course, the extent to which business can do this successfully will probably minimize the extent to which the government will enlarge its control and increase the regulation of business activity in the future.

Many business people go a considerable distance beyond even the "publicly accepted standard" of business responsibility. They have found through careful study that willingness to accept responsibility has proved profitable; has enhanced the prestige of the firm; and has created a better atmosphere for sales, employee relations, and similar factors that help toward business success.

Perhaps one reason for these changes in attitude has been the separation of ownership and management in modern business and the consequent gradually increasing influence of professional management. In addition, the modern professional manager is undergoing change. We are now beginning to feel the impact of higher education at all levels of management. Each year our universities send some 20,000 M.B.A.'s into business corporations, and many thousands of managers already in corporations receive additional formal management training. The consequence is that today's manager has been exposed to theories of corporate responsibility not available to previous generations. The modern professional manager is trained to examine business problems in the widest possible context and to show concern for both the long-range and the short-range effects of business policy. Although short-run gains cannot be ignored, the long-range effect of policy carries more weight with the modern professional manager than it did with a predecessor who owned the firm. Because of the importance attached to long-range policy, American business is today better led and hence in a better position to accept and carry out its responsibilities than it was in the past.

Responsibilities in today's world

The general responsibility that business people must assume for world affairs—an obligation to humanity, in a sense—is gaining more and more recognition with each passing year. The United States is a major world power, with interests that encompass the globe. As a vital part of American society, the business person shares with fellow citizens the general responsibility for the country's conduct of its affairs. In a more special sense, American business has its own worldwide interests, for there are sources of vital raw materials as well as lucrative markets in almost every part of the globe.

The market for goods is the whole world and not just one country. The United States must be able to compete, economically as well as politically and militarily, with other nations of the world in a more unified market system.

This challenge raises many problems. For example, the American worker is the highest-paid worker in the world but not necessarily the most productive. American goods tend to be more expensive than comparable items manufactured by other countries, and the principal reason for the price differential is found in the cost of labor and the physical state of production equipment. It is foolish to expect to compete on a world market unless productivity, new ideas, or cost of finished product makes American goods more desirable than competitors' products.

Public responsibility

That American business has responsibilities to the public cannot be doubted, for many of these responsibilities have been defined by law: they are legal responsibilities. How far beyond the strict terms of legal obligation ought the business person to go? Again, this is a difficult question to answer, for much will depend upon the individual's ethical beliefs or moral code. He or she will consider some policies right and others wrong, and find it impossible to state clearly why they are one or the other. Our conceptions of right and wrong stem from custom, religion, intuition, reason, past history, and tradition. They change with time and do not remain static for any long period.

Business ethics fills the gap between legal requirements and the actual decisions that business leaders must make. Is it right to fire on short notice a worker who has spent 40 years with the firm, even though there is no legal limitation to prevent his being thus discharged? Should the firm charge the public $10 for an item which cost only 50 cents to make if it can get away with it? People in business make decisions of this type every day; there is no legal guideline, yet the decision involves questions of right and wrong. The guidelines are provided by the ethical code that the business person accepts. The code itself changes constantly as business people evaluate the results of their own decisions and alter future decisions to produce different results.

Specific responsibilities to the public

Some business people still take the view that the sole function of business is to earn profits; others adopt the philosophy that business exists for the betterment of mankind. Between these two extremes, there is a wide range of responsibilities that are accepted by some if not all American business people. The responsibilities listed below are not all-inclusive, but they do suggest the direction in which modern thought on this question is moving.

Preservation of basic institutions Most business people accept the need to maintain the basic American institutions which make possible our system of free enterprise. Private property, freedom of contract, and freedom of investment are essential features of our business environment, and abuse of these institutions will certainly weaken them and reduce the probability that they will continue unchanged. By accepting the need to exercise his or her rights in a responsible manner, the business person can contribute substantially to the preservation of these basic institutions.

Increased standard of living Since business is the major source of income in this country, and the goods and services that business provides set the basic standard of living for every member of the society, business has great power to increase or decrease the standard of living. A dynamic and expanding business system can make a genuine contribution to the betterment of human life here and everywhere. In the past, business has fulfilled this responsibility in a dramatic and forceful way, and it is likely that American business will continue to pursue this goal in the future.

But there is another way to look at our standard of living that has been largely ignored. When members of society had to sweat, toil, and suffer all sorts of hardships and inconveniences in order to exist, the goal of more material possessions was quite realistic. Most people today enjoy a rather high material standard of living, and efforts to improve it often involve diminishing returns. Many people today believe that we must change our values so that the quality of life will include more than physical possessions. The fact that we now have much more leisure time can be in itself an increase in our standard of living if we learn how to put it to good use.

Preservation of resources Goods cannot be produced without raw materials and the supply of many vital resources is fixed and cannot be increased. Hence business has a responsibility to use these resources efficiently and to create as much wealth with as little waste as possible. But if the consuming public continues to demand more and more material possessions, the resources problem cannot help but worsen. Power shortages, fuel shortages, and the like may at first glance appear to be the result of poor business practices. A closer look will reveal that they are caused by our gluttonous appetites for more. The issue of social responsibility does not rest on business alone; it encompasses every institution and every person.

Economic operation The continuous striving for efficiency which is characteristic of American business is a necessary element in the business person's responsibility to self and to society, for efficient operation makes more goods available at lower cost, thus aiding in the conservation of resources and contributing to an increased standard of living.

Regard for others Business people must conduct their affairs in such a manner that the rights of others, whether in business or not, are not interfered with more than is necessary for healthy competition. This does not imply that free competition should be abolished but that monopolistic and unfair competitive methods should be avoided.

Social responsibility More and more business people are coming to accept the need for a broader conception of business responsibility to the community. No law forces business to contribute to education or entertainment or the beautifying of the community. Business sponsors entertainment and sometimes educational or cultural programs on a large scale through radio and television. It plays an important part in sponsoring research work and provides fellowships and scholarships for college students. Though these efforts need not be entirely altruistic, many of them contribute to the betterment of society. Progressive management looks forward to an even greater expansion of these activities.

Responsibilities to the government

Business exists as private enterprise in the United States because the citizens of this country, acting through their governments, allow it to take this form. This point is fundamental, for business could not operate if the legal system was antagonistic to it. Further, the most important form of business ownership, the corporation, is completely dependent upon state charter for its existence. Other laws permit business to operate and own property, to build in certain zoned areas, and so on. In return for these privileges, business has an obligation to government.

One of the most obvious of business's responsibilities to government is to provide the financial support needed to maintain the governmental system. Businesses must also obey the laws and must help develop a system of law which provides the best possible climate for business enterprise. When business people fail to accept such responsibilities, a conflict between business and government ensues that is detrimental to the long-range interests of both.

Responsibilities to the owners

A sole proprietor has no responsibilities to other owners, but in a partnership or a corporation, business leaders must consider the interests of those who have given them their authority and responsibility. American business is owned by millions of stockholders who are very dependent upon the integrity and sense of responsibility of management. In general, the law protects the stockholder from injury caused by management only in cases of gross fraud or negligence. In any event, though the law can often punish, it cannot force retribution on a mismanaged business once the assets of the firm have been lost. An important principle of business ethics has developed out of this interrelationship among owner and stockholder, management, and government.

The prime responsibility of management in this regard is to secure the stockholder's investment and to endeavor to provide a reasonable return on his money. Of course, a careful balance must be maintained between the long-term needs of the firm and the need to pay current dividends. Some stockholders are concerned only with their current earnings on stock; they want the bulk of the annual earnings to be distributed as cash dividends. Other stockholders are willing to forego dividends or accept nominal payments in the interests of long-term expansion. With the reinvestment of earnings in the firm and the growth that may result, they hope that the value of their stock will increase greatly.

The leaders of business must establish sufficient communication with the stockholders to permit them a reasoned judgment of the best interests of the firm in any given year. This is particularly important when a corporation has stockholders spread over several continents. Some firms hold regional meetings which give management a better opportunity to explain current policy objectives to the stockholders and to establish better rapport between owner and manager.

Responsibilities to the customer

The customer is a member of the general public and shares the benefits of those obligations which business accepts in its relations with the general public. Business people also have a more specific obligation to the customer as such.

First and foremost, business must fulfill its contractual obligations to its customers, whether they are private consumers or other business firms. The firm which fails to keep its promises soon finds its markets diminished, a development which reflects the failure of management responsibility to both the owner and the consumer. Business should also take pride in satisfying the needs and demands of the customer as efficiently and economically as possible. Even the retail merchant who relies primarily on self-service has the obligation to place before his customers only such goods as he himself believes are not only satisfactory in quality but also satisfactory in dependability.

Responsibilities to the workers

What is desirable in labor-management relations is difficult to define because of the accumulation of antagonisms and resentments arising from past conflicts. The law identifies certain aspects of the business person's responsibilities to labor, and business certainly has the obligation to accept this minimum responsibility. However, it takes more than a series of laws to create the difference between "good" jobs and "poor" jobs. An individual's work is usually the sole means of earning a living for himself or herself and any family and is a primary source of satisfaction. Because of the significance of employment in the lives of millions of workers and the human problems that can follow from the failure of business to accept responsibility for this complex relationship, the obligations of business to the worker are in a slightly different and more urgent category than other phases of business responsibility. Unlike these other phases, business responsibility to the worker is always immediate, direct, and consequential because the worker's life is entwined with his or her employment.

Perhaps the first task for the business person when making policy is to attempt seriously and honestly to take into consideration the effect of these policies upon the lives of the workers. This thinking must go well beyond material benefits and wage plans. Insofar as possible, management ought to be clearly aware of the physical, the psychological, and the social implications of personnel policy. That is, human relations ought to be an important aspect of managerial responsibility.

The problem is particularly serious in an age when management is moving further and further away from direct personal contact with the production worker and when such relationships as exist are more and more with groups of workers rather than with individuals. The problem is easily stated in general terms, but it is extremely difficult to put into effect any program considered to be a reasonable program through which management can accept and fulfill its responsibilities in human relations.

Specific responsibilities to the workers

Although it would probably be impossible to obtain complete agreement among managers on the actual responsibilities of a firm to its workers, it is possible to indicate the scope of these responsibilities very briefly as they are currently accepted in well-managed companies. Again, the conception of responsibility here is a dynamic and not a static condition, and an adequate definition for today will probably be quite inadequate in a few years' time.

Wages Business has the responsibility to pay its workers a living wage; this is required by law. But "living wage" does not mean just a subsistence income—a wage on which the worker can barely keep himself and his family alive. Wages should provide more than bare necessities. In fact, wage policies should aim to make life as full as possible for the worker, at least to a degree compatible with management's other financial responsibilities. This principle has meant in the past a steady increase in wage rates and a decrease in the number of hours worked in a normal week. The exact level of wages depends on a number of variable factors, of course, but the general principle is fairly well established.

Vacations No law in this country requires the private employer to grant paid vacations to employees. But workers feel that they are entitled to paid vacations, and business has for the most part agreed. The time allowed for vacations was formerly one week per year; today the standard is generally a two-week vacation with pay. In the future this may increase to even more. Why should business accept this responsibility? Perhaps the simplest way to answer such a question is to ask yourself whether or not you would accept employment with a firm that did not consider paid vacations one of its obligations to its employees.

Job satisfaction The implications of management's responsibility for job satisfaction go well beyond the "good job" concept. Our economy is very productive, and people have more goods and services today than ever before in history. But there is ample evidence that Americans as a rule obtain far too little satisfaction from their work. The achievement of great material prosperity has been accomplished at great human cost. The individual worker has too often become a mere production number, a nameless entity without either personality or identification. Many of the tasks in industry are menial, providing little or no opportunity for either creative thinking or skilled physical manipulation. To many workers a job means "Put four pieces in here, press the button, and when the machine stops, take the pieces out and repeat the process." The individual worker is a smaller and smaller cog in a mechanism whose size increases steadily.

Psychologists have long recognized the need for adequate self-expression. Since work occupies more of a person's time than any other function, and since it is, or should be, fundamentally creative, it potentially offers more opportunity for self-expression than any other human activity. The role of the job in the psychological satisfaction of an individual, then, is preeminent even though that satisfaction may be difficult to define and to achieve within the existing industrial framework. Most people have one talent or another, and when their talents are not used and appreciated, they naturally feel frustrated. Worse, there is a waste of talent that might be used fruitfully in industry. Making the most of a worker's abilities in granting him or her satisfying creativity is perhaps the greatest future responsibility of business, and one of the most difficult problems it must face.

Miscellaneous Management is nowadays considered responsible to its workers in a number of other ways. Injuries sustained at work are today the responsibility of management according to law (workmen's compensation), and business accepts at least some responsibility for the worker during a period of unemployment (unemployment compensation). There has recently grown up the additional obligation, as yet voluntary in many cases, to provide retirement funds, met in part by the worker, in part by the employer, and already available to some degree through the social security laws.

These basic areas in which business has responsibility to and for its workers are only a small element in a problem that we are barely beginning to grasp. If we are to maintain our present business structure, then business must discover how to create within its own framework a worker-job situation that is adequate to meet human needs—"needs" defined in the broadest possible sense of the word.

POLITICAL RESPONSIBILITIES OF BUSINESS

Should business people engage in and encourage political activity? It sometimes seems as if business leaders have abandoned political action to the lobbyist and professional politician. Yet management theory shows clearly that the qualities required for business leadership and those needed for political leadership are basically identical. Further, there is a definite need for active business participation in government, if only because business is affected drastically by government action. As a matter of self-interest, and as a responsibility to society, business people ought to be prepared to take an active part in political matters, even at some personal cost to themselves.

The self-interest motive for participation in politics by business leadership is easily demonstrated. Laws regulate and control the interplay of competitive forces in the American economy. Social legislation, which affects business people perhaps more than any other group in society, is a consequence of political action. Taxation falls most heavily on the business community. Labor unions have been moving steadily in the direction of political activity, particularly since the passage of the National Labor Relations Act in 1935. Even if the influence of unions has been somewhat diminished by more recent labor legislation, labor remains a powerful political influence, able to make its weight felt in governmental circles.

Legislation is in a very real sense the outcome of the interplay of pressure groups with goals that are sometimes mutually exclusive. Business must make its voice heard in the same way. A democratic society depends upon each citizen to pull his own weight in matters affecting the general interest, and we commonly make our decisions by weighing the numbers on each side of an argument. By avoiding political action, the business people lose the opportunity to make themselves heard and felt in government, and therefore the decisions made by government often do not give adequate consideration to the business person's views. The businessman should consider whether he is not defaulting on an obligation, both as a citizen and as a member of the business community.

Nor should business interest in government be confined to national matters. In local and municipal government there is a crying need for managerial talent, financial expertise, and the ability to make maximum use of available resources. These abilities and capacities are found behind all sound business practice.

Democracy and free enterprise are no more than sets of conditions within which individuals are permitted to work out their own destinies. They may be used fully, or they may be ignored.

It would indeed be shortsighted, however, to ignore the opportunities that our political institutions offer if business people will choose to take an active part in them, and equally shortsighted not to see the intimate association between the political and the economic sectors of our society.

Expansion depends upon a clear view of the needs of the time, efficient management of our affairs, and a firm sense of responsibility that is wider than the immediate confines of a particular business enterprise. In the long run, the sense of responsibility of the American business person will probably determine the manner in which the problems of a rapidly changing civilization are solved in the foreseeable future.

This view of business' political responsibility does need to be modified or further defined. Involvement by business in the political arena is fine up to a point. In too many instances during recent years large business corporations, as well as other large institutions, have used their power and financial resources to further their own selfish interests. Frequently their actions are completely legal, if not responsible, but too often we see instances of arrogance and defiance of the law. When a firm donates several hundred thousand dollars to a political campaign it is hard to believe that its purpose is simply to further the democratic process. The use of powerful lobbies financed by business to influence legislation is another type of political involvement that is suspect. Because of this, we, society, need to draw much clearer lines between responsible and irresponsible involvement by business and business people in the political process. This will not be easy because business will use all its influence to ascertain that the new lines will not be drawn too tightly.

CURRENT PROBLEMS AND BUSINESS RESPONSIBILITY

The decade of the sixties graphically introduced the American people to a wide range of long-standing national problems. Unless these are solved, we face the promise of a bleak future for many groups if not for all the people of this nation. Millions of citizens and thousands of business people are joined in their concern and are making efforts to deal with such current and worsening problems as poverty, urban blight, pollution, and crime. These, more than improved productivity or profits, represent the real challenges of the 1970s. The nature of the problems is clear; the pathway to their solutions is less clear. Every individual, whether privileged or not, and every business person has a stake in the improvement of the many areas of blight brought about by individual avarice, self-concern, and disregard for the rights of others. Where does the concept of business responsibility fit into the scheme of correcting these obvious problems?

In many cases, business contributes directly to these problems by being overly concerned with the immediate or short-run profit and thereby committing itself to practices which in the long run have proved to be destructive of resources and environment. Pollution of air and water are specific illustrations. Many individual firms are voluntarily responding to the problems, but overall there is no clear reason to believe that their efforts will move us very far along the road to solution. The business person, in general, needs a rational approach to the commitment of his corporate energy and funds. It is difficult to find the appropriate rationale which will encourage greater participation on his part in the quest for a solution to these problems, for there is no short-run possibility of the profits which impel the business person to action. Unless the belief that what is good for all in the long run will eventually benefit the business firm develops and is accepted by the business community, the alternatives available may be an increasing government role in the control of industry. Even in this prospect, there are many who feel that government power has reached its limits in forcing business to take positive actions to prevent or correct conditions which contribute to social problems. Implicit in this attitude is the threat of altered government structure wherein freedom may be limited and sanctions imposed to force compliance.

A convention of American scientists meeting in Boston in December 1969 focused not only on the scientific and technical aspects of our environment but also on the social facets. Their reactions to the problems of environmental pollution ranged from a pessimistic 35 years to an optimistic 100 years as the range of time within which it is imperative that the pollution problems be eliminated. Otherwise, they predicted, there will be no problem at all.

QUESTIONS

1 Should business people be expected to assume an increasing measure of responsibility as time goes by? Discuss.

2 Should business people be forced by law to assume an increasing measure of responsibility as time goes by? Discuss.

3 It is agreed that businesses do have a responsibility. What is this responsibility and to whom is it owed?

4 Distinguish between and describe a *legal* and a *self-imposed* obligation.

5 Has the rise of professional managership changed the concept of business responsibility? Discuss.

6 Compare the views of Friedman and Ford on social responsibility of business. Justify Friedman's stand.

7 Illustrate why it might be difficult to ascertain why an action by business might be considered both responsible and irresponsible.

8 What differences exist between the business person's responsibility to the public and to customers?

9 What is business ethics and what specific purpose does it serve?

10 What are the major responsibilities that United States Steel and General Motors owe the American public?

11 What responsibilities do these firms have to the government?

12 What major problems arise in establishing a business person's responsibility to the owners of business, i.e., the stockholders?

13 It is said that business people have a responsibility to provide job satisfaction for workers. What does this mean and what does it imply?

14 Why should business people engage in political activity? How should they participate?

15 What role has business played in creating our environment? How many ways can you suggest that business can improve our environment?

TWO ORGANIZATION AND MANAGEMENT: THE INTERNAL ENVIRONMENT

In Part 1 of this text the reader developed an understanding of the overall environment within which business must operate. To a great extent this defines what business can and must do and what it cannot do. This in turn has a significant impact on you, the person who is or will be an employee of business. Business people have little control over the environment and at times they will be frustrated by the environment. Business can prosper and grow in this environment, but success will depend largely on the way the business is set up, organized, and managed—the way it adapts to the environment.

In this section of the text we will be dealing with the things that compose the internal environment of business—the specific environment with which you will be involved. Here, business people can exercise a significant amount of control over the conduct of business affairs. Since the external environment is common to all business firms, an understanding of the variations that are possible as regards the internal environment takes on added significance. Here, we are concerned for the environment within which you will be working on a day-to-day basis.

The relation between the owners of a business and the business itself can take several forms, and the role of a given owner in the conduct of business affairs can vary significantly. In a proprietorship or partnership, the owner or owners are as a rule directly involved with business affairs; they are apt to be in direct contact with customers, bankers, and suppliers. They are directly responsible for all actions of the firm. In larger corporations, an owner, as a stockholder, has no direct involvement in the conduct of business.

The two most important ingredients of business success, however, are organization and management. Organization is important because it provides the mechanism for achieving enterprise objectives. The approach a firm uses to organize can be important to you, the employee, because it greatly influences the types of jobs that will be available. The annals of business history note countless instances of business success which can be attributed to excellent organization and too many failures that resulted from poor organization. Proper organization should be a first consideration for all business executives.

Organizations provide the means for doing something, but management is the activating and energizing force that moves people to do their jobs and achieve objectives. Without management, organizations fall apart. Management is people, and people have the capacity for overcoming deficiencies in organization; but this does not mean that poor organization should be condoned.

Organizations and managements vary, and they can have a significant impact on jobs. Whether the job you will have in business provides the rewards and satisfactions you demand will depend more on these two factors than on anything else.

The purpose of this chapter In this chapter the different approaches to business ownership are examined. Because society depends on business to provide for its needs, the legal forms of ownership must be sufficiently adaptable to allow for all sorts of businesses. Small business can satisfy a portion of our needs but these are primarily in the service area. It requires large-scale business to provide us with most of the goods we consume—automobiles, TV sets, petroleum, and the like. Proprietorships (single owner) and partnerships (several owners) do not have the capacity to engage in mass production and mass distribution. Large-scale business generally requires large-scale ownership. / In America, therefore, a business may be owned by one person or by several million people; there is no maximum number. Obviously the role of an individual owner in governing the affairs of a business will vary in importance depending on the total number of owners. A proprietor has complete authority over his or her business, but a single shareholder in American Telephone and Telegraph may own less than a millionth of the business and consequently has virtually no voice in the affairs of the company. Ownership of business takes many forms and people become owners of business for a variety of reasons. In this chapter we will identify and examine the basic forms of business ownership and indicate the situations where each can be best applied. / Questions raised in the chapter include:

1 What must a person do to start a business under each of the various ownership forms?

2 What are the factors that affect the choice among the various ownership forms?

3 How do the principal forms of ownership both limit and enlarge the scope of a business person's activities?

4 What is the extent of authority of owners in a proprietorship, partnership, and a corporation?

5 Why is the proprietorship the most common ownership form and the corporation the most economically important ownership form?

FORMS OF BUSINESS
OWNERSHIP

Ownership is a legal relationship between a person and some object. (Bear in mind that a corporation is considered a legal person.) The meaning of ownership—the rights which an owner may exercise over his possessions—is determined by law. Usually, ownership implies the exclusive right to possess and use property, always, of course, within the limits of the law. The law may allow ownership of a pistol, but that does not carry with it the right to shoot another person. Ownership also implies responsibilities on the part of the owner for the activities of the owned property; the owner of a dog or a business is responsible for its behavior, and the courts will enforce that responsibility with suitable penalties.

In any business it is important to establish clearly and precisely who is the legal owner or owners, for this determines who is to benefit or suffer from the activities of the business. The form of business ownership decides the sharing of profits, the responsibility for debts, the responsibility for illegal activities, and all similar questions.

FORMS OF OWNERSHIP

When a new business begins, the ownership may be established in any manner that is not prohibited by law, following the basic legal principle that any action not prohibited by law is acceptable. Virtually all American businesses, however, exhibit one of three basic patterns of ownership:

1. *Proprietorship*—individual or single ownership
2. *Partnership*—a legal arrangement between two or more owners
3. *Corporation*—a special type of ownership which is chartered by the state

Each of these forms of ownership has advantages and disadvantages, to be identified later in this chapter. The choice of the form of ownership is one of the basic decisions the business person must make. For one thing, each form of ownership is subject to different tax provisions; in addition, the legal responsibility of the individual owner differs with the form of ownership.

117

ORIGIN OF OWNERSHIP FORMS

No one knows precisely when or how business began on this earth, but it is certain that the forms of business ownership are as old as business itself. These forms have been modified over the course of time to keep pace with business needs and the customs of society.

Business organization to be legal must be sanctioned by laws that either provide for them or do not prohibit them. Law that sanctions our forms of business ownership is either common or statutory law.

Statutory law, as pointed out in Chapter 2, refers to that body of law which has been enacted by our various legislative bodies. For example, the state of Illinois has enacted laws which provide for the creation and control of the corporate form of ownership. Every state in the Union has a statute pertaining to corporate ownership. Without such statutes there could be no corporate ownership.

Common law, as we have seen, has an entirely different origin. We are aware that all actions of individuals are legal unless prohibited by law. Over the years, the people of a society come to do things in such a well-defined and acceptable manner that society and the courts look upon them as being legitimate. When the courts uphold and recognize such unwritten rules of conduct, they become a part of our common law. Early in history, courts recognized and upheld the right of an individual to go into business for himself, and the proprietorship form of ownership had its legal birth. Later the courts recognized and upheld the right of two or more individuals to go into business as co-owners, and the partnership type of ownership was born.

Proprietorships and partnerships are unique forms of ownership because documented sanction by a government is not necessary for their creation; they are common-law institutions. The most significant feature of these ownership forms is the fact that the business and the owner(s) are one and the same; business assets and liabilities are personal assets and liabilities. The meaning is explained below.

THE PROPRIETORSHIP

The word "proprietor" denotes exclusive ownership of something. Thus *proprietorship* describes that business which is owned by one individual. This is the very oldest form of business ownership. It is also the simplest; there is little difficulty about organization and operation of a proprietorship since it can be established quite informally. Today there are more proprietorships in the United States than any single form of business ownership, but these firms are small.

Starting a proprietorship

An illustration will show how quickly and easily a proprietorship can be established as a new business. Let us suppose that a man named Charles Jensen is employed as an accountant by a large firm, but that he wants to strike out on his own. He finds a number of small businesses willing to employ him to do their accounts, and he begins working on these accounts in his spare time. The moment this work begins, Jensen is the sole proprietor of his own business. He need take no legal action; there are no organization expenses; and there is no formal requirement for publicity. Any person who engages in business activity—buys, sells, or provides a service—under his own name is the proprietor of a business. It may be part time or full time, and may be small or large without altering the legal status of the firm.

However, if Jensen wishes to enter business under a different name, say, Middlesex Accounting Service, he must record the fact that this is his business, usually at the city hall. There is a small registration fee for recording the title. This has the effect of making Jensen's position as owner of the business a matter of public record, but it does not change the fact that Jensen is the proprietor. Perhaps the reader has seen how the relation between the owner and the business is expressed in a situation like this: Charles Jensen, d/b/a Middlesex Accounting Service, where d/b/a means "doing business as."

Some businesses cannot be established without a license or permit. For example, a permit is usually required to sell gasoline, tobacco products, liquor, and similar items. In some states, a license is required to practice as a public accountant. Professions such as medicine, architecture, and dentistry require a license as a matter of course. But these restrictions are placed on all forms of business ownership; they are not limits on the proprietorship.

Advantages of the proprietorship

The proprietorship has many advantages, particularly for the small business person. It can be established quickly and easily and with very little cost, since there are no organization fees and the services of an attorney are not generally required. The individual proprietor is subject to very little governmental regulation. The individual proprietor sets his own goals and directs his business toward them in any way he sees fit so long as he does not violate the law.

The profits earned from the business belong to him, and he is personally responsible for business losses. Proprietorship rewards the owner directly for efficient and profitable operation and punishes him directly when he manages his affairs badly. It is a highly individualistic and personalized form of business ownership.

The proprietorship does not pay taxes as a business; the profits from the business are the personal income of the owner and are declared on his individual income tax return.

Finally, the proprietorship can be liquidated as easily as it is begun. The proprietor can merely stop doing business, for his assets and liabilities are his personal responsibility. Even though the proprietor goes out of business, he is still legally entitled to any money owed to him as a businessman and is legally liable for any debts he incurred while doing business.

Drawbacks to the proprietorship

The same characteristics that make the proprietorship an advantageous form of business can also be a serious handicap under certain circumstances. Since proprietorship is personal, the owner has a great deal of freedom, but he is also exposed to certain hazards that need to be considered. First of all, business debts are personal debts, and if business assets are not sufficient to cover claims against the business, the personal property of the owner can be taken to satisfy these claims. This could lead to financial disaster. It is possible to take some measure of protection against such personal losses by disposing of personal assets prior to going into business; that is, a proprietor can "give" his personal assets to his wife and family and thus limit his potential loss. Nevertheless, the unlimited liability feature is a serious handicap to the proprietorship form.

A second major drawback to "personal" businesses is that the life of the business ends when the life of the owner ends. It is possible to arrange for the business to be continued by the heirs, but legally a new business, with new owners, must then be established, and there are legal steps to be taken before the heirs can use the estate.

Money problems   It is usually rather more difficult to attract outside capital into a proprietorship than into other forms of business ownership. For the most part, the capital invested in a proprietorship comes from the personal savings of the individual. Since there is much more risk attached to the proprietorship than to a partnership or corporation, financial institutions are more reluctant to lend their funds, and this makes it difficult for the business to expand or to take advantage of opportunities that require additional capital.

The importance of the proprietor

The success of a proprietorship rests with the proprietor. This can be considered an advantage in that it personalizes the challenge to business success. But it is also a drawback to successful and expanding business. Successful business demands a wide range of talents, and the larger a business grows, the broader the talents needed for operation. In a one-person business, this can be a significant limitation on expansion. A corollary disadvantage of a personal business is the effect of illness or serious injury to the owner. In the absence of

TABLE 6-1   The proprietorship summarized

Advantages	Disadvantages
1. Simplicity of organization	1. Unlimited liability of owner
2. Minimum legal restrictions	2. Life of business limited to life
3. Individual accountability	of owner
4. Business gains are personal gains	3. Difficulty in raising additional
5. Freedom to terminate business	capital
6. No business income tax	4. Success heavily dependent on
7. Freedom from government control	a single individual

Suitable applications	Questionable applications
Barber shop	Heavy manufacturing
Medicine, dentistry, and accounting	Amusement center
Small retail store	Supermarket chain
Repair shop	Construction contracting
Service station	Automobile sales
Boardinghouse	Hotel
Writing	Wholesaling

organized direction, the business may well collapse when the owner is incapacitated, particularly in the critical early years. Table 6-1 summarizes this discussion of the advantages and disadvantages of the proprietorship.

Applications of the proprietorship form

When is a proprietorship desirable? Obviously, the person with a little capital who wishes to begin a small business has little choice other than the proprietorship. In cases where the need to get started quickly is urgent, when limited life—the risk of the business lasting a short time—is not a serious problem, or when the skill of the individual is the basic ingredient of the new business, then the proprietorship will work well. But if much capital is needed, if risks are high and extended life is essential, or if the business requires a wide variety of skills, then the proprietorship form may not be adequate.

From a social standpoint, the proprietorship is in general a desirable form of business ownership. The smallness of the proprietorship unit carries no danger of concentration or monopoly. Small business is usually more flexible and adaptable than very large-scale business and can adjust to new conditions with less disturbance. It can adjust but whether it will depends not on the ownership form but on the individual involved. A small scope of business operation is more conducive to individualized or personalized production; therefore, in many cases it can supply the consumer with precisely what he wishes rather than with a standardized product. Finally, small business is an important source of new ideas, new products, and new materials.

THE PARTNERSHIP

A *partnership* is an association of two or more individuals who enter business as co-owners to share in profits and losses. The word "partner" is a contraction of the two words "part" and "owner." There have been partnerships in business at least since the days of the

Roman Empire. Partnerships are common-law agreements, though there are statutes that control special aspects of partnerships. The partnership resembles the proprietorship more closely than it does the corporation because of the unlimited liability feature but it has certain advantages over the proprietorship which make it more desirable for some business situations.

The partnership is a means of bringing into a business more capital, or more skills, which can be used for expansion. It is also, within limits, a means of spreading the risk of loss among several persons. Unlike the proprietorship, which has no special body of law, the partnership can be regulated by the Uniform Partnership Act, a model code which the majority of our states have adopted, thus unifying to a great extent partnership law throughout the nation.

Forming partnerships

A partnership is the result of an agreement between two or more competent persons, and like many agreements, it can be created either by express consent or implied consent. That is, there may be a formal written agreement regarding partnership (see Figure 6-1) or merely an oral agreement that covers the same ground. It is also possible to create a partnership even if there is no intention to do so, since the courts will rule in certain cases that two parties who give the impression that they are partners can be held legally liable as partners. In all but a few cases, however, partnership rests on the intent of the parties involved, whether or not the intention has been formalized.

The partnership agreement

It is always wise, when a partnership is formed, to have the terms of the agreement placed in writing and notarized (see Figure 6-1). This provides a basic legal document which can be used to decide many issues that might arise in the future about the rights and duties of each partner. The agreement cannot, of course, provide for every possible contingency that may arise, and some element of trust is needed to make it work. People who have no trust whatever in one another ought not to enter a partnership in the first place. No agreement can guarantee that one of the partners will not act in a way that is detrimental to the interests of the other or others, but it can provide some safeguard against bad faith, and some protection for the injured partner.

Buying into a business

Not all partnerships come into being as shown in Figure 6-1 and not all partnership agreements are as simple. Here, things are quite clear because each partner invested $10,000 in cash. It is not uncommon for people to buy into a going business where a proprietorship becomes a partnership or a partnership adds another partner.

ARTICLES OF COPARTNERSHIP

This contract, made and entered into on the ___seventh___ day of ___August___, 19__ by and between Robert P. Grayson and George Stockton both of Elgin, Illinois

WITNESSETH: That the said parties have this day formed a copartnership for the purpose of engaging in the ___manufacturer's representative___ business under the following stipulations which are made a part of this contract:

First: The copartnership is to continue for __15__ years from above date.

Second: The investment of each partner shall be __$10,000__ in cash.

Third: The business shall be conducted under the firm name of ___Grayson and Company___ at __19899 Cottage Plaza, Elgin, Illinois__.

Fourth: All profits and losses shall be shared ___equally___.

Fifth: A systematic record of all transactions is to be kept and made available to each partner for inspection. On __June 30__ and __December 31__ hereafter a statement of the business is to be made, the books closed, and each partner credited with his gain or charged for his share of the loss.

Sixth: Each partner will devote his entire time and attention to the business and engage in no other business enterprise without the consent of the other.

Seventh: Each partner is to have a salary of ___$1,500___ per month, the same to be withdrawn at such time or times as he may elect. Neither partner is to withdraw an amount in excess of his salary without the consent of the other.

Eighth: The duties of each partner are as follows: Robert P. Grayson is to have general supervision of the business, have charge of the office and all records, and handle all relationships with manufacturers. George Stockton is to have charge of all field work, hiring all field personnel and having charge thereof and any other duties that pertain directly to the contact of customers or potential customers.

Ninth: Neither party will become surety or bondsman for anyone without the consent of the other.

Tenth: In the event of the death, incapacity, or withdrawal of either partner, the business is to be conducted for the remainder of the fiscal year by the surviving partner, the profits for the year allocated to the withdrawing partner to be determined by the ratio of the time he was a partner during the year to the whole year.

Eleventh: In case of dissolution, the assets are to be divided in the ratio of the capital invested at the time of dissolution.

IN WITNESS THEREOF:

Robert P. Grayson ___Robert P. Grayson___

George Stockton ___George Stockton___

FIGURE 6-1   A partnership agreement

If you were buying into an existing business such as the one shown in Figure 6-2, you would be buying a share of owner equity. There are a number of ways this can be done, such as:

```
                 Cadillac and Mountain

          Statement of Condition, July 1, 19___

Assets                        Liabilities and equity

Cash                 $ 5,500   Owed to suppliers      $ 3,500
Due from customers     9,500   Owed to bank (loan)      6,000
Merchandise inventory 21,000   Taxes payable            1,500
Equipment              7,000   Total                   11,000
  Total              $43,000   Owner equity            32,000
                                 Total                 $43,000
```

FIGURE 6-2   A statement of condition

1 Buying the entire interest of a partner by paying him an agreed-upon sum

2 Buying part interest from both partners by paying each an agreed-upon sum

3 Buying an interest by paying money into the partnership, thereby increasing the total partner equity.

Regardless, how much should you pay for an interest in a going partnership? Partner equity equals the value of all assets minus amounts that must be paid. In our illustration, if certain customers default on their payments to the firm, if inventory turns out to be unsaleable at planned prices, if the equipment should become obsolete, and if the amounts owed by the firm are actually understated, it is easy to see that owner equity could be far less than the $32,000. The partnership agreement necessary to cover all the contingencies facing the new investor would be far more involved and complex than the document illustrated in Figure 6-1.

Legal features of the partnership

The legal status of the partnership is very similar to the status of the proprietorship. Both are common-law institutions, and they share many advantages and disadvantages. Both are personalized forms of business ownership; that is, the business is personal and its profits and losses, its assets and liabilities are also personal. The partners are, with some exceptions, personally liable for their business and its operation. The chief legal difference between a partnership and a proprietorship is that the former has a multiple ownership.

The liability of partners

The extent to which each partner is liable for the actions of a partnership is one of the most important and interesting aspects of the law of partnerships. Jointly, the partners are liable in the same sense that a proprietor is liable, but since there are two or more partners, the liability of each must be defined and established clearly. For example, suppose you became a partner in Cadillac and Mountain (see Figure 6-2) and it was later found that liabilities amounted to $15,000 instead of the $11,000 as shown. Should you be liable in any way for this additional $4,000? You could be. Ascertaining liability is also accomplished by defining the various types of partners and establishing the extent of the liability of each. Three types of partners are commonly found in American business, each with a different degree of liability:

1 *General partner.* He has unlimited liability, and may be personally responsible for the debts of the partnership. Unless otherwise stated, all partners are considered general partners.

2 *Special partner.* The obligations of the special partner may be limited by agreement; in such cases, the authority of the special partner in relation to the management of the partnership is also limited.

3 *Dormant or secret partner.* He is a silent partner, whose association with the firm is not known to outsiders; he has no voice in the management of firm affairs. But if the association is discovered, he may be treated as a general partner by the courts.

In law, partners are jointly liable for the debts of the partnership, and a creditor who sues to collect debts will sue the partners as a group. However, if the assets on the partnership are not adequate to meet the obligation, creditors may sue any one, or all, of the partners as individual persons to gain satisfaction.

For the partner with large personal assets, this financial liability can be a serious handicap; he may find himself obligated to pay the entire debt of the partnership. The injured partner could always, in such a case, bring a suit against the other partners and attempt to collect a part of the obligation from them, but if the remaining partners have no personal assets, the entire business loss does legally fall on the solvent partner. Since the actions of any one partner automatically affect the liability of all the others, a partnership can be quite a dangerous legal arrangement. It is often said, and with much wisdom, that a person should exercise the same care in selecting a business partner as one would in selecting a spouse.

Dissolution of partnerships

One of the prime disadvantages of the partnership form of ownership is the uncertainty about the duration of the business that may be involved. A partnership may be legally terminated for any one of several reasons, and this possibility can be very awkward in some situations. First, there may be an agreement that limits the life of the partnership; this is not a serious problem, for then everyone concerned is at least aware of the date of termination. Second, the death of any partner automatically ends a partnership, and this cannot be anticipated. Third, if one partner withdraws from the business, the partnership is automatically dissolved. Fourth, and finally, the bankruptcy of one partner or a legal declaration of insanity of one partner suffices to end the relationship. There are steps that can be taken to minimize the shock of dissolution, but the possibility that the partnership may terminate at any time is a limiting factor on the desirability of this form of ownership.

Management of partnership affairs

If there is no special agreement to the contrary, each partner has an equal right to take part in the management of the affairs of the partnership, regardless of the portion of the business he may own. This is an express provision of the Uniform Partnership Act. In most cases, decisions are made by majority agreement, though unanimous agreement may be required for certain special decisions such as admitting a new partner into the firm.

When partners agree on management, a partnership can proceed with little confusion. But when partners disagree, their disagreement can bring the business to a halt. Two heads are better than one so long as the two heads are cooperating. In the event of a complete stalemate, the only solution to the problem may be to dissolve the partnership, though some partnership agreements contain special provisions for settling disputes through the mediation or arbitration of a third party. However, this type of third-party action seldom occurs, and in the nature of a partnership it cannot be very successful. Partnerships demand cooperation and agreement among the partners as a fundamental condition of successful operation.

Applications of the partnership form

When moderate amounts of capital and diversified managerial talents are needed, the partnership may be an ideal choice for the form of business ownership. In general, partnerships work well in the areas where proprietorships work well, but a partnership is usually somewhat larger than a proprietorship, for there are more mouths to feed. A common application of the partnership is found in law firms where one partner may specialize in trial work, a second in probate, a third in criminal law, and so on. Accounting firms, law firms, real estate brokers, and the like, which have a *fiduciary,* or *trustee,* relation with outsiders, must be formed as partnerships or proprietorships in most states.

The partnership will not function well in a very small business that cannot provide enough income to make association worthwhile. Nor is partnership really adequate for a very large enterprise, where the corporate form of ownership is more suitable. Table 6-2 briefly summarizes partnership strengths and weaknesses.

The limited partnership

The form of partnership that has been described above is called a general or ordinary partnership; in this case there are no special

TABLE 6-2 The partnership summarized

Advantages	Disadvantages
1. Diversified managerial talents	1. Unlimited liability
2. Greater financial resources	2. Divided authority
3. Simplicity of organization	3. Limited and uncertain life
4. Freedom from government control	4. Difficulty in finding qualified and agreeable partners

provisions governing the relation of the partners. It is possible, however, to enter into a limited partnership agreement which reduces the liability of one or more of the partners. Since the concept of limited liability is not a feature of the common law, a limited partnership must depend on statute law for its validity, and limited partnerships can be formed only in those states whose statutes contain provisions for this form of ownership.

In a limited partnership one or more of the partners must be general partners with unlimited liability, but the remainder may have their liability for business debts limited to the amount they have invested in the firm. The limited partner takes no active part in the management of the business, but anyone who has business dealings with a limited partnership is entitled to know which partner is limited and which is not. If this information is not disclosed, the limited partners may be considered the same as general partners, with full liability, by the courts. Of course the limited partners share in the profits of the firm on terms set forth in the agreement.

On the surface the limited partnership seems a very satisfactory type of organization. But if the statutes that govern limited partnerships are not complied with very strictly, the courts may void the limiting agreement and treat all partners as general partners, with full liability, thus nullifying the effect of the special agreement. Further, limited partnerships are formed under authority granted by the statutes of a particular state, and they cannot do business in other states on the same basis.

THE CORPORATION

The corporation is without question the most important form of business ownership in the United States, whether the standard on which it is judged is sales volume, number of employees, wages paid, or physical property owned. Although only about 20 percent of American business is incorporated, corporations dominate the economic system and account for a large part of the national income.

Of course, not all corporations are giant industrial firms; in fact, most corporations have only a moderate amount of capital, for it is possible to incorporate a business in many states with $1,000 or less in capital. Even some private individuals have incorporated themselves, largely because of the legal advantages that accrue to corporations.

A corporation is in essence a fiction—a legal "person" created by law. A corporation comes into being when a charter is granted by the state. As Justice John Marshall stated, a corporation is ". . . an artificial being, invisible, intangible, and existing only in the contemplation of the law. Being a mere creature of the law, it possesses only those properties which the charter of its creation confers upon it. . . ." The corporation is created by statute law, not by common law as is the case with proprietorships and partnerships.

Except for a few special purposes, the federal government does not charter corporations; this is left to the individual states. Since each state enacts its own laws to govern the organization and operation of corporations, there are significant differences in the statutes controlling corporate activity. Some states have enacted laws which make incorporation easy, require few reports, and levy few taxes; other states have very stringent requirements. Because there is no uniform code governing corporations, there may be a real advantage to incorporating in one state rather than another.

A corporation is a "citizen" only in the state in which it is incorporated. At law a corporation is foreign in any state other than that of incorporation. Thus a New York corporation has no rights in Illinois until it has registered as a foreign corporation and complied with Illinois law. For example, a New York corporation can conduct business in the state of Illinois but it cannot bring legal action against a person or business in Illinois, say, for the nonpayment of a debt, unless it has registered as a foreign corporation.

Characteristics of the corporation

The corporation differs in many respects from any other form of business ownership. The business in this case is an entity separated completely from the owners. The owners often have no part in the actual management of a corporation. The corporation, being a creature of the law, can have unlimited life. The liability of the owners of a corporation is limited. Corporations are taxed differently from other businesses. Each of these advantages must be weighed when a new business is being established, to determine whether or not incorporation is desirable.

Permanence One of the reasons why the corporation is so popular as a form of ownership is that it does not terminate with the death of the owner. In fact, corporations can only be dissolved with the approval of the state that granted the charter. A proprietor or group of partners actually own the assets of their business; they can dispose of them as they see fit. The stockholders of a corporation do not own the corporation in this sense. Stockholders do not own the assets of the corporation; rather, their ownership of stock is evidence that they possess certain rights such as the right to a share of the profits, the right to vote on certain issues, or the right to a share in the remaining assets if the business is dissolved. These rights can be transferred from one person to another without affecting the corporation at all. Millions of shares of stock are traded every business day. Strictly speaking, the stockholders have given money to a "person"—the corporation—in return for these rights.

Limited liability Another important asset of the corporate form of ownership is that with few exceptions the liability of the stockholder is limited to the amount he has invested in the corporation. The personal property of stockholders cannot be sold to pay the debts of a corporation in which they have invested. The risk of investment is limited, yet the possibility of profit may be very large.

For the investor, this limitation of his risk is most attractive, and it is the main reason why corporations are able to attract the enormous amounts of money needed for large-scale enterprise. Table 6-3 shows the original investment of several people in the Ford Motor Company, then a risky enterprise, and the return on this investment. This is certainly atypical, but such returns are always possible when new businesses are highly successful.

Taxation of income Incorporation, as compared with other forms of ownership, often confers a real tax advantage on the business person. The proprietor and the partner pay no income tax as business people; their business income is personal income and is taxed accordingly just as our wages are taxed. Since the corporation is a person in law, it too has income and must pay a tax on that income, but there remains an advantage to the owners in spite of this. The federal government levies a tax of 22 percent on the first $25,000 of corporate

TABLE 6-3 Original investors, and the return on their investment, in the Ford Motor Company

Name	Investment	Reported return
James Couzens:		
Cash	$ 900	$39,500,000
Notes	1,500	
His sister	100	355,000
Alex Y. Malcomson	7,000	175,000
Dodge Brothers	10,000	34,871,500
J. S. Gray	10,000	36,605,075
Horace Rickham	5,000	17,435,750
John Anderson	5,000	17,435,750
Albert Stretlow	5,000	25,000

TABLE 6-4   Comparative tax burden

As a proprietorship		As a corporation	
Business profit	$50,000	Income before salary	$50,000
Jones's gross income	50,000	Jones's salary	25,000
Estimated deductions	5,000	Corporate net income	$25,000
Taxable income	$45,000	Corporate income tax	5,500
Income tax	$14,560	Jones's salary	$25,000
		Estimated deductions	5,000
		Taxable income	$20,000
		Income tax	$ 4,380

Comparison

Tax as proprietor		$14,560
Tax as a corporation		
Corporation tax	$5,500	
Personal income tax	4,380	
		9,880
Saving through incorporation		$ 4,680

profits, and 48 percent on any income in excess of this amount. Individual taxes, on the other hand, vary from 0 on low incomes to 70 percent on taxable incomes of $100,000 for single persons and $200,000 for married persons.

A technique used by a number of corporations is to split a single corporation into several corporations. If a firm has taxable income of $100,000 it must pay an income tax of $41,500. If the same venture is operated as four corporations each with income of $25,000, the total tax on the venture is reduced by $19,500 to $22,000.

The tax advantage that may be gained from incorporating can be illustrated very easily. Ms. Jones runs a successful proprietorship but wants to investigate the advantages of incorporating. Last year the business earned $50,000, but Ms. Jones took only $25,000 for her services as a manager, leaving the remainder in the business. An estimate of the tax burden on the business when it is organized as a proprietorship, and as a corporation, is given in Table 6-4, which shows that a savings of over $4,600 results from incorporation. In both cases the business profit not taken by Ms. Jones remains in the business. Of course, incorporating does not always bring tax advantages, but the question usually bears investigation.

Double taxation   The corporation, a legal person, must pay income taxes, as we have seen. These taxes are paid on net profit, which includes the money paid later to stockholders as dividends—the return on their stock. A corporation with a net profit of $100,000 must first pay a federal corporation tax of $41,500 on its profits. The $58,500 remaining after taxes may be distributed to the stockholders as dividends. Despite the fact that an income tax has already been paid on this money, the individual stockholder must also pay a tax on what he receives. This is a form of double taxation, but the advantages of incorporation frequently offset this drawback.

Formation of corporations

If the corporation is small and simple it may be formed for a few hundred dollars, but if it is large and complicated, the process can be both expensive and time-consuming. The first step in the formation of a corporation is to obtain a charter from the state. This step is performed by a promoter or promoters who request the right to engage in a particular type of business and to issue a specific number of shares of stock. The application for a charter also includes such information as the corporate name, location of the business, the officers of the corporation, and perhaps the intended life of the business.

The sale of stock The fact that the promoters of a corporation are successful in obtaining a charter does not guarantee that the corporation will become a viable entity. All businesses need money and other resources. The corporation must raise these at the outset through the sale of stock. Attempts are usually made prior to incorporation to obtain preincorporation subscriptions; that is, to get people to agree to buy stock if and when it can be issued. But frequently new corporations must rely on the investing public to provide the resources necessary to get the corporation going.

The promoters may prepare a prospectus which outlines in detail the investment opportunity or they may simply contact anyone who they feel would be a willing investor. It is not uncommon to have a prospectus mailing in the magnitude of tens of thousands of copies. If enough people are interested in buying the stock, all well and good, but if there is not an adequate response, the corporation may fail before it gets started. There is no guarantee that the stock authorized by the charter will be sold.

The stock of a corporation can have a *par* or *stated value* printed on its face or it can be stock having no par value. Par value may have no relation at all to its true or market value. Stock having a par value of $1 could have a market value of $10 or 10 cents. Usually par value is stated much lower than anticipated market value, primarily for psychological reasons. When a corporation issues stock it must estimate the price at which it can be sold. This involves considerable risk because if the asking price is too high the stock will not sell and it is virtually impossible to change the asking price once a commitment has been made.

When a person buys stock, he pays the corporation and receives a certificate indicating the number of shares purchased. Unless restricted by corporate bylaws, the owner of stock may sell it to anyone he chooses and at any price he can get. Thus the actual ownership of a corporation can be in constant change.

If there is active trading of a stock, the management of the corporation may apply to have it listed and traded through one of the exchanges such as the New York and the American stock exchanges. A stock exchange is not in the business of buying and selling stocks. Rather, it provides the facilities whereby member stockbrokers buy and sell shares for their clients. There is a limit to the number of brokers who may belong to an exchange and a "seat" on an exchange may sell for $100,000 or more depending on the demand.

A corporation receives its money when the stock is first issued. The millions of shares traded on the exchange each day involve investors only, not the corporation. When the value of a share of IBM stock rises or falls ten points in the market IBM is not directly affected. However, if the market value of a stock continues to decline, the possibilities of the corporation's obtaining additional funds through new stock issues is diminished.

Operation of the corporation

The supreme authority in a corporation is the body of stockholders. They have the right to determine corporate policy, to elect officers, to approve corporate bylaws; in short they have the right to approve or disapprove any and all corporate actions. In fact, they can run the company if they want to. In corporations where there are few stockholders this actually happens. In theory, each stockholder has a voice equal to his portion of the total amount of voting stock. This is a *vested right*—a right that cannot be taken away. In practice few stockholders in large corporations exercise their rights and for a number of reasons:

1 Many stockholders such as you and I do not understand the workings of a business well enough to know how to vote in our best interest.

2 Many and perhaps most individual stockholders are not at all interested in voting. As long as the market value of their stock stays up and as long as dividends keep coming in, they are satisfied with the way others are voting.

3 The "owners" of millions of shares of stock cannot exercise the voting right. Mutual funds, pension funds, investment trusts, and the like hold stock which they purchased with "our" money, but of course we have no chance to vote.

4 Many stockholders prefer to assign their right to vote to an officer of the corporation by signing a *proxy form;* the officer who holds these voting rights is said to be the proxy, or agent, for the stockholder.

The management of a corporation

The management of a corporation can be identical to the management of a proprietorship or partnership. One person may own all the stock in a corporation and run it as he or she sees fit. For many years Henry Ford held all the stock in the Ford Motor Company and ran the business as a one-man show. Two stockholders each holding 50 percent of the stock in a corporation and having equal authority in business matters would function as a partnership.

However, in larger corporations there usually is a group that has the controlling interest and this group has the power to determine who will be involved in the firm's management. Oddly, this group may not need to have 51 percent of the votes in order to maintain control.

All authority in a corporation rests initially with the stockholders. They in turn can delegate as much or as little of this authority as they see fit or as much as the law allows. They cannot delegate the authority to elect a board of directors or to authorize a new issue of common (voting) stock, for example. But if the stockholders want to select the president, vice president, treasurer, and so on, this is their right.

Similarly, the board of directors may be actively involved in the management of the corporation if they see fit. More likely, they will delegate authority to the next lower level of organization, the president, to manage the affairs of the firm. There is no single pattern of who will do what in a corporation. In some instances the board is all-powerful with its chairman acting as chief executive officer; in others, the board is a rubber stamp of the president. The locus of authority identifies who really manages a corporation.

In many of our highly scientific or complex corporations the locus of power may be several organizational levels below the board of directors. It becomes impossible for the board or the president to understand or see at firsthand all the ramifications of corporate operations. Top management is forced to rely on the upward flow of information to have a basis for decision making—information which may not be adequate or appropriate. A consequence is that top management's role is often reduced to an approve-disapprove action rather than an initiating action.

The corporation—An assessment

The forms of business ownership discussed this far can be described as natural and unnatural. The proprietorship and partnership forms are natural because they are common-law institutions. The corporation, because of its limited liability feature, the separation of owners from the business, and the need for a charter, is an unnatural form of ownership. Initially, the corporation was viewed as a special-purpose form of ownership to be used only in those necessary situations where the needs of society could not be fulfilled by proprietorships and partnerships. The need to construct railroads, canals, and communication systems was so imperative that a workable ownership form had to be utilized.

At one point in time each request for a corporate charter required the submission of a special bill to the state legislature and only after legislative approval could a charter be granted. As time passed by the restrictions on the use of the corporate form of ownership gradually disappeared to the point where a person can incorporate himself if he has reason to. This opening up of corporate ownership is largely responsible for our giant industrial, commercial, and financial institutions. Bigness has many advantages, as has been pointed out earlier, but bigness also allows for the concentration of tremendous amounts of power in the hands of very few individuals. Power, if properly used or directed, can be good for society but it carries with it the possibility that those with power will use it for their personal gain and to the advantage of the corporation. Society can also be hurt because of bigness.

Applications of corporate ownership

In the previous paragraphs the corporation has been discussed in such fashion that its applications are quite obvious. In summary, the corporate form of ownership can be applied in any and all situations not prohibited by law, although it may be a cumbersome arrangement for many very small firms. Table 6-5 summarizes the favorable and unfavorable aspects of the corporation.

The corporate conglomerate

Technically, the *corporate conglomerate* is not a distinctly different form of ownership but because this approach to ownership applies a different philosophy and because it is so important today, it is considered separately.

A conglomerate such as International Telephone and Telegraph (ITT) is a combination of many diverse businesses which have been purchased by ITT. Some of these businesses are small such as the Hammel-Dahl-Conoflow division which deals in valves and control mechanisms. Sheraton Hotels and Continental Baking are by comparison quite large.

Traditionally businesses have merged along more related lines such as General Motors' acquisition over the years of AC Spark Plug, Harrison Radiator, Saginaw Steering, and Delco. The products of each of these acquisitions are used in the manufacture of General Motors

TABLE 6-5 The corporation summarized

Advantages	Disadvantages
1. Limited liability of owners	1. More government controls
2. Specialized management	2. Lack of uniform corporate code
3. Greater ease of raising capital	3. Double taxation
4. Ease of transferring ownership	4. No legal status outside state where
5. Permanence of organization	formed; becomes a foreign corporation
6. Possible tax savings	

TABLE 6-6   Types of holdings of two conglomerates

ITT	Brunswick Corp.
ITT Canteen Corp.	Mercury Division (outboards, etc.)
ITT Grinnell Corp. (sprinklers)	Bowling Division
Hartford Insurance	McGregor Division (sports equip)
ITT Rayonier (paper)	Sherwood Medical Products
ITT Sheraton (hotels)	Technical Products Division

Note: This is but a sample of United States holdings. A complete listing of the holdings of these two conglomerates would require more than a full page.

Source: *Moody's Industrial Manual,* 1972.

automobiles. Normally a firm grows in this fashion to increase efficiency and lower costs. This, as we have seen, is consistent with our philosophy. But conglomerates, such as the two described in Table 6-6, acquire companies for purely financial reasons—to improve the value of the conglomerate's stock. If a firm, regardless of its line of business, can help the parent company by providing a good tax-loss write-off or by having a surplus of cash, for example, it might make a good acquisition. Consequently, the direction and speed with which a conglomerate will grow are quite unpredictable.

When a firm such as ITT acquires another company it may do so without spending a penny. What happens is this: The parent company, ITT, will pay for the company being acquired by issuing additional shares of its stock. The acquired company may operate exactly as it did prior to the takeover. It is not uncommon for employees of an acquired company to be completely unaware that ownership has changed. There is one difference. The head man of the acquired company has a new boss at ITT headquarters.

Reaction to the conglomerate movement   In 1963 there were fewer than 1,500 mergers and acquisitions in this country; in 1966 there were about 2,400; in 1967 there were about 3,000; in 1969 there were 6,132; and for the latest year there were 2,544.

Several officials in government and business have expressed concern over the continuing conglomerate trend and its ''radical restructuring'' of the nation's economy. About half the nation's manufacturing assets acquired in 1969 were purchased by companies that ranked in the top 200, and as a result of mergers, this group's share of total United States industrial assets rose to 60 percent. The 100 largest corporations own about 48 percent of manufacturing assets. Twenty years ago this was the percentage held by the top 200.

These figures are indicative of a significant change in the structure of ownership of industry. The important question to be answered is what social, political, and economic implications are there in this restructuring? The antitrust division is so concerned over possible effects of the conglomerate movement that efforts are underway to prevent conglomerate-type acquisitions among the nation's 200 largest companies. In addition, laws to regulate and standardize incorporation of companies engaged in interstate commerce have been suggested at the federal level.

Since, by definition, conglomerates operate without apparent horizontal or vertical relationships among their parts, and since they appear to be principally concerned with financial structuring and improvement in the market value of stock of the conglomerates, the old tests to establish anticompetitive tendencies in the structure are inadequate. Finding the right answer to this enigma will provide one basis for successfully challenging conglomerate acquisitions.

SUMMARY

Broadly speaking, a person has the choice of three approaches to business ownership: the proprietorship, the partnership, and the corporation. The best approach can be found after considering the following six points:

1 Costs and procedures in starting Corporations are the most complicated to form because they are created only by following strictly the legal procedures of the particular state in which the corporation is being set up. Proprietorships are the easiest and cheapest to get started and partnerships are only a little more involved.

2 Size of the risk A proprietor cannot restrict his liability in any way. Likewise, each member of a partnership is himself fully responsible for all debts owed by his partnership irrespective of the amount of his own investment in the business. Corporations have a real advantage in this respect because an owner's liability is limited to his investment; he cannot lose any more. The degree of risk in a business venture is a cardinal consideration in the selection of an ownership form.

3 Continuity of the business A corporation can have unlimited life but proprietorships and partnerships die when an owner dies. The impact of a sudden termination of business must be considered before adopting an ownership form.

4 Management Frequently the talents of one person are adequate for business success but there are many cases where a combination of talents is essential. Both the corporation and partnership provide the means for using the abilities of more than one person at the owner level.

5 Impact of laws There are no laws governing the proprietorship form of ownership and any laws governing partnerships are not burdensome. A partner or proprietor, being a private citizen, is recognized as such in each of the fifty states. The corporation is a citizen only in the state of incorporation and may be treated differently in each of the remaining forty-nine states.

6 Attracting additional capital The limited-liability and unlimited-return-on-investment concepts that apply to the corporation are a great advantage in attracting new capital. However, any business that is successful will be able to attract new capital regardless of ownership form. A corporation that is not successful will have as much trouble getting new capital as any other business.

QUESTIONS

1 Why is it important for the person going into business to be careful in choosing the ownership form?

2 Under what conditions is the proprietorship the most desirable form of legal ownership?

3 Why is the proprietorship so very widely used? Why is it a socially desirable approach to ownership?

4 How are proprietorships and partnerships alike? How do they differ?

5 If partners disagree on the management of their business, what are the alternatives facing them? How can they resolve their differences?

6 Distinguish between the liability of a general partner, a silent partner, and a limited partner.

7 Why is it that the limited-partnership approach to ownership has not become popular?

8 What are the consequences of a company doing business in a state other than the state of incorporation?

9 What are some of the implications of the fact that the owners of a large corporation are not likely to be the managers?

10 What is the function of the stockholders in the operation of a corporation?

11 A corporation pays a federal income tax, but a partnership does not. Why?

12 What is a conglomerate? How does the conglomerate differ from the traditional pattern of business growth? What are the consequences?

13 When the price of a share of stock rises in the market, what impact does this have on the firm that issued the stock? Why?

14 How do the promoters of a new corporation sell its stock? How do they determine the value of a share of stock?

The purpose of this chapter Every business organization should have goals and objectives, to explain the reason for its existence. These goals give rise to a number of functions that must be performed, such as production, marketing, and finance. These functions vary in importance from one firm to another, and it is vital not only to recognize them but to give them an appropriate assignment in the organization structure. This is the basic purpose of organization. / Organization structures can develop along a variety of lines. It is important that the structure be tailored to the specific needs and philosophy of the firm. The danger is that certain functions may go undone, others may be overemphasized, and communication may become ineffective. The test of a sound organization is that it achieves goals and objectives in effective fashion. / Questions raised in this chapter include:

1 Why is organization so important to effective business operation?

2 What are the different organization structures and how do they develop?

3 How are different functions made a part of the organization structure?

4 Why do organizations become decentralized?

goals
objectives

7 ORGANIZATION THEORY

The business environment in the United States is determined by our legal, social, and economic institutions; they establish the basic framework in which business is carried on. In general, laws and customs are not directive in nature; rather, they are limiting. They are more concerned with eliminating unfair advantage and ensuring fair competition than with prescribing the specific direction a business must take. This can be likened to a professional football game wherein the league determines the rules and penalties of the game but does not interfere with its progress. Also, the rules and penalties are applied without discrimination.

Success in business depends mainly on the skill with which business people make use of the resources available, just as success in football depends on the skill with which the players on the roster are used. The key to success is the efficient and effective use of the available people, materials, and machinery or plant. This calls for a sound and efficient organization of the factors of production and for good management to ensure that the aims of the organization are sound.

Both elements—organization and management—are essential. It is useless to establish any goal if the organization needed to achieve the goal is not available. It is also useless to have an efficient and competent organization that is directed toward the wrong goals. The most effective organization in the country would fail if it produced goods that no one wanted; on the other hand, production of goods for which a ready market existed would not produce a profit if the business were so poorly organized that the goods cost more to produce than the price at which they could be sold.

WHAT IS "ORGANIZED"?

In the main, when we speak of organization, we are concerned with human resources, for this is the most important of all business resources. The organization of physical and financial resources cannot take place until human resources are organized, and the effectiveness of the organizational scheme depends on the manner in which human resources are utilized. Everything hinges on human resources.

In a sense, therefore, we do not organize physical and financial

139

resources; we organize people who in turn are responsible for the utilization of resources. Yet we must apply the concept of organization to all resources or face the probability that their use will not be maximized. "Money in the bank" and "sparkling new equipment" are nice-sounding phrases, but neither is worth a great deal by itself. A $10,000 bank balance used to maximum advantage may accomplish more for a firm than a $50,000 balance that is only partially utilized. The same idea applies to all resources. What is "organized"? All the resources available should be organized, with emphasis on those that are most closely related to the purpose of the firm.

The size and complexity of business

Organization and management are relatively simple in a business where the owner-manager is the only worker and only one kind of goods and services is produced, as in a one-man barber shop. But as a business grows in size, the work force may swell into thousands and tens of thousands of workers; dozens or even hundreds of pieces of raw material must then be handled and coordinated; millions of dollars' worth of machinery and equipment comes into use; the various parts of the firm become geographically separated; in short, each problem faced by the owner-manager of a small shop is magnified a thousand times. The organization required to weld all these separate elements into an efficient and productive system becomes immensely complex.

A simple way to demonstrate how the complexity of personnel relationships increases as the number of people involved increases utilizes the data in Figure 7-1. In the first instance there are only two people involved and only two possible relations. The supervisor and the worker know the extent of their involvement and can plan accordingly. By adding just one person, the number of possible relations jumps by ten. Thus the supervisor can be involved in a wider variety of relations which can consume more of his time and reduce his effectiveness. With three employees, the number of possible relations is fifty-four.

THE ESSENCE OF ORGANIZATION

Every joint human endeavor, whether in the field of business or government or sports or any other activity, requires organization. There must be a recognition of the functions that must be performed if the firm is to achieve its objectives and each function must be brought into proper relationship with the other. This is the essence of organization—functions and their relationships. Through organization the individual parts are brought together and made a working unit, just as assembling the parts of a machine produces a unit that functions as a whole.

Organized groups, whether people, beasts, or inanimate parts, can

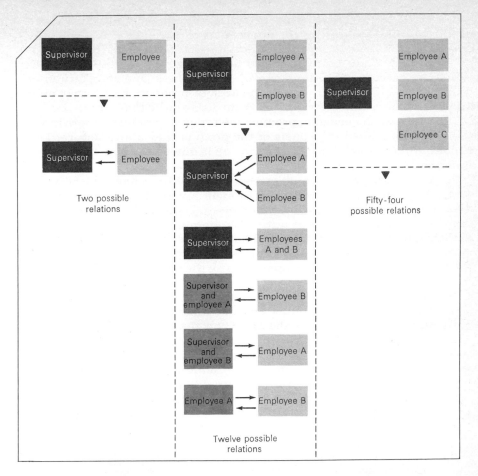

FIGURE 7-1　How the task of management grows in complexity

As personnel increases, the possible number of relationships grows geometrically, and the complexity of management's task grows correspondingly.

do things which the individual parts cannot do by themselves; no single part of a watch can keep time, but the whole watch performs this function if each part runs properly. Again, this is the essence of organizational problems in business. Each part must be assigned a function which will fit into the operation of the whole business, and each unit in the business must perform its assigned function. Organization is what makes large-scale business possible.

Organization and purpose

A statement of the goals, objectives, and purposes of an enterprise is a necessary prerequisite to the development of any organizational structure, for not until the purpose of a firm is established can the requirements for meeting the purpose be established. Once the purpose is established, the specific functions that must be performed can be identified. Then using purpose as a basis, the appropriate relationships between functions can be established. One company may find that its significance lies in the area of production; another may emphasize sales and distribution. Some firms build their organization around the skills needed to produce the product, whereas others build their organization on the basis of the product they manufacture. The fundamental nature of any organization is determined by the purpose it serves.

In effect, organization establishes relationships among the persons and things involved in business in such a way that the purpose of the organization is accomplished efficiently. In any sizable firm, this involves the distribution of authority among the various major elements in the business structure. The type of structure that is created varies a great deal from one business to another. The diagrams in Figure 7-2 show two ways of approaching the problem of organization in the same firm.

At the left, the organization was patterned by the functions performed, making sales, production, and finance the three basic subdivisions of the system. At the right, on the other hand, it was assumed desirable to structure the organization into three divisions corresponding to three separate products. In this situation, each division is responsible for its own sales, production, and fiscal administration. Both types of organizations provide a clear and definite line of responsibility, but the scope of responsibility varies considerably.

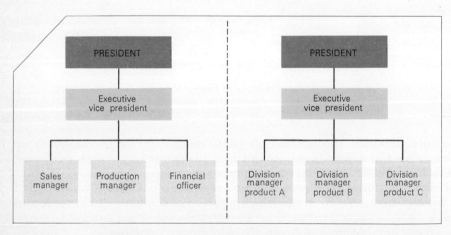

FIGURE 7-2 Organization according to specialized function or according to product

In the same business firm the organization structure could be set up according to the various functions, as at the left, or according to the several products that are made and sold.

Either type of organization may prove satisfactory, depending on the particular circumstances within the firm.

Organizational needs vary

The significance of any given function inside a firm depends largely on the goals of the firm—the type of activity involved. An assembly plant which depends on the uniform flow of parts from many different suppliers may attach great significance to purchasing, and a maker of precision instruments of high quality may assign relatively little importance to purchasing but great significance to quality control. Because there are great differences between the goals of one business and the goals of another, it is impossible to lay down a single organizational pattern which will produce optimum results in every case. The pattern of organization will generally be different in firms engaged in different kinds of businesses and even among firms which produce the same type of goods.

Further, there may often be changes in organizational structure, since a kind of organization which is adequate for a small firm may prove inadequate when facilities are expanded. Business firms may add new product lines or acquire subsidiaries, and it cannot be assumed that the organization which proved suitable to the parent company will be adequate for manufacturing a new line of products. A change in ownership may call for an organizational change if the existing system is not suited to the aims or methods of the incoming managers.

THE CLASSICAL THEORY OF ORGANIZATION

To better understand what organizations are and why they are structured as they are, we need to turn back to the beginning of our industrial era. Organizations have always existed but business organization in a democratic society is a relatively new discipline.

Our shift from an agricultural society to an industrial society came about in a relatively short period of time. Almost overnight we experienced the new phenomenon of hundreds of people working under a single roof performing mostly menial tasks in the production of goods. This presented a new problem in organizing. The business of agriculture was primarily family centered and the time-tested principles of family organization provided the necessary unity for effective operations. Operating a factory like a huge family just would not work; some alternative was necessary.

Frequently when we are faced with a new problem we look for similar circumstances to learn what to do. Over the years there have been a number of very effective large-scale organizations. Certainly the building of China's great wall and the great pyramids were large-scale operations. Also, the Roman Catholic church and the Prussian army were successful large-scale organizations. The apparent logic was to borrow a number of ideas from these nonbusiness institutions and apply them to the organization of business enterprise. Consequently, there are many elements of the classical theory of organization that have nonbusiness origins. Some of these elements are:

1 The idea that the organization is more important than any member of it and each member therefore should subordinate his own interest to the interest of the organization. There is much wisdom in this idea, but taken to the extreme, which too frequently happens, this reduces a person's role to a mere cog in a huge gear.

2 The idea of hierarchy and chain of command. We decided at the outset that there would be superiors and subordinates in organization and that superiors would deal only with immediate subordinates. In addition, superiors dealt with subordinates as they saw fit.

3 The idea of the infallible head. What a superior says is right must be accepted as right and subordinates should not question the wisdom of their superiors.

4 The organization's only responsibility to its members is economic. As a result, workers should expect no satisfactions from their employment other than the agreed-upon pay.

These concepts were the backbone of our organization theory until midway through this century, and as you move from one business organization to another today, you will see that many of these concepts are still applied. When you hear such common statements as, "Working for this outfit is like being in the army" or "In this company there is only one right way, the supervisors'" or "The boss really reamed me today for a mistake he made," you know that the classical theory is still with us. This approach to organization, although subject to much criticism, remains with us because it is a much more certain approach to organization than alternative approaches, and we must agree that it has produced outstanding results. In the discussions that follow, you will see the classical theory in operation and also how this approach has been modified.

THE THREE-ORGANIZATION THEORY

Up to this point reference has been made several times to "the" organization of a business. We should recognize that in virtually all situations where numbers of people are brought together to achieve a common goal there will be three distinct organizational structures operating side by side. At this point we will merely identify them and leave the more complete discussion until later.

1 The formal organization The formal organization created by management is best pictured at this point as the organization chart that hangs on the wall. It is an expression of the functions that must be performed and the relations that should take place to achieve enterprise objectives as viewed by management. This is the model for organization, and it frequently emphasizes the classical approach.

2 The operating organization The formal organization with people assigned to each function and each job is the operating organization. "Marketing manager," to illustrate, is a logical business function, but what will be the specific role of this function and how will it relate to other functions such as production and finance? The answer lies not in the formal organization plan but in the people involved. Functions do not relate to other functions; people must relate. Functions have no vitality of their own; people give vitality to functions, and people carry out functions. Every function in business has some of the "personality" of the people who are involved with it. Therefore, the operating organization, in essence, may cancel out the formal organization in part.

3 The informal organization The people in organizations have their personal goals and objectives that must be fulfilled. If the formal or operating organizations do not provide for this fulfillment, people will establish, in an informal organization, the functions and relationships that are needed to achieve personal goals. These additional functions can involve communication, socializing, or even status symbols.

In conclusion, the organization structure for any group endeavor may begin in very formal fashion, but it will be modified by the people who head up the recognized functions and the informal functions and relations that are created by the members of the organization. Moreover, these changes will continue as the views of organization members change and as new faces are brought on the scene.

FUNDAMENTAL PATTERNS OF ORGANIZATION

Regardless of the fact that the ultimate design of an organization may be unknown at the outset, there must be some structuring, some discernible form to organization. Although there is no single organizational structure that is suitable to all businesses, we do find that there are three basic patterns of organization which can be used alone or in combination when organizations are being created. They are:

1 Line structure
2 Functionalization
3 Line and staff structure

In smaller organizations, we sometimes find these patterns in "pure" form, that is, not combined with other patterns. But in most large organizations various combinations modify these basic patterns.

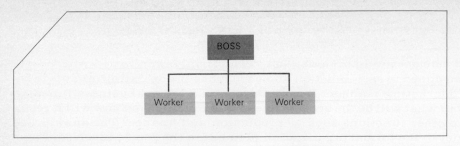

FIGURE 7-3　A simple line organization

This organization structure is usually found in a small business or in a firm that cannot afford the staffing costs of a more complex form of organization.

Line structure

Line structure, the simplest and oldest of the three types, signifies an organization in which there is a direct flow of authority from top to bottom. Figure 7-3 shows a graphic illustration of line organization in two levels. This structure can be used if the business is not overly diversified and the number of personal relationships is reasonably low. There is one manager, one final authority, and one line of authority. All that happens within the firm takes place in this one line. This can be modified, if the business grows too large for one manager to supervise properly, by adding an intermediate level with foreman or supervisors, as shown in Figure 7-4. The boss will then be the focal point for two or more lines of authority.

By adding more lines of authority, the boss can delegate greater responsibility to the foreman, leaving his own time free for other tasks. This structure is not necessarily limited to use in small business. We can easily duplicate the organization shown in Figure 7-4 several times and place a higher boss in charge of the entire opera-

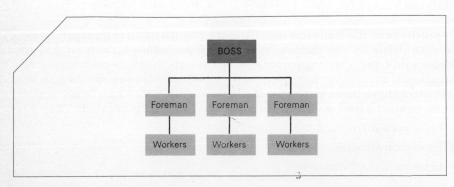

FIGURE 7-4　A line organization with an intermediate level

In this case the boss delegates authority to the foremen, who, in turn, direct the workers. The boss's job thereby becomes less involved.

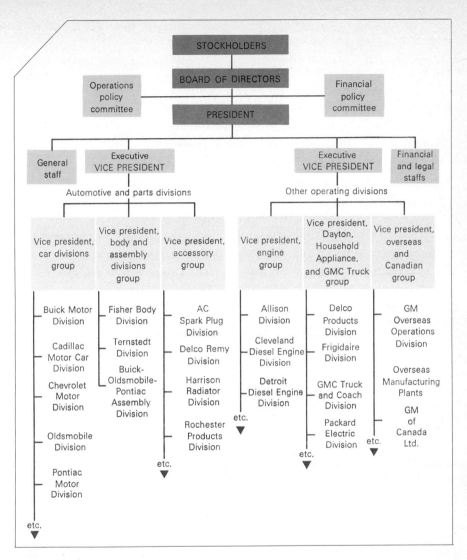

FIGURE 7-5 Organization of General Motors Corporation

Although this illustration does not show G.M.'s complete organization structure, note that the line relationships shown in Figures 7-3 and 7-4 apply even in the largest of industrial corporations.

tion, thus creating a pyramid of authority that may take in a number of subordinate lines. Figure 7-5 shows a large corporate organization structure built upon a foundation of the line.

Advantages and disadvantages Before management adopts a line structure for its organizational plan, the relative advantages and disadvantages of this type of organization need to be weighed carefully. The principal advantages of line structure are:

1 It makes for easily understood relationships among individuals in the firm.

2 It eliminates confusion by fixing the flow of authority and responsibility in a direct line from top to bottom.

3 It simplifies the problem of discipline.

4 It minimizes "red tape" and "buck passing."

5 It makes possible quick action by top management.

The disadvantages are fairly obvious:

1 The organization depends much more on the persons at the top than is the case with other structural patterns.

2 The growth of business may overload some of the supervisors.

3 There is little room for specialization in this pattern.

4 It is possible to assign too much authority to a few people.

Functionalization

The functional approach to organization begins with the special skills and talents needed to operate a business, and creates a structure which makes maximum use of these skills. Its foundation is thus basically different from that on which line organization rests. In a line organization the foreman and boss are assumed to have all the necessary managerial skills; all too often this assumption cannot be justified in large business concerns. The boss who is expert in one or two areas of business activity may find that his expertness is not adequate if the business expands to include other functions with which he is not familiar.

Pure functionalization

In an organization based on functionalization alone, every person who performs a particular type of work falls into a single division. Thus there is a direct line of authority from the head of accounting to every accountant in the firm; every electrical worker is responsible to the supervisor of electricians. The arguments in favor of this type of organization are based on the view that an electrician is better able to understand the problems electrical workers face and to evaluate their performance than someone who has no electrical experience.

The problem created by functionalization, however, is the diffusion of authority and loss of effective control, the reason being that workers cannot be grouped functionally in the actual production system. Figure 7-6 shows the effect of functionalizing the line of authority in an organization where production is organized on a line basis. The individual worker may find himself under the direction of two or more supervisors and uncertain of the extent to which each

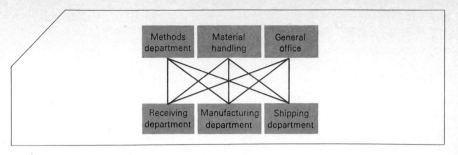

FIGURE 7-6   Pure functionalization

Pure functionalization may create a maze of interrelationships that are hard to follow. A worker here has divided responsibility, i.e., different bosses as different situations arise.

of them should control his actions. To illustrate, the manager of the Methods Department can exercise authority over all departments in matters pertaining to work methods. This type of divided responsibility produces confusion, poor personnel relations, and friction. For this reason, we seldom encounter pure functionalization in the business world.

Practical functionalization   Nevertheless there are real advantages to permitting a certain amount of functionalization in a business organization, and management attempts to gain this advantage by assigning certain well-defined work areas to specialists, while retaining a fundamental pattern of organization which is not functionalized. The chief problem is to prevent the overlapping of authority or divided responsibility that functionalization often produces.

For example, a production specialist may be used to manage production, a marketing specialist to supervise marketing, and so on, as illustrated in Figure 7-7. This approach to organization achieves a number of objectives:

1 It makes possible the effective use of special skills.

2 By narrowing the work area, it simplifies training.

3 Its manpower requirements can be readily determined.

4 It encourages the division of labor, which usually increases efficiency.

5 The system is flexible in conditions of growth; it can be adapted to expansion with a minimum of delay and upset.

Line and staff organization

Both the pure line and the pure functionalized approaches to business organization are extremes. Line organization concentrates authority; functionalization tends to disperse authority. Neither is a complete solution to modern organizational problems.

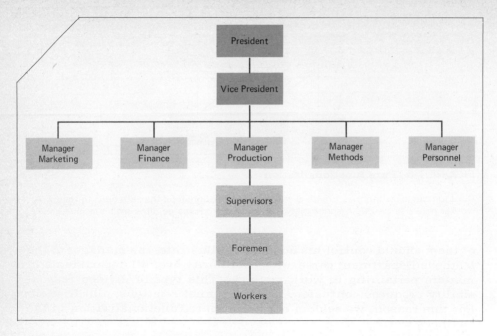

FIGURE 7-7 Practical functionalization

If methods is a functional division, it can dictate to the foremen, for example, the particular work methods that will be employed.

By combining the best features of both the line and the functional approaches to organization, we produce what is called the *line and staff organization.* The flow of authority proceeds, for the most part, along fixed channels as in line organization, but suitable provision is made for the use of specialists by the creation of staff positions in which they act in an advisory capacity to the line officers. Figure 7-8 illustrates this type of organization. The staff positions are advisory to the president of the firm in this case, but there may be further staff positions attached to the various subordinate divisions of the company as well. It is the role played by a particular office, however, that decides whether the office is line or staff, not its location in the organization. Notice in Figure 7-8 that it is the president, not his staff, who holds authority, so that the authority flows in a clear channel from top to bottom. The staff offices provide the president with information, but the final decision about action is his alone. This gives the firm the use of expert advice while preserving the integrity of the basic channel of authority.

Departmental organization

In addition to establishing the appropriate pattern of organization—line, staff, or functional—for each area of activity, we must also consider the organization within each area. Purchasing as a function, for example, may be established as a staff division or a functional division as it relates to other parts of the organization. The purchasing department itself can be set up as line, functional, or line and staff. Not to confuse the issue but it is quite possible that a staff portion of a functional division could be organized on a line basis. The overall organizational plan does not dictate the organization of divisions and subdivisions.

Staff versus functional

In one respect the work of the staff and of the functional divisions is the same. Both are specialists, and each group exists to assist or serve other segments of the organization. These two groups differ in one very important respect. In theory, at least, the staff is a source of ideas. It advises other segments of the organization on such matters as the best source of supply (purchasing), the best way to do a particular job (methods), or the best person to hire (personnel). The staff has the authority to advise but does not have the authority to force compliance.

The functional division does everything that the staff does but goes one step further. The functional division can say "We will buy from this source," "This is the way the job will be done," and so on. Functional divisions, unlike the staff, have the authority to act.

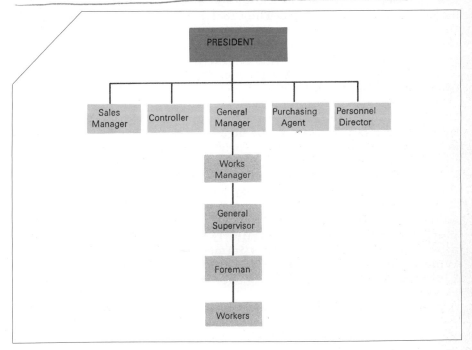

FIGURE 7-8 Line and staff organization

A line and staff organization combines the best features of the line and the functional organizations. The basic channel of authority remains in the line, while the staff provides advice and service.

Fact or myth? Is this distinction a fact in practice, or is it a myth? Does the staff always refrain from attempting to force compliance and does the functional division utilize all the authority that it can command? Again, we must rid our minds of "staff divisions" or "functional divisions," for they exist in title only. The character of any organization depends on the people assigned to different positions. If a person holds a staff position for an extended period, it will naturally take on some functional characteristics. Picture a manager of purchasing who by management definition is a staff officer. He or she performs a service for other segments of the organization; he relieves line management of many purchasing problems. Over the years he performs so well for line management, becomes such an authority on purchasing matters, and does the whole job so much better than line people, that he is permitted to make all purchasing decisions. Line management welcomes the relief. If he makes all purchasing decisions he is in effect the manager of a functional division. An aggressive and competent staff person can change the character of his function. Conversely, the very weak head of a functional division who cannot use his authority may in time become no more than an adviser.

Another consideration that affects the character of organization is the fact that many people want greater responsibility and greater authority, and they take it. They feel perhaps that their status will improve if their area of responsibility increases. The following is a case in point. One of the two authors had just completed giving a management development course to a group of first-line supervisors at a plant employing 1,200 people. During a review session with upper management following the course, it was brought out that many employees had no idea what the company made or what went on in the shop. All agreed that it would be a good idea to do something about a bad situation, but no decision was made as to whether or not there should be a product-orientation program.

A few days later the cost manager received a memo from the personnel manager (both had attended the review sessions) requesting that he release one-third of the cost department personnel for a 2-hour product-familiarization session which was being conducted by Personnel the following Tuesday afternoon. The balance of the employees were to be released similarly on Wednesday and Thursday afternoon. The cost manager's immediate response was negative. What right did Personnel have to ask for a release of workers, and how come Personnel was taking over the role of product familiarization?

Yet the following Tuesday afternoon one-third of the cost department workers reported for their familiarization session. When they returned to their work area they were very pleased and they showed their enthusiasm in conversations with fellow workers. Their main question was why their own boss, the cost manager, had not had enough imagination and drive to do this long ago. The second and third groups followed with equally good results. Then the estimating department, billing department, and so on were given the same treatment. Did the personnel manager have the authority to do what he did? This is purely an academic question because he did it and became recognized as the authority in this new area of activity—employee familiarization. We shall see more and more as this subject develops that organizations, functions, and jobs cannot be dictated by a central authority; they are each susceptible to change by the people involved.

BUILDING THE ORGANIZATIONAL STRUCTURE

The organization chart which hangs on the wall in the boardroom tells very little about the organization or the process of organizing. It does not reveal how the organization came to be, what authority is vested in each office, or what personal relations take place during and after office hours. A great deal can be learned about organization by following its development from a one-person operation into a firm employing a large number of people.

The line

A number of functions are common to all business organizations. Every business has a production function, a distribution function, a finance function, a legal function, a record-keeping function, and so on. In a one-person business, one person is responsible for every function. With growth, the same functions, perhaps enlarged, are split among a number of people.

The line portion of a business must be the first to develop because line activity relates directly to the generation of income. Production and distribution as a rule are line-type functions. Service functions, whether staff or functional divisions, must be a later development because their purpose is to serve the line. In a one-person business there is no true organization because everything is the responsibility of one individual. Even after the firm has grown to two or three employees there may be no real organization, for every member of the group may be involved with the same functions.

If a business does not grow beyond the one- or two-person operation there will, of course, be no organization problems. Eventually, if the business grows, the sheer volume of activity will force the owner-worker to leave the work bench or the machine. The pressure of planning, directing, and coordinating the work of subordinates along with selling, record keeping, and other tasks will more than occupy an 8-hour day. At this stage, the organization chart might resemble Figure 7-3. As the business grows and the need for more production people increases, the burden of supervision will become more than the owner can handle. The best course of action may be to delegate the task of worker supervision to a foreman or foremen. Thus a new level of organization is born as shown in Figure 7-4.

If the business continues to grow, this process will be repeated over and over—more workers and more foremen. Eventually, there will be more foremen than the owner can effectively manage, and another level, the supervisor, must be added. Thus the pattern continues as growth continues. We can now see that the line portions of an organization have natural evolution which is based on the number of operative employees (workers) and the ability of a superior to effectively manage subordinates, or the manager's span of control. The line portion of an organization can be likened to a pyramid (see Figure 7-9); the broader the base, the greater the number of layers it contains and the taller it becomes.

There may be several lines in a good-sized organization, but each will develop according to the pattern described above. The production "line" described above could just as well be a distribution "line" wherein workers are called sales people and foremen are called district managers. The process is the same. The size of the firm and the types of activity performed affect the number of lines.

A natural question at this point would be: If the above analysis is correct, will not the time come when the number of workers at the bottom (see Figure 7-9) will be so great that it will require so many levels of organization that it will become unwieldy? The answer would be affirmative if no action were to be taken regarding the managers' span of control.

Span of control

Span of control or span of management is of great significance in building and operating an organization. "Span of control" refers to the number of subordinates that a superior can effectively manage. It applies to managers of all functions and all levels of organization. There is no ideal or set number of subordinates that a given manager can effectively handle; there are too many variables. We do know that a manager's span decreases as we go up the organizational ladder. A foreman can effectively manage more subordinates than the president, for example. We shall see why later on.

Management must attempt to extend every manager's span of control. If this is not done and the firm grows there will be more man-

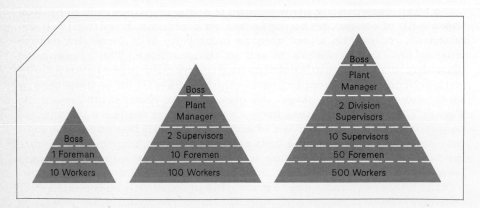

FIGURE 7-9 The evolution of an organization

agers than the firm can afford. Managers are necessary in any group effort, but this does not justify having more managers. A principal role—the reason for being—of a manager is to make it possible for subordinates to be more effective. If there are no workers on the production line there is certainly no need for a production foreman. In a sense managers do not make money for a firm; they are not directly involved in the manufacture and selling of goods. Production-line workers and field sales persons are directly involved in creating income for the firm, but all other workers are engaged in "helping" activity. Thus if a manager's span is extended he can be a more helpful person.

Extending the span Obviously, if a manager's span of control can be extended, the number of levels in the organization can be reduced. Refer to the left pyramid (Figure 7-9) and see the impact on organization if the foreman's span of control could be increased from ten to twenty workers. Not only would the need for managers at many levels be reduced, but levels of organization—division manager, for example—may be eliminated with no loss of organizational effectiveness. Apart from the savings in manpower costs that may result, communication is facilitated through a lessening of the "distance" from the top of the organization to the bottom.

We can best approach the problem of extending a manager's span if we look first at those factors that tend to limit it. The fundamental limitation is time. Expressed differently, a manager's span is limited by the frequency and variety of relations he or she has with subordinates. Conceivably, one or two subordinates could eat up all their supervisor's time. The key to extending a manager's span is to reduce the need for contact and reduce the variety of decisions that the supervisor must make.

Reducing the need for contact Both the manager and the subordinates can be responsible for excessive contact—the subordinate by failing to accept self-responsibility and the manager by listening to problems that should be handled by the subordinate. This points out the need for identifying beyond doubt the responsibilities of every person in the organization.

A manager can extend his span of control by careful delegation to subordinates provided of course that subordinates have the capacity to act on their own. Staff assistants may be employed to act on the more routine decisions that cannot be made at the subordinate level. Many managerial decisions involve repetitive situations, and it is quite possible that policy statements can be prepared to provide answers for subordinates. Finally, at certain levels of organization the computer—the information provider—may eliminate the need for personal contact in order to obtain the desired data and thus conserve the manager's time.

Reducing the variety of contacts If the range of decisions that a manager must make is narrow, he may be able to handle a very high volume of contacts. However, if decisions involve diverse and inter-related areas, the time required to think through the problem will be much greater. If the organization is designed so as to reduce the variety of activities for which a manager is responsible, his span can thereby be increased. This is another instance where the application of specialization benefits the organization. Note that this option is not open to the president because his responsibility is for all activity.

Impact of growth Most organizations grow, and the rate of growth has a bearing on a manager's span of control. If growth is moderate and does not involve new functions a manager may be able to double or triple his span. Over time a manager learns the details of his operation so fully that problems that once took many minutes to solve can be handled at the snap of a finger. Thus he is able to assume a larger area of responsibility.

The service divisions

As the line develops, the need arises for specialized assistance. When production divisions are small the foreman may be able to handle the purchasing function, personnel, quality control, and other aspects of operations. Eventually, the combined volume of activity will be more than one person can handle. Because the foreman's prime role is getting workers to produce goods he will ask for help in such areas as those described above. Thus service divisions are born. They exist not to be directly involved with income generation but to make it possible for the line to operate more effectively. Service divisions can be staff or functional in nature (refer to previous discussion of staff and functional organization), but to simplify this discussion service divisions will be referred to as "staff."

Staff divisions come into being and develop quite unlike the line. The line develops based on units of production and the span of control of managers—a relatively precise basis. The only justifiable reason for adding workers to the line is that more units are being produced. Service divisions are designed to help the line and other service divisions, and as we all know one person may need, or use, a significantly larger or smaller amount of help to get a job done than another will use.

Development of service divisions What is the normal pattern of development for service divisions? Unlike the line, service divisions have no normal pattern. Frequently, which service division first becomes a part of the organization will depend on who asks for what at the most opportune time. Considerable "selling" of need goes on in organizations, and all too often it is the squeaking wheel that gets the lubricant.

Once a decision has been made that a particular service function is needed, two questions remain, either of which could have a number of answers. First, where will the function be assigned, and how broad will be the scope of this function? Second, how many people will be "needed" to perform this service? The help that line management asks for in the personnel area could involve mere record keeping, or it could involve all the activities required to recruit workers and prepare them to go to work on the production line before the foreman sees them. Personnel might serve only the production area, for example, or it could cover all employees at all levels.

The consequence is that service divisions are often out of balance with true organizational needs. Bear in mind that the manager of a service division is concerned for his job and his development; he wants his division to grow. As a result service divisions may decide unilaterally that they should provide certain services and may attempt to impose them on other segments of the organization.

FUNCTIONS AND THEIR ASSIGNMENT

The essence of organization is functions and their relationships. From the various organization charts above, such as Figure 7-8, we can learn what functions are and that they are placed above, below, or beside other functions. A great variety of activity is also present in any organization that is not identified as a specific function. There is a definite distinction between an *activity* and a *function* in business. A function is an area of activity that has been accorded a specific organizational position and for which some individual is responsible. For example, in every business firm where there are employees there is personnel activity. Every foreman or every supervisor may be expected to take care of "personnel" activity in his area along with his other duties. When management creates a personnel department and makes someone responsible for personnel activity, then it becomes a function. Activities become functions when management recognizes the need to make them a formal part of the organization. New functions also come into being as a result of expanding a firm's scope of operation.

Importance of assignment

All functions must be assigned somewhere in the organizational structure, but there is no cardinal rule that states where each function belongs. Many factors must be considered, including the goals of the firm and the philosophy of management. But the proper assignment of functions is a most important consideration. A poor assignment will result in overemphasizing or underemphasizing the function, thereby distorting its intended purpose. Whenever a function is to be assigned, management should consider the alternatives available and should make an assignment which is consistent with the goals or objectives of the firm.

To illustrate this point, let us take a hypothetical situation which we will call Excaliber College (see Figure 7-10). This is a relatively small liberal arts college located in a city having a population of about 20,000. Excaliber, whose organization chart is shown in Figure 7-10, is the only institution of higher learning within 100 miles of the city. To satisfy local needs primarily, the board of trustees has decided that the college should offer a program in business administration and has instructed the president to incorporate this function into the organization. Where should the president assign this function? Several alternatives are available and each is apt to yield different results.

Because there is a significant element of economics in business administration, a logical assignment might be shown in position 1 of Figure 7-10. In this assignment, no matter what title is given to the head of this function, the role played will be subordinate to and dictated by the head of the department of economics. It is quite apparent that business administration will never be as important as economics at Excaliber with this arrangement.

Position 2 puts business administration on an equal plane with other departments. Here, business administration could enjoy the same status as other departments and be in an equal bargaining position with the dean for its share of college resources. Position 3 puts business administration on a higher level. Here the head would report to the president. Another possible assignment of this function could be to create a College of Liberal Arts and a College of Business Administration.

There are many job titles that sound good, but titles per se are quite meaningless. A good job allows for independent judgment and an opportunity to grow. The above illustration proves that the specific assignment of a function in the organization is of far greater importance in indicating what a job really is than its title.

Bases for assigning functions

There are a number of bases, or justifications, that managers apply when assigning functions. Executive interest always enters the pic-

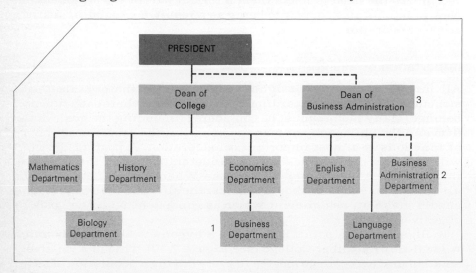

FIGURE 7-10   The assignment of functions at Excaliber College

ture. If the president likes the idea behind a new function he or she may assign it high in the structure. Similarly, the function may be assigned in such fashion that it can compete or not compete with other divisions of the firm. If the Mercury division of the Ford Motor Company was a part of the Ford division, Mercury cars could compete with Ford cars only to the extent desired by the manager of the Ford division. By setting up two distinct divisions, Mercury is in a much better competitive position.

CENTRALIZATION AND DECENTRALIZATION

The organization charts of two firms could be identical in their appearance, yet fundamentally different in their meaning. We know that there is more authority in high organization levels than at low levels, but there can be varying amounts of authority at any managerial level. If the chief executive decides to retain most areas of authority, the organization is described as centralized. If, however, the chief executive assigns significant areas of authority to relatively low levels, the organization is described as decentralized.

Thus the true significance of any managerial position depends on the extent to which authority is centralized or decentralized. Centralization tends to make every position below the top much less significant; decentralization tends to increase the importance of subordinate positions. When we speak of centralization or decentralization, we are always speaking of degree, for no organization can go 100 percent in either direction. If all authority is held at the top, there effectively is no organization. Complete decentralization would result in the loss of control.

Decentralization eventually takes place in most firms because at the outset they are highly centralized. In Figure 7-3, all authority rests with the boss; in Figure 7-4 some authority rests with the foremen —all managers must have some authority. Each new level of management results in further decentralization. Centralization can offer the advantage of flexibility and adaptability because only one or a few persons are involved in the decision-making process. Centralization is practiced in large and small firms although a higher degree of centralization would be expected in a small firm. Much depends on the capabilities of the people who hold the high positions.

The General Electric Company is a prime example of decentralized organization. GE is made up of a large number of diversified and dispersed businesses ranging from consumer credit to computers. GE uses decentralization to create a large number of semiautonomous businesses, each playing its part in the overall company plan. Properly applied, decentralization can yield a wide range of benefits to the user. Among them are:

1 It puts authority for making decisions close to the point where the decision is to be applied.

2 It allows managers at lower levels to be responsible for decisions on matters that affect them; it is democratic.

3 It gives managers a sense of accomplishment and importance.

4 It creates a pool of managers who are experienced in the decision-making process.

5 Because authority is not centralized and because there is a pool of trained managers, the organization should be more adaptable to growth.

6 It minimizes the ability gap between top management and subordinate managers, thereby facilitating the process of succession.

Impact of growth on organization

Most American businesses have a philosophy of growth and it is imperative that this be considered in the design of an organization structure. But there are a number of reasons for business growth and there are variations in the ways that organizations grow. Also, there are differences in the rate of growth that firms experience. Consequently, the impact of growth on a particular firm could range from insignificant to significant depending on a number of variables.

Reasons for growth The following is an indication of some of the reasons for business growth:

1 To broaden the profit base. Profit is generated by the sale of goods and services. Frequently, increased sales lead to increased profits.

2 To spread fixed costs. If the fixed costs of operation can be spread over 2,000 units of activity instead of 1,000 units, the unit cost of the activity can be cut in half.

3 Competition demands growth. Firms may have to grow simply to keep pace with competition—to maintain their share of the market. If Sears, Roebuck decides to grow, it behooves Montgomery-Ward to grow—otherwise it will become a lesser institution in the field of retailing.

4 People in organizations grow. Over time, people master relatively complex tasks and look for new worlds to conquer. Growth and change can provide the challenge that many people seek.

5 To gain control over markets. The huge investment required by higher levels of technology and the increased time span between the inception of a product and the marketing of that product make it necessary for firms to have some control over markets—some assurance that their product will be purchased. Firms such as Procter & Gamble and General Motors are strong enough to influence the market's reaction to their new products.

As we look at the above, we can detect how reasons for growth can impact on an organization. If the impetus for growth comes from members of the organization, one could expect a greater degree of cooperation and involvement in the growth effort. If the reason for growth is to lower costs, members of the organization could be expected to respond with varying degrees of enthusiasm.

Nature of growth Growth can be described as <u>internal</u> or <u>external.</u> Internal growth means that the management team is involved with greater amounts, and perhaps with a greater variety, of activity. Here, growth springs from what is already there in the organization and everyone is a part of this ongoing process. External growth always involves the acquiring of an existing business. But the impact of acquisition on the parent firm can vary. If one book publisher acquired another and expected the editing, marketing, and production divisions of the parent firm to absorb this work previously done by the acquired firm, there could be a significant impact on the managers of the parent firm. On the other hand, if the autonomy of the acquired firm was preserved, and only the president of the acquired firm was responsible to the president of the parent firm, the impact of growth on the parent-firm organization could be minimal.

Patterns of growth Growth is further classified as <u>horizontal</u> or <u>vertical</u>. When a firm grows by doing more of the same thing—a supermarket chain adding another store—we describe this growth as horizontal. Vertical growth always involves new areas of activity. Firestone decided to broaden its area of activity from tire manufacturing to the ownership of rubber plantations on the one hand, and retail outlets on the other. Both these new areas of activity involved vertical growth.

Putting this all together, we can see how different combinations of factors impact on organizations differently. If growth is internal, involves more of the same activity (horizontal), and is encouraged by the existing management team, the impact can be minimal. If growth involves the acquisition of a firm engaged in a different line of endeavor, and if existing personnel are expected to manage the new area of activity, the impact could be significant. Despite any problems that growth may create, most of us would prefer to be associated with a growth firm than one that is content with the status quo.

SUMMARY

Every joint endeavor requires organization whether it relates to a family, a church, a government, or a business. The purpose of any organization is to facilitate the achievement of the group's goals. The achievement of goals requires a plan of action which identifies the things that must be done (functions) and places them in their appropriate relationship. However, "appropriate relationship" does not imply that there is a single or best order of relationships. Organizations can center around the products or services it produces and sells, or around the functions involved in producing and distributing goods and services.

Another significant feature of organizations is the amount of authority that top management delegates to subordinate levels. Two firms whose organization charts are identical may have quite different organizations because one retains at high levels most of the authority for doing things (centralization) and the other gives lower-level managers the right to act on their own (decentralization).

The most important part of any organization is the people involved because the character of people dictates the character of the group they make up. Such terms as "line," "staff," and "decentralization" help to describe organizations, but human characteristics such as the desire for power, authority, status, or individual development are the fundamental determinants of organizations. The significance of people in organizations is explored further in the following chapter.

BUSINESS ITEMS

The garment trade: Organizational changes

The garment trade as exemplified by Manhattan's Seventh Avenue garment district still includes many family-owned and -operated units in this industry which sports a failure rate of 4 to 5 percent of the total number of companies each year.

The industry does more than $50 billion of business annually and is quietly reorganizing its marketing approach and relying far less on intuition and seat-of-the pants judgment. Many of the companies have passed from first generation to college-educated second generation. With this change has come an awakening to the realization that the industry would no longer dictate fashions to its customers. As a result, the product mix of both large and small companies is broadening; more companies are diversifying their lines, such as covering both men's and women's wear instead of just one. The approach to style is more classic so as to appeal to a broader market. And backward integration into textile manufacturing and some forward integration into retailing are more the order of the day. This both cuts costs and gives the apparel makers greater control over product and service quality.

Whereas many apparel companies were formerly run purely on intuition, now they are doing much more with information systems and marketing planning.

An unstructured management

Koppers Co., a Pittsburgh-based manufacturer of industrial equipment and materials, has a management structure best described by its chairman as "loose."

In essence, decision making is pushed down to the level where the change is taking place. The result is a great degree of decentralization and a stimulation of subordinates to do their own thinking and make their own decisions. Managers are rated on their willingness to make such decisions and their success later in convincing the chairman or the president that the decision was reasonable.

To avoid anarchy in such a loose organization, a great deal of communication is essential. Actually, the close personal relationships established among the senior officers are the key reason that this relatively nonstructured management works.

Some executives wonder whether this structure will hold up as the company continues to grow. They feel that more control from the top may be necessary. The chairman, however, believes that the structure will still serve the company's needs when it is larger if more sophisticated sensing devices are utilized, such as computerized communications systems that more efficiently analyze and distribute management information.

QUESTIONS

1 What is meant by the statement that physical and financial resources are not organized? Discuss.

2 Organizational needs vary. Discuss the meaning of this comment.

3 Define organization. Explain how organization establishes relationships.

4 Point out the advantages of functional organization. What are its drawbacks? In what business situation might a functional organization be preferable to other structure patterns?

5 Staff and functional divisions are similar in some respects yet basically different in others. Explain.

6 "The distinction of staff and functional pertains more to theory than practice." Do you agree? Discuss.

7 Describe the line and staff type of organization. How does one distinguish between line and staff responsibilities?

8 Distinguish between centralization and decentralization in organization.

9 The line portion of an organization has a natural evolution, but the staff does not. Discuss the reasons why this is true.

10 Refer to the organization chart of Excaliber College. What difference does it make where the business administration function is assigned?

11 What is meant by "span of control," and why is it essential that every manager's span be broadened?

12 Explain how a manager's span of control can be broadened.

13 What is the difference between an activity and a function in the organizational sense.

14 Why is it generally true that decentralization takes place in all organizations?

15 A firm can grow quite rapidly and make only a minor impact on organization. Explain why this could be true.

The purpose of this chapter   The essence of organization is functions and their relationships. Management expresses its organization in the form of a chart, as shown in the previous chapter. It does this to provide some assurance that the things that need to be done to achieve objectives can be done. / The true character and potential of an organization do not emerge until people have been assigned to manage each function. Because no two managers are alike, the specific contribution any function makes toward achieving enterprise objectives cannot be predicted. It all depends on who is assigned to manage the function. If a function is managed by a young, eager person who has high expectations, it will contribute something quite different than the function headed by a person who feels that he or she is being put out to pasture. Whether there is little or great similarity between the organization that is planned and the organization that actually exists depends on the people involved. / In this chapter we will examine a variety of ways that people influence the course of organizations and point out how management can best cope with these influences. / Questions raised in this chapter include:

1 How does the operating organization differ from the formal organization?

2 How do people in organizations broaden their authority?

3 What is the informal organization and how does it develop?

4 What can management do to minimize the impact of people in organizations?

5 How can management control the cost of organization?

THE DYNAMICS OF ORGA-
NIZATION

In a sense the use of an organization chart to depict the organization structure of a firm is misleading because it implies a fixed situation. We should not conclude that the structure of organization has not changed simply because the chart which hangs on the wall of the corporate office is the same as it was years before. The organization structure of any group is subject to constant change. Change may be necessary because the firm has altered its objectives which in turn required additional functions or affected the relative importance of existing functions. Change takes place in the organization structure each time a different person is assigned to a task and change takes place also simply because the people in an organization change in terms of their goals, aspirations, and drive. The previous chapter, therefore, tells us only a part of the organization story. Perhaps that chapter is best described as a theory of organization, or a theory of the formal organization, or a theory of how the organization looks today on paper. In this chapter we will explore the dynamic nature of organizations by identifying some of the causes and consequences of change.

CHANGING OBJECTIVES

The objectives of a firm dictate the functions that must be performed and the relative importance of these functions. Consequently we should expect that changing objectives may necessitate changes in the organization structure. What do we mean by changing objectives, and how might they affect organization? Suppose that a business has for a number of years produced and sold a line of standard electrical connectors. These were produced in large volume and sold to distributors who in turn sold them to manufacturers. Because the company dealt in standard products it had no special identity in the marketplace, and the effects of competition made the business unprofitable. The directors of the business decided to change the firm's objective from mass production and mass distribution of standard products to products engineered and designed for the peculiar use of specific customers. How would the importance of functions change? Would new functions be needed? Would incumbent managers still be able to carry out their functions effectively? Without attempting to answer these questions it is obvious that the distribution, production, and engineering functions would change drastically, and there may be some question about whether incumbent managers could handle the changed function.

THE OPERATING ORGANIZATION

The formal organization which was described in the previous chapter is the starting point for the operating organization. The formal organization which is commonly expressed in chart form identifies the functions management deems should exist, and places each in its appropriate relation to the others. The operating organization is defined as the formal organization with people assigned to each "box"—June White, manager of marketing, for example. Operating organizations are groups of people charged with the responsibility for carrying out established functions and maintaining certain relations with other parts of the organization.

However, we cannot predict how a person will act as part of a group, and the nature of relations that will develop within any group cannot be prescribed by the lines on an organization chart. We cannot completely separate organizational relationships from personal relationships. If personal relationships between individuals are strained, their relationships as members of the organization are bound to be affected. The consequence is that the organization cannot function according to the plan.

Some misconceptions about organizations

Figure 8-1 will be used to point out additional reasons for differences between the planned organization and what might be expected in

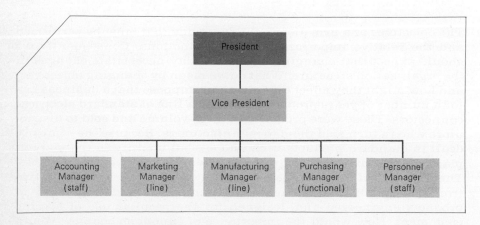

FIGURE 8-1   Organization of upper management

practice. First, we tend to visualize an organization as consisting of a number of well-defined and separate areas of activity; we imagine that manufacturing, for example, has specific starting and ending points, and is separate and distinct from all other functions such as purchasing and personnel. It would be very unusual if this were the case. The responsibilities of manufacturing and purchasing may be clearly defined by management, but such definitions are based on what management expects the departments to do. It is difficult enough to divide work and responsibility on paper so that all work is assigned and overlapping is avoided, but it becomes a nearly impossible task when people become involved. Production and purchasing by nature are not completely separate; hence divided responsibility exists, and when there is divided responsibility it becomes difficult to place accountability if the need arises.

Second, we view the established line of communication in our illustration as manager of marketing to vice president to president or the reverse. Again, this may or may not happen, depending on the people involved. The president, for a number of reasons, may permit the manager of marketing to bypass the vice president—because the two just do not get along, because the vice president never has the answers that the manager of marketing needs, or because the president and the manager of marketing belong to the same club and are golf partners. Yet he may not permit this freedom to other third-level managers. This practice, which is all too common, has its negative consequences. The first is that as lines of communication change, so do the jobs of the people involved. Each time the president permits the bypassing of his vice president, he is adding to his job and subtracting from the vice president's job. The consequences of this practice if carried to the extreme should be obvious: there would be no need for the vice president. The reason why a situation like this comes about is not a weakness in organization but a characteristic of the people involved.

Third, every function—every box—in the organization chart identifies something that needs to be done to achieve enterprise objectives. Ideally, the specific responsibilities that make up each function are identified, and it is expected that each manager will discharge his responsibilities. We can visualize that each box contains a number of responsibilities and that a person with just the right amount of qualifications nicely fits into the box. However, people seldom fit perfectly into these boxes because of their changing abilities, because of changes in responsibilities, or because of the way a person interprets his or her responsibility. The consequences of this situation are described by the following illustration:

In A the responsible manager has interpreted his role as something less than planned. The dark area represents a portion of his function that for some reason is not being performed. It could be, for example, that A is the purchasing function and the dark area represents the value analysis part of the function, which is not being performed. Perhaps the manager does not have the time, the skill, or the interest in this portion of his job. What are the consequences of this common situation? The task may go undone and therefore impair the possibilities of achieving objectives—assuming that the task is necessary— or some other manager might decide to do it. In either event, the result is a change in organization.

In B the manager sees his job differently than planned. In this case the dark area represents an enlargement of his role in the organization. This is a common occurrence because many managers like to enlarge their area of responsibility and their value to the organization. Actions such as this take place with and without the consent of upper management. In this instance the enlargement could be the part of function A that was left undone, or it could be that B is the purchasing function and the manager decided on his own that it would be a good idea to have a value analysis program. C illustrates another common practice in organizations, in which one manager simply takes on a part of another manager's job. This could happen if the manager of job 2 was slow to respond to the needs of job 1 or did not provide 1 with the services needed. For example, 1 may need a computer programmer; after several weeks, 2, Personnel, fails to come up with a qualified candidate and the manager of 1 goes out and hires a person.

The extent to which these variations in organization will take place cannot be predicted because each depends on the characteristics of the people involved. If the president exercises a loose control over the organization variations may happen frequently, but if his control is tight they will be less frequent. We must also consider that some people want more responsibility than the job is designed to have and that others want less. Some people by nature will respect the formal organization more than others. Some people by nature are very aggressive and others are not. These are but a sampling of the many reasons why the operating organization may differ considerably from the planned organization. They are also reminders that the organization chart cannot tell a person just what his job will be.

THE INFORMAL ORGANIZATION

In the process of creating an organization the designers attempt by logical and rational processes to provide the mechanism for achieving enterprise objectives. The structure thus created is facilitative in nature (it helps people to be more effective), yet at the same time it must be restrictive. Organizations demand a degree of conformity on the part of their members—conformity as regards objective, lines of communication, and the role each person is expected to play. It is quite possible that the nature of organizations and the nature of their members will at times be in conflict. People are not always logical and rational and they are creatures who constantly change.

Chris Argyris[1] suggests that there are a number of basic developmental trends present in all people who live in our culture, such as:

1 As youngsters we tend to have a passive attitude toward life, but with age we develop a need to be involved in—to be an active part of—the factors that affect our lives.

2 We develop from a state of complete dependence on others as children to a level of relative independence as adults. This is a paramount drive in most people.

3 As we mature physically we mature intellectually. We shift from satisfaction with shallow interests and superficial knowledge to a demand for more rigorous mental exercise.

4 We live our early years as subordinate members of a family and a social circle and expect to assume the role of superiors in our adult years.

Each of these developmental trends is common to the makeup of all people, yet not all people develop to the same degree or at the same pace. Therefore the impact of each trend on a particular individual at a specific point in his life is an unknown.

Let us apply some of these known characteristics of people to some known characteristics of organizations to see the consequences that can be expected. The logical organization applies the specialization concept wherein work is broken into smaller and smaller job units. It is generally true that the longer a person remains with a given growing organization, the narrower will be his area of responsibility. This may lead to a greater total responsibility and greater income, but the narrowing effect of this phenomenon may be contrary to a person's natural process of development.

All organizations have their hierarchy with countless superior-subordinate relations, and most of us are forced to live the subordinate role. The more formal the relations the greater is the feeling of dependence by the subordinate on the superior. The subordinate must depend on his superior for pay increases, promotions, and perhaps even his job. In summary, there are many things we as humans wish to do and many goals we wish to achieve, and the typical organization tends to hinder rather than assist their accomplishment.

When the organization prevents the development of natural tendencies a number of consequences can be expected. Many people will leave the organization only to be caught in the web of another organization; others will leave to create their own organization so that they need answer only to themselves. It is possible but not probable that people generally will submit to the demands of the organization. Whether they will depends largely on the alternatives that are avail-

[1]Chris Argyris, *Yale Scientific*, February 1960, pp. 40–50.

able. Most likely, people will stay with the organization and develop, outside the formal structure, the means for satisfying their desires through the informal organization.

Development of the informal organization

The informal organization comes into being simply because people get together, talk about common concerns, and decide to take action or refrain from taking action. Within a single office there may be several separate groups each dealing in its own way with its area of concern. Informal organizations have no structure except for the person who may emerge as the recognized leader. This leader has only that authority which members of the group permit, and he will remain leader only as long as he is so recognized by the group. The life of an informal organization may be as short as minutes or as long as years depending on its purpose. Since the informal organization has no specific purpose or direction its actions could be in harmony with the formal organization or in direct conflict.

Purposes of the informal organization

The purposes of the informal organization can be inferred from the previous discussion. They are twofold. The first purpose is to develop the means whereby workers can satisfy certain personal goals such as status, social interaction, and knowledge of the firm's operation not forthcoming through the formal structure. The second purpose is to establish a set of norms to govern output, behavior, dress, or other areas of concern. Such norms may be consistent with those established by management, or they may be in conflict.

Functions of the informal organization

The impact of the informal organization on the formal structure is a direct result of the functions performed by the former. Since informal organizations are unstructured it is impossible to identify what functions they will be concerned with in a given situation. However, the following functions appear to be common to most situations.

Communication The formal organization structure provides the means for people at all levels to communicate with each other. But this is no guarantee that communication will take place or that the pattern of communication will be satisfactory to all people. Communication cannot be built into a structure; only the means for communication can be built in, because the people involved are the source of communication. People in organizations want and need to know certain things, and if the information does not flow through established channels, they will create new channels—through the president's secretary, the telephone operator, the mail boy, or anyone in the know. Part of the problem stems from the fact that you and I, occupying positions of authority, have too little comprehension of the things people one, two, or three levels below need and want to know. Too often we assume that because we are aware of events others are also aware. Informal lines of communication may also develop simply because the formal line acts too slowly.

From management's point of view, one drawback of informal lines of communication is that there can be no control over the information that enters the line. If the head of this function happens to be a rumormonger, a great deal of damage to morale can result. The persistence of rumors can be an indication that management is doing a poor communication job.

Status The formal organization chart identifies the status of each function and consequently identifies each individual: A is above, below, or equal to B in status. As long as a person holds a given job his status as a member of the organization is fixed. But the accounts-payable clerk who is at the bottom level of office organization may be dissatisfied and may seek ways to raise his or her status. Status may be obtained by either doing something or knowing something special. The lowly accounts-payable clerk may achieve high status with fellow workers by being the first to know what is going to happen or by taking the lead in the establishment of new norms.

Establishing norms Members of an organization are expected to live up to a number of standards which may be formally stated or implied. These norms may or may not be acceptable to the group. If not, a probable outcome will be an attempt to establish and enforce new norms. For example, management issues a memo stating that henceforth the morning coffee break will be limited to 15 minutes instead of the current 15- to 30-minute break. If no one is concerned there will be no action, but if one person, especially an aggressive one, decides that an injustice has been done, he or she may campaign to win supporters and organize to sabotage the "establishment." The group decides that 20 minutes is a better norm and gets everyone to take a 20-minute break. The group's attitude is that if everyone takes a 20-minute break, management can do nothing about it, and therefore it is worth a try. If management does not set reasonable norms, explain their purpose, and enforce them, it is certain that norms will be set by the workers.

Benefits of informal organization

Informal organizations can be powerful forces that have positive or negative consequences; much depends on how well managers manage. But a number of benefits may accrue if managers understand the roles played by informal groups. The roles are as follows:

1 Filling gaps in the formal structure. No organization can provide for all eventualities, and strict adherence to the formal structure could prevent important things from being done. An attitude that can lead to a more complete organization is: If you see something that needs to be done, do it.

2 Acting as a breeding ground for future leaders.

3 Acting as a useful channel of employee communication.

4 Forcing managers to be better managers.

5 Causing worker productivity to rise because of a more satisfied workforce.

PLANNING THE ORGANIZATION

Much of the previous discussion implies that there may be significant differences between the organization that is planned and what the organization becomes—differences that have both positive and negative connotations. Differences will always exist but there is a need to minimize them or the organization may get out of control. While there is no way to predetermine how an organization will work, we are certain of a number of features which should be a part of all organizations. Those who are responsible for organizational planning, which should be a continuous process, should ask whether each of the following has been attended to:

Clarity
Completeness
Authority commensurate with responsibility
Coordination
Flexibility
Consideration of the human factor

If the planned organization is lacking in any of these areas, the spread between actual and planned organization can render the organization ineffective.

Clarity

The aim of clarity is to ascertain that every member of an organization clearly sees his area of responsibility, to whom he is responsible, and who is responsible to him. With clarity every individual knows his range of authority and the authority limits of those about him. The pattern of organization has a bearing on the probability of achieving clarity. The line organization incorporates clear flow of authority and simple lines for communication. A functional organization creates an octopus of authority wherein a person during a single day may be responsible to a number of different people representing different areas of activity. It is not that the functional feature is bad, but rather that the consequences of functional organization must be considered and that the means for overcoming the inherent lack of clarity must be developed. The use of staff divisions should not impair clarity, but staff people, like all people, like to exercise authority. Whenever there is a question about who is responsible and who has authority, clarity is lacking.

A common pitfall of the operating organization, as indicated above, is what is called *overlapping authority*. This refers to actions that are contrary to expressed lines of authority. An instance of overlapping authority occurs when an individual oversteps his area of expressed jurisdiction and acts in a position of authority in an area which is not organizationally expressed as being within his province.

Completeness

We may define completeness of organization as that situation which exists wherein routine or anticipated areas of business procedure have been assigned to specific channels of action.

The attempt to build into the organization a procedure for coping with every possible situation which may face a business is not the means by which completeness of organization is to be had. Regardless of the extent of the rules and procedures which may be elaborated upon in organizational structure, there eventually and inevitably will arise some occurrence for which specific handling instructions have not been formulated. Completeness in this case is achieved by providing a means whereby such unique and exceptional matters may be brought to the attention of those who are best prepared to analyze the problems and present the possible solutions.

This situation is amplified by the establishment of the *exception principle*. The principle states that repetitive matters are best handled via established routines and channels, and therefore only those situations which are exceptional, or beyond the scope of customary activity, need be channeled to top echelons for evaluation and disposal. The need for practicing this principle becomes quite apparent when one visualizes the picture of top-management people constantly plagued with small, repetitive details of business operation and, therefore, restricted in the amount of their costly time that they can devote to the more important aspects of their business. The higher the level of management, the greater the amount of time that should be spent looking ahead and the smaller the amount of time that should be devoted to current operating problems. But if the structure does not provide for dealing with all situations they will be passed up the ladder and possibly involve top management. The details of operations should be an increasingly larger part of the jobs assigned to progressively lower rungs on the ladder of organizational structure.

Authority commensurate with responsibility

The failure of an organizational pattern may usually be traced directly to the fact that responsibility for some activity has been placed in the hands of an individual, but at the same time this individual has not been given sufficient authority to allow him to exercise command or control over personnel and machines so that the task can be accomplished as management desires. It seems foolish that such a situation can exist. The following illustration shows how easily this type of situation can arise and points out the weakness of inadequate authority.

Assume that an individual has the final responsibility for supervising a given production schedule. Whether the product is goods or services is of minor importance in this illustration. Furthermore, assume that management has assigned a rigid deadline for the accomplishment of this production. If the deadline approaches and it becomes clear that the goal cannot be reached, is it not reasonable to assume that the individual responsible for the work output should have authority at his disposal to authorize overtime, to reassign tasks, or some other suitable device, in order that the rigid schedule be met? It is not consistent on the one hand for management to establish tight rules for performance and at the same time restrict the performer by limiting his authority.

Coordination

Since any and all areas of work within a business enterprise have a common goal, that is, the success of the venture, it is necessary that the efforts of these various areas be concerted and coordinated. However, an organizational structure caters to the many specialized areas of activity in which the firm is involved, and the problem of coordination among these several areas becomes aggravated. If only two of the divisions of a typical manufacturing firm, such as the sales and production departments, are to be considered in the light of their respective and immediate goals, it may be said that the sales department concerns itself primarily with the volume of sales, and the production department defines its first concern in terms of a quantity of acceptable production achieved with the greatest practical economy. The fact that these separate goals may be incompatible is demonstrated in the case of the sales force which constantly seeks new products or variations in old products to compete successfully in the market and woo its share of customers. The production unit, with its eyes ever focused on efficiency in production volume and costs, rebels at the fact that such product variation as the sales force may seek can be accomplished only with at least temporary losses in both productive and cost efficiencies. We have not lost sight of the fact that the ultimate goal of either department is overall business success, but in terms of respective and immediate goals and successes, the two divisions are in opposition.

Organizational structure must, therefore, have built into it some device which will help mold the many specialized unit problems into the shape of a common problem and by so doing preserve the unity of goal. This effort presents a difficult problem in terms of finding the correct or even a workable solution. Attempts are made in industry to bridge this gap by employing such devices as the committee and conferences. By these means a common area of discussion, understanding, and evaluation is set up, wherein it is hoped that the individual goals set by each respective department or division may find a place in the overall goal of the enterprise.

Flexibility

When the element of flexibility in organizational structure is considered, two features should be kept in mind: first, the ability of the structure to mold itself to suit changing business needs, and second, the inclusion within the master plan of organization of the need for succession and accession of personnel. As to the first feature, since the patterns of business activity are potentially ever-changing, they must be subject to scrutiny and change if the organization is to best serve its purpose. A pattern once established should be considered as merely the start of a series of revisions, each of which is originated by the existence of some new need. The pitfall in organizational practice which may exist at this point lies in dependence on the attitude that an existing organization can shoulder additional or changed duties by simply adding or changing assignments. If there is either art or science in the scheme of building an organization, haphazard or makeshift delegation of work is a certain means of destroying its value. Flexibility may be achieved by reassignment, additional assignments, innovation, or elimination. Whatever the means, the desire is that it be accomplished only with due consideration of the final effect that it will have on personal relations and overall organizational performance.

The second feature which we consider in connection with flexibility is that of succession of personnel. Succession refers to promotion in the organizational ranks. Accession refers to additions to the organizational ranks. There are various reasons why men vacate posts within a company, but these reasons do not immediately concern us. Rather, we are concerned with the task of replacing the men who leave.

Good policy in organizational procedures involves selection of individuals to fill vacated posts or newly created posts from existing personnel whenever possible. If, of course, after careful consideration of available personnel it is found that the necessary talents are not available, the company must resort to new employees.

The chart of organization must be viewed as a device which will indicate areas in which the future need for promotion activity will arise. Every position will eventually need to be refilled. What operational procedures have been instituted which will aid in filling these needs? Some companies recognize that junior management will eventually replace senior management and that the positions of foremen will eventually be refilled from the worker ranks, and so forth. The need here is that positions of preparation be assigned to the areas from which promotional material will be drawn.

Therefore, if management recognizes that a feature of every job is that it is serving as a preparation ground for promotion, then establishment of the organizational environments which will best serve this purpose must follow.

Consideration of the human factor

The organizational chart posted on the wall of the executive's office is an impersonal thing. However, when the master plan is put into operation, the chart gains significance in terms of people and action. A good plan is of little avail unless the right persons are placed in the right positions. To accomplish this, there must be a means to correctly evaluate and orient available personnel. The basic desire is that the organizational ranks be filled as competently as possible. Personal evaluation will have its shortcomings since the subject, human beings, and the object, human beings, are nonscientific. This fact should not be allowed to stand as a deterrent. The goal of evaluation is clear; the means of evaluation will become clearer.

The human factor must be recognized for what it seeks. Those employed, in any capacity, seek the answers to these questions:

1 What am I within this organization?

2 What status is available within the organization? What must I do to attain this status?

3 Who knows of what I do, and to what extent is there commendation or criticism due me for my work?

The office boy or the company executive should ask these questions of himself. If there are answers available, we may consider that the organization has cognizance of the human factor. Each of these questions points to an area of human need and, if unanswered, to an area of human frustration.

The first question recognizes that all people, regardless of lot, want to know where they stand in relation to others. They desire and need a fundamental feeling of being part of something. Workers need to be a part of a team, a recognized and specifically assigned element in the structure of the organization.

The second question points to the need for a company policy of publicized information available to the workers regarding promotional opportunities and the necessary attainment qualifications. If this policy is fostered, the company has a better assurance of a workforce which will be interested and active in the area of self-improvement. It is simply a case of indicating the goals and specifying the means of attainment. Any policy which arouses the worker to the task of self-improvement in the hope of acquiring a better position results in a gain to management. As a result of learning, the worker is better able to serve management.

The third question is raised because of the desire on the part of the individual to be recognized in terms of his or her own worth. Any organizational scheme which does not consider individual recognition must be considered deficient. Very few, if any, workers are of the type who get their confidence or assurance from within themselves. Everyone needs the pat on the back, the badge of achievement, the posting of exceptional production records, the hourly wage raise, the promotion, or some such device, all of which are tools of recognition. The worker, a sensitive being, is not, however, contented with continual praise which is not at some point materialized in terms of rank or monetary increase. Praise alone becomes insignificant and eventually spells out defeat as far as the employee is concerned. Eventual recognition must come in the form of improved status. Otherwise, all the verbal praises are lost in the worker's attitude that the criticism which was not forthcoming must have greatly outweighed the expressed commendations.

Recognition and eventual promotion many times may cause a person to reveal capabilities heretofore not clearly recognized. On the other hand, promotion may bring about unfortunate results if it is not recognized that the very interests which cause someone to do an excellent job on one level may be too strong or too specialized to satisfy the necessary qualifications for a succeeding position. For example, a salesperson extremely capable in the activity of selling the company products may possibly be incapable of performing adequately as a sales manager or an executive whose task may be to exercise authority and control over a sales organization. The necessary activities of a sales manager may be beyond the field of basic interest of the salesperson.

The answers to the three questions raised above will provide some of the means necessary to assure management of a more contented and a more productive working organization.

Communication within the organization

The need for communication within the organization starts with the need for something to communicate. The nature of company policies, managerial philosophy, the objectives of the enterprise, and the company's principles of operation are subjects which may provide worthwhile information and establish a bond of understanding between the company and the workers as individuals. Inadequate communication with the workers may interfere with performance on the job because the worker is uncertain what to do in a given situation. It may also leave the workers unaware of their significance as members of the workforce simply because they have not been included within the communicative system which could have provided them with such a basic understanding.

Organizational structure is activated by communication. The success of operations is very much centered in the nature and adequacy of communication. The specific details of organizational relationships and operational procedures may be transmitted via channels, but the performance of individuals on the job depends upon the extent to which consideration of the human element has been included. Communication cannot be separated from employee relations, nor can it be separated from organizational relationships. It is vital as the connecting link between plans and action and as a very significant determinant of the quality and adequacy of performance.

COST OF ORGANIZATION

The cost of organization can be divided into two parts. The first is the cost associated with the process of organizing—planning and designing the structure. The second is paying salaries to and providing services for members of the organization. Obviously, if objectives can be achieved with periodic rather than continuous organization planning or if objectives can be achieved with a smaller staff, so much the better. The goal should be to make the costs of organization proportionate to the utility of the organization, but this is a goal that is very hard to achieve.

One might expect that as time passes, fewer people would be required to run an organization because of the opportunity the people have had to absorb knowledge and because with time the difficult task should have become routine. Offsetting this idea is the fact that organizations over time employ more and more specialists with the hope of more efficient and more effective operation. Thus the organization grows. But organizations also grow merely because staff tends to beget staff, as pointed out in the well-known Parkinson's Law.

Organizations have a tendency to grow at a rate disproportionate to the volume of production and sales—the sources of income. The proper size of a manufacturing or selling organization is relatively easy to establish. If the addition of a production supervisor increases output by $100,000 over his cost, and if a market research function costing $45,000 a year causes sales to increase by $1 million, it appears that these two additions to the organization are justified. But beyond these two areas—producing and selling—the appropriate organization and the appropriate cost are hard to predetermine. The reason for this is that no other part of the organization actually produces something that must be sold or actually sells products to make a profit.

If a firm employs 1,000 people there is obviously a need for a personnel function, but the appropriate size and budget allowance for such a function cannot be predetermined. Should the personnel function include separate divisions for community relations, wage and salary administration, personnel research, testing and counseling, industrial relations, and so on? There is a need to do some work in each area, but how much time, talent, and money should be allocated to each? Since each of these areas contributes to profit only indirectly, if at all, there is no precise yardstick that can be used. If a wage and salary administrator is hired, for example, the odds are that he can make a full-time job of it and ultimately involve several people.

Controlling cost

Although we may not be able to tell the specific value of more people in an organization, it is possible to measure the consequences of fewer people and less organization. This is the basic means for controlling the cost of organization. If we eliminate or reduce the size of our legal department, the savings in salaries, office space, and services can be accurately measured. Over a period of time we can measure the cost, if any, associated with this action, such as hiring lawyers on a consulting, as-we-need-them basis. If savings exceed these costs and it appears that the same will hold in the future, the action is justified.

Controlling the cost of organization requires a constant appraisal of all functions. A firm should retain only those functions whose value exceeds their cost.

SUMMARY

There is no way in which an outsider can look at an organization and know for sure that it will or will not work. There may be some telltale signs such as a very broad span of control for a manager or too few or too many levels of management, but the only logical test for an organization is how well it gets the job done.

People make or break all organizations. They have the capacity to make a "poor" organization operate efficiently and effectively. They can also make a "good" organization fail. A person may play several roles in a given organization. He may play the role assigned by upper management, or he may enlarge on this role because he sees things that must be done and plays a role that will provide him and his associates with job satisfaction.

The formal organization is the starting point for spelling out the functions that must be performed and the relations that should take place. But it is not until the organization operates that we can see how these functions and relations are interpreted. One very common mistake is to assume that organization once created will operate effectively in a changing environment.

BUSINESS ITEM

Love makes the wheels go 'round

At Texas Instruments, Inc., the Dallas-based semiconductor maker, there is a long history of tinkering with the human element in the management equation. Job enrichment and team-planning programs have produced results.

In its continuing efforts to maximize the effectiveness of the individual employee, the company has experimented in psychoanalyzing employees to learn what turns them on to the job. Another experiment prescribed the early retirement of most executive vice presidents by age fifty-five to make room for younger men.

These and other efforts, all part of a program called "People and Asset Effectiveness," have produced phenomenal results. Although it is difficult to pinpoint which of the many programs has contributed most to Texas Instrument's productivity gains, the Director of Corporate Personnel believes that what makes it all work is very simple. "There are two things in life that people want," he explains. "They want to achieve and they want to be loved. If you can provide an atmosphere where these things can occur with a minimum amount of structure in the work flow, you are going to get what you want."

QUESTIONS

1 How can changing objectives affect organizational needs?

2 How does the operating organization differ from the formal organization? Is the difference important? Discuss.

3 Why is the operating organization considered an ever-changing organization?

4 The space between the boxes on an organization chart is more important than the box itself. Do you agree? Why?

5 What is the informal organization and how does it come into being?

6 There is something contradictory in the human makeup and the structure of organizations that will be a constant source of friction. Do you agree? Explain.

7 Identify the basic functions of informal organizations.

8 In what ways can the informal organization actually help management?

9 What is meant by clarity in organizations?

10 Do all organizational forms promote the clarity concept? Explain.

11 What is overlapping authority, and what are its causes?

12 Why is it difficult to maintain completeness in organization?

13 What does the concept "authority commensurate with responsibility" imply?

14 Why is it nearly impossible to apply this concept?

15 What is meant by the cost of organization? How can it be controlled?

The purpose of this chapter Management and organization are inseparable because the organizational structure is the framework within which management must operate. It is inconceivable that a business can prosper and grow with either poor organization or poor management. / Management is the energizing force that welds together the separate functions of a business to make them a cohesive whole. Management is also the leadership that directs and motivates people to work toward the goals of the firm. Management is the force that can maximize the value of the firm's human and physical resources. / In the past, managers were often referred to as the "bosses" of an organization, but we shall learn in this chapter that management in modern business involves quite a different approach. Managers today must be far more concerned with planning than with the mere overseeing of workers. / Questions raised in this chapter include:

1 What types of work are included in the manager's job?

2 To what extent are all managerial jobs the same?

3 What skills do managers use in performing their jobs?

4 What principles do managers apply to increase their effectiveness?

5 Who really runs the modern business corporation?

for management personal skill are better than technical skill.

MANAGEMENT

Every organization —social, business, political, or otherwise—has at its head a manager, a person who is responsible for its leadership. Without leadership, organizations flounder about, having no direction and little purpose. In a large business there may be several organizations—for production, marketing, finance—each with a manager or leader. In business, any person who "heads up" or is responsible for a function is a manager. The president of the firm is a manager, as are the production supervisor and the foreman.

Management is not confined to the business organization; rather it exists wherever there is cooperative endeavor. Wherever and whenever the actions of several people must be directed toward a common goal, there is a need for management. The process of management is universal to all cooperative endeavor whether it be the corner filling station or a giant corporation.

MANAGEMENT AND ORGANIZATION

Management and organization are interrelated functions; they are also joint functions, for one cannot take place without the other. Leadership or management is required for the development of an organization structure, but at the same time organization structure delineates the relationships between managers and establishes the responsibilities of each manager. Organization is discussed prior to management in this text to point out that the former provides a framework within which the process of management must take place. Without the organizational framework, it would be impossible to identify the types of managers needed to operate the business firm.

What is management?

Most readers of this text are probably headed for managerial jobs—jobs that stress personal skills rather than technical skills. Management jobs vary in importance and in the opportunity they offer, based on two primary considerations. First, management jobs exist at various organizational levels; in fact, every person above the lowest level of the organization is a manager of sorts. Second, managerial jobs have different amounts of authority for reasons other than their position in the hierarchy. We learned in Chapter 7 that centralization in organization makes all jobs below the top level less significant. We also learned that some jobs are simply advisory in nature and therefore void of meaningful authority.

Being a manager, therefore, can mean many things depending primarily on the freedom a person has to act or initiate. A former student took employment with a bank upon graduation. Within 5 years he was named manager of a newly opened branch of the bank. In less than two years he quit the job because it paid him less than $175 per week. Was this person overpaid or underpaid? Could it be that all decisions of any significance were made at the home office and the branch manager merely had to follow orders? This was the case.

True Job titles frequently do not reveal the importance or nature of managerial positions. What comes to your mind when you think of a job called "cashier"? In many firms, cashiers are primarily money takers, but in certain banks the cashier is a high management position. In many insurance companies the position of "secretary" is a very important managerial post. The meaning of any job depends on the role it is expected to play in the overall operational plan.

We must also recognize that the term "management" and the role of the manager will change as time goes by because the nature of business will constantly change. Management is often called the function of executive leadership, but the personal qualities required for effective management in the past may be wholly ineffective today or tomorrow. A survey of American business history will reveal a host of practices that were effective in the past but are unacceptable today because of changes in the moral and legal environment of business management.

Management defined

It is universally agreed that management is important, that good management can make a business prosper and grow, and that poor management can lead to its demise. Good management can be recognized, though it is hard to say precisely what it consists of—there are different management styles. It is like the undefinable characteristic called leadership; we can name a number of great leaders of the past, but there is little that can be generalized about the qualities that made them great leaders, for each is individual and different, and each operated in a different environment. Good managers are also individual and different, and the qualities that make a good manager are highly diverse.

Over the years, authors and practitioners have developed hundreds of definitions to describe and explain management. Two are presented here. Lenin has described management as "the extraordinarily simple operations of watching, recording, and issuing receipts, within the grasp of anyone who can read and write and knows the first four rules of arithmetic." For the small, bureaucratic businesses in Russia during Lenin's time this perhaps was a realistic expression of management. But is it a realistic expression of management today? It could very well be and we need only to refer to our branch manager above for verification.

A more appropriate definition for our purposes is that management is "the process of getting things done through people." A manager magnifies his own capabilities through the effective use of his subordinates. A manager, then, is a person who makes it possible for his subordinates to produce. A manager is a person who must decide what should be done and then initiate the actions necessary for accomplishment. We will see how this definition applies in a number of discussions that follow.

This definition of management is quite adequate for the recent past, the present, and most likely for the future. This does not mean that the process of management is at all fixed, because the means for ascertaining what should be done are in a constant state of change—the computer, for example, has already made a terrific impact on the process of management and will continue to do so—and the manner in which human resources may be utilized is constantly changing. Thus, though management will exist as long as there is cooperative activity, a particular manager may find that he can become obsolete if he fails to keep pace with changing times.

THE FUNCTIONS OF MANAGEMENT

A good way to understand management as it is practiced today is to examine the types of work that make up a manager's job. It is impossible to identify management-type jobs in terms of specific duties, for each management job may be different. The job of president of United States Steel is not the same as the job of president of General Electric, nor are these two jobs necessarily the same today as they were 5 years ago. Yet, common threads that run through all management jobs can provide us with a basis for determining what business managers do. Management always involves one or more of these seven primary functions:

1 Planning for the work of the business
2 Building and maintaining an organization
3 Staffing the organization with competent people
4 Directing the work of subordinates
5 Controlling business activity
6 Coordinating activity
7 Representing subordinate personnel

If a person's job, regardless of title, involves these functions, then it is a managerial job and he is a manager. He need not divide his time equally among these functions to qualify as a manager, nor need he perform all functions. But the bulk of his time must be consumed by some combination of these functions. The meaning and significance of each function are described below.

Planning

Planning, which is basically selecting the best course of action from the alternatives available, is the core function of management. Every business firm should have some goal or objective; otherwise, it will not know where it is going. The plan identifies the course of action that will lead to the attainment of the goal.

Managers at all levels of organization and in all areas of activity—production, marketing, finance—have a planning job to do. At low organizational levels such as the bottom rung of the production ladder, the foreman plans for his subordinates. Planning at this level is characterized by (1) a relatively short time span—a day, a week, or perhaps a month, (2) a relatively narrow range of activity, such as the stamping of automobile trunk lids, and (3) the involvement of a relatively small number of individuals.

As we move up the organization ladder the nature of planning changes; it involves longer time spans, broader areas of activity, and more people. At the top, the chairman of the board engages in long-range planning for all areas of the firm's activity, and his plans may affect people outside the firm as well as its employees.

Planning is an important and continuous management function. It is important because it indicates how a particular goal is to be reached—it is a standard of sorts—and it is a continuous function because goals change and because many elements of a plan are based on assumptions that may not be realized.

The planning process Planning is a mental process, and consequently the quality of the plan rests on the mental capacities of the planner and the adequacy of the information needed for planning. Intelligence, experience, perception, judgment, and conception are mental tools for planning. However, they must be used in effective fashion, or the real value of the tool may be lost. There are steps to follow in deciding the proper course of action—the plan.

The first step is to determine the objective that the organization should attain. This is not a simple task but there are certain guidelines to follow. The primary objective should always be to create the maximum value for "customers" at the lowest possible cost. "Customers" in this context includes more than those who purchase the firm's goods and services. Every function has the purpose of creating values. This is easily seen in the production and distribution functions, but it also applies to purchasing, personnel, maintenance, and the like. Their "customers" are another part of the organization.

Note that we have not considered profit as the primary objective and for good reason. Profit is a residue—revenues minus expenses. There can be no profit unless adequate revenue is generated. The business person who sets his sights on profit rather than on generating revenue through creating values will usually end up in trouble. A firm must have a profit objective, a return-on-investment objective, and perhaps a share-of-market objective. But these objectives must be considered secondary because they can be achieved only if values are created for the customer group and also for members of the firm—those who create customer values.

A second step is to consider what might be done to achieve the primary objective and secondary objectives. What courses of action are available? What are the possible solutions? This phase of planning is most demanding of the manager's imaginative and conceptual powers, for without good alternatives there cannot be a good plan of action. The best of several poor alternatives may be a poor solution.

A third step is to examine each possible solution. Each hypothesis should be judged in terms of its strengths and weaknesses, its chances for success, its adaptability to changing conditions, and the potential rewards that it offers.

The final step is to select the plan. There will be times when one possibility is clearly superior to all others. Very often the manager is faced with several solutions that have the same merit. The final choice may require the introduction of new variables. Let us not overlook the possibility that none of the alternatives is acceptable and that the planning cycle must be repeated.

Planning—an illustration Back in the 1950s the Ford Motor Company established a policy of having a line of cars in every price category covered by General Motors cars. A void existed in the Ford line between the low-priced cars and higher-priced cars. Because General Motors was successful in the intermediate price range, Ford reasoned that there would be a market for Ford cars. Thus we had the birth of the Edsel which was no more than a different-looking Ford. The car was a dismal failure because it had no unique market value. This was a car that Ford needed, not the market. At a later date, market studies revealed that there was a market for a sporty, small, low-priced car. Not wanting to get burned twice, Ford approached this situation with great care. A maximum retail price was set and the company went to work to give the most value at that price. The result was the original Mustang which was a very successful venture. Over the years the Mustang grew in size, horsepower, and price. Larger cars bring in more profit. It became apparent after a few years that the public did not want this type of Mustang and in 1974 Ford went back to the sporty, small, low-priced car, Mustang II.

Organizing

Organizing for business means simply arranging men, materials, and machines into the best possible relationships for the attainment of business goals. It involves the selection of materials, the assignment of specific tasks to specific individuals and machines, and the delegation of the right amount of authority to those who will be responsible for the operation of the organization. The essential factor in organization is the pattern or system to be imposed upon the component parts of a business. Without some kind of overall pattern to establish a chain of command and an orderly allocation of responsibility, chaos will follow, for there can be no certainty of the function that each individual is expected to perform.

A business organization must be subjected to constant review, for business is a dynamic process and the interrelation between the parts of the organization changes constantly, partly from pressures within the organization (such as personnel changes and similar factors) and partly from pressures outside the organization (such as the development of new machinery, new products, and the like). The basic aims of management are the simplification of organizational structure and the attainment of a higher level of coordination and efficiency among the various parts of the organization. Since each new employee, each new government regulation, and each technological advance produces some change in the operation of the system, the need for organizational change is a constant factor in management. The belief that a good organization can continue unchanged throughout the life of the company has been responsible for the collapse of many business ventures.

Staffing

The importance of the staffing function in good management has increased steadily in recent years as it has grown to include much more than the simple hiring and firing of employees. It now involves the selection and training of workers, adequate supervision of their activities, and the maintenance of sound human relations.

The staffing problem begins when management sets out to determine the number and types of personnel needed to carry out company plans. A system of replacement must also be worked out, employee advancement must be provided for, and all other contingencies that arise in handling personnel must be dealt with.

A business is no better than the people who operate it, and no business can run without people. The success of a business depends primarily on the caliber of its personnel, and businesses which are inadequately staffed, either at the managerial level or in subordinate positions, have little hope of success. The staffing function is discussed in some detail in Part 3 of this text.

Directing

Management also has the function of providing direction for all subordinate levels of workers and of accepting responsibility for the work they perform. The effectiveness of the supervision which management provides for its workers is a good criterion for judging the effectiveness of management; it is also the key to more efficient and effective operation. Workers ought to be accustomed to looking to management for direction. First, such a clearly established pattern of guidance makes for better personnel relations within the organization. Second, it provides management with a more effective tool for implementing plans. And finally, if there is not adquate direction from management, the workers are likely to turn in other directions for their instruction—to the union, to fellow workers, or to their own personal preferences—upsetting the balance within the organization and perhaps introducing objectives which are at odds with those management proposes to achieve.

Control

The purpose of the control function is to ascertain that what is actually taking place conforms to the plan. Delegating authority without the means for control is a dangerous practice. Control is necessary because of the inherent variability of people and things and needs to be applied to all management functions. Control is a relative concept, and a basic management problem is to determine how much control should be exercised over any function. This is important because control costs money yet does not directly add to revenue. The value of control must be measured in terms of loss control—loss of money, loss of customers through poor service or quality, or loss of inventory items.

How much control? In theory, at least, management has a number of options regarding the degree of control it will exercise over an activity, ranging from 0 control at one extreme to 100 percent control at the other. Seldom will there be no control and seldom will there be absolute control over any activity; it would be too costly. Determining the appropriate degree of control to be applied involves two basic pieces of information:

1 The cost of exercising additional degrees of control. This is relatively easy to estimate because we know how much an additional inspection would cost or how much it would cost to recount the cash, and so on.

2 The value to the firm when additional control is exercised. This is more difficult to estimate because it may take time to measure the value of an action. Improving quality may result in increased sales, but only time will tell by how much.

These data can be expressed in the chart form as in the illustration on page 190.

The cost of control tends to be low at first but increases eventually at an increasing rate as absolute (total) control is approached. As a rule it takes more refined and costly techniques to maintain higher levels of control. The value curve rises quite rapidly at first and eventually levels off. For example, customers may not be willing to pay

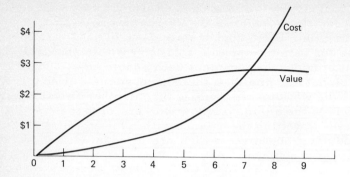

any more for an item that has been inspected at 20 points than they would for an item inspected at 15 points. And, as we can see, it is possible to spend more for control than it is worth.

The degree of control that should be exercised lies somewhere between 0 and 7. There is a point where the spread between the two curves is the greatest. Assume that it is 4. At this point $1 invested in control yields a value of $4.50. No other amount of control will yield as great a gain. When you buy a new car and note any number of defects, it is because automobile manufacturers, and all producers, apply this concept. A manufacturing system that would guarantee that every unit produced would be perfect would be prohibitively expensive. Most Americans would prefer to own 5 Chevrolets to 1 Rolls Royce.

The control process The control process involves four distinct steps. The first involves the establishing of standards. Standards define the condition that should exist. A standard can be quite precise such as a material-cost standard of $9 per unit or it could be a standard that permits variation. Seldom does a blueprint specify that a shaft diameter be 1.000 inches; rather it would specify 1.000 ± .005. This is a precise standard but it does not require the same attention to detail as a standard of 1.000 inches and it would not be as difficult to reach this standard.

A second step in the control process involves the measurement of what actually happened, or what is. Again, it is possible in some instances to measure what actually happened with precision or it may be better to have a less-than-precise measure. Measuring the actual cost of production can be precise. But visualize the problem of determining precisely what is in inventory at your local A&P supermarket. The only method for determining what is in inventory is to physically count every item. Since human beings must do the counting, there exists the possibility of error.

If what should be (standard) agrees with what is (actual) we conclude that the situation is under control. If they do not agree, a third step is necessary: the variance must be analyzed. Suppose there was a $2,000 material cost standard for a batch of production. This was expressed as 1,000 units costing $2 each. The actual cost was $2,091 because 1,020 units costing $2.05 each were used. The $91 variance is accounted for in two steps. Using 20 extra units costs $40 and paying $.05 per unit more than standard accounts for $51. This step provides the basis for taking the final step which is corrective action. The production foreman must explain why the extra units were used so that the situation will not recur. Similarly, the cause of the price variance must be explored.

Coordination

Coordination—the bringing together of a number of separate elements to form an organized and coherent unit—is an essential task at all levels of management. Any unit of organization that involves more than one person, product, or machine requires coordination, and large businesses involving many separate units may depend on very close coordination to prevent a serious stoppage of production. Although coordination is a management function, achieving it by simply ordering that coordination take place is often impossible. When everyone concerned understands and appreciates the relationship of his own task to the work of others and accepts the need for joint effort, then the firm is likely to obtain the coordination it needs.

Representation

Every manager has the responsibility for representing his subordinates. A review of the organization charts in Chapter 7 will be a reminder that workers who wish to communicate with higher levels of management do so through their foreman. He or she is the communication link between the workers and upper levels of management.

There are many situations in business that workers seek to improve, remedy, or learn more about, and that are beyond the foreman's control. If a foreman fails in his duty to bring such matters to his superior, he is, in the eyes of his subordinates, a poor manager. The manager who is close enough to his subordinates to understand their needs and who is willing to act when action is in order is, in reality, helping himself as well as his subordinates. Refusal by management to represent workers is a common cause of outside representation—the union.

THE UNIVERSALITY OF MANAGEMENT

In this discussion of management functions no attempt was made to relate them to the type of activity being managed—manufacturing, retailing, or education—nor were any functions designated as the exclusive province of a particular level of management. The reason for this is that the functions of management are universal; that is, managers of steel mills must perform the same functions as managers of banks or managers of an airline. Also, managers at all levels of organization from foreman to chairman of the board are concerned for the same functions. Planning, organizing, staffing, etc., make up the manager's job irrespective of what or who is managed. Because of the universal nature of management functions, a good manager can put his talents to work managing various types of activity. A former president of the Ford Motor Company became dean of the graduate school of business at Stanford, and the former dean became chairman of the board at Wells Fargo bank.

A former vice president of the Ford Motor Company described this situation very well by saying:

What impresses me is how much the requirements for various jobs have in common—particularly at higher levels—and how easy it is in most instances to pick up the specialized knowledge in a particular field. . . . What I am emphasizing is that most careers require the same basic skills and abilities and that in many such careers these basic skills and abilities constitute a substantial part of the requisites for success. . . .[1]

MANAGERIAL SKILLS

Because of the universal nature of management functions, there is a high degree of universality as regards managerial skills. That is, the same basic skills are required of all managers. The degree of universality is greatest among top-management people and least at the foreman level.

The skills needed in the operation of a business may be classified as technical or managerial. Technical skills relate to the performance of a specific task such as programming and operating a computer or machining a gear blank to close tolerances. Managerial skills, as shown below, are those skills needed in the process of getting things done through people. As a rule, managers do not need to exercise technical skills on their jobs, although they must know what skills their subordinates should possess. We should modify this generalization somewhat and consider particular levels of management. Foremen, for example, will possess greater technical skill than the president of the firm because their job is but one step removed from the technical area. There may be a strong urge for foremen to maintain their technical skills—if they were the best-skilled workers prior to promotion, they may hate to lose what they have developed. However, unless technical skills are applied directly to management-type work—planning, for example—a manager is performing nonmanagerial work. Before leaving this topic, we should note that there is a great difference between having technical knowledge or technical awareness and actually having a technical skill. Some of the finest

[1]Theodore O. Yntema, "The Transferable Skills of a Manager," *Journal of the Academy of Management,* August 1960, pp. 79–80.

and most successful managers in professional athletics never excelled at their game. An excellent statement of managerial skills was developed by Yntema in "The Transferable Skills of a Manager."[2] They are summarized below.

1 The ability to see and solve problems. This requires the ability to discern between a situation that requires managerial action and a circumstance that should be ignored.

2 The ability to deal with people effectively. This should be self-evident since management is the process of getting things done through people. Yet it is a skill that is too often lacking. This skill requires some understanding of the nature of the people with whom the manager must associate. A manager must be flexible so that he can adjust to different behavior patterns. Every person has good days and bad days and a manager who can instantly diagnose the mood of his associates will accomplish much more than the manager who cannot.

3 The ability to communicate effectively. Effective communications requires different approaches in different situations, as implied above. Communication is effective when the message gets across. This is a most important skill because the best ideas in the world have value only to their creator unless communication takes place.

4 The ability to organize. Few managers have all the resources they would like to have to work with. The ability of a manager to get the most out of what he has to work with is therefore a very important managerial skill.

5 Persistent effort. This is important because a principal weakness in people generally is their inability to follow through to completion what has been started. Many projects or ideas fail to materialize simply because the person in charge has not developed the capacity to completely dedicate himself to the task.

6 A good memory. Managers should develop the ability to recall facts, names, and relationships that are a part of their work. This ability not only saves considerable time in the decision-making process but increases the confidence others have in him. Such replies as "I don't know" and "I will look it up" have their place, but using them too frequently can cause others to ask, "What does he know?"

Note that each of the above is a personal skill, not a technical skill, and that each has application in all types of managerial situations.

MANAGEMENT STYLES

Management has always been considered the process of getting things done through people, but this tells us nothing about how individual managers operate. We are certain that no two managers are exactly alike and we should expect that no two management styles are exactly alike. Every manager must adapt his own peculiar per-

[2]Ibid.

sonal qualities to the situation and to those he is managing. Managing a group of scientists engaged in research is a process quite different from managing workers on an assembly line. However, this does not preclude the existence of detectable management styles.

Scientific management

Scientific management was in vogue up until World War II, at least. We say "at least" because there are many managers who apply this approach today. Frederick W. Taylor was the father of this movement which was born out of his concern for the waste he saw in industry during the latter part of the nineteenth century. Many of the tasks performed were quite menial and could be carried out by almost anyone who was physically able. Because of this, little care was exercised in the selection of workers and few job instructions were ever issued. Taylor made a number of observations about management but two stand out as representative of his management style.

1 Taylor proposed that there was a science to each element of a person's work—there was *a* best way to do any job. It made no difference to Taylor whether it was a pick-and-shovel job or a machinist at a lathe; there was one best way to do the job. Taylor broke each job down into its basic elements, studied them, and then developed that sequence and combination of body motions that would yield the greatest output per period of time. The result was to standardize the way each job was done. Every worker was required to perform a given job in the same manner. By standardizing the way a job was done, Taylor was able to ascertain how much time, on the average, a person should take to complete a task. For the first time, the means was available to determine whether a person was doing the day's work for which he was paid. If the standard time for a job was 10 minutes, a worker was expected to repeat the job 60 times in a 10-hour day. This provided management with a far greater degree of control over the worker than it had ever been able to exercise. Further, Taylor reasoned, why pay a person by the day? Why not pay him for each task he completes? Rather than pay a person $3 per day, why not pay him 5 cents for each job completed? This would reward the worker who wanted to produce more than 60 units a day and penalize workers who produced less. Basically, this management style says produce or you will not get paid. It was a hard-nosed approach.

2 Taylor also reasoned that there were people who were "best" suited for any job. Because of his analysis of jobs he was in a position to determine the personal qualities that would lead to a high level of job performance. This matching of people with jobs coupled with the incentive to produce, inherent in piecework, would rid industry of much of its inefficiency.

Scientific management yielded fantastic increases in productivity. One illustration shows that Taylor increased the amount of pig iron handled in a day from $12\frac{1}{2}$ tons to 47 tons per man. Scientific management tends to drive a person and it forces a worker to stay with it or suffer. Obviously, unions were very much against Taylor and in many instances were successful in preventing an application of Taylor's style. Scientific management is practiced in modified form today in many situations where repetitive manual tasks are being performed. It has the advantage of providing a high degree of control over production costs and output.

Bureaucracy

Scientific management provided the much-wanted solution to the problem of increasing efficiency in the production of goods. Increased production causes an increase in the volume of administrative work necessary to support production. Eventually, the administrative function grew to such proportions that then-existing management approaches could not cope with it. Max Weber, a German sociologist, advanced the concept of bureaucracy or management by bureaucrats, and business people immediately adopted it as *the* way.

Bureaucracy requires the breaking down of a total administrative task into a number of clearly defined and easily learned jobs. Then calculable rules are developed to govern the carrying out of each job. Thus every worker knows exactly what the job entails and is provided with a set of rules to follow. The rules tell the bureaucrat what to do in every circumstance that is anticipated. This can be a very efficient approach to management and because of this permits the payment of relatively high wages.

Bureaucracy was and is applied in those situations where change is not anticipated or where the direction and rate of change can be predicted. We generally associate bureaucracy with government but it has widespread use in most public utilities and in many large businesses.

There are several shortcomings to bureaucracy and you may have been witness to them. It is impossible to foresee every event that might take place and consequently there will be events for which there is no rule. As a result, you get the response, "Sorry, I can't do anything about it." Departments in a bureaucracy tend to make work for each other, which can result in mountains of red tape. Employees under a bureaucratic system are apt to spend many years at the same job. Too frequently, they lose interest in what they are doing.

The human relations emphasis

The amount of sacrifice a person is willing to endure to make a living is, in part, a function of the labor market. When labor was abundant and unorganized, managers handled their workers in ways that now seem overly severe and strict. Workers had to accept this condition because there was always someone in line at the employment office waiting for an opportunity to work even under adverse conditions.

In the 1940s the labor market changed dramatically. Wartime production requirements and a reduced labor force resulted in the need to restructure labor-management relations. For the first time, managers had to face the hard fact that if they did not offer employees something more than a place to work they would lose them to an employer who would provide additional benefits and privileges. Aided by social scientists, the most notable of whom was the Harvard Business School's Elton Mayo, a theory was developed that contented employees are more productive employees. Rather than driving workers, as scientific management required, Mayo would build an atmosphere within which workers would want to produce more. More specifically, Mayo concluded that:

1 Logical factors (more money) are less important than emotional factors in determining production efficiency. (To this Taylor would say "hogwash.")

2 Work performed by individuals must satisfy their goals as well as the goals of the firm.

3 Management must learn to develop cooperative attitudes and not rely on the concept that it has the right to command subordinates to do as they are told.

4 We must rely more on group endeavor and less on individual endeavor in the process of getting things done through people.

The management-by-pressure era

The human relations approach to management was subject to much criticism in the late 1940s and early 1950s. It became more and more evident that it would require something more than a nice atmosphere and harmonious working conditions to maintain high levels of productivity. Management by pressure[3] combines some aspects of scientific management and human relations. This approach to management requires great skill and an understanding of what makes a particular employee tick. The same types of pressure cannot be applied effectively to every employee, and different degrees of pressure must be applied based on circumstances. However, managers today are far better schooled in human behavior than managers of the past and this approach, therefore, can be quite effective.

Management by objectives

"In brief, the system of management by objectives can be described as a process whereby the superior and subordinate managers of an organization jointly identify the common goals, define each individual's major areas of responsibility in terms of the results expected of him, and use these measures as guides for operating the unit and assessing the contribution of each of its members." [4]

This approach to management provides each manager with considerable operating freedom but it can be a hard-nosed approach as well.

[3] This term is borrowed from George S. Odiorne's *Management by Objectives,* Pitman Publishing Corporation, New York, 1965.
[4] Ibid., pp. 55–56.

Each manager agrees on what he will accomplish and he either makes it or does not. Emphasis here is not on the number of hours a manager works but on what he can accomplish over a period of time. Management by objectives requires competent managers and each manager needs to know the strengths and weaknesses of other managers on the team. In some respects this approach to management incorporates some features of the profit-center concept and the decentralization concept. Good managers generally like this approach because of the free hand it provides, because they can be rewarded for their efforts, and because it permits rapid individual development.

MANAGEMENT PRINCIPLES

The term "principle" can be defined as a fundamental truth, a basic law—the ultimate basis or cause. Principles are valuable in any area of study because they provide a firm basis for action: a given effort yields a given result. Principles are best seen in the field of physical science where, for example, it is known that a given force on one end of a lever will always produce a specific force on the other end, depending on the location of the fulcrum.

In the fields of social science of which management is a part, there are also principles, but they are not so absolute as in the field of physical science. We know for example that incentives (the cause) can stimulate worker productivity (the effect), but this principle does not tell us the effect of a 25-cent-per-hour wage increase on the productivity of a particular group of workers. A certain amount of experimentation must take place before management can determine the best type of incentive to yield the desired result. In management, therefore, we must expect that principles will be more generalizations and guides than absolute bases for action.

The development of management principles is a slow and continuous process. Principles have their origin in theories. When a theory has been developed and refined to the point that it always applies, a new principle is born. Some well-known principles, developed through years of observation, are presented below to point out both the substance and the nature of management principles.

Division of work

It has long been known that the most efficient way to get a task completed is to divide it into several segments so that workers can concentrate on narrow areas of activity and thereby develop maximum skill in the minimum amount of time. However, this principle does not reveal what the ideal breakdown should be in a given instance. Rather, it reminds management that it should seek the ideal.

Authority commensurate with responsibility

A manager's authority should be commensurate with his responsibility, as explained in a previous chapter. If, for example, the foreman of a cabinetmaking shop is responsible for the production of a given quality of cabinet but has no control over the quality of raw materials or manpower which he must use, then responsibility and authority are not in proper balance. For best results, management must seek the appropriate balance. The means for doing this are given below.

Unity of command

Employees should receive orders from and be responsible to only one superior. This means that a worker should receive orders only from his foreman, not from the supervisor, the production manager, or even the president. The significance of this principle lies in the fact that if orders come from more than one source, they may be in conflict and the worker will not know what direction to take. This is bad from a human relations point of view and from an organizational point of view.

Subordination of individual goals

The goals of every member of an organization, from stockholder to worker, should be subordinate to the goals of the firm. Every member of an organization should have goals that he seeks through his association with the organization, but he should not attempt to achieve such goals at the expense of organizational goals. The ball player who has a goal of hitting as many home runs as possible, the hockey player who has a goal of getting as many scoring points to his credit as possible, or the salesperson who increases her income by padding her expense account are each violations of this principle. In all instances, the goals of the firm should provide the framework within which each member of the firm seeks his or her personal goals.

Authority and responsibility

These two terms have been used several times in a general sense in prior discussions. At this point we will discuss them in greater detail because they are very important concepts.

Authority is the right to command. In business it is the right of a superior to command that subordinates do certain things or refrain from doing certain things. Every manager must have authority to do his job—getting things done through people. A manager gets authority when it is delegated to him by a superior.

Responsibility is similar to accountability; a manager is made responsible for conducting prescribed activity. The relation of responsibility to other functions is set forth in Figure 9-1.

For a firm to achieve its goals there are certain functions that must be performed. Functions become the basis for establishing responsibilities. Thus the goal of producing 120,000 units necessitates a production function. The production function has the responsibility

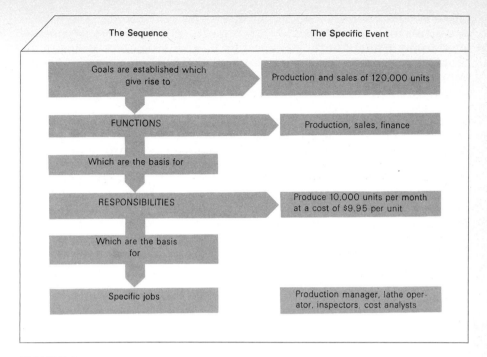

The Sequence	The Specific Event
Goals are established which give rise to	Production and sales of 120,000 units
FUNCTIONS	Production, sales, finance
Which are the basis for	
RESPONSIBILITIES	Produce 10,000 units per month at a cost of $9.95 per unit
Which are the basis for	
Specific jobs	Production manager, lathe operator, inspectors, cost analysts

FIGURE 9-1 The relation of responsibility to function

for producing 10,000 units per month at a cost of $9.95 per unit. Once the responsible person decides how he will carry out his responsibility, specific jobs are created. In theory, the sum total of responsibility in a firm should equal the sum total of functions that must be performed. Not until responsibilities have been defined can the appropriate amount of authority be delegated.

Sources of authority In the United States the ultimate source of authority in business is the owner group—proprietors, partners, or stockholders. The members of the owner group have the right to command because of the right of private property. The person who owns property has the right to dictate how it will be used. Note that in a communist country there must be a different basis of authority— the state.

There are other sources of authority in American business. Some people will assume authority and exercise it until told to refrain by higher authority. When one manager fails to carry out all his responsibilities, another manager may pick them up and thereby assume additional authority. In the final analysis, a person in business has as much authority as he can make others believe he has. A manager may have the right to command but when he does, no one listens. The acceptance theory of authority states that a superior has only as much authority as his subordinates are willing for him to have. This idea has considerable merit because authority that cannot get things done is worthless, and a person who can get things done in the absence of a formal grant of authority actually has considerable authority. In terms of day-to-day activity, the acceptance theory is very important, but when vital decisions must be made, "You are fired," the ultimate source of authority must enter the picture.

Balancing authority and responsibility This seems simple enough; identify a person's responsibility and then delegate to him or her the necessary authority. Now if we apply this idea to a bank teller it can work. The teller is responsible for a given amount of money and is given complete authority over the cash drawer. We can also apply this idea to inventory or other types of physical property. But how much authority must be delegated to a foreman who is responsible for a particular volume of production? Does he need the authority to fire or otherwise discipline workers? One foreman might need it and another not. Authority is a personal thing and one person may carry out his responsibility with no apparent exercise of authority while another may fail even with complete authority. Since it is difficult to measure the amount of authority that a particular manager needs to carry out a responsibility, significant imbalances commonly exist.

Policy

A manager is basically a decision maker—one who decides what to do in a wide variety of situations. Many of these situations can be anticipated, especially at lower managerial levels, and many of these situations are bound to be repeated in the normal course of business. Personnel turnover must be expected and a firm may have a policy of promoting the next in line to fill such vacancies. Sears, Roebuck knows that customers will return merchandise they have purchased and has a policy of: "Your money refunded with proof of purchase."

In the absence of policy, upper levels of management might need to be involved to resolve certain situations. With policy, the routine and anticipated situation can be handled by low-level personnel. Policy can be viewed as a predetermined answer to a recurring question; it is management's decision when a particular event takes place. Policy relieves management from the routine and anticipated situation; it provides for like treatment in similar situations; and it makes management's attitude regarding a variety of activities a matter of record. Management then needs to be involved only with the exceptional case. Policy can be a great time-saver.

Policies are a tool of management but they must be developed with care. Policies should facilitate the conduct of business, not hinder it. Policy development requires a clear understanding of what is routine and what is exceptional. If policy is so established that every event is an exception, then the policy is meaningless. Finally, policy is not a substitute for good management; policy is merely a tool of management.

THE FUTURE OF ORGANIZATION
AND MANAGEMENT

Organization and management will always be the heart of any business because they establish what will be done, how, and by whom. Over the years we have witnessed many changes in the approach to effective organization and management. Today we expect even greater changes in these areas as the computer becomes more universally accepted and applied.

One of the primary tasks of middle managers is to collect, process, and analyze information that their superiors will use in planning, controlling, and coordinating activity. As organizations have grown, additional layers of management have been added to facilitate the flow of information up and down the organizational ladder.

Much of the information that flows through middle management can be processed by the computer more quickly, more completely, more accurately, and at less cost. The principal impact on management, therefore, will be the combining and/or eliminating of many functions. Many middle managers, and managers at higher levels too, will see their jobs disappear because of the work the computer will do. This trend is already established. Upper management is relying more on reports from the information center than on time-consuming conferences with subordinates. Organization structures will become flatter as layers of management are abolished.

The process of management will also be affected. This will be primarily in terms of the depth and frequency of planning and decision making. Before making a plan or a decision, a manager gathers relevant information. But there have always been limitations on the amount of information that can be gathered. Both the time factor and the cost factor have been serious deterrents to gathering all the information that could be used to make an intelligent decision. The information system is overcoming these prior handicaps. We should expect, too, that it will be much more feasible to reappraise plans more frequently than in the past. Cycles of information flow are being shortened through integrated data processing systems.

Another outgrowth of this speedup in information flow is that change will take place more frequently and in greater magnitude. Uncertainty is the great obstacle to change, but uncertainty is often the result of not having the necessary information. We are approaching the point where the manager in need of information will simply press a combination of buttons and have the needed information in seconds. All in all, the future will make great demands on both organization and management—demands that can and will be met.

SUMMARY

Management is often referred to as an invisible force that welds the diverse functions of an organization into an effective operating whole.

Through sound management, the resources of an organization, human and otherwise, can be made to produce far more than they could without management.

In a very real sense, managers have the responsibility for multiplying their own talents through the effective use of subordinates. Thus it is extremely important that managers understand and develop these requisite skills. Managerial skills, by and large, are personal in nature, not technical; thus it can be said that managerial skills have universal application. Managers at all levels of organization or managers in different organizations are involved with the same basic tasks.

BUSINESS ITEMS

Changing needs for management skills

Pepsi-Cola claims to have more than 20 percent of the soft-drink market and is convinced that it will catch up with number one—Coca-Cola—which has more than a 30 percent share of the market. This hope is pinned on Pepsi's shift from a brand management to a "functional" management organization form. What this adds up to is a change from a single brand manager who coordinates all jobs to separate managers who specialize in advertising, promotion, planning, and other marketing duties for all brands.

Since most companies started with a functional form of organization, this move looks like a step backwards. Pepsi's answer to this is that marketing has changed so much since the 1950s that the functions existing then which favored the brand manager organization are totally different now. Fifteen years ago, Pepsi looked for people who were strong on advertising and publicity skills. Today they are looking for people with skill in the areas of planning, distribution, finance, and economic analysis.

Good guesses make a good executive?

When a tough decision faces the businessman he often consults with experts and uses a variety of analytical techniques, some computerized, which provide him with market studies, projections, and other information which he uses in making his decisions. This information is seldom perfect or complete and the executive generally ends up guessing at the unknowns before deciding. This process is called judgment, but some businessmen readily admit that they rely on their intuition or play their hunches.

Since some executives are regularly more successful in the results of their decisions than are others, researchers are led to believe that a sixth sense may exist for these executives—an inexplicable ability to predict the future. After 10 years of research, experiments, and testing of hundreds of people for precognition, these researchers are convinced that superior decision makers are superior precognitors.

In a significant number of cases involving executives who had held the top-level decision-making post for at least 5 years, the highest scores in the precognition tests were achieved by those executives whose companies, under their direction, had achieved the best records of profit growth.

With research results such as these, better tests are certain to be developed which could help companies select the best executives from a group of well-qualified candidates.

QUESTIONS

1 "Without the organizational framework, it would be impossible to identify the types of managers needed to operate a business firm." Explain the meaning of this statement.

2 Why should profit not be the primary objective of a business? What should be the primary objective of every business?

3 Contrast Taylor's approach to management with Odiorne's *Management by Objectives*.

4 Do you agree with Taylor that "there is a science to each element of a man's work"? How about a ditchdigger?

5 How does planning differ at the various organizational levels?

6 Outline the steps involved in the planning process.

7 Identify and explain the principal tasks of management. Illustrate their application in the operation of a retail store.

8 What criteria can be used to determine whether a particular job is managerial?

9 What is meant by "universality of management functions"? Discuss the applicability in the case of a company president who becomes dean of a college of business administration.

10 What is authority? How much authority does a given manager have?

11 How do the skills of a manager differ from the skills of a nonmanager?

12 What must be done to control an activity? Apply these concepts to the control of material cost.

13 What is policy? What purposes is policy intended to serve?

14 What changes in organization and management can be expected in the future?

THREE

THE BUSINESS FUNCTIONS AND THEIR PERFORMANCE

Parts 1 and 2 of this text presented a picture of (1) the general framework within which business operates and over which it has little control and (2) the internal environment of business over which the business person has a great amount of control. Now we can examine the basic functions of business enterprise to learn about what types of tasks business people are concerned with and why. Specifically we need to know about the four basic business functions: the process of getting goods and services into the hands of the consumer (marketing); the creation of goods and services (production); the process of obtaining and retaining the personnel needed to carry on the business (staffing); and the process of providing money for the business (financing).

The marketing function is examined first because in theory, at least, the production function depends on market factors. An understanding of market demand should be prerequisite to planning for the other functions. What does the market want? In what quantity, and at what quality and price? These market questions must be answered before intelligent production, personnel, and finance decisions can be made.

The production of goods or services requires the use of resources: people, money, materials, and facilities. The success of business is closely related to how well these resources are organized into smoothly operating and efficent units.

People are the most important ingredient of business success and finding the right people at the right price is a major staffing task for any business person. The specific manpower requirements are dictated by the manner in which goods or services are created and sold.

Although businesses generally have most of their dollars tied up in the investment in the plant and in inventories, there must be a continuous flow of funds into and out of the business if it is to remain alive and healthy. This flow of funds represents the blood-stream of the business system. Depending on what activities the business is engaged in the requirements for funds will vary both in the amount needed and in when it is needed. For these reasons, keeping close tabs on the financing function is all the more important.

The basic format of Part 3 is first to describe the particular business function in terms of its organizational structure and general characteristics and then to discuss how business people go about carrying out the specific tasks that are involved.

The purpose of this chapter   Distribution encompasses the activities involved in moving goods from the manufacturer to the consumer. This is a most important function, for goods sitting in the manufacturer's warehouse do not satisfy any human want until they reach the hands of the consumer. / In this chapter we shall analyze the very complex system of distribution to determine precisely what factors are involved in the process. Distribution involves many of the same factors found in any other facet of business—funds, personnel, equipment, and so forth—but the organization and arrangements required for distribution are different from those needed for other types of business operations. / Questions raised in this chapter include:

1 How do the functions performed in the distribution of goods and services create utility?

2 What are the problems involved in buying and selling at the manufacturing, wholesale, and retail levels?

3 What are some of the channels of distribution?

4 How is the sale of goods and services effected?

5 Are distribution costs too high? How can they be evaluated?

THE MARKETING FUNC-TION

The variety of goods and services available to American consumers is almost endless, and it increases day by day. The variety of routes used by business people to bring goods and services to the consumer also seems endless. Consequently a tremendous number of people—perhaps as many as 25 percent of the work force—performing a wide variety of tasks, make up the total marketing function. Let us see why this is so.

During our winter months small green pods appear on the limbs of certain trees on a South American plantation. Inside the pods there are a number of small seeds. Months later, a small boy in the United States buys a 10-cent bar of chocolate in the corner store and eats some of these small seeds. Of course, the seeds are now chocolate, for the tree is the cacao tree, and the seeds, when processed, yield a fatty oil used in the production of chocolate. The cycle of production, distribution, and consumption is completed when the chocolate is all eaten. Between the plantation and the corner store the little seeds in the cacao pod are processed, moved, stored, sold, and resold many times over. Each step in the process is a unified, steady movement from one step to the next until the cycle is completed.

PRODUCTION AND DISTRIBUTION

For convenience, we usually divide the economic cycle described above into two major parts: production and distribution. In the production part of the cycle, the raw materials are transported, processed, stored, sold, and resold until they achieve the form in which they are to be used by the ultimate consumer. All the activity that transports and processes the cacao beans until they are part of a bar of chocolate candy, ready to be eaten, makes up the production process.

Then the distribution system must move the bar of candy from the manufacturer to the final consumer—the small boy. The manufacturer sells the candy to a wholesaler who transports and stores it until it can be sold to a jobber. The jobber again transports and stores the candy until he packs and ships it to the corner store. The candy remains in the corner store until it is bought and eaten. Each step in the process of transferring the candy bar from the manufacturer's plant to the small boy's grimy palm is part of the process we call distribution.

CONSUMER WANTS AND NEEDS

The task of the marketing effort is to create an environment which results in the consumer's feeling a need for a given product or service. The need may be real or imaginary; often what we describe as a "need" could be better described as "something nice to have." There is perhaps a real need for air conditioners in automobiles that travel the streets and highways of the southern United States in the summertime. The need is less real in New England, but this does not deter business from trying to convince automobile buyers everywhere that air conditioning is needed.

Once the concept of need has been established, the task facing business is to get consumers to convert their dollars into products and services—to translate need into want. Business is often criticized on the grounds that it takes unfair advantage of the consumer, that it creates imaginary needs. But who is to say? Of what increased value are whitewall tires over blackwall tires? Of what value is the extra-cost bumblebee stripe on the back of a sports car? Perhaps they are needed just to satisfy owner ego, and consequently they become wanted items. Out of want comes new business with increased opportunity for employment, investment, and better living.

At this point, the distribution process and all that it entails is a necessary service to move the goods in a manufacturer's warehouse to us as consumers. The longer they remain in the warehouse the higher the costs of business operation become. The economic cycle is not complete until goods are actually in the hands of the consumer—this is the task of the distribution system.

DISTRIBUTION COSTS

The distribution process described above—buying, selling, storing, creating consumer demand—involves many people and consequently is a costly process. The cost of distribution is defined as the difference between the price which the producer or manufacturer charges for goods and the price paid by the consumer, disregarding any taxes that must be paid along the way. If a loaf of bread is sold by the baker for 16 cents but costs 35 cents at the supermarket, the cost of distribution is 19 cents. This cost may seem high, and the cost of distribution does make up a large portion of the price we must pay for goods. Still, it would cost us a lot more than 19 cents to run to a central bakery every time we needed bread. Spark plugs for automobiles cost a few cents each to the manufacturer but may sell for a dollar or more at the garage. Ball-point pens which cost a few cents to produce may sell for a dollar or more. A number of reasons why distribution costs are so high are identified below.

First, the production of goods is mechanized or perhaps automated and is generally far more efficient than the distribution process, which still relies heavily on expensive manpower. Visualize what is involved in getting a can of B&M beans from the Burnham and Morrill bakery in Portland, Maine, to your car in an A&P parking lot in Albany, New York, and you can see how distribution costs mount up. First the can must be moved from the warehouse to a truck or freight car. Next it must be moved to an A&P distribution center, where it is unloaded, transported to a storage area, unloaded again, and placed in stock. (Note: we must not forget all the paperwork that each step of this process involves.) It waits in storage until ordered by an A&P supermarket. Then it is loaded on a pallet and moved to a delivery truck. It is placed in the truck and transported to the store. There it is unloaded and placed in the basement storage area. Later it is brought upstairs where it is marked and placed on shelves. Still later it is handled at the check-out booth, put into bags, and taken by a bundle boy to your car. Compare this process to the automatic and continuous movement of materials down an assembly line, and the inefficiency in distribution is obvious.

Second, distribution costs include expensive inventory and storage costs. The costs of carrying an item in inventory can range between 20 and 30 percent of its value when measured on an annual basis. Thus it may cost between $1,667 and $2,500 per month to carry a $100,000 inventory. Why does it cost so much to carry an inventory? Inventory investment is a money investment, and money is worth 8 to 10 percent. Inventories must be insured, they depreciate, and they deteriorate; this costs money. In some instances, inventories are considered taxable property and taxes increase the cost. Maintaining inventories is a mandatory part of the distribution process, and therefore the costs associated with inventory are inescapable. They may be lowered through efficient management, but they cannot be eliminated.

In addition, distribution entails a considerable element of risk for which there is no insurance. The greater the risk involved, the greater must be the compensation for assuming the risk. The basic risk that every business person faces is that the goods he buys or produces may or may not be sold at a price that will yield a profit. Generally, the amount of risk that a business person assumes varies directly with the perishability of the merchandise involved—pig iron, low; fad items, high.

Distribution is comparatively expensive in this country and it is certain to take more of management's time in the future as it seeks to reduce costs to the consumer and to increase sales. An extensive and highly complex distribution system is absolutely essential to the maintenance of our high standard of living, and from this point of view it may not be too expensive at all. Some specific conclusions regarding the cost of distribution can be more appropriately drawn later in this chapter, after a discussion of the distribution functions.

DISTRIBUTION FUNCTIONS

The basic functions or processes in distribution are buying and selling, transporting and storage. Buying, selling, and storage especially may involve financing, which may be considered a fifth function. At each stage of the distribution process the business person must assume risk in varying degrees. The cost of this sixth function, risk taking, must be assessed by the distributor when he is calculating the profit he hopes to make on his transactions. Figure 10-1 diagrams the stages, the functions, and the people involved in the distribution process. Had this paragraph been written 50 years ago or more, it would have been appropriate to the times. The basic functions remain the same but the manner in which they are carried out is subject to constant change.

Buying

The goods that you and I purchase at the store have probably been bought and sold several times before they get into our hands. Few manufacturers deal with the consumer directly, although there is a trend in modern distribution toward a reduction of the number of middlemen involved in the transfer of goods from manufacturer to consumer. Large-scale or chain-store distribution enhances the feasibility of removing some middlemen. There are several types of buying in the distribution process, but the two that are the most significant are buying at the wholesale level and buying at the retail level.

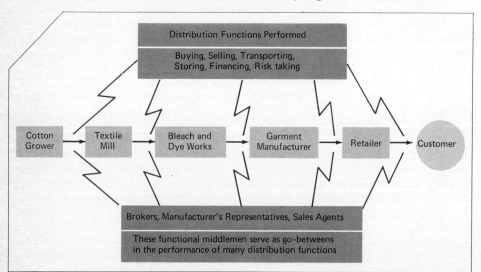

FIGURE 10-1 A distribution process

The distribution process for goods destined for further production is generally shorter than the process shown here.

Wholesale buying

A *wholesaler* is a business that provides a source of supply for retailers. This definition brings to mind the retail stores where we trade and may lead us to feel that selling to these stores is the extent of wholesaling. However, we must include in our group of retailers such business people as the plumber, the electrician, and the home builder, each of whom buys at wholesale and sells at retail, if we are to have the correct perspective of the wholesale function.

Wholesale buyers, in general, purchase stocks of goods from manufacturers, hold them, and sell them to retailers. A single wholesaler may service a hundred or more retailers spread over a broad geographic area; he covers a large market. In general, wholesale buying is more specialized then retail buying. For example, a wholesaler may deal only in automobile parts, canned goods, or appliances, whereas a large department store may carry all these items and more.

Wholesale buying involves the same considerations as would be used by a manufacturer, retailer, or any business buyer: selecting the kinds of goods to purchase, determining the appropriate quality or suitability of goods, determining the appropriate quantities to purchase, and selecting a source or sources of supply that will permit achieving the first three considerations. The price that must be paid for a particular item is determined largely by its quality or suitability.

If we visualize a wholesaler as basically a storehouse for certain retailers, then we can begin to pinpoint the problem. Retail customers prefer to deal with wholesale sources that can provide them with whatever goods they want at any time and at a reasonable cost. This permits the retailer to operate with minimum investment in inventory and, at the same time, to provide customer satisfaction.

Kinds of goods

The time lapse between the decision to buy a particular product from a given source of supply and its availability for sale may be weeks or months or longer. During this time span a number of things can happen to improve or destroy the marketability of the product. Competition may come out with a vastly superior product, consumer taste may change, prices may change, or laws may be enacted that require or prohibit its use. Every time a wholesaler, or any businessman, buys, he gambles that market conditions will not change or that he has accurately measured the changes that will occur. Because the wholesale buyer deals with finished goods, he does not have the alternative open to the buyer of raw materials, sheet steel for example, who may be able to use his stocks for other purposes if demand for the intended item of manufacture should fail.

To overcome this problem the wholesaler can divide his inventory investment into two classes of goods: (1) more or less standard items that history shows are consistent performers and (2) items whose sales performance is unknown but whose profit potential is high. The larger share of inventory investment should be in the first category to ensure an acceptable volume of sales. Also, within certain limits most wholesalers find their choice of merchandise fairly well defined by their clientele and competition. Knowing this will be of value to the wholesale buyer only if he understands his clientele and competition.

Quality or suitability Again, knowledge of clientele and competition is essential to intelligent decisions on the quality or suitability of merchandise. If a wholesaler of hardware items has a clientele of discount stores, merchandise of low quality is suitable, but if the clientele is full-line hardware stores, such merchandise would most likely be inappropriate. Buying right makes selling easier, and this should underscore the idea that one must know one's customers before one can buy intelligently.

Quantity How much to buy is determined from the sales plan— provided there is such a thing. Without a sales plan, which is a reflection of customer needs, there is no logical basis for ascertaining the amount to buy. The process of sales planning is discussed in Chapter 11.

Source of supply The source of supply may or may not pose a problem for the wholesaler. If the wholesaler decides to handle brand-name goods—Black and Decker power tools, for example—there is only one choice of supplier. The problem of source is associated with unbranded merchandise. In selecting a source of supply, consideration should be given to such factors as dependability, accessibility, and the net cost of acquisition. If a supplier has been in business for an extended period of time, it should not be difficult to ascertain how well he measures up against these criteria.

Retail buying

More than any other buyer the retailer is at the mercy of consumer demand. The problem is complicated because manufacturers in an effort to be different offer dozens of variations in the style, quality, or design of merchandise to be purchased. The consumer may give some advance indication of what he will purchase, but often he does not express a willingness or unwillingness to buy until the merchandise is actually on display; then it may be too late. That some retailers are forced to buy from specific wholesalers because of availability or credit restrictions adds to the problem.

Small-scale retail buying especially is very wasteful. Here, the buyer will spend but a fraction of his time on buying activity and will buy in a limited buying market. Therefore he will have little opportunity to become proficient. The combination of buying errors and inability to buy at maximum discounts is the main source of waste.

Large-scale retail buying Buying for large-scale retailers such as Sears, J. C. Penney, or Zayre resembles wholesale buying more than small-scale retail buying. In such cases, a single buyer purchases merchandise that might be sold in a hundred stores or more. The principal difference is that the buyer here has captive retail outlets not available to the wholesaler. The trend today is toward large-scale retailing, and one of the main reasons for it is the economy of large-scale buying. Large-scale retailers can afford full-time professional buyers who become specialists in a particular line of merchandise. Because they are specialists they are in an excellent position to understand the markets in which they will buy and the markets in which they will sell. The resulting reduction in buying errors plus the economy of large-scale buying provides advantages unavailable to small retailers.

Specification buying Many large retailers such as Sears contract with selected manufacturers to have goods made to their specifications. Through research and market analysis Sears determines the kinds of goods that it wants. This permits the retailer to order from the manufacturer exactly what he wishes to have in his stock and often gives him a price advantage. There is no middleman to deal with, and the manufacturer may be able to operate more efficiently by producing to a known delivery schedule. The producer may also be able to make delivery of goods in smaller amounts over a period of time, thus relieving the retailer of high inventories and allowing the manufacturer flexibility in his production schedule. In some cases, only a few samples of merchandise will be carried in the retailer's stock, and delivery will be made directly to the consumer from the manufacturer's warehouse after the sale is consummated.

Selling

The business person's inventory may represent thousands or even millions of dollars in investment, but it can earn nothing until it has been sold. This is true of the manufacturer, the wholesaler, and the retailer alike. Selling is the ultimate satisfaction of the consumer's desire for goods. Obviously, the greater the number of products from which the consumer may select and the greater the number of outlets where goods may be purchased, the more difficult and expensive the sales process is for a specific business person. Advertising and promotion, free samples, free trial use, and countless other devices are employed to induce the potential buyer to spend his funds on the seller's product or in the seller's establishment.

Advertising and promotion

Advertising and promotion are essential features of our distribution system. Business people have been criticized many times because of the vast amounts of money that they spend on telling consumers about their products. The feeling expressed is that advertising adds to the price of goods on the market, and that with less advertising savings would accrue to the consumer. Obviously there is poor or ineffective advertising and good or effective advertising. But all in all we are able to record a number of benefits that have accrued to society through advertising, and other benefits may be added in the future.

1 Selling the consumer Advertising's chief role is conditioning people to buy. For a particular business, advertising's role is to condition consumers to buy its brand instead of another and to continue the purchase of its brand. There are other means for achieving this end, but advertising is the most effective and efficient approach for most businesses. There are many businesses that make no specific allocation of funds for advertising, but obviously we know very little about them.

Advertising is the most effective and efficient means for informing people about product or service characteristics because it reaches vast numbers of people over and over and enables the use of a variety of appeals to the consumer. It costs as much as $80,000 per minute to advertise on television but if 4 million families are exposed to the commercial the cost of bringing a message to each family is only 2 cents. This is far less than it would cost to reach these families by mail and, for many types of products, is far more effective.

Selling to the consumer can be accomplished through personal contact wherein the salesperson attempts to convince the consumer that his product is superior to all others. Generally, this approach cannot be used for low-cost or low-markup items because it is highly inefficient. When it is used it is generally accompanied by advertising.

2 Creating new markets Advertising informs and advertising can educate. Through advertising business people can multiply the need for their product. Food manufacturers especially bring to the consumer's attention through advertising the variety of ways their products can be used and perhaps substituted for other food products. Advertising can make a person want something to the point he feels he needs it and finally ends up buying it.

3 Lowering cost to consumers Although advertising adds to the cost of business operation it can result in lower costs if properly used. Advertising creates mass markets which are essential for lower-cost mass production techniques. In addition, advertising can stimulate demand for products during seasons when they normally would not be purchased. This enables the manufacturing and distribution systems to operate with greater efficiency.

4 Increasing competition One of the requisites for competition is an informed public. Without advertising we would know very little about the products and services available for our use; we cannot determine whether product X is the best buy unless we know about competing products. Advertising provides us with this knowledge and makes it possible for us to get more of what we want for the dollars we spend. To be sure, some advertising is no more than meaningless words and illustrations, but by and large, considering all types of purchases, it provides an effective basis for making a buying decision.

5 Aiding research Procter and Gamble has been advertising its products since 1882. Over the years it has developed the confidence of millions of buyers by bringing them consistently good value. As a result, any new product advertised by Procter and Gamble is certain to receive customer attention. This capacity to get the eyes and ears of the consumer, developed in part through advertising, reduces the risk of not being able to get a new product "off the ground." Management is more willing to invest in new-product research when there is assurance that it can quickly reach the market with a new idea.

Advertising media The methods or media for advertising and promotion are many. The specific responsibility for the advertising function in business varies from a part-time assignment for one person to full-time work by large departments of nationally known advertising agencies. Advertising takes so many forms and utilizes so many variations in terms of responsibility that we just do not know how many people or how much money it involves.

Some indication of the magnitude of advertising is given in Table 10-1. The total amount spent on television, magazine, and newspaper advertising is shown, along with the major industry users. Newspaper advertising still leads the field, and the relatively young medium, television, holds second place.

Note that several industries stand out as heavy spenders in both television and magazine advertising. These two media tend to be national in coverage, whereas newspapers are quite local. Note also that we can account for almost $1 billion in advertising for the automotive plus drug and toiletries categories in just these three media.

The specific medium that an advertiser uses depends on the people

TABLE 10-1 Advertising expenditures by medium, 1971

Totals (in millions) by medium

Newspapers, national and local	$6,215
Television	1,398
Magazines	1,251

Totals (in millions) in selected categories by medium, 1971

	Newspapers	TV	Magazines
Automobiles	126	101	111
Drugs	—	96	38
Toiletries	16	154	121
Food	9.7	304	98
Smoking materials	35.5	5	118
Beer, wine	—	78	88

Source: *Statistical Abstract,* 1972.

he needs to reach. Thus *The Wall Street Journal* is an effective medium for locating executive talent and promoting the fleet sale of automobiles but probably would be a poor means for advertising toothpaste.

Merchandising

Merchandising is the process of "adjusting" to consumer demand the merchandise that is produced or offered for sale. It is concerned with getting the right merchandise to the right place at the right time and presenting it to potential customers in the right fashion. Each time we enter the automobile showroom, the department store, or the supermarket, we see merchandising in action. The location of merchandise in the selling area, the way it is displayed, the emphasis on price, and the services available to the customer are all parts of the merchandising function. This is a most important function which should be coordinated with other aspects of the sales plan. Through advertising, people are drawn to a place of business. Whether these people become customers or just observers hinges on the quality of the merchandising effort.

Although the merchandising function is performed by manufacturers, wholesalers, and retailers, it is a most critical function in retailing. The retailer has far less leeway in merchandising than do manufacturers and wholesalers. There is, for example, little opportunity in modern retailing to bargain with the customer over price. If the set price is not to the customer's liking, then the sale is lost. For manufacturers and to a lesser extent wholesalers, much bargaining often takes place to arrive at the right price—a price that is mutually satisfactory to both buyer and seller. Because the ultimate consumer generally buys for immediate consumption—retailers and wholesalers frequently do not—the retailer has far less opportunity to make adjustments once merchandising decisions have been made.

Many large retail stores employ merchandise managers, who are located high in the organization structure, to supervise the activity necessary for effective merchandising; it is that important. The merchandising function is repeated in each retail outlet. The merchandise manager has the responsibility for developing the merchandising plan which may be modified in each store depending on local conditions.

Wholesale selling

There can be no wholesale selling unless there is retail buying. Therefore, the discussion that follows should be considered with the problems of retail buying in mind. Whether wholesale selling will be a routine process or will call for skill depends basically on the merchandise involved. The selling of appliances, foods, and other consumer goods is much simpler than the sale of automobile parts, plumbing supplies, and the like because far less understanding of the product is needed to satisfy the buyer.

The goods that you and I buy may be identified as brand-name goods such as Frigidaire, Kelvinator, or Motorola; private-brand goods such as Grant's Bradford; and unbranded goods. Unbranded goods usually have a name that has little meaning to the consumer. Brand-name goods are associated with a specific manufacturer, are promoted by the manufacturer, and often carry the warranty of the manufacturer. These features are an advantage to the wholesaler whose own name means little to the consumer. Some national or regional wholesalers have successfully developed private brands, but with the possible exception of food products, they are in the minority. Many unbranded goods or goods with a yet-to-be-established name must be sold solely on the basis of price and consequently will be low-profit items.

Wholesale selling attracts a higher caliber and a more stable type of sales personnel than retailing because wholesale selling, as a rule, is more difficult and challenging. Wholesale salespeople have the responsibility of locating and developing customers to the point where mutually profitable relations are maintained, whereas retail salespeople characteristically simply wait for customers to come to them. It is far easier to measure performance and hence value of salespeople in wholesaling, for each salesperson may have a distinct territory and line of goods for which he or she is responsible.

Retail selling

Retail selling may soon become a lost art. Once important in the retailing of foods products, it has virtually disappeared and been replaced by self-service establishments. In soft goods, housewares, automobiles, and other lines, very little sales effort takes place at the point of sale. There are several reasons for the demise of retail selling. It has been found that making the sales pitch prior to the time a customer enters the store is far more productive and economical than making it in the store. Through advertising and promotion, helped significantly by television, manufacturers and retailers are able to get consumers to decide on a particular purchase beforehand, and the store serves as a convenient place to pick it up. Retail sales forces generally simply do not have the time or knowledge necessary to convince a potential customer to buy this or that. The scarcity and high cost of competent sales help make it imperative that the time spent on each sales transaction be kept to a minimum. Thus, some retailing becomes more and more self-service: a warehouse with a place to pay.

The above description characterizes a great many retail stores but certainly is not true of all. The sole-proprietor retailer will in all probability make a greater attempt to sell than would an employee, because he must sell if he is to stay in business. Furniture, musical instruments, fine jewelry, and other relatively high-cost and high-markup items may be sold more effectively in the store by sales personnel than through conventional advertising and promotion channels.

Sales force productivity

When a sales organization is confronted with increasingly higher costs, much greater emphasis is then usually placed on methods of increasing the productivity of the sales effort—that is, taking those steps which will bring in more sales dollars for every dollar spent in the selling effort. In an industry such as retailing where payroll and fringe-benefit costs may amount to 60 to 70 percent of operating costs, the emphasis on greater productivity is especially important.

Various approaches may be used to spur the sales-force productivity. Diversification of products, expansion of outlets or territories, and intensive efforts at extracting maximum sales results are some of these approaches.

Sales personnel In addition to the need to shape up all activities relative to the sales effort, such as buying, merchandising, and distribution, it is extremely important that the quality of the sales force be subject to continuing examination and control. In many areas of business, and particularly at the retailing level, the weakest link in the sales effort is in the quality of the sales personnel.

Transportation and storage

The transportation facilities available to a business person have a significant impact on the scope of his operations and consequently on his profit. If the transportation system permits the movement of goods for great distances at reasonable cost, the business person gains in two directions. First, he can increase his sources of supply and thereby increase the competition for his business; he is not at the mercy of one or a few local sources. Second, he can offer his goods for sale in more markets, expose them to more types of consumers, and increase the probability that his goods will be sold at a profitable price. This concept applies to all business whether it be a market gardener selling perishables, a steel manufacturer, or a petroleum company.

Transportation is important for another reason: it is a major contributor to the high cost of distribution. Increases in efficiency and productivity are basic to our philosophy; we see ample evidence of this in manufacturing enterprises. Our transportation system, however, has not increased its productivity and efficiency at the same rate as manufacturing enterprises. Labor unions are in part responsible for this because of a number of restrictive practices aimed at preserving work opportunities for its members. Lower costs of transportation are still a basic goal of the industry and of those who use the transportation service, but, at most, we should expect only a gradual reduction in the portion of our sales dollars that goes for this service.

Good transportation must satisfy several conditions. First, it must be comprehensive; it must be able to serve all areas of the country. In China and in Brazil, for example, where the major portion of the transportation system is concentrated along the coastline, there is a significant difference in the standards of living of those serviced with transportation and those in the poorly supplied interior. Second, transportation must be capable of handling almost any size or type of object in almost any quantity. Finally, the system must be flexible. A system that depended primarily on railroads or waterways would not be considered flexible. The combination of highways, waterways, airways, and railroads that supplies the United States, together with such specialized transportation methods as gas and oil pipelines, is unequaled in any other part of the world. We may wish to brand our transportation system backward and inadequate when compared to the state of the art in manufacturing industries, yet it does satisfy a major portion of the extreme demands that are made upon it.

Storage A good transportation system can reduce the need for storage facilities, though it cannot wholly eliminate the need. For the business person, good transportation facilities may mean a reduction of inventory needs from several months' supply to weeks' or even days', resulting in a real savings in the amount of funds invested in stored goods, plus a saving in storage cost. The fantastic degree of coordination between the delivery of materials and production schedules at General Motors assembly plants permits the unloading of many component parts directly to subassembly lines. Although this is an exceptional circumstance, it does point out the possibilities.

Most storage requirements in this country, however, are not caused by the lack of transportation facilities. Some of the major reasons for needing storage are the following:

1 Some goods are not produced to meet current demands. There is the obvious illustration of crops harvested in a short time span but consumed year-round and the less obvious case of manufacturers who seek the economies of stabilized production though market demand is highly variable.

2 Transportation facilities can be affected by season or weather. Iron ore cannot be transported across the Great Lakes year-round, but steel must be produced year-round—hence the need to store iron ore.

3 Some goods, such as tobacco, cheese, meats, and alcoholic beverages, must be stored before sale while being ''aged'' to reach a marketable condition.

4 Goods may be stored for speculative purposes. Business people frequently buy in excess of current requirements to make certain that they will have goods when needed or, perhaps, to buy at a lower price than they would pay later on.

Using credit to finance inventories

Credit, or the deferred payments for goods or services, is used at almost every stage of distribution and is a vital ingredient in our distribution system for manufacturer, wholesaler, retailer, and individual consumer alike. In some instances credit is used for convenience, but it is also used because buyers just do not have the necessary cash.

Credit, which is a form of borrowing, is considered necessary and useful. Probably the most important function of credit from the business person's point of view is to increase the demand for goods. If everyone had to pay cash for all the things they buy, sales would be much lower than they are. Credit is used extensively today in the purchase of goods, even those costing only a few dollars—it is easier to buy on credit even if this increases the cost of purchasing.

Most wholesalers and retailers need credit to maintain inventories at reasonable levels. Credit terms of 30, 60, or 90 days or longer are common in the business world. This means that business people may be able to sell the goods before the payment is due. If this happens, they could maintain and pay for inventories without investing their own funds. However, to do so probably means that cash discounts have been forfeited and, since the extension of credit by suppliers adds to the cost of operation, this added cost must be reflected in higher selling prices.

If business were to operate without any inventory, that is, as goods were produced they were sold, there would be no problem in supplying customers as long as the demand was at a constant level. If demand fluctuated widely, in order to keep pace with demand, production would also have to fluctuate widely. The result would be that at times when demand was low, production capacity would be idle. At other times when demand was high, the production facility would be strained to produce enough. Inventories serve as a sort of reservoir or buffer to handle the differential which occurs between supply and demand at any given time and as a result provide for more efficient and economical use of production facilities and less reason for price fluctuations.

Finally, credit plays a vital role in establishing new businesses in distribution, as it does in production. Credit fills in the time lag between purchase of goods and their subsequent sale. Few individuals have the resources needed to enter business without the assistance of credit. Even a limited deferral of payment—30, 60, or 90 days—can enable the small retail store owner to begin operations.

Risk Distribution, like all other forms of business enterprise, contains a variable element of risk. The type of risk and the degree of risk vary from one business to the next, but most distributive risks fall into one of the following categories:

1 A reduction in demand due to changes in style or buying habits or price

2 Government action limiting business activity

3 A reduction in the value of inventory due to falling prices

4 Losses from theft, breakage, pilfering, etc.

5 Losses because customers default on payments

6 Losses due to calamities such as weather or fire or death of key personnel

It is possible to insure against—pass to someone else the responsibility for—some of these risks, especially the last four, but insurance seldom offers complete protection against risk. There is no way to insure against the first four risks. But this does not imply that a business person cannot protect himself from these risks. If one is ignorant of consumer wants, the trend of the economy, and pending legislation affecting business, one can be hurt severely.

Although "risk" has an ominous sound, it is an important ingredient in any free enterprise system. In a state-dominated economic system the concept of risk is not present, because consumer demand is not the determining factor in production and distribution. The government makes the decisions about what and how much will be produced and the price at which it will be sold, and the consumer must accept what is offered, since there is no alternative source of goods. In a free enterprise system, risks tend to affect the poorly managed business first; in other words, poor management increases the risk element in business. Many business risks are incurred through dependence on faulty information or through poor use of available information—essentially poor management.

CHANNELS OF DISTRIBUTION

The distribution system consists of all those who are involved in the buying and selling functions which occur as the goods move through the distribution channels from the producer to the ultimate consumers. These intermediaries include wholesalers and retailers and also a variety of people known by such titles as agents, brokers, manufacturer's representatives, and so on. These are all independent business people whose function is to move the goods along an additional step in the distribution process.

Sometimes middlemen are covered by agreements such as franchises or distributor contracts which protect their sales territories from intrusion by other distributors of the products which their suppliers handle.

Since the supplier's goal is to reach his ultimate customer at as low a cost and as efficiently as possible, he will use middlemen or set up his own sales organization, whichever best serves this objective.

The process of distribution involves the marketing functions discussed above. The number of times each function is performed and who performs it depends on the manner in which these functions are organized. Buying, selling, transporting, etc., cannot be avoided, but the question of how many buys, sells, and moves will be made and who will make them depends on how the system is organized. The principal question is who will carry out these functions rather than what functions will be involved. The answers depend chiefly on the role which the manufacturer chooses to play in the distribution of his products. A given manufacturer may use several channels of distribution depending on the needs of his customers.

Some firms, including Avon Products, Inc., the Fuller Brush Co., and the Electrolux Corp., control distribution completely by selling directly to the consumer at home. In other cases the manufacturer may want no part of the distribution of goods, and he may sell his entire output to wholesalers who then pass the goods along to the retailer. Between these two extremes there are varying degrees of control of distribution by manufacturers.

WHOLESALE SERVICES

The wholesaler buys goods from the manufacturer and he sells them to retail outlets. In the process, he may provide a variety of services on behalf of the producer or the customer.

What services do wholesalers perform? Much depends on the product concerned. In the vegetable-canning industry, the wholesaler is the key figure in distribution because he grades, stores, advertises, and delivers the food to the retailer. Wholesalers in this business must finance a very extensive set of operations. In the distribution of automobiles, on the other hand, there are virtually no wholesale functions. The retailer orders directly from the manufacturer, and the manufacturer arranges transportation and finance. There are no middlemen.

Some factors affecting the use of wholesale services

Small producers can seldom engage very extensively in the distribution process, if only because of the costs involved. They usually employ the services of a wholesaler. Millinery and garment makers, novelty and toy makers, and plumbing-supply producers make extensive use of wholesalers. In some cases, small producers may band together to create a distributing organization as in the case of the California Fruit Growers Exchange (Sunkist).

Larger producers may choose to market their own products through their own facilities. Many times this is prompted by their desire to maintain control over each step in the distribution process or simply because by eliminating the middleman their costs are reduced.

Products of exceptional quality or reputation are often distributed or promoted by their producers. These products often are identified by a well-known trademark or registered name.

Sometimes the relative locations of the producers and their customers influence the way in which distribution is handled. Large customers who are centrally located and easily reached may be serviced directly by the manufacturer. For example, the garment industry is centered in New York City; the grain trade in Chicago; the furniture trade in Grand Rapids, Michigan; tobacco production in North Carolina; and the automobile industry in Detroit. Manufacturers who produce for these particular markets may deal directly with the companies without having to search too far or wide for their customers.

There are also times when the large customer is in a better position to take over the performance of the services usually performed by the wholesaler. This is particularly true when the customer's name is better known than the producer's and is a better drawing feature. The companies which supply Sears, Roebuck and Co. with paint, appliances, or tools need not advertise these products, for Sears' retail customers are attracted primarily by the Sears name and the trade-names which are applied to the products. Much the same holds true for stores like Macy's or Neiman-Marcus.

FUNCTIONS OF THE RETAILER

Today, it is sometimes difficult to make a clear distinction between the functions of wholesaler and retailer. Many retailers now perform some of the tasks traditionally listed as wholesaling activities. However, certain functions are clearly the responsibility of the retailer and are not performed by either the manufacturer or the wholesaler:

1 Determining his customer demand. The manufacturer and the wholesaler are, of course, concerned with total consumer demand, but not so specifically as the retailer. The retailer who cannot determine what his customers will purchase, at what price, at what time, is in difficulty.

2 Offering goods for sale at convenient locations and in adequate supply.

3 Making credit available to the customer.

4 Delivering and installing goods.

5 Offering advice on purchases.

6 Honoring guarantees. Although manufacturers commonly issue warranties on their products, the retailer is often called upon to assume the responsibility for goods purchased through his firm, particularly the class of goods we call durable. Retailers of automobiles, television sets, refrigerators, and the like must expect their customers to look to them for service and adjustment.

DISTRIBUTION COSTS

A number of inferences can be drawn from the material presented in this chapter relative to the costs of distribution. There are many things that must be done to bring goods to the consumer, and it takes considerable time to complete the process. All this costs money. But to fully appreciate the complexity of the distribution-cost problem we must look deeper; after all, this has been of concern to business people for decades, yet significant reductions in the cost of distribution are not yet a reality.

There are three principal factors that bear on the increase in distribution costs: a general increase in the cost of everything, a significant increase in the variety of goods which the distribution system must handle, and constant changes in the buying habits of consumers. If the price level, the variety of goods, and consumer buying habits were to remain constant for a period of time—a year or more—distribution costs would probably decline.

Price increases

Price increases affect every facet of the distribution process, and after experiencing an increase in costs, business people frequently organize cost-reduction campaigns. But what do they find when they examine the total array of distribution costs?

Self-service retailing was introduced to cut the cost of retail store operation, and little can be done to further reduce costs here to any great extent. Transportation and inventory are two major distribution costs, but little can be done to reduce them without reducing the level of service to customers. There are two approaches to the reduction of transportation cost, each with negative consequences: (1) adopt a slower-moving mode of transportation or (2) ship goods in larger quantities. Either approach adds to cost in some ways as it decreases cost in other ways; and the usual experience, especially with consumer goods, is that the net cost will rise. Longer delivery time results in greater inventories in transit and requires larger reserve stocks to maintain a given level of customer service. Bulk shipments result in larger maximum inventory and a slower rate of inventory turnover. Because the cost of maintaining inventory, in transit or on warehouse shelves, often equals $2\frac{1}{2}$ percent of the inventory value per month, it is easy to see that savings in transportation costs must be tremendous to warrant a lower grade of service.

Product-line proliferation

"In the good old days" the Ford Motor Company produced a line of cars which included a sedan, a touring car, and a single-seat roadster. A customer could request any color he chose as long as it was black. There was no such thing as extra-cost options, and the roadster sold for $295, FOB Dearborn, Michigan. The effects of this policy on the costs of production and distribution were fantastic. A dealer could display the entire product line in his showroom with a total inventory investment of about $1,000. At the manufacturing level significant savings were possible because the only difference in the production line was the body.

Since we, as customers, demand the right to select from a wide variety of products, the consequence is a multiplication of inventory. Suppose that a manufacturer of typewriters produced elite and pica models in a single color, black. If a retailer maintained an inventory of two—one of each—he could satisfy any customer who wished to buy a typewriter. If the manufacturer added a maroon and a green typewriter to the line, to maintain the same level of customer service would require an inventory of 6 or an increase of 200 percent. This would lead to increased inventory cost which may or may not be offset by the gains from a larger sales volume.

Manufacturers, wholesalers, and retailers have been able to keep the costs associated with product-line proliferation from rising out of bounds by lowering the level of customer service, that is, by making the customer wait. The waiting period may be minutes or weeks. But every time a business person does not have what the consumer wants on his shelves, he runs the risk of losing a sale. As proliferation continues, the odds decrease that a given business person can satisfy a specific customer's wants and make a profitable sale unless he is able to carry a very large and diversified inventory with all its added costs.

Changes in buying habits

When a business person decides to produce and distribute a product he visualizes that at a particular point in time it will roll off production lines, go through the distribution channel, and be accepted by the consumer. He hopes that this process will be a continuing one that will benefit all parties involved. Both the product and the channel of distribution are created with the assumption that the manufacturer knows who the consumer will be and also knows his buying habits. Our buying habits, however, are conditioned by a number of factors that neither the manufacturer nor the distributors are able to predict. The consequence may be that instead of a flow of goods through the channel there is inadequate consumer acceptance, and the goods back up at every stage of the distribution process. The result is several types of waste whose cost must be borne by the business activities that are profitable.

SUMMARY

The distribution of goods requires the performance of certain basic functions, regardless of the type of goods being distributed. These functions may be performed by the manufacturer, the wholesaler, or the retailer. The goods must be sold by the manufacturer, transported, stored, financed, and sold to the final consumer. All such economic activity requires organization. The organization may be based on the product, the geographical area, the function performed, or any other suitable factor, so long as it carries out its appointed task. The cost of distribution is high, often higher than the cost of production—but this is not necessarily to the disadvantage of society as a whole. The high costs are due to a number of causes, some of which are beyond the control of the distributors themselves.

BUSINESS ITEMS

Productivity is also a retailer's problem

The second-largest department store chain, Allied Stores Corporation, which operates an array of 16 discount stores and 142 department stores in 28 states, considers both its and its industry's biggest and most challenging job as retailers to be the task of boosting productivity.

Productivity is the buzz word in almost every business, but it is particularly significant in the retail field where payroll and fringe benefits make up 60 percent to 70 percent of operating costs. It is most significant to Allied, for whereas other store chains have shown gains in labor productivity over the past years, Allied, because of a long history of stiff and stodgy management, is running to catch up and doing this under new leadership.

Compounding the problem is the diversity of Allied's operating units which range from tiny Missoula Mercantile in Missoula, Montana, to bigger and better-known operations such as Jordan Marsh in Boston and Miami; Gertz in New York State; Bon Marche in Seattle and Lowell, Massachusetts; Maas Bros. in Florida; and Stern Bros. in New Jersey.

The strategy for improving productivity involves a revamped management structure; spruced-up merchandising, buying, and distribution; and upgrading the quality of sales help—one of the customers' single biggest complaints about retailing today.

The product recall—reverse distribution

Some people are almost seriously suggesting that a new course will soon be found in the curriculum of any worthwhile business school. Students of marketing are currently taught the intricacies of the distribution process—that series of steps that gets the product from the manufacturer, through wholesaler, dealer, or distributor, to the ultimate consumer. The new course is one which will be concerned with reverse distribution—getting the product back to the manufacturer from the customer.

Since the Consumer Product Safety Act became law in 1972 and a five-person Consumer Product Safety Commission was formed to administer it in 1973, an increasing number of products have been involved in recall situations. Manufacturers, as a result, have had to establish contingency plans covering the best way to recall substandard merchandise and effect the necessary repairs.

Civil fines of up to $500,000 for a related series of violations and criminal penalties of up to a year in prison and a $50,000 fine can be leveled against manufacturers who knowingly market a "noncomplying" consumer product.

To handle recalls usually means that a system of product identification must be set up so that the product can be tracked throughout the distribution process. It would not be too difficult to keep track of some heavy industrial machinery units but it would not be easy to keep track of the owners of 30,000 TV sets which are recalled for checking a defect which exists in only 2 percent of the sets.

Other approaches to deal with the problem require the involvement of the quality-control people so that they may more closely watch the quality of supply items which might cause product defects or on the other extreme establish a quality control situation in the plant so as to produce products with "zero defects."

QUESTIONS

1 If a 10-cent bar of candy costs 4 cents to manufacture and distribution eats up the other 6 cents, are the costs of distributing a bar of candy too high? Discuss.

2 Point out the reasons why the retailer's buying problems are more involved than the wholesaler's buying problems.

3 What are the principal benefits of buying to specification?

4 Retail selling may soon become a lost art. Do you agree? Discuss.

5 Advertising is wasteful and consumers would be better off if less money was spent for it. Do you agree? Explain.

6 Since advertising costs money and this cost must be covered by the selling price of the goods advertised, how can advertising lower costs to consumers?

7 Discuss the significance of this statement: The transportation system determines the limits of both the business person's sources and his markets.

8 What constitutes a good transportation system?

9 Comment on this statement: A good transportation system will eliminate the need for storage by, in effect, providing storage.

10 Discuss the importance of credit in distribution.

11 What are the primary areas of risk in distribution? What can be done about them?

12 What services do wholesalers provide?

13 What factors influence the amount of service that wholesalers must provide?

14 What services do retailers provide?

15 What conditions contribute to the high cost of distribution?

The purpose of this chapter   Chapter 10 dealt with general marketing issues; this chapter considers the specific steps that management must take to move goods to the customer in an efficient and effective manner. It deals with the organization of a sales force and with the issues of planning for and controlling many aspects of the marketing effort. / The chapter is specifically oriented to the business which has a product for sale, although the principles expressed are just as well applied to the firm which sells services, such as an insurance company, a trucking firm, or a uniform-rental business. / Distribution is costly, and one reason for its high cost may be an ineffective sales program. Experience has shown that many sales personnel, for example, spend a great deal more time traveling and waiting to see prospects than they do in actual selling and that the dissemination of product information to customers could often be better handled via other media. / A number of considerations ranging from the sales organization to paying the sales force are examined in this chapter. / Questions raised in this chapter include:

1 What is involved in developing a sales organization?

2 In what ways are sales organizations specialized? Why?

3 What is a sales plan and how is it developed?

4 With what sort of measuring sticks does a company appraise the performance of its sales force?

5 How can a sales salary plan help in achieving sales goals?

11 / PLANNING AND CONTROLLING THE COMPANY SALES ORGANIZATION

Sales organizing, planning, and control are necessary functions at each stage of the distribution process. However, the role of each party in distribution will vary depending primarily on the role that the manufacturer decides, or is forced, to take in getting goods and services to the consumer. Consequently the nature of sales organization, planning, and control will vary from situation to situation. In the distribution of automobiles, the manufacturer dominates the process to the point of dictating a minimum-sales plan for every retail outlet. Hence little or no sales planning takes place at the retail level. But a retailer of clothing, furniture, or appliances will not have a manufacturer who will provide him with the sales plan.

At every level of distribution top management must decide the role that the sales division will play in achieving the overall goals of the firm. This is an essential first step because it provides the basic guidelines for the sales effort. On the surface it may seem that there is only one goal for a sales division—selling as much as possible—but there are other justifiable goals such as market penetration, profit making, or inventory liquidation. The particular charge given a sales division has a significant bearing on the organizing, planning, and control of the sales effort.

FACTORS DETERMINING THE SALES ORGANIZATION

The sales organization is the means for carrying out the sales plan, but the plan is usually formulated within the framework of an existing organization structure. The scope and complexity of the selling organization vary greatly from one company to the next and with the passage of time. Some firms exercise great control over the sales function while others do not. The factors that determine the nature of a sales organization are the volume of sales needed, the competition, the market, the current trade practices, and the type of consumer for whom the goods and services are intended.

231

Sales volume

The sales organization must be capable of distributing the output of the firm it serves. Therefore, the volume of sales that must be generated is a paramount consideration in building the sales organization. There are many small firms that have no formal sales organization because the necessary sales volume can be achieved without one. This is not true for larger business firms. Since every business has an optimum production level—that level where unit costs of production are lowest—it is not uncommon to find that production managers have a greater voice in establishing sales levels than sales managers. However, whether a firm operates at the optimum level of production over an extended period of time or at some other level is determined by the efficiency of the sales organization.

Price field

The extent of competition in the price field in which the firm manufactures also has an important influence on the character of the sales organization. The manufacturer who produces large quantities of low-priced goods does not have the same sales problem as the business person who produces limited quantities of high-quality prestige items. To develop and maintain a prestige item requires much more careful control over sales than is necessary in the marketing of mass-produced materials. For one thing, the relation between cost and selling price is much closer in the case of mass-produced goods, and the markup for wholesaler and retailer is consequently much smaller. With prestige items, particularly those in which there is a substantial margin between cost and selling price, an elaborate set of controls can be employed to maintain the public image of the product.

Location of the market

One manufacturing firm located in Cleveland, Ohio, produces and sells $1 million worth of goods each year; all its customers are located within 10 miles of the plant. An industrial valve-packing manufacturer located in Everett, Massachusetts, also produces $1 million worth of goods each year and sells them in every state in the Union.

The sales organizations of these two firms will differ. The national market requires coverage by sales representatives or company salespeople, each assigned to a different area. Communication between the firm, its sales agents, and its customers may be slow. The local market may be serviced by a small number of salespeople, and there should be greater ease of communication. Obviously, every manufacturer must tailor his sales organization to meet the requirements and cope with the problems posed by the nature and extent of the market he wishes to reach.

Trade practices

The selling practices of other firms in the same trade will often influence the selling practices of a particular manufacturer. When purchasers have been accustomed to buying in a particular way, they are often unwilling to accept new selling methods and different levels of service. Of course, it is sometimes possible, and profitable, to inaugurate a new selling approach in an established trade, but this can be hazardous and requires careful preliminary study.

The nature of the product

The type of sales organization that best suits a particular firm will also depend on the type of product that is manufactured. Producer goods, which are sold to other businesses, require quite a different sales organization than do consumer goods sold to the general public. Producer goods may be raw materials, supplies, equipment, tools, and the like. But in nearly every case, the buyer is primarily concerned with technical and economic considerations, and the salesperson must be able to answer the buyer's questions. Further, the sales force needs a technical understanding in order to be able to point out new uses for the firm's products to prospective customers.

Consumer goods do not generally require a high level of technical skill in the sales force. But the type of consumer goods produced will affect the sales program of the producer. Convenience goods—goods that are relatively inexpensive and purchased often—are generally sold to local retailers. This takes a concentrated distribution system since there is a very large number of potential customers for the product. Therefore, to take full advantage of the potential market, a wide variety of retail stores should carry the product. Bread, milk, candy, and tobacco products are only a few examples of convenience goods.

Shopping goods—items which are not usually found on a shopping list and for which there is usually a brand preference—do not appeal to any particular buyer group, and many of them are best sold in areas where there is a large volume of pedestrian traffic. Examples of this class of goods include electrical appliances and automobiles. For the manufacturer, reaching this market poses a different problem from that of reaching the convenience-goods customers. No single system distribution is satisfactory, and the manufacturer must devise the selling organization best suited to the particular product he is marketing.

Types of purchaser

The complexity of the business person's sales problem and the nature of his sales organization will depend, to some extent, on the type or types of buyers he wishes to reach with his product. There are industrial and commercial buyers. wholesalers and jobbers, retailers, foreign buyers, and exporters, to name but a few. If a manufacturer wishes to trade with several of these different buyers, his sales organization must be flexible enough to cater to their varying needs.

Number of customers

With some exceptions, the number of customers that the sales force must serve has a direct bearing on the size and complexity of the sales force. It is possible, of course, to reach a mass market by using vending machines that require very few salespersons. It is also possible that the existence of a few customers who require extensive services may increase the size of the sales force considerably. Much depends on the personal contact needed for selling the product. If advertising and promotion can reduce selling to routine transactions, the sales force can be kept small. If the product must be sold by personal contact with the customer, a large sales force is usually needed.

FORMS OF SALES ORGANIZATION

An efficient sales organization can affect both the consumer's price and the manufacturer's profit very significantly, for, as we have seen, the price of goods to the consumer is quite often more than double the actual cost of manufacture. When sales costs are reduced by efficient organization, it should be possible to increase profits substantially or to pass part of the saving along to the consumer. In either case, the competitive position of the firm will be enhanced. Obviously, no single form of sales organization is "best." But most selling organizations are built around a sales territory, a product, or a particular group of customers.

Organization by territory

The sales force is organized according to geographic area or territory more often than any other basis. Such organization is clearly practical when the sales force must cover a large part of the United States. It avoids the duplication of territory coverage by salespeople from the same firm merely because they handle different products that might just as well be handled together and permits a certain measure of adaptation to local conditions, which is highly desirable. In special cases, like overseas operations, it is almost impossible to organize efficiently on any other basis.

Organization by product

When sales are organized by product, a selling unit must be arranged for each item, or class of items, which the firm produces. For example, one sales division may handle refrigerators, another electrical appliances, and a third household wares, if these are the three basic products of the firm. When specialized knowledge of the product is an advantage to the salesperson, this can be a very useful type of organization.

Organization by customer

When selling involves special problems, such as fitting the product to the particular demands of the customer, it may be desirable to assign salespeople to particular groups of customers. Advertising agencies commonly assign their employees to particular customers of the firm since the services being sold are closely related to the operation of the buyer, not the seller.

These three basic types of sales organization are shown in Figure 11-1. A cigarette manufacturer might make use of the territorial organization, but obviously he could not use an organization based on customer class. A paper bag manufacturer might employ organization based on customer class but find it difficult to use an organization based on product lines. Each type of organization has its own advantages and disadvantages, and management must choose the form best suited to its own product and its own customers.

SALES PLANNING

Sales planning means laying out a program for the selling of goods and services. It should begin with a sales forecast to show how much of the firm's goods is likely to be sold, when they are to be sold, and in what area. The sales plan then shows exactly how these goods will be distributed.

The plan in Figure 11-2 shows the manufacturer as the chief motivating force in the sales program. Advertising and promotion flow from the manufacturer to the wholesaler, to the retailer, and directly to the consumer. The wholesaler in turn exerts pressure on the retailer to press for higher sales levels. The retailer adds his advertising and promotion pressures to influence the general public. Frequently retailers receive promotion allowances from manufacturers to ensure that a "local level" sales effort is made. This is a common approach to large-scale selling when the manufacturer is the prime influence. But a sales plan is no guarantee of success; it can do no more than ensure sound coverage with tested tactics.

If the manufacturer does not play a dominant role in distribution, the sales plan would differ. The manufacturer's sales effort would be directed at the wholesaler or other middlemen who in turn would aim their efforts at retailers. In such cases, the success of the sales plan depends much more on retailers. Thus in the sale of refrigerators, toothpaste, automobiles, and other brand-name goods the manufacturer plays the important role; but whenever the manufacturer's name is not known to the consumer, the retailer must play the dominant role.

The sales forecast

A sales forecast is a prediction of the volume of sales that a company can expect during some definite period of time in the future. It is the

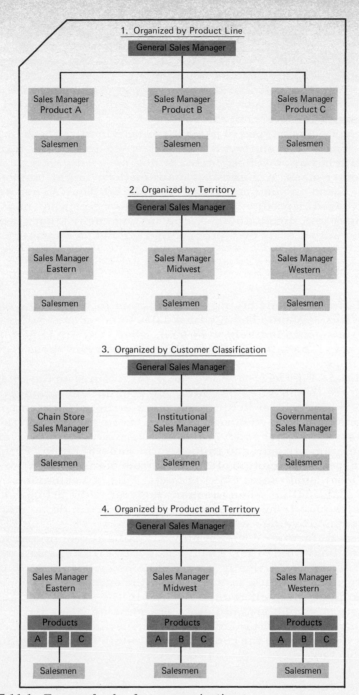

FIGURE 11-1 Forms of sales force organization

Sales organized by territory is the most common form, but the need for specialized knowledge of the product or of the customers' problems often makes other forms of organization preferable. Form 4 indicates that sales are specialized within each territory according to product. In form 2, each salesman in each territory handles all three products. The choice as to organizational form would be made in terms of which form best serves customer and company needs.

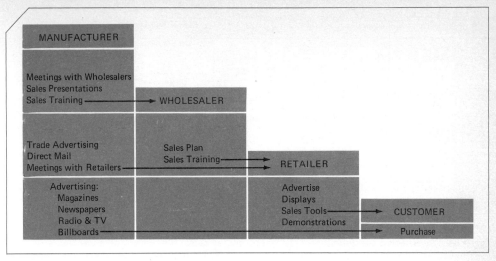

FIGURE 11-2   A sales planning guide

logical starting point for many aspects of business management, for the sales forecast is a necessary prerequisite to production planning, purchasing, financial planning, and marketing. The forecast may be made for a period of weeks, months, or years depending on the use that will be made of it. Long-range forecasts must be more general in nature and may be expressed in such terms as "the anticipated sales volume" 5 years hence. The forecasts which cover a shorter period of time—a few months—consider anticipated sales item by item and are the most useful for sales planning and production planning.

The sales forecast is produced by assembling all available information about the firm, the market, the state of the economy, and the future of the entire industry in which the firm operates. It should include social, political, and economic factors that bear on the future activities of the company. Such factors as total sales by all firms offering this product on the market, trends in market prices, relevant legislative action that is likely to take place, the status of competing firms and their future plans, and tax rates must all be taken into consideration for a good forecast.

Methods of forecasting

There is no single approach to forecasting. The techniques employed range from complex statistical analysis based on masses of data to intuitive "hunches" based on experience or perhaps based on nothing at all. The information needed for forecasting comes from a variety of sources. Government agencies, economic associations, university research bureaus, salespeople, market research, customers, and company records all provide material helpful to the forecaster. Once the data are gathered, various techniques or kinds of information are used for the actual forecasting (see Figure 11-3). Some of the more common forecasting methods are discussed below.

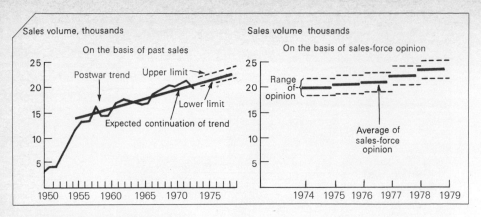

FIGURE 11-3 Forecasting

In the expected continuation of the past trend of sales, the upper and lower limits of the forecast are based on the extent to which past sales have fluctuated about the trend line. Since opinions in any group usually vary, the average of informed opinion may serve as the basis for future plans. The range of opinions is shown because, along with strongly favorable opinions, there were many which were less optimistic.

Opinions of management The opinions of the top executives of the firm or of an industry may be "averaged" to produce a forecast. It is common practice for the heads of our major automobile manufacturing firms to establish unit sales goals each year. Such forecasting is not precise—it does not forecast sales of Plymouth Dusters—but it does establish the ball park within which the firms are likely to operate.

Past sales For a large percentage of businesses, especially retail establishments, the sales forecast is made by applying a growth factor to past sales records. The growth factor, say 10 percent, is determined by observing the trend of sales over a period of years. This approach to forecasting is fine provided the conditions that created past sales continue into the future. Since this is unlikely, using past sales as the basis for future sales is a precarious approach to forecasting.

Sales-force opinion The views of individual salespersons are often combined to produce the sales forecast. The wisdom of using this approach hinges on the salesperson and his or her understanding of market conditions. Certain of General Electric's sales engineers are required to make sales forecasts item by item for their entire line. Since the sales forecasts are apt to be their sales quotas, salespeople are forced to study their market and to know their customers. Management may require that a growth factor representing new or additional sales be incorporated into the sales forecast.

Customer estimates In the industrial market the estimated requirements of the firm's customers can be used as a forecasting base. Thus a customer may indicate that it will purchase 10,000 electric motors for washing machines during the coming year. This is no guarantee of sales, but it does indicate what is possible if the customer's terms can be met.

Market research Market research is important in providing the basis of information with which management can make informed decisions. In utilizing market research to assist in the process of sales forecasting, many complex dimensions of the market must be accounted for. Competition; government policies and regulations; consumer attitudes; growth expectations of the economy, of the market, of the industry; and many other factors which pertain to the future size and quality of the market for particular goods or services are measured and analyzed.

The process of market research, carried out in a scientific manner, must still be viewed in respect to its inaccuracy, inadequacy, and lack of timeliness, for there is no way possible to get up-to-date, complete information pertinent to business activity. At best, the results of market research are analyzed and evaluated with a large dose of good judgment thrown in.

Market research is, in effect, a starting point for all business activity—not just for sales. Business produces in anticipation of demand and the research in the marketplace is an attempt to find and measure that demand as well as to devise means of stimulating it.

One illustration of market research utilizes a random sample of 15,000 households which are surveyed every three months to determine consumer buying expectancies. For example, a question may be asked to determine the probable number of households wherein a new car will be purchased in the next 6, 12, or 24 months. This information is then used as a basis for forecasting new-car sales. Major auto manufacturers then have a forecast which they can analyze in the effort to determine their respective volumes of car sales.

Correlation analysis Frequently a basis for forecasting may be found in the close relationship which may exist between two sets of data. For example, the sales of golf clubs are related to the sales of golf balls and to attendance at golf courses. The sales of electrical appliances have a relationship to the sales of electric energy; birth rate and infant furniture and clothing are related; the number of motor vehicles on the road is related to the need for fuel, accessories, and servicing; the estimates of automobile production provide a basis for forecasting requirements for steel, tires, etc.; the estimates of how much disposable income the American people may have is a basis for forecasting future expenditures for leisure and other nonessential activities.

The key to successful correlation analysis is to find the perfect relationship which provides a firm basis for forecasting. The only problem is determining where the individual firm fits into the forecast. Knowing the total volume of cars on the road may provide us with a forecast of the number of replacement tires which will be required in a given time period. However, it does not tell Firestone, or Goodyear, or Pirelli how many of these tires each will sell. The process to determine this specific answer depends on the company's policy in respect to maintaining or improving its sales position in the industry and the success of the methods whereby it attempts to achieve its goals.

ESTABLISHING SALES TERRITORIES

The sales forecast should provide the information needed to establish the territories for each salesperson or group in the sales force. The data should include the total number of customers, their geographic distribution, the sales history of customers, an estimate of potential sales to each customer, and the estimated service that must be given to each customer. In addition, prospects for new accounts should be estimated and included in the data used as a basis for dividing the sales market; otherwise future changes in the sales pattern may render the division unsatisfactory. The area need not be divided by geographical location and size of area, though these factors in combination are a common basis for sales assignments. The market is made up of customers, not geographic areas, and the best basis for dividing the market is the distribution of customers.

A useful guideline for dividing sales territories is to assign each salesperson an approximately equal portion of the potential sales of the firm. Since each salesperson must earn his cost to the company by providing service to customers, a salesperson assigned to an area that contains only 2 percent of the sales potential of the firm may be a poor investment if five other salespeople must divide the remaining 98 percent. The same principle can be used by the salesperson when he divides his own time among the customers in his territory. A group of accounts which provide 5 percent of his total sales should not be allocated much more than 5 percent of his service time unless there is a possibility of expanding the account by doing so.

Advantages of planned sales territories

A well-planned organization of sales territories is highly advantageous to the producer seeking to market his goods, for the following reasons:

1 An organized approach to territory division ensures adequate coverage of the entire market and prevents unserviced gaps in the overall sales area.

2 Well-divided territories ensure full use of sales personnel.

3 Territories allocated according to estimated sales potential provide a standard for judging the performance of the sales force.

4 Organized sales territories are more easily controlled than those not systematically covered; trouble spots are quickly located and corrected.

5 Salespeople are usually more contented when the sales potential has been fairly divided.

In some circumstances, however, it is better not to allocate specific sales territories. If sales are based on personal or social relations between salesperson and customer, as in insurance selling, or if sales involve highly technical and specialized consultation, it may be preferable to allow salespeople to seek out their own customers without regard to territory.

Allocating sales territory by frequency of calls

Individual accounts are usually classified according to the number of calls that must be made on the customer in a given year. Accounts that must be serviced every month are placed in class A; accounts that are serviced every 2 months are in class B; accounts serviced every 4 months are placed in class F. Classifying the accounts makes it possible to measure the amount of service that a salesperson must render the customers in his territory more accurately than is possible when each account is assigned the same value. In Table 11-1 it is clear that territory I demands many more customer calls than either territory II or territory III. In fact, the number of calls made annually in I is about the same as the number made in II and III combined. On this basis, if one salesperson can just comfortably manage the whole of territory II or territory III, then two salespersons ought to be assigned to territory I.

Of course, we must first be sure that it is possible for one salesperson to handle all of territory II or territory III alone. Travel conditions, the type of service rendered to customers, the location of customers, and other factors may make it impossible for one person to

TABLE 11-1   Determining territories by sales calls

Territory	Account class	Calls per year per customer	Customers in territory	Total calls per year	
I	A	12	50	600	
	B	6	140	840	
					1,440
II	A	12	30	360	
	B	6	40	240	
	F	3	60	180	
					780
III	A	12	18	216	
	B	6	50	300	
	F	3	50	150	
					666

Accounts are classified according to whether sales calls should be made every month, bimonthly, or quarterly. If one salesman can handle territory II or III, then two ought to be assigned to territory I.

service these areas, and the number of salespersons will have to be increased. Other considerations to be taken into account when assigning salespeople to territories are:

1 The amount of competition in the field.

2 Business conditions in the area covered by the territory.

3 The ability of the individual salesperson.

4 The degree of sales coverage desired in the area.

5 The time needed to develop new customers. This will depend on the estimated potential sales in the area.

Sales territory allocated on the basis of the number of calls actually made may not provide adequately for the sales potential of the area. Room for future expansion must always be allowed, for the potential of new accounts is difficult to anticipate, and errors in allocation can be made when the possibility of growth is not taken into consideration. The expansion of sales may turn out to be greater or less than planned, in any case, and the fairness of the allocation will suffer accordingly. When this happens, allocations must be readjusted to meet changed conditions.

ESTABLISHING SALES QUOTAS

A *sales quota* is the measure of the volume or value of sales that each salesperson employed by the firm is expected to achieve in his or her territory. It is derived basically from the total sales potential established by the sales forecast, responsibility for which is divided as equitably as possible among members of the sales force. The quota of a single salesperson will depend on a number of factors: past sales in the area, the sales forecast, general sales policies, the potential anticipated for the territory, and the amount of competition in the territory.

The quota is also a standard for judging the performance of the individual salesperson, though it must be used with great care. If the quota is not being met in a particular territory, it may have been set too high and may need to be revised. In any case, a careful investigation is required to determine why the quota has not been met; the investigation itself may provide the firm with extremely valuable marketing information.

Types of quotas

Most quotas are set in terms of value of sales or volume of sales. The salesperson, or group, is expected to make sales of a certain value or sell a specified number of units of the company's product in a given time period. The sales quota may be set for a full year or broken down by months or even weeks. When it is broken down into short periods, it must be adjusted for seasonal variations and other factors that cause fluctuations.

Not all quotas, however, are stated in terms of value or volume. Some are expressed in terms of the number of calls made in a given time period. In other cases, the salesperson must install a specified number of displays, or produce a certain level of profit from his territory.

However the quota is set, it is intended as a standard of sales performance and a tool for management control of sales. It is often used as a basis for bonus or other incentive payments and is also useful as a device for discovering the weak spots in a sales organization. Although the sales quota is not infallible or even very precise as an index of sales efficiency, it is accepted by most business people as a better means of control than no standard whatever.

ROUTING AND SCHEDULING THE SALES FORCE

Once the territories have been assigned to the sales force, the actual performance of the selling function must be planned. The aims are to keep improving coverage of the territory, to achieve the set quotas for each territory, and not least, to give management some measure of control over the movement of the sales force. *Routing* and *scheduling* involve planning sales calls in detail—working out, respectively, the order in which calls are to be made and the time at which calls will be made. Before routing and scheduling are possible, it is necessary to define the territories, list all customers and their locations, survey the transportation facilities available, and approximate the number of calls that must be made on each customer in a given time.

Factors that influence sales routing and scheduling

Routing and scheduling depend fundamentally on certain characteristics of the sales area and of the product being sold. If the product is a standard item that requires frequent calls on each customer and little actual "selling," so that the time involved in each call is brief and predictable, then the salesperson's schedule may be planned very closely. But if the product is not standard and the necessary calls are infrequent or likely to be lengthy, close scheduling is not worthwhile, since a close schedule will invariably be broken by the salesperson.

Detailed routing and scheduling are most commonly used by driver-salespeople and wholesale salespeople of groceries, drugs, hardware, or tobacco products. In these cases, sales are routine and servicing is frequent, so that a detailed schedule is generally practical. Even where tight schedules are not possible, however, it is advantageous to the firm to set a broad general schedule that will provide some measure of control over the individual salesperson, and at least ensure broad coverage of existing accounts.

Such a schedule, once made, should be revised periodically to adjust to new conditions, for the salesperson's job is continually changing as new accounts are added or old accounts closed. A fixed schedule can seldom be maintained for any long period of time unless sales of the product involved are exceptionally stable.

TABLE 11-2 Customer classifications

Class	Characteristics	Frequency of calls
A	Large customers and prospects where the company product is the principal item of consumption of equipment	Monthly
B	Large customers and prospects where the product is a major item of consumption or equipment	Every 2 months
C	Average customers	Every 10 weeks
D	Small-volume customers	Every 3 months
E	Seasonal customers	In season, every 2 weeks
F	Rare-demand customers	Every 4 months

Customer classifications are the basis for planning the efficient use of a salesman's time.

Classifying customers

When plans for routing and scheduling are being made, it is necessary to prepare a classification of the customers or accounts in each territory based on the frequency of calls required. A typical classification is shown in Table 11-2.

The sales schedule

A simple sales schedule can be devised by dividing a territory into smaller area units that can be covered in 1 week. If four subterritories, each containing about the same number of accounts, can be devised, the salesperson can cover his complete territory in a 4-week cycle. Such planning is also helpful to the customer, who can then anticipate the call and plan his own needs accordingly.

If the classifications of customers in an area vary greatly—if some require weekly servicing while others need no attention for weeks at a time, for example—this simple plan will not work. It may be necessary instead to base the salesperson's schedule on his prime accounts and attach a given number of secondary accounts to the main route so that complete coverage is maintained over a given time period. Such a plan usually involves more travel for the salesperson, and therefore secondary customers must be visited only on alternate trips, or perhaps only once every third trip. The added expense and time required for coverage are presumably justified by the importance of the prime accounts.

In Figure 11-4, the salesperson must service two classes of customers. Class A customers are visited once each month; class D customers are visited once every 90 days. The salesperson can work out a monthly route providing complete coverage of the territory every

Territory __33__   Salesman __Havers__

Customer class	January	February	March	April
A	All	All	All	All
D	Accounts 1-40	Accounts 41-80	Accounts 81-120	Accounts 1-40

FIGURE 11-4 A sales call schedule

By dividing class D customers into equal groups for monthly calls, the salesman systematically covers the entire list of accounts every 3 months.

90 days by a fairly simple breakdown of class D accounts into three equal monthly groups. According to this schedule, all class A customers are visited monthly; in addition, one-third of the class D customers are visited each month. When the cycle is completed, the entire list of accounts has been covered.

SALES CONTROL

The best sales plan will be useless unless every member of the sales organization understands and applies it. The salespeople must be convinced that the sales plan will not only improve the company's services to its customers but will also provide the salespeople themselves with added time, less drudgery, and more earnings. From management's viewpoint, it is essential to have some means of ensuring that the sales plan is carried out and to be able to learn as quickly as possible when the sales plan is not working properly. That is the function of sales control. Various devices are used for sales control. Some of the more common techniques are sales reports, quota analysis, and sales compensation linked to a control system.

Sales reports

Virtually every firm requires regular reports from its sales force. Although the report can be considered as a primary control device, it is also an essential channel for communicating information from the field to top management. Data taken from sales reports are widely used in planning production, expansion, etc., in the company. Some of the reports required of sales personnel are:

1 Progress reports

2 Expense accounts

3 Reports on lost business

4 Records of complaints and adjustments

5 Prospect reports

6 Demonstration reports

7 Record of daily calls

8 Credit and collection information

9 General reports that include comments on the product, comments on the prospects for further sales, lists of prospective customers, suggestions for improvement in product design or advertising, etc.

As a rule, salespeople dislike paperwork, and the number of reports required should be kept to a minimum. Well-designed report forms can also help reduce the work involved to a minimum. In general, the degree of control that management wishes to exercise over its sales force determines the amount of reporting salespeople must do.

Like all control systems, reporting is expensive in that it takes the salesperson's time from actual selling and requires time for auditing. It must, of course, be justified by the effectiveness of the control it provides for management. To be useful, reporting must be accurate, up to date, and clear. Further, reports must be reviewed carefully and used as a basis for action before they can justify themselves. In most cases, they are helpful as a basis for follow-up programs to correct deficiencies revealed by the reporting system.

Quantitative control measures

There are various means of appraising quantitatively the performance of a sales force. Quota analysis will show which sales areas are reaching or exceeding their quotas and which are not and whether the quotas were realistic to begin with. It will thus be possible to locate weak spots in the sales organization. The relationship between volume of sales and selling expenses is also a useful index to performance. The net profit on sales in particular territories is another helpful measuring stick. Some of the common standards used for quantitative measurement of sales performance are:

1 Cost per order

2 Cost per customer call

3 Ratio of sales expense to sales volume

4 Ratio of sales volume to quota

5 Profit or gross margin per territory

6 Time and frequency of customer calls

7 Ratio of calls, or of time, to order size

Qualitative control measures

The number of calls and the immediately resulting volume of business are not, however, a sufficient measure of good selling. Often the efforts of the sales force do not bear fruit at once, and qualitative

factors should not be overlooked in a justly administered sales organization. Some of the points to be considered in the qualitative measurement of sales performance are:

1 Record of salesman-customer relations

2 Extent of customer servicing

3 Product knowledge on the part of salespeople

4 Initiative in presentation to the trade

5 Reporting of timely competitive data

6 Preparation of thorough sales reports

7 Sound personal conduct and good appearance

8 Generation of goodwill

Sales-compensation plans as control devices

Sales-compensation plans may also be used to control the sales function, but they must at the same time meet other fundamental objectives of the firm. Combining the various criteria for compensation is
apt to become extremely complex. For example, sales compensation
should secure a satisfactory volume of sales, thus helping to achieve
the profit goals of the firm. It should be considered as a factor in the
control of selling costs and yet provide an adequate incentive for the
sales force. If compensation plans can be worked out within this
framework, they are often effective for purposes of control. A good
sales-compensation plan has its own basic requirements. It should:

1 Compare favorably with the terms offered by competing firms.

2 Stabilize the earnings of the sales force, either by setting aside a
"reserve" from current earnings to meet periods when earnings
are low or by some other device.

3 Be easily understood. If a plan is too complex and requires extensive accounting and statistical treatment, it can become costly
to administer and hard to comprehend. Employees are under-
standably suspicious of compensation plans that are difficult to
calculate.

4 Be flexible enough to take into consideration differences in the
experience of salespeople, in the conditions in different territories,
and in the types of product handled. Some goods sell easily; others
are difficult to move. Some salespeople are young and lack experience; others have been in the same territory for years and handle
selling easily there. These differences must be adjusted equitably
if the firm is to retain a satisfied and effective sales force.

Types of sales compensation

Sales compensation may be based on the amount of time spent on
the job, on performance, or on a combination of both. There are many
different plans in use; the basic compensation methods are explained
below.

Straight-salary payments Payment is made solely on the basis of time spent on the job. Salespeople are assured of an income as long as they perform satisfactorily for the stipulated period of time. The principal weakness of straight-salary payments to salespeople is that salary cannot be easily adjusted to differences in actual performance. There is little incentive for better work if there is no differential to be gained by increasing sales volume.

Commission plans A common method of paying salespeople is by a fixed percentage of the dollar sales volume. The commission rate may vary on a sliding scale depending on volume, the product sold, or the type of customer. The salesperson achieves a high degree of independence under this plan because his earnings are dependent on his own sales results. The chief difficulties are irregularity of earnings, lack of cooperation among salespeople, and absence of management control over the sales force.

Drawing and commission A variation on the straight-commission plan allows the salesperson to draw a basic salary as an advance against expected earnings. When commissions are not adequate to cover the amount withdrawn, the excess is taken from future earnings. This plan favors the new salesperson by allowing him a reasonable salary during his training period even though his actual commissions at the time do not warrant the payments. In some instances, though, salespeople must sign a promissory note for their advance to assure that the firm will not be left holding the bag.

Salary plus commission This plan combines regular salary with commission on dollar volume of sales. It attempts to overcome the disadvantages of both straight-salary and straight-commission plans.

Sales-bonus plans Many firms offer a bonus as extra compensation for specific achievements by the sales force. Bonuses may be given on a number of different bases, but the most common are:

1 Increased sales or quota achievements
2 Savings in selling costs
3 Sales of specific products
4 Company profits
5 Overdue-account collections
6 Securing new accounts
7 Volume of cash sales

SUMMARY

Effective selling requires the same careful planning, organizing, and control as does every other phase of business activity. The sales plan should consider both long-term and short-term objectives of the firm, current economic conditions, and any other factors that may affect future sales.

Sales planning begins with a forecast, which is used to allocate sales territories among the sales force. Allocation of sales territories may be based on geographic location, on the product, on the customers, or on a combination of bases.

A sales quota is established for each territory and later adjusted on the basis of actual performance. To, meet the quota, a carefully organized schedule is prepared for each territory. Customers are classified according to the amount of service they require, and the classifications of their distribution are used as a basis for scheduling and routing the sales force through the territory. But salespeople cannot do the entire selling job by themselves. Through advertising and promotion the way can be cleared to make their selling efforts more productive.

Management seeks to establish adequate controls over the operation of the sales force through written reports, sales conferences, quantitative and qualitative controls, and payment plans of various sorts. The object of this activity is to establish sales policies that satisfy both the needs of the firm and the needs of sales personnel.

QUESTIONS

1 What considerations are there in building a sales organization?

2 How does the type of product manufactured influence the sales organization of the firm?

3 Can the same salesperson or form of sales organization be used effectively in dealing with a retail outlet and with a government purchasing agency? Why?

4 If you were a salesperson, would you think it best to establish sales territories on the basis of geographic area or number of customers or both? Why? Suppose, instead, that you were a sales manager and were responsible for establishing sales territories. Would you feel differently on the matter? Why?

5 A salesperson sells and any salesperson should be able to sell to any type of purchaser. What do you think?

6 Would you say that the more statistically involved the method of sales forecasting becomes, the more accurate and reliable the forecast is likely to be? State the reasons for your answer.

7 Is it always desirable to allocate specific sales territories? Why?

8 What are the factors that influence sales routing and scheduling? What are their influences?

9 Why must sales performance be judged qualitatively as well as quantitatively?

10 What compensation plan would you recommend for: (*a*) life insurance salespeople, (*b*) sales engineers employed by an electronics firm, and (*c*) automobile salespeople?
Indicate why in each instance.

The purpose of this chapter The production of goods for distribution to the general public or to other businesses requires a very complex organization of management, facilities, and personnel. In this chapter we shall consider the various resources involved in production and show how they are integrated into productive business units. This survey will include examination of the characteristics of the physical facilities and systems which produce goods; the materials that are used for processing or resale; and the organization of the purchasing function to supply these material needs in the right quantity, of the right quality, and at the right price and time. We shall also consider the role of labor in the production system insofar as the nature of physical production systems has its impact on the demand for various personnel classifications. / Questions raised in this chapter include:

1 What is a manufacturing system and what determines the particular system which will be used?

2 How does a manufacturing system dictate the type of production facilities which are required?

3 What are the basic characteristics of production systems?

4 In what ways do manufacturers gain from diversification? Standardization? What do they lose?

5 What is the significance of the purchasing function?

6 How does this function differ between the manufacturer and the wholesaler or retailer?

7 How does the nature of the manufacturing system determine the classification of labor which is employable in the system?

12 / THE PRODUCTION FUNC-
TION: MACHINES, MATE-
RIALS, AND PERSONNEL The pro-
duction of goods is by far the single most important activity in the American economy. No other single sector of our
economy contributes as much to employment and income as does
manufacturing. Many other industries, such as transportation,
power production, retailing and wholesaling, rely heavily upon
manufacturing for the goods or equipment which they use to earn
their profits. To a great extent, the prosperity of the nation depends
on the success of the manufacturing sector. The success of other sectors such as construction and services is impossible without the
flow of income generated by the manufacturing sector.

PRODUCTION, MANUFACTURING, AND ASSEMBLING

The terms "production" and "manufacturing" are quite often used
interchangeably. However, we should make a distinction. *Production*
has the much broader meaning and includes all activity wherein
something of value is created; therefore, we can talk about services
such as those provided by hospitals, insurance firms, universities,
and others. We use *manufacturing* in reference to the production of
tangible goods such as cars and food products along with many thousands of other items produced for individual and business uses. In
this chapter the emphasis will be placed on the production of goods.
  Manufacturing means changing raw materials into finished goods
by some chemical or mechanical process. It is carried on in physical
facilities called plants or factories or mills. It is characterized by the
extensive use of power machinery to handle materials and to process
them. The result of manufacturing may be a product which is ready
for the final consumer, such as a light bulb, a pair of shoes, or a piece
of household furniture, or it may be a machine or tool which will be
used by another manufacturer to produce other goods. Products which
are ready for consumption by the individual consumer are called
consumer goods; products which are to be used for further manufacturing are called *producer goods.*

To further clarify the broad area of production, a distinction should be made between manufacturing and assembling. In a strict sense, a Ford assembly plant is not a manufacturing establishment. This plant and many others like it in the automobile and appliances industries are not making goods but are engaged in putting component parts together into a finished product. The management of an assembly plant involves quite different and fewer production problems than the management at a manufacturing facility.

CLASSIFICATION OF MANUFACTURING

We are all familiar with the endless variety of consumer goods available in retail stores. The list of producer goods which are available to manufacturers is also very long. The general classification of

TABLE 12-1   The manufacturing division of industry, 1970

	Value added by manufacturing, adjusted* (in billions of dollars) 1967
Food and kindred products	31.9
Tobacco manufactures	2.5
Textile mill products	9.3
Apparel and related products	11.6
Lumber and wood products	5.9
Furniture and fixtures	4.8
Paper and allied products	11.5
Printing and publishing	17.3
Chemicals and allied products	28.0
Petroleum and coal products	5.4
Rubber and plastic products	8.5
Leather and leather products	2.8
Stone, clay, and glass products	9.9
Primary-metal industries	21.4
Fabricated metal products	20.7
Machinery, except electrical	31.8
Electrical machinery	27.8
Transportation equipment	28.9
Instruments and related products	7.9
Miscellaneous manufactures	10.6
Total	298.5

* Value of shipments less cost of materials, supplies, fuels, electric energy, and contract work, plus net change in finished goods and work-in-process inventory and value added in merchandising activities of manufacturing establishments.

Source: U.S. Bureau of the Census, U.S. Census of Manufacturers: 1970.

manufacturing into consumer and producer goods, however, is too broad. For accuracy and convenience, manufacturing enterprises are usually divided according to the materials they use or the type of goods they produce. A typical classification of this kind is found in Table 12-1. Some of these industries, such as electrical machinery producers, produce both consumer and producer goods.

The significant advances made in scientific knowledge during the past two decades have influenced the classifications of industry. Structures have changed, and new enterprises and industries have come into being, such as those in the electronic, nuclear, and chemical fields. New discoveries have had their effects on the technology of manufacturing and brought about new production equipment and techniques.

THE DESIGN OF MANUFACTURING SYSTEMS

In a free enterprise system, manufacturing aims to earn a profit by producing goods which individuals or other industries will buy. The purpose of a manufacturing system is to produce goods of the right quality, in the quantity needed, at the right time, and at a reasonable price. This is a big order, and the design of the manufacturing system must be examined very carefully by management to ensure economic operation. The system used for manufacturing must be suitable both to the raw materials used and to the product manufactured; the system must be as economical and efficient as possible within the limits imposed by materials, product, and labor force.

There are three basic manufacturing systems in use today, each with its advantages and disadvantages. They are mass production, custom production, and process production.

Mass production

The basic definition of *mass production* is the manufacture of uniform products in large quantities. Making a uniform product out of uniform interchangeable parts began with Eli Whitney more than 150 years ago in the manufacture of firearms. Modern mass production techniques, however, go beyond this simple conception of uniformity of product.

In a modern mass production firm, a careful analysis of each of the firm's products is made to determine what common characteristics or parts they possess. Even with a widely diversified line of products it has been found that standard parts could be developed for use in more than one product. The idea is to be able to make the greatest possible number of different products while using the fewest possible number of different parts or components. Of course, to get a variety of products from a limited number of parts requires a versatile assembly process, but business firms have been successful in doing it. As a matter of fact, in the designing of new products, it is customary that standard parts are an initial consideration.

Modern mass production—or standardized production, as it is sometimes called—involves repetitive operations. That is to say, a series of operations is performed repeatedly to produce large quantities of standard items. When the system operates around the clock, it is sometimes referred to as a continuous system.

The great advantage of mass production is, of course, the low cost of manufacturing each unit. The chief disadvantage is the risk of obsolescence involved in the very large investment in facilities needed for mass manufacturing. There is also a tendency for mass production to limit the range of products, and this restriction can be a handicap. Finally, mass production demands a mass market and steady demand; otherwise the flow of production will accumulate and create inventory problems.

Custom production

To satisfy the customer who wants variety or products made to particular specifications, the manufacturer must turn to *custom production* or job-order production. A custom manufacturer may produce "one of a kind" or he may produce a substantial volume but certainly nowhere near the quantity typically produced by a mass production system.

Because of the intermittent nature of its operations, custom production presents a number of difficulties for the manufacturer. Each product, being unique, will require its own special sequence of operations. Planning and coordination of these operations to achieve maximum efficiency in the use of facilities are a constant task. The key to custom manufacture is general-purpose equipment, able to do many varied operations, and a flexible organization of manpower and machines. To make effective use of general-purpose equipment, the workers must be more highly skilled. Operating cost, as well as production cost per unit, will generally be much higher than comparable mass production costs, but the purchaser of custom products is willing to pay the higher price to get exactly what he wants.

Process production

Certain kinds of manufacturing are peculiar in that the process and the product cannot be separated. For example, sugar refining, blast-furnace operation, petroleum refining, and chemical production all involve the application of processes to raw materials. The process determines the product obtained from the material. The term *process production* indicates that the product can be produced only by a carefully controlled sequence of operations. Once the process is begun, it must be continuous for physical as well as economic reasons. For instance, a blast furnace is not shut down after an 8-hour shift but runs continuously for months at a time until the furnace must be relined.

Often the entire production cycle can be enclosed and controlled automatically. In the case of petroleum refining, the design of the cracking tower actually determines the products obtained from the refining process.

ACTIVITIES INVOLVED IN MANUFACTURING

Obviously, the major division in any manufacturing concern will be the production division. This part of the firm is concerned with the acquisition of raw materials and the fabrication of the end product. In most cases, production is the largest part of the firm in that it employs more people and requires more capital and equipment and housing than other divisions.

Production alone will not make a successful business. For one thing, the goods which the manufacturer produces must be sold. Therefore every manufacturing firm has a vital interest in marketing; buyers must be found for the goods which the division turns out.

Again, the production division must be given a product to manufacture before it can begin working. That is, there must be a branch of the firm which supplies the design for the product that is to be made. This is often called the *research division,* or the *research and design division,* for a great deal of fundamental investigation is needed before a new product can be placed on the market. The product must be worth producing, it must be producible with available facilities, and it should be a product which the firm can afford to produce.

Finally, behind all this activity there must be a sound financial policy. No business firm operating in a free enterprise system and dependent on profit for its existence can afford to ignore the cost factor for any length of time. Funds necessary for initial or additional investment must be procured. Prices must be established. Raw materials must be bought. The cost of operation must be watched carefully and continuously. All these fiscal matters are generally concentrated in the finance division, yet they influence the operation of every other part of the firm.

MANAGEMENT'S JOB IN MANUFACTURING ACTIVITY

The management of a manufacturing firm is responsible for integrating and combining the activities of these basic divisions—production, marketing, research and finance, and operation. Obviously a wide variety of skills and abilities is needed to make the firm operate efficiently. Personnel must be selected, trained, and coordinated into a smoothly operating group. Since it is generally desirable to subdivide the total operation of the firm into basic administrative units, some authority must weld their efforts together, and this is the task of management.

Although it might appear that every subdivision in a firm is working toward a common goal and that therefore there is little cause for conflict, this does not always turn out to be the case in practice. Since the organization is specialized, particular interests develop within each specialized division that may conflict with one another or even with the general interest of the firm. For example, the sales department is concerned primarily with the volume of sales, and the production department is interested chiefly in economic production of an acceptable quantity of finished goods. Although the two functions serve the same overall purpose, they may conflict sharply in particular areas.

Sales is constantly seeking new products that will increase the competitive position of the firm. Production dislikes drastic changes in product since the necessary alterations in production methods lower the efficiency of the division. One of the principal tasks of management is reconciling these particular interests and charting a course of action which is to the best advantage of the entire firm. Just as the federal government must attempt to reconcile differences among the states in a manner that serves the best interests of the whole country, management must reconcile differences among its primary divisions so as to promote the general interest of the firm.

THE PRODUCTION DIVISION ORGANIZATION

In a firm devoted to manufacturing, the production division is generally the most complex as well as the largest division. The degree of its complexity depends on such things as the type of manufacturing process, the scale of operations, and whether the organization is centralized or decentralized.

If the manufacturing process is repetitive, organization may be simple. The more varied the operation, the more complex the organizational structure. Ordinarily, as the size of plant or volume of production increases, the organization of the production department becomes more complex. The more centralized the organization of a firm, the more the operation of the production division is devoted to carrying out detailed instructions rather than engaging in the complex planning which precedes actual production.

Figure 12-1 is a simplified organization chart of the production division in a typical manufacturing firm. The chart shows the type of work performed at each level of the organization. The works manager has divided production into five basic areas, each supervised by a single manager. Notice that this is a line-and-staff type of organization, with the main line of authority running from the works manager through the superintendent of production down to the individual foremen.

The supervisor or foreman

The terms "supervisor" and "foreman" are generally used interchangeably, though some firms distinguish between them by limiting

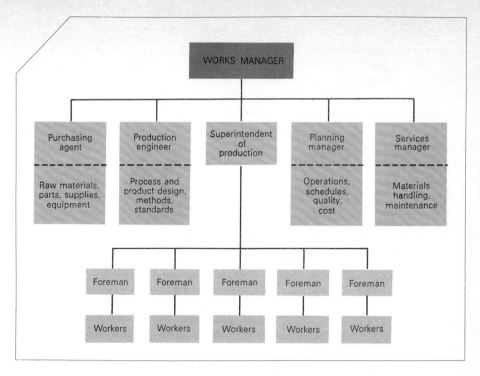

FIGURE 12-1   Organization of a production division

the term "foreman" to those persons who actually work in direct
contact with other workers and by using the term "supervisor" to
designate positions which have advisory functions. If a foreman
heads a large department and requires assistance, he may be called
a "general foreman" and have the assistance of several group leaders.

Duties and responsibilities of supervisors   The supervisor or foreman
is a key figure in most manufacturing firms. He stands between the
actual production workers and the general management of the organization; his duties and responsibilities extend in both directions. He
is responsible to management for a number of functions, and he also
has responsibilities to the workers he supervises. The best way to
grasp the scope of the foreman's job is to examine some of his principal responsibilities.

He must maintain a constant check on quantity of production, be
mindful of costs, and be alert to discover more efficient means of
operations.

He is responsible for working conditions in the shop and keeps
management informed of the need for facilities.

He keeps records of various production activities and makes periodic reports to management on these areas.

He must safeguard company property and ensure the health and safety of his workers to the best of his ability.

He serves as a model for his workers and is the prime figure in any morale-building program.

He is generally responsible for the administration of company policies and the enforcement of work regulations.

He must train and place new workers properly.

He prepares efficiency ratings on the workers in his employ.

He is the primary channel of communication between worker and management.

Worker grievances usually come through the foreman, and company policies are explained to the workers by the foreman.

This list, though not complete, indicates the extent of the foreman's responsibility. Obviously, the foreman must be highly skilled and experienced in the production process and in the handling of the machinery and equipment used for production. He must also be skillful in his relations with other people. He acts at various times as planner, adviser to management, counselor to workers, inspector, training director, disciplinarian, ambassador of goodwill, and technological expert. This is indeed the most formidable job in any production department, and a firm which has good foremen is well along the road to successful operation. Poor foremen can be catastrophic.

PRODUCTION CHARACTERISTICS

The production process in a manufacturing firm varies according to the product being made, the process used, the type of equipment available, and so forth. Whatever the specific nature of the enterprise may be, there are nevertheless certain basic characteristics of operation common to all manufacturing systems. They are simplification, diversification, and standardization.

SIMPLIFICATION

Simplification means eliminating items in a company's output, or reducing the number of products manufactured. Manufacturers, wholesalers, and retailers all engage in simplification. When studies reveal that some items handled by a firm are not selling rapidly or are not needed any longer by the bulk of the firm's buyers, such items can be dropped from the business with little or no loss, and sometimes even with profit.

Simplification also applies to the actual production process, where it may mean the elimination of certain tasks or the merging of several jobs into a single operation.

Whether simplification is applied to products or to jobs, the process should always be the consequence of a careful analysis of the existing system. Usually, the benefits derived from simplification are best expressed as savings. Fewer products, or fewer working operations, usually mean greater efficiency and concurrent saving in cost.

DIVERSIFICATION

Diversification is the opposite of simplification. It means adding new products, or a wider variety of products, to the company's output. Simplification occurs when management expects to reduce costs without affecting profits; diversification occurs in the hope of gaining additional profits by selling new and different goods in addition to the regular line. Some reasons for diversification follow.

Consumer demand for variety The automobile industry is a good example of the diversification resulting from consumer demands for variety. It would be almost impossible to produce a single model that would satisfy all the uses that people have for automobiles. Hence diversification has occurred to meet the variety of demands.

Price appeal Diversification of products can increase sales by enabling the manufacturer to offer the same product in different qualities at different prices, thus appealing to different groups of consumers. Any number of products are illustrative of this.

Quality demands Many people buy on the basis of quality rather than price. Hence manufacturers often diversify in an effort to obtain as customers those who demand high quality in addition to those who are more concerned with price. Of course, a high price does not necessarily guarantee a high-quality product, but it is usually taken as a reasonable guide.

Avoiding a limited market Manufacturers will often add another line of products to reduce the risk element in their business. A single line means that company success depends on a single market. It is better to have additional products or markets so that the loss of any one market will not be disastrous.

The extent of diversification

Diversification, then, is expected to produce a balanced line of products that covers a wide demand area and to maximize the efficient utilization of raw materials, manpower, equipment, etc. However, there is always the danger of overdiversification—producing too broad a range of products. When a company produces a single item, production techniques can be standardized and the greatest operating economies may be realized. As the line of products grows and requires constant change in the application of facilities, it is possible that manufacturing methods will bring about relatively high costs of operation.

Cost of diversification

Diversification can increase the cost of manufacturing very rapidly if it is not controlled. Four basic operating costs particularly tend to increase rapidly with growing diversification.

Inventory and storage costs Although better utilization of raw materials may result from diversification, larger quantities of finished goods must be kept in stock to supply orders. This additional inventory will also increase storage costs if more space is needed than that originally available. These factors increase the operating capital required to run the firm.

The equipment and personnel needed to control and safeguard increased and diversified inventory can be substantial. Handling costs may also increase, particularly when the new products cannot be handled with the same equipment used to handle other items in the firm's inventory.

Increased production cost Diversification may mean using the same equipment and personnel to produce several different products. The resulting shorter runs of production, the time spent in setting up for new production, and the training of workers for new tasks add to production costs.

STANDARDIZATION

Standardization means the use of common or standard parts in every unit of one product or the use of the same part in many different products. The aim of standardization is to reduce the great number of parts or components in inventory. It also aims at the simplification of work methods, of tools and equipment used for production, as well as at uniform quality of product along with other things. Manufacturers standardize to reduce the number of tools needed for manufacture and to reduce investment in inventory. The chief goal of standardization is economical production with a concurrent increase in profit margin.

Standardization of work methods, which is also significant, results from careful study of the various tasks involved in manufacture to arrive at the most efficient possible means of using personnel, equipment, and plant for the production of a particular item. Once a standard work method is devised, training is simplified and supervision is made easier, since the sequence of operations is settled and the supervisor need only make certain that the worker is following the predetermined pattern.

PRODUCTION PROCESSES

Some manufacturing systems turn out a finished product; others refine raw materials and prepare them for manufacture; still others assemble parts to produce a new product. One of the most important parts of any production process is the method used to handle materials. This can affect the cost and quality of production—the efficiency—of the firm very significantly. Material-handling facilities are often considered an integral part of the manufacturing process.

The classic illustration of manufacturing involves some combination of production, fabrication, and assembly of parts. Of course, not all three may be done in the same plant, or even by the same company, but industries producing machinery and related equipment are based on these three processes.

Metal production includes such operations as those performed by blast furnaces, steelworks, rolling and finishing mills, iron and steel foundries, and smelting or refining facilities. The production group is in this case actually involved in the preparation of a raw material for further manufacturing. In metal fabrication the materials are converted into products which may be either consumer goods, such as cans, wire, and tools, or parts that will be used for further manufacturing. The firms concerned with assembly take the parts produced by the fabricating industries and construct larger and more complex units, such as automobiles, machine tools, or appliances, by bringing the parts together.

Analytic and synthetic processes

To *analyze* means to break down; to *synthesize* means to put together. These definitions offer a clue to the use of the processes of analysis and synthesis in industry. Some industries, such as oil refining, produce by breaking down raw materials into component parts and making use of the parts; these are analytical processes. Other industries, such as the steel industry, combine a number of raw materials to arrive at the finished product; these are synthetic processes. Considering whether a process is analytical or synthetic can often provide us with useful insights into the nature of a particular manufacturing operation.

Conditioning processes

If a piece of thermoplastic is placed in a warm mold and compressed, it will take on the shape of the mold. Pocket combs and many other plastic products are made in this way. Nothing is added to the original plastic material; instead, the material is given shape and form—we say it has been *conditioned*. The shape, dimensions, or density of the material may be altered by various means, depending on the product that is desired. The conditioning process is very important in modern manufacturing, since technological progress has produced many new machines for conditioning materials of various sorts. A huge press can shape a whole section of automobile body in one operation, for example.

Conditioning adds to the value of a material by giving it a useful form. This can be done by forming, pressing, molding, turning, and shaping on a lathe, cutting (cloth or other soft materials) with shears, or any one of a number of means, so long as the result is to add to the value of the material by altering its shape or characteristics.

The physical properties of plastics and the various techniques of the conditioning processes have been combined to displace the use of metal for parts in many products. Each year, for example, more plastics are used in the manufacture of automobiles and appliances to displace metal die castings.

PRODUCTION FACILITIES

Before manufacturing can be carried on, it must be planned. Assuming that funds are available, the owners must select a suitable location for manufacturing, provide adequate housing for the equipment to be used in production, select the equipment most suitable to the product, arrange for a supply of materials, and employ the necessary manpower. The decisions involved in taking all these steps are highly significant for the future, since they entail a considerable expenditure of money. Each decision will have some effect on all the others. A poor choice of location, for example, may lead to a serious shortage of manpower or to high transportation costs for moving raw materials or finished products. Despite the recognition of the importance of location of plant, site selection is often handled poorly.

LOCATION AND HOUSING

Selecting an ideal location for a new plant is a complex matter, for there are dozens of different factors that have to be taken into consideration. In practice, the location actually selected is usually a compromise, rather than the ideal spot. Choosing a location in a heavily populated area, for example, may provide a large labor market, banking facilities, adequate power, and so on, yet result in higher labor costs, higher plant costs, and higher transportation costs. Many factors influence site selection. Among these are:

Labor supply

Highway system

Utilities—power, light, etc.

Raw material availability

Educational facilities

Airport

Climate

Railways

Tax rates

Over the years the general list of factors influencing plant location does not change too much. However, the relative importance of the respective factors does change. During the past decade, for example, railway service declined in importance while airport facilities increased. The availability of utilities, particularly energy and water, is continually increasing in importance.

Not long ago, manufacturing concerns were virtually forced to locate in or near large urban areas in order to find adequate services and labor force. Today, nearness to the urban center is of less importance. Modern transport facilities can move both goods and employees over long distances with speed and efficiency. The various service-oriented businesses such as banks and insurance companies still prefer to locate in urban centers but with the extension of broad systems and the general availability of private transportation in the form of the automobile, suburban locations or branches have become more attractive locations at which to serve the enlarging suburban population.

Production and transfer costs

One method used to simplify the task of selecting a suitable location for manufacturing is to reduce all these factors to a statement of the costs involved. The total burden of cost placed on a business by a particular location is termed production cost; the cost of moving the goods to market is referred to as transfer cost. The sum of these two costs as they apply to each of several possible locations will provide the business person with a helpful guide in determining where to settle. This approach underscores the effect of location on operating costs, and cost must be the fundamental consideration in any business decision. To build a factory on a "pretty" site, or in an area near the owner's home, can be very poor business.

Housing

The structure that houses a business enterprise must be considered from three different points of view:

1 As a fixed cost imposed on the business

2 As a factor in the organization of efficient production

3 As a means of creating a favorable impression on workers and customers

Worker morale is strongly influenced by the physical appearance of the company's building. Business people need housing which will convey a suitable impression of the profession and will serve to invite the prospective customer. The expenditure for housing is increased by this approach to construction, but the value of appearance may be sufficient to override the additional cost. In many cases structural standards and conditions must also meet legal requirements which affect both appearance and cost. However, although housing must primarily be suited to the operation of the business and at the same time must meet legal requirements and make a good impression on the workers and customers, it should not impose an undue burden of costs on the enterprise.

Most commonly, industrial housing must meet four basic requirements:

1 Adequate size for storage. The structure must provide adequate storage for raw materials, machinery, and stocks of finished materials. It must also, of course, provide office space.

2 Adequate size and arrangement for freedom of movement. Materials, paperwork, people, etc., must be able to move freely within the housing area.

3 Reasonable cost. It may be necessary to temper the size and arrangement of housing in order to bring costs within the limits that can be borne by the enterprise.

4 Attractiveness. The physical appearance of the housing facilities must be adequate for worker morale and customer and general public approval.

Modern factory construction, which leans heavily on steel, plastics, glass, and aluminum, is ideally suited to today's manufacturing needs. The appearance of new buildings, inside and outside, is usually very good. Lighting is usually excellent. Movable partitions and similar devices produce a measure of flexibility of internal arrangements that is highly desirable.

Industrial site developments

The promoters of industrial site developments seek to attract business enterprises to their locations. These industrial locations are often ideal sites for manufacturing plants since their transportation, sewage-disposal facilities, power and water, and the like are developed according to a comprehensive plan that may provide cheaper rates to the manufacturer. In many cases, business can be housed in leased buildings, sometimes designed and constructed specifically for the enterprise that takes the lease. These "package-plan" methods of housing industry can be of great assistance to the new firm which lacks sufficient capital to develop its own site fully.

These advantages to the firm sometimes result in disadvantages to the transportation system of the area. The concentration of firms in suburban areas, reached by high-speed highways which loop through bedroom communities, has created traffic snarls and frustrations on double-barreled highways. The solution to such jams is often in the form of additional high-speed highways. This solution makes new land areas accessible and desirable as locations for new industrial site developments. This all adds up to more traffic, more snarls, more relief needed and supplied in the form of more roads. Thus the cycle repeats itself, and problem begets problem.

The economy of the large plant with hundreds of thousands of square feet of area under a roof and with parking spaces for thousands of cars must be evaluated along with transport costs, transport systems, and the elimination of natural environment. A significant question being raised currently is whether it is time to reconsider the advantages of moving people to jobs versus moving work and materials to workers. Implicit in this question is the suggestion that many smaller, specialized-task plants should be used in a system of production in which the parts and components are transported from plant to plant until the product is completed.

EQUIPMENT

Equipment includes everything used in manufacturing except materials and housing. The term "plant" is usually taken to include both the equipment and housing of an industry, but housing, strictly speaking, is not equipment. Machinery, tools, dies, fixtures, furniture, and so on are the equipment needed for manufacturing.

Equipment may be operated by hand or powered by an engine or motor. It may be self-regulating or it may require an operator. Some machines perform only a limited number of functions; others can do a wide variety of tasks, depending on the skill of the operator. Four classes of equipment can be identified in manufacturing, each having its own uses and applications: general-purpose equipment, special-purpose equipment, building-block machine tools, and numerically controlled machine tools.

General-purpose equipment

Machinery which can perform basic operations on a variety of products is called general-purpose equipment. Such standard equipment as the lathe, milling machine, grinder, planer, shaper, drill press and borer, and shearing and pressing machine are found in this classification. The drill press can bore holes of various diameters and varying depth in a wide variety of materials with little change in the machine. Such a machine is not product-centered but is designed to carry out a particular kind of operation. General-purpose machines are those built to perform functions that have wide application to a variety of products.

Special-purpose machinery

Machinery that can perform only one or a very limited number of operations, involving a few materials or only one material, and which produces many pieces of identical shape and size is called special-purpose equipment. A special welding machine that performs only one operation in automobile or aircraft assembly is an example of a special-purpose machine. If the machinery is correctly designed, it may be possible to speed production immensely by using precisely the right tool for the job. Usually, special-purpose machinery is easier to operate than general-purpose equipment and requires only a semi-skilled operator. Special-purpose machinery is efficient if the product is standardized and if its sales volume is sufficient to absorb the cost of special equipment without undue burden on profit. But this consideration is generally true of all equipment.

Building-block machine tools

The building-block machine tool is made up of several parts which can be changed depending on the particular job to be done. This is the great advantage of such a machine for when a change is to be made in the product all that needs changing on the machine are the forming tools and the attachments necessary for holding the work in place. All other parts of the machine remain the same. These building-block machine tools consist of six major sections:

1 A tool that forms the metal

2 A tool holder

3 A motorized assembly that powers and controls the tool

4 A carriage

5 A base

6 A bench that holds the metal in place while it is being formed

Numerically controlled machine tools

The latest device to hasten production is the controlling of machine tools by magnetic tape or punched paper tape instructions that are "read" and "translated" by an electronic computer. A wide variety of intricate adjustments or operations can be controlled very carefully in this way, since repetition is always perfect and there are no "human" errors due to fatigue or carelessness.

Tape-controlled machines have revolutionized short-run production and inventory control. They enable a manufacturer to turn out parts quickly, when needed, instead of requiring inventories to fill orders. They also help to eliminate waste and reduce personnel-hours required in production. Tools such as these, however, are only a small part of the machine tool population.

MATERIAL-HANDLING SYSTEMS

Manufacturers spend countless millions of dollars every year moving materials into, around, and out of their plants. A significant part of the cost of manufacturing is the cost of handling materials. Every plant contains some handling equipment, ranging in size and complexity from the simple crowbar to the enormous automatic crane and to the computer-controlled integrated handling system.

As a material-handling system grows more complex and expensive, the need for manpower declines. The old catch phrase "untouched by human hands" can sometimes be applied to the operation of an entire plant if material-handling equipment is fully automatic and self-controlled. The labor requirement is reduced to a minimum in such a system, which does call for, however, a very heavy investment in specialized and costly equipment. Such an integrated system is as advantageous where the material being used is hot, very heavy, or in some way dangerous to people (in rolling mills and in parts of the chemical industry, for example) as it is in the movement of small parts or components (in the drug industry, for example).

Handling must be flexible

The basic requirement of any material-handling system is that it move materials through the production process in an efficient manner. The mass production industries, with their great volume and high speed of operation, need an orderly and balanced flow of materials moving into and away from the system to avoid a bottleneck at which production piles up.

A good handling system, however, may be asked to do much more than just move goods. Often in production the position of the product must be changed between operations; the unit may be reversed, inverted, etc. This prepositioning may be automatically accomplished by the handling system. A conveyorized handling system may be used to sort the products riding along it, directing the proper products into designated channels for further processing or other operations. An inspection system may be built into the material-handling operation to measure and control quality between the various processing stages. Each of these features may be incorporated into a handling system as long as there is justification of the added investment by savings in production time, manpower, and other costs, which contribute to the efficiency of the operation and the quality of the product.

The "necessary evil"

The need to handle materials has always been considered a "necessary evil" by manufacturers. This is particularly true in connection with manual handling of goods and in those cases where the only accomplishment is the movement of products rather than an improvement in the overall process of production. Manual handling may be both costly and wasteful of product and manpower, since expensive breakage is likely to occur and extensive use of manpower is involved in the moving of bulky and heavy materials. Today the machinery available for handling materials has been refined to the point where the handling system can be a distinct asset to the firm and quite capable of justifying the investment in it. The use of the handling system as a basic control of the entire manufacturing process and as an inspection facility of great accuracy is now possible.

Not every industry is adapted to automatic integrated handling, of course. In the leather-tanning industry, manual operation still predominates, though this limitation may eventually be overcome by technological advance. In most of the large-scale industries, however, material handling has become more and more efficient and useful. In fact, the handling process has become so thoroughly integrated into the production process that it is no longer realistic to consider handling and production as two separate operations: they have been integrated into a single inseparable function.

Return on equipment

Before the manufacturer invests heavily in equipment, he must assess the potential profit to be earned by its use. Each new machine must pay for itself, and more, during its own lifetime; otherwise there can be no profit. Of course, any machine represents only a potential capability—inefficient use may reduce its performance, and efficient use may produce high returns. Management can only measure a machine's potential and attempt to relate that potential to the efficient operation of its own firm.

MATERIALS AND PURCHASING

The cost of materials varies from one industry to the next. Figure 12-2 shows the relationship of materials cost to the total value of the finished product in several manufacturing industries. The category

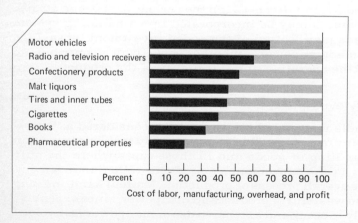

FIGURE 12-2 Cost of materials as percentage of value of product shipped

Source: Calculated from U.S. Bureau of Census, Annual Survey of Manufacturers, 1971.

"materials" includes raw materials, semifinished parts, parts, components, containers, supplies, fuels, and the cost of purchased power. Roughly speaking, industries using high-cost material add little to its value by manufacturing; manufacturers who use low-cost material add substantially to its value by manufacture or processing. The material in a long-playing phonograph record is worth only a few cents; the finished record may sell for $5 or more.

Purchasing is performed in virtually all organizations whether they are profit-making or not-for-profit, manufacturing or service. It is difficult to imagine an organization that does not invest in raw materials, goods to be traded, parts and supplies, and machinery and equipment. All such items must be purchased from some other business enterprise. Since these purchases may account for a large portion of the firm's expenditures, the efficiency and effectiveness with which the firm does its buying may well determine the margin of profit which the business produces. Good purchasing can reduce the investment in materials required for economic operation, the danger of obsolescence, and the incidents of needless purchases. Good purchasing can enhance the possibility of maintaining a high level of customer service and eliminate unnecessary expense. In this way purchasing and inventory control contribute to more profitable operations.

Most large manufacturing concerns achieve economy in purchasing by assigning the function to one centralized department that buys for the entire firm. Of course, purchasing departments do more than buying. They maintain inventory levels, control the volume of materials coming into the firm, prevent duplication of orders, arrange for lower prices through bulk purchases, help standardize purchases, and maintain records of the operation. Although the purchasing function may grow very elaborate, it is generally more efficient to have only one agency charged with this responsibility, despite the extra size.

As the cost of materials increases relative to the total cost of a product, the significance of the purchasing function increases, for if a greater percentage of company funds are to be spent on materials, the risks and gains of purchasing increase. The prime criterion for purchasers is cost, though other factors also play a part in the decision as to where, when, and at what price to buy. The need for volume may alter price structure, as may the scarcity of supplies and the bids made by competitors for existing stocks. Purchasing is in practice an intricate business which requires long experience of market conditions, knowledge of suppliers, and familiarity with the operation of the firm for which buying is done.

PURCHASING AND PROFITS

The significance of the purchasing and inventory-control function varies from firm to firm based on the sheer volume of activity involved and the importance of materials in the generation of profit. If the cost of materials represents but 5 percent of the sales dollar, improving performance in the materials area will have little bearing on profit. But in the "typical" manufacturing firm, where 50 percent or more of each sales dollar is spent for the cost of materials, small savings in material costs can exert great leverage on profit. Suppose a firm has costs and income as shown below. A saving of 10 percent in material costs will increase profit to 50 percent.

	Present		With 10 percent material saving	
Sales		$100		$100
Materials	$50		$45	
Labor	20		20	
Overhead	20	90	20	85
Profit		$10		$15
				50% increase

In the wholesale and retail trade purchasing provides the major, if not the only, avenue for earning profit. Consequently this function is delegated to high levels of management and often is regarded as a line function. In a typical year General Motors will spend $10 billion or more purchasing tens of thousands of items from some 25,000 sources of supply. To this company savings of one-hundredth of a cent on certain items is significant. On the other hand, an experimental machine shop may spend as little as 4 or 5 cents out of each sales dollar for purchases.

FACTORS IN PURCHASING

In any purchasing transaction, the buyer is concerned with four primary factors: quality, quantity, price, and delivery date. The basic task for the purchasing agent is to balance these four factors to obtain the exact combination he needs at the cost most advantageous to the company.

Quality

Materials that cannot be used by a firm are wasted. Therefore every purchasing agent must first consider the quality of material he is buying. Quality is, of course, closely related to cost in most products, since it is a characteristic that is built into the product during processing or manufacture.

While too low quality in purchases is a mistake, too high quality can also be a purchasing error. Quality in excess of that for which the consumer is willing to pay is also waste. The quality required for each purchase must, of course, be determined by the person making the requisition, not by the purchasing agent. Once the quality requirement is set, the purchaser ought to buy quality as close to the level stated in the requisition as the market permits.

Quantity

Though having excess material on hand is generally considered better than running short, excessive inventory too may be a poor investment of the firm's capital. A balance must be struck between the cost of running out of inventory and the saving that accrues when lower inventories are kept. Attention must also be given to the order size which gives the best price and the size necessary to satisfy the production needs of the firm. However the decision is made, it must balance the gains from bulk buying against the additional cost of superfluous inventory. Excess buying is hard to justify unless there is a substantial saving in cost, or unless special conditions, such as an impending strike, demand increased inventories.

Price

Although price often governs choice of supplier, the buyer must ask himself whether the seller of low-priced goods is skimping on quality and whether such a vendor will provide adjustments or other services that may be needed at a later date. There is also the possibility that the low-cost vendor may not be able to make delivery at the time goods are needed.

Reputable dealers generally build their reputations on the quality of their goods and on the services they offer their customers, not on the bare price of their product. Suppliers that stand behind their products and guarantee quality and service prefer not to trade with firms that are interested only in the lowest price possible. High quality and excellent service are not compatible with low price in a competitive market.

Delivery

A dependable source of supply is often cheaper in the long run than a source that offers goods at lower cost without dependability. Some suppliers operate with a very small inventory; they may be in no position to guarantee rapid and efficient service. The supplier who carries a varied inventory and a good stock of each item can generally promise better service in terms of volume, variety, and timely deliveries.

Purchasing objectives

Management must make decisions regarding each of the purchasing factors every time a purchase is made. Such decisions must take into consideration the basic purchasing goals of the firm. If the goal is simply to meet the production requirements, the purchasing plan will be a reflection of the production schedule. If the goal is to attain the lowest cost of acquisition, economic factors will need to be considered. If the goal is to be assured of an adequate source of materials, other factors will need consideration. Purchasing practices must be geared to and appraised in the light of purchasing objectives.

DECENTRALIZED PURCHASING

In a decentralized purchasing system each department in the firm is responsible for its own purchasing activities. A budget allocation is given each department based on planned purchases for the period. Thus a shop foreman makes purchases for his area of concern, as do the office manager and the sales manager. Most organizations have or have had decentralized purchasing because in the early stages of business only the line managers are qualified to make purchases; the firm cannot afford to employ purchasing specialists. Decentralization makes for flexibility since purchasing may be tailored to the exact requirements of the department concerned. In addition, upper levels of management are relieved of responsibility for purchasing functions and therefore left free for other tasks—a questionable advantage.

The basic weakness of decentralized purchasing is the loss of managerial control. Other disadvantages can be inferred from the discussion of centralized purchasing which is presented below. Decentralized purchasing has its best application in situations where the volume of purchases is low or the nature of the purchase is highly specialized.

CENTRALIZED PURCHASING

If the purchasing function is centralized, one person—one office—is responsible for making all purchases.

Centralized purchasing has the potential for offering a number of advantages but whether they will be realized depends on other organization considerations. First, if purchasing is established as a strict staff or service department, its authority is limited. Very often we see the title "purchasing agent." The implications are significant. An agent, by definition, is one who acts in place of another. Thus a centralized purchasing office may do little more than serve as an order-processing area, recording purchase orders initiated by the user of the purchase. In this role, the centralized purchasing approach adds little advantage over decentralized purchasing.

On the other hand, purchasing can be established as a functional division vested with the authority to make a number of important purchasing decisions. The decision areas may relate to sources of supply, the timing of purchases to achieve cost savings, or even the decision to standardize all typewriters. The precise role of a functional purchasing department will depend on the range of authority granted to it. In some institutions, purchasing is given production schedules and from that point on has complete authority over purchases and materials to meet the schedule.

Advantages of centralized purchasing

If the manager of a centralized purchasing office is given adequate authority, there are a number of benefits that may accrue to the firm:

1 Control over liability A purchase order once accepted by the seller is a legal contract to which the buyer can be held. In centralized purchasing only a few persons who should be versed in contract law are permitted to enter into contractual relations with suppliers.

2 Specialized purchasing Each year thousands of new materials come into the market. Some of these are for new purposes but a large number are less costly substitutes for materials currently in use. It would be impossible for a line foreman or any person devoting only a part of his time to purchasing to keep up with changes that are taking place. A centralized system can make use of purchasing research and value analysis. The result can be lower cost and/or more advanced design.

3 Property control Centralized purchasing provides a single location where information relating to acquisitions is kept. The purchasing manager will be able to avoid making a duplicate purchase if the information that the firm has the item somewhere in inventory is readily available.

4 Greater Standardization Standardization of parts, supplies, and equipment yields a number of advantages to a firm. It reduces the variety of purchases, it allows for the economies of larger-scale purchases, and it can reduce the cost of maintenance and service. Complete standardization is perhaps a poor policy because purchasing should continually test new products in an attempt to improve operations.

5 Lower administrative cost Lower administrative costs are possible because a small centralized purchasing office can make a tremendous volume of purchases. Part of the economy stems from the fact that a single negotiation may satisfy annual requirements of an item for the entire firm. The "conventional" approach to the processing of a purchase involves creating a purchase requisition (see Figure 12-3) which is transmitted to purchasing via interoffice mail. From the requisition, purchasing will determine the source of supply and

```
                    PURCHASE REQUISITION
                       ABC Company

    To _____     Requisition number_____

    Order for department _____     Date_____

    Date wanted_____     Requested by_____

    Ship via _____     Approved_____
  _____
  |           |                      |               |             |
  | Quantity  |    Description       |     Price     |   Remarks   |
  |_____|_____|_____|_____|
  |           |                      |               |             |
  |           |                      |               |             |
  |           |                      |               |             |
  |           |                      |               |             |
  |           |                      |               |             |
  |           |                      |               |             |
  |_____|_____|_____|_____|
             This space for purchasing office

    Date ordered_____     Purchase order number_____

    Vendor_____     Approved by_____

    Charge to account number_____

    Remarks:
```

FIGURE 12-3 A purchase requisition

This form, filled out, tells the purchasing department what it needs to know for intelligent buying.

process a purchase order (see Figure 12-4) which travels by mail to the source of supply. There the information is used to complete the sales order and packing slips. The entire process may require a week or more. Automatic reordering systems which use computers for inventory control and ordering reduce the time cycle considerably.

6 Reduced cost of goods Large-scale buying results in lower base prices, larger discounts, and lower transportation costs. Purchasing specialists with intimate knowledge of the market know the best time and best place to buy.

7 Professional buying Finally, centralized purchasing has the potential for creating a group of professionals—people who will make

PURCHASE ORDER
Barber-Dowell Corp.
19 8th Street, Omaha, Nebraska

Purchase order number
S-4975

TO
Carter Supply Company
284 Pine Street
Denver, Ohio

Date	Delivery date	Ship via	Job number	Account number	Terms	F.O.B.
6/5/7-	7/15/7-	Truck	K-3658	K-14763	2/10	Denver

Please enter the following order and ship to above address.

Item	Quantity	Part number	Description		Price
1	500	B-4059	Baffle plate	@ $3.50	$1,750.00
2	500	B-4060	Box cover	1.10	550.00
3	1,000	B-4061	Spindles	0.49	490.00
				Total	$2,790.00

Acknowledgement required

Conditions:

Barber-Dowell Corp.

J. B. Dowell

FIGURE 12-4 A purchase order

After a supplier is located, and price, quality, delivery date, and other conditions are agreed to, a purchase order is made out.

purchasing a career or a steppingstone to higher office. The prestige and power of a professional group are certain to reap rewards for the firm.

RESEARCH ON PURCHASING

The aim of good purchasing is to obtain maximum value from company expenditures through cost reduction or increased efficiency. Since market conditions change constantly as prices fluctuate and new products appear on the scene, the task of choosing the best market is becoming increasingly more complex. Purchasing research is a relatively new field of management that attempts to cope with this problem. By collecting information, planning purchases, and analyzing transactions from the standpoint of gain to the company, purchasing research provides management with information that can be used to increase efficiency. Often, for example, the purchasing department learns of new developments in machines, materials, or processes that can replace those now used by the company and reduce costs or otherwise result in savings.

Value analysis and the learning curve

Two relatively new techniques now widely used in purchasing departments are value analysis and the learning curve concept. Each has as its purpose a lower overall cost of materials and services. The logic behind each of these techniques is not at all new, but the application of the techniques is of recent origin.

As the term implies, value analysis is an examination of every purchased good or service in terms of its real value to the firm. It is concerned with the question: Is every expenditure of one dollar worth it, or could the dollar be better spent?

Value analysis is needed because of human reluctance to change. We become so accustomed to and engrossed in doing things in a particular way that we forget that there can be a better way. Value analysis is also needed because of the accelerated rate of technological change. New products and new methods which can lead to lower costs must be examined by a trained eye to keep the firm in a sound competitive position.

Often the same parts are ordered from the same supplier for a period of years. In a situation like this it is expected that the supplier will "learn" to produce such parts better and at lower cost as more units are produced. A learning curve is a graphic portrayal of the reduction in time or cost that can be expected as the quantity produced of a given item increases. The idea behind this concept is not new. What is new is that management now pays specific attention to this rate of "learning" and thereby has another criterion for measuring the performance of the purchasing department and its suppliers.

TYPES OF PURCHASE

The list of goods which purchasing departments are asked to buy is endless. The purchasing agent for a circus may buy an elephant or a tiger or the services of a bearded lady. In a manufacturing firm the list may be more conventional, but it is likely to be extremely varied. Most of the items purchased, however, can be classified into four main groups: goods to be used by the firm, goods to be processed by the firm, goods that the firm will sell again, and services of various sorts. Each class of goods produces special problems for the purchasing department.

Goods purchased for use

Any item which the firm uses in its business—machinery, office supplies, equipment, and the like—is defined as "use" goods. In some cases these goods are of minor importance to the firm, and little damage follows from a poor purchase. However, the cost even of office supplies and clerical equipment can reach a significant total in a large insurance firm, for example, or in any business with extensive correspondence and record keeping.

Major items of equipment, such as machine tools, data processing equipment, and packaging equipment, are most significant, and the requirements imposed on the purchasing agent are in these cases usually exacting. Such purchases involve large sums of money, and the goods bought are usually intended to last for many years. Obviously, great care must be exercised with this type of purchase, and senior management personnel should consult closely with the purchasing department before a final decision on purchase is made.

Goods purchased for processing

In manufacturing, the goods used for processing are probably the most important single item on the purchasing department's list, once the basic equipment has been purchased. Goods in this category may include raw materials and also component parts such as nuts, bolts, transistors, and complete generators to be installed in a large product.

Purchasing goods for processing can be extremely complex. Each of the purchases made from outside sources must be of the right quality and quantity and must arrive at the right time. Since the lack of a single item may retard production in one or more departments of the firm, careful supervision of purchasing and delivery becomes an important part of steady and efficient production.

Goods purchased for resale

The purchasing of goods for resale is perhaps the most risky and complex form of purchasing. This is especially true at the wholesale and retail levels of distribution. The buyer of materials for processing is told exactly what type and amount of material are needed and when it is needed. But goods that must be resold depend on factors other than production, and the most important question facing the buyer is what to buy. The answer to this involves a prediction of future demands by the firm's customers, which introduces a larger measure of risk into buying for resale than is present in buying for manufacture.

Purchase of services

Nearly every business must purchase services at one time or another, whether it is the minor repair of a time clock or typewriter, the collection of bills long overdue, the rental of automobiles, or a multi-million-dollar advertising campaign. The skill required by the purchaser and the significance of the purchase depend on the nature of the business and the service purchased.

One of the more interesting trends in modern business is the growth of many specialized companies that handle services once performed by the company for itself. For example, delivery services are often contracted out to specialized transportation companies. Other firms will carry out advertising campaigns; supply automobiles; paint, clean, and maintain equipment; keep books; etc. This type of purchase can be very important, and the decision to employ another firm to supply a particular service may be a major policy decision for management.

PURCHASING SPECIFICATIONS AND PROCEDURES

Most products come in a variety of shapes and sizes and qualities and these features pose the first problem in purchasing. It is necessary to establish the specifications or standards for each item according to its proposed use. The more rigid the specifications, the higher the costs and the greater the difficulties in securing adequate supplies. Often it is desirable to standardize the specifications for items such as equipment and supplies rather than purchasing a variety if for no other reason than to simplify the servicing, parts, and maintenance of such equipment. An important task of purchasing is to reduce the variety of products used by the firm whenever possible without imposing negative effects on operations.

The formal purchasing routine generally begins with a written request or purchase requisition which details the specific items wanted. Usually approval of the requisition by management is required. The level of management which approves requisitions depends on the dollar value or the nature of the item being requisitioned. A new machine tool or a maintenance contract would be approved by upper management. A department head may approve minor purchases such as supplies or those items within a stipulated dollar amount limitation.

Purchase order

The purchasing department locates the supplier who can best satisfy the specifications as well as cost considerations. Once the supplier is located, and the price, quality, quantity, and delivery date are agreed on, a purchase order, similar to Figure 12-4, is prepared and sent to the supplier. After his acknowledgment, a contract is in effect between the buyer and the seller. Among other considerations in the contract are the terms of payment.

Receiving goods

When the goods are delivered, the receiving clerk checks the delivery against the order, notes discrepancies, and adjusts the inventory balance to reflect the delivery.

Other considerations

A number of questions may arise during the period between the issuance of the purchase order and the payment for the goods:

1 What are the obligations of the buyer and the seller if goods are not shipped as agreed? If goods are damaged in transit?

2 What liability does a supplier have if a faulty component part he has supplied causes a malfunction or extensive damage to personnel or materials in the buyer's plant?

3 Does the buyer have any liability if his supplier ships him goods which are an infringement on somebody else's patent rights?

It should be evident that there may be times when a purchase order cannot be well prepared without the assistance of competent legal counsel. It is not always possible to foresee and cover all possible contingencies.

WHOLESALE PURCHASING

Since the wholesaler's buying problems are quite different from those met in manufacturing, his purchasing is usually handled somewhat differently. Most of the wholesaler's purchases are trading goods— goods meant for resale. His basic functions are to buy, store, sell, and perhaps deliver or transport.

The factors that determine need are much more variable in wholesaling than in manufacturing. The purpose of the wholesale firm is to supply the needs of retailers, and the wholesaler is not always able to predict retailer demands. In some lines of goods, prediction is reasonably simple (for example, candy, tobacco products, canned goods, sugar, and coffee). But the wholesaler who handles goods such as women's dresses has a more serious problem. He can easily determine the range of sizes and perhaps the total quantity of dresses needed, but style, fabric, color, etc., are all subject to wide variation. A well-managed wholesale house studies its own past records and current market conditions very carefully in order to reduce the substantial element of risk involved in wholesale purchasing.

Wholesale requisitions and purchase orders, if they are used at all, are generally very similar to those used in manufacturing. There is seldom any question about the best source of supply when the wholesaler handles brand-name goods, but if the wholesaler handles unbranded goods, or makes use of his own brand name, he faces somewhat different problems. He must choose from the wide range of qualities and prices available, and choosing the source of supply may be an extremely important decision.

PURCHASING FOR RETAILERS

The retail buyer shares many of the problems of the wholesale buyer. Both must make a profit on the goods they buy, and hence purchasing is an extremely important function in both industries. In practice, the retail buyer, particularly in the small establishment, lacks the skill and experience in purchasing found in large establishments or manufacturing enterprises. The retailer must attempt to make use of sound procedures in his purchasing in order to realize his hopes for success. To establish his needs, the retailer must know the customers he serves and their likes and dislikes, for customer likes determine retailer's needs. One method commonly used in retailing is to prepare a basic stock list of items little affected by style changes. A minimum inventory can be set for each item, and a regular buying policy for these items can be created from past experience. This technique can bring some measure of order to retail buying.

The model stock

Goods that cannot be included in the basic stock list are much more difficult to identify. Even past records do not always indicate what customer demands will be. Instead of depending solely on the past records, the retailer may attempt to establish a model stock which, in effect, is his best estimate of those items of merchandise categorized by style and price which will produce effective sales under normal conditions. Then the retailer must consider the impact of current market conditions as to how they will affect his business and modify his model stock accordingly. This procedure for determining stock requirements may result in a reasonably accurate purchasing plan.

The merchandise budget

Many retail establishments operate on a merchandise budget, based on planned sales, controlled inventory, and planned purchases. As an illustration, suppose a retailer planned—probably on the basis of previous sales—to sell $50,000 worth of men's shirts in a given month. If his inventory was worth $110,000 at the beginning of the month and he needed an inventory of $120,000 at the end of the month, $60,000 worth of shirts must be purchased during the month. The merchandise budget begins with inventory levels as a base and takes into consideration the general level of sales for each item carried by the store. If the firm is not overly specialized, this may prove quite a useful means of establishing the purchase quantity.

MANPOWER

Manufacturers, like all other business people, must give great care and consideration to their manpower requirements. The problems they face can be divided into three general categories:

1 Problems concerned with the composition of the workforce, that is, with age, sex, skills, and other characteristics of the firm's employees

2 Problems that deal with availability of workforce—with numbers, location, and mobility

3 Problems concerned with the effectiveness of the workforce

Each of these problems has a direct and immediate bearing on the manufacturer's cost of production.

MANPOWER CLASSIFICATIONS

Manpower in general is classified as unskilled, semiskilled, and skilled. Unskilled work is defined as the performance of simple manual tasks which can be learned in a short time and require little or no independent judgment by the worker.

Semiskilled work is usually defined as the performance of routine tasks which require skills in a narrow area only. Training for semiskilled work is usually limited both in time and in scope. That is, semiskilled workers perform particular operations that may require skills but generally form only a part of the total work process.

Skilled workers are usually those who have had long periods of formal training or experience, often beginning with apprenticeship. They possess a thorough knowledge of the work processes involved in their skill area, are capable of exercising independent judgment, and have a very high degree of dexterity in all the operations that make up their skill.

The skilled worker

The old craftsman, capable of carrying out the complete manufacturing process for a product, declined rapidly in numbers after the advent of the machine age. In their place the factories developed skilled machine operators to replace the machinist and tools and assembly-line workers to replace other craftsmen. The composition of the skilled-worker category changed drastically. Now, the introduction of automation and even more highly mechanized production systems threatens to change the meaning of "skilled worker" once again. With automation comes a new kind of factory worker, the skilled technician, to twist the dials and maintain the machines.

The trend toward progressive elimination of skilled workers, which occurred in the manufacturing industries early in the century, still continues in some areas such as baking, milling, and tailoring. But in recent years the trend has turned once again toward increased employment for skilled workers.

SPECIALIZATION OR DIVISION OF LABOR

Specialization—the division of labor—means simply that each worker concentrates on a single function or a small area of production. The concept is probably very old, for we learned long ago that it was more efficient for one man to perform a single function in society than for each man to attempt to do everything. That is why ancient cities had blacksmiths, pottery makers, weavers, and other "specialists." Specialization makes it possible to achieve high skill levels in comparatively little time, since training is confined to a small area of activity. The essential element in specialization is the repetition of a single task that can be made very simple and routine. It is, of course, an essential feature of any mass production system.

Forms of specialization

Although specialization always aims at increased efficiency, it may take place at various levels, depending on the industry concerned. Some of the common forms of specialization are:

1 By trade. Workers specialize in a single trade: they become mechanics, machinists, plumbers, etc.

2 By function. Specialization depends on the type of work performed: maintenance, assembling, welding, etc.

3 By specific task. This is more detailed than functional specialization, for the worker may be limited to a single task such as sealing envelopes, folding cartons, etc.

4 By operation. This is the most highly specialized division of labor found in industry. Men may be limited to tightening a single bolt on automobile frames moving down an assembly line. At this point the job is usually open to mechanization, for machines are ideally suited to high-speed performance of simple repetitive operations.

Specialization makes the production process highly complex, for each operation is broken down into successively smaller parts, and men are trained to perform only a single part of the total production job. All these units of work must then be combined, each in its right time and place, to provide a finished product. This makes industrial processes and workers highly interdependent. Each element in the chain of production depends on some previous element: the assembler depends on the worker who supplies parts, and the machine operator depends on the setup man. The problem of coordination can be serious when specialization is carried to extremes in a large and complex production process.

SUMMARY

Production, as a day-to-day task, consists of the organization of personnel, materials, and equipment to perform work efficiently. The facilities needed for manufacturing goods include housing, equipment, materials, and manpower. Various aspects of these facilities, such as the location of housing, the adequate provision of materials, the skill levels required of manpower, and the type of equipment, should also be considered. The need for continual improvement in productivity via more effective use of manpower and better equipment represents the most significant challenge to the managers of production.

Purchasing is a primary function in most enterprises. It requires sound organization and is usually centralized to ensure management control over expenditures and stock. The function begins with a clear statement of the need for goods and upon receipt of the goods which satisfy the buyer's requirements in terms of quantity, quality, price, and delivery, becomes involved with inventory control. The purchasing operation varies considerably among manufacturers and wholesalers and retailers because of the differences in characteristics and purposes of their respective operations.

Each of the various factors on which the business person has to act wisely must be evaluated in terms of cost and potential advantage in production. The chief task of management in the manufacturing industries is achieving the integrated and balanced combination of these factors that will produce goods at a price, quality, and volume which ensure effective competition with foreign products both at home and abroad.

BUSINESS ITEMS

What happens when marketing and manufacturing are not in balance?

Skil Corporation, one of the largest producers of portable power tools, several years ago brought in a new president to solve a burdensome 50-percent overcapacity problem. Three years later, as a result of reorganization and an aggressive marketing program, the situation was completely reversed and the company found itself with an order rate far in excess of its ability to produce.

At the root of the problem was the inability of the manufacturing department to keep up with the pace set by the marketing department. What a shame to have sales potential but be unable to keep up with it! Problems centered in production bottlenecks. Attempts to ease this situation by turning to outside suppliers resulted in costs which were three to four times higher than standard costs. Other problems involved significant increases in the amount of unfinished goods tied up in inventory because of shortages of parts ranging from switches to shipping containers and problems with labor turnover of both skilled and unskilled workers. The annual rate of labor turnover doubled in each case to 100 percent.

The net effects of these problems were reflected in a lower market price for the company stock and in its reduced earnings. In the hopes of curing its ills, management brought in new talent to fill key manufacturing posts and thinned out its product line. Lawn and garden and air tools are being eliminated and Skil's domestic line of power tools will be thinned by some fifty overlapping models, or about 15 percent of its entire line.

In process is the installation of a large-scale computer system to help the company keep track of its in-process materials which are located in four plants scattered around Chicago and a new plant in Arkansas which is expected to be available in 1974.

Volvo locates in the United States

In September 1973, Volvo announced that it would construct a $100-million auto plant in Chesapeake, Virginia. With a planned annual capacity of 100,000 units by 1977, Volvo would rank as the fifth largest American auto producer.

There were several reasons given for this move.

1 No room for Volvo to grow at home in Sweden. It already has twenty-two plants there.

2 Labor is scarce in Sweden and wages are virtually the same as in the United States.

3 Seventy-five percent of Volvo's sales are exports. This makes the company very vulnerable to international trade restrictions and makes foreign expansion necessary.

4 Volvo must get closer to its important markets and feels it can do this by moving its assembly and manufacturing into these markets.

QUESTIONS

1 Why is manufacturing activity important in the United States?

2 What are the differences between manufacturing and assembling?

3 Cite some illustrations of new industries which have come into being during the past two decades as a result of technical discoveries.

4 What are the respective product and production characteristics that are associated with each of the three basic manufacturing systems in use today?

5 What are the activities involved in manufacturing? What is the role of each?

6 What features contribute to the complexity of the production division?

7 What is the role of a supervisor or foreman in a manufacturing firm?

8 Simplification and diversification are opposite but common characteristics of all manufacturing systems. Explain how these opposites may exist together.

9 When is diversification advantageous? When is simplification advantageous?

10 Explain the manner in which the concept of standardization is applicable both to products and to production.

11 Although specialization may simplify the task of the worker, it makes the production process highly complex. Why does this occur?

12 What factors must be considered in selecting an ideal location for a new manufacturing concern? Do these factors vary in importance with the nature of the firm and its products? How?

13 Compare the housing requirements of a retail clothing merchant with those of a clothing manufacturer.

14 How is plant location related to economic use of resources? To conservation? To transportation?

15 Identify and give the advantages of:
  a general-purpose equipment
  b special-purpose equipment

16 Explain the relationships which exist among the following:
  a numerical control
  b computers
  c machine tools
  d quality and quantity of production

17 Why is material handling referred to as the "necessary evil"? Is it?

18 Illustrate a situation where a small increase in purchasing efficiency (pricewise) may significantly enhance a company's profit.

19 Under what circumstances is the purchasing function more likely to be designated as a line function rather than a staff function?

20 What is the role of the purchasing agent in a centralized purchasing department? In one which is decentralized?

21 Discuss the relative importance of the four primary factors in purchasing.

22 Which of the following is more difficult or exacting: purchase for use, purchase for processing, purchase for resale? Explain.

23 What documents are involved in the purchasing procedure? Who prepares them? Who authorizes them?

24 How does the process of establishing purchasing specifications differ among manufacturer, wholesaler, retailer?

The purpose of this chapter   A carefully prepared plan is the first step in the successful achievement of any goal. In this chapter we shall examine the steps involved in production planning. These include planning the process, the methods, the material needs, the time it should take to do work, the appropriate quality standards, and the effective use of the resources of the firm. / No business person wants more inventory than is absolutely necessary because it represents idle money. Consequently there must be a high degree of coordination between production and inventory control. We shall examine some of the basic inventory control techniques which are basic to sound materials management. / A great deal of the work in the area of production is not directly involved with producing goods, for many people are involved with the planning and controlling activities. Their goal, of course, is to plan and control in such a fashion that resources are used efficiently and the production effort is maximized—no more, no less. / Questions raised in this chapter include:

1 What sort of planning should precede production?

2 What influence does the physical layout of a work area have on production efficiency?

3 To what extent can it be determined how a man should do his work and how much output he should produce?

4 What factors affect the planning of the quality of a product? How is quality maintained?

5 How does inventory control relate to purchasing and production?

6 What special inventory problems confront the retailer?

PLANNING AND CONTROLLING PRODUCTION

Planning is a vital element in the successful operation of any business enterprise. Whether the firm is just beginning or is already producing and distributing goods to the consumer, a planned approach to the problem involved is essential. Plants must be located properly; sources of supply must be determined; personnel and materials must be organized to carry out the firm's activities; the distribution of the product must be efficiently undertaken. All these tasks require planning.

In addition, there must be some means of controlling operations so that the plan will be fulfilled. Planning and control supplement each other, for a plan without controls is worth little. The purpose of production planning and control is to regulate and coordinate production facilities, by following a definite plan, so as to meet a set delivery date, and all to be done at a satisfactory cost.

FUNCTIONS OF PRODUCTION PLANNING

Production planning covers a wide variety of activities. The basic operations include:

1 Planning future production from sales forecasts

2 Translating these plans into personnel, machinery, and material requirements

3 Estimating the costs involved in each of these areas

4 Determining the specific operations required for each phase of production, and scheduling them in the correct sequence

5 Assigning specific jobs to personnel, machines, and departments so that the combined effort will produce the planned results

6 Making any necessary changes in designs, schedules, output, etc.

7 Arranging the administrative apparatus, paperwork, etc., needed to carry out productive operations

287

8 Maintaining a constant check on work progress and correcting any discrepancies between plan and actual operation

9 Altering plans when necessary

10 Keeping the sales department informed of output relative to delivery schedules

11 Controlling inventories of materials, parts, goods, etc.

Not all these functions need to be assigned to a single department. The original planning may be given to the engineering department, and the purchasing department can assume responsibility for procurement, and a quality control section can maintain a check of the quality of the firm's output. But the responsibility for coordinating all this activity must be centralized in some part of the firm's management structure, and management must have sufficient authority to induce conformity to the agreed plan. A typical arrangement for dealing with production planning is found in Figure 13-1. Notice that every major unit in the firm's management is directly involved in the program.

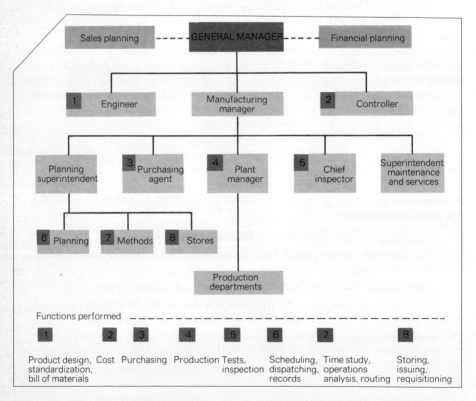

FIGURE 13-1   An organization for production planning and control

PRODUCTION PLANNING INVOLVES
INTERRELATIONSHIP OF FUNCTIONS

The interrelationship of business functions is most clear when the decision of what and when to produce is made. The continuous cycle of making and selling a product runs the full gamut of all functions within the firm. Decisions about what to make, its quality, price, raw materials, labor, process requirements, and investment in inventory must be made. The involvement of the sales, purchasing, finance, personnel, and production functions of the business firm is required to answer the questions which are raised.

As usual, any decision which the business person must make is proved to be good or bad only after the experience. Decisions about production rate, work-force requirements, and other matters are made with varying degrees of uncertainty. Uncertainty is a normal feature of planning in the business environment, for the controlled, laboratory circumstances of the scientist are not characteristic of the environment in which business problems are analyzed. A decision made by the business person is more often than not only the first of a sequence of decisions which will have to be made at successive points of time. Since business activity takes place within a dynamic environment and new information is constantly becoming available, a necessary feature of planning is the ability to reopen the issue and make changes in direction and objectives from time to time.

PLANNING THE PHYSICAL SETUP OF PRODUCTION

Production planning must include every phase of business from the conception of the product to its delivery to a customer. A *production plan* is meant to achieve the basic objectives of the firm. It will aim at optimum use of facilities, low production costs, the meeting of production dates, flexibility of output, and other general goals, plus any special conditions that management may establish.

The principal elements in the production plan are the sequence of operations to be used in the production cycle, the layout of plant and facilities, the methods to be used to perform each fundamental operation in the productive process, the time schedule to be followed in production, and the control system to be used.

Process analysis

Process analysis is the procedure used to determine which operations are necessary for production and to place them in their proper sequence. Each step in the production process must be carefully defined and its relation to every other phase of production established. In most cases, process analysis provides the planner with:

1 A list of materials and parts to be used in production, called the *bill of materials*

2 A list of the equipment and machinery needed for production

3 A list of the labor skills required

4 A sequence of operations to be followed in production, together with the time allotted for each function or schedule

Process analysis is clearly the first step in sound production planning since it produces the basic information on which a production plan is based.

Plant layout

Plant layout refers to the arrangement of the facilities used by an enterprise to produce goods and services. It may mean the arrangement of counters and display cases in a retail store or the location of machines and personnel in a factory. In either case, the important point is to obtain a smooth and efficient coordination of personnel and materials as the work of the firm is carried on.

Material-handling problems can be reduced to a minimum if layout is designed to give proper attention to the flow of materials through the plant. Making a good layout involves selecting the right equipment, the right method for doing each job, and the right location for each activity. The goal is to produce goods and services of stated quality in the shortest possible time and at least cost. A sound layout should enable the business person to achieve:

1 Lower-cost operations

2 A shorter production cycle

3 Maximum output from existing facilities

4 A reduction in the requirement for working capital

5 Improved morale among the workers

A poor plant layout is, of course, a handicap to the worker, to the efficient use of equipment, and to the activity of the whole enterprise.

Line layout and process layout

The type of layout used by a firm depends on the processes used in production and the variety of goods produced. When the firm uses one major process, or makes one principal product, a layout pattern very closely fitted to that specific requirement may be used. This is called the "line layout." The firm that produces a variety of goods is wise to adopt a layout pattern that is flexible and easily changed about. This form is called the "process layout."

Line layout, or production-line layout, is advisable when the firm engages in a repetitive or continuous activity. Line layout is generally found when a large volume of similar or identical products must be produced; it involves a fixed sequence of operations through which each unit of product proceeds. Thus each unit produced by the firm passes along the line and emerges as a completed product, ready for market. The line and its facilities are devoted to the specific product.

Process layout is a system for organizing physical facilities in such a way that equipment is located according to the nature of the operation it performs rather than according to the sequence of operations required in the production of a particular item. In process layout, all equipment performing the same operation, such as drill presses, or grinders, or spray-paint booths, is grouped together, so that any product which must be spray-painted is sent to the part of the plant where the spray-painting equipment is located. Process layout may be efficiently used when the items to be produced are not highly standardized, when a variety of products is to be made, and when the quantity of production may range from one of a kind to some larger number.

Process charts A useful way to plan a layout is first to show the details of the manufacturing process on a chart or graph. A typical operation-process chart is shown in Figure 13-2. Here a manufacturing and assembly plant engages in the production and assembly

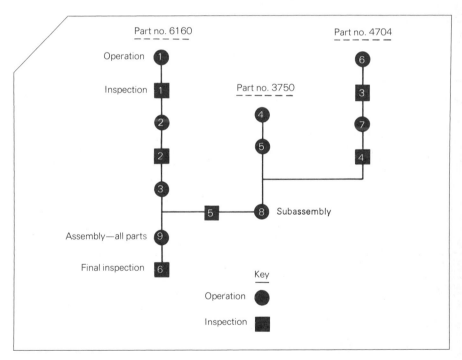

FIGURE 13-2 Operation-process chart

This chart diagrams the sequence of the operations and inspections involved in manufacturing three parts and assembling them into an electrical component.

of several separate items that are brought together to make up the finished product.

The flow-process chart in Figure 13-3 presents a different graphic portrayal of a process. The nature and frequency of each operation are shown along with the time and distance involved in each step of the process.

Both the operation-process chart and the flow-process chart are aids to management when layout is being planned or improved. Once a manufacturing process has been outlined clearly on such charts,

PROCESS: Finish operation on part X
LOCATION: Department 42

LOT SIZE: 100 units

Operation number	Symbol	Explanation	Time, minutes	Distance, feet
1	■	Incoming material inspected for quality and quantity	30.0	
2	●	Truck transport to work station 304	0.4	40.0
3	●	Rough-finish operation	50.0	
4	●	Transport to inspection	0.6	50.0
5	■	Inspect for quality	20.0	
6	●	Transport to work station 405	0.6	50.0
7	●	Fine-finish operation	50.0	
8	●	Transport to inspection	0.6	50.0
9	■	Inspect for quality	40.0	
10	●	Transport to elevator	0.4	30.0
11	■	Wait for elevator	3.0-3.5	
12	●	Transport to storage	0.4	Vert. 30.0

TOTAL TIME/LOT 196.0-196.5

TOTAL DISTANCE/LOT   220 Hor. 30 Vert.

SUMMARY ▶   ● 2 Operation   ▼ 0 Storage   ■ 3 Inspection   ▶ 1 Delay   ● 6 Transport

FIGURE 13-3   Flow-process chart

management can examine each phase of the overall operation to learn whether some steps can be eliminated, combined with others, or perhaps simplified and divided into smaller units.

Flow diagrams The development of the final plant layout is the outcome of careful planning, testing, and improvement of the suggested process sequence. Every process involves a flow of materials through the plant; the pattern in which the work flows can be charted in a flow diagram. By graphic delineation of the actual routing of materials through the plant, management can locate errors in the placement of equipment and personnel and can anticipate bottlenecks. Weak traffic arrangements, or poor spatial relations among the various machines and materials, can often be spotted by this technique.

The result of process revision through the use of flow diagrams is demonstrated in Figure 13-4. The "before" diagram represents the layout plan that is being considered for improvement. The excessive hauling distances, the backtracking of the product during manufacture, and the potential traffic problems are readily apparent. The "after" diagram shows the revised layout which seeks to eliminate several sources of inefficiency and introduces an orderly flow of materials through the manufacturing system. Of course, the new flow of production requires a revised layout and will have to be tested under working conditions to iron out any problems that the study of the flow diagram could not pinpoint.

Factors affecting work flow The flow pattern inside a plant depends on a number of conditions. The greater the number of individual parts

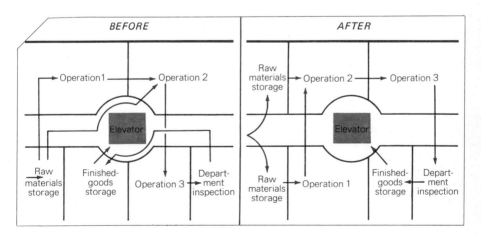

FIGURE 13-4 Flow diagram

Diagraming the flow of production (before) suggests improvements in the layout (after) to increase efficiency.

in the manufactured product, the more complex the flow pattern is likely to become. When fewer operations are used in manufacture, the pattern of flow is simpler. A concern which assembles parts may find that the storage problem increases the complexity of the flow pattern. Some types of raw materials that require special handling because of weight or dimensions influence the flow of work inside the plant. Plants with large numbers of workers must allocate more space for the movement of personnel inside the plant and so on. Each of these special conditions must be taken into consideration when the flow pattern is being designed.

Templates and models The use of scale models or templates to show the distribution of personnel and equipment inside a plant helps in the development of an efficient work flow. Three-dimensional scaled models or two-dimensional templates can be shifted about readily on a scaled floor plan to show the effect of different layout combinations on the flow of work. (In most industrial plants the actual equipment cannot easily be moved about to try out different layout suggestions.)

With these techniques it is possible to make photographs of the several proposed layouts for purposes of comparison. Such comparison demonstrates spatial relationships and helps to locate potential trouble spots. Skill and experience combined with these various aids to planning should then be able to produce a trouble-free flow of work throughout the plant.

PLANNING WORK METHODS AND TIME STANDARDS

One of the primary goals of any business concern is efficiency—doing the best job possible with the facilities available. The "best job" must be defined, however, and this means that business must have performance standards that will tell management whether or not the best job is being done. In modern industry, methods have been developed for determining the standards business must have to do its best work.

Does management wish to know how a particular job can be accomplished most efficiently? Techniques such as process and operation analysis or motion study can provide a standard.

How long should it take for an individual or a machine to do a particular job? A time study can supply the answer to that question.

How should the work be checked or inspected to provide satisfactory output? Standards of quality control answer this type of question for management. Proper use of these valuable tools is an important part of good management.

Motion study

Motion study is the attempt to establish scientifically the best possible sequence of motions that can be used to accomplish a particular task.

Motion study as applied in manual work divides worker movements into five basic classifications:

1 Finger movements

2 Finger and hand movements

3 Finger, hand, and lower-arm movements

4 Finger, hand, lower-arm, upper-arm movements

5 Finger, hand, lower-arm, upper-arm, and shoulder movements

The general principle followed in motion study is to reduce worker movements to the lowest possible classification in order to lessen fatigue and speed the rate of activity.

By analyzing the way in which a worker actually performs a job and attempting to establish the best or most efficient way of doing it, motion study contributes significantly to industrial efficiency. Motion study does not, of course, confine itself entirely to the movements of the worker. It also considers the worker in conjunction with his tools, materials, machines, and work area. The basic principle, of eliminating to whatever extent is practical the time periods during which the worker's hands are not in use, cannot be applied without considering the complete working environment.

By making motion studies and adhering to the principles of motion economy, management is able to set a standard method of doing a job. The standard method is not simply the most rapid possible means of accomplishing a job, but one that also takes into account factors such as worker fatigue and the need for accuracy. In general, management seeks a fixed method of work that makes training easier, makes the job easier to perform, and lessens the cost and time required for producing each unit of goods.

Time study

Time study is a procedure that records the exact time it takes to do a given task and then uses this information to develop a time standard—the period of time that it should take an average worker to perform a particular job. Time study may be applied to a particular job, a particular machine operation, a complete process, or any aspect of production that concerns management. Time study combined with motion study can determine the quickest of several methods of doing a job—the method of maximum efficiency. Once a time standard has been established, it may be used as a basis for production and work schedules, as a standard for worker quotas, and as a check on the production activity of a particular department or of the entire plant.

In practice, time study and motion study are generally combined. Motion study establishes the best means of doing a job; time study establishes the time required to do the job by this best means. Combined, these studies may produce accurate work standards for almost any job, or any combination of jobs.

Stopwatch time-study procedure The purpose of time study is to establish the time period that the worker will be allowed to do a specific task. Workers should be clearly informed of this purpose, especially any worker who is selected for time-study observation. The job or work cycle to be timed is customarily broken down into its component parts. This permits detailed time analyses of the parts or elements of the job so that allowances may be made for those elements which should receive special consideration in the time-study procedure.

Making the time study The time study involves making a large number of observations, recording the actual time taken for each element of the job, and then determining the average time required for one cycle. If the job has a short time cycle—say, 1 minute—a study 15 to 30 minutes long will provide enough observations to produce a satisfactory norm for a particular worker. But if the work cycle is longer, hours or even days may be needed to establish the norm. A stopwatch or a time-study machine called the Marstochron may be used for timing purposes. High-speed motion pictures of the work may also be used to facilitate detailed motion analysis.

Grading the time study When a sufficient number of work cycles have been timed and an average or norm has been arrived at for the worker in question, the study must be graded or adjusted to make up for any differences between the particular worker studied and the "average" worker. This involves an appraisal of the tested worker's performance and a judgment of his skill, of the effort put forth, of the consistency shown by results, and of the effect of working conditions during the study. Since it is always possible that one worker may be better or worse than the average, some allowance of this sort is needed.

Adding allowances Even when grading is finished, additional allowances may be made in the time standard for the job. The short time period in which the job was studied may not have been representative of ordinary work conditions. The worker may have been performing under ideal conditions, with no shortages of material or equipment breakages, though normally time must be allowed for these contingencies. Generally, allowance is made for the following factors not included in actual performance time:

1 Personal allowance. The time that is necessary to attend to personal needs.

2 Fatigue allowance. As the workday progresses, the worker will lose some of his speed and efficiency. The amount lost depends on the nature of the job studied.

3 Delay allowance. Time allowed for breakage, faulty materials, and other delays that are not the worker's responsibility.

Table 13-1 illustrates the calculation of a time standard.

TABLE 13-1　Determining a time standard

Number of cycles observed	10
Total time for 10 cycles	72 minutes
Average, or selected, time per cycle	7.2 minutes
Grading of performance	5% above average
Graded time per cycle	7.56 minutes (7.2 x 1.05)
Allowances	10%
Allowed, or standard, time per cycle	8.32 minutes (7.56 x 1.10)

On the basis of this allowed time per cycle or unit of production, an average worker is expected to turn out close to 58 units in the course of an 8-hour day.

Other methods of setting time standards　Time standards are sometimes set on the basis of experience rather than of stopwatch studies. Personnel who have supervised or worked on particular operations may be able to accurately estimate the time which a particular job should take. Sometimes, the experience may be with similar work rather than with the exact job for which the standard is being set. Nevertheless, on the basis of experience and know-how, a satisfactory time standard may be set. A shop which handles a great variety of low-volume work may find it more practical to use similar experience as a basis for setting standards rather than specific time studies. The time-study procedure costs money and takes time. As in so many other areas of business practice, it is desirable to measure both the gains and the cost involved as a guide to the decision to use a particular device or procedure such as time study.

Another means of arriving at time standards involves the classification of time data in the form of a manual of element times. Studies of different jobs will provide much basic data for this manual. An operation for which a time standard is to be set may not involve the same product or overall process as other jobs which were actually time-studied, but it may involve some elements of work which are common. Many if not all the element times of a new job may be available in the time-data files. The procedure for establishing the time standard requires a search of the time-data files and the combining of element times which fulfill the detail of the job for which the standard is being developed. If certain elements are not found in the manual, time studies may be taken or estimates made to fill in the missing pieces.

A third method, called MTM (methods-time measurement), is based on the conclusion that all normal human activities are combinations or sequences of unvarying basic motions. MTM classifies these basic motions and applies time standards to them. With such data it is possible to take any task, regardless of product or process involved, and classify the human activities into basic motions. The motion pattern is recorded, and then by reference to the basic timetables the time values of the motions are added to equal the time standard.

QUALITY STANDARDS AND CONTROLS

Production plans always include a set of standards for judging the quality of the product. The overall quality standard should not be set either too high or too low. It is possible, of course, to make too good a product as well as too poor a product. A foot rule accurate to a few thousandths of an inch can be made for a few cents; an absolutely accurate rule would cost thousands of dollars to manufacture. A manufacturer cannot expect to continue in business very long, however, if the goods he produces do not meet the standards which the firm claims publicly for its products.

Quality standards are set by considering the relationship between the cost of production and the selling price of the product. The selling price roughly determines the quality of the product that can be produced, for the costs of materials, labor, machinery, overhead, and profit must all be met from selling price. Quality standards must be clearly stated for each part of the productive process, so that workers will clearly understand the required characteristics of their output, and to provide the basis for determining whether a unit of product is acceptable.

Ultimately, the quality standards are determined by the characteristics required in the final product, which may have to conform to certain dimensions, may have a specified degree of smoothness, malleability, viscosity, or weight. The product may also, of course, be required to meet performance characteristics. An electric motor, for example, may have to produce a given amount of power and to continue doing so for a definite period of time without wearing out.

Inspection

Production quality is checked by inspection, which may be either manual or automatic. Once standards have been established for the quality of the product, management must decide how often inspection will occur, at what points in the production process inspection is needed, and which standards will be used at each inspection point. It may be necessary to inspect every item produced (100 percent inspection) or only a small sample of the output (sample inspection). For example, it may be important to test every electric sewing machine before sale, but in the manufacture of electric light bulbs such care is not necessary; only a controlled sample is tested for performance.

Inspection does not always take place during the actual production process; it may occur only when the product is completed. It would be pointless, for example, to test a portion of a light bulb, but in the manufacture of expensive items, it is often desirable to test each part as it is produced to avoid excess costs. In either case, inspector or worker must know what features of the product to inspect, how to make the inspection, when to inspect, and what defects to look for. When inspection is controlled by machine or electronic equipment, these questions must be answered before the inspection equipment can be set.

Quality control

The quality of production may be checked by inspection. However, if the inspection is made after the product or a part is completed, the only possible result is an accepted or a rejected unit. This is not really a control over quality, for quality control is the attempt to prevent defective production. It seeks to determine as quickly as possible, during the production cycle, when quality is slipping, so that corrective action may be taken before the occurrence of real loss in the form of defective items. A good quality control system must include inspection. In this case, however, the basic purpose of such inspection is not to isolate good and bad units, but to play watchdog over the production process, thereby providing the control required to keep performance within acceptable limits.

Statistical quality control One of the most difficult problems in quality control arises from the great speed and volume of modern manufacturing. Suppose that a particular machine is set to produce parts 0.258 inch in size. Naturally, the machine cannot be expected to produce precisely this size every time; therefore a set of limits or tolerances is established for the completed product. If the tolerance is ± 0.004 inch, the part is satisfactory if it is up to 0.004 inch larger or smaller than the specification, no more.

Now, must the worker assigned to the machine measure every part that comes out of it to be certain that the machine is not "wandering"? This could be expensive and time-consuming, and it is not really necessary. Instead, a few items of the output can be inspected periodically. If these units are satisfactory, then it can be assumed that the machine is working properly. This is called *statistical quality control,* and it is based on modern sampling techniques. The procedure followed when applying statistical quality control is generally as follows:

1 Tolerance limits for the product are established.

2 Samples of the product are tested periodically.

3 The results of sample inspections are recorded on a quality control chart.

4 The records are interpreted to determine whether any correction of machinery is needed.

Figure 13-5 shows a typical quality control chart. Every half hour, samples are taken from a machine, measured, and recorded on the

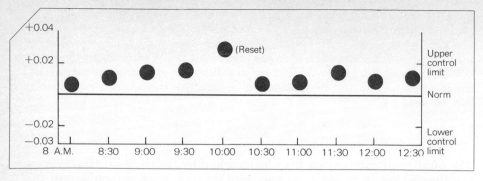

FIGURE 13-5 Quality control chart

chart. If the measurements approach the tolerance limits, the machine is stopped immediately and adjusted. The chart shows that the machine was functioning properly at 8 A.M. but by 10 A.M. the sample showed a definite trend away from desired quality. The machine was stopped at this point for adjustment, and then production was resumed. For the remainder of the morning, the machine produced goods of the right quality. Some machines have a mechanical or electronic adjustment built into them that automatically stops the machine if the output varies significantly; that is, the machine measures its own output and stops when the measurements are wrong. In still more complex systems, the measuring device is connected to the control board of the machine, and adjustments in quality of output are made automatically while production continues.

Other considerations In matters affecting quality, management must always attempt to strike a balance between quality and cost. As the tolerance limits on a product are narrowed, more adjustment is required, more inspection is needed, and more rejects appear. High quality is expensive. And naturally, the tolerance limits set must be within the capabilities of the machine. Very fine precision work may be possible on a new machine, but normal wear will produce small variations in quality of output in a relatively short time. In the case of most mass produced goods, tolerance limits are quite broad; otherwise, it would hardly be possible to maintain high-speed production for long periods of time.

INVENTORY PLANNING AND CONTROL

In planning for materials and parts needed for production, two questions must be answered: when are the materials needed and how much should be ordered? Let us first see how these questions can be answered when the objective is simply to ensure having on hand enough material to satisfy production requirements. Before we can answer these questions, the following types of data are needed:

Units of the item on hand today	14,000
Weekly consumption, units	2,000
Maximum inventory allowable	14-week supply
Delivery time required, weeks	2
Safety stock, weeks of supply	3

Maximum inventory allowable is prescribed because of space and money limitations. Safety stock is a reserve inventory that is needed to cover variations in the actual rate of use and delivery time. Obviously if there were no variations in the actual rate of use and delivery there would be no need for a safety stock, but using the above data we can draw the following conclusions:

1 This item should be reordered when stock on hand drops to 10,000 units, or in 2 weeks. This represents usage during delivery time plus safety stock.

2 The amount that should be ordered at a time is 22,000 units. This is the quantity needed to bring inventory up to the prescribed maximum. When an order is placed there are 10,000 units on hand. When delivery is made 2 weeks later there will be 6,000 units on hand. The 22,000 units will restore inventory to the 28,000 maximum.

Economic purchase lots

Under certain conditions it is economical to buy more than is needed to meet current production requirements. Quantity discounts, transportation and handling economies, and a reduced probability of stock-outs are the types of savings that can accrue through buying in large quantities. But large purchases result in larger inventory carrying charges.

Inventory carrying charges

Measured on an annual basis, it costs about 25 percent of the cost of an item to carry it in inventory. The inventory carrying charge includes interest on the investment, taxes, insurance, storage, handling, depreciation, and the like, and is applied to the cost of the average inventory. Obviously there are tremendous variations in the suitable carrying charge depending on the material—pig iron versus sterling silver—but 25 percent is an average figure commonly used.

Suppose a firm plans to purchase 100,000 units of an item during the next year. The minimal feasible purchase lot is 10,000 units, but the item could be purchased in five lots of 20,000 units each or two lots of 50,000 units each. Which lot size is most economical if the costs per unit are $1, $.95, and $.93, respectively, and the inventory carrying charge is 25 percent per annum? Figure 13-6 illustrates how this question can be answered:

The most economical alternative is to make five purchases of 20,000

	Ten lots	Five lots	Two lots
Price per unit	$ 1.00	$ .95	$ .93
Acquisition cost	$100,000	$95,000	$93,000
Inventory carrying charge	1,250	2,375	5,813
Totals	$101,250	$97,375	$98,813

Calculation of inventory carrying charge applied to average inventory:

	Ten lots	Five lots	Two lots
Maximum inventory, units	10,000	20,000	50,000
Average inventory, units	5,000	10,000	25,000
Value, average inventory	$5,000	$9,500	$23,250
Inventory carrying charge	$1,250	$2,375	$5,813

FIGURE 13-6   Purchase lot size determination

units each. Here the reduction in the cost of acquiring a unit is greater than the increased carrying charge. This does not hold true in the third situation.

Safety stock determination

The above discussions are oversimplifications of basic purchasing decisions and serve only to identify relationships. In practice, variations in the rate of use and delivery are as much the rule as they are the exception. This is the reason for safety stock. The size of safety stock depends on a number of factors. If management establishes a policy of never running out of stock, safety stocks of necessity must be higher than with a policy of occasional stock-outs. The trick is to operate with both a minimum safety stock and a minimum stock-out record. A second factor that bears on safety stock is the variation in the rate of use and delivery that may be anticipated. (Remember that if there are no variations, there is no need for a safety stock.) Without these two values safety-stock determination must be hit or miss.

Maintaining safety stocks can be a costly endeavor, and the only way to cut the cost is either to reduce the level of service by permitting more stock-outs or to reduce variations between what is planned for and what actually takes place. Automobile assembly plants operate with virtually no safety stock. They can do this because of precision planning, and they must do it because the cost of maintaining safety stocks for more than 10,000 items is prohibitive.

INVENTORY CONTROL

Control, by definition, is a process whereby events are made to conform to a plan. Control is lacking when actual performance deviates from the plan, and thus, to control inventory there must be a plan. Planning includes determining how much to buy, when to buy, and the safety stock question discussed above. Good inventory control depends on "controlled" purchasing so that the size of inventory is no greater than is needed for production requirements, giving due consideration to economies of purchasing, and on management's having all the information it needs for good inventory management. A second aspect of good inventory control relates to material in the storehouse. Control of inventory is facilitated if it is broken down into manageable parts that are treated separately. A common breakdown of inventory in industry is:

1 Raw materials. This group includes all materials that eventually will be made into a finished product. Sheets of steel used for refrigerator panels and crude rubber used for tire production are typical items in this type of inventory.

2 Finished parts. Materials already manufactured by a firm or its supplier, and ready to be included in the finished product—such as spark plugs for an automobile—fall into this category.

3 Supplies. These are materials that are necessary for operation but not a part of the goods being produced. Oil, cutting tools, and cleaning materials are a part of this inventory.

4 Work in process. Any material used in manufacturing on which some work has been expended is included in this category. Knowledge of work in process is essential for the measurement of production activity.

5 Finished goods. This category includes all items that are completely manufactured and presumably available for sale or shipment.

Purposes of inventory control

Inventories are directly related to the purchasing function, but they may also influence selling, production, and all other phases of business. Management needs to know not only the size of its inventory and its classification breakdown but also its value, it age, and its relation to established inventory needs.

Inventory must be related to production needs to ensure against delays due to lack of materials. It must be related to sales to avoid undue storage costs or failure to deliver goods because of inventory shortages. The age of goods in inventory is particularly significant when goods can spoil quickly or become obsolete.

There are two basic approaches to inventory control: unit control and dollar control. Unit control is based on the units of various materials that move into and out of inventory, whereas dollar control is based on the dollar value of items that move into and out of inventory, with no reference to the specific units involved.

Unit control illustrated

Unit control consists of a record of authorized additions and withdrawals of materials from stock. Authorized additions are recorded from information contained in the receiving slip. Authorization for withdrawals comes from a variety of work orders. The work order may be for the production of goods, maintenance projects, or office supplies. The idea is that nothing will enter or leave the stockroom without formal authorization. Unit control utilizes the perpetual inventory concept. Figure 13-7 illustrates this concept. In practice these records may be maintained by hand entries or by modern data processing systems which can handle this type of work more accurately, faster, and at lower cost.

Looking at Figure 13-7 again, we see that on March 27 there are 1,400 units on hand and that none have been "reserved" for future use. This figure tells us only how many units should be in stock, not how many are actually there. For a number of reasons such as pilferage, breakage, spoilage, or "I'd better take two more just in case," the actual count may be lower. We can never be sure that inventory is in control until a physical count is made.

Unit inventory control requires four distinct steps:

1 A standard. How many units should be on hand?

2 Measurement of actual. How many units are on hand?

PERPETUAL INVENTORY RECORD

Item _____Condenser_____ Standard order quantity _1,200_

Item number ___456 J___ Maximum ___1,600___ Reorder point _300_

ON ORDER			ON HAND				RESERVED			AVAILABLE	
Date	Quantity	Unit cost	Date	Quantity	Unit cost	Value	Date	Requisition number	Quantity	Date	Quantity
			3/1	1,000	.50	$500.–				3/1	1,000
							3/6	496	600	3/6	400
							3/9	499	200	3/9	200
3/10	1,200	.52									
			3/16	400	.50	200.–					
			3/24 {	400 / 1,200	.50 / .52	200.– / 624.–				3/24	1,400
			3/27 {	200 / 1,200	.50 / .52	100.– / 624.–					

FIGURE 13-7 A perpetual inventory record

A perpetual inventory provides a written record of every item added to or subtracted from the stock of materials on hand.

3 Analysis of variances. If there is a difference between what is and what should be, we must find the causes.

4 Corrective action if necessary.

Unit control involves a tremendous amount of paperwork and can be quite costly. It could very well be that this amount of control should not be exercised over all items. Picture the problem involved in applying unit control to all the materials used in the manufacture of an automobile. Careful unit control is kept over radios, air conditioners, and the like, but virtually no such control over the lugs used to hold on wheels.

RETAIL INVENTORY CONTROL

Retailers employ both unit control and dollar control. A retailer of furniture, appliances, automobile tires, and the like can effectively use unit control, but the local supermarket generally cannot. Basically, if the number of transactions is relatively low and the variety of goods sold is limited, unit control will work. But when a large volume or a large variety of merchandise is involved, perpetual inventory may be impossible.

Inventory control is far more difficult in retailing than in wholesaling or manufacturing. Retailers have a great problem in trying to measure consumer demand with the consequent inventory overstock or stock-out problem. Also, since the retailer's merchandise is exposed to public handling, there is a strong possibility of loss through damage, pilfering, and the like.

A principal inventory task facing the retailer is to determine accurately what has been sold during a given time period. This determination is facilitated by the extent to which such devices as sales slips, split price tags (see Figure 13-8), and computerized sales recording devices are used.

The retail method: Dollar inventory control

The nature of retail store operations makes it difficult to apply a perpetual inventory method; this is especially true of food retailers and self-service department stores. Many retailers, therefore, make no attempt to record the quantity of goods sold. Rather, they rely on dollar control of inventory, in which accurate records of purchases, receipts, markdowns, and sales must be kept for each department or line of goods. The figures can then be used to estimate the value of inventory as shown in Figure 13-9.

The retail method of inventory, then, depends on the total cost and the total retail value of goods as the bases for inventory control. The store manager is responsible for the total retail value of goods available for sale, and the sales and authorized markdowns show the movement of goods from inventory. The difference between the value

SALES STORES INCORPORATED	DATE 3/14/6-	CLERK NO. 14	DEPT. NO 933

SOLD TO _Mr. Jason Smith_

STREET _4739 Carbon Avenue_

CITY & STATE _Barksville_

CUSTOMER SIGNATURE _Jason Smith_

CIRCLE TYPE OF SALE

2743-9	Cash	C.O.D.	Regular charge	P.B.A.	Three-month	Budget

Quantity	Code	Merchandise	Amount
1	F126-10E	Shoes	14 95
			14 95

AUDITOR'S VOUCHER	DATE 3/14/6-	CLERK NO. 14	DEPT. NO. 933
		AMOUNT	14 95

CIRCLE TYPE OF SALE

2743-9	Cash	C.O.D.	Regular charge	P.B.A.	Three-month	Budget

	SPLIT	TAG
	F126 10 E	F126 10 E
	Black Men's	Black Men's
	$14.95	$14.95

FIGURE 13-8 A sales slip and a split price tag

Either of these records will provide the information needed to record all sales from inventory.

	Cost value	Retail value
Merchandise inventory, Jan. 1	$180,000	$ 300,000
Purchases for January	500,000	820,000
Total value accounted for	$680,000	$1,120,000
Sales for January (retail)		$ 850,000
Authorized markdowns (retail) on sales		30,000
Total retail value accounted for		880,000
Merchandise inventory, Jan. 31 (retail)		240,000
Total retail value to be accounted for		$1,120,000

Inventory is the difference between these two figures

FIGURE 13-9 Retail method of inventory control

The retail method provides dollar control, instead of unit control of inventory.

that had to be accounted for and the amount that has been accounted for through sales and markdowns should be in inventory. Thus in this illustration the value of the inventory on January 31 was $240,000.

PRODUCTION ROUTING AND SCHEDULING

The general planning and layout of physical facilities are accomplished before production begins. During the course of production, however, the generalized plan must be translated into the specific set of operations needed to convert an order into a batch of goods ready for delivery. Since day-to-day modifications occur, the actual operation is seldom precisely like the original plan. For example, one machine may not be functioning properly and therefore may be unusable for orders that require very high-quality work. A shortage of one type of raw material or parts may force production changes until the shortage is removed. The skill and efficiency with which these production problems are solved are an important factor in the success of any manufacturing concern.

Routing

Any order to produce requires the selection of a sequence of operations that will give the desired end result. This is called *routing*. It begins with a list of the operations and equipment needed, selected from the facilities available in the plant. Obviously, the routing function is most complex in the manufacture of a wide variety of items, and relatively simple in repetitive production. Routing fixes the sequence of operations to be used, and then fixes the equipment and the manpower allocated to the task. It may even indicate the precise machine and operator responsible for each step in the manufacturing process.

Routing also involves the allocation of time. Each step in the process of filling an order must be timed properly. Otherwise the order will be delayed between production processes or will cause delay to other orders. Time and motion study usually provides the information needed for this part of the routing function. All this information is recorded on a route sheet (see Figure 13-10).

Scheduling

Routing establishes how production will occur. *Scheduling* determines the time when each part of the process should begin in order to meet the delivery date specified in the order. Usually scheduling works backward from date of delivery to determine when production must begin. When a job calls for the manufacture and assembly of many different parts, the complex procedure involved may require the coordination of virtually every department in the plant.

Scheduling obviously cannot be done until the production rate of each department, machine, and individual worker in the plant is

Part	Pinned face plate		Job no.	1234
Part no.	1407-AB		Drawing no.	317-408
Material	Aluminum			
Quantity	150			

Operation number	Department	Description of operation	Machine	Time (decimal–hrs)		
				Setup, hours	Run, hours per piece	Total hours
30	135	Face surfaces	Lathe	0.50	0.03	5.00
47	140	Drill	Gang drill	0.25	0.05	7.75
45	140	Counterbore	Mill	0.30	0.02	3.30
38	101	Press pin	Press	0.50	0.01	2.00
40-A	100	Inspect	Bench	0.30	0.03	4.80
60	100	Deliver to Stores				1.00

FIGURE 13-10   Route sheet

This sheet lists the time requirements, the sequence of operations, their nature, and the departments involved in the production of part no. 1407-AB.

known. Time study provides the basic data from which these figures can be calculated. Often these data are combined in a master schedule (see Figure 13-11), showing the working capacity of the plant, department by department, or even machine by machine. This is an invaluable aid to the scheduling officer.

Since the schedule arranges the time at which steps in the manufacturing process should begin and end, it is a useful check at any given time on whether the plant is on schedule. However, every schedule must contain some element of flexibility to allow for the emergencies which always occur in normal operations and for the possibility of interruptions caused by priority orders.

In some companies, scheduling is done by the production control department. In other cases, the function is decentralized, and each foreman is responsible for the output of his own department. In either case, management must ensure proper coordination among the departments to be certain that commitments for delivery of goods can be met on time.

The routing and scheduling of part no. 1407-AB on job no. 1234 are demonstrated in Figures 13-10 and 13-11. The sequence of operations and the required time for each as shown on the route sheet (Figure 13-10) are posted to the master schedule (Figure 13-11) along with details of several other jobs being run in the shop. Job 1234 is scheduled to start on the morning of September 12 in department 135. On the morning of the thirteenth, the next operation, number 47, will

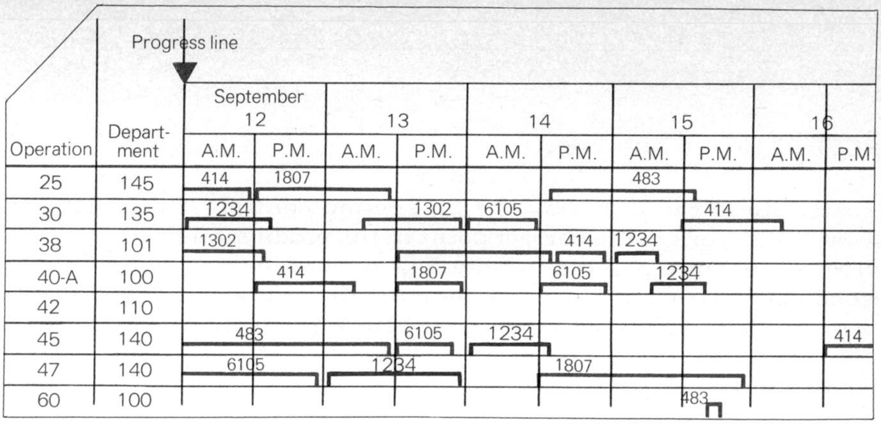

FIGURE 13-11   Gantt chart: Master schedule

This graphic scheduling device displays the planned use of departmental time. For example, job no. 1234 (see Figure 13-10) is scheduled to start in production the morning of September 12, and inspection is scheduled to be completed in department 100 during the afternoon of September 15. From there the inspected parts are delivered to stores. The movable progress line (∇) shows the current time of day. By relating the planned schedule to reports from production areas, it can be ascertained whether actual production is on schedule, as indicated by the position of the progress line.

start in department 140. As the operation is finished in each department, the job moves on to the next department in accordance with the sequence set up on the route sheet and at the time set on the master schedule.

COMMUNICATION IN PRODUCTION

Communication is vital to any business. For the most part, business depends on written communication because it provides a permanent record of information sent and received and can be readily referred to. Writing everything out is costly in personnel and in materials; sometimes the quantity of paperwork in a concern appears to involve more effort than the production it stimulates or controls. Yet paperwork is a necessary part of modern business life, and so long as its cost does not exceed its value it will be retained.

The amount of communication required in production is enormous. Authorizations for work, material movement, material use, equipment use, etc., must all be reduced to writing, both for clarity and for control. When materials must be moved, purchase requisitions, reservation orders, movement orders, etc., are required. Job tickets, time tickets, or work orders are used to allocate the use of personnel and machinery. Inspection orders, rework orders, and completion schedules control the quality and rate of production of the final product.

Paperwork is used to authorize, to instruct, to obtain information, to order, to clarify, and to do all the thousand and one things required of any communications system.

PRODUCTION CONTROL

Dispatching is the first stage of production control. It controls the allocation of work to the correct point in the production process at the correct time. Once the manufacturing process begins, follow-up is needed to keep track of the movement of orders, to anticipate difficulties or conflicts, and to resolve them before production is affected.

Dispatching

Control of the flow of work orders to and from the various areas in a plant is called *dispatching.* In effect, the dispatcher puts the machinery of production in motion, for these written orders are authorizations to the departments to proceed with specific tasks. Orders from the dispatcher move materials, load trucks, start machines spinning, and set personnel to work. As each job is handed out or completed, the dispatcher informs the central control office, so that progress is recorded steadily on a master control system. In some companies the dispatcher may actually be responsible for establishing the work sequence and assigning jobs to the workers available. In small firms the foreman is often made responsible for the dispatching function, but in very large organizations the dispatcher allocates work according to a predetermined plan that he is responsible for putting into effect.

In some plants, each department assigns responsibility for follow-up to particular men within the department. It is their task to make certain that the work entering the department is properly routed and that it leaves the department on schedule fully completed. In other cases, one person may follow up on a particular order throughout the production process until the order is entirely completed. In either case, the follow-up person is an aid to production and a control on production.

It is also possible to make use of reporting systems of various sorts to control the movement of work through the plant. The reports made by the dispatcher are usually an important part of such paper control systems. The tighter the paper control system, the less need there is for personal follow-up activity, though many companies make use of both follow-up personnel and extensive paper controls.

COST OF PRODUCTION

Cost is the accumulation of all expenses incurred in the manufacture of a product. It includes the costs of services rendered to the company—materials, facilities, and manpower. Not all these costs originate in the production division, of course. Therefore, any attempt to measure and control cost must involve all basic divisions in a manufacturing firm. To create a better cost structure in a firm, management must know how much each division contributes to overall cost, as well as how changes in the structure of one division affect costs in another.

Just as in the physical sense it is necessary to plan and control production, so it is also necessary to plan and control costs. The best-conceived production plan is of no use unless it is able to turn out products at an acceptable cost.

TYPES OF COSTS

Manufacturing costs may be classified in a number of ways. Management commonly makes a distinction between short-term costs and long-term costs and between fixed costs and variable costs. *Short-term costs* are those which arise out of the day-to-day operations of a going concern. Included are such items as payroll, payments for materials, and power and light. Fundamentally, these are the items which are needed daily and for which a commitment is not made over a long time period. If we need less labor, we lay off or do not replace workers who leave; if we need less material delivery, we do not reorder. For these items the commitment at any time is short-term. Long-term costs are the burden on the enterprise brought about by the investment in machinery, buildings, plant, etc. These make up the capital investment which is prorated and charged against the business over a number of years and constitutes a long-term commitment.

Fixed costs may include such items as rent, the payment of interest on outstanding loans, certain salary costs, and any other item which continues as a cost whether the plant is operating at full speed or not at all. Variable costs are those which change according to the level at which the plant operates. They include such items as the cost of labor, which varies with the number of workers employed, and the cost of materials, which varies with the volume used in production.

Effective production planning requires an understanding of the basic nature of the costs which may be encountered in the production system. This is necessary in order to establish cost estimates and controls. Without estimates it is possible to learn too late that actual production costs are excessive. Estimation, at least, provides a preview of what actual costs may be. Without adequate cost controls it would be impossible to keep actual costs within the limits necessary for profitable production.

Once the nature of costs is understood, we should then be able to establish the cost estimates. This process is not an absolute one, for the determination of production costs is not completely scientific. There are times when the business person must use his best judgment to determine the cost of his output. Since he is not infallible, his judgment may sometimes lead to disaster, for he may set a selling price based on an inaccurately determined cost.

A good example of the type of decision which the business person must make is shown in connection with the cost associated with the fixed assets of the firm. The cost is called *depreciation*. It is a long-term cost.

Depreciation and long-term costs

The fixed assets of a firm—buildings, machinery, and so on—are customarily used for a number of years before they are replaced. The initial cost of these assets cannot be charged against the business in the first year of their use, for it is unrealistic for one year's production to absorb the cost of assets which still have many years of production left. Instead, the initial cost is spread out over a number of years. In this way, the cost is spread out over the productive life of the asset. For example, assume that a firm purchases a machine for $5,000 and expects to use it for a period of 5 years. At the end of that time the machine can be sold for $1,000. The machine will then have "cost" the company $4,000 for a 5-year period. The value of the machine depreciates as it is used in production through the years. The question faced by the business person is: How much depreciation cost is to be charged periodically against production? Depending on the method by which the asset is depreciated, different amounts of depreciation may be charged against production each year of the machine's life. Different methods are used in business to depreciate assets. One, called the *straight-line method,* divides the total cost into equal parts and charges off one part each year (see Table 13-2). Another method, called *reducing-fraction method,* subtracts a different and lesser amount each year (see Table 13-3). A third method, called *production-unit method,* subtracts a proportionate amount of cost, determined by the amount of annual production of the machine related to its predetermined total production volume potential (see Table 13-4).

TABLE 13-2 Straight-line depreciation

Original cost of asset	$5,000
Expected residual value at end of useful life	1,000
Amount to be depreciated	$4,000
Anticipated useful life	5 years
Amount to be depreciated per year $4,000 ÷ 5 = $800	

This is both an easy and popular method of depreciating assets.

TABLE 13-3 Reducing-fraction depreciation

Original cost	$10,000	Depreciation Program:		
Residual value (selling price)	1,000	First year	40%	$3,600
Amount to be depreciated	$9,000	Second year	30%	2,700
Anticipated life: 4 years		Third year	20%	1,800
		Fourth year	10%	900
		4-year total	100%	$9,000

This method is used when equipment depreciates greatly during its early life, but much less in its later years.

TABLE 13-4 Production-unit method

		Depreciation program		
Original cost of asset	$5,000			
Residual value	1,000		Units produced	Depreciation
Amount to be depreciated	$4,000	First year	1,500	$ 600
		Second year	2,000	800
		Third year	2,500	1,000
Anticipated life	10,000 units	Fourth year	2,000	800
		Fifth year	1,000	400
Unit depreciation	$\dfrac{\$4,000}{10,000 \text{ units}} = \$0.40$	Sixth year	1,000	400
		6-year total	10,000	$4,000

This illustration indicates that the asset is fully depreciated. If, however, there is still useful life in the asset, it means that our original estimate of its production life was in error.

Prime costs: Labor and materials

As production increases, the cost of materials and parts actually used in production increases in total amount, but the cost of materials used in each unit of production may decrease. For example, in Table 13-5 look at the unit cost of materials for the firm when it is operating at 60, 75, and 100 percent of its capacity. Notice that the total cost of material increases steadily, but the unit cost drops. The reason for this may be savings effected by bulk purchase of materials. In many cases, savings in material cost per unit may be little or may be none at all.

The labor that is actually used in making a product is termed *direct labor*. The cost of this factor of production may be either fixed or variable, depending on the formula used for wage payment (see Table 13-6).

TABLE 13-5 Direct materials cost

Capacity, percent	Production volume	Total cost of materials used	Unit cost of materials
60	12,000	$24,000	$2.00
75	15,000	28,800	1.92
100	20,000	36,000	1.80

TABLE 13-6 Direct labor cost

Capacity, percent	Production volume	Total cost of direct labor	Unit cost of direct labor
1. Time basis of wage payment—40-hour week at $2.00 per hour; 50 employees			
60	12,000	$4,000	$0.33
75	15,000	4,000	0.27
100	20,000	4,000	0.20
2. Performance basis—Piece-rate system, $0.20 per unit; 40-hour week; 50 employees			
60	12,000	$4,000	$0.20
75	15,000	3,000	0.20
100	20,000	4,000	0.20
3. Performance basis with minimum wage guarantee— Guarantee of $1.50 per hour regardless of output and piece rate of $0.20; 40-hour week; 50 employees			
60	12,000	$3,000	$0.25
75	15,000	3,000	0.20
100	20,000	4,000	0.20

Manufacturing overhead

The various costs included in manufacturing overhead—depreciation, salaries, supplies, maintenance, indirect labor, repairs, insurance, etc.—should also be separated and treated in the same manner to arrive at a realistic appraisal of the burden these costs place on each item of production, as well as on the overall operation of the business. Let us consider the treatment of one item of manufacturing overhead, the fixed costs. These costs arise out of long-term commitments and the same cost must be assessed each month, regardless of the amount of production. A high level of production reduces the amount of fixed cost that must be covered by the selling price of each unit of production. For example, if fixed costs are $5,000 per month, the cost per unit will be $5 if 1,000 units are produced but only $1 if 5,000 units are produced. The selling price in the latter case can be set at $4 lower per unit; or the company's profit on each unit can be increased by that amount.

Marginal costs

An aspect of cost which is little understood by business people is called "marginal cost." This is the increase in total cost which occurs as more units are produced. If the total cost to produce one unit is $1,000 and the total cost to produce two units is $1,800, the marginal cost to produce the second unit is $800. If the first unit can be sold for $1,400, it will return a $400 profit. The second unit can be sold for as little as its marginal cost, $800, without diminishing the profit made on the original unit. Therefore, there appears to be some justifiable basis for considering additional production even when the market will not buy it at the same price which it was willing to pay for the original output. The relationship of the marginal cost concept to product pricing is discussed more fully in Chapter 19.

Summary of costs

The business person must learn to live with and control the costs involved in his enterprise. The main task, certainly, is to have a clear view of the elements of the business that contribute to cost and the amount that each contributes. From that point, the nature of the business operations will determine the classification of costs as fixed or variable. Cost figures are used by the business person in a thousand different ways. They help him to decide when to expand his business, and in which direction. They help him to locate soft spots in the enterprise and correct them. They set the level of activity on which the achievement of all business goals depends. One prime goal of business is profit, but profit cannot be determined until cost is known. In fact, we might almost say that business is guided by its costs rather than by its profits as it seeks expansion and growth.

The process of determining costs is by no means completely scientific. An enterprise which uses common facilities to produce a variety of goods may resort to arbitrary or estimated bases for determining the cost of the respective products. As a matter of record, there have been many instances in industry where the selling price of a product has been set too low or too high because of errors of omission in the process of costing the product. A too-low price may cause profit losses, and a too-high price may cause customer losses.

OTHER ASPECTS OF PRODUCTION

There are other ways of viewing a production system than through the medium of cost or efficiency. The concepts of capacity, seasonality, and productivity are particularly important to manufacturers and may significantly affect costs and profits.

Capacity

A production system may be said to have a certain capacity to produce. This is a measurement of its potential output, which may be expressed in units of production, hours of operation, dollar value of output, and so on. Such measurements are very useful indicators of the status of a business enterprise. They may be stated in terms of hours, days, years, or any period of time, depending on the nature of the business.

Capacity is in a sense a measure of the potential output that may result from an investment in a production system. Failure to reach this potential is thus a waste of investment. However, there may be good reasons for not working at peak potential, or peak capacity. When we consider the effect of idle potential on the fixed cost of the business, we begin to see how important this conception of capacity can be, for if not every unit of investment can pay its own way, then the whole may prove a poor investment. On the other hand, excessive load on a manufacturing system may result in vastly increased cost due to excessive wear, overtime payments, and similar items of additional expense.

Normal capacity

Rated capacity or normal capacity is the level at which the plant or machine or department operates in normal circumstances. Thus when the normal workday is 8 hours, and operations go on for 8 hours, the rated capacity or normal capacity is being used fully. If the workday went into overtime, the operating level would be in excess of 100 percent normal capacity.

Optimum capacity

Average speed in an automobile does not mean peak speed. And normal capacity in a plant or machine does not mean peak capacity. But average speed also does not mean the most efficient or optimum speed. The optimum capacity of a plant is the level of production when all the factors are considered. Figure 13-12 shows how the range of optimum capacity can be determined.

Actual operating level

Of course, the actual level of production at which a factory operates may not be the average or the peak or the optimum rate, just as the

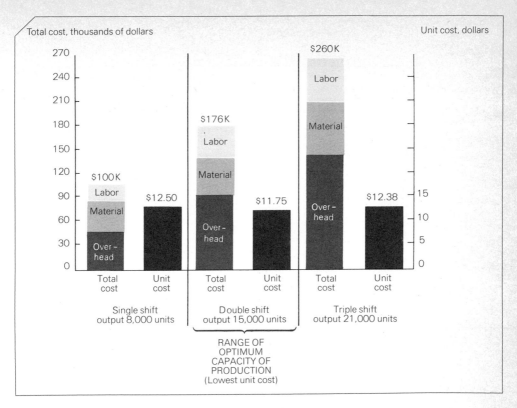

FIGURE 13-12 Illustration depicting optimum production level

Typically, the total cost increases as larger quantities are produced. The average cost to produce a unit at each level of production also varies; it tends to move from higher to lower levels as production becomes more efficient, and to return to higher average cost levels as production passes the optimum capacity level.

speed we drive at may not be average or peak or optimum. The workers may not wish to work the optimum number of hours. Competitors may force the plant to operate near or at peak capacity to meet their challenge. The pressure to provide employment, the desire to use equipment at high speed to gain maximum output before obsolescence, and similar considerations determine the actual level at which the factory produces. Again, management must take into account the long-term effects of actual operations on the life of machinery, on labor costs, on breakage, and on similar cost items. Figure 13-13 diagrams the relationship between actual operations and capacity levels.

Capacity problems

Perhaps the first problem for any plant manager is to determine the actual capacity of his plant. Once this is done, putting the capacity concept to use demands careful control of all the factors that enter

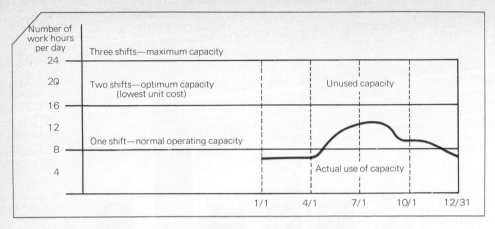

FIGURE 13-13 Capacity utilization—an illustration

Although various levels of capacity may be stated, most firms will never operate at the theoretical maximum capacity. Many reach optimum capacity, although most hope to operate at least at the level which is normal for their type of business. Seasonal factors cause the level of activity to vary at different times of the year.

into the productive process. Management may find that too much capacity is being left idle, and then must search for a means of using it effectively. In another case, the work load may be in excess of capacity; some means of increasing capacity or reducing the load is needed. Although excess work would seem a desirable problem for the business person, actually it may not be. Extensive overtime operations place a strain on workers and equipment alike, and such operations may defeat their own purpose if fatigue results in lower production rates, or even in excessive illness or absenteeism.

Human capacity

In every plant the capacity of personnel as well as machines needs to be calculated, and here management faces a real problem, for human capacities differ enormously. Although management has only a slight amount of control over human capacity in individual terms, it can control some of the factors that affect human capacity to produce, particularly the following:

1 Regularity of work volume. Workers produce best when the work load is steady and even, not irregular.

2 Availability of materials. A steady flow of materials helps to prevent interruption of work and loss of efficiency.

3 Clarity of instructions. The orders must be clear enough to maintain operations at a steady pace without interruptions to determine what ought to be done next.

4 Planned transitions. Transitions to new phases of production must be planned, to avoid excessive loss of work time.

5 Clear standards of performance. If standards are unclear, an excessive amount of production may be rejected at the final inspection. Further, uneven standards may overburden some phases of production and leave others with idle capacity.

Other, more general aspects of personnel management which affect human capacity to produce are discussed in Chapters 14 and 15.

Seasonality

Business firms which are affected by *seasonality*—the requirement for more or less commercial activity according to the time of year—are particularly conscious of the relation of capacity to usage since there may be very great differences between normal level of operation and peak operation during certain seasons. Irregular use of facilities is costly, and if the facilities are highly specialized, the excess cost may be unavoidable. This seasonal factor handicaps the firm that is seeking to balance productivity and capacity over the long run.

Stabilized production

Ideally, business firms should stabilize their production level at some norm that can be maintained on a year-round basis. This makes it easier to maintain a constant labor force and steady inventory levels, and is considerably more efficient than having alternate peak and idle periods. Stabilized production is possible only under certain conditions, however, and they cannot be met by all businesses. The principal reasons for failure to achieve stabilized production are:

1 Seasonal availability of raw materials, such as foods for canning or freezing.

2 Fluctuating demand, which produces storage problems. Perishable goods, for example, cannot be manufactured and stored until they are needed; they must be produced according to current demand.

3 Style changes, which make it undesirable to produce an excessively large inventory. Women's clothing, for example, cannot be produced too far in advance for fear of style change or obsolescence.

4 Manufacture of custom-made goods, which are produced to specifications and obviously cannot be made in advance.

Sometimes it is possible to make use of diversification as a device to achieve stabilized production. If the production of one line of goods is seasonal, it may be possible to add another product which will use the existing capacity during the off season.

Productivity

The search for higher output per unit of input—higher productivity—is constant in every manufacturing firm, and indeed in every business. Research departments and production planners spend a good part of their time looking for new methods and techniques to improve the rate of output of the firm. The usual method of measuring productivity is to relate the value of output to the input of labor and the investment in facilities. American industry has, over the years, increased productivity at a rate of about 3.5 percent each year; that is, a constant annual input of labor and investment in facilities results in an output that increases by 3.5 percent each year. This increased efficiency may result from new methods, new machinery, improved morale, or more efficient use of capacity. The key factor in productivity is cost, and the aspects of cost that we have already considered play an important role in the efforts of management to achieve higher productivity and a greater volume of output.

SUMMARY

A master plan is always needed to coordinate the personnel, materials, and equipment used for production. The chief task of production planning is to produce this master plan. The plan should ensure a continuous and efficient flow of work through the plant at minimum cost. This calls for the careful arrangement of materials, parts, equipment, personnel, storage space, etc., and for full control of production times, processes, and methods of work. A poor plan leads to additional cost, loss of output, inefficiency, and perhaps faulty products.

A control mechanism is needed to ensure conformity to plan when the business is actually operating. Controls must first detect variations from planned production and inventories and then introduce necessary corrective action. Inspections systems and paper control systems are usually essential parts of the control mechanism.

The optimum use of plant facilities, once they are planned and laid out, demands good routing and scheduling of work. Personnel and machines must be kept busy at all times. This means a steady flow of raw materials into all departments, good coordination among departments that contribute to the final product, and adequate preparation for emergency periods or rush orders.

Finally, a follow-up system, which may make use of either personnel or paper controls, or both, provides the means by which management can gauge the progress of particular orders through the plant. A useful index to the state of efficiency within the firm can be obtained by comparing these progress reports with the planned operation of the plant.

Fundamentally, the production of goods requires active consideration of numerous functions and costs, as well as their interrelationships. Efficiency may be measured in terms of volume of output, speed of production, achievement of schedules, and least cost.

QUESTIONS

1 Explain why production is accomplished in two stages: planning and control.

2 In what ways is the sales department involved in the planning and control of production? The purchasing department?

3 Process analysis is fundamental to plant layout. Discuss the validity of this statement.

4 How does the nature of the product or production process influence the physical layout? Illustrate such influences from your own experience.

5 What is the objective of motion study? Of time study?

6 Would you say that there are interrelationships among time study, motion study, and methods study? What is the nature of the interrelationships?

7 The grading of a time study is often pointed out as an inherent weakness in the time-study procedure. Why do you think this is so?

8 What is the difference between inspection and quality control?

9 Before inventory can be controlled, some specific planning must be done by management. What is it that must be planned?

10 Discuss the importance of good inventory control.

11 Under what circumstances is unit control of inventory preferable? Dollar control?

12 Identify the production planning activities which must occur before production routing and scheduling can be done.

13 Out of what circumstances do short-term and long-term cost arise?

14 Production costs will differ depending on what method of depreciation is used. Are the costs resulting from one method more valid than the costs resulting from some other method? Why?

15 Differentiate between variable and fixed cost features. Illustrate the features of each type.

16 What is meant by "spreading fixed costs"? Why is it an important consideration? Can variable costs be spread? Why?

17 What are the prime costs of production? What items of cost are included in manufacturing overhead?

18 What is meant by the marginal cost of production? How does it compare with the average cost of production?

19 Describe the various concepts of capacity. When should each concept be used?

20 Optimum level of production and most efficient level of production mean the same thing to many people. Define each so as to make their differences or similarities clear.

The purpose of this chapter   On many occasions, when a new business is formed or an older firm is expanded, management tends to concentrate its attention on the products, processes, and facilities required and gives very little attention to other matters. This is understandable, for the physical needs of an organization seem more pressing and more urgent during this phase of business activities than the quality of the personnel who will ultimately staff the organization. This is precisely the point at which management may commit a serious error by neglecting to adequately consider the work-force requirement and by devoting most of its energies to setting up plant facilities and processes. / Many external as well as internal factors play a role in staffing decisions. Government, union, and social pressures have a significant impact on the whole task of getting together and keeping a workforce. The specific work-force skills needed today may undergo change as the organization grows through the years and continuing attention must be paid to the staffing process so that both present and future staff requirements are kept in focus. / In this chapter, we shall examine the goals that management seeks in its overall personnel operation and shall consider the many factors which bear on the staffing activity. / Questions raised in the chapter include:

1 What goals does management seek through its personnel activity?

2 What does the worker seek through his employment?

3 How do government and unions influence the staffing situation?

4 How does management determine its work-force requirements?

5 How does the problem of staffing for management differ from the problem of staffing for the general workforce?

6 What are the work-force costs?

7 Is there a human side to staffing which must be considered?

14

THE STAFFING FUNCTION

Many of the more significant and perplexing problems that executives must face have their origin in the employees of the organization. Although we have developed machines that reduce the need for manpower, this does not mean that the need for manpower has declined, for every machine made in the past and every machine that may be developed in the future is the product of human thought and effort. The value of manpower is greater today than ever before.

STAFFING

Staffing has a number of meanings in business, but in its broadest sense it includes the recruitment, selection, training, promotion, retirement, and any other such action pertinent to all personnel from president to the lowest-skilled worker. It also includes all those activities required in planning work-force requirements. It is in this broad sense that staffing is discussed in this text. We are concerned with every company policy and every consideration which has something to do with the employees, whatever their functions. Not all aspects of staffing are matters that can be decided by management alone. Management decisions are tempered by federal or state law and by the activities of labor unions as well as by the opinions and desires of the individual worker. Nor should we forget that social change, which has raised the status of even the lowest-skilled worker, makes a significant impact on personnel policies. The staffing policies of even the largest organizations, then, are a result of the interplay of many pressures from government, unions, workers, society, and, of course, the pressures of the goals and objectives of management.

BASIC FACTORS

Perhaps the chief cause of staffing problems is that although people are employed to help achieve the organization's goals, the workers really seek employment to achieve their personal goals. When the goals of the organization are not compatible with those of the workers,

323

conflict and poor personnel relations result. There are bound to be certain areas of conflict, if only because high labor costs may reduce the size of business profit as well as increase the costs of goods and services. The basic personnel policies of any business should be designed to produce a working compromise between the goals of the organization and the goals of the workers.

MANAGEMENT GOALS AND PERSONNEL POLICY

From the management point of view, one basic goal is to control costs, and management will attempt to manipulate its personnel policies to achieve this goal. This does not mean, however, that management is concerned only with reducing labor costs. On the contrary, management has often found that it can achieve its goals and at the same time satisfy the demands of the legal, social, and economic environments if it seeks other goals such as the following:

1 Achieving the maximum development of each individual worker.
2 Using to the maximum the available human resources.
3 Creating harmonious working relations.

If an organization can increase the skills of its workers, use these skills effectively, and create working conditions and relations which foster these achievements, and, in addition, if its overall objectives are well conceived, then the realization of these objectives is much more likely to occur.

Maximum development of each worker

Good personnel management requires that at both work-force and managerial levels each employee's skill and efficiency be developed to the highest state possible. Doing so maximizes the contribution that the individual worker can make to the enterprise and to himself. It also reduces the possibility of having to use unqualified persons in responsible positions, for it creates a reserve of skill and ability that can be drawn on to fill important vacancies as they arise. The responsibility for the development of skills must rest with management, for many individuals lack the motivation for self-development.

In organizations where a philosophy of growth and change prevails there is both a need and an opportunity for individual development. In organizations with a high degree of decentralization, there can be a maximum opportunity for individual growth. Today, for example, we find that more managers and potential managers have achieved high levels of education and are seeking opportunities to better their positions. The more successful enterprises will be those which make a concerted effort to guarantee maximum individual development by providing opportunities.

Efficient use of human resources

For the most efficient possible use of worker skill, management must be able to decide how, when, and where the services of each individual are to be used. Flexibility in the placement of a worker is important to management but just as important is the need to put the right person on the right job. Too frequent shifting of a worker may have a negative impact on his relations with other workers. In some situations, the provisions of the union contract may govern when and where a worker may be shifted.

Harmonious working relations

Experience tells us that harmony in the workforce is too often the exception rather than the rule; therefore, a primary task of all those concerned for the organization's personnel is to eliminate as many causes of friction and discord as possible. Conflict within the workforce produces inefficiency, harmful internal competition, and other deleterious effects that should be avoided whenever possible.

WHY DO PEOPLE WORK?

Although many people do work because they must, this certainly is not the only influence on their choice of vocation. In general, people work to achieve satisfaction of their various personal needs. For example:

1 Subsistence—food, clothing, and shelter. Few workers are content to work for subsistence alone.

2 Security. This is an important psychic need of all individuals. Having a job or "working" is important in satisfying this need.

3 Self-development. Many people judge their job by the amount of opportunity it provides for their growth. Not all workers, however, care about growth or self-development.

4 Status. Social status, self-confidence, etc., are very strongly tied in with the job a person holds. A job which carries a title or one which coworkers hold in high esteem provides status for the jobholder.

Of course, the above are highly simplified examples of the forces which motivate workers. In fact, a satisfied workforce is not easily achieved. It requires that some balance between good and bad aspects of work be arrived at so that good aspects predominate.

WHAT MAKES A JOB A GOOD JOB?

Worker attitudes as to what constitutes a good job will vary depending on the worker's age, level of skill, background, and other factors. In any event, management should be concerned with what its workers consider to be the characteristics of a good job and use this information as a guide in establishing personnel policy.

Specifically, workers are usually concerned about the following job factors:

1 The physical environment of the job

2 Adequate and equitable wages

3 Fair treatment in matters other than wages

4 The degree of independence associated with the job—how much a man is on his own as opposed to being supervised

5 The feeling of satisfaction that comes from doing important work

THE GOVERNMENT ROLE IN PERSONNEL MATTERS

The needs of the American workers are a major governmental concern. However, prior to the early 1930s, very little was done by government to improve the lot of the working person. Since that time, the government has established a basic policy which it hopes to implement through legislation and the cooperative efforts of business. Specifically, it aims to accomplish the following goals:

1 To encourage the practice of collective bargaining; that is, to encourage and make possible the unionization of more workers

2 To raise the standard of living of all wage earners

3 To increase the productivity of the workforce

4 To provide greater security for the worker both off and on the job

5 To broaden the area of worker rights

The National Labor Relations Act (1935)

Our basic law governing labor-management relations is the National Labor Relations Act of 1935. We refer to it as the basic law because it establishes the American philosophy for labor-management relations: free collective bargaining. To enable free collective bargaining the law prohibits certain "unfair labor practices" on the part of employers:

1 Interference with labor efforts to form a union or to engage in concerted activity for mutual aid or protection.

2 Employer domination of labor organization or financial support of unions by employers. (This was aimed at the then popular company union which was sponsored and dominated by management.)

3 Discrimination in hiring or tenure or any other term of employment against workers who were members of labor unions.

4 Discharge of any employee because of his activities under the terms of the act. A worker cannot be fired simply because he charged the company with discrimination or with interference in workers' attempt to organize a union.

5 Refusal to bargain in good faith with the duly elected union representatives.

The National Labor Relations Board was also established to administer and enforce the provisions of this act. The act was somewhat one-sided, since it restricted the employer but placed no significant restrictions on the union. It led to the rapid growth of unions in the years that followed, and management complained bitterly that the unions abused their rights under the act. In consequence, the National Labor Relations Act was amended in 1947 by the Taft-Hartley Act, which attempted to secure a better balance between the rights of labor and employer.

The Taft-Hartley Act

The Taft-Hartley Act retained the basic restrictions on employers outlined in the National Labor Relations Act but placed new limits on labor union activity, for which it was heartily denounced by labor. The composition and responsibilities of the National Labor Relations Board were also amended. The *closed shop* (making union membership a condition of employment) was outlawed, although the *union shop* (requiring workers to join after a trial period) was permitted. Union contributions to political funds were forbidden, and a list of "unfair" union practices was added to the law, including:

1 Coercing or restraining any employee who exercised his rights under the act

2 Causing an employer to discriminate against an employee

3 Refusing to bargain in good faith with the employer

4 Engaging in unlawful strikes or boycotts

5 Requiring excessive initiation fees of members

6 Requiring employers to pay for services which were not actually performed (a practice known as *featherbedding*)

The Landrum-Griffin Act

The Labor-Management Reporting and Disclosures Act of 1959—known as the Landrum-Griffin Act—arose out of congressional investigations of union activities. These hearings led Congress to the conclusion that the governing bodies of labor unions were too often corrupt, and that too many union officials flagrantly abused their authority and neglected their responsibilities. It was found that collusion between management and labor unions resulted in abuses. The major provisions of this law relate to such matters as the rights of union members in the conduct of union affairs, the responsibility of union leadership to keep its members informed, free and open elections, and the reporting of certain financial information to the Secretary of Labor.

The Civil Rights Act

The long-debated Civil Rights Act, passed by Congress in July 1964, has a section devoted to employment practices. The basic purpose of this section is to eliminate discrimination in employment. The law specifies certain unlawful practices for employers, labor organizations, and others. Specifically it provides:

1 That an employer may not refuse to hire a person, or a labor organization refuse him membership because of his race, color, religion, or national origin

2 As above, that a person may not be deprived of employment opportunities, such as promotions, for the same reasons

3 That an employment agency may not refuse to refer a person for employment or discriminate against a person, for the same reasons

This law has had a far-reaching impact on employment and worker relations. More types of work will be available to specific groups of workers than ever before. Jobs previously restricted to males are now open to females unless the job requires the physical strength of males. Conversely, jobs once the sole province of females must now be open to males.

Wages and hours legislation

Laws to control the hours of work and amount of wages paid to American workers first appeared during the Depression years—the 1930s. Their purpose was to spread employment and eliminate low wage rates and excessive working hours. The two basic federal laws (with amendments) in this area are the Fair Labor Standards Act of 1938 (the Wages and Hours Law) and the Walsh-Healy Government Contracts Act of 1936.

The wages and hours law

The Fair Labor Standards Act, as amended, includes four basic provisions and applies to all persons employed by firms engaged in interstate commerce, or producing goods for such commerce, unless they are specifically exempted by the act. The law applies to workers paid by the hour, by piecework, by salary, by commission, or by any other standards. Its provisions are:

1 It prescribes a minimum rate of pay.

2 It requires payment of 1½ times the base rate for all work in excess of 40 hours per week.

3 It sets a minimum age of 16 years for general employment.

4 It requires all employers to maintain records of hours worked and wages paid to their workers.

The Walsh-Healy Act

The Walsh-Healy Act applies to workers employed by firms that have contracts with the United States government in excess of $10,000. Since the federal government spends tens of billions of dollars each year for the purchase of goods and services, this law affects a substantial number of workers. The act has two basic provisions, one affecting wages, the other affecting the hours of work:

1 All work in excess of 8 hours per day must be compensated for at a rate not less than 1½ times the regular rate.

2 The minimum wage is based on the prevailing wage rate in the community for the type of work involved.

Social security laws

Social security laws, though not strictly speaking labor laws, are closely related to employment and play an important role in personnel administration. The basic Social Security Act was passed in 1935 and has been amended several times since. It contains three major programs: social insurance, public assistance to the needy, and services for children.

Social insurance

For millions of Americans, the most important provisions of the Social Security Act are those concerned with old-age and survivors' insurance. One section of the law provides for pensions for retired workers and benefits for the survivors of workers who were covered by the act. The dollar amount of the benefits is controlled by Congress and is subject to change at any time.

Younger workers are usually more concerned with the provisions of the act which provide benefits for survivors rather than those provisions which provide for retirement. The survivor benefits amount to a type of "life insurance" which, in the event of the death of the worker, will provide benefits for his survivors. As the worker approaches retirement age, he or she becomes more concerned with those provisions of the act which provide an income during retirement and, if the worker is married, also provide benefits for the survivor.

Old-age and survivors' benefits are an important concern in industrial relations because a firm's fringe benefits program is usually tied to the provisions of the Social Security Act. In general, the more generous the retirement benefits provided by the act, the less that must be provided as retirement income from alternate sources. In addition, few workers can afford to carry enough life insurance to provide for all their families' needs in the event of death or disability and in this respect the provisions of the act make substantial amounts of income available to the family.

Unemployment benefits

The Social Security Act was passed when unemployment was society's greatest concern. The act has continued to benefit the unemployed worker during good and bad times. Unemployment insurance is a provision which creates credits in a fund which may be drawn out by the worker during periods of unemployment. This fund is created by a payroll tax which is levied on the employer by both state and federal governments. The program is actually administered by each state, and benefits paid to unemployed workers vary from state to state.

Health and safety of the workforce

In many firms, health and safety activities are the responsibility of the personnel or industrial relations department. There are several reasons why this is so. First, the personnel department, in a sense, oversees each job as to its content, physical requirements, and working conditions. In addition, the department is responsible for recommending for employment only those applicants who meet the required physical standards.

The health and safety of the workforce have long been recognized as a management responsibility. This is ensured by a variety of laws, such as Workmen's Compensation laws, as well as by an enlightened management philosophy which recognizes the responsibility of the employer to safeguard life and limb of the employee. In many instances, the mechanization or automation of processes has been initiated to provide safer working conditions. As a rule, management carries insurance to cover the costs of accidents and impaired health.

THE IMPACT OF LABOR UNIONS ON PERSONNEL POLICY

The growing impact of labor unions on personnel policy is partly a corollary to government regulation of business, for the growth of unions is chiefly due to the policy of encouragement on the part of the federal and state governments. The Wagner Act of 1935 showed plainly that Congress strongly desired the development of powerful labor organizations. The act states in its preamble:

It is hereby declared to be the policy of the United States to eliminate the causes of certain substantial objections to the free flow of commerce, and to mitigate and eliminate these obstructions . . . by encouraging the practice and procedures of collective bargaining and by protecting the exercise by workers of full freedom of association, self-organization, and designation of representatives of their own choosing, for the purpose of negotiating the terms and conditions of their employment. . . .

Today some 18 million of more than 80 million United States workers belong to one labor union or another. The benefits which these workers obtain for their labor in the way of wages, working conditions, pension rights, and so on are largely determined by union-employer negotiations. During the past decade the number of workers employed by the manufacturing sector of our economy has declined. Traditionally this group of workers has been the prime source of union membership. The result has been a decline in the percentage of the total labor force which is unionized, which may be offset someday by the increasing union membership among those workers in the "public sector," such as firemen, policemen, teachers, and other public sector employees.

WHAT ARE UNION GOALS?

We cannot reasonably talk about the goals of the "average" union since some are organized on the basis of crafts or skills and others are organized by industry. Some unions have membership which consists largely of skilled workers while others include a wide variety and level of work skills. Over the years, however, a pattern has developed, and we can at least make some general statements as to union goals as follows:

1 To limit the exercise of authority over labor by management
2 To participate more fully in the formulation of business policies which are of concern to labor
3 To maximize the development of the entire membership rather than the development of individuals
4 To stimulate the growth of union membership as well as spheres of influence

ARE UNION GOALS THE SAME AS WORKER GOALS?

The answer to this question has to be both yes and no. Both the union and the individual worker want higher standards of living, better working conditions, more job security, and a stronger voice in the formation of company policy. But since the union is primarily concerned with progress in the status of the total membership rather than with that of the individual member, the result of union activity sometimes is that the individual worker is held back and that those with greater seniority move ahead or reap benefits.

WORK-FORCE REQUIREMENTS

The number of personnel and the variety of skills and experience which make up a workforce depend principally on the volume of products or services which the firm supplies and on the type of manufacture or the process used. A job-order machine shop must hire highly skilled men. A large assembly plant needs workers who can be trained in a few hours to perform some relatively simple repetitive tasks. A hospital requires the services of a broad spectrum of semi-skilled to very skilled personnel, some with limited training and experience, others with extensive training and lengthy experience.

How many workers are needed?

The number of workers required depends mainly on the volume of activity to be performed, whether it be production of goods, sales, or services. An activity forecast is a typical starting place for determining personnel requirements. The types of skills and the number of workers are not determined solely by the forecast, however, for the way in which work is performed and the extent to which machines, advanced technology, automation, and computers are utilized has a distinct bearing on both the quantity and quality of manpower needed to get the work done. As any one of these features is introduced or changed in a work situation there is bound to be an impact on the workforce requirement, which may result in certain jobs being eliminated and other jobs being created.

Another significant factor affecting work-force requirements is the variation which may occur from year to year in the level of business activity. In general, the features described in the paragraph above as influencing the work-force size are important whether activity levels are high or low. However, the real or total impact on total workforce is determined by the general economic level of the country.

Manpower sources

Most businesses have a continuous need for new personnel. This need may be due to growth, which creates new jobs, or to normal labor turnover from retirement, death, disability, separation, or worker dissatisfaction with the job or the company. Depending upon the type of business activity, normal turnover may be high or low. For example, the turnover of clerks in the retailing field is high compared to the turnover of personnel staffing a bank. In any event, work-force requirements involve both a consideration of the need to replace individuals as well as the need to fill newly created positions.

Management does not always find it possible to plan its future manpower requirements precisely. Additional workforce may be needed on short notice to fill needs which were not anticipated. To cover such a possibility, the personnel department must attempt to locate a source of workers that can be used to fill the needs, skilled and unskilled, as they arise. That is, it must create what is known as a "labor pool."

STAFFING FOR MANAGEMENT

The types of managers needed by a firm depend on the way it is organized. But unlike staffing for the workforce, which can be defined in terms of specific skills required to do the job, management skill requirements are difficult to pinpoint. Two managers may be equally effective in similar jobs, yet may use entirely different styles of management with different emphasis on the specific managerial skill requirements. The rapid changes that are taking place in business, coupled with changing views about what the process of management should be, also make it more difficult to quantify requisite skills and abilities.

Management specialists and generalists

Modern organizations require both specialists and generalists as managers. Specialists are needed to provide specific skills necessary to carry out business functions. But specialists tend by nature to be narrow in their viewpoint and tend to isolate their function from all other functions. They tend to make decisions for the benefit of their function and position, rather than for the benefit of the overall organization.

Therefore, there is the need for generalists who can provide leadership for a number of related or interdependent functions. A generalist is needed in the marketing function, for example, to blend the specialized but related functions of the market researcher, advertising manager, and sales manager into a unified marketing effort. There is similarly a need for a generalist who is capable of unifying the interdependent activities taking place in the functional areas of marketing, production, finance, etc.

The basic skill of a good general manager is a conceptual skill: the capacity to see the impact of changes on all segments of the organization and to see the impact beyond the local and immediate to the ultimate point of the decision.

WORK-FORCE COSTS

Although the efficiency of many organizations depends primarily on their ability to control and limit the cost of labor, it would be unwise to assume that high labor costs are indicative of inefficiency. Some enterprises have inherently high labor costs and others do not. On a job-order machine shop, the cost of labor may represent 75 cents out of every dollar spent; a self-service retail store may spend as little as 5 cents of each expense dollar on labor; a legal firm or a hospital has large labor costs. The extent to which labor costs are relatively high depends on the type of enterprise and the product or service it provides.

Labor costs include more than the dollars paid to employees. The total labor cost must also include the dollar costs of vacations, sick leave, paid holidays, insurance, pensions, workmen's compensation, unemployment benefits, social security, and many other benefits. A company may have relatively low payroll cost and still have a much higher labor cost than its competitors because of a variety of benefits which it provides its workers.

Company labor cost may be low, and yet the cost of producing a unit of goods or services may be quite high. The opposite is also possible; that is, even though labor cost may be high, the unit cost of labor may be low. Since the unit cost is one of the determinants of the selling price of goods and services it must be obvious that to the customer who buys these goods and services unit labor cost is very important.

The worker's view of labor costs

To the worker, the company's labor cost consists of his wages and whatever other benefits he receives. He is equally concerned with the pay that he takes home and the other benefits he receives. In particular, however, workers wish to be paid wages that are adequate and equitable.

Adequacy of wages refers to the number of dollars needed to maintain or improve the worker's economic status. *Equitability of wages* refers to the concept of equal pay for equal work. The worker's desire for an equitable wage can be satisfied by careful job analysis and evaluation on the part of the employer. See Chapter 15.

The union and labor costs

Union leaders take a great interest in labor costs. Their thinking goes well beyond the considerations of adequacy and equitability that are the primary concern of the worker. Union leaders feel that the worker ought to receive an increasing share of the total earnings of business, and they have pressed constantly toward this goal. They also feel that workers are entitled to wages 12 months of the year just as management is, and they are making gains in this direction.

The consumer and labor costs

The general public—as consumers—has a vital interest in labor costs because they affect the price of every item of goods and services bought. Rising labor costs may force the price of goods up beyond the reach of the consumer. Communities, be they towns or cities or states, suffer when the local businesses on which they depend for tax revenues, employment, etc., are forced to close down because high cost makes it impossible for these businesses to compete effectively with other domestic or foreign producers.

Labor cost and foreign trade

An increasingly well-understood effect of labor costs is their influence on the course of American international trade. American labor's jobs can be protected by imposing tariffs or import duties on goods brought into this country and produced by foreign competitors in countries where wage rates are lower. Tariffs may bring about at least two results: the cost of the imported goods is increased in the American market, and the foreign countries may retaliate by placing import duties on American goods which may, in effect, bar these markets to American producers.

The effect of labor cost on the United States international trade cannot be ignored. Over the long run we must export more than we import to protect our financial strength in world markets.

THE HUMAN SIDE OF STAFFING

Human relations is not a new problem of organizations, but it is a problem that has grown in complexity and it warrants special attention. There have been a number of changes in the organizational environment of enterprise that bear on human behavior.

Traditionally managers have approached human relations from the "economic man" concept. That is, an individual's basic motivation is economic, and through the application of economic sanctions and rewards, management can shape workers into the type of behavior pattern that suits managerial objectives. However, the price a person must pay for being out of work is gradually declining and, along with this, the threat of unemployment is not as potent a weapon in achieving high levels of efficiency and in building effective work teams. Unemployment insurance, severance pay, and a significant change in the philosophy of welfare tend to cushion the economic blow of even fairly long periods of unemployment.

The size of an organization also contributes to the problem of human relations. When organization is small, work groups are small, there is a close working relationship with the boss (who is perhaps also the owner), and there are fewer problems of coordination and communication. Increased size, however, makes possible a number of technological and economic advantages which cannot be ignored, for large organizations have greater capacity for doing more to alleviate the major causes of poor human relations. They can afford to employ the specialized skills necessary to develop better plans to stabilize employment, to provide better wage and salary administration, and to provide for a broader range of fringe benefits to reduce the worker's dependency on himself now and in the future. The large organization need not be overwhelming in structure, for it may be advantageously organized as a large number of small operating units instead of as a small number of large operating units. Large work units are not absolutely necessary to achieve economies of scale and with many smaller work units the lines of communication to coordinating managers can be shortened so that people have access to those who can make the decisions.

SUMMARY

Management will continue to face the general problem of staffing the enterprise in the years ahead; however, the nature of the problem will change as mechanization and automation, social change, and a better-educated workforce make their full impact.

As a result of a continuing educational effort and more responsible collective bargaining, unionism has gained a much wider acceptance by society as a whole. Groups that felt unionization was beneath them a decade ago, such as public school teachers and college professors, are now an active part of the union movement. The government seeks to improve worker income levels by enacting minimum wage laws, by encouraging annual wage increases, by "suggesting" wage rate settlements in certain collective bargaining situations, and, of course, by supporting unions and collective bargaining.

Our various social security laws, aimed primarily at the unemployed and retired worker, have set the stage for other types of worker security programs financed largely by the employers. These include life insurance, hospital and medical assistance, payments to support further education, severance pay, and assistance in finding employment when layoffs are necessary.

The question of worker rights will always be with us, for there is no firm basis for enumerating what are and what are not worker rights; the concept of worker rights is constantly changing. The law guarantees certain rights such as the right to join a union, and there is legislation relating to discrimination against employees because of sex, race, religion, and so forth.

The internal and external factors which influence personnel policy making within an organization are bound to be more difficult to cope with in the years ahead. Perhaps the most significant factor in recent decades has been the increasing limitation of management's freedom of action in the personnel field. Restrictions have been imposed by government action, by the force of public opinion, by social pressures, and by the workers themselves banded together in organized groups.

We must expect additional staffing problems as the workers' economic goals become more easily and more completely attainable by the combination of wages and other benefits and as the workers then seek more satisfactions of a social nature.

BUSINESS ITEM

Swedish workers have a safety valve

Even in Sweden, vaunted bastion of industrial democracy, there are problems of worker discontent akin to those in the United States. For some time, the Swedish Employers Federation, believing that two-way communication in the company increases a worker's satisfaction with his job, has pushed for a new style in employee publications. The idea proposed is that company house organs carry articles written by employees, controversial or not, as well as the articles which express the company's viewpoints.

The advantages of such an open press are believed to far outweigh the disadvantages in that criticism about the company comes out in the open rather than showing up in discontented employees who wander about grumbling. The Swedes admit that their executives at first took exception at published criticism and controversial issues but can become used to it and even get to like it. There is not a universal acceptance of this idea in Sweden and, of course, many companies still have employee publications which reflect only what the boss is thinking.

United States executives do not yet seem ready to accept the Swedish proposal. They prefer not to editorialize in the employee publication and feel that other channels are available for dealing with worker discontent.

Management on the move

Many business corporations have a policy of transferring managers from place to place every few years. The reason for this is that multiple exposure is a good way to build top executives. Today, business managers are looking beyond the mere benefits of such a policy and are assessing the costs it imposes on the company and the people involved.

Businesses suffer because they lose the potential benefits of an executive's ability to establish connections in a community, to influence local political decisions, and to build a corporate image. When executives know that their stay in a community is short-lived, they are apt not to become involved in local affairs. Much the same is true of the executive's family. Wives lose much of the opportunity to develop a career of their own and the continual interruption of a child's education imposes a cost that is high.

QUESTIONS

1 What is perhaps the chief cause of staffing problems? Explain why this is so.

2 Why are decisions relating to manpower seldom made by management alone? What forces prevent such unilateral actions?

3 Who should be responsible for individual worker development? Why?

4 Specifically, how does an employer achieve the maximum utilization of human resources? Can this be a unilateral action? Explain.

5 What satisfactions does the worker seek through employment? What do you believe to be the order of importance of these satisfactions? How may this order or list be modified in the next decade or two?

6 To what extent are worker goals and union goals alike? Dissimilar? Does it matter whether the worker is considering himself as an employer; as a customer for goods and services?

7 Picture yourself as:

    a A part-time worker while attending school

    b A graduate looking for your first "career" job

    c A person approaching retirement years

For each case, what are the features which you feel would constitute a good job?

8 What reasons does the government have for playing a role in personnel matters?

9 Compare the National Labor Relations Act with the Taft-Hartley Act.

10 What are the goals of the Civil Rights Act?

11 Explain the provisions of the Wages and Hours Law.

12 How does the Walsh-Healy Act differ from the Wages and Hours Law?

13 Social Security legislation provides security for workers in a variety of circumstances both present and future. What are the various provisions of the law which provide such security?

14 How do the goals of management, government, and the union compare in respect to matters regarding the workforce?

15 What factors enter into the determination of work-force requirements?

16 Which are easier to define, work-force skills or the management skills required to do the job? Why?

17 Is the cost of labor (wages) too high? Answer this from the viewpoint of each of the following:

a A worker

b An employer

c A customer of the business

d The union business agent

e A government economist

f A foreign producer of competing products

g A foreign user of the product produced in the United States

18 From a human relations point of view which would you rather work for—a large organization or a small organization? Why?

The purpose of this chapter The proper selection, orientation, and training of personnel are the first steps in carrying out the staffing function. In addition, since the day-to-day relations of the work environment are very important, the workers want to know what opportunities there are for advancement and how people will be selected for the new opportunities as they arise. They want to know how wages are determined and what they must do to move up on the wage scale. / In this chapter we shall examine the various techniques and methods used to carry out the personnel operations of an organization. Emphasis will be on the techniques employed in personnel work, the goals of personnel work, and the methods of selecting and placing personnel most effectively. In addition, the various methods used to distinguish between the performances of workers, the bases for promoting and transferring workers, how jobs are rated, how management determines its pay scales, and other related topics are covered. / Questions raised in this chapter include:

1 What is the appropriate organizational status for the personnel function?

2 How does a personnel department carry out its function in selection and placement?

3 What are the basic steps in the selection procedure, and what aids are available?

4 What training methods facilitate the matching of personnel with jobs?

5 What factors does management consider when rating workers?

6 What is seniority, how is it measured, and how is it used?

7 How does management determine what a job is worth?

8 What are fringe benefits? How important are they to the worker?

15 PERSONNEL MANAGE-MENT

MENT This chapter will emphasize the activities that make up the work of the personnel department. Management, as we learned in the previous chapter, must determine the number and types of workers that are needed in the enterprise. Once these decisions have been made, the tasks of locating, recruiting, selecting, and training, as well as arranging other personnel matters, generally fall on a personnel department. To achieve the maximum efficiency in the use of human resources, the workforce must be properly assigned and reasonably contented. Personnel policies must be soundly based and fairly executed, particularly in the vital activities of promotions, wages, and ratings. The company must be aware of the human aspects of the labor force and must be prepared to make adjustments in its own goals in order to achieve and maintain a well-adjusted work group.

THE ROLE OF THE PERSONNEL DEPARTMENT

The actual personnel functions performed will vary from one firm to the next; they depend on the size, complexity, and activity of the business. The state of the personnel department within the firm also varies. Some managements attach great importance to personnel work and make the director of personnel a vice president or a major executive of the firm. Others consider personnel work of less importance and assign it accordingly. A large personnel department will normally carry out some of or all the following functions:

1 Formulation of basic personnel policies and procedures which become basic guidelines for employer-employee relations

2 Acting as clearing houses for information about employee conduct and attitudes toward management, the job, and the firm

3 Recruiting and selection of new employees

4 Orientation and training of new employees

5 Supervision of employee-rating programs

6 Assisting line managers with employee problems, such as promotion, demotion, transfer, discharge, etc.

7 Preparing a job analysis and a job evaluation for each position in the firm

8 Assisting in the establishment of an equitable system of worker compensations and benefits

9 Assisting management in collective bargaining negotiations

10 Advising management on the laws governing employer-employee relations

There are, of course, many additional operations—such as notifying company people of publicity about personnel policies, and health and safety control—that sometimes fall to the personnel department. In all these areas, specific techniques or methods based on special knowledge need to be developed and used efficiently.

THE ORGANIZATION OF THE PERSONNEL FUNCTION

The personnel function as carried out in a line organization differs from the way that the function is carried out in a line and staff type organization. In the line type organization there may actually be no separate personnel department. In Figure 15-1, the personnel responsibilities are taken over by the line manager. Since he is primarily concerned with supervising production from his unit, he may deal with personnel matters summarily as a "necessary evil." In a line and staff type organization, such as that suggested in Figure 15-2, the personnel department operates as a specialized staff agency, advising both top management and the line managers in all matters related to their personnel.

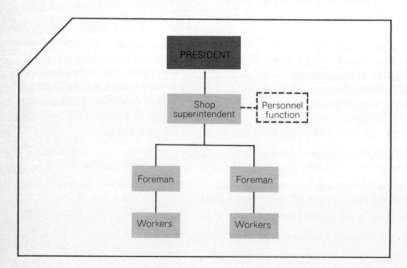

FIGURE 15-1   Personnel function in a line-organization structure

Personnel responsibilities are assumed by the shop superintendent.

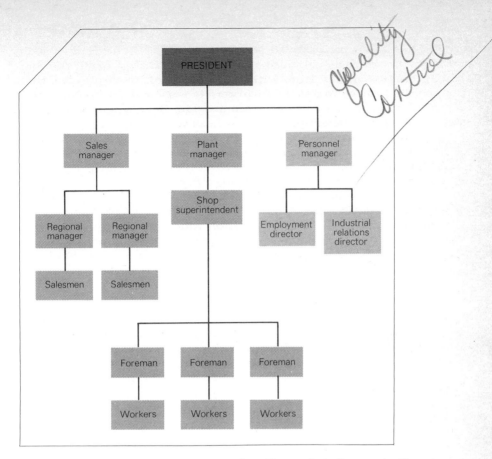

Quality Control

FIGURE 15-2   Personnel department in a line and staff organization

As a specialized staff agency the personnel department advises top management and line officers on personnel problems.

THE NEED FOR PERSONNEL POLICY

A personnel department cannot operate and the personnel function cannot be carried out properly until management has established a clear set of personnel goals and the policies which are to be adhered to in order to achieve these goals. Of course, the personnel department may assist management in preparing these policies.

The basic personnel policy of the firm defines the general attitude the firm takes towards its workforce. Are the workers to be considered "partners" in the enterprise or merely an added cost to the business? Will the firm recruit actively for new personnel? Are promotions to be made from within the firm? Will the firm hire only skilled personnel or will it establish facilities for training new personnel? All these and many other questions should be answered by a well-conceived personnel policy.

Company policy and labor requirements

The type of labor pool needed by an enterprise will depend in some measure on company policies on promotion, training, etc. If the company promotes chiefly from within the ranks of its employees, then the need for recruiting skilled workers is lessened, for usually only a lower-level job will be filled from outside. Such a policy makes it very necessary to select initially workers who have a high potential for growth, but it does not make the selection process independent of the outside availability of skilled workers.

On the other hand, few business establishments can promote exclusively from inside the firm. Often the men available for promotion from within are less capable than those who could be obtained from outside the firm. Further, if workers are assured of promotion from within, there may be less competition among them for improving their position and the possibility of lax performance increases. Before any policy is set, both the good and bad features must be considered.

SELECTION OF EMPLOYEES

Many personnel problems result from the faulty selection of employees. Good selection does not mean simply finding and hiring an available person who has the skills needed for a particular job. Good selection is concerned with the long-run as well as the immediate problems of staffing. It asks whether the new employee is suited to advancement in the organization and whether he or she will fit well into the existing organization.

Business people cannot afford to look at the selection process causually, nor can they work on a trial-and-error basis as was commonly done in the past. In many union contracts the right of an employer to release or transfer employees is severly limited once the worker has completed the probationary period of employment which may be as short as 30 days. Employers cannot always fire a person simply because he does a poor job, or because a better employee is available. Sometimes the only way to be rid of an undesirable employee is to eliminate his job completely; and even in such an event there is no guarantee that this method will work.

Recruiting

The modern relationship between employer and employee, which limits the once-complete freedom of the employer to hire and fire as he pleased, has led management to attach much more significance than previously to the process of selecting employees. For example, many firms no longer rely on simply employing the best of the voluntary applicants for a position. Instead, they actively seek out prospective employees and encourage them to apply; this is called "recruitment." Although recruitment is expensive in one respect, it creates more competition for jobs, offers the employer a much wider range of selection, and to some extent reduces the possibility of making a poor selection. When compared with the costly results of poor selection, the cost of recruitment is considered well justified by many firms.

Internal and external labor supplies

The labor supply already available within a firm is a good source of manpower even though it should not be the only one. If the personnel department maintains adequate records of each employee's performance on the job, these records are probably the most complete and accurate evaluations available and can be used to determine the growth potential and the capacity of the workers. This method of singling out employees for advancement in position is usually favorably looked on by both the employees and the union.

External labor sources may provide greater variety and in this respect may be better. However, recruitment outside the firm has the disadvantage of being costly and time-consuming. If it is company policy to engage in external recruiting there are various techniques for obtaining higher-caliber employees.

Some firms deliberately seek to hire top-level or other desirable employees away from competing firms. Such "pirating" is usually accompanied by offers of higher wages and other benefits as bait. Many firms use public and private employment agencies to provide manpower, and some of these agencies perform a valuable screening service that simplifies the selection process by eliminating workers who are not suited to the prospective employer's needs. Colleges and universities, technical schools, and labor unions are other important sources of workers. In each case, the employer has the advantage of securing an employee whose ability and skill are reasonably well-known in advance. A student with a degree in mechanical engineering or accounting and an adequate academic record or a union bricklayer or carpenter should be able to perform the duties of his specialized field of education or training.

Centralized and decentralized selection

In a small organization, each group or department often selects its own new employees, and there is usually no centralized employment office for the firm. The current trend, however, is in the direction of a centralized selection system that uses the specialized skills of a personnel department and entrusts it with the responsibility for the selection process for all the organization's work-force requirements. For the large firm especially, the advantages of centralized selection far outweigh any possible disadvantages:

1 Centralized selection eliminates the duplication of activity and thus reduces administrative costs.

2 It frees the line manager from the details of hiring, leaving him with more time for the direct supervision of the work of his area.

3 Centralized selection has the potential for making selection more accurate and scientific. A skilled personnel specialist, armed with the latest tools of the profession, can produce a better analysis of the applicant than can be arrived at through "personal judgements" made hastily by line managers who are burdened with other duties.

4 It permits the development of a centralized manpower pool in which the caliber of the potential employees is known.

5 Centralized selection permits a wider range of placement opportunities within the firm. An applicant for a position in one department may not be well suited to that job but he may be well qualified for another job which is open in a different department.

6 Centralized selection helps to eliminate favoritism in the selection process.

THE TOOLS FOR PERSONNEL SELECTION

Personnel selection normally begins when a new job is created or when a vacancy occurs in the workforce. The personnel department is informed of the vacancy and is requested to find a new employee to fill the job. Clearly, before the process of locating, screening, and hiring can begin, the personnel department needs to know exactly what the new employee is expected to do on the job and the skills and any other special requirement he must possess.

Figure 15-3 outlines the steps in the personnel process which attempts to match a man to a job. Orientation and training, which complete this initial matching of the individual and the job, will be discussed later.

The job description

In a great many businesses, large and small, the position to be filled is outlined in some detail and written up as a formal job description

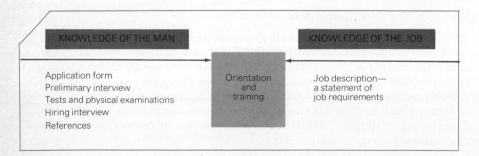

FIGURE 15-3 Matching the man and the job

CLEVAX ENGINEERING COMPANY

Job Description

Job title: Engine lathe operator   Job number: P-454

Departments where used: Tool room, maintenance, machine shop, foundry

General description:

This job requires the operation of a variety of lathes up to 16-inch capacity. Operators are expected to perform any and all work that the machine is designed to do. This is not a production job, rather a job-shop type of work.

Allied jobs:

   Screw machine operator, milling machine operator

Job requirements:

1. Eyesight corrected to 20/40
2. Average to good strength
3. Ability to work from blueprints, sketches, or models
4. Ability to set up own work
5. Ability to use micrometers and other inspection devices

Job conditions:

1. Operator works with minimum supervision
2. Job requires standing for prolonged periods
3. Accidents are rare but workers must wear safety glasses while operating machine

Employment terms:

1. Regular shift work (except maintenance department)
2. Wages paid on hourly basis
3. Job pays from $2.35 to $3.80 per hour
4. Maintenance department employees are expected to work on weekends and holidays when emergency conditions warrant

Promotion:

Promotion may be to toolmaker, assistant foreman, or foreman

Additional requirements:

Height: 5 feet 4 inches to 6 feet 2 inches

FIGURE 15-4   A job-description form

which describes only the position, not the person who will fill the job. Typical job descriptions are shown in Figures 15-4 and 15-5. A job description will usually include:

1 The name and title of the job

2 Departments which use this job

3 Allied or related jobs (as possible sources of substitutions)

CLEVAX ENGINEERING COMPANY

Job Title __Factory auditor_____ Job No __A-591_____

Department __Factory cost_____ Date __October 6, 19--____

Summary

Directs supervisors engaged in all accounting activities. Prepares and issues accounting reports and determines internal accounting procedures whenever necessary. Represents the accounting department in meetings with government representatives regarding cost matters.

1. Responsible for the control and the direction of the following departments: bookkeeping, cost-billing, invoicing, timekeeping, payroll, comptometer, and telephone service

2. Responsible for the issuance of all reports and correspondence and for the signing of checks controlled by and demanded of the factory auditor

3. Responsible for the preparation of special accounting reports

    A. Directs the preparation of reports showing forecasts of sales, expected costs of sales, and expenses by contract

    B. Directs the preparation of special burden studies when requested

    C. Directs the preparation of reports for the Bureau of Aeronautics and for the Naval Cost Inspection Service

4. Responsible for reviewing the minutes of labor relations and plant-union shop meetings to determine if any wage adjustments are to be made

5. Responsible for the analyzing and the follow-up of all government contracts to determine accounting procedures for approval of division comptroller

6. Responsible for representing the accounting department when matters of contracts and accounting procedures are discussed with the government

FIGURE 15-5   A partial job description for a management position

4 Conditions pertaining to the job (skills needed, supervision available, working conditions, hazards, etc.)

5 The job responsibilities

6 Employment terms (pay rate, holidays, bonuses, benefits)

7 Qualifications required of person filling job (physical abilities and characteristics)

8 Any other special conditions which must be satisfied by the job-holder in order to adequately fulfill the job requirements

Preparing the job description

Job descriptions should be prepared for each job as soon as the job is created. On many occasions, however, a job description may not be written up until some time after a job has been created. In such a case, information about the job can be obtained from the workers, from supervisors, and from direct observation of the job. All three sources should be used and questions should be raised in a person-to-person situation, particularly if the job is in industrial production where workers generally dislike filling out forms or questionnaires. A completed job description is the first step in the process of filling the job with a satisfactory employee. Other steps follow.

The job application form

Most workers applying for jobs in industry must complete a form or application. The purpose of the application form is to make available in a convenient arrangement all the information that the personnel department needs in screening applicants for employment. It will usually include questions about the applicant's personal history, work history, and educational history, plus requests for any additional information that the firm considers important.

Briefly, the application form gives the worker an opportunity to tell what he can do to assist the firm. If the form is well designed and the information carefully recorded, the personnel department can eliminate unsuitable applicants in a very short time, thus reducing recruitment costs substantially.

The preliminary interview

The application form is a limited selection tool that can do no more than help narrow the field of job applicants and give management some indication of conditions in the labor market. Before the selection process can proceed, the firm needs more information about the applicants, and the applicants need to know more about the firm. This is accomplished through a preliminary interview in which each applicant for the position who has not been screened out is brought to the personnel office for an interview. It is of the utmost importance that this initial interview be carefully organized and conducted. Poor interviewing may end in poor selection or even in rejection of a good prospect. As a rule, the initial interview involves only the applicant.

Test and examinations

Increasing numbers of firms are making use of a variety of pre-employment tests in the process of screening applicants. Although these tests cannot be the sole criteria for employment, they can indicate a range of aptitudes and capabilities that is helpful to the employment manager. Tests are an accepted means for distinguishing among people, and even though they cannot provide a definite answer about who should be hired, they may provide good evidence about who should not be given further consideration. Some of the more commonly used tests are discussed briefly below.

Intelligence tests Although intelligence is hard to define, a convenient and fairly accurate meaning is "the inherent ability to learn." It is important to the firm to have some idea of a job applicant's general ability to learn and to use ideas, since his intelligence helps assess his growth potential. Well-kept records may show, for example, that workers with intelligence test scores below a certain level do not perform well on particular jobs; such information can be very useful when job assignments are being made. Again, we must bear in mind that tests are only one factor in job assignment or employment.

Ability or achievement tests Achievement tests measure current ability to perform. A trial period on a job is, in effect, a sort of achievement test, and probably one of the best available. But since it is not always possible for reasons of time and money to try out a person on a job, the availability of a test which will indicate a person's ability to perform in certain areas of work is a very helpful device.

Aptitude tests Young people seeking their first job usually need training and development, but the question of which line the training ought to take is not easily answered. People are often interested in positions which require skills for which they have no particular aptitude. It would be foolish for a person with poor coordination to begin training as an acrobat even though his interest level was high, and it is equally foolish to train for business skills when the necessary aptitude is not present.

Aptitude tests can differentiate between those best adapted to learn, say computer programming, and those whose aptitudes favor sales work. There are tests that indicate aptitude for sales work, for routine assignments, for personal contact with others, and for work in a variety of other categories.

Other tests A wide variety of specialized tests are available to the personnel department to use in screening and categorizing job applicants. Some of the more widely used are:

1 *Dexterity tests.* These tests measure the skill with which an individual manipulates objects; controls muscular movements of the arms, legs, or body; and performs physically.

2 *Interest tests.* These tests attempt to measure the degree of interest an individual has in a given type of work. This is an important test, for without interest in his work an employee may never perform above a mediocre level or may not remain on the job for any reasonable period of time.

3 *Personality tests.* Such tests measure some of the emotional characteristics of the person tested. They help estimate the ability of the individual to get along with others and to respond favorably to difficult situations. Personality tests are useful for workers required to work closely with others over long periods of time.

In addition, other tests have been developed to measure even more highly specialized personal traits for particular purposes. Revere Copper and Brass for many years has used a test designed to help weed out applicants for employment who are "accident-prone," that is, those who tend to be involved in accidents quite frequently.

We must bear in mind that men are complex creatures and that no tests have been devised to measure many of their characteristics. Testing does not, for example, measure loyalty, reliability, or courage. Within their limits, tests are very useful indicators, but they must be treated with caution and used by qualified persons who understand these limits.

The hiring interview

The applicants for a particular position are usually screened in a final interview before selection is actually made. This interview should be conducted by the supervisor who requested the worker and may also include the personnel department representative. Since the purpose of the previous steps in the selection process is to eliminate all applicants who do not meet the job requirements, the applicants called in for a hiring interview should be fully qualified, assuming the personnel department has done its job. All that remains is to select the applicant who seems best fitted for the position. It is possible, of course, that none of the applicants will be selected, and that the personnel department will have to look further for a suitable worker.

If an applicant is chosen for the position, the exact terms of the job should be very clearly understood by everyone concerned. The worker needs to know his responsibilities and duties; his hours, wages, and other benefits; the amount of overtime that may be demanded of him; and any basic company policies that may affect him while he is employed by the firm. A good reason why a personnel department representative should be at the hiring interview is to make certain that the terms of the job are understood. Many companies provide general information on personnel policies in a booklet or brochure that is presented to the new worker. Whatever the particular situation, the worker should go into his new job with full knowledge of what his employer expects of him and what he can expect from his employer.

WORKER ORIENTATION

Orientation, when it is properly carried out, will acquaint the worker with the operations of the firm and with the position of his department inside the firm. More than that, it will tell him exactly what job he is expected to do. Finally, it should clarify the relation of the new worker to the other members of the department. This kind of orientation is an absolute minimum.

A good orientation program will leave the employee firmly established in the new job, comfortable and relaxed in his relations with other members of the department, and content with his position in the firm. Though orientation takes a small amount of time from productive activity, it repays the firm many times over in better personnel relations.

WORKER TRAINING

The goal of training is to help employees to contribute their maximum usefulness to the firm in the shortest possible time. In a sense, orientation is part of the training program of a firm, but training is usually limited more strictly to the task to be performed by the employee.

Every new employee requires some training. The length of training needed will depend partly on the past experience of the worker. A skilled machinist may move from one shop to another and attain maximum production after a few hours of coaching. Achievement tests, mentioned earlier, are helpful in indicating the amount of training a particular employee needs to measure up to standards. Some formal training programs, like those of General Electric and International Business Machines Corp., may last up to 3 years and represent a very sizable investment by the company.

A second aspect of training goes beyond introducing the new employee to his immediate job and involves training to upgrade the worker's skill. Since the growth of the firm is contingent on the abilities of its employees to develop their own capacities more fully, this type of further skill training is a vital need in an expanding business.

Remember that the fundamental goal of any personnel policy is to obtain the maximum utilization within the firm of the potential abil-

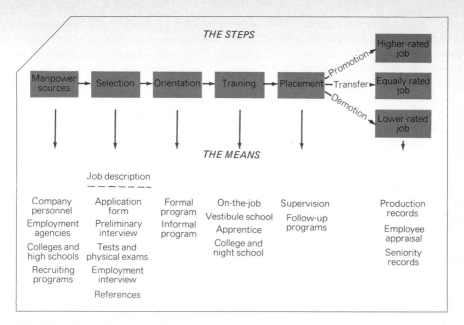

FIGURE 15-6   The overall selection process

ity of each individual worker. To achieve this goal, a sound training program is mandatory. Figure 15-6 points up the importance of orientation and training in the overall selection process.

Training may be brief and informal or very extensive and formal, depending on the skill level of the worker, the job to be done, and the particular circumstances of employment. Some of the more common training methods are on-the-job training, apprentice training, the "vestibule" or practice school, and management training in its various phases.

On-the-job training

Probably the most common method of training workers today is on-the-job training. In effect this means giving the trainee an opportunity to practice the job under intensive supervision until he is skilled enough to work satisfactorily under a normal degree of supervision. The employee is placed in the job for which he is employed; the job is explained carefully and demonstrated; then, under supervision, the employee performs the functions of the job. If the new worker has the necessary capacity, he should respond satisfactorily under work conditions.

Instructors for on-the-job training must also be selected carefully. The experienced worker with a desire to instruct and with careful work habits is often a good teacher. But it cannot be assumed that every experienced worker is a good instructor; some will be unable to teach successfully. The firm must make certain, too, that workers used for training others have an adjusted work load, and earnings must be adjusted so that the trainer is not penalized for his necessarily reduced production.

Supervisory personnel are also widely used as instructors for on-the-job training, and the same considerations apply to them. If training means the serious interruption of some other type of activity for which the foreman or supervisor is responsible, both jobs will suffer. This factor must be considered when the overall work load is being planned.

If the firm is large enough, a professional training staff may be maintained. In this case, training will not usually be on the job but will be in vestibule schools or in a classroom.

Vestibule training

When on-the-job training is not feasible and when there is enough staff to provide the necessary instruction, training can be carried on in simulated work areas or vestibule schools. Since the goal of the work done in these schools is training, not production, more time can be spent in planning and in thorough learning than is possible in real on-the-job training. Supermarket cashiers are often trained in a mock-up of a checkout station where they learn to operate registers like those used in the store under conditions like those met in the store. For the worker there is much less pressure involved in learning at vestibule schools than in on-the-job training. This method is, however, generally more expensive to administer since it requires extra facilities and the necessary supervisory personnel to conduct the school.

Apprentice training

Many trades, the building trades and machine-tool trades especially, still make use of the apprentice system for training workers. The younger worker is assigned as an assistant to a skilled craftsman for a period of time that may vary from several months to several years. During that time the apprentice learns by watching, helping, and doing. The apprentice generally signs a contract with the employer in which he agrees to perform certain tasks and the employer agrees to provide instruction in the craft or skill. In the early stages of training the apprentice performs only simple tasks or merely observes and lends a hand. In time he passes to more difficult tasks according to a regular plan or according to the speed with which he masters the basic skills. At the end of the apprenticeship, the worker is a journeyman craftsman, a skilled worker. During the training period his earnings gradually increase as he becomes more and more skilled in the trade. Few employers make use of apprentice training, because it is so time-consuming and wasteful, unless they are forced to do so by a labor union. In many trades the only means for acquiring a skilled-worker rating is to complete an apprentice program. The apprentice system will prevail as long as trade unionism remains strong.

MANAGEMENT TRAINING

Although worker training has been going on since man first acquired job skills, management training is a recent development. This is partly due to lack of knowledge of what constituted good management training, and partly to general apathy and lack of interest in the business world. Traditionally, management skill was learned by working under an experienced manager. Not until this century were techniques of management explored. The urgent need for trained managers in World War II production accelerated the development of management training considerably; up to then only a few firms had an active program of this kind. Many firms still have no formal training program for managers at any level.

The goal of management training is to provide managers with the skills essential for their task. This requires knowing what these skills must be. Then the areas in which a given individual needs additional training must be determined. Finally, methods for raising the levels of skill in these areas must be devised.

Foreman and supervisor training

Foreman trainees are often selected from the work group which they will eventually supervise. Since technical competence is an essential requirement of the foreman's job, it is a reasonable basis for selection. However, the worker being trained for a foreman's position will also require skill in communication, in coordinating the work of others, and in the proper exercise and delegation of authority. In addition, the foreman's job requires a thorough understanding of company policy and the organization structure of the firm. It is most helpful, too, if foremen have a basic understanding of budgeting and cost procedures. Most foreman-training programs, then, concentrate on these managerial skill areas rather than on technical competence.

Since training foremen or supervisors involves the first line of management—the group that is in direct contact with the workers in the firm—it affects the largest group of managers in business and in some ways the most significant. Training at the supervisory level often aims primarily at the development of leadership capability and the ability to coordinate the work of others. In certain firms there is a growing tendency to go outside the existing workforce to find supervisory trainees. Many firms make strong recruiting efforts for supervisory trainees among college seniors.

Junior management training

Trainees in junior management programs are generally recruited from among new college graduates who are intelligent, trained to study, and highly motivated. They are generally well equipped with communication skills. Their chief instructional needs are in the technical aspects of the new position and in areas of work planning, exercise of authority and judgment, company policies and procedures, and personnel relations.

Senior management training

Senior management trainees are commonly taken from the lower ranks of management. It can be assumed that they are proficient in company operations, in company policy, and in the exercise of managerial authority with all its ramifications. Their instructional needs are usually in the areas of interplant or interfirm relations; in knowledge of governmental regulations; and in the relationship between the firm and the community—between the firm and its distributors, suppliers, and customers. In addition, senior management training must take into consideration the fact that the senior managers are the public "character" of the firm; therefore, a broad cultural or educational program is often included in their otherwise firm-oriented training.

Management training methods

Perhaps the oldest method of training managers is simply to place them in positions close to incumbent managers so that they can watch and learn by experience and thereby develop their intuitive abilities. Unfortunately, this type of training is seldom clearly defined or systematic. Managers who have not themselves been trained formally often fail to realize precisely how they go about making decisions. Formal training, however, has the great advantage of systematizing operations, and judgment based on systematic activity is more easily learned and applied than "intuitive" judgment.

A good management training program should be a blend of theoretical and practical training that produces a manager able to do things but also aware of the impact of the things that he does.

JOB EVALUATION

In many smaller businesses the value of any particular job is set by management on the basis of "experience and judgment." If the duties

of each job are clearly understood by management, a satisfactory
structure which shows the relative value of each job to the other jobs
in the enterprise can be created in this informal way. But to serve
the needs of larger firms, a more scientific method called "job evaluation" has widespread application. It is used to measure the relative
value of each job in the entire structure of jobs in the company.

The basis of job evaluation is simple. Jobs are studied carefully and
classified according to their contribution to the firm. For example, one
job may be given a rating of 70 while another has a rating of 140;
the value to the firm of the second job is twice as great as that of the
first. Job evaluation does not necessarily establish the precise rate
of pay for a job but it does provide a sound basis for that determination. Furthermore, job evaluation does not rate the worker on the
job; it only establishes a grade or rating for the job. Although there
are several methods for evaluating jobs, the three most common
methods are the point method, the factor-comparison method, and the
ranking method.

Before any particular position can be evaluated, a complete analysis
of the position must be made. This analysis includes the preparation
of a job description, job specifications, and a brief definition of job
requirements. This information is necessary to the evaluation process.

The point method

All job evaluation methods make use of the same basic concept—that
every job involves a number of different factors such as physical
effort, mental effort, responsibility, education, and working conditions and the attempt is made to measure the amount of each of these
factors present in a given job.

In the point method, each factor identified with a job is assigned
a maximum point value representing the relative importance of that
factor in the job makeup. The number of points is then scaled to
represent several degrees of importance of each factor. As a result of
this procedure, a table is drawn up as in Figure 15-7 which is used
in the process of establishing a total point value for a job based on
the relative importance of the several factors considered.

Figure 15-8 shows how two jobs, A and B, are evaluated under a
point system. This illustration shows that job A is worth 245 points
and job B is worth 290 points. It we translate these points into an
indication of job worth, it follows that job B is worth almost 20 percent
more than job A.

The factor comparison method

The chief difference between this method and the point method is that
the factor comparison method begins with a number of key jobs whose

Factor	Maximum points	First degree	Second degree	Third degree	Fourth degree	Fifth degree
Skill, mental	100	30	50	70	90	100
Skill, physical	60	20	30	40	50	60
Physical effort	70	25	35	45	55	70
Responsibility	80	10	30	45	60	80
Education	40	5	15	25	35	40
Working conditions	50	10	20	30	40	50

FIGURE 15-7   Point-method rating chart

A point-method rating chart lists the job factors and the values or points for each degree of each factor. The chart above shows that mental skill is the most important factor and therefore has the largest point value. This table would not be used if the jobs being evaluated required a lesser degree of mental skill. Another chart would be prepared for such jobs.

wage rates are established and agreed to by all parties concerned and also the factors which enter into these jobs are well known. These jobs are, therefore, for all practical purposes already evaluated and rated. A rating table like that in Figure 15-9 is prepared for these key jobs and all other jobs are rated against the key jobs and their respective factor values. For example, job A in the figure has a mental skill requirement the equivalent of the machinist job, responsibility re-

FACTOR	JOB A Degree	JOB A Points	JOB B Degree	JOB B Points
Skill, mental	3	70	5	100
Skill, physical	5	60	2	30
Physical effort	5	70	2	35
Responsibility	1	10	5	80
Education	1	5	4	35
Working conditions	3	30	1	10
Total points		245		290

FIGURE 15-8   Evaluation of two jobs

In job evaluation the degree to which each factor is present in a given job is rated by the corresponding points in the chart. Jobs A and B, both subject to the same scale of rating factors, are evaluated above.

FACTOR	KEY JOBS					
	Machinist	Toolmaker	Janitor	Latheman	Inspector	Welder
Skill, mental	40	50	10	20	30	25
Skill, physical	40	50	10	30	30	30
Physical effort	20	20	30	30	10	30
Responsibility	40	80	15	20	100	30
Education	20	30	5	10	30	15
Working conditions	10	10	20	15	5	25
TOTAL	170	240	90	125	205	155

FACTOR	JOB A		
	Type	Points	
Skill, mental	Machinist	40	JOB A is evaluated by comparing each factor with the one it most resembles in the key jobs that have already been evaluated and rated.
Skill, physical	Inspector	30	
Physical effort	Toolmaker	20	
Responsibility	Welder	30	
Education	Latheman	10	
Working conditions	Janitor	20	
TOTAL		150	

FIGURE 15-9 Factor-comparison rating chart

quirements are the equivalent of the welder job, and working conditions on the job are as good as those found in the janitor's job, and so forth. The value of this method of job evaluation is that each job is compared to an existing, real-life position rather than having its position in the scale of jobs determined from a fabricated rating table as is the case with the point method.

The job ranking method

This is the simplest of the three evaluation methods but is also the least accurate. In effect, it ranks jobs in relation to one another by arranging all jobs in the order of their complexity and responsibility. Whoever has the responsibility for job evaluation must consider the same factors that are considered in any other evaluation system, but in this case, there is no attempt to construct any sort of point scale. Instead, the jobs are listed in order from lowest to highest, and then divided into general classifications or grades. In the federal civil service, for example, jobs are classified as grades GS-6, GS-7, etc., each grade level representing jobs more complex and demanding than the previous level. Each grade level may contain many different jobs, all graded the same and each having the same wage rate. This plan is fairly simple and does not take too much time to work out. On the other hand, it shows that one group ranks higher than another, but it does not show by how much. This can be a real handicap where there is a wide range of skills involved in the operation of the business.

Uses of job evaluation

Job evaluation, if complete, is a very useful management tool. It provides assurance to management that pay rate is consistent with the value of the job to the firm. For the worker, it means that the principle of equal pay for equal work is in operation. Because job evaluation ranks jobs, it provides a clear picture of the job assignments which constitute promotion and also minimizes the possibility of promoting a worker beyond his or her capacity. By indicating skill requirements for jobs, evaluation is very useful in the process of employee selection, placement, and training. It also makes it easier to determine the rate of pay for newly created positions.

The process of job evaluation is both costly and time-consuming but it is more than likely to repay its costs many times over in the form of efficiency in personnel procedures and in assurances to the workforce that an equitable system of personnel assignment and pay is in effect.

WAGES AND THE WORKER

When management prepares its wage policies it must keep in mind the significance of wages to the individual worker. Wages are a prime factor in job selection. The size of the wage package determines the worker's basic standard of living. Wages also are a symbol of achievement in our society. Again the size of the wage package tends to establish status in the community.

Wages, in the broad sense, are a stimulus to greater productivity and are a means of attracting workers to the enterprise. Of course, this does not mean that on every occasion a worker is attracted to the job which pays the highest wages or that more money automatically induces the worker to produce more.

Finally, the wages the worker receives for his services tend to identify his status inside the business organization. As the worker rises in the organization and assumes greater responsibility, he normally receives higher wages. Since it is often impossible to directly compare one job with another, wage payments tend to be accepted as an indirect way of measuring or comparing jobs.

A sound wage structure is essential for good employer-employee relations. High wages and the best of working conditions do not

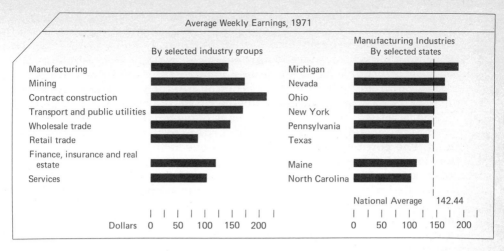

FIGURE 15-10   Wage differentials

Although the trend is toward more equitable wage payments, wage levels vary from industry to industry and from state to state.
Source: U.S. Department of Labor, Bureau of Labor Statistics.

always guarantee a contented and productive workforce. However,
low wages and poor conditions will almost certainly produce labor
dissatisfaction and unrest.

Wage levels

"Going rates" or average rates of pay vary considerably from one
industry to another. The result of such differentials may be more or
less pay for exactly the same labor skills, depending on the employing
industry. The average pay rates also vary from one section of the
country to another. Thus the wage level or going rate for a skill or
job depends on the industry and its location. See Figure 15-10.

CREATING THE WAGE SCALE

When a general management policy on wages has been set which
considers workers and going wage levels and job evaluation has taken
place, the tools for creating the actual wage scale in a firm are available. Where the industry is strongly unionized, of course, the wage
scale is created in part through collective bargaining between union
and management, and the scientific method of scaling wages cannot
be the only method used. Unions do accept the idea that there should
be differentials in pay based on skill requirements and are not opposed to job evaluation.

To some extent, the way in which the wage scale is determined is conditioned by the method used for job evaluation. The factor comparison method uses several key jobs which by definition would be those jobs for which there is agreement on wage levels. In effect, the relating of other jobs to these key jobs really establishes the wage scale. A non-key job which is evaluated higher than a key job would have a higher wage assigned and vice versa. If a classification method is used, a wage rate is assigned to each class of jobs and the individual jobs are then assigned to classes according to their respective evaluations. The point system of evaluating jobs assigns a point score position to each job and wage rates are presumed to be related to these point scores. If a wage curve is developed by plotting the point-wage position of several key jobs and then the point values of all other evaluated jobs are plotted along this curve, the wage rates of each of these jobs may be determined by interpolation. Usually, however, this procedure is used to determine whether an established wage scale is appropriate, that is, whether some jobs are overpriced or underpriced. See Figure 15-11. Plotted points which fall below the curve or are above the curve represent job wage levels which are out of line. If the job is underpaid, wages should be raised. If the job is being overpaid

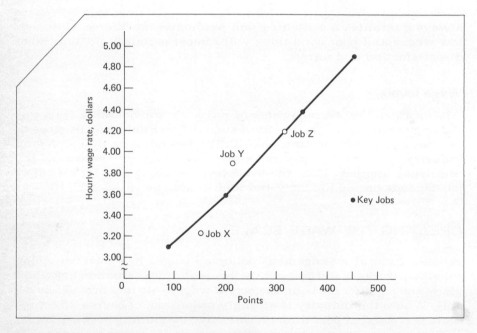

FIGURE 15-11 Wage curve and job prices

The wage curve is determined by the key jobs. The plot of job X indicates it is out of line and underpaid. Job Y is overpaid and job Z is in line with the wage curve.

this represents a more difficult situation to resolve. It would probably be unwise to reduce these wages, and other corrective actions may be taken such as:

1 Increase the duties and responsibilities of the job so as to increase its value.

2 Withhold future wage rate increases until the job rate falls in line.

3 Continue the rate with current employees but adjust it for all newly hired employees.

4 Set a definite future date for rate adjustment, inform the workers, and give them opportunity to upgrade their positions before the adjustment takes effect.

RATING EMPLOYEE PERFORMANCE

Every employer, consciously or not, rates his employees. The most basic personnel questions are: ''How well is the employee doing?'' ''Is he developing as expected?'' In a small business, the informal rating that takes place is not adequate for the larger firm which has large numbers of people. A fair rating system requires a systematic and objective evaluation of the way in which the employee meets the standards of his job. Clearly, these standards must be well defined and fair. Not all jobs can be rated easily, but, in any event, the need exists for a just, impartial system acceptable to both employers and employees.

Purposes of rating or evaluation

Employee rating, or evaluation, is very valuable as a management tool. It is widely used for many purposes.

Promotion A good rating system provides the best basis for identifying the most qualified candidates for promotion. Sometimes unions insist that promotion be based on seniority. Management, therefore, if it wants to override union pressure and establish a merit system as the basis for promotion, must produce acceptable evidence that it can measure performance accurately.

Determining individual pay rates Payment for any job should depend on both the nature of the job and the manner in which the job is done. Individual pay is frequently considered as being divided into two parts: part of the pay is for meeting the minimum requirements of the job; part of the pay is based on how well the job is done. The latter portion represents the reward for the worker contributing more than the bare minimum to the job. A good rating system provides a sound approach for paying workers what they are worth. If no rating system exists, increases in wages will depend on seniority.

Correcting worker weaknesses A good rating system will identify worker weaknesses as they relate to skills and abilities. Thus, management can see where increased efforts at training or supervision may be required. Correcting these weaknesses means creating a better workforce which is consistent with personnel objectives.

Locating talent in the workforce Rating can be used to identify persons with outstanding abilities, thereby pinpointing workers entitled to rewards or promotion.

Creating competition Some competition between workers is good. A rating system gives each worker a "score" which identifies him in relation to the other workers.

   The above are some of the ways in which a good rating system may be used by management for both current and long-range planning.

RATING SYSTEMS

Rating systems may be formal or informal. Informal ratings are made every day in all fields of human activity. Students get rated in school, neighbors are rated as good or bad, and so on. These informal ratings are usually made without reference to a known standard and they are likely to be too much influenced by recent events. If workers are rated informally, it can be quite by accident that on the day the boss checks up on the workforce, the busiest person may be the biggest loafer of the crew who just happened to see the boss approaching before any of the other workers were aware of what was going on.

   Formal rating programs are more desirable and advantageous. First, they make use of standard measurements which are defined. Second, each measurement is given a weighted place in the overall rating scheme and in this way each aspect of a man's performance is given its relative worth. Finally, in a formal program, ratings are made at definite intervals so that the rating process is continuous.

   Rating is time-consuming. Ratings under pressure or at inopportune times for the rater may result in inaccurate ratings. Accuracy is a necessity. A poorly run formal rating plan is no better than a haphazard informal rating system.

THE POINT METHOD OF EMPLOYEE RATING

Most formal rating systems make use of some variation of the point rating method. A chart is prepared, similar to that in Figure 15-12,

Clevax Engineering Company
Employee Rating

Worker _____ Job Title _____ Date _____

Characteristic	Maximum points	Excellent	Above average	Average	Below average	Poor	Rate
Quantity	20	20	16	12	8	4	
Quality	20	20	16	12	8	4	
Cooperativeness	30	30	24	18	12	6	
Initiative	40	40	32	24	16	8	
Dependability	20	20	16	12	8	4	
Job knowledge	25	25	20	15	10	5	
Capacity to develop	35	35	28	21	14	7	
Attitude toward work	20	20	16	12	8	4	
Attitude toward others	30	30	24	18	12	6	
						Total points	

Rated by _____

Remarks:

FIGURE 15-12 Employee rating chart

Also called a merit rating or performance rating chart. The rater checks the appropriate column for each characteristic and totals the result.

which lists the performance characteristics considered important and assigns maximum points to each characteristic as an indication of their relative values. This maximum point value is then scaled to represent several levels of performance from excellent to poor for each characteristic. In practice a written description of each level of each characteristic is prepared so that the person doing the rating will understand, as clearly as possible, the meaning of poor or average or any other level of performance. In some cases, objective measurements may be made to determine whether performance is excellent or something less. For example, in cases where quantity or quality of work is being rated, units of production or percentage of rejects can be readily translated into a level of performance. In other cases, judgment must be exercised by the rater.

Training of raters

Personnel responsible for rating workers must be sufficiently trained to be able to apply the rating standards. Raters, who usually are the supervisors and foremen, should carry out the rating program on a long-term basis rather than on the evidence of a single performance by the worker. To develop proficiency in the raters, a brief training and practice program is usually all it takes to produce a rating system which is basically sound.

Along with the training program it is good practice to periodically evaluate the rating system both to indicate its weaknesses and short-comings and to indicate that it is valid and does effectively do its job. The validity of a rating program must be shown if workers are to place any faith in the system and if management is to be convinced that it is at all worthwhile.

DETERMINING INDIVIDUAL RATES OF PAY

Most jobs will not have a single *rate* of pay assigned but will instead be assigned a *range* of pay, such as from $4 to $4.80 per hour. The question of what rate, within this range, to pay the worker may be determined on any of several different bases.

The first approach may be the use of performance ratings as discussed above. Once the performance rating is established, the point value can be converted into a dollar value to determine the individual's pay. Figure 15-13 illustrates the use of performance ratings to show the difference between rates actually being paid and rates that should be paid if performance is to be rewarded. If performance is not used as a basis for wage increases, the pay rates are apt to get out of line with the actual value of the workers to the company.

A second approach may be that everyone's wage moves together based on the passage of time. This is often referred to as "lock step" and is evidenced whenever everybody gets a raise periodically and the dollar amount is fixed in accordance with some predetermined schedule rather than with an individual performance appraisal. This method, a uniform wage policy, has sound application in a number of situations:

1 Some production processes require that jobs be done on a rigid time schedule and there is no way for the worker to alter this schedule. Under these conditions, the volume of work produced by each worker would be identical and, unless quality intervened, all should receive the same pay. Examples of this circumstance would be when a machine sets the pace of work such as in an assembly line, or when the process requires a fixed amount of time to be completed such as in chemical processing.

2 Some jobs are so variable that it is very difficult to determine just how long they should take. Any job which does not occur re-

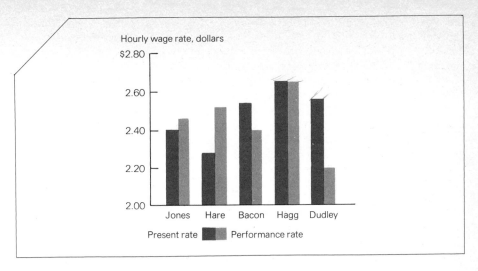

FIGURE 15-13 Employee performance chart

Except for Hagg, the wage rates are not consistent with the performance ratings. Dudley's performance rate is worth $2.20 per hour, not the $2.56 he is being paid. Hare's performance rate is $2.50 and he is being paid $2.28.

petitively and which occurs under varying circumstances is a difficult task for which to establish a time standard.

A third approach is that of setting wages on the basis of the worker's productivity, that is, on the basis of the number of satisfactory units produced. To set wages on this basis requires that the worker alone must be responsible for his output. That is, he must not be paced by a machine or another worker. Management must provide a continuous supply of work and maintain the conditions under which the job is done. A common example of this basis for wage payment is found in the piece-rate system wherein a worker receives wages directly related to the number of "pieces" he produces. This wage practice is found in many industries where manual skills are used, such as in the garment and shoe industries, and also in other quite different fields, such as sales, where production consists of selling and wages are based on the volume of sales made (sales commissions).

FRINGE BENEFITS

No discussion of wages would be complete without some mention of fringe benefits—the services provided for the worker by the employer in addition to the wages paid and definitely considered part of the total wage package. These benefits consist of such items as life and medical insurance coverage, vacations with pay, birthday holidays, sick leave, educational benefits, price concessions on the company's goods, severance pay, retirement plans, and other benefits which accrue to workers in addition to their wages.

Benefits such as these are often the means of enticing workers onto the company payroll as well as the reason why many workers prefer to stay with a firm. The worth of the fringe benefits to the worker is a strong attraction. From the employer's viewpoint, fringe benefits add a significant dollar cost over and above those dollars paid as wages. These benefits easily exceed 10 percent of the wages paid and more often exceed 25 percent.

As costly as these fringe benefits may be, they are less costly when purchased on a group basis than they would be if each employee were to personally buy or provide each benefit for himself. In this respect, a dollar of benefits is worth more than a dollar of wages. This alone is a good enough reason for labor to press for more fringe benefits in preference sometimes to pressing for an increase in wage rates. It is less costly to buy group insurance than individual insurance and it is also more efficient to expend money in large amounts for a large number of workers than in small amounts by the individual worker. In addition, these benefits do not appear as taxable income, thereby saving the worker a certain amount of income taxes.

PROMOTIONS, TRANSFERS, AND LAYOFFS

Promotion is defined as the transfer to another job with greater responsibility and higher financial or other rewards. Traditionally promotion should be a great incentive for a worker to deliver top performance and ideally, a sound rating system should produce promotions based on performance. This is not always the case in practice. Promotion is not always the reward for efficiency; sometimes it is used as a device to remove a problem by "kicking upstairs" some person who is a source of friction or inefficiency. At times, the workers may not desire to be considered for promotion regardless of their satisfactory performance levels simply because they have no wish to take on the added responsibilities which come along with promotion. Sometimes it is simply the case of the worker not wishing to leave the "gang" and move into a new environment among new faces.

Ability and promotion

Ideally, from management's point of view, promotion should depend on the individual's ability and the enterprise's needs. Sometimes it is difficult to measure ability or to distinguish between two people in this respect. However, setting minimum requirements for a position is possible and when more than one person meets these minimum requirements some procedure is then necessary to differentiate between the candidates for the promotion. One means of doing this requires the use of a "point-rating" system to evaluate each worker's performance. This evaluation would consider such features as the quantity and quality of performance, cooperativeness, initiative, attitudes, dependability, and other characteristics considered essential to an adequate appraisal of the worker's performance. As in the case with job rating, point values would be assigned to each characteristic in accordance with its relative importance and a point score could then be established for each worker being evaluated. If one candidate earns a point total significantly higher than the others, it would appear that he should receive the promotion. If point differentials are not significant, the point system would not suffice as a basis for distinguishing between the parties and management would then have to resort to further discussions, tests, interviews, and possibly even consider other candidates before making its promotion decision.

Seniority and promotion

The oldest basis for distinguishing among employees is that of seniority. The standard on which seniority is calculated is time. Therefore the oldest in service is generally the "senior" member of the group. Time, however, is interpreted on different bases. Seniority may refer to chronological age, length of service in the enterprise, length of service in a particular plant or job, or the length of time a worker has been a member of the union. A worker could have top seniority on one basis, length of service with the company, and rank at the bottom of the seniority list on some other basis, time on the job, if he had just changed jobs in the firm.

There are many technical aspects to the definition of seniority under different bases as identified above, but nevertheless, once defined, seniority ratings are easily measured and labor unions prefer them as a basis for distinguishing between workers because they give preference to the older workers—those who have contributed to the union over longer periods of time. Despite the problems which may be involved, unions and many workers prefer seniority rather than so-called "merit" or performance ratings as a basis for actions.

For example, at one extreme we find that some firms simply promote the senior man in the department when a vacancy occurs just above him. At the other extreme, seniority may only come into play when all other factors being considered are equal.

The following paragraphs extracted from a work agreement illustrates one use of seniority:

The parties recognize that promotional opportunity and job security in the event of promotions, decreases of forces and rehiring after layoffs should increase in proportion to length of continuous service, and that in the administration of this Section the intent will be that wherever practicable full consideration shall be given continuous service in such cases.

A much stronger seniority provision is part of a contract between a union and a public utility:

In cases of promotion within a department, the Company agrees to apply the principle of departmental seniority and provided the senior employee is reasonably well qualified for the promotion, he shall be given a thirty-day (30) trial. In cases of promotion involving plantwide bidding, the bidding employee having the longest seniority will receive first consideration, provided that he has reasonable qualifications for the promotion.

Whether seniority is the best basis for personnel actions depends on one's philosophy and values. Those who support seniority as a basis argue the following:

1 It provides an easy and objective measurement. Ability measurements are much more difficult to arrive at.

2 It rewards long service which the general public feels is certainly worth special consideration.

3 If management has done a proper job of personnel selection, training, and development, then the senior man will be well qualified.

Critics of seniority argue that seniority can be gained by simply meeting minimum performance requirements and as a result the less capable workers may have a better chance for promotion than the excellent workers. There is also the possibility that younger workers will show less initiative because they realize that time and not exceptional performance will bring them rewards.

Layoffs

Layoff rights are the worker's most jealously guarded possessions. Next to firing, layoff is most drastic from the worker's point of view. The financial impact may be lessened by unemployment compensation provisions in the law. The basis for determining who is to be affected by layoffs is much more specific than that used for promotion or transfer. Generally, those with the lowest seniority are the first to be laid off and the last to be recalled.

SUMMARY

Two of the primary functions of the personnel department in any organization are the selection of personnel and the adequate training of personnel. The aim is to produce workers who can make a maximum contribution to the goals of the firm.

Worker selection should begin with the establishment of a labor pool either from within or from outside the firm. In the selection process, various testing procedures are used to screen the applicants and to measure such attributes as intelligence, aptitudes, and abilities. All this effort is directed at reducing the risk of poor selection.

After selection, the employee should begin a continuous training program aimed to develop his potential to its maximum. Each type of training program, whether for operational or managerial positions, has its own special requirements.

Each working day, events transpire which affect each worker's relation with the firm. Procedures are necessary to assist management in making decisions related to the workers on matters such as wages, promotions, layoffs, etc. And the workers should be made aware of these procedures. There are a number of excellent techniques available for these purposes such as job evaluation, employee performance rating, and wage rate determination. The range of these techniques includes highly formalized systems as well as informal procedures for making the appropriate decisions. Each has its place.

BUSINESS ITEMS

Some reactions to job boredom

Worker discontent is basically nothing new so why should job dissatisfaction be so critical a problem today? Some say that this problem is really a "creation of the pundit," whereas others believe that the issue may be magnified but should not be ignored.

Whether worker discontent, which some see evidenced by poor productivity, deteriorating work quality, use of drugs, absenteeism, high labor turnover, and sabotage, is really a phenomenon of our times brought about by job boredom or whether the dissatisfactions are due to insufficient pay has not really been resolved. There are adherents to both views. In any event, many companies have turned to behavioral scientists for help in such techniques as job enrichment. The idea is to satisfy and motivate the worker by systematically giving him greater responsibility, autonomy, and feedback on his performance. Another technique applied is organizational development which fosters communications between workers and supervision. Groups of employees informally hash over problems, propose solutions, and set mutual objectives with their supervisors.

Skeptics are not at all sure about the validity of these techniques and whether they will endure as solutions. The social scientists believe that more pay and job enrichment are short-run answers to the problem. For the long run, they feel that the significant answer lies in better understanding about people and what is really going on.

How to pay an executive

Many goodies have been used to reward executives, such as stock options, deferred pay, etc. But with a poor stock-market situation and with prospects of long-term inflation, these goodies are not attractive.

Cash—or something readily convertible to cash—is the "in" thing today.

Coming on strong is the idea of extra compensation tied directly to the performance of the top brass and middle managers. In addition, more is being done in the way of perquisites—"perks"—as an offset to the diminished value of most stock options. More companies are making cars and space in the company garage available to key people; paying for club memberships, all-inclusive major medical coverage, and fancier physical examinations. And there are almost never any taxes to be paid on these fringe benefits. Coming up are extras such as more paid vacation time and long sabbaticals every 5 or 7 years.

These changes in the executive compensation package have been dictated by changing economic conditions, in part by tax law changes, and in part by the attitude of today's crop of younger corporate managers.

QUESTIONS

1 What are the functions with which a personnel department gets involved? Does most of the work of the department have to do with wages?

2 What difference does it make whether the personnel function is assigned to the line manager or is organized as a specialized staff agency?

3 What sort of questions are addressed by a personnel policy?

4 How does the promotion policy of a firm bear on the need for a labor pool?

5 What are the advantages of an active recruiting program?

6 How do internal labor sources compare to external sources?

7 What benefits accrue to the practice of centralized selection?

8 What is a job description? What does it contain and what are its uses?

9 Should an employer always use tests when hiring or promoting an employee? Why?

10 Distinguish among an intelligence test, an aptitude test, and an achievement test. What is the value of these tests? Limitations?

11 Suppose you have just hired a number of workers who are to be placed on jobs which require only a moderate amount of skill. What variety of training opportunities would you make available to these men? Is one preferable?

12 How does the nature of the specific training change as one proceeds from foreman to junior manager to senior manager?

13 What is the purpose of job evaluation? How is it done? What are its limitations?

14 How is job evaluation involved in the process of setting wage rates?

15 How is employee evaluation or rating involved in the process of setting wage rates?

16 What are some of the areas in which a good employee rating system may be useful for management planning?

17 Once the job's wage rate range has been set, what are some of the ways of arriving at the specific wage rate to be paid to a worker?

18 List as many items as you can which are classified as fringe benefits for a worker in a plant; for a senior manager of the plant.

19 What advantage is there to the worker in receiving fringe benefits? Would it be better for him if he were paid higher wages and purchased these "benefits" on his own?

20 Under what circumstances would you consider promotion according to ability to be synonymous with promotion according to seniority?

21 Define seniority. Do you believe it to be a valid basis for pay and promotion? Explain.

The purpose of this chapter Like most major functions of business, finance can be broken down into several subfunctions. It involves obtaining the necessary funds for buildings, machinery, inventories, payrolls, and the like, but it also involves obtaining them from the best source. Financing a payroll through an issue of capital stock can rarely, if ever, be justified. Finance also involves the management of funds. Management, as we now know, includes planning, organizing, control, and the like. / In this chapter, we shall consider the financial requirements of normal business operations, the sources of funds to meet them, and the impact of alternative sources of funds on the firm. This chapter will also explain much of the vocabulary that is necessary for an understanding of the finance function. The managerial aspects of the financing function are discussed in the following chapter. / Questions raised in this chapter include:

1 For what purpose does the business firm need money, and how are these purposes categorized?

2 What are the sources of the required funds?

3 Is borrowing the only way for a business to obtain needed funds?

4 What does borrowing cost? What are other factors to consider in borrowing?

5 How much money does a firm need? For how long?

16 / THE FINANCING FUNC-

TION The problems of business finance are a matter of interest to everyone, even to people who are not directly involved in business. Students of business are naturally concerned with finance and its effect on business policy. Other future members of the business community, who will one day have to make decisions about financial matters as either owners or managers of business firms, are also well advised to acquaint themselves with financial affairs. There are now millions of persons who have investments in stocks or bonds that give them a lively and personal interest in business finance. Nor can we ignore the millions of wage earners employed by business, for business finance affects their earnings in a direct and immediate way. In short, almost everyone comes into contact with matters of business finance and should know something about them.

The expansion in public and professional interest in finance in recent years is due to a variety of factors. From the public's point of view, the diffusion of stock ownership in our society has produced stockholders in almost every community. Second, the actions of government, regulatory agencies, and trade unions have continually drawn attention to the area of business finance. The questions of business size and financial power, profit and ability to pay higher wages, the increasing need for capital, and the rapid growth seen in many areas of business and reflected in stock market activity and prices have all combined to stimulate the interest of more and more people. The communication of matters related to business finance is much more adequately handled these days by means of press, radio, and television than it was earlier. And with this communication comes understanding and interest as well as participation.

FINANCING AND THE FIRM

All aspects of a firm's operations have financial implications. Even before the firm is in operation, it has financial involvements, and certainly, once it gets under way, there is no phase of operations which does not require funds. These funds may come from various sources. However, before the funds are sought, the amount required must be established, the manner in which the funds will be allocated to the various planned uses must be determined, and a system for managing the efficient use of the funds must be devised.

The money supply of a firm may come from investors, lenders, or be generated by the operations of the firm—profit. Thus, it arises from either internal or external sources or from both. In dealing with external sources of funds, the business person does business with banks, insurance companies, and other business firms. The internal generation of funds occurs as a result of the sale of products and services by the firm. If the sales are made at a profit to the company, funds are thereby provided which may be used to finance the growth of the business or to provide dividends for the owners. In this respect, management must establish a policy on the payment of dividends which both satisfies the stockholders' desire for return on their investment and makes certain that enough profit is retained in the business to support planned growth. Of course, not all growth is or can be financed from profits alone. Additional owner investment and borrowing from other sources may provide the required funds. From time to time, a firm as financially strong as General Motors will borrow hundreds of millions of dollars. In such cases, it is the expectation of profit from the business operations which induces investors and lenders to make their funds available to the firm.

What does the financing function include?

The financing function includes the day-to-day concern for the use and control of funds as well as the long-range planning which is involved with determining future requirements for funds and optimum uses to which they may be put. The financial policies of the firm are exemplified in its basic decisions about methods of financing growth, dividend distribution policy, relations with lending institutions, economic evaluation of alternative investments in plant and equipment, and other activities involving uses or sources of funds.

A partial listing of financing functions is as follows:

1 *Planning and forecasting*—operations, changes, and growth

2 *Coordinating and controlling*—accounting and budgeting

3 *Financing*—availability and use of funds

4 *Cost analysis*—measuring and controlling capital costs and company costs

5 *Pricing*—relation of prices and profits

6 *Credits and collections*—liquidity and security of customer accounts

7 *Asset management*—optimizing investment in fixed assets and inventories

8 *Insurance, pensions, and welfare plans*—administration and control

9 *Taxes*—measuring and minimizing impact

Increasing complexity of the financing function

As a company increases in size and complexity of operations, its financing function broadens significantly in scope. Increased size may result from merger or acquisition or from self-generated growth. With increased size come an increased need for funds, an increased complexity of taxation problems, a greater variety of investment opportunities and need for their evaluation, and a greater need for close financial control. In this respect, the use of automatic data processing and computers has been of an inestimable value in providing the means whereby information that is pertinent to financial planning and control has been made available for use by management.

Capital, investment, lending, and borrowing

Though "capital," "investment," "lending," and "borrowing" are common terms, the student of finance needs to know their precise meaning in business. The term "capital" is used in a number of different ways. When the business person speaks of capital, he is usually referring to the assets he needs to operate his business. When he uses the term "equity capital," he means the amount of original investment in the firm plus any permanent investments that have been made since the firm began. The capital of a corporation, on the other hand, is the amount of money received from the sale of stock that the corporation has issued. An accountant speaking of capital defines it as net worth, the excess of business assets over business liabilities. Capital goods are those used to produce other goods; they are sometimes called producer goods. Net working capital is the excess of current assets over current liabilities; it is a good indicator of the ability of the firm to meet its current obligations without financial difficulty. Each time you meet the word "capital," look carefully to discover the exact meaning of the word, for it does not always mean assets needed to operate a business. In this text it is always used with an explanatory modifier.

An "investor" is an owner who provides funds for a firm, usually for a long period of time. His two main concerns are security of his funds and the amount of return—dividend—he gets on his investment. A corporation is under no obligation to return or repay this investment. The "lender" provides money for a business but usually for shorter periods of time and not as an owner, but as a creditor. He too is concerned with the security of his funds and with his return, which is interest. Whereas the corporation is under no obligation to repay the investor, the lender will be repaid the funds he has provided the firm as specified in the loan agreement. A dividend is a share of profits whereas interest is a business expense that must be paid irrespective of profit. Both the lender and investor expect a higher return from their funds if the business is risky.

FINANCIAL PLANNING AND POLICIES

Before the business person can acquire funds, he must determine as accurately as possible the amount required and the use that will be made of them. Financing a business involves different problems at different stages of company development; there is also a great difference between starting a new business and purchasing a going concern.

Management usually establishes basic policies to guide its financial planning. These policies relate principally to:

1 *Maintaining control of the enterprise.* Limitations may be set by management on the extent to which the company may incur debt. This is done to avoid restrictions on financial operations which may be imposed by those to whom the company is indebted.

2 *Financing company growth.* Management may specify that expansion will occur primarily from retained earnings (self-generated expansion) or from new investment rather than by incurring debt. A policy of this type may restrict dividend payout.

3 *Maintaining financial structure.* A policy may be established which sets certain restrictions as a means of maintaining the financial structure of the firm. For example, the capital structure of the firm may have limitations imposed on it, and a specified working capital position may have to be maintained. The ratio of earnings to sales, the amount of dividends to be paid, and other financial matters which have a bearing on successful operations may also be subjected to limitations by policy statements.

For the moment we will deal with the problems involved in beginning a new business. The first task is to decide on the amount of funds needed. Then the funds must be properly used to achieve the objectives for which they were obtained. This overall financial plan is a necessary prerequisite to the business person's attempt to raise money.

FUNDS AND THE NEW ENTERPRISE

Long before a new business has found a location and begun to build its facilities, certain costs have been incurred, and funds must be available to meet these costs. Legal fees, the cost of incorporation, patent expenses, promotional or organizational expenses, and many other costs arise in the founding of a new business. Then there are investments in real estate, plant and equipment, and salaries for the key personnel who supervise the construction of facilities. Finally, funds are needed with which to conduct business operations (working capital) since there are payrolls to meet, materials to purchase, and plant expenses, such as electricity and repairs, to be paid as soon as the enterprise is functioning. There is a constant flow of funds through any business enterprise, and the speed with which they flow is of vital importance. If funds flow into the firm slowly, large cash reserves will be needed. In general, the investments needed by a new concern fall into four major categories:

1 Funds to cover cost of organization

2 Fixed-asset or capital investment (plant, machinery, and other long-life equipment)

3 Working capital (for current expenses)

4 Excess funds to cover early losses, emergencies, etc. (sometimes called a *reserve*)

FINANCIAL REQUIREMENTS BUDGET

A very necessary step, which requires great detail in planning, is to prepare a budget of financial needs. The budget is only an estimate and it may prove inaccurate; but it should be calculated as closely as possible. A budget is an orderly statement of the amount of funds needed, the time at which they will be needed, and the use that will be made of them. Another budget may be made up to show capital expenditures in the new business. These budgets are used when the business person attempts to borrow the funds needed for his enterprise. Budgeting is discussed in greater detail in the following chapter.

TYPES AND SOURCES OF FUNDS

The new enterprise has need for two different types of funds or credit: first, it must have long-term funds or credit that will provide the fixed assets of the firm; second, it must have short-term funds or credit that will provide the necessary working capital and initial expense money. Short-term funds are usually obtained from commercial banks, and the relation between the bank and the owners or managers of the new business is often a personal one that continues for many years. Long-term funds are usually available initially from investments of the owners and subsequently from retained earnings. However, long-term credit is also obtained in the form of loans and mortgages or from the sale of bonds to institutions such as banks or insurance companies and to the general public. Table 16-1 summarizes the nature and sources of business funds.

Capital investment

The amount of money that must be invested to establish the physical plant and facilities needed to do business is called "capital invest-

TABLE 16-1   Nature and sources of business funds

Nature	Sources
Equity capital	
Stocks: common, preferred	Ownership investment
Retained earnings	Reinvested profits
Long-term debt	
Bonds: collateral trust, debenture	Insurance companies
Mortgage loans: real estate, equipment	Pension funds
Term loans	Banks
	Government agencies (e.g., Small
	Business Administration, Federal
	Reserve banks)
	Trade creditors
	Individuals
Short-term debt	
Open-book accounts	Trade creditors
Credit instruments: notes, drafts,	Banks
acceptances, commercial paper	Finance companies
	Commercial paper market
Pledged receivables and factoring	Factors

Equity capital and long-term debt make up capital investment; short-term debt makes up working capital.

ment.'' Ordinarily, this investment is not converted into cash within a year, for it is a long-term expenditure of funds. Capital provides the plant and facilities, and the value of capital investment lies in its potential for producing goods which can be sold for profit.

Variations in capital requirements   The fixed capital needed to do business depends to some extent on the type of enterprise. Service and merchandising concerns may be started with relatively limited amounts of capital. In general, the larger the enterprise, the greater the capital investment needed.

In heavy industries such as steel production very large investments are required to provide the facilities used for processing raw materials. Investment in a steel company may range from several million dollars to as much as several billion dollars in the case of a really giant business like United States Steel, for example. The chemical industries vary greatly in their capital requirements. If the firm merely buys chemicals and mixes them to produce a different product, investment may be relatively low, but a primary producer of chemicals may need to make a large investment in processing plants.

The manufacturer, too, finds that his capital needs vary according to the type of manufacturing done. In general, a manufactured product that is large, complex, and made up of many separate parts will require a large capital investment. Simpler products may be fashioned with much less equipment, thereby lessening the need for capital. Again, manufacturers who must operate at very high volume levels to meet their competition will also have high investment requirements, since this type of manufacturing generally requires costly, specialized equipment.

THE SOURCES OF FUNDS

There are various sources that can be tapped for funds to provide fixed capital for a new firm. In most cases, the primary source of such funds is the owner or owners of the firm—the proprietor, the partners, or the stockholders. Funds can also be obtained from a bank or insurance company that invests in business enterprise. Finally, some trade creditors—firms which supply goods or services to other businesses—will lend capital to potential customers to assist them in starting their business.

Money borrowed from sources outside the ownership must be returned by a fixed date, and the borrower must pay a fixed return on the loan at specified intervals. In some cases, the lender will require the firm to pledge particular assets as security for the loan. If the firm fails to make the scheduled repayments, these assets may be sold to pay the creditor firm.

Funds supplied by the owners of a business—stockholders, partners, proprietors—fall into a different classification. For one thing, the firm has no obligation to pay a fixed return on these funds. Second, there is no fixed date on which the funds must be returned. Third, owner-invested funds carry the right to take part in the management of the firm, either by direct owner management or through the selection of top managers for the firm, as in a corporation.

Capital-investment funds are, of course, needed when the business is first established. But this does not end the necessity for capital. Throughout the life of the firm there will be need for additional capital, either to permit expansion and growth or to replace fixed assets that are no longer usable. This additional capital may be available from past profits, but it is often necessary for the firm to borrow funds to meet these requirements.

Stock investments

Investment in a corporation through the purchase of stocks is somewhat different from other types of capital investment. A corporation is authorized in its charter to issue stocks up to a specified limit. Each share of stock is in effect a share in the ownership of the corporation. The shares are assigned a dollar value and sold to the investor, who may be a private person, a bank, or some other source. The purchaser receives a stock certificate from the corporation showing the number of shares that have been purchased. Sometimes a stock certificate is completed for a single share of stock, or one stock certificate may be used to show ownership of thousands of shares of stock in the corporation.

The proceeds from the sale of stock are available to the corporation for investment purposes. Usually the corporation will not issue or sell all the stock that has been authorized by the corporation charter. The stock held unissued leaves the corporation with a further source of funds for growth or replacement. Should the authorized issue of stock prove inadequate, it is always possible to have the charter amended to raise the authorization.

Not every corporation places its stock on the market for public sale. A few persons may join together to form a corporation and purchase all the stock themselves without selling a single share to the general public. This is called a *private* or *close corporation*. Until the 1950s, the Ford Motor Company was a close corporation; all the stock was held by members of the Ford family. Many other family businesses are close corporations, as are numbers of small business corporations. For the small business, the cost of floating securities—that is, making them available to the public—is prohibitively high. In other cases the desire to maintain control of the corporation in a few hands leads to the formation of a close corporation.

Investors who purchase stock in a corporation may buy either common stock or preferred stock. Each type of stock has advantages and disadvantages which should be weighed carefully before the investment is made.

Common stock The common stock in a corporation usually, but not always, carries with it the right to participate in the control of corporate affairs. That is, common stock carries voting privileges, each share of stock being entitled to one vote. The ordinary stockholder does not generally exercise this right in person but delegates his votes to an agent or proxy, who is usually a major stockholder or officer in the corporation. The proxy may cast a large number of votes if he is delegated this authority by stock owners.

Holders of common stock are also entitled to dividends, to the right to subscribe to new issues of stock—called the *preemptive right*—and to the right to share in the assets of the corporation if it is liquidated. They may inspect the company's books, and they may sell their stock whenever they please.

Although the holders of common stock are entitled to dividends, there is no guarantee that dividends will be declared by the corporation, and the common stock may pay no return whatever. For this reason common stock bears the higher risk of the two types of stock. In addition, common stock receives its dividends only after the holders of preferred stock have received their payments, and this fact adds to the risk element involved.

Preferred stock Preferred stock is so named because it carries certain priorities in the distribution of company profits, or in some cases in the distribution of company assets if the corporation is liquidated. If a dividend is declared, payment is made to the holders of preferred stock before any payment can be made on common stock. This reduces the risk of investment considerably, for holders of preferred stock will profit before any investor in common stock. On the other hand, there is usually a limit on size of payment that can be made on preferred stock, while common stock carries no upper limit. When great sums of money remain after the dividend on preferred stock has been paid, the holder of common stock may receive a very large dividend.

Stocks versus bonds and notes Persons wishing to invest in a corporation need not necessarily buy stock in it. They can purchase *bonds*—in effect, notes or promises to pay made by the corporation—or they can accept *notes*. A share of stock is actually a sign of ownership interest; a bondholder is not an owner, he is a creditor—a person who has loaned money to the corporation.

A bond is a promise to pay, very much like a note, but the bond is more formal and has a longer maturity; it is repaid over a longer period of time, usually 10 years or more. Both bonds and notes are instruments of credit, which contain a promise to repay principal and an agreement to pay a definite interest rate at fixed intervals.

There are many differences between stocks and bonds; generally these differences make bonds a much more secure investment. Stocks have no maturity date; a bond is payable at a specified time. Stocks receive dividends only from surplus and only after the board of directors has decided that a dividend is in order; bonds bear interest at regular intervals, which must be paid whether or not the company is earning a profit. Interest on bonds must be met within a definite time period; otherwise legal action can be taken to force payment.

In many cases, bond issues are secured by mortgages on the physical assets of the corporation. These loans are made by commercial banks or insurance companies, and they carry higher interest rates than other loans. The amount that can be borrowed on industrial property is comparatively small, seldom greater than 50 to 60 percent of the appraised value. Such mortgage bonds are usually made out for a short term; payments must be made within very narrow time limits. Another variety of bond is secured by other stocks or bonds; such bonds are called *collateral-trust bonds*. A bond issue which is unsecured is called a *debenture bond*.

The issuance of bonds is rather complex, for there are always three parties involved. One is the corporation that is borrowing money, a second the lenders or bondholders, and the third the trustee, who acts as a go-between and in effect represents the bondholders. The sale of bonds, and of stocks as well, is usually handled by an investment banker, who purchases the securities from the corporation at a discount and sells them again to financial institutions or individual customers.

Indebtedness to creditors

Any contribution to a firm's fixed capital that does not come from owners or stockholders or from retained earnings comes from creditors. Creditors lend money to a corporation and take notes or bonds as security for their loans. These securities are, therefore, evidence that they have contributed to the capital of the firm, and they constitute a fixed claim on the firm's assets. Interest is usually paid on these notes at specified rates and at definite times. There is also a schedule for the repayment of the principal—the amount loaned—over a definite time period.

Investment of retained earnings

Business profits are not always returned to the owners of the business. They may provide an important source of investment funds; that is, profits can be reinvested in a business to provide further capital. If profits are very large, it may be possible to return some dividends to the stockholders and still retain enough to provide a substantial amount for further investment.

The decision to retain earnings for further investment is determined by the financial policy of the firm. The stockholder is, of course, interested in the largest possible return on his investment, and the payment of a reduced dividend or the failure to pay a dividend at all may cause him to sell one kind of stock and change to another. On the other hand, further investment of retained earnings in the business may lead to increased profits and a consequent increase of the value of the stock.

WORKING CAPITAL

"Working capital" is the term applied to the assets which are converted into cash within a year of normal business operation, that is, the assets which are bought and sold in the everyday operating routine of the firm. We must make a clear distinction here between fixed capital, which is the amount of long-term investment in a firm, and net working capital, which is the excess of current assets over current liabilities. Roughly speaking, working capital is the amount of liquid assets available to the firm for such purposes as meeting the payroll, paying transportation costs, paying for raw materials, and taking care of other expenses that must be paid in cash. In addition, these current assets provide the funds necessary to pay off long-term obligations when they come due.

Working-capital requirements

The amount of working capital required by a firm depends on a variety of factors, but the main consideration is the length of time it takes for a dollar spent today to return to the firm—with profit. If a firm must carry large stocks in inventory to meet customer demands or the varying needs of production, working capital requirements will be high. Furniture retailers frequently must carry inventories equivalent to one-half their annual sales volume, but a newspaper dealer gets rid of his inventory every day. If a firm extends credit to its customers it will take longer for dollars to return to the firm and thereby increase working capital requirements.

Another important consideration is the time it takes to make a product. The production of a sophisticated special-purpose machine may require a year or more and involve the expenditure of several hundred thousand dollars for payroll, materials, and plant operations. The firm may not receive a penny until the machine has been installed and the bugs have been worked out. On the other hand, an automobile manufacturer may receive component parts starting on a Monday and have a completed car in a dealer's yard before the week is over. In this case, the firm may get its money before it has to pay its bills.

Working-capital requirements are often divided into two classifications: (1) normal requirements and (2) seasonal requirements. The normal requirement is the minimum needed to support the firm at any part of the year; the seasonal requirement is the extra capital needed during periods of peak activity in production and shipments. A canning factory, for example, may have a relatively small need during the winter months but a very large requirement during the canning season.

The business person is apt either to overestimate or to underestimate his need for working capital. In the first case no harm is done, and the overestimate may even prove beneficial, since the extra funds available may be used to replace equipment or for other emergencies and short-notice needs. Underestimating the need for working funds can be hazardous, since the business person may have to search for additional capital under great pressure and be forced to accept terms less favorable than those he might otherwise obtain.

Sources of working capital

The funds needed for current operations are not always available as cash in the firm's account; in fact, the company may have much of its cash frozen as inventory or as unpaid bills due from other companies (that is, accounts receivable). The need for short-term funds can be satisfied by borrowing from finance companies, factors, banks, or other institutions that make a practice of lending for short periods of time in relatively small amounts. As far as possible, the business person ought to estimate his needs for working capital and include this amount in his long-term financial plan, limiting short-term borrowing to seasonal needs, unforeseen developments, or the purchase of new facilities.

Line of credit   One of the most common devices used by business firms to obtain working capital on short notice is the line of credit. This is an arrangement whereby a bank will agree in advance to provide funds up to a certain maximum. Once the line of credit has been established, the business person simply informs the bank that he will need to make use of this credit and signs promissory notes for the amount advanced by the bank. In some cases, the borrower must keep a certain portion of the loan, perhaps 20 percent, on deposit with the bank. This has the effect of decreasing the amount of money actually advanced by the bank, though the interest must, of course, be paid on all money borrowed.

Short-term loans   Short-term loans must be repaid within 1 year from the date of borrowing. Borrowers are expected to repay the full amount of their obligations annually so that at some point in the year all accounts are closed. This rule is not always enforced strictly. Most short-term loans are secured, though a substantial amount of money is loaned to business firms without security. The security offered to the bank or lending agency may be in the form of inventories, accounts receivable, stocks, bonds, equipment, or plant.

Factoring and pledging accounts receivable   Another method that a firm can use to obtain cash for current expenses is by factoring accounts receivable. The accounts receivable are sold to a company called a factor; the factor then collects the accounts receivable. The firm pays interest and a service charge on the accounts outstanding. This procedure is used instead of borrowing or seeking trade credit in meeting financial requirements. The services of the factor are used by members of the textile, lumber, shoe, paper, and other industries.

The arguments against factoring are based on the fact that it separates the firm from its customers, since normal procedure calls for monthly statements of account which maintain some relation between customer and producer. The system is also believed to limit the freedom of the firm's sales arrangements, for the sales must be on a basis which the factoring company will accept. Further, the use of factoring demands that a firm pay greater attention to sales risk than is normal practice. If, instead of being factored the accounts receivable are discounted—sold for less than face value—or used as collateral or security for regular loans, then the firm maintains its own accounts and the drawbacks to factoring are at least partly removed.

Commercial credit As a substitute for borrowing, the business firm may be able to make use of commercial credit—credit extended by the companies with which it does business. Instead of borrowing money to meet a bill, the firm may ask the creditor to extend credit terms which will defer the need to borrow. This point is discussed further in Chapter 17.

EVALUATION OF SOURCES OF FUNDS

Financial requirements will obviously vary from one business to the next. Figure 16-1 shows the diverse financial bases of three corporations, reflecting not only the differing nature of their operations but also their evaluation of the available sources of funds. When the business person must borrow, he will do well to consider the factors involved in each type of borrowing before he decides which is best suited to his enterprise. In particular, he should note:

1 The burden of cost and repayment

2 The effect of borrowing on business control

3 The flexibility of the financing

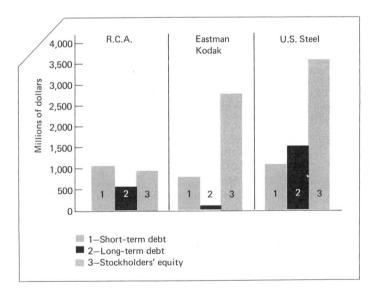

FIGURE 16-1 The financial bases of three corporations

Source: Annual reports, fiscal 1969.

Cost and repayment burden

The old maxim, "Never borrow what you cannot repay," applies with full force to the business person; overborrowing is one of the most common errors in business. However, nearly every firm must borrow at some time, not merely to produce greater profit but to prevent embarrassment, to avoid carrying charges or penalties, or to maintain satisfactory relations with suppliers. The method of repayment may considerably affect the ability of the firm to repay the loan without difficulty.

If funds are obtained through the sale of bonds, the interest charge is fixed and the repayment of the principal takes place in regular steps. Money obtained from stock sales, on the other hand, has no fixed interest charge and no maturing date when it must be repaid. However, it is necessary to attract investors, and one way of doing so is to provide guaranteed interest rates and definite repayment times, reducing the risk to the lender. This procedure, of course, also changes the basis for repayment so that it no longer is related to the firm's ability to pay. Each of these conditions must be weighed before borrowing occurs.

In general, bond issues and loans can be financed more cheaply than stock sales, for lenders will usually accept a lower interest rate in exchange for the promise of regular interest payments and assured repayment of principal.

Influence on business control

If additional funds are obtained by issuing stock, which carries the privilege of voting, the number of owners in the corporation is increased and there is, therefore, a possibility of dilution of control. The same problem occurs when new members are admitted to a partnership which needs additional funds. This does not mean that control of company affairs is automatically placed in different hands. But the new shareholders of a corporation, if there are enough of them, may exert a substantial influence on corporate policy and may even be able to select directors of their own choice.

Bondholders, noteholders, or other creditors of a business are not owners and have no voting privileges; yet they too may, in the last resort, influence company policy. If the terms of a firm's debts cannot be met, the law provides that creditors may take over control of the business, or else take steps to place the firm in bankruptcy. Further, the enterprise may, at the time of borrowing, find that it must alter its policies in order to satisfy lenders; this tends to give the lending agency some element of control over company affairs. Of course, this development may provide the basis of a sound and desirable relationship, particularly for a young firm which lacks the business experience to evaluate its own policies wisely.

Flexibility of the financing plan

Because the cost of financing is a variable that changes from year to year, a business should have some flexibility in its obligation which allows it to take advantage of favorable changes in financing costs. A substantial decrease in the interest rate is of no use to a firm if it cannot replace its high-interest debts at the new rate. Such replacement can be accomplished by issuing stocks and bonds which are callable, that is, which can be called in by the company and replaced by new securities at a lower interest or dividend rate.

Another technique used for this purpose is the open-end mortgage, that is, a mortgage which is not limited to a loan of a specified amount. This source is very useful when borrowing costs increase, for the firm can then increase the sum borrowed on the mortgage at more favorable terms than are usually otherwise available.

The company may also adopt a flexible policy toward dividends, retaining profits within the firm and using them for the retiring of high-cost obligations in order to reduce the fixed drain on current earnings. If the entire surplus is distributed as dividends and the company is forced to rely upon long-term borrowing for needed funds, the fixed charges on the business may become a serious burden when earnings drop. Further, the failure to retain some surplus may limit the ability of the firm to borrow and to take advantage of opportunities for expansion and growth.

FINANCING THE SMALL BUSINESS

Both large and small firms usually need to find additional funds when first beginning, and often, during the course of normal operations. Like the large firm, the small firm must begin with a well-thought-out financial plan and budget. The sources of investment capital open to the large firm are not always useful to the small firm, for they are often too expensive. The personal savings of the owner and his friends or relatives are likely to be the main source of funds in the early stages of growth of the small business. Other funds may come from suppliers, banks, or other loan agencies such as those licensed by the Small Business Administration (SBA). The SBA was authorized by Congress in 1958 to provide equity capital and long-term loans to small businesses through private and government-financed firms. A small business is defined as a firm with fewer than 1,000 workers, a retail or service company with yearly sales of less than $1 million, or a wholesale or construction company with annual sales below $5 million. Incorporation, involving the sale of stock or bonds, is usually not a good policy for small businesses because of the expense involved in fees, etc., and because this procedure cannot guarantee that buyers will be found for the stock in any case.

ALTERNATIVES TO FINANCING

Long-term leasing of equipment or facilities is a means of avoiding purchase and of minimizing the amount of funds that must be invested in the business. Since plant machinery and equipment are usually available on a lease basis, it is possible to undertake a substantial business venture with only the financial backing necessary to secure the lease arrangements and to establish credit with firms that supply materials. The amount of working capital needed by the firm will depend on the turnover of finished goods and the speed of the production cycle. In the short run the extra cost of leasing may be justified by the fact that the leasing makes it possible to establish a firm for which normal financing arrangements would not be available.

Another means of minimizing investment and working-capital requirements is to subcontract work to other firms. In an extreme case the business person may operate without either fixed capital or working capital if he can arrange to have all his work done by subcontractors and defer paying his bills until he has been paid by the firms he supplies. In any case, if some part of a firm's work can be subcontracted, it takes less fixed investment and working capital for the firm to do business. Subcontracting is particularly useful when exceptional orders place a burden on current facilities and when management is not certain that permanent expansion can be justified over the long run.

SUMMARY

The business firm may obtain capital from four main sources: the owners of the business, lenders such as bondholders and banks, trade creditors, and internal sources such as retained profits and depreciation allowances. The ownership is usually the major source of funds, particularly in small business. Owner investment is usually of a long-term nature and places little burden on the business during its growth stages. Owners may contribute funds directly by purchase of stock or indirectly by allowing profits to remain in the business.

Because all firms find it necessary at one time or another to obtain extra funds, business people commonly borrow on a short-term basis from banks or other institutions. The decision to borrow should be made only after careful consideration of costs, anticipated income, risk, and the flexibility of terms. The effect of borrowing on the control of the business needs to be examined with great care, for dilution of control commonly follows from borrowing.

When a firm borrows, it must give its assurance that the loan will be repaid and often must pledge a part of its assets as security for the loan. Loans are always for a definite time period and at a fixed interest rate, and the business person must plan for the repayment of these sums out of working capital. Long-term borrowing may extend 5, 10, or even 50 years, and is generally used for the purchase of fixed assets.

As alternatives to borrowing or investment, the business person may choose to lease plant and equipment or to subcontract work, thereby reducing the amount of capital required for the enterprise.

BUSINESS ITEMS

Can the small business person find venture capital?

A few years ago, most venture investors preferred to put their money into "high tech" types of companies. Recent surveys show that financiers are favoring other types of ventures. Among the top favorites are medical products, communications equipment, and service industries.

Good advice to those seeking financing is to look close to home and to be prepared to present more facts than words to the prospective investor. In addition, it appears that more investors are interested in the firm which has a year or more of operations behind it and can point to track records as well as prospects.

It pays to know what the investors are interested in and to develop a shopping list of organizations that provide the most likely sources of funds. Among these consider the investment banker, insurance company, and small-business investment company.

Will United States industry find the money it needs?

A source of funds for business is the equity market in which stocks are offered for sale to investors. For many companies, the equity market no longer is a ready source of funds, and as an alternative these companies must borrow money at ever-increasing interest rates to meet their needs.

Behind this failure of the equity market to provide funds for thousands of corporations is the dominance of institutional trading concentrated in the high-priced, high-visibility securities. Except for these institutional favorites, stock issues have effectively ceased. Suggestions have been made that the institutions (banks, insurance companies, pension funds, etc.) should be allowed only limited holdings of any particular stock so as to force a spread of their holdings among many stocks. In this manner, it is felt, support for many additional stocks would be forced and maybe this would restimulate the equity market for the thousands of stocks which are not institutional favorites.

An indication of the concentration of investments in these favorites was cited late in 1973. At that time the ten top United States banks had concentrated $27 billion of investments funds in the grand total of just ten sacred cows.

The laws are very kind

There are more people waiting in line for a World Football League (WFL) franchise than there are franchises available. On the surface, this may seem to be an unlikely situation in view of the low attendance during the 1974 season.

But tax laws are very kind to owners of professional football teams. For one thing, player contracts are subject to depreciation—the same depreciation that applies to machinery. It seems certain that most WFL teams will lose money in 1974, but if the owners can hold on for another year, the prospects are that they will come out ahead by selling the franchise. When a team is successful, its returns are similar to those found in a real-estate deal that generates cash flow, tax benefits, and long-term appreciation.

QUESTIONS

1 Explain why public interest in business finance has increased in recent years.

2 Compare the relationship to business of an investor and a lender. Which would you rather be? Why?

3 What types of investment are required by new firms? Why? Does the type of enterprise have any bearing on these requirements?

4 Distinguish between long-term and short-term funds.

5 What is the difference between interest and dividends?

6 How do stocks differ from bonds?

7 How do bonds differ from notes?

8 What are the features that make common stock different from preferred stock?

9 As an investor, which would you prefer, stocks or bonds? Why?

10 If you were a creditor of a firm, would you have any interest in its working-capital position? How would this interest differ if you were the owner?

11 What are the differences between bank credit and commercial credit? Explain why the business person may prefer one over the other.

12 Discuss the influences of types of borrowing on each of the following:

    a cost and repayment burden

    b business control

    c flexibility of financing

13 What are the alternatives to financing?

14 What financing arrangements are available to the small business person, and how flexible are they?

The purpose of this chapter   Ultimately, all the activities of the firm are stated in terms of dollars and cents. The measure of business success or failure is made in terms of dollars of profits or losses. This chapter is devoted to exploring some of the specific procedures and techniques used by financial managers who are responsible for preserving and enhancing the company's financial position. / As a portrayal of financial results, the statements of condition and income and expense are provided for managerial review and analysis. These statements identify the firm's financial condition and summarize the events that caused the firm to achieve that condition. The statistical yardstick commonly used in this analysis is the ratio—a measure of relationship between two figures. / The financial operations of the firm encompass much more than the safeguarding of company cash. Every business activity generates a cost or an income or both and the impact of these activities should be measured and judged. To do this requires an intimate knowledge of the cost structure of the firm; a familiarity with the interaction of cost, volume, and income; and the use of a budgetary system for planning and controlling financial activity. / Questions raised in this chapter include:

1 How are accounting and finance related?

2 What do financial statements portray? What is ratio analysis?

3 What are the different cost concepts of which the financial manager should be aware?

4 How is the budgetary process used as a tool of financial management?

5 What factors affect the flow of cash in a firm?

THE FINANCIAL OPERA-

TION OF THE FIRM

Much of the information needed to make financial decisions comes from the firm's accounting system. In many firms there is no clear line of demarcation between accounting and finance, and in many firms the areas of accounting and finance are the responsibility of a single manager. The accounting system should have the capacity to provide answers to such questions as:

1 How much profit has Division X earned this year to date?

2 Are inventories too high in relation to sales volume?

3 Will there be enough cash available to pay bills falling due 3 months from now?

4 Are labor costs in line with the volume of production?

5 How much money is owed to the firm and when can payment be expected?

6 How much is the business worth to the owners?

THE ROLE OF ACCOUNTING

Accounting deals with a formal system for recording and summarizing business transactions such as the sale of merchandise, the receipt of cash, or the payment of wages. Accounting is not directly involved in the making of transactions; these result from business operations.

In general terms, the purpose of the accounting function is to assist business managers by providing them with the data required for effective decision making. But there may be several groups apart from management who are interested in the accounting function. An accounting system that is adequate for one group may not be adequate for another. The Internal Revenue Service is interested in a firm's accounting system, as are managers, stockholders, and creditors. Because of this, a firm may keep more than one set of records for the same transactions.

WHAT DOES ACCOUNTING INVOLVE?

For accounting purposes, transactions are business events than can be given an exact dollar value. The hiring of an employee is not a transaction, but the payment of wages to an employee is. There are always two sides to a transaction in which something is given and something received. The following are examples:

Received	Given
Worker services	Cash (wages)
Merchandise purchased	Cash
Merchandise purchased	A promise to pay
Cash	Merchandise sold
A promise to pay	Merchandise sold
Cash	Promissory note

Whenever a business transaction is recorded, each entry is assigned to the appropriate account. Thus every entry involving cash is assigned to the cash account and every entry involving the sale of merchandise is assigned to the sales account. The balance of any account at any point in time is the net effect of all the plus and minus activity in that account up to that point in time. The balance of the cash account at year's end, for example, is the difference between the cash balance at the start of the year plus all cash received and less all cash spent.

Types of accounts

Most business transactions involve one or a combination of five types of accounts. These accounts, described below, provide a means for classifying business transactions. The accounts are:

Assets An asset is some form of property whose value can be measured. Cash, inventory, equipment, and buildings are common business assets. Assets are further classified as current and fixed. Current assets include cash, merchandise inventory, and receivables: cash or assets that normally will become cash within a year. Fixed assets are long-term assets such as land, buildings, and equipment. These have no short-run debt paying potential unless sold, whereas current assets do.

Liabilities Liabilities are obligations or debts that arise from business activity. Like assets, liabilities are classified as current or fixed. Current liabilities must be paid within a year. Amounts owed to suppliers, taxes, and short-term notes are illustrations of current liabilities. A 20-year mortgage on a building is a fixed liability.

Ownership As the term implies, this account shows the owner equity in the business. Owner equity always equals the value of assets minus the value of liabilities.

Income Every business transaction ultimately affects in some way assets, liabilities, or ownership. These are the three basic types of accounts. Income accounts record revenue from business operation such as the sale of merchandise or the performance of a service. If merchandise costing $600 is sold for $1,000 cash, the cash account increases $1,000, merchandise inventory decreases $600, and $400 is added to the ownership account. If expenses are incurred in the process, they would be subtracted from the ownership account.

Expenses Expense accounts are used to record the costs of doing business such as purchases of materials, payroll, taxes, advertising, and the like. Not all expenditures of cash are considered expenses. Only that which is consumed in the process of doing business during the period involved is considered expense.

Basic financial statements

The users of accounting information are interested primarily, but certainly not exclusively, in two financial statements. They are the statement of condition and the operating statement. The statement of condition, also called the balance sheet, shows the firm's financial position at a given point in time. As shown in Figure 17-1, it is concerned only with assets, liabilities, and ownership. The operating

Assets			Liabilities and ownership			
Current assets			Current liabilities			
Cash	$190,000		Due to suppliers	$86,000		
Due from customers	200,000		Due to banks	74,000		
Inventory of goods	90,000	$480,000	Taxes payable	14,910	$174,910	
Fixed assets			Fixed liabilities—mortgage		150,000	
Equipment	$320,000		Total liabilities		$324,910	
Land and buildings	240,000	560,000				
Total assets		$1,040,000	Owner equity			
			Capital stock		$640,000	
			Retained earnings:			
			Previous balance	$45,790		
			Net profit	69,300		
			Total	$115,090		
			Less dividend paid	40,000	75,090	715,090
			Total liabilities and ownership			$1,040,000

FIGURE 17-1   Johnson Sales Corp.

Statement of condition, December 31, 19___

Income from sale of goods		$1,000,000
Less: Cost of goods sold		
Inventory, January 1	$110,000	
Purchases of goods	459,700	
Total	$569,700	
Inventory, December 31	90,000	479,700
Gross profit on sales		$520,300
Less: Operating expenses		
Selling expenses	$185,000	
Administrative expenses	205,000	
Miscellaneous expenses	10,000	400,000
Net profit before taxes		$120,300
Provision for income taxes		51,000
Profit after taxes		$69,300

FIGURE 17-2   Johnson Sales Corp.

Operating statement for the year 19___

statement is concerned with income and expense. In a sense, the statement of condition answers the question, Where are we? and the operating statement summarizes how the firm got there (see Figure 17-2).

Statement of condition   The statement of condition (Figure 17-1) shows the owner equity as of December 31, 19—. In addition, it reveals that owner equity increased $29,300 during the year. Owners are also interested in what they own—the nature of assets. Johnson Sales has 46 percent of its assets in a current state and 54 percent in a fixed state. Moreover, the owner's equity amounts to about 69 percent of the total assets.

Operating statement   Management needs to know how much profit was earned and how much it costs to operate at varying levels of activity. From Figure 17-2 we learn that it cost $400,000 to generate $1 million in sales. To be sure, a single operating statement may not be a good indicator of cost—volume relations—but a series of operating statements covering several years of operations can provide the necessary information.

Using financial statements—ratio analysis

A ratio is a commonly used yardstick to express the relationship between two figures. This relationship may be expressed as a percentage, a rate, or a quotient. Financial ratios, as a control device, are only as good as the ability of the financial managers who analyze them. Ratios may be developed to meet particular needs. Because several such ratios have proved practical in business, we will illustrate several which are useful in depicting the use of assets and in showing the ability of the firm to meet its obligations.

Ratios: Use of assets

Business people show the relation between plant investment assets and sales in the form of a ratio. A high ratio is indicative of management's ability to use its tangible assets effectively. The assets which make up inventory or receivables may likewise be related to sales, to provide other ratios which are valuable in monitoring assets and their use.

Plant turnover ratio The plant turnover ratio shows the relationship between the physical facilities of the firm (land, buildings, equipment) and the income from sales. It is an excellent index to productivity. In the Johnson Sales Corp. (Figures 17-1 and 17-2) $560,000 worth of facilities produced $1,000,000 in sales income. The plant turnover ratio in this case is 1.8 to 1 ($1,000,000 × $560,000). Every dollar invested in plant created $1.80 in sales. By comparing current plant turnover ratio with the ratios of previous years, management can provide itself with a very useful tool for measuring and improving plant efficiency. A high income from each dollar invested is a desirable goal under almost any circumstances.

Inventory turnover ratio Inventory turnover shows the relationship between average inventory and total shipments of goods during a specified period of time. In the Johnson Sales Corp., the average inventory was $100,000 and $479,700 worth of products were shipped in one year (computed at cost to the company). The inventory turnover ratio is $479,700 to $100,000, or 4.8 times per year. This shows a complete inventory turnover approximately every $2\frac{1}{2}$ months. This information is quite significant, for inventories represent invested funds, and a low rate of turnover means relatively low earnings, in most cases. On the other hand, the inventory turnover rate alone is not an adequate measure of efficiency. A very high turnover rate can be achieved by selling merchandise at giveaway prices, for example.

Turnover of receivables A comparison of the amount due from customers and the credit sales of the firm gives us the turnover rate of receivables. This ratio indicates the speed with which accounts are collected; it may also be used to determine the average age of unpaid accounts.

If all the Johnson Sales Corp. sales are credit sales, the turnover ratio is 5 ($1,000,000/$200,000) times per year. Another conclusion is that 20 percent of the year's sales were not paid for at year's end. On the average, the unpaid accounts are 2.4 months or 72 days old. If credit terms for this firm are net 60 days, we may conclude that on the average these accounts are 12 days past due. To be sure, some accounts are older than this and some are not nearly as old, but this measure provides a good general indicator of the status of unpaid accounts.

Ratios: Ability to meet obligations

Management must also make use of ratios that show the ability of the firm to meet its obligations as they fall due. The current ratio and the acid-test ratio are most commonly used for this purpose.

The current ratio The current ratio compares the current assets of the firm with its current obligations. Cash and items that will become cash in a relatively short period of time make up the current assets. In Figure 17-1 for example, current assets total $480,000 (cash, receivables, and inventory). Current liabilities total $174,900. The ratio is 2.7 to 1. The most desirable ratio will depend on the type of enterprise involved and a number of other factors. Companies that invest heavily in physical plant may have low ratios compared with firms that have a large investment in inventory. A firm that leases its plant will usually have a higher current ratio than a firm that owns its plant.

The acid-test ratio The acid-test ratio measures cash on hand together with amounts due from customers against the firm's current obligations. This eliminates inventories that for some reason may not be converted into cash in the immediate future. Consequently this is a very conservative measure of the ability to meet current obligations as they mature. The 2.2 to 1 ratio of Johnson Sales is quite high (good).

Other ratios There are other financial ratios that are helpful in making an analysis of a firm's performance. Good indicators of effectiveness include the relationship of gross profit to sales, which, in turn, affects net profits on sales and earnings per share. Table 17-1 gives some of the many ratios that are computed by Dunn & Bradstreet for various-sized firms in different lines of business.

The use of ratios is not limited to financial statements. Sales, production, and personnel executives find ratios a convenient and reliable index to the status of their activities. The reader should note that no ratio can by itself provide the business executive with a complete diagnosis of the firm's business health, but it can indicate problem areas, and further investigation of these areas will usually reveal the causes of changes in a basic ratio.

PROFIT-VOLUME RELATIONSHIPS

The data generated by the accounting system are used in a number of ways by the financial staff. Some of the more important elements of financial management deal with such issues as the impact on profits when the volume of activity (sales or production, for example) increases or decreases; the impact on profits when selling prices are raised or lowered; and the volume of activity that is necessary just to break even. Not that breaking even is a satisfactory objective; rather, management needs to know where this critical point lies. Increasing sales volume does not necessarily lead to higher profits. In the early stages of its "WEO" promotion, A & P food store sales increased significantly but the cost of operation increased at a more rapid rate and losses resulted.

The impact of volume changes on profit depends primarily on the cost structure of the firm. The costs of doing business fall into two categories: time or fixed costs and activity or variable costs. In some instances a given cost may have both a fixed and variable element. The $30 charge for renting an automobile could be $16 per day plus 14 cents for each of the 100 miles driven. Real estate taxes, depreci-

TABLE 17-1 Some typical ratios

Business	Net profit to sales, times	Current ratio, times	Sales to inventory, times	Collection period, days
Manufacturing:				
Auto parts, etc.	4.55	2.52	5.8	40
Industrial chemicals	6.08	2.09	7.3	44
Drugs	5.93	2.94	6.5	44
Machine shops	2.08	4.28	11.7	43
Wholesalers:				
Auto parts, etc.	1.65	2.68	4.6	35
Drugs	1.64	2.58	6.7	34
Fruits and produce	0.90	2.72	50.5	15
Groceries	0.58	2.17	10.9	14
Hardware	1.48	2.98	4.6	41
Retailers:				
Department stores	2.18	3.37	5.4	*
Lumber and building	1.89	3.72	5.0	57
Women's specialty	1.91	2.45	6.7	*
Groceries, independents	1.30	1.97	16.6	*
Furniture	2.39	3.19	4.8	110

* Insufficient data, with both cash and charge account sales, to obtain average collection period.

Ratios, such as these, are based on industry experience over a period of years and serve as rough comparisons in analyzing business data.

Source: Adapted from *Fourteen Important Ratios* prepared by Dun & Bradstreet, Inc.

ation of property, rent, and interest are examples of time or fixed cost. These costs are the same in total whether the firm operates at 0 or 100 percent of capacity. Because these costs are a fixed total, unit costs become variable. If fixed costs are $5,000 and 2,500 units are produced, the unit fixed cost is $2. But if 5,000 units are produced, the unit fixed cost drops to $1. Thus, to the extent that a firm's costs are fixed, there is always a cost advantage to increasing the volume of activity.

Activity or variable costs come into being only because something is being produced. These costs increase and decrease in direct relation to the volume of activity taking place. The labor and material that are a direct part of the production process are considered variable costs. Unlike fixed costs which are measured originally in total, variable costs are measured on a per unit basis. This is shown in the illustrations given below.

Thus in the hypothetical situation where all a firm's costs are variable, there is no cost advantage in increasing the volume of activity because total cost is a function of volume. If this firm is profitable, it earns the same profit on the first dollar of sales as on the last. The firm with fixed costs will not earn profit until these costs are covered.

Illustrations The following examples demonstrate the type of analysis in which financial management should engage if it is to make sound decisions on matters involving cost-volume relationships.

We will assume that product X is one of several produced by a manufacturing firm, and that it has the following characteristics:

Present sales volume	2,500 units
Selling price per unit	$ 10
Variable costs per unit	$ 6
Fixed costs assigned to X	$4,000

Several questions may be raised:

1 How much profit did product X earn? (*The answer:* Profit equals sales revenue minus costs. Therefore profit is $25,000 minus the variable cost of $15,000 (2,500 times $6) and the fixed cost of $4,000. Profit earned was $6,000.)

2 At what volume of sales did the firm begin to earn a profit, or what is the break-even point? (*The answer:* Six dollars is needed to cover variable costs leaving $4 to cover fixed cost and profit. Since we are concerned only for break-even, the question boils down to the number of units needed to absorb $4,000 when the unit contribution is $4. The answer is 1,000 units. The profit of $6,000 came from the sale of the last 1,500 units at the rate of $4 per unit.)

3 With no change in volume, how low can the selling price go before a loss is sustained? (*The answer:* The total cost to be covered is $19,000. $19,000 ÷ 2,500 units = $7.60.)

TABLE 17-2 Unit costs at various volumes

	Volume	Selling price	Variable cost per unit	Fixed cost per unit
	2,500	$10	$7	$1.60 or $4,000/2,500
Plus 10%	2,750	9	7	1.45 or $4,000/2,750
Plus 20%	3,000	8	7	1.33 or $4,000/3,000

4 Market research indicates that for every $1 reduction in selling price, unit sales will increase by 10 percent. How low can selling price go before profits are eliminated? (*The answer:* Table 17-2 indicates that the answer is $8 per unit. Actually, a profit can be earned at this price but a loss would result with a selling price of $7.)

5 If an advertising campaign costing $5,000 is launched, what increase in sales volume would be needed to maintain the original profit? (*The answer:* An additional 1,250 units must be sold to cover the additional fixed cost $5,000 ÷ $4.)

COSTS AND DECISION MAKING

The business person is concerned first with the day-to-day costs incurred. These costs are a specific burden and must be allocated to production and covered by the revenue from sales. Other costs, associated with opportunities and future profits, are the costs that must be evaluated for each long-range venture or new product considered. They are very significant in planning and unless carefully considered may lead to business losses rather than profits.

Costs associated with opportunities and future profits are not current costs but anticipated costs. They are really cost concepts which are used in the decision-making process. There are several such cost concepts which management finds useful, among them marginal costs, differential costs, and sunk costs. Each of these concepts contributes information which is used by the financial managers when they are considering the financial implications of an operating opportunity or investment.

Marginal cost

Marginal cost is the addition to the total cost brought about by the production of additional units. If we were producing toothpicks, it would not be reasonable to assume that the cost of an additional toothpick could be isolated. The concept of marginal cost becomes applicable only in the production of large items or batches of items for which specific costs and revenues can be isolated. The additional unit of product whose costs we are seeking must be a unit large enough to be capable of practical measurement.

How is this concept applied? In its simplest terms, as long as the sale of the added unit of production brings in more revenue than its added cost, profits are increased. If the added cost exceeds the added revenue, profits are decreased. A simple illustration is as follows.

The costs and revenue of 1,500 units of product X are:

Total fixed cost	$ 4,500
Total variable cost at $4 per unit	6,000
Total cost	$10,500
Total revenue at a $10 selling price	15,000
Net profit	$ 4,500

The producer of product X has unused production capacity and can produce up to a total of 2,000 units without incurring additional fixed cost. What would be the total cost of producing 1,501 units? What would be the total revenue for 1,501 units? (Assume a unit selling price of $10.)

Total fixed cost	$ 4,500
Total variable cost	6,004
Total cost	$10,504
Total revenue	15,010
Net profit	4,506

This illustration points out the additional cost of $4 for the additional unit; this is the marginal cost. In this case marginal cost equals variable cost because this is the only additional cost associated with the additional unit.

The concept of marginal cost cannot be applied unless management is well informed of production cost characteristics. Marginal cost analysis is unknown to most business people; the notion of a costing basis other than average cost is quite alien to them. Because of their lack of understanding, they may not recognize available profit-making opportunities.

To illustrate this, let us assume that Sears, Roebuck & Company is in the market to buy 2,000,000 tires for a special promotion. Sears engineers have established the necessary specifications and their tire buyer is looking for the best price. One possible source of supply is the Good Tire Company which has a capacity of 8,000,000 tires but plans to produce only 6,000,000 during the period in question.

If the manufacturer does not apply the marginal cost concept, he may analyze his production costs using Table 17-3. At the 6,000,000-unit level, the average cost per tire is $11 and at the 8,000,000-unit level it is $9.75. If the Sears buyer offered to pay $9 per tire, Good probably would turn him down.

The best decision in this case depends on the alternatives open to Good for utilizing its excess capacity. Obviously, if someone will pay

TABLE 17-3   Total and average cost of production at various volumes

| | Cost to produce | |
	6,000,000 tires	8,000,000 tires
Total fixed cost	$30,000,000	$30,000,000
Total variable cost	$36,000,000	$48,000,000
Total cost	$66,000,000	$78,000,000
Average cost per tire	$11	$9.75

more than $9 per tire, it is better than the Sears offer. Suppose that Sears is the only bidder for this excess capacity. What impact will acceptance of the Sears offer have on profit? The only additional cost to Good to produce tires for Sears is the $6 variable cost per unit. Since each tire sold will bring in $9 in revenue the Sears offer will add $6 million to income and profit.

The marginal cost concept has many applications in business and in other areas. A final illustration relates to the experience of three college students who planned a camping trip by automobile. All costs were to be determined, and each would pay one share. Shortly before the trip was to start, they agreed to invite a fourth person to join them. Because the fourth person's financial situation was not so sound as that of the original three, the decision was made that she could come along provided she financed the costs which she added to those already covered by the three. This is marginal costing and pricing, for the added member purchased the trip at a price equal to the marginal cost. The marginal cost in this case did not include any charges for transportation, as the original party of three had already absorbed the automobile expense, and adding one more to the party did not increase the total cost of transportation. The marginal cost consisted primarily of such expenses as food and accommodations.

Differential costs

There are times when the business person must make a decision on whether to modify methods and equipment even though there may be no significant changes in revenue. Often, new machinery is introduced into the production process because it provides better control over quantity or quality of output, or because it reduces cost of production. Before the decision to change is made, the differences in costs between the existing situation and the proposal (differential costs) should be examined. Although the change may not bring in additional revenue, if there are any cost savings as a result of the change, they represent the eventual net effect on revenue.

The term "differential costs" is not standardized, and sometimes these costs are labeled incremental costs. Nevertheless, decisions

TABLE 17-4 Comparison: old and new		
Illustration	Present method	Proposed method
Output	1,000 units	1,000 units
Total cost	$9,500	$8,200
Investment in new equipment		$7,800
Desired rate of return on investment in new equipment		10% per annum

relative to changes in production processes, sales promotion, wage payment plans, and the like should be made in terms of differential costs.

When considering the desirability of changing from the present method of doing a job to a proposed method which requires investment in new equipment, certain details must be investigated. As an example, let us assume that a proposal is being evaluated in comparison to a present method, and that the details in Table 17-4 are available. Although no increase in output is indicated in the table, there is a potential cost saving of $1,300 per 1,000 units. This represents the differential costs and is composed of the savings made in the various elements of total cost. One way of evaluating this saving is to relate it to the dollar investment in equipment which made the savings possible. If the savings are sufficient to meet management's stipulation of rate of return on new investment, this is a point in favor of the investment.

In Table 17-4, the $1,300 saving is well in excess of 10 percent of the $7,800 investment in new equipment. The saving passes the rate of return test. Other considerations of a financial nature involve the disposition of the investment in the displaced equipment, the availability of funds to finance the investment, and the long-term security of the new investment. Some of the nonfinancial considerations involve the effect of change on the workforce, the quality and reliability of machine output, and the availability of servicing in the event of breakdown, etc.

Cross-over points

The break-even concept, discussed earlier, can be applied to many decision-making areas. Management is constantly trying to lower the cost of doing things. Just about every task in business can be done by a variety of methods each of which has different cost implications. When applying break-even analysis to processes for doing things, we are in essence trying to determine at what volume of activity one process is better than another. When the volume of an activity is low, generally manual processes are used, but as volume increases, the reliance on machine inputs increases. This is due to the fact that labor costs are basically variable costs which do not offer a cost advantage with increased volume. Machine costs are fixed in total and offer savings through growth.

Suppose a firm starts out with five employees and the decision is made to perform the payroll function manually—the only "machine" is a 49-cent ball-point. Assume that the entire payroll function requires 1 hour at a cost of $5. A payroll involving fifty employees would require 10 hours for preparation and cost $50 to complete.

A salesperson comes by and tries to sell a payroll system that reduces labor (variable) cost to 20 cents per employee but involves a fixed cost of $40 per week for up to 100 employees. How many payroll transactions are needed to make the machine method better than the manual method? We know that at some point the machine method will be less costly because of the 80-cent saving in variable costs per transaction. The cross-over point is found by dividing the unit variable cost saving into the increased fixed cost. The answer is that when the number of payroll transactions exceeds fifty per week, the machine method becomes more economical.

Sunk costs

The saying "There's no sense crying over spilled milk" is very sage advice even for the person in business. Too often the business person is hampered in making a sound decision because he insists on bringing past financial outlays to bear on future actions. This is like the person who refuses to buy new shoes to replace those which are uncomfortable because the soles of the old shoes have not yet worn through. Many people in business feel compelled to resist making expenditures on something new or better because they already have an investment in an asset. Similarly, offers to buy goods or equipment are often refused because the vendor only considers what the goods cost him and not the realistic opportunities for their disposal.

Once a given expenditure has been made, its size, whether in dollars or thousands of dollars, should have no effect on management's decision relative to the use or nonuse of the asset purchased. This expenditure, called *sunk costs,* should have no bearing on decisions about future actions.

Illustration The ABC Company accepted a foreign customer order for the manufacture of special-purpose machinery. It had expended $200,000 on the manufacture of this equipment when it was notified that the government to which the customer was subject had issued an order nulifying all import contracts. The scrap value of the equipment was $45,000, and no purchaser could be found for the equipment except for one firm which offered a price of $120,000 if certain modifications were made. The cost to make these modifications was $60,000.

Questions What bearing does the $200,000 sunk cost have on the alternatives facing the ABC Company? The alternatives are:

1 To scrap the equipment. There would be no additional cost incurred. There would be a revenue of $45,000.

2 To accept the offer and modify the equipment. In this case there would be additional cost of $60,000 and additional revenue of $120,000 which leaves a net revenue of $60,000.

Neither of the alternatives considers the past outlay of $200,000. This is the sunk cost and does not enter into the decision process. There is no question that the company will suffer a substantial loss regardless of the decision, but the correct decision is obvious. The ABC Company should accept the offer to modify the equipment and take the larger net revenue even though neither alternative comes anywhere near covering the total costs. To do otherwise would increase the net loss to the company.

BUDGETARY PROCEDURES

One of the prime responsibilities of management is the development of new techniques which will reduce the element of uncertainty in making business decisions. Budgeting, certainly, is not a new technique. It has had wide application even before the advent of large-scale business, but it has not developed to the point where it serves business as it should. There still exists in business a great lack of understanding of what budgets are and how they can be best utilized to serve management. As the process of managing increases in complexity and as the forces of competition increase the risks in business, budgeting should play an increasingly important role.

In its final form a budget is a collection of figures showing such things as planned sales, production, costs, and asset changes. This plan may be set up week by week, month by month, or for longer time periods. It is a formal and quantitative statement of management's plan for the period ahead. It is not necessarily a fixed plan, in the sense that it cannot be altered. Most budgets need to be changed after they have been once approved, because the bases upon which the budget estimates were originally made also change. If budgets were not accordingly adjusted to meet changing circumstances, they would be more of a hindrance than an aid to management.

Budgeting is often viewed as an accounting function. This is perhaps due to the fact that a budget contains statements of income and expenses, assets and liabilities, and the like. The accounting function is very close to the budget function since, among other things, it provides the historical data needed for budget preparation, and it prepares periodic reports showing the relationship between budgeted figures and actual performance. However, budgeting is much more than accounting. First, the budget is a plan. Second, actual performance is recorded and compared with the plan. Finally, necessary actions are initiated whenever planned and actual performances differ significantly. Because budgeting is such a comprehensive operation and involves planning, control, and coordination, it is realistically a management function and falls within the authority of the financial officer of the company.

Certain advantages accrue to budgeting, including:

1 Budgeting forces managers to plan.

2 Budgeting requires that activities be coordinated.

3 Budgeting forces the keeping of adequate records.

4 Budgeting pinpoints efficiency and inefficiency.

Budgeting also has its limitations, including:

1 All budgets are based on estimates.

2 The budget is only a tool and cannot take the place of management.

There are two kinds of budgets: operating budgets and financial budgets. The components of an operating budget are sales, production, materials, and personnel (see Figures 17-3 to 17-6). In the preparation of the operating budgets a forecast of sales is made and serves

ABC Corporation

Sales Budget for Six Months Ending December 31, 19___

Product	Total		Eastern Division		Western Division	
	Units	$ Volume	Units	$ Volume	Units	$ Volume
Refrigerators	6,000	1,200,000	3,000	600,000	3,000	600,000
Freezers	2,500	750,000	1,200	360,000	1,300	390,000
Air conditioners	4,000	520,000	2,500	325,000	1,500	195,000
Water coolers	500	50,000	300	30,000	200	20,000
Total		2,520,000		1,315,000		1,205,000

FIGURE 17-3   Sales budget

This sales budget must be further defined to be useful to the other divisions of the firm. Details on the volume of each model of refrigerator, freezer, etc., as well as the timing of the sales, must be spelled out.

ABC Corporation

Refrigerator Production Budget for Six Months Ending December 31, 19__

		Model No.		
	Total	203	303	403
Units for inventory at end of year	1,500	200	500	800
Units required for sales	6,000	1,000	3,000	2,000
Total	7,500	1,200	3,500	2,800
In inventory at start of year	1,000	300	200	500
Units to be produced	6,500	900	3,300	2,300

FIGURE 17-4 Production budget

Although this budget indicates the volume of production required to satisfy sales estimates and inventory policy, it does not indicate when production will take place and in
what quantity the product will be made from month to month. This information must be
detailed for production planning purposes.

ABC Corporation

Refrigerator Direct Materials Budget
by Material and Model for Six Months Ending December 31, 19__

Model	Units produced	Steel (lb.)		Paint (gal.)		Insulation (lb.)	
		Per unit	Total	Per unit	Total	Per unit	Total
203	900	30	27,000	0.20	180	28	25,200
303	3,300	40	132,000	0.25	825	36	118,800
403	2,300	50	115,000	0.30	690	40	92,000
Totals			274,000		1,695		236,000

FIGURE 17-5 Direct materials budget

This budget shows certain materials requirements for the refrigerator models. The next
step would be to establish a detailed purchases budget which would show in detail when
the materials should be purchased to ensure availability for production.

ABC Corporation

Refrigerator Direct Labor Budget by Department
for Six Months Ending December 31, 19__

Model 203					
Operation	Units produced	Labor hours per unit	Total hours	Labor rate	Total labor cost
Stamping	900	0.25	225	$2.40	$ 540
Painting	900	0.20	180	2.50	450
Fabrication	900	0.40	360	2.30	828
			765		$1,818

FIGURE 17-6   Direct labor budget

A simplified direct labor budget form which would be prepared for each product model. Estimates of the amount of labor required and its cost provide guides for comparison and control purposes.

as the basis for determining the production schedule. The production quota is determined by relating existing inventory to projected sales and setting the production level at that point which will satisfy inventory requirements. The production quota determines the materials and personnel requirements. Other operating budgets cover manufacturing overhead, distribution expenses, administration, and research and development. Manufacturing overhead expenses include indirect labor, supplies, and other factory costs. Distribution expenses cover salespersons' salaries, advertising, warehousing, and storage. The administrative budget covers salaries of executives and the costs of service departments such as accounting. The research and development budget is a very important function these days because such large amounts of money are usually involved; it covers the costs of labor, materials, and other expenses associated with research projects. Although the research and development budget may be considered an operating budget, it is not usually directly related to the immediate operating plan of the firm. Current sales and production, for instance, have little influence on these budgets.

The financial budgets include the cash budget, the capital expenditure budget, and the final projections of the profit and loss statement and the balance sheet. These budgets reveal the effect of the operating budgets on the firm's financial position and earnings potential. They concern matters which are of primary interest to the financial officer.

Cash budget

Most business transactions involve a flow of cash either into or out of a business. The purpose of a cash budget is to plan for the net effect of all budgeted transactions. Management can then plan for those times when there will be too little cash to meet obligations. It is also important to plan for the proper utilization of any surplus monies. Obviously, more cash must flow into a business over time than flows out or there will be no way to pay cash dividends or support growth.

For the going concern, the prime source of cash flowing into the coffers will be from the sale of goods and services and the major outflow will be to cover the costs of creating these goods and services. Figure 17-7 describes the cash-flow process for a manufacturing firm and identifies the areas where the flow may become dammed up. Cash is expended to purchase the labor, materials, and facilities needed to produce goods. If the production process is slow, the cash-flow cycle is extended because any waiting defers the time that goods produced will become cash. Once completed in production, goods move into inventory where they may remain for short or extended periods. The longer goods remain in inventory, the slower will be the flow of cash. Eventually, the inventory must be sold. Some sales will be made on a cash basis, and to the extent that this happens, the cycle is completed. If a profit is made on these sales, more cash will return to the firm than was originally expended. The bulk of all sales in our society are for credit and this means that most often businesses have to wait for their cash. How long this will be depends on credit terms and the firm's collection policy.

This discussion of the cash-flow cycle identifies several problem areas in cash budgeting. If actual sales and production levels conform

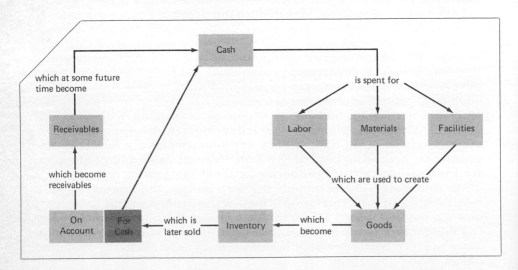

FIGURE 17-7 A cash flow cycle

	January		February		March	
Cash on hand, beginning of month		$1,400		$ 350		$ 250
Receipts:						
Cash sales	$1,100		$1,000		$1,400	
Account collections	1,200		1,600		1,900	
Total receipts		2,300		2,600		3,300
Total cash available		$3,700		$2,950		$3,550
Disbursements:						
Expenses	$3,350		$3,700		$2,200	
Repayment of loans	---------		---------		1,000	
Total disbursements		$3,350		3,700		3,200
Net cash balance (deficit)		$ 350		($ 750)		$ 350
Required borrowing		---------		1,000		--------
Cash balance, end of month		$ 350		$ 250		$ 350

FIGURE 17-8   Budgeting financial needs—an illustrative cash budget

The estimated cash available for February is not sufficient to meet payments; hence, borrowing is necessary. The total cash available for March, however, is expected to be large enough to cover disbursements for expenses, to repay the loan, and to provide a cash balance at the end of the month.

to the budgeted figures and if collections hold true to form, then the process of cash budgeting is quite easy. If the delivery of a component part is delayed one week, thereby delaying production, sales and collections may be deferred.

Figure 17-8 shows a simple cash budget for a 3-month period. Some firms may find it advantageous to budget cash on a weekly or daily basis. The cash budget is a logical document. It simply records anticipated receipts of cash and planned disbursements and indicates the cash surplus or deficit that can be anticipated. A great advantage to the cash budget is that it forewarns management of money needs and permits making loan arrangements well in advance and often on the most favorable terms.

It may not seem a problem to the reader but many organizations must plan for the effective use of surplus money. A university that takes in one-half of its annual income during September and the balance in February must face this problem. A large number of businesses fail to make good use of their unneeded cash. Each year there are 52 weekends or 104 days when most firms have cash balances sitting in a vault at the bank. There exists, for those in the know, a weekend money market where millions of dollars are loaned from Friday at 5 P.M. to Monday at 8 A.M. It is a sound objective to operate with as little cash as possible. The object is to keep cash working. On December 31, 1972, General Motors had a cash balance of $380 million. This is a lot of cash, but GM spends an average of $100 million each working day. Thus GM had on hand enough cash to last 3.8 days. Obviously a high degree of control over cash flow is maintained.

Capital expenditure budget

The capital expenditure budget presents the company's plans for replacing, improving, or adding to the capital assets. No plan of capital budgeting can forestall technological change or alter the rate of obsolescence, nor can it guarantee that all capital expenditures will be profitable. It can force management to pay proper attention to all the factors that should be a part of the capital-equipment decision and thereby to reduce the possibility of a poor investment.

Capital expenditures may be a significant element of the financial program of a firm. For one thing, outlays for equipment, unless their extent and timing are carefully planned, could prove to be a serious drain on the working-capital position of the company. Funds to obtain additional assets may not be available from internal sources. Budgeting is the means whereby this information can be learned in advance, allowing sound planning of the means of financing the capital acquisitions. If plans for growth cover a long term, they should be set up well in advance to allow the company to take advantage of low-cost periods and favorable money-market conditions.

SUMMARY

There is no aspect of business operation which excludes financial implications. Because of this, no textbook treatment of financial operations can be satisfactorily presented in a chapter or two. However, certain aspects of financial operation are basic regardless of the specific area of business dealt with. Consideration of the effect of transactions on profits is fundamental. Whether a contemplated business transaction may have an adverse or a beneficial influence on profit is very desirable information; it does not guarantee success, but it does provide a sounder basis on which to make financial decisions. An understanding of the complexities of the cost structure of the firm and the significance of the concepts of marginal and differential costs is helpful to management in making the type of financial operating decisions which are expected of good management. Because the flow of cash is vital to the conduct of everyday business, and because neither creditors nor employees can be expected to exercise patience when payment is due, sound financial operation demands that cash-flow analysis be a continuous aspect of financial planning.

QUESTIONS

1 What are the nature and purpose of the statement of financial condition? The operating statement?

2 How are ratios constructed? How are they used?

3 How scientifically are profits measured? Cite your proof.

4 What is meant by a "loose" basis for cost determination?

5 All costs vary in one respect or another. How do fixed costs vary? How do other costs vary? Why is this knowledge important to the financial officer?

6 What relationships may exist between volume and income? What is the significance of the marginal cost and marginal revenue concept in relation to changes in volume?

7 What is a standard? How are standards utilized?

8 Define opportunity costs. Why are these costs always associated with future profits (or losses)?

9 Under what circumstances is it feasible to sell goods at less than the average cost of production?

10 What is the purpose of a budget? What are some of the advantages which accrue to budgeting?

11 In outline form, indicate the budget organization which may exist for:

    a A small manufacturing firm

    b A sales organization

    c A municipality

    d A social club

12 What factors have the effect of slowing the flow of cash in a firm?

FOUR

SELECTED BUSINESS CONSIDERATIONS

Certainly there are many more areas than those explored in the first three parts of this text which are very worthy of consideration in any study of business administration. Some of these topics are everyday elements of concern to some businesses and of minimal, if any, importance to other firms. How and when any of these elements are considered is a function of the environment in which the firm operates and the style of its management.

The first two chapters of this Part 4 are both concerned with the element of funds. Doing business on credit, collecting accounts from customers, and the considerations which enter into the setting of prices all, it is hoped, end up in a movement of dollars which may finally resolve itself in terms of dollars of profit. The more one understands some of the characteristics of these processes, the better equipped one is to make a reasonably good business decision.

Because so much of business activity is capable of being quantified, reduced to numbers, and then subject to analytical techniques, it is only natural that as often as is possible, the business person should seek to analyze data by means of these techniques. With the advantage of greater insight and understanding which we presume will result from applying analytical procedures to the business data, the result may be the difference between making good and bad decisions. Any procedure which adds to the business person's storehouse of applicable information may provide significant benefits.

The whole concept of information in a business setting is fundamental to all the material discussed in this text. As a matter of fact, the business unit and the entire economy are representations of information systems which depend on the availability and the processing of data. The flow of information serves to integrate the many activities of business to the end that each function operates to achieve the objectives of the organization. In many business situations, because of the volume of information processing and the need for speed, the process may be automated by using computer technology.

Despite all the information which may be readily available to the business person to assist him in rendering better decisions, he finds it impossible to avoid the incidence of all the risks which confront business in its operations. In the attempt to minimize the possible unfavorable impacts of some of the risks which must be taken, the business person turns to insuring against the consequences.

And finally, because these days an ever-increasing number of firms are directly or indirectly influenced by what is called international business activity, it is a good idea to have some understanding of this area of business activity so as to be able to anticipate in what ways a business may be helped or hindered by it.

The purpose of this chapter   A substantial portion of all business transactions are made on credit. Therefore, extension of credit and collection of debts play a vital part in the administration of any business. In this chapter, we shall examine the factors that are involved in the extension of credit, and the types of credit transactions that are common in business. Finally, we shall deal with the various techniques that may be used in collecting business debts and the considerations that must be borne in mind when collection policies are being formed.

Questions raised in this chapter include:

1 What is the nature of credit, and how important is it?

2 What is involved in the granting of credit? What credit instruments are most commonly used and why? How is the credit cycle completed?

3 How does business credit differ from consumer credit?

4 What does credit cost the creditor? The customer?

18 / DOING BUSINESS ON CREDIT

The word "credit" is derived from the Latin *credere,* which means "to believe" or "to trust." *Credit* is time allowed for payment for goods and services already delivered to the customer. From its Latin origin we see that credit implies trust, or the belief that payment will be made. The seller must have faith in the buyer's willingness and ability to pay within a given time for the goods delivered; the buyer must have faith in the value of the goods he is purchasing. There is also an element of risk in credit, for since there is a lapse of time between delivery and payment, there can be no absolute certainty that payment will be made.

THE NATURE OF CREDIT

The business person is involved with credit in at least two dimensions. First, he must obtain credit, or time, in which to pay his debts to his own suppliers and all the business firms who provide him with goods and services and do not demand "cash on delivery." Second, he extends credit to his customers, who may be other businesses or individuals.

Business credit

Credit extended to others in the manufacturing and selling industries is called *business credit.* This credit, usually extended for a short period of time, is granted to some other business person who may be purchasing materials for manufacture or goods for resale. Business credit is available from suppliers or from commercial banks which will lend the funds to the business person so that he may make his purchases.

A common form of credit is the *open* or *book account.* The seller keeps a record of credit advanced to the buyer and the terms of payment. He sends a bill to the buyer when payment is due. Written instruments such as promissory notes and bills of exchange are also used as credit instruments.

Consumer credit

The credit that a retailer or manufacturer extends to a purchaser who is not another business person is known as *consumer credit*. Business credit facilitates and promotes either production or distribution; consumer credit is meant only to ease the terms of buying for the individual. Some common forms of consumer credit are installment payments, open accounts or charge accounts, and consumer loans.

Consumer credit, although less direct as an aid to business than business credit, plays a very important role in the sale of consumer goods, particularly of heavy items such as appliances, automobiles, and houses, which are too expensive for most consumers to pay for all at once in cash. Usually the use of credit means an increase in the cost of goods to the consumer, but credit makes it possible for the consumer to begin using costly goods before he has saved enough cash to purchase them. Consumer credit has the effect of increasing the demand for goods at a particular time and acts as an encouragement to buy.

CREDIT MANAGEMENT

It is estimated that 90 percent of all the sales made by manufacturers and wholesalers involve the use of credit. In the retail field about 30 percent of all sales are made on credit. Of course, there are differences in policy from one firm and one industry to another. Some companies sell only for cash; others deal almost entirely on credit terms. Credit management has become an important feature of the business scene because of the great increase in credit sales in recent years. Business encouragement of consumer credit buying has promoted a vast new flow of goods and services through the economy, and in many ways the present total volume of business activity depends on the smooth flow of credit operations.

The aim of *credit management* is to allow the maximum practicable dollar value of credit sales while expending a minimum for collecting accounts—that is, minimizing both the losses from bad debts and the costs of credit operation. Credit management, like all other aspects of business, must strive for efficiency. Since it is no longer possible in most cases for businesses to extend credit on the basis of personal knowledge, a large number of published reports, information bureau services, and other facilities are now available to help expedite the credit manager's work. Some firms make use of credit specialists within their own organization; others employ specialized agencies to operate the entire credit side of the business.

THE CREDIT DEPARTMENT

In small firms, credit activity may be a part-time function of some member of the staff. In large firms, it is usually carried out by a large, well-trained staff under the supervision of credit manager. The primary functions of a credit department are to help the business make a profit and to advise management on its credit policy. In practice, this means supervising the extension of credit and the safeguarding and collection of debts.

In general, it is sound credit policy to avoid extremes. A too liberal credit policy may lead to rapid losses if many customers turn out to be bad risks. On the other hand, it is unwise to apply such stringent credit standards that applicants are rejected without adequate reason.

Another goal of the credit department is to promote goodwill for the firm, for increased goodwill is usually a result of sound credit policy. If credit is extended in a reasonable manner and the collection of accounts is carried out with skill and tact, customer reaction will be favorable. On the other hand, poor collection methods or an unclear or inadequately applied credit policy may create an immense amount of ill will and damage the reputation of the firm. While an overly liberal credit policy can be bad business, a credit policy that is too stringent can also reduce the volume of business considerably. Good credit management, therefore, often leads to more business.

Another aim of the credit department is to provide a clearinghouse for credit information. The credit manager must offer as well as receive credit information about his customers, and maintaining good relations with other firms is an essential part of good credit management. Again, a clear policy is needed, for it is unwise for a credit department to give information insufficiently grounded in fact or in some other way unjust to the person it concerns.

SOURCES OF CREDIT INFORMATION

Sound credit decisions must be based on adequate information. When the financial status or previous credit experience of the buyer is known, the credit manager is likely to make a wise decision about extending or withholding credit. In fact, it is hard to see how any decision at all can be made without this information. The safe extension of credit has been limited, until now, by the ability to get accurate credit data. However, the availability of the computer is finally being felt in the credit bureau industry, and computer systems designed to provide immediately available credit data on individuals are becoming increasingly available. Many sources of credit information are open to the credit manager, and some of the more important are the following:

1 Mercantile agencies. Firms like Dun & Bradstreet, Inc., supply information about any business that makes use of credit.

2 Credit bureaus. Local branches of the National Association of Credit Men will provide information regarding the manner in which an individual has met his obligations in the past.

3 Group interchanges. These are regional meetings sponsored by the National Association of Credit Men for exchange of information about credit.

4 Other firms that extend credit. Often a direct or personal exchange of information between the credit departments of two firms will provide essential information about a prospective customer.

5 Banks. Banks can supply information about a customer's financial status, such as his account balance, his performance with regard to credit the bank may have extended to him in the past, or other pertinent data.

6 Sales reports. Salespeople often come into close contact with customers and may acquire information of use to the credit department. Such reports should be verified, of course, before they are acted upon, as should any informal credit report.

7 The customer. Interviews and application forms can supply the basic information about a customer's credit, such as his financial position and his references.

8 Miscellaneous. There are other less formal sources of credit information. Newspapers, annual financial statements, records of legal proceedings, etc., may all provide the astute credit manager with information he can use in his work.

EXTENDING BUSINESS CREDIT

Business credit, which does not involve the consumer, plays a very large role in economic activity in this country, as we have seen. The credit department of a manufacturing firm or wholesale house has as its general aim the achievement of company goals, stated in terms of sales volume, profits, etc. Within that context, however, credit policy must spell out the specific objectives the department seeks to achieve in its day-to-day work.

Credit policies, to repeat, vary from one firm to another and from one industry to the next. Some companies are extremely conservative and exercise great caution in the extension of credit. This reduces losses through bad debts, though it may also act to decrease sales volume without significantly reducing risk. Others follow a more liberal credit policy, which will usually lead to greater sales plus some increase in the risk of loss. Credit policy must attempt to balance the two elements of gain and risk and arrive at the decision most favorable to the company in any particular case.

Much depends on the business customer who requests credit. In any given case, the type of industry, the importance of goodwill, the past history of the firm, etc., must all be weighed carefully. Obviously, sound credit policy would not refuse credit to a good risk and should not extend credit to bad risks, but the application of this principle often calls for very skillful judgment based on sound organization, good information, and well-considered policies. Particular attention must be paid to the collection of obligations, for this aspect of credit work is often more difficult to handle than the extension of credit. "In God we trust; all others pay cash" is a credit policy that has been facetiously suggested because of the many factors involved in the extension of credit and in the subsequent collection.

CREDIT TERMS

Every credit transaction involves the promise to pay for goods or services at some future date. *Credit terms* refer to the method of payment, in particular the time at which payment must be made and the amount of the payment. Credit terms may be defined and enforced either loosely or rigidly, depending on the firms involved, the customs of the industry or trade, the relation between buyer and seller, and similar factors. Some firms use terms as a competitive device, since loosely applied credit terms may be a genuine incentive to buy for some customers.

Various credit terms are offered in business, depending on the goods being sold, the risk involved, etc. Generally speaking, raw materials, particularly those which have a rapid turnover rate or are perishable, carry short credit terms. Heavy equipment and other durable goods carry longer credit terms. Such terms may also depend on the season of the year or the credit rating of the buyer. If a buyer is engaged in a seasonal enterprise, sellers will often allow more time for payment during off-season months.

Buyers who are poor risks are usually given shorter credit terms; a substantial prepayment may also be required, thus reducing the amount of credit extended. Finally, the financial position of the seller may affect credit terms. If the seller is pressed financially, he cannot afford to offer easy credit terms. On the other hand, if the seller badly needs to dispose of his stock, he may offer very generous terms in order to unload his goods at the current market price. Credit terms are an instrument of management policy that can be used to achieve many different ends.

The credit terms generally offered by certain selected lines of business are listed in Table 18-1. They are representative of the entire industry indicated, of course, and do not necessarily define the actual credit terms of any particular company.

CREDIT INSTRUMENTS

A *credit instrument* is some evidence that credit has been granted; it classifies or describes the terms of the transaction. Every credit instrument, regardless of form, involves futurity or date of payment, an element of risk, and a debtor-creditor relationship. In domestic business three credit instruments—the open or book account, the promissory note, and the trade acceptance—are most commonly used in extending business credit. In the export or import trade, the bill

TABLE 18-1 Common terms of sale

Manufacturers

Industrial chemicals	n/30
Agricultural equipment	2/10; n/30
Boxes	COD and n/30
Clothing—men and boys	n/30 and n/60
Confectionery	2/15; n/30
Drugs	2/10; n/30
Furniture	2/30; n/60
Hardware and tools	2/10; n/30
Shoes—men, women, and children	n/30

Wholesalers

Confectionery	2/30 or n/30
Drugs	1/10 EOM
Hardware and tools	2/10; n/30
Shoes—men, women, and children	n/30
Plumbing and heating supplies	2/10; n/30

The terms of sale 2/10, n/30, for example, mean a 2 percent discount provided this bill is paid within 10 days; otherwise the full amount is due in 30 days. Thus if a retail hardware merchant buys goods costing $100, he can take a 2 percent discount and send a check for $98 if he pays the bill within 10 days. COD means cash on delivery; EOM means end of month. Source: Roy A. Foulke, *Terms of Sale Generally Used in 90 Lines of Business Activity*, Dun & Bradstreet, Inc., New York, 1956.

of exchange, the banker's acceptance, and the draft on letter of credit may also be employed for credit purposes.

Open or book account

The *open account* is perhaps the oldest and simplest credit instrument. In many cases, the only evidence that credit is being extended is an entry in the seller's books. (Long ago it was a chalk mark on the back bar of an inn.) A credit agreement may be entirely verbal. Once agreement is reached, goods or services are exchanged and the buyer is indebted to the seller. A book entry does not establish a debt in the same legal sense as a promissory note does, but correspondence about a sale, purchase orders, invoices, shipping documents, etc., may be used to verify a debt if any questions arise.

The open account is extremely flexible, and that is its chief advantage. It is also relatively simple and inexpensive to maintain. But the very flexibility of open accounts can also be a disadvantage, since disagreement about the terms of the sale may easily develop, and as a result the collection of accounts may be seriously impeded.

```
$  1,000.00                              Boston, Mass., April 1, 19--

        Ninety days
_____ after date, ____I____ promise to pay to
the order of _____ J. J. Smith Co. _____

One thousand and 00/100 - - - - - - - - - - - - - - - - - - - - - - -dollars

And interest at _____
                                            Robert Janus
Value received
                                        196 First St.
No.____ Due_____
                                        Boston, Mass.
```

FIGURE 18-1 A promissory note

Janus, a jeweler, buys goods from J. J. Smith Co., a manufacturer, and makes a promissory note to pay the amount 90 days hence.

The promissory note

The *promissory note* is an unconditional promise to pay a specified sum of money to a specified person at a definite future date (see Figure 18-1). The promissory note is always written and signed by the maker. This is a major instrument in credit practice, and most installment sales, for example, are based upon a promissory note.

Poor credit risks may sometimes obtain credit by persuading a good credit risk to guarantee payment by cosigning the promissory note. Should the buyer default, the cosigner is, of course, liable for the amount due on the note. A promissory note may be used when a customer requests and is granted an extension of the payment date for goods or services already delivered. The promissory note, signed by the debtor, establishes the new date of payment.

The trade acceptance

A *trade acceptance* is a draft drawn by the seller against the buyer for the amount of credit extended to him (see Figure 18-2). It directs the buyer to pay a specified amount to the order of the seller at a specified date. The buyer accepts the terms by signing the face of the draft and indicating the bank or other location at which payment will be made on the due date. The obligation to pay is then absolute.

The trade acceptance is widely used by manufacturers and merchants, for it allows business transactions to take place when the buyer does not have the necessary cash in his possession. Further, the seller can readily convert the trade acceptance into cash, and the buyer does not have to produce the funds for payment of the obligation until the due date printed on the acceptance.

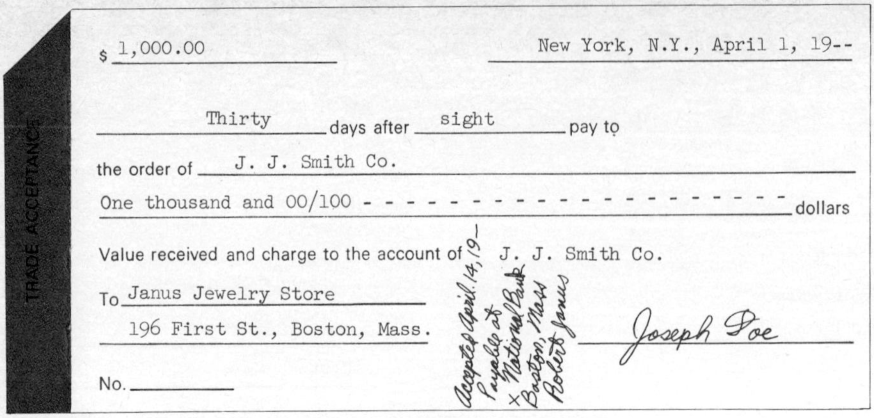

TRADE ACCEPTANCE

$ 1,000.00 New York, N.Y., April 1, 19--

Thirty days after sight pay to

the order of J. J. Smith Co.

One thousand and 00/100 - dollars

Value received and charge to the account of J. J. Smith Co.

To Janus Jewelry Store

196 First St., Boston, Mass.

No.

Accepted April 14, 19—
Payable at
X National Bank
Boston, Mass
Robert Janus

Joseph Doe

FIGURE 18-2 A trade acceptance

J. J. Smith Co. draws a draft against the buyer, Janus, for the credit extended. Janus accepts by signing the draft and indicating the bank where payment will be made on the due date.

Other credit instruments

In the export trade, the draft on letter of credit and the banker's acceptance are used. The major portion of American exports are financed by export *letters of credit.* An American bank acting as agent for a foreign bank issues a letter of credit to the American exporter. Under the terms of this letter of credit, the exporter presents his draft, which is an order to pay, to the American bank and receives payment for the goods which he is exporting to the foreign customer. The American bank is reimbursed by the foreign bank which, in turn, collects from its foreign customer who made the purchase from the American firm.

The banker's acceptance is a time draft, due at a later date, arising out of export transactions. Once the bank has "accepted" the draft—that is, agrees to pay it when due—it may be immediately sold at a discounted price to the bank or to others rather than be held until the due date. This procedure is a convenience to the exporter who has immediate use for the funds.

APPLICATION FOR CREDIT

In most cases, applications for business credit take the form of orders from one business person to another. Since most business orders are shipped on credit, an order in fact amounts to a request for credit. If credit is extended, the goods are shipped; if credit is refused, the firm placing the order may be offered definite terms, such as partial or complete prepayment, or the order may be refused completely.

If the application involves only a small sum, a decision may be made quite arbitrarily. The credit manager may even have a general policy for dealing with applications for small amounts of credit. In such cases the cost of investigation may actually outweigh the possible loss involved, whatever the risk, and therefore many requests for small amounts of credit are not closely investigated.

If a large order is received, however, a thorough and systematic analysis of the buyer's credit history is usually made prior to the extension of credit terms. In some cases a buyer will ask that a line of credit be granted for all his dealings with the firm; he will be investigated with similar thoroughness. The points that interest the credit manager most are the character and experience of the applicant, his fiscal position, and the references he gives to provide information on his past transactions.

Credit analysis

Credit analysis begins with the collection of data relevant to credit standing. The information may consist of balance sheets, income statements, bank statements, or other financial reports, as well as letters of reference, reports from mercantile agencies, reports from other businesses, or reports from a local credit bureau. These data give the credit manager a picture of the applicant's credit history and current credit status. Using this information the credit manager evaluates the risk involved and makes the decision to grant or withhold credit.

Credit lines

Once credit has been extended to a customer, the seller needs a systematic and efficient means of handling any subsequent requests for credit from the same buyer. A common device used for this purpose is to assign a line of credit to the customer. The line may be used simply to authorize credit for normal purchasing by the customer. If an order exceeds the normal figure, the order will be referred to the credit manager for approval before goods are shipped. Sometimes the line is arranged so as to establish a maximum permissible balance of indebtedness. When a new order would exceed the maximum, the order is referred to the credit department for approval. The maximum credit the firm will extend to a customer is called a *credit limit*.

The credit line is established only after a number of factors have been considered carefully. The volume of goods that the customer buys regularly is one significant factor. The willingness of the customer to supply financial information is usually taken into consideration as well. Finally, the customer's ability to pay—his financial status—is crucial. If the customer is listed with a firm like Dun & Bradstreet, Inc., the task of evaluating his credit standing may be much simplified, since that company verifies most carefully the information it publishes about a given business enterprise.

COST OF CREDIT OPERATIONS

Credit operations may be very costly to a firm or may bring it profit. The cost of operating the credit department is, of course, basic. Losses may come about through bad debts, the legal expenses of collection, and the difficult-to-measure cost of ill will toward the company incurred through poor operation of the department. On the other hand, efficient credit management may bring additional sales and increased goodwill for the company. It may be possible, too, to pass credit costs on to the consumer, which will aid in balancing the total account of the credit department.

COLLECTIONS

The credit cycle begins with the granting of credit and the delivery of goods. It is not completed until payment has been received, as shown in Figure 18-3. The collection department has the task of collecting payments for goods sold on credit.

Ideally, the goal of collection is the prompt payment of obligations in an atmosphere of friendliness between the two parties. Collection of the debt less promptly is still preferable to noncollection. Similarly, if the debt cannot be collected without the loss of customer goodwill, it is still desirable that collection be made. The ultimate goal is collection. It is not always fair, however, to measure the efficiency of collection services solely in terms of the percentage of accounts collected. By using drastic methods, it is possible to approach 100 percent collection, but the measures involved may in the long run have an undesirable effect on the reputation of the firm or frighten off prospective customers.

The importance of collection policy

Collection policy may be very lenient, or it may be quite severe. One firm will prefer to move slowly, giving the customer every opportunity to make payment; another will resort to severe measures when the first payment is late. In either case, collection policy has significant effect on the success of the business. Ways that it may affect success are as follows:

1 Policy affects profits. Credit terms determine the actual rate of capital turnover in the firm. If too much of a firm's investment is tied up in uncollected debts, the firm may be obliged to borrow, adding payment of extra interest to operating costs. The turnover rate is important, for a slow turnover rate reduces the opportunity for profits.

2 It is obvious that collection policy is a determinant of losses through bad debts. A lenient credit policy, one that allows buyers to accumulate excessive and old debts to the firm, increases the

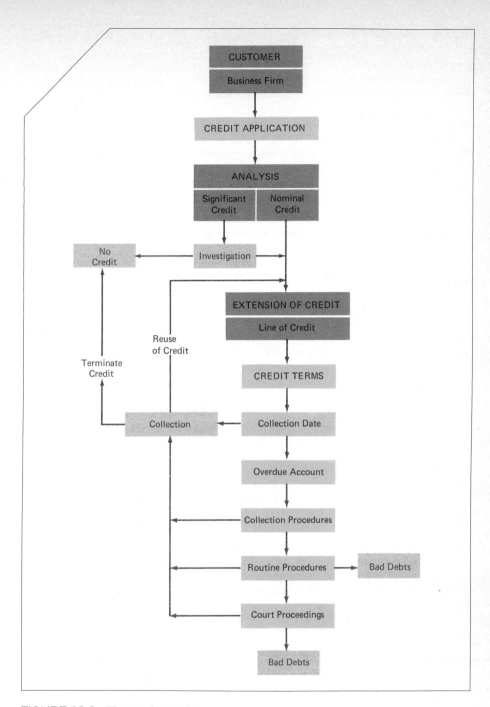

FIGURE 18-3   The credit cycle

risk of loss and increases the actual amount of loss should the buyer fail to make payment.

3 Indirectly, collection policy influences business volume, for a buyer overly indebted to the firm is less likely to make further purchases than a buyer whose account is current.

4 Collection policy certainly affects collection costs, since bills that are long overdue are invariably accompanied by expensive efforts to collect the account. The longer the account continues unpaid, the greater the accumulated cost of collection.

5 Finally, collection policy tends to determine the attitude of the buyer. Most people respect a realistic credit policy firmly applied; ill will is not necessarily generated in the process.

Like other business policies, collection policy must be clear and easily understood, and it should be applied equitably if it is to be effective.

The collection system

The system used to collect credit obligations depends on a number of factors but chiefly on the customer, the competition, and the profit margin.

1 *The customer.* The same collection system cannot be applied to good and poor credit risks, to regular and infrequent customers, or to private and institutional buyers. Each major customer type requires a slightly different approach to collection.

2 *Competition.* If competition is severe, credit collection is likely to be more lenient, just as credit terms are likely to be more lenient. Credit and collection terms are competitive devices that may have important effects on the volume of business.

Profit margin. The collection system adds to the cost of business operation, and this cost must be balanced against the risk of losses from noncollection. It is uneconomical to press too strongly for collection in cases where the added cost of doing so is greater than the loss involved in nonpayment.

The collection system depends, of course, on a well-organized account system within the firm. Each customer account must be accurate and up-to-date, and sales personnel must be aware of the account status of each customer if friction between the collection department and other parts of the firm is to be avoided.

Collection techniques

A careful method for dealing with credit accounts is absolutely necessary for any collection system. There must be a *collection cycle,* a regular pattern of activity for handling all the normal accounts—those which are paid promptly and without difficulty. In addition, regular methods for handling exceptional accounts are needed. These may include collection by draft or by personal calls, the use of collection agencies, and recourse to legal action in rare cases. Such accounts must be classified and the sequence of collection actions specified for each type of account.

In every case, policy should determine how far collection efforts should be carried, which steps should be taken first, and how different collection situations are to be handled. The extent to which these matters have been thought out and organized will largely determine the efficiency of the collection system.

Automated collection systems

Because of the large-scale distribution and use of credit cards by individuals in the United States, pressure has been developing over the past few years for automating the entire process of collection of debts via computerized systems which will deal in "electronic money." The dawn of a virtually checkless, moneyless society is with us, according to those who are promoting the idea of using computers to keep track of a consumer's bank deposits and the payment of bills directly from his bank account.

The computers would be used to maintain an up-to-date credit rating and to maintain the current bank balance of each individual enrolled in the system. Paychecks would be automatically deposited by companies in cooperating banks, which would credit the appropriate individual accounts and also handle payments of all bills from these accounts. The bills would be communicated to the bank by computer hookup between the bank and the merchants with whom the depositors did business.

Before the collection process becomes as automatic as indicated above, significant problems will have to be solved. Among these are the problems of interbank and business firm cooperation in the system of reporting, for not all customers will limit their transactions to the same few banks and merchants.

CREDITOR RIGHTS AND REMEDIES

When the usual current methods for collecting accounts fail, the business person may simply write off the account as a complete loss or may resort to his legal rights and attempt to obtain the assistance of a court in collecting money due him. The laws that protect the creditor are state laws, except in the case of bankruptcy, which is a federal matter. Most states have uniform laws relating to such matters as negotiable instruments, sales, and conditional sales, but other aspects of commercial law vary in detail from one state to the next. Generally, state law provides the creditor with the following possible lines of action:

1 If the unpaid-for goods have not yet been delivered, they may be retained under a seller's lien. If shipment has been made, but the goods have not yet reached the buyer, the process of delivery may be stopped, as a seller's lien applied to the merchandise.

2 If the goods have already been delivered, the seller may sue the buyer for the amount of the obligation, or if the goods have been delivered but not used, the seller may sue either for the return of the goods or for their money value.

In practice, a firm planning to use legal measures against a buyer should consult a competent attorney. Credit managers must know the fundamentals of commercial law in their own state, but legal action is best left to an attorney.

CONSUMER CREDIT

The individual consumer who makes use of credit may have a charge account at a local store or make installment payments on his large purchases, both of which involve borrowing from the seller. In other cases, loans may be obtained from finance companies, credit unions, or banks. It is also possible to obtain credit cards of various sorts that give the bearer credit in hotels, service stations, restaurants, and many other different facilities. The use of consumer credit is widespread and is growing rapidly, as shown in Figure 18-4.

Purposes of retail credit

Merchants extend credit to their customers for the several reasons we have described. Credit is a convenience to the customer, and hence it produces goodwill. It is often necessary as a competitive device. Finally, it tends to increase the volume of sales, since the credit customer tends to buy more extravagantly than the customer who pays cash, partly because the immediate outlay of cash is small compared with the total price of large items, and easy-payment schemes are an attractive lure to the customer who desires to purchase but cannot command ready cash. When payment is spread over a period of time, the customer often fails to notice the added cost of merchandise in credit buying—the so-called "service charge."

Retail credit policy

Consumer credit is extended on a slightly different basis than is business credit. Business credit is actually a source of future income to the buyer; consumer credit is really a drain on future income, or a claim against future income.

Credit policy and procedures follow the same broad pattern, however, whether the seller is granting consumer credit or business credit. An adequate investigation of the customer is needed, credit terms must be carefully defined, and collection procedures must be established. The investigation of the applicant for credit is virtually the same in both cases. The sources of information about the con-

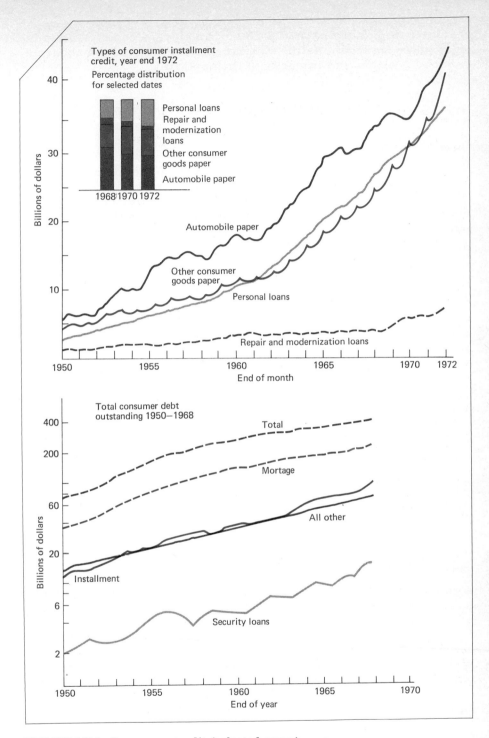

FIGURE 18-4 Consumer credit (selected years)

The lower chart shows the increase since 1950 in total consumer debt outstanding. The graph above shows the components of the installment debt portion of consumer credit outstanding at the end of 1972.
Source: *Federal Reserve Bulletin.*

sumer of retail goods are more numerous than those about the commercial customer. Retail credit bureaus, employers, banks, landlords, other stores, and loan institutions can provide information about the financial position and integrity of the applicant.

TYPES OF CONSUMER CREDIT INSTRUMENTS

Charge accounts

A charge account is considered a convenience to the customer rather than an extension of credit, and terms of payment are often quite short—10 days after billing is the common requirement. It is also customary for the seller to set limits on credit buying through charge accounts. The charge account is really a substitute for cash purchases. It provides the customer who wishes to purchase beyond the limits of his ready cash with a convenient method of making payment.

Installment accounts

The installment account differs from the charge account in the payment terms. Most installment accounts extend the payment period over a period of months rather than days. Although this, too, is a convenience, it is also a genuine case of granting consumer credit. Installment plans may require the buyer to prepay a part of the purchase price; the remainder is paid over a period of months in regular installments to which a carrying charge is usually added.

There is little standardization in installment buying, but it is a general rule in the soft-goods field that the payment period should not exceed the life of the goods. This rule ensures that the debt is paid before the item purchased has been completely used up or worn out. It would be foolish, for example, to pay for a pair of trousers over a 3-year period. The rule is not usually applicable to the purchase of durable goods, since it is assumed that the life of the article exceeds the terms of the installment contract by a considerable amount.

Personal loans

A number of credit agencies extend personal loans to consumers. The more important of them are personal finance companies, credit unions, commercial banks, and pawnbrokers. Personal loans are made for minor business purposes, for the purchase of expensive goods, for home improvement services, and for emergency expenses of many kinds. The loan is an alternative to installment buying and the terms of payment may be easier for the buyer. All personal loans are based on promissory notes signed by the borrower, and in some cases co-signed by another person.

THE COST OF CONSUMER CREDIT

The cost of consumer credit to the business person may be measured by the bad debts incurred, by the cost of administration and collection, by inventory costs, and by the amount of merchandise returned to the seller. Part of these costs is offset by the interest or carrying charge paid by the customer. There are other "costs" that are more difficult to calculate, such as the good or ill will generated by credit policy, or the social "cost" of a credit system that permits consumers to go into debt beyond their ability to pay.

The cost of credit to the consumer is often overlooked by those who engage in extensive installment buying. Carrying charges, or interest, which must be paid for most installment purchases, often amount to a substantial addition to the actual price of the goods concerned. For example, suppose that installment purchases involve a 10-percent carrying charge when the debt is repaid over a 12-month period. The details of the transaction are shown in Table 18-2. The sum owed at

---

TABLE 18-2   Credit cost—an illustration

The installment contract

Purchase price of item	$270.00
Less down payment	30.00
Balance to be financed	$240.00
Carrying charges for 12 months at 10 percent	24.00
Total balance to be repaid over 12 months	$264.00
Monthly payment	$ 22.00

The real rate of interest

Average unpaid balance for whole year (because monthly payments reduce the debt from $240 to $0 in 12 months)	$120
Carrying charges paid	24
Interest rate ($24 ÷ $120)	20%

Although carrying charges are stated as being at the rate of 10 percent, since the rate is applied to the original balance to be financed, the fact that the debt is reduced by monthly installment payments results in an effective carrying charge rate of 20 percent.

the beginning of the contract is $240, and 10 percent interest for 1 year on this sum is $24. But the consumer does not actually borrow the full $240 for a full year. Each month $20 of that sum is repaid. At the end of the first month, the debt has been reduced to $220; at the end of the second month, it is only $200; and so on. Yet the rate of interest, 10 percent, is calculated as though the $240 were to be repaid in a lump sum at the end of the year.

A simple determination of the average amount of indebtedness may be arrived at by taking the original amount of the debt and dividing it in half. Thus, half the original $240 is $120, which represents the average indebtedness during the course of the 12-month term of credit extension. A charge of $24 made by the creditor for this extension of credit is, then, the equivalent of 20-percent carrying charge ($24 is 20 percent of $120). We have seen, however, that if the total debt were paid in one lump sum at the end of the 12 months, the charge of $24 would represent a 10-percent carrying charge. The effect of the installment payments is to double the interest rate.

OTHER CONSUMER CREDIT DEVICES

The several sources of credit previously mentioned are usually adequate for the short-term requirements of borrowers. In the event of major purchases of homes, land, and business properties, however, credit is available in the form of long-term mortgage loans. These loans, involving a large amount of money, are secured by a mortgage on the property involved and are repayable over periods ranging up to 30 years. The interest charges vary and, because of the large principal amount of the obligation and the long term of the debt, add up to a considerable sum over the life of the loan.

A similar source of credit is the secured loan. In this case the borrower pledges certain property as security for the loan. The security may consist of land, furniture, stocks and bonds, or other items of negotiable value.

SUMMARY

The majority of business transactions involve the use of credit, and about one-third of all consumer purchases also involve credit. It follows that the expansion or contraction of credit facilities can have a very important effect on the amount of buying done in the economy. The credit policy of a firm is the amount of business or consumer credit it will extend under particular conditions.

Credit policy and credit activities based on that policy are carried out in most large firms by the credit department. The department advises on the extension of credit and carries out necessary credit

TABLE 18-3 Credit summarized		
Nature and purpose of credit	A source of business income by facilitating production and distribution	Facilitates the purchase and immediate use of goods and services but is a claim on future income
	Constitutes 90 percent of sales by manufacturers and wholesalers	
Sources of credit	Open-book accounts and credit terms	Charge accounts
	Credit instruments: promissory notes, trade acceptances; also bills of exchange, banker's acceptances, and drafts or letters of credit	Installment accounts Loans Mortages

transactions. In the process it hopes to promote goodwill and expand sales, thus furthering the best interests of the firm. Sound credit decisions require a variety of information, and numerous agencies provide such information.

The instruments of credit vary with the product, the customer, the industry, and the business firm. The most common instruments of business credit are the open or book account, the promissory note, and the trade acceptance. Consumer credit is extended mainly through charge accounts, installment buying, and personal loans. A line of credit is often set by business people for one another to facilitate credit transactions, but only after credit has already been established (see Table 18-3).

Collection policy is an important part of any credit system since collection completes the credit cycle. The measures used in collection systems depend on the type of customer, the amount of competition, profit margins, and various other tangible and intangible factors. The ultimate aim of a collection system is to achieve payment for goods, but the drive toward collection must be tempered by other considerations. With the advent of a "moneyless" society, the problems of current collection systems would be replaced by new issues.

The granting of consumer credit has much the same purpose as the granting of business credit, though it does not add to potential productivity. The cost of consumer credit is felt by both the firm and the customer. For the customer, installment buying may involve high interest charges, and the firm, of course, takes the risk that the customer may default on his payments.

BUSINESS ITEM

Creditors lose some legal clout

Special state laws which have allowed business people to more easily collect their bills are being struck down by the courts. The United States Supreme Court declared unconstitutional the laws under which merchants are allowed to repossess merchandise sold on credit before the customer gets to give his side of the story. As a follow-up to this action, many judges are voiding the statutes which allow businesses to resell repossessed merchandise to pay overdue bills. A New York law letting hotels seize the baggage of a guest who has an unpaid hotel bill has been jettisoned.

QUESTIONS

1 Credit implies trust and has implicit risk. Explain this statement.

2 Indicate in what respects business credit differs from consumer credit.

3 Are increased credit sales and minimum cost of credit operation consistent with each other? Explain.

4 What part does goodwill play in the credit operations of the firm?

5 Credit terms vary according to the goods being sold. Why? Credit terms also vary according to the customer. Why?

6 The open, or book, account and the promissory note are customarily two-party credit instruments. The trade acceptance and the export letter of credit involve more than two parties. Explain this difference.

7 Would you, if you were a business person, closely investigate all requests for credit made of your firm? What factors would influence your decision?

8 What is a credit line? How is it used?

9 The only realistic collection policy is that 100 percent of outstanding debts be collected. Do you agree? Why?

10 If a "checkless" society develops, and automated debt collection occurs, what are the implications for the business person who uses terms of sale as a pricing device? What about the business person or individual who writes checks in anticipation of his deposits?

11 What factors influence the system used to collect credit obligations? Justify each of the factors considered.

12 What alternative actions does the creditor have at his disposal if a credit customer refuses to make payment?

The purpose of this chapter   To the average person, price setting often appears to be a simple question of deciding how much profit is desired, adding it to the cost of goods, and thereby setting the selling price. For most business people, if not all, the process is not this simple. Many additional considerations are involved. This chapter deals with the basic function of price in an economic system, with the involvement of the consumer and the producer, and with the concepts of real income and purchasing power as features which enter into the understanding of price setting. We are also concerned with the degree of freedom or nonfreedom which the business person has in setting prices. / Questions raised in this chapter include:

1 How involved is the government in the price-setting process? Why?

2 What are some of the factors involved in setting price levels?

3 How do price levels and purchasing power influence business operations?

4 What is price policy?

5 What is the relationship between prices and profits?

6 What methods are available to a firm in setting prices? Why or when is each used?

7 What is the importance of price level in relation to individual earnings?

THE ROLE OF PRICES IN BUSINESS

The price of goods and services affects, both directly and indirectly, the producer, the distributor, and the consumer. The volume of production within the economy is influenced greatly by price. Price helps determine how people will spend their incomes, since the price of goods often influences the decision to buy. Prices fix costs and the level of profits. For the consumer, prices control the standard of living, since the relation between wages and prices is a measure of the purchasing power of the buying public. The business person cannot always control the price he receives for his goods, but even within the areas where business people can set their own prices, this function is often haphazardly performed.

PRICES AND COMPETITION

How are prices determined in a free market? Essentially, a free market contains a number of producers trying to sell their goods and a number of consumers seeking goods to purchase. Each producer sets a price for his own goods; each consumer makes up his own mind what price he will pay for the goods he wants. That is, the producers compete for the consumer's dollar, and the consumers compete for the producer's goods. This competitive condition is the essence of a free market.

Out of competitive bidding for goods and services comes the price of goods. The price depends on the willingness of producers to sell and the willingness of the consumer to buy. Only when the two reach an agreement and the goods change hands can we truly say that a price has been set. Actually, the price of the goods is set before they enter the market, but the principle remains the same, for the price does not mean anything until the seller finds a buyer for the goods at the stated price.

GOVERNMENT AND PRICES

The government has a great influence over prices, and there has

443

been a tendency for this influence to increase in recent years. In some cases the government may set prices directly. For example, services offered by government corporations such as utility companies or the postal services have their rates set by government action. Government legislation or the action of government agencies may also control the rates that may be charged for particular goods or services. Interstate transportation rate changes must be approved by the Interstate Commerce Commission or the Civil Aeronautics Board. The Federal Power Commission makes the decision on natural gas prices. The Federal Communications Commission controls interstate telephone and telegraph rates. In each case, the government sets the price of goods or services directly.

Since the federal government is the nation's biggest single customer, its contracting and procurement practices have an impact on price levels of many products. Automotive, communications, food, and construction activity are among the many areas in which the government has the power to influence price levels and movements by its buying policies.

Indirectly, too, the government has enormous influence on prices. Excise taxes affect the prices to the consumer of items included in the tax schedule. Labor legislation influences the cost of labor to business, and this cost is passed along to the consumer as an addition to the price of the goods or services produced. At times, it is not easy to pass the price along, and the producer may have to absorb part or all of cost increases by reducing the margin of profit. Antitrust legislation has been applied to price-setting agreements in business in an effort to prevent business combinations that reduce competition. Any expressed or implied agreement which directly or indirectly sets the quantity of production or the prices of goods is illegal and subject to prosecution. However, exclusive dealerships, price discrimination, and tying clauses are not considered illegal unless the effect is to restrict competition. These indirect influences of government on prices can make a great deal of difference to both the consumer and the business firm. Sale or the threat of sale of materials from government stockpiles is another method whereby significant pressure may be imposed to forestall anticipated price increases by the private vendors of these materials. The principle of additional supply offsetting the threat of higher prices would apply in this case.

DEMAND, SUPPLY, AND PRICES

The quantity of goods and services offered on the open market at a given price is the available supply; the amount of goods or services that the consumer will buy at a given price is called the demand for goods and services. In a competitive system, the relation between supply and demand tends to determine the amount of goods and services sold.

Demand

The demand for a particular product is the amount of this product that the customer will buy at a given price. It is very important to note that demand implies a real purchase, not "wishful buying." If goods can actually be sold at a given price, then, and only then, is there a demand for them. Price can be looked upon as an obstacle to purchasing; with most goods, when the price rises the demand for the product declines. As the price falls, there is more and more demand for the product. We say that demand increases. See Figure 19-1.

To construct the graph in Figure 19-1, we begin with a selling price and determine the number of units that can be sold at this price. In the figure, 200 units will be sold at a price of $3; 400 units will be sold if the price drops to $1.50; and 460 units will be sold if the price is only $1. Each of these points is located on the graph, and a line, called a demand curve, is drawn connecting the points. The demand curve shows the number of units that can be sold at each price level.

The principle on which the demand curve is based is quite simple. Suppose that all new automobiles sold for $10,000 each. Obviously only a few would be sold each year. On the other hand, if new automobiles sold for $100 each, millions of people would purchase new vehicles. For each price level in between these extremes, a different number of sales can be expected. The change in the expected sales that comes with a change in price sets the points on the demand curve.

Demand elasticity The effect of a change in price on the demand for the item is not the same for all goods and services. For some goods, a reduction in price does lead to a large increase in demand. For example, if color television sets were reduced to a small fraction of

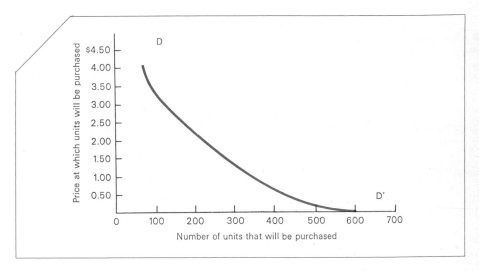

FIGURE 19-1   A demand curve

their present price, a much larger number of sets would be sold. This is an example of an elastic demand—it changes significantly as the price changes.

Other goods are inelastic—a change in price does not change demand a great deal. If the price of household salt, for example, were to be cut in half, it is not likely that more salt would be used by the consumer. Nor is it likely that doubling the price would significantly reduce the demand for household salt, whereas a large increase in the price of color television sets would almost certainly reduce the demand for them. This does not mean that the producers of salt are not competing. It means simply that demand for this type of salt is fixed, and since salt is a household necessity, people will continue to demand salt so long as price remains within reason. If the price of the salt rose to $50 a box, on the other hand, many people could not afford the price and the demand would fall.

Demand and utility Demand implies the ability to pay and the willingness to buy. It is thus a measure of the usefulness of the goods to the consumer, which is called the utility of the goods. Goods for which the consumer is willing to pay a high price have a high utility for that person. Again, we must remember that the utility that individual customers see in a particular product varies considerably.

A multipurpose tool has greater usefulness and may command a higher price than a single-purpose tool, but this usefulness, or utility, has little meaning in terms of demand unless a customer requires the additional features of the multipurpose tool. If he does, and the price is right, he will buy it.

Utility is involved in the decision to buy. However, we should recognize that potential usefulness of a product does not by itself increase the demand for the product. For the demand to increase, there must be a consumer who recognizes the utility and is willing to pay the price to gain it.

Supply

The quantity of goods or services offered on the market at a particular price is the supply of that product. Like demand, supply depends primarily on the price of goods and is essentially a measure of the producer's willingness to sell his product. The supply curve shows the number of units that will be made available for purchase at any given price. The relation between supply and price is shown in Figure 19-2. Obviously if the price is well below the production cost, no goods will be offered on the market. As price rises, the supply of goods becomes increasingly available. The supply curve is thus the exact opposite of the demand curve. As prices increase, the supply increases but the demand decreases; as the prices decrease, the demand increases but the supply drops. This relation can be shown by combining a supply curve and a demand curve on a single chart, as in Figure 19-3.

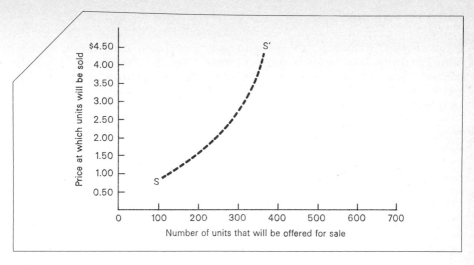

FIGURE 19-2   A supply curve

The graph shows one very significant fact about the relationship of supply, demand, and price. There is one price, and only one price, at which the number of sellers and the number of buyers are equal. That is, at one specific price, supply and demand are in balance. In Figure 19-3, suppliers are willing to sell 300 units at a price of $2.50; buyers are willing to purchase 300 units at this same price. At this price level, supply and demand are equal.

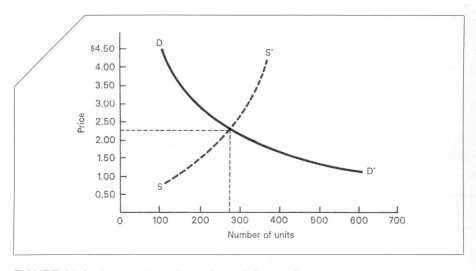

FIGURE 19-3   Interaction of supply and demand curves

THE LEVEL OF PRICES

Historically, prices of goods and services have fluctuated widely, though there has been a general trend in the direction of higher prices. Inflation is the term used to describe a condition in which most prices are rising; deflation occurs when most prices are falling. Price changes result from a change in the relationship between goods available and purchasing power, or money available for spending. This is another way of saying that prices change as a result of the relation between supply and demand. When there is a strong demand for goods, and the supply is not adequate, prices will rise until supply and demand are approximately even. On the other hand, if there is a large supply of goods and little demand, price will tend to drop.

We must bear in mind that other conditions may change this tendency for supply and demand to balance. If goods that are in heavy demand and short supply are controlled in price, then no price increase will follow. Further, a period of rising prices does not necessarily mean that every product increases in price. Quite often the prices of farm products, for example, have fallen during a period of inflation or risen during a period of deflation.

Prices and purchasing power

Purchasing power is a measure of the relation between income and price. Obviously, the meaning of a rise in prices cannot be determined until the general level of income is known. For example, a price increase of 5 percent during a period when income remains stable means in effect a decline in purchasing power, since the same number of dollars will buy fewer goods and services. On the other hand, a large rise in income may result in an increase in purchasing power even at a time of moderately rising prices. And, of course, if prices remain steady while income drops, the effect is a decrease in purchasing power. Purchasing power relates income to prices by measuring the amount that a dollar will buy at different times.

The significance of prices or price changes, then, can only be judged when the relationships between supply and demand, price and income, and price and purchasing power are taken into consideration. In practice, still other factors must be taken into account before the true significance of a particular price level can be determined.

Prices of consumer goods

The price paid by a consumer for a particular item may vary considerably, depending on the brand purchased, the location of the store, and various other circumstances. Virtually identical products often sell for a different price in the same store if one brand has the advantage of skillful advertising. An item with a particular brand name may be priced higher in a local grocery store than in a supermarket at an area shopping center, without affecting sales in the local grocery, since it has the advantage of convenient location.

The price paid for goods is not always high, of course. The business person may lower the price of goods to attract customers and increase his volume of sales. Producers often lower their prices when they are introducing a new product to the market.

Prices of producer goods

The price range of producer goods is generally more limited than the price range of consumer goods. Producer goods are sold to industrial buyers who are little affected by advertising and promotion. They buy mainly on the basis of technical data and specifications. In general, goods of the same quality will tend to stress the service they can provide their customers rather than the points stressed in consumer-goods advertising.

THE INFLUENCE OF PRICES

Prices have an enormous effect on the operation of the economic system. The ultimate goal of business is to use labor, materials, and equipment in such a way that products can be sold for more than the cost of producing them. In any economic system, business or government must determine:

1 What goods are to be produced and in what quantity

2 The method by which the goods are to be produced

3 How much is to be paid as the price for labor, capital, and materials

It is, of course, possible for a dictator to answer these questions arbitrarily, without regard to costs, profits, or prices. In a free economic structure, however, the price of goods on the market at a given time—as determined by supply and demand—will tend to answer these questions without dictation in a manner to be modified only by the exercise of individual choice and judgment.

What to produce

In our economic system, any individual is free to produce anything he wishes. Since business is conducted for profit, business people produce those goods which can be sold at a profit. This is determined by the cost of production (the prices of the factors of production) and by the selling price or demand for the product. A would-be producer compares the profit that can be earned by producing different types of goods or services and chooses those which will earn the greatest profits, other things being equal. For example, when television first began to expand in the 1940s many different firms began to manufacture television sets because they believed, rightly, that a good profit could be earned from their sale. When it is no longer possible to earn a profit from the sale of particular goods, then production stops or is greatly diminished.

How to produce

The method of production, as we have learned, depends on the cost of production and the price for which goods can be sold. In general, business people strive to determine which method of production will mean lowest costs and highest profits. Obviously the price that can be obtained for the product is crucial.

The relationship among prices, costs, and profits is easily demonstrated by considering the position of a firm that is seeking a profit from manufacturing.

If the company must sell its product for no more than $3.50 per unit, or lose sales to its competition, the relation between cost and profit is that shown in the first part of Table 19-1. If sales drop below 2,000 units, the company will suffer a loss. The demand for the product must equal at least 2,000 units at a price of $3.50 for the company to break even.

TABLE 19-1   Prices, costs, and profits

Conditions	Units produced and sold	Total cost	Total sales income	Profit (or loss)
At price of $3.50 per unit	1,000	$ 3,800	$ 3,500	$(300)
	2,000	7,000	7,000	0
	3,000	10,100	10,500	400
	4,000	13,300	14,000	700
At price reduction to $3.37 per unit because of competition, and no change in costs	1,000	$ 3,800	$ 3,370	$(430)
	2,000	7,000	6,740	(260)
	3,000	10,100	10,110	10
	4,000	13,300	13,480	180

	At the 3,000-unit volume		
	Present unit cost ($10,100 ÷ 3,000)		$3.366
To restore profit margin at reduced price for *3,000 units*, what change in cost is necessary?	Total income at $3.37 price	$10,110	
	Desired profit margin	400	
	Maximum allowable total cost	$ 9,710	
	New unit cost ($9,710 ÷ 3,000)		3.236
	Necessary cost reduction per unit		$0.13

Now we can examine the effect of a reduction in price from $3.50 to $3.37, assuming that competition has forced the company to reduce its price. The cost and income relationship has now changed, as shown in the second part of Table 19-1. The effect of this relatively small price change is quite significant:

1 The break-even level is now approximately 3,000 units.

2 The profit potential at each level of production has dropped.

3 The risk of loss has increased sharply.

4 To preserve the original profit margins, costs within the firm must be reduced substantially.

If the selling price of $3.37 is retained, and the company wishes to restore its profit margin, the company is forced to take drastic action. At the 3,000-unit production level, before price reduction, the excess of income over cost, or profit, is $400; after price reduction it is $10. The profit margin has been reduced by $390. To restore this margin, costs must be reduced by the same amount. In effect, as the last part of Table 19-1 indicates, the production cost of each item must be reduced by 13 cents, from $3.37 to $3.24. Cutting 13 cents off the cost of such a low-priced item may not be very easy to do.

PRICES AND THE FACTORS OF PRODUCTION

Table 19-1 shows clearly the relation between price and the total cost of the factors of production. Since price determines the cost level at which business must operate, management will obviously select the combination of labor, materials, and equipment that will produce the desired merchandise at the least cost. If labor is expensive, management may replace labor with equipment that will reduce the cost of the goods to a more desirable level.

PRICE POLICY

The amount of influence that a business person can exert on the price of goods depends on a number of variable factors. Small firms that make goods similar to those sold in large quantity in the market and whose output is not a significant part of the overall volume of goods offered for sale have little or no control over the prices of their product. The monopolist, who has complete control of a single product, has complete price control over the product, within the legal limits imposed by society. Most firms lie somewhere between these two extremes. The price they ask for their goods depends partly on their own policy and partly on factors they cannot control. Large-scale producers may be able to set prices for the entire industry if they command sufficient respect in the market. When there are two or more large producers, the extent to which they enter into competition will help determine the market price for all the firms manufacturing a particular product. This is described as price leadership.

In cases of price leadership, such as that in the United States steel industry where per-ton steel prices are uniform, there are a variety of ways in which a particular company's price is made better than that of competitors. Examples are shipping a better grade of product at the lower price of another grade; better finishing of the product before it leaves the mill; and delivery of materials well ahead of normal waiting periods.

It is quite clear that delivered price is but one of the factors which determine sales. The dependability of the supply source, the service, and the quality standards applied are factors as significant as price itself. Dissatisfaction with any of these product features may result in loss of sales. For example, U.S. Steel, the nation's largest steel company, felt the wrath of General Motors, the largest United States manufacturing firm, when, late in 1969, subsequent to a hefty price increase by U.S. Steel, General Motors reallocated some big steel orders to other companies. Other product features besides price were involved in this decision by General Motors.

Product and price policy

The reputation, quality, distinctiveness, usefulness, or convenience of the product offered for sale will have a direct effect on selling price. The price of merchandise may be influenced by its appearance, by the manner in which it is packaged for sale, or by advertising. If the product is meant for industrial consumption, the principal factor in pricing will probably be its quality, whereas the price of goods meant for the consumer's market may depend more on other factors. In either case, the producer will have to take into consideration a number of points about the product before deciding upon its correct price.

Pricing competing products

Most products must compete with other goods for sales on the open market, and the general level of prices will affect the price that can be asked by a particular product. If the price is set above the competitive level, some of the market may be lost, particularly when there is little qualitative distinction between competing goods.

When goods are priced below the market level, on the other hand, more goods will be sold, but this likelihood does not guarantee greater profits. Unless production costs are lowered by the increase in production volume, the sales increase may affect profits very little, if at all.

The third alternative is to price goods at the competitive price level—to play "follow the leader." Although this pricing policy is not very enterprising, it has some advantages. It does not encourage price cutting by competitors, and it generally produces optimum prices for a particular production level. However, the firm that adopts this policy also relinquishes its opportunity to maximize its own gains by active pricing.

Products that need not compete directly with other goods occupy a special position in the market. There is no necessary limit on price for these products except what the customer is willing to pay. A product which is truly unique, or can be made to appear unique, may be priced at any level that the market will accept. The problem here is to determine the price which the market will accept and then to substantiate this price by active promotion of the product.

On the other hand, products that are in distress because of changing styles, deterioration, heavy storage charges or inventory costs, and similar factors make up another special group. In cases such as these, the important thing is to minimize the losses and forget profit altogether. The price level should move to any point at which the goods can be sold and stop the drain which these products constitute on the firm's resources. It is better to sell at a low price and lose 50 percent of the cost of the goods than to keep the price high and not sell, and thus lose 100 percent of the cost plus the additional charges of storage.

Pricing new products

When a new product is brought into the market, special consideration must be given to pricing. This is particularly true when the new product does not have a competing item which can be used as a guide to price selling.

In these cases, the price of the product may be set to:

1 Maximize profits as quickly as possible. This method is often used to price "fad" items whose popularity dies out quickly.

2 Discourage competitors. A low initial price will often accomplish this result.

3 Recover development costs and investment within a given time period.

4 Yield a regular rate of return, despite any new competition that may appear, or future market changes.

5 Gain speedy acceptance of the product.

In general, the manufacturer of a new product must bear in mind that his product is likely to change in the future as improvements are suggested and that his asking price should be set with this possibility in mind. In addition, he should note that:

1 Pricing on the basis of cost alone is questionable, since it is often difficult to determine the exact cost of a new product before having had some extended production experience with it.

2 Price cannot be established on the basis of demand either, since estimating demand for a new product is highly speculative.

Essentially, the price of new products must take into consideration all the changes that may appear in the future. They include the development of better design, the growth of competition, and changes in public taste.

Price and profit

The profit the seller desires is the most important factor in determining price policy when the seller has the ability to influence the price level. Although the seller's general aim is maximum profit, there is a limit to the amount of profit that can be earned, and most producers must determine what they consider a reasonable profit on the investment in the enterprise.

Management may be satisfied with a small profit if it can produce goods which involve slight risk of loss, but when the possibility of loss is high, a large profit is usually considered necessary to make up for the greater risk involved. Management does not always set its sights on immediate, large-scale profits. In fact, a business person is often satisfied if he is able to break even, or he is even willing to suffer a small loss when introducing a new product to the market. It is important that management state its profit requirements, however, both in the short run and in the long run, before attempting to fix the selling price of its merchandise.

The pricing problem is less severe in wholesaling or retailing than in manufacturing. A simple markup formula may be quite satisfactory for nearly all the goods handled by distributors. Of course, the distributor must also consider the risk element and the investment required of him before he sets the markup that will give him an adequate return. In cases where the price of a product is fixed by the manufacturer under fair-trade laws, the price which the distributors obtain for the goods has already been set, and there is no pricing problem for the distributors to solve.

Effect of price levels

Price rivalry among large firms is not really very common. A competitive struggle actually works to the disadvantage of the firms that take part in price cutting. Large firms tend to seek price stability, to reduce the risk to themselves and to large-scale buyers as well. They may, however, stabilize prices at either a high or a low price level.

If prices stabilize at a high level, the effect is often peculiar. While profits are maximized for the large firms, the effect of high price levels is to increase competition as other firms seek to take advantage of the high potential gains. In addition, high price levels tend to protect inefficient firms producing at high cost from the full effects of competition.

On the other hand, keeping the price levels low will tend to discourage the entry of new firms into the industry. If maintaining a low price becomes the principal goal of the producers, the resultant low level of profit discourages further investment in production, thus stifling creativity. Of course, low price levels can also mean good

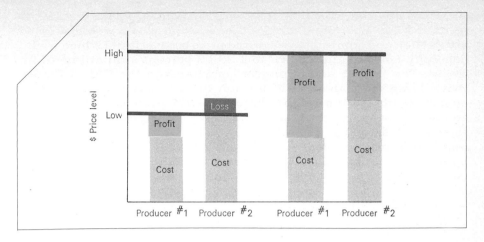

FIGURE 19-4   Price umbrella

With price stabilized at the low level, producer 1 is able to operate at a profit, while the less efficient operator, producer 2, finds that the low level of the price is not enough to cover his costs. This may cause producer 2 to withdraw from the market. If price, on the other hand, were to stabilize at the higher level, both producers would be able to cover their costs and make profits. Thus, the higher price level provides an "umbrella" under which the inefficient (high-cost) producer finds it profitable to operate and which at the same time increases competition because more producers are in the market.

value for money for the customer, depending on the product being marketed. Figure 19-4 shows graphically how the maintenance of a low or high price level effectively excludes or permits added competition from higher-cost, less efficient producers.

Price agreements

Price agreements are arrangements between two or more competing firms to maintain stable price levels. The effect of price agreements is to stifle competition, and laws against such "price fixing" have therefore been enacted, though it is probable that a certain number of such agreements are still made privately and illegally. It is very difficult to prove the existence of a price agreement made in secret, and the extent to which price agreements are in force today is not easily established.

GOVERNMENT PRICE CONTROLS IN ACTION

During the early 1970s, in response to inflation, the United States government imposed a wage and price control program which progressed through several phases. In phase I, during 1971, all wages and prices were frozen for a period preparatory to the start of phase

II. As phase II came into being it brought along with it the establishment of a Pay Board and a Price Commission which were designed to establish and administer wage and price boost criteria which would hopefully hold inflation down to a 2 to 3 percent annual rate of increase. The largest and strongest companies in the United States, those doing more than $100 million of business per year, which meant anywhere from 500 to 1,000 companies, were required to report any price movement in advance. Major wage changes were also to be reported. A second group of some 6,000 to 10,000 companies were required to make periodic reports of what they were up to. The remaining some 10 million enterprises in the United States would have to follow the criteria which the commission lay down and their records would be subject to spot checks. This phase allowed price hikes within limits that left a lot of discretion to the business person.

After 14 months of phase II, phase III came into existence. The Pay Board and Price Commission disappeared as such and became part of the Cost-of-Living Council which is a Cabinet-level group. This council was intended as a step back toward an uncontrolled economy and was to be directly involved in the decision-making process and exercise direct intervention by means of formal wage and price controls. Such public control is, in reality, a trend away from the market system which makes its decisions on the basis of feedback from the profit mechanism and which is an essential feature of capitalism. In mid 1973, phase III was faltering as a program of wage and price controls and gave way to a second price freeze as a preparatory step to the introduction of phase IV. Wages were excluded from this freeze because of the relatively moderate union settlements which had occurred. Other items, namely, rents and raw agricultural products at the farm gate, were also exempted from the freeze. In addition, a limitation on agricultural exports was instituted. Phase IV was intended to exert greater control over the economy on a sector-by-sector basis rather than on a generalized basis. Like phase II, depending on size, companies were required to give prior notification of price hikes and file quarterly or annual reports. Unlike phase II, there would not be any across-the-board rulings but each sector would be handled independently with the possibility that some sectors of the economy would be decontrolled. A schedule of decontrol was established with the idea that whenever the supply-demand situation had returned to reasonable levels as evidenced by a lack of shortages or by dropping prices, the sector would be decontrolled. There was hope that by the end of 1973 controls would be ended and there would be a return to a free market.

Even as phase IV got underway, business people were confused by the policy governing it and by evidence that this phase was not holding together. Controls were loosened over several industries and price increases were approved in several basic areas, as were wage hikes in major union areas. In effect, in this case, the program was not successful, but it does serve as an example of government efforts at control.

PRICE DETERMINATION

There does not appear to be a standard method whereby the American business person determines the price of goods. Of course, the selling price should always be greater than the cost of the goods in the long run; otherwise, there will be no profit for the seller. But even this rule is sometimes violated, for the Ford Motor Company has stated that it sold its Mark I Continental at a price below cost because of the prestige value of the product to the firm. Such a practice as this is not recommended for the firm which does not have rich relatives in the form of profit-producing goods for sale, the profits from which are available to subsidize the "loss leader."

Selling prices may also be pegged at high levels to enhance the quality of the product in the customer's eyes. Because the customer assumes that there is a direct relationship between price level and quality level of the product, he is often willing and happy to pay the higher price. Such a higher price is by no means always justified by quality.

Firms that are attempting to enter a new market may well price their goods lower than usual in the attempt to attract sales.

Finally, competition plays a significant part in the pricing process. Prices must meet competition, both direct and indirect, if the product is to be sold.

SPECIFIC PRICING POLICIES

Four common techniques used by business firms to price their products are as follows:

Cost-plus pricing

This is probably the most common pricing method in use today. Management determines the cost of the goods to the company, adds a percentage of its cost to cover expenses and profits, and arrives at a selling price. A retailer, for example, buys a suit of clothes for $70, adds 40 percent for his expenses and profit, and sells the suit for $98. A manufacturer buys raw materials for $10, uses labor and equipment to turn the materials into a finished product at a cost of $50, adds 100 percent to cover overhead and profit, and sells the output for $120. Very few pricing systems can completely ignore the actual cost of the goods to the seller.

Follow the leader

In many lines of business, there is a leader who sets the price pattern for the industry. In the automobile industry, for example, the price of Chevrolet has seemed to be a guide to other manufacturers of full-sized cars, while the price of Volkswagen seems to be a guide to the manufacturers of compact vehicles. Pattern pricing can be found in the prices of a number of products which are manufactured by more than one firm.

Less-than-cost pricing

It is sometimes desirable to sell goods at prices below the cost to the seller. Once the goods have been produced, any sale is better than no sale at all unless the product can be refashioned. Perishable goods are often sold below cost simply to get rid of them before they deteriorate to the point where sale is impossible. Manufacturers may deliberately produce goods that will have to be sold at a loss if the loss thereby suffered will be less than the operating loss involved in not producing at all. In any event, below-cost pricing is always a temporary expedient or an emergency measure. In the long run, for obvious reasons, price must always be greater than cost.

Intuitive pricing

Occasionally, a business person will set the price of his goods simply by estimating how much people will be willing to pay for them, and without regard for cost. This is particularly true for pricing of fad items or other goods that people buy on impulse and seldom purchase a second time.

TERMS OF SALE

When a buyer purchases goods, he is interested in two basic points: when the bill must be paid; and how much he can deduct from the bill by paying early, that is, the discount he can get. These two conditions constitute the terms of sale and are important constituents of the pricing of goods. The longer the time period allowed for the payment of a bill, the longer the buyer is able to make use of the seller's funds. This, in effect, lowers the cost of the goods to the buyer, for to have had the use of funds without a cost is a savings. The common terms of sale are that a bill which must be paid in 30 days may be discounted 2 percent if paid within 10 days. These terms are written 2/10; n/30. Although 2 percent sounds like a small figure, it amounts to $200 on a $10,000 purchase. If buying in the amount of millions of dollars annually, one could save a considerable sum by taking advantage of the 2 percent discount. These terms are commonly referred to as the cash discount terms. Other terms of sale frequently used in business are listed below.

1 Season dating. Goods that are purchased early are not billed to the customer for weeks or even months after purchase. Dry goods, for example, may be purchased in January and not billed until May. This encourages early buying and allows the manufacturer to plan his production more carefully, thus reducing his risk and cost.

2 EOM terms. Under EOM (end of month) terms, the credit period begins at the end of the month in which the goods are purchased. The buyer is usually given the benefit of the cash discount as well.

3 ROG terms. Under ROG (receipt of goods) terms, the credit period begins when the goods are received. This can be a valuable feature when goods must be shipped long distances.

4 Extra dating. This means allowing extra time for payment. For example, "2/10; 60 extra" gives the buyer 70 days to take advantage of the 2 percent discount. Some of these terms may sound unwise, but their use is widespread, and convenient sales terms encourage buying by making payment easier. In each line of goods the sales terms are more or less uniform, and no seller can alter the terms of sale current within his industry without affecting the volume of his sales.

There are other terms of sales, of course, some of which are made up of combinations of the above. In price lining, for example, the basic idea is that the business person wants the best price possible and at the same time wants to preserve a certain margin of profit. Once he establishes the desired price level, he adjusts costs by altering the quality of the product to preserve the profit margin between cost and the desired selling price. If he must change the selling price, his profit margin is maintained by varying the product quality up or down.

PRICE LEVEL AND THE PUBLIC

It is almost impossible to predict the public reaction to a particular price level. A high price may attract customers who believe that high price guarantees high quality, but it may also attract competitors who seek to share the profits to be earned from high prices. High prices may, on the other hand, discourage customers who shop principally on the basis of price. A low price will generally increase sales volume, depending on the elasticity of demand. Low prices tend to discourage competition and to promote efficiency.

PRICES AND THE INDIVIDUAL CONSUMER

Consumption, which is the satisfaction of demand, depends on the amount of money generally available in the economy for the purchasing of goods and services. When large amounts of money are available, a wider variety of goods is purchased, and more goods of each type can be purchased. When average money income is small and prices are high, fewer goods are purchased. This relation between prices and income is expressed in terms of purchasing power. The purchasing power of the individual members of society effectively determines which goods are consumed by which persons. Each rise in prices that reduces purchasing power limits the number of people who can enjoy certain goods. We say that certain things become "luxuries" or "too expensive." As purchasing power increases, the number of people who buy particular goods increases and yesterday's luxuries become commonplace in many more homes. When purchasing power is low, only a few people may feel that they can afford new automobiles each year; when purchasing power increases, many more persons buy new automobiles each year. And along with this variation in purchasing power we have the creation of problems for the supplier industry, the automobile producers, who, as sales decrease, cut back production and lay off workers.

PURCHASING POWER AND REAL INCOME

In illustration, suppose that Ms. Jones has a take-home income of $92 per week in a particular year, and that she can satisfy her family's needs by purchasing "consumption units"—a combination of food, clothing, shelter, and services—at a price of $18.40 per unit. We can then measure her standard of living as being at a level of five units in this particular year. Let us also assume that her neighbor, Mr. Smith, also has a five-unit living standard.

Five years later Ms. Jones takes home $144 per week, and Mr. Smith takes home $288 per week. The price of each combination consumption unit has also increased to $36 per unit. Jones now has a four-unit standard of living, whereas Smith has improved his position to an eight-unit standard. Both individuals have received increases in take-home pay, yet the purchasing power and standard of living of Jones have dropped while those of Smith have increased. We have actually measured the real income of the two persons by looking at the purchasing power they possess after both wage and price changes have been taken into consideration.

Another way of viewing the same problem is to calculate the percentage of increase in prices and in income and to compare them. For the real income to remain the same or be maintained, the percentage of increase in income must equal the percentage of increase in prices. As we can see from the first three lines of Table 19-2, Jones's income increase percentage was less than the price percentage increase, and thus, her real income decreased. Smith's case is just the opposite. His income increase percentage exceeds the price percentage increase, and his real income took a jump.

An alternative way of measuring purchasing power is to restate the dollar income of a given period in real income terms. This will allow a direct comparison of the real income of various periods. The conversion of dollar income into real income is accomplished by dividing the actual dollar income by an appropriate price index and multiplying by 100. In Table 19-2 the consumption-unit price index shows that the price levels of consumer goods have almost doubled in the 5-year period. If prices double, it takes twice as many dollars to buy a given item as it did during the base year. Jones's real income declined by 20 percent during the period, and she has at the end of 5 years less purchasing power and less real income.

TABLE 19-2 Income and real income

	Base year	Five years later	Percentage of increase over base year
Actual dollar income:			
Jones	$ 92.00	$144.00	+ 56.5
Smith	$ 92.00	$288.00	+213.0
Actual price per "consumption unit"	$ 18.40	$ 36.00	+ 95.7
"Consumption-unit" price index	100	195.7	+ 95.7
Real income:			
Jones	$ 92.00	$ 73.60	− 20.0
Smith	$ 92.00	$147.20	+ 60.0
Real price per "consumption unit"	$ 18.40	$ 18.40	

Real income is a measure of purchasing power. It is derived from the percentage changes in income and prices as compared with a base period.

Real income is a measure of purchasing power, and purchasing power determines the amount of goods that can be bought for consumption. Changes in real income, then, establish the amount of goods and services which we shall consume. This has the effect of deciding who will consume goods and services, or in effect, amounts to a system of rationing production.

Prices are inextricably involved in this relationship of income and purchasing power. The income represents the prices paid to labor for its services. The price of the consumption unit represents the prices set by industry for goods and services. The direction and extent of movement of these "prices" determine the changes in real income and purchasing power.

SUMMARY

Prices affect, and are affected by, a wide range of conditions in our society. Fundamentally, price is determined by the rule of supply and demand, by the amount of goods offered at a given price, and by the amount of goods purchased at a given price. Many additional factors, however, may act to alter this basic relationship.

Historically, prices fluctuate between inflationary periods, when prices are rising, and deflationary periods, when prices are falling.

The relation between prices and income, which is measured in purchasing power or real income, determines the standard of living of the population and the manner in which goods and services are distributed among the members of the community.

The chief function of the price mechanism in a free economy is to determine what will be produced, how it will be produced, and how the goods will be shared. Since price affects cost and profit as well as purchasing power, the pricing system answers all three of these fundamental questions without difficulty.

Pricing policy in any industry will depend on the product being manufactured, on the general price level in the industry, on government policy, and on a wide variety of local conditions. Government has a significant effect on prices, both by direct control over the prices charged for goods and services and through indirect controls such as taxation, legal regulation of competition, and large-scale procurement.

The methods used for pricing an item offered for sale are usually related to the cost of the goods. Most prices are set on a cost-plus basis, but it is sometimes necessary or desirable to sell goods at less than cost for short periods of time as a means of minimizing losses or to gain entry into a market.

QUESTIONS

1 What is the significance of price to the consumer, producer, labor force, retailer, government, investor, banker?

2 Why is it possible for a price range to exist for virtually identical items in the same general market area?

3 How much influence do you as an individual have on prices? Why? How much influence do prices have on you? Why?

4 What is demand elasticity? How may it work in the cases of (a) trouser belts, (b) houses, (c) spats, (d) diamonds, and (e) steaks? Is the answer to this question different for a wage earner, an entrepreneur, a bon vivant?

5 The more utility an item has, the greater is the demand for the item. Discuss.

6 If the price level of a product is high, the less efficient producers are able to continue operations. How is this related to the fact that the higher the price, the greater the willingness to supply goods and services?

7 How are the following interrelated: (a) real income, (b) purchasing power, (c) price level, (d) dollar income, (e) inflation, and (f) deflation?

8 What influence does price have in determining what is to be produced and how it is to be produced?

9 How may prices serve to ration goods and services? What personal experience have you had to support your answer?

10 The small firm has no influence on the price policy of the industry in which it operates and usually is content to follow the leader's pricing policy. Does this mean that the small firm has no role or leeway in setting the prices for its own products? Discuss.

11 Discuss the many direct and indirect ways in which government influences prices.

12 Terms of sale are price determinants. Explain.

The purpose of this chapter   The cost of a poor decision increases as business becomes larger and more complex. As the margin for error becomes smaller and smaller, business people must develop and apply techniques that will facilitate more accurate planning and control. In the field of physical science, mathematical analysis is essential for measuring the impact of a set of variables. Business people have learned a lesson from the scientist and are now using various types of quantitative analysis to help solve their problems. / In this chapter we shall discuss a variety of elementary techniques that are used to solve common business problems. / Questions raised in this chapter include:

1 How does a business person estimate the volume of activity necessary to earn a profit?

2 How does a business person determine the least costly production schedule?

3 How can a business person optimize the use of his production facilities?

4 How does a business person determine when to shift from one process of production to a more sophisticated one?

5 How much control should be exercised over a particular business activity?

20 / QUANTITATIVE ANALYSIS FOR BUSINESS DECISIONS

Good management is well-informed management. The manager who must make decisions on the basis of inadequate or inaccurate information can hardly be surprised if the decisions prove to be in error. At the very least, sound business decisions depend on current conditions within the firm; in most cases, management is well advised to look beyond the firm to local conditions, the status of the industry, and the general trends of business activity within the whole economy. The necessary information is usually available to management, but management has to see that the data needed are collected and used. Businesses suffer far too often because management has failed to make adequate use of the information available to it.

BUSINESS DATA

The data available to the business person comes from a variety of sources. We can better understand some of the problems involved in the use of data if we first categorize the various types of data. There are several ways of classifying or describing data, each of which identifies some of the uses and limitations of data.

Secondary data

Secondary data have, by definition, already been gathered and published, and they are generally quicker, easier, and cheaper to use than primary data. Sources of secondary data include company records, government agencies, banks, trade associations, and universities. These sources should always be explored first. Many of the statistical data in this text came from secondary sources; in Figure 20-1, later in this chapter, the sales and payroll data came from the annual report of the General Motors Corporation.

Primary data

Primary data are gathered by the person or group studying the problem. Suppose you are asked by the company president to determine the cost of processing a purchase order. You explore all sources of published data in the firm and cannot find an answer. You are now forced to go to original sources, research the problem, and come up with an answer. This is primary research, and the result is primary data.

Primary data are costly to gather, and the collection process can be very time-consuming. Obviously, this source should be avoided until it is evident that secondary sources will not suffice. As desirable as it may be to avoid primary investigations, most firms have a continuing need for primary data. One goal of a firm's information system is to provide needed data, but change in business is so frequent and often so drastic that a given system can seldom be complete.

The collection of primary data in business presents a number of special problems, particularly in terms of the money and time consumed plus the special skills required in the fairly elaborate procedures of primary investigation. In most cases, at least four basic steps are involved:

1 *Locating the sources of information.* In many instances, a preliminary study may be necessary simply to determine where the desired information can be found. If Chrysler wants information indicating why people purchased the current Chrysler models, the source of information is readily available because every purchaser can be identified. But if Black and Decker needs information regarding an increase or decrease in the sale of three-eighth-inch electric drills, the source of information is less clear because purchasers or potential purchasers are much more difficult to locate.

2 *Designing a method of collecting data.* After the source has been identified, a decision must be made as to the method that will be used to obtain the necessary data. Mail questionnaires are frequently used but the rate of return is usually very low and there is no way to ascertain who actually provided the data on questionnaires that are returned. Personal interviews are frequently used by Gillette to gather data on shaving habits and preferences. This approach can cost $10 or more per interview and many firms cannot afford this approach. Gillette finds it a very effective approach. The method used must consider time, cost, and reliability. Cutting the time and money available for gathering data generally reduces the reliability of the data.

3 *Conducting field investigations.* In almost all cases, a certain amount of field work is needed in primary investigations. As the term implies, people must go out into the "field" and observe what is going on. Without such supervision, little credence can be placed on the data that comes in.

4 *Analyzing and interpreting data.* It is useless to analyze and interpret data unless the data are accurate and representative of the situation under study. The first three steps of this information-gathering process are very important. A primary investigation generally produces a mass of raw data which, as it stands, is useless. It must be tabulated, compared, arranged, and brought together so that it has meaning. Very often such data are subjected to a number of statistical procedures such as those discussed later in this chapter.

Internal data

Internal data are fundamental to all business decisions. Every business organization is to some extent unique, and the particular circumstances of the individual firm should be the starting point for sound management. Basic business decisions usually begin with the question: Where do we go from here? Unless the management of an enterprise has accurate knowledge of its present state, it cannot give a satisfactory answer to this question.

The adequacy of internal data depends largely on the collection and recording system used by the firm. A management that keeps only enough records to meet legal requirements will usually find that it is unable to determine basic conditions inside the business without additional information. When management recognizes the need for adequate information and assigns the information system a high priority, its business records will meet the firm's present and future informational needs. A sound data-collection system must be carefully planned so that future need for certain kinds of information is anticipated.

Desirability of using internal data If a firm's business records are complete and accurate, internal data have several advantages over external data in addition to those mentioned above:

1 Time and money are saved in the data-collecting process because it can be made an adjunct to the company's record system.

2 Internal data are more up-to-date than data obtained from external sources.

3 The accuracy of internal data can be verified. Regardless of the source from which external data are obtained, one cannot be completely sure of their accuracy.

External data

Internal data alone, however, do not usually provide a sufficient basis for all business decisions, and most firms make some use of external information in their planning. It is highly desirable in this case, too, that management seek the most accurate and up-to-date written material and not rely on personal feeling, hearsay, or incomplete reports. Business information available in regular publications can be a gold mine for the business person. The principal problems encountered in the quest for external data are the identification and evaluation of sources. Where can data be obtained? How far can they be trusted? Some of the answers are given below.

Ascertaining needs

It would be impossible for a business person to maintain a complete collection of all the business data available today, as the yearly output would fill a number of large rooms. The business person must be selective about the material he keeps within the firm; otherwise he will soon be overwhelmed with storage, handling, and identification costs. For most firms a few basic sources of information published at regular intervals should be sufficient. When further information is needed, it can be obtained from libraries and from government and private sources quite efficiently. The vast bulk of information that is available forces management to decide precisely what its needs are before it begins to assemble external data. The more precisely the needs of the firm can be defined, the more efficiently and cheaply the information can be collected.

SUMMARY

A business enterprise generates a steady stream of vital information in the normal course of its operation. Data concerning payroll costs, production, productivity, sales, personnel, etc., are always present in the firm for collection, classification, analysis, and use by interested parties. Whether this information will be used is another matter, for if people are unaware that certain information exists, or if it is not made available to them, it will not be used. Internal data are extremely important to the decision-making process because they describe both the past and the present state of business. This information when combined with relevant external data provides a solid foundation for predicting future business needs.

THE USE OF BUSINESS DATA

Data as generated in the normal course of events, or as obtained outside the firm, are seldom ready for use in evaluating performance and planning activities. They are usually collected in the form of total sales, total payroll costs, or total accessions to the payroll. As a result, most business data must be processed before they are in usable form. The modern business manager must have a basic understanding of statistical and mathematical techniques that will enable him to make full use of the data available.

In the balance of this chapter several statistical and mathematical techniques are discussed with specific reference to their use in solving financial, staffing, marketing, production, and other types of problems. Of necessity, the discussions are quite brief and elementary.

GRAPHIC PRESENTATION

A list of numbers about sales volume, accounts receivable, factory output, or payroll over a period of time is quite meaningless to the manager who must evaluate it and use it for planning purposes. A simple line graph such as Figure 20-1 often gives a much clearer view

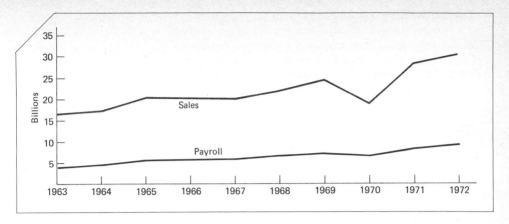

FIGURE 20-1   General Motors Corporation, annual sales and payroll, 1963–
1972

of activity than a list of numbers. There is greater need to chart data
when two or more sets of data are involved. In Figure 20-1 a clear,
but general, comparison can be made of sales and payroll for a 10-year
period. If this form of graphic presentation does not do the job, there
are many alternatives that are explained in all business statistics text
books.

STATISTICAL MEASURES

Graphs and charts are very helpful in making simple comparisons
or noting the trend of activity over a span of years, but often the
manager needs to have a single value that is representative of an
entire group of data. For example, he may need a single value to
describe the age of equipment, typical earnings, typical sales transaction, or typical time to complete a unit of production.

Averages

An average is a single value that can be used to represent a series
of values. For example, the average time required to assemble a unit
of production may be 43 minutes. Each of us has used the term
"average," but more likely than not we have used it as a generalization such as, "The traffic is about average for a Tuesday morning."
In statistics, however, the term "average" has three explicit meanings: the mean, the median, and the mode.

Averages and ungrouped data Business information can be presented
in two distinct forms—ungrouped data, used in this section, and
grouped data, illustrated in Table 20-1. Most students have used the

arithmetic mean many times as they compute their average earnings or average grades. The concept is simple, and can be readily explained by an example: If a student receives scores of 82, 75, 88, and 79 on four equally weighted exams, his mean score is 81. The sum of the four values (324) is divided by the number of items (4).

The median is the middle value in a series of numbers that have been arranged in order of their magnitude. Thus if five students took an exam and their scores were 75, 79, 80, 86, and 90, the median score is 80. Note that had the lowest score been 20 or 60, for example, the median would still be 80. This feature of the median is a strength in measuring central tendency because the median is not affected by extreme values.

The mode is the most frequently mentioned item in a series. Thus the shoe retailer who sold 20 pairs of size 7 shoes, 45 pairs of size 8 shoes, 27 pairs of size 9 shoes, and 15 pairs of size 10 shoes has a modal size of 8.

These illustrations of the three types of averages are simple, and yet they contain the basic concepts. The mean is the sum of all values divided by the number of values; the median is the middle value in an array of items; and the mode is the most frequently mentioned item.

Averages and grouped data   Frequently the number of items in a set of data is so great that they must be grouped or classified to facilitate analysis. A list of the earnings of 1,500 employees, for example, is a meaningless mass. Such a large number of values can be assigned to appropriately selected classes as in Table 20-1. In the process of grouping, the identity of the individual items is lost, and we must assume that the mean value of the 160 items in the $80 to $90 class, for example, is $85. In practice, the midpoint of each class probably will not be the arithmetic mean of all items in each class. Thus, some accuracy may be lost in the grouping process, but with proper attention to grouping, a high level of accuracy can be maintained.

The arithmetic mean of grouped data, as in Table 20-1, is obtained by multiplying the number of items in each class (f) by the midpoint of each class (x), totaling $f \cdot x$, and dividing by the number of items in the series. Thus in our illustration total wages of $158,900 are divided by 1,500 and the arithmetic mean is $106. This becomes a representative value for this set of data.

The business person might be interested in knowing the earnings of the middle wage earner rather than the mean wages. If so, he needs to calculate the median earnings. Since the median value is the value of the halfway point, we are interested in the value of the 750th item in the series. To find this value we must first cumulate the frequencies (Σf). Next look down the list of cumulated frequencies until the 750th item is reached. It falls in the $100 to $110 class interval because the sum of f up to this point is 480 and the class ends with the 980th item. To determine the precise location of the median, we reason that it is 270 (750 minus 480) "steps" into this class. Since the class has 500

TABLE 20-1 Earnings of 1,500 factory employees, week of March 4, 19—

Class interval	Number (f)	Midpoint (x)	Σf	f · x
$70 to $80	60	$75	60	$ 4,500
80 to 90	160	85	220	13,600
90 to 100	260	95	480	24,700
100 to 110	500	105	980	52,500
110 to 120	240	115	1,220	27,600
120 to 130	180	125	1,400	22,500
130 to 140	100	135	1,500	13,500
	1,500			$158,900

The mean equals $158,900 divided by 1,500 or $106.

steps, the median is 270/500 into this class, or 54 percent of the way through. The dollar span of the class is 10; therefore the median is $5.40 above the starting point of the class ($100). The value of the median, then, is $105.40. We can conclude that an equal number of workers earned more than and less than $105.40 during the week of March 4. In a situation where there are many extreme values, the median is a much better measure of "average" than the mean. In this illustration the mean is greater than the median because there are more workers earning relatively high wages.

The mode is more difficult to understand than the mean or the median, but from observation we can see that it falls between $100 and $110 because this class has the greatest frequency (f). If the frequency in the next higher class and the next lower class were equal, the modal value would be the modal class midpoint. Therefore in our illustration we can reason that it falls a little below $105 because the frequency in the next class (240) is less than the frequency in the preceding class (260)—there is a pull effect. Specifically, the value of the mode is estimated by relating the frequency of the modal class (500) to the frequency of the preceding and following classes. The modal value in this illustration is 240 (500 minus 260) divided by 240 plus 260 (500 minus 240) times the dollar value of the class (10) added to $100. The modal value is $104.80. We can conclude that more workers earned $104.80 during the week in question than any other amount.

Measures of dispersion

Averages, also called measures of central tendency, are single values that describe a number of values. As useful as they are, they may present an incomplete picture of events, and this tends to destroy

TABLE 20-2   Minnesota Vikings defensive team, standard deviation of the mean

Position	Weight X	Mean X̄	X−X̄	(X X̄)²
D.L.	265	226	39	1,521
D.L.	255	226	29	841
D.L.	248	226	22	484
D.L.	240	226	14	196
L.L.B.	226	226	0	0
M.L.B.	231	226	5	25
R.L.B.	231	226	5	25
L.C.B.	195	226	31	961
R.C.B.	200	226	26	676
S.S.	195	226	31	961
F.S.	198	226	28	784
	11 2,484			6,474
Mean weight	226			

Standard deviation equals $\sqrt{\dfrac{6,474}{11}}$ equals 24.2 pounds.

their usefulness. Suppose, for example, that the mean temperature on Cape Cod during the month of July is 72 degrees. Based on this picture of temperature, what sort of wardrobe is in order for next July? How much bedding should one plan to take on vacation to Cape Cod next July? From this picture of temperature little can be concluded.

Measures of dispersion tell how the individual items in a series are spread out. Some of the common measures of dispersion are described below.

The range   The range is the difference between the low and high values in a series. The range of weights of the Minnesota Vikings as shown in Table 20-2 is 70 pounds; the lightest player weights 195 pounds and the heaviest player weighs 265 pounds. The range of wages shown in Table 20-1 is assumed to be $70. If experience indicates that the range of temperatures on Cape Cod is from 60 to 84 degrees in July, we have a much better basis for making the wardrobe decision.

Quartiles   When the items in a series have been arranged according to their magnitude as in Table 20-1, it is possible to divide the series into groups such as quartiles or deciles. When computed, quartile 1 lies at a point on the scale which divides the series so that 25 percent of the items are below it in value. Quartile 2, which is also the median, lies at a point where one-half the items are below it and one-half the items are above it. Quartile 3 is the value which is exceeded by 25 percent of the items. From the data presented in Table 20-1 we can reason that the value of the three quartiles will be the value of the 375th, 750th, and 1,125th items. These values are calculated in the same way as the median, for they too are position values, and they are $95.96 for the first quartile, $105.40 for the second quartile, and $116.04 for the third quartile.

From this, we can reach several new conclusions about wages earned during the week of March 4. Twenty-five percent of the workers earned less than $95.96, and 25 percent earned more than $116.04. Another interesting observation is that the middle 50 percent of the workers earned between $95.96 and $116.04. These values give a clearer and more complete picture of worker earnings than either of the averages described above.

Standard deviation   The statistical measure, standard deviation, is a means for learning about all the items in a distribution. It is determined by comparing the mean with each item in the group to determine how far, "on an average," each item is from the mean. Table 20-2 shows the calculation of the standard deviation of the mean weight of the Minnesota Vikings defensive team. What we have done is to take the difference between each player's weight (X) and the mean ($\bar{X}$), disregarding plus and minus signs because the values are later squared. The squared values ($\bar{X}$ minus X)^2 are totaled and divided by the number of items (11), and the square root is extracted. The standard deviation is 24.2 pounds. All that this simple illustration is designed to do is explain a concept. Now, suppose that we had used a similar process to calculate the standard deviation of the mean wages in the previous illustration and found it to be $8. With this we can draw some valuable conclusions. (Calculating standard deviation from grouped data is deemed too involved at this point; therefore it is assumed.)

The normal curve   When a large number of items are included in an analysis, they tend to follow a normal distribution such as Figure 20-2. The center vertical line denotes the mean. The curve has a distinctively characteristic shape. We know for example that 68.27 percent of all the items in a normal distribution are included in an area ±1 standard deviation, that 95.45 percent are included in an area ±2 standard deviations, and that 99.73 percent are included in an area ±3 standard deviations. These relationships hold true no matter what the magnitude of the mean or standard deviation.

Returning to our illustration on earnings, we can conclude that slightly more than two-thirds of the workers earned $106 ± $8, and that fewer than 5 percent earned more than $122 or less than $90. These figures tell us much more about wages in general than a simple measure such as the mean. Tables are available that enable us to calculate the range of earnings for any portion of the group.

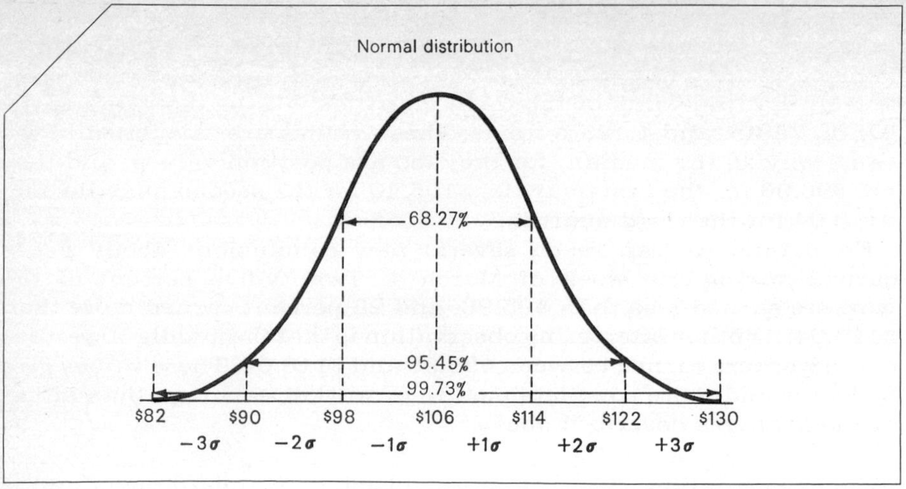

FIGURE 20-2 Normal distribution

The trend

The trend is a very important statistical technique used to measure the growth or decline of activity over an extended period of time. Management is concerned with trends in sales, costs, accidents, and many additional types of activity. The trend measures average growth or decline of activity for the time period involved. The calculation of the trend is explained in Table 20-3.

The underlying concept in "fitting" a trend is that there is a line that best depicts growth or decline. Several methods are used to cal-

TABLE 20-3 Calculation of trend

Year	*Sales Y*	*X*	*X^2*	*XY*	*Trend*
1969	460	−3	9	−1,380	446
1970	580	−2	4	−1,160	524
1971	520	−1	1	− 520	602
1972	640	0			680
1973	800	+1	1	+ 800	758
1974	830	+2	4	+1,660	836
1975	930	+3	9	+2,790	914
	7 | 4,760		28	+5,250	
	Mean sales 680			−3,060	
				2,190	

Average annual growth is 2,190 ÷ 28 or 78.

culate trend values, including a method for calculating a freehand trend. The method used should depend on the data itself and the use to which trend measurement is put. The method described below and illustrated in Table 20-3 is called least squares, and it can be proved that a least-squares trend line runs precisely through the middle of the plotted data (see Figure 20-3). Calculation of the least-squares trend involves the following steps:

1 Determine the arithmetic mean of the values in the time series. This is the midpoint or focal point for the trend line.

2 Identify each year as ±1, 2, 3, etc., from the middle year, X.

3 Multiply each X by the corresponding Y value, noting positive and negative quantities. This is done to determine the slope of the trend line. Higher values in early years result in a downward trend; higher values in later years result in an upward trend.

4 Square and total the X values.

5 Divide the sum of XY by the sum of X. This is the average annual rate of growth or decline.

6 Add to or subtract from the mean found in step 1 the average growth or decline starting with the middle year. Note from the Trend column of Table 20-3 that the difference between successive values is 78.

These trend values can be plotted and compared to actual activity as in Figure 20-3. One use of the trend is to project it and obtain an indication of what can be expected in future periods. Once the trend has been calculated, it is possible to measure any seasonal influences that may exist, that is, movement of activity that can be expected

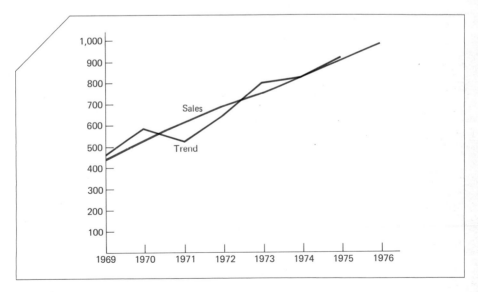

FIGURE 20-3 Plotting of trend

away from the trend each month because of seasonal changes—Christmas, Easter, school openings, etc.

Correlation

There are many situations in business where management is concerned with the relationship that exists among two or more variables. For example, what change can be expected in sales if advertising expenditures are increased by 10 percent, or what, if any, increase in spoilage can be expected if the work week is extended to 44 or 48 hours? Correlation studies can identify the extent to which there is a cause-and-effect relationship between different aspects of business operation. Obviously this can be of great help to management in the planning process.

The sales manager of the Apex Corp. spent a great deal of time in the development of a sales aptitude test. The purpose of the test was to obtain an index of probable success of newcomers to the sales force. Each of the company's ten salesmen has been on the job for a minimum of two years and his test score, recorded when he was hired, is compared to his last-year's sales in Table 20-4. We would like to know whether there is a significant relationship between the two variables.

The extent to which two or more variables are related can be shown graphically by the use of a scattergram. Figure 20-4 is a scattergram of the data given in Table 20-4. The fact that the points scatter diagonally across the chart from lower left to upper right is evidence of a positive relationship; that is, higher sales is a function of higher test scores. If the distribution was from upper left to lower right, a negative relationship would be indicated.

The closer the points on a scattergram fall in a straight line, the more direct is the relationship between the variables. If the points were scattered all over the chart, no correlation would be indicated. It is possible to measure correlation mathematically. A coefficient of correlation of $+1$ indicates a direct positive relationship and a coefficient of correlation of -1 indicates a direct negative relationship. If, in our illustration, the coefficient of correlation was $+.9$ we know that sales aptitude is a good measure of sales success.

TABLE 20-4 Apex Corporation test scores and sales volume

Salesman	Score	Sales (000)	Salesman	Score	Sales (000)
Abbott	60	$400	Fardy	80	$600
Barnes	40	300	Goldman	50	400
Carey	70	420	Harvey	90	500
Daniels	50	360	Irving	40	350
Epstein	60	380	Johnson	60	420

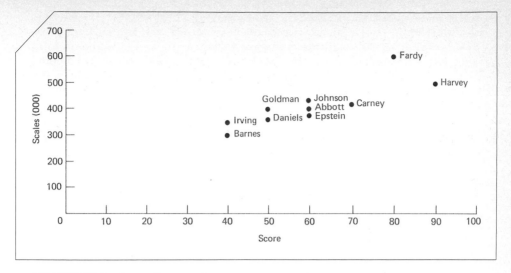

FIGURE 20-4   Apex Corporation scattergram of test scores and sales

MATHEMATICAL ANALYSIS

Modern business management relies heavily on mathematical analysis when making decisions because of the precise nature of mathematics. To be sure, mathematics is not a substitute for sound judgment, but there are many situations in which a manager's view can be sharpened by this type of analysis. Of necessity, mathematical devices are feasible only in those instances where the pertinent factors can be expressed in numerical terms. The techniques discussed below are quite elementary and can be developed in more sophisticated fashion, but they do provide an insight into the nature of mathematical analysis.

Break-even analysis

This technique, referred to in Chapter 17, is used to determine the level of business activity at which the firm neither earns a profit nor suffers a loss—it "breaks even." Break-even is seldom a goal of business; rather, it establishes a reference point or a point of departure. This type of analysis is very helpful when selling prices are being set, equipment replaced, production methods selected, or production volume determined.

The data required for break-even analysis are a measure of income expressed as a unit selling price or a total sales volume, fixed costs of operation, and variable operating costs. Fixed costs are the costs that will not change as levels of activity change, within reason, of course. Variable costs are the costs that increase and decrease in direct proportion to changes in activity. The break-even level of activity is determined by dividing the contribution of each unit sold into the total fixed cost. For example, let us assume that the selling price of an item is $6.50, variable costs are $2 per unit, and fixed costs total $40,000. The contribution that each unit sold makes to the fixed costs is the difference between selling price and variable costs. Here the contribution is $4.50 per unit and 8,888 units must be sold to break even ($40,000 ÷ $4.50). We can rephrase this information to reach another conclusion. If sales volume is estimated at 8,888 units and the same costs will be incurred, the selling price per unit to break even is $6.50.

This information is shown graphically in Figure 20-5. The total cost line shows the operating cost at different levels of activity. Note that the fixed cost is the same for every level of activity being considered, while variable cost increases at a constant rate. The intersection of the income line with the total cost line marks the point where income is equal to cost. In addition, a quick estimate can be made of the profit that will result for any level of activity above 8,888 units.

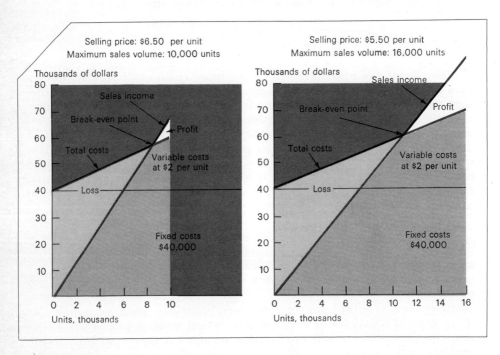

FIGURE 20-5 Break-even charts

With fixed costs of $40,000, and variable costs increasing at a constant rate of $2 per unit, the manufacturer finds the break-even point at the intersection of the total cost line and the sales income line. At that point costs and income are equal, and there is neither a profit nor a loss from operations. Profits will be larger with a sales forecast of 16,000 units when the selling price is reduced to $5.50 than with a forecast of only 10,000 units sold at a price of $6.50.

A break-even chart is a handy tool for measuring the impact of a price change on the break-even point. In the right-hand diagram of Figure 20-5 everything is the same as in the left-hand diagram except the selling price which has been reduced to $5.50 per unit. Note that the break-even level increases to 11,428 because of this reduction. If sales are sufficiently stimulated by the price decrease, the higher break-even point presents no problem. One can easily determine the volume necessary to improve on the profit attainable at a selling price of $6.50.

The basic break-even concept can also be applied to retail operations. A store owner reads his financial statements and learns that a profit of $200,000 was earned last year on sales of $4,000,000. He is interested in learning when, in terms of sales volume, this profit was made. The answer will indicate to the retailer just how vulnerable his profit is to changes in sales volume. As before, fixed and variable costs must be known before any analysis can take place. If variable costs were $2,800,000 (70 percent of sales) and fixed costs were $1,000,000, the break-even point is $3,333,333 of sales, and the contribution was 30 cents of each sales dollar because variable costs are 70 cents. This means that all profit was earned on the last $666,666 of sales at the rate of 30 cents on each sales dollar. The retailer can conclude that a reduction in sales of $666,666 would wipe out his entire profit.

Whether break-even will be an effective tool for management depends on the ability to pinpoint costs. There is no question about it; with variable costs of $6, a selling price of $10, and fixed costs of $80,000, break-even volume has to be 20,000 units. But costs are not always fixed or variable as described earlier. So-called "variable costs" may rise or fall faster or slower than the level of activity, and many of the determinants of fixed cost are variable. Consequently, break-even analysis is not always as precise a measure as we may have implied.

The economic-lot concept

The economic-lot concept is used in business to help in making a variety of decisions such as the best lot size for production, production runs, and movement of goods. The basic idea surrounding the application of this concept is that there are many choices open to the business person and each presents a different combination of costs. The problem is to determine the point where the sum of the costs involved is the lowest.

Suppose a firm plans to use 200,000 units of a product during the coming year. Consumption will be at an even rate throughout the year. The agreed-upon price is $5 per unit, the cost to process a purchase is $30, and the inventory carrying charge is 25 percent of its average value. The question is: Should the year's supply be purchased at one time, weekly, monthly, or what? This problem can be solved by a formula such as the following:

$$\text{Economic lot} = \sqrt{\frac{2 \times \text{the number of units used per year} \times \text{the cost of placing an order}}{\text{unit cost} \times \text{carrying charge (\%)}}}$$

$$= \sqrt{\frac{2 \times 200,000 \times \$30}{\$5 \times .25}}$$

$$\doteq 3,100$$

Considering only the factors that are a part of the formula, the most economic purchase lot size is 3,100 units, approximately.

Without doubt few readers will understand why the formula works. Basically it considers the relationship of two costs. As the size of the purchase lot increases, the fixed cost of purchasing goes down because fewer orders will be placed. At the same time, increased lot sizes create larger inventories and increase their carrying charge. The economic-lot size is the point at which the sum of these two costs is the lowest. Table 20-5, which can be used in place of the formula, explains this concept in greater detail.

The assumed lot size, which could be any quantity not over 200,000, is divided into 200,000 (total to be purchased) to give the number of purchases necessary for each lot size. This number times $30 gives the total purchase cost for each alternative. However, each lot size creates a different inventory; the larger the lot, the larger the inventory. The inventory carrying charge (ICC) is 25 percent of the value of the average inventory.

Note that the total cost drops and reaches its lowest point at the 3,000-unit lot size. This is close enough to the 3,100 determined by the formula to prove that each method reaches the same conclusion. Often, management is concerned with the best of several alternative choices, as in this illustration, rather than the precise quantity. This

TABLE 20-5 Determination of economic-lot size

Assumed lot sizes	1,000	2,000	3,000	4,000	5,000
Number of purchases required	200	100	67	50	40
Purchase cost at $30	$6,000	$3,000	$2,000	$ 1,500	$ 1,200
Inventory carrying charge	625	1,250	1,875	2,500	3,125
Total cost	$6,625	$4,250	$3,875	$ 4,000	$ 4,325
Average inventory in units	500	1,000	1,500	2,000	2,500
Value of average inventory	$2,500	$5,000	$7,500	$10,000	$12,250
Inventory carrying charge	$ 625	$1,250	$1,875	$ 2,500	$ 3,125

approach also indicates how much cheaper one lot size is than another.

Linear programming

In many firms a single group of facilities must be used to produce a variety of products. Convertibles, station wagons, and sedans may use the same stamping facilities; several grades of gasoline may be processed by a single refinery; or a bakery may use a single facility to make cookies, brownies, and pastries.

Linear programming may be used to determine the best product mix when alternate uses of facilities are possible. This is a relatively simple concept to apply if only two products (variables) are involved, but it becomes extremely complex when the number of products increases to five, ten, or more.

To illustrate this concept let us assume the following:

	Capacity per day	
Department	Product A	Product B
Casting	1,200	800
Machining	1,000	1,400
Finishing	1,500	1,500
Painting	1,800	2,400

Two products, A and B, are produced via a process that uses the services of these four departments. The problem is to determine the best balance between the two products, that is, how many of A and how many of B. The best balance to maximize profits may not be the best balance to maximize production or to achieve some other objective. Let us assume here that we want to maximize profit and that each unit of A produces a profit of 5 cents and each unit of B produces a profit of 6 cents.

We shall solve this problem through graphic analysis, although it can also be solved mathematically. Figure 20-6 plots the capacities of each department for each of the products. This plotting allows us to narrow the alternate product mixes to the solid area in the lower left corner. In other words, no more than 1,000 units of A or 800 units of B can be made; but this is not necessarily the best product mix. If we produce 1,000 units of A, we cannot produce any of B; or if we produce 800 units of B, we will not be able to produce any of A. But we can produce 600 of A and 400 of B or 300 of A and 600 of B plus many other combinations. (These values can be read from Figure 20-6.) Given any quantity of A, merely move over to the right to the limit of the solid area. Drop directly to the base line and read the quantity of B that can also be produced.

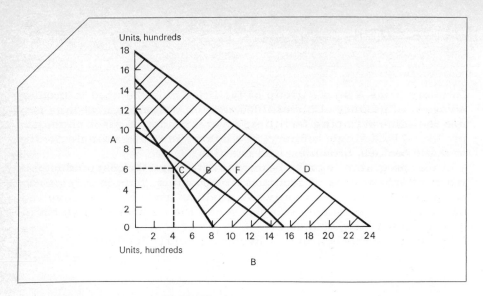

FIGURE 20-6   Linear programming

   Table 20-6 presents several, but not all, possible combinations (the B quantities may not be exact) together with the total profit for each combination. Note that total profit rises and then falls. Profit is maximized at 800 units of A and 270 units of B.

Investment decisions

For a number of reasons, business people are involved with investment decisions. Old equipment and facilities must be replaced, demand for the firm's products may dictate greater capacity, or improved methods of production may be developed. In most firms there are many more proposals to use funds for these purposes than there are funds available. If management receives requests for $5,000,000 to finance new investments but can raise only $3,000,000, some method must be available to identify the relative merit of each pro-

TABLE 20-6   Profit for varying product mixes

Production A	B	Profit A	Profit B	Total profit
1,000	0	$50.00	0	$50.00
800	270	40.00	$16.20	56.20
600	400	30.00	24.00	54.00
400	530	20.00	31.80	51.80

posal. There are two approaches that are widely used for this purpose. They are the payback method and the internal-rate-of-return method.

Payback Payback refers to the number of years it will take an investment to pay for itself either through savings or profit. It is widely used to determine whether particular pieces of equipment should be purchased. The production manager has proposed that existing equipment be discarded and that new equipment requiring a net investment of $100,000 be purchased. His estimate is that the new equipment will generate average annual savings of $20,000. This would give a 5-year payback. The technique is simple but estimating what savings will be in the years ahead is not a simple task.

A 5-year payback cannot be judged as good or bad by itself. Some firms establish payback standards and reject any proposals that exceed the standard. Thus 5 is good if the standard is 6, but poor if the standard is 4. Also, a 5-year payback might be acceptable if all other proposals involved longer periods.

Although payback is a widely used method for ranking investment proposals, it does have its limitations. A major limitation is that it does not consider the period after payback. Payback is a type of break-even point, and savings which continue to accrue beyond it are profit. Thus a machine having an expected life of 4 years and a 4-year payback may not be as good an investment as a machine having a 6-year payback and the promise of savings for several additional years.

Internal-rate method This method, like payback, requires an estimate of savings (net income) that will accrue from an investment. By trial and error, the interest rate that equates the present value of the expected future savings to the cost of the investment is determined. This is the rate of return. In the following illustration this is shown as a one-step process, the final step.

Year	Factor	Savings	Present value
1	0.83	$1,000	$ 830
2	0.69	2,000	1,380
3	0.58	3,000	1,740
4	0.48	4,000	1,920
5	0.40	5,000	2,000
6	0.33	6,000	1,980
			$9,850

In this illustration, the proposed investment is $10,000 and it promises savings of $1,000, $2,000, $3,000, $4,000, $5,000, and $6,000 over a 6-year period. The process shown in the illustration is repeated using progressively higher interest rates. This illustration assumes that the rate of return will be 20 percent. The "factor" is the present value of $1 for each of the 6 years at 20 percent. "Present value" is the product of savings times the factor. The total present value of savings of $9,850 approximates the $10,000 investment. Thus we conclude that the rate of return is about 20 percent. Again, whether

20 percent is a good rate of return depends on company standards and the return that other proposals promise.

SUMMARY

Business information as collected in the normal course of operation has limited value to the business person. Data on sales, for example, that are adequate for accounting purposes may be wholly inadequate for sales forecasting. Data must be classified, measured, and analyzed before they can be used to best advantage. This demands the application of a variety of statistical and mathematical techniques.

Statistical measures range from simple graphic presentation to specific and sometimes complicated measures including probability and the normal curve, standard deviation, and correlation.

The quality of decisions can be improved through use of mathematical techniques such as break-even and linear programming. One significant advantage of mathematical techniques is that they force the business person to attach specific values to the pertinent factors; they require thinking in specific rather than general terms. The application of statistical and mathematical techniques will increase in the years ahead because of the need for more precise planning and evaluation.

QUESTIONS

1 Why must internal data be considered fundamental to all business decisions?

2 For what reasons are internal data more desirable than data from other sources?

3 Discuss the role of external data in the decision-making process.

4 Distinguish between the mean, the median, and the mode.

5 Distinguish between grouped and ungrouped data. Illustrate a situation where each could be utilized.

6 What is the purpose of correlation studies?

7 What is a scattergram and what is its purpose?

8 For what reasons might a business person be interested in break-even analysis?

9 Specifically, what factors are involved in the economic-lot concept? Why is there an economic-lot point?

10 Under what circumstances is linear programming a useful tool for the business person?

PROBLEMS

1 A firm produces a product that sells for $4. The variable cost associated with this product is $2.50 per unit regardless of the quantity produced, and total fixed cost is $225,000.

a How many units must be sold just to break even?

b What profit will result if sales are 160,000 units?

c Suppose that it is possible to sell 170,000 units and that the costs shown above do not change. What unit price must be charged in order to break even?

2 Prepare a chart and plot the two sets of values listed below. What conclusions can you reach?

Year	No. taking bar exam	No. passing bar exam
1967	2,200	1,330
1968	3,100	1,580
1969	2,650	1,420
1970	2,250	1,350
1971	2,620	1,450
1972	2,860	1,720
1973	2,800	1,680
1974	2,700	1,670
1975	3,000	1,820

3 From the following distribution of wages calculate the mean, the median, and the mode.

Earnings	No. of workers
$ 80 to $ 90	3
90 to 100	9
100 to 110	15
110 to 120	27
120 to 130	18
130 to 140	12
140 to 150	9
150 to 160	7

4 The sales of the Chartier Company for the past seven years were:

Year	Sales (000)
1	$ 6,000
2	7,000
3	7,600
4	8,000
5	8,800
6	9,200
Current	10,000

a Plot this data on a chart.

b Calculate and plot the least squares trend.

c Based on this data, what would you estimate next year's sales to be? Why?

The purpose of this chapter   The basic business functions discussed in the previous chapters are not and cannot be independent functions. Each, of course, is completely dependent on the others. Yet many business people who realize this fail to provide the means whereby each segment of the firm knows what the other is doing. Communication of information often is too late to be useful, often is incomplete, and many times is inaccurate. Poor communication always results in waste, but in the past the sheer volume of information generated in a firm made it impossible to put it to good use. With modern data processing facilities, management need not live with this situation any longer. / In this chapter we shall discuss how a communications system is developed, how it influences company organization, and how it is used to aid the solution of business problems. In addition, we shall explore briefly the components of a computerized data processing system. / Questions raised in this chapter include:

1 What is a business system and how is it organized?

2 How do data become a part of an information system?

3 What types of reports come from the information system?

4 How is the information system used to control activities?

5 How may the information system affect managerial roles?

6 What is the role of computers in data processing?

21 / BUSINESS INFORMATION SYSTEMS AND COMPUTERS

The functions common to a business organization were discussed in several preceding chapters. Repeatedly, the point has been made that the operation of the firm depends on the efficiency with which each function is performed and the extent to which all functions are integrated as a coherent whole. It makes no difference whether we consider the larger or smaller business as an example, for in all cases the functions to be performed are similar. There is an apparent difference, however, in the number of people usually involved in the organization of a small versus a large business enterprise. The small firm operates with few people filling managerial positions, and commonly the responsibility for each of the various business functions is not clearly spelled out. Because of this, there may be a great deal of overlapping of activity on the part of different people. In the large firm, organizational planning results in graphic displays, called organization charts, which show the assignments of workers to specific responsibilities. In the large firm with its many managerial people, the organization is usually along functional lines, and according to the chart, each individual has his sphere of responsibility and activity. However, what is never apparent either in the formal organization chart of the large firm or in the simple pattern of relationships of the small firm is the complex pattern of interrelationships and communications which exists throughout the company structure. These relationships do not necessarily adhere to any lines of authority and responsibility, but follow the paths dictated by the needs of day-to-day operations.

For example, an organization chart may show that the authority and responsibility for the production of goods are vested in a specific division; but no production division can by itself generate all the answers to the many questions which must be raised before production is initiated. In reality, the decisions on the production function influence and are influenced by overall company policy; by the dictates of the sales, finance, personnel, and other company divisions; as well as by demand for the product. This type of interrelated responsibility exists in every area of company activity. The bond among many interrelated functions is the goal of common business objectives.

It happens not uncommonly that a sales policy decision must be made before a production decision can be rendered. The question whether to add to a company's line of products so as to strengthen its competitive position may have to be answered even before any questions are raised about production implications. In another case, just the opposite may hold true, and production considerations may override any proposal to add to the line of products. Physical or financial limitations may be barriers to change. In any event, the age-old question of which came first, the chicken or the egg, is analogous to such cases as these. Inevitably, all divisions become involved in the decision-making process even though the initial question or problem may have been raised in a particular functional area.

A BUSINESS SYSTEM

The word "system" by itself is likely to cause more confusion than revelation these days. It is applied with increasing frequency to a great variety of circumstances. Time was when it conjured up nothing more romantic than a plumbing or heating arrangement; among certain people it was used to refer to a method of beating the horses or the roulette wheel; by others it was used in reference to the political machine of the city or state. Of course, we are all familiar with the circulatory and nervous system, missile guidance systems, and possibly even systems people.

During the past 10 or 15 years much greater emphasis has been placed on the role of systems and procedures in the business enterprise. This area of work is, in part, concerned with the methods of handling the paperwork and clerical processing which are involved in running a modern business. Actually, the personnel engaged in systems work find that their services are required in all the areas of the business enterprise, whether marketing, production, personnel, accounting, materials handling, or any of the several departments where the flow of data and work are involved. The objectives of systems activity are to plan the how of getting things done and the methods of doing the various jobs. This is a general statement of the systems and procedure operation.

A *system* may be defined as an organic or organized whole. Your body and mine are systems in total, and they include a number of subsystems such as the nervous and circulatory systems. Each subsystem performs an activity which is vital to the total system functioning. In general, the term system may be applied to any activity or any collection of facts, ideas, or principles which are so arranged as to present a coherent whole. We expect, by definition, that the operation of a system will be methodical, thorough, and regular—all according to plan.

This concept of the system holds true when applied to the business world. In this case, the system refers to the many divisions of the

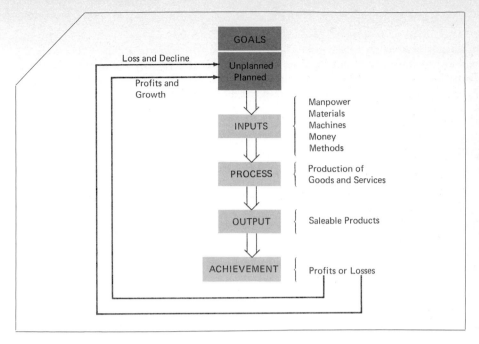

FIGURE 21-1   The business system: A total plan

The coordination is the task of management. Control and evaluation via standards. Communication via organization.

enterprise which are organized into and act as a coordinated whole in the pursuit of the objectives of the firm. Individual objectives are in tune with the common, overall goal, and the operation is planned and scheduled.

In the business world, as in the human body, some systems work more effectively than others. A malfunctioning subsystem or a poorly coordinated system does not give the best results. Figure 21-1 portrays a general model of a traditional system within a business organization.

DESIGNING THE SYSTEM

To apply the concept of system in the operation of the business enterprise, we must recognize four generally accepted business functions which in their entirety and interrelationships may be considered the system for systems design. These functions, planning, organization, control, and communication, are discussed below.

Planning

As the first stage of planning, the business person must state the objectives of the system which he intends to establish. This accomplishes two results: it gives direction to the planning activity and it provides the standards of achievement for evaluation of the accomplishments of the system and, if required, for the introduction of corrections.

Dramatic illustrations of this feature have been readily available to us during these days of space exploration and missile operations. During space flight, the adherence to the planned trajectory must be measured, and if necessary, the course must be corrected.

Just as significant to owners and employees, but not universally accepted as being so dramatic, is the case of the business enterprise which embarks on a program of product development and promotion aimed at eventually achieving a stated volume of sales or dollars of profit. These goals have their impacts on the design of the system which is to be set up. If the plan does not seem to be working out, the system should be designed so that management will be informed of this fact as quickly as possible and so that corrective actions, if deemed necessary, can be taken.

In the development of a system, planning is important at the overall level of operations and at the many intermediate or basic subsystem levels of activity. A system involves the development and coordination of many interrelated aspects of a task in order to achieve the goals. We see the extent of specialized interrelationships especially in the record-keeping and accounting procedures of business. The details involved in handling a customer or creditor account and the data processed in connection with inventory, production, and payroll records are illustrations of the many subsystems which exist within the overall information system of the business organization.

Organization

It is an obvious truth that, regardless of plans, nothing will get done without adequate organization. Furthermore, despite the sophistication of machinery which replaces human beings, we still rely heavily on the individual in organization. Organizing people to get a job done is a very fundamental activity, and its elementary nature is even recognized by children at play when they say, "You're the bad guy, and I'm the good guy." Organization pervades the structure of a business and goes beyond merely assigning responsibilities to individuals. Organization is concerned with the structure of activities, with the structure of communications channels and the data which flow through them, and with the structure of the system within which all this takes place. Thus it is easy to see how organization must exist at various levels of operation. Some of these organizational efforts are directed toward accomplishing results through the use of people; other efforts are directed toward getting results from machines or physical plant and facilities; still other organizational efforts are directed toward setting up paperwork systems or other forms of communications systems which provide details and control information. In effect, organization deals with intangible situations, for sound organization promotes goodwill and efficiency and enhances the flow of communications. Each of these areas is vital to healthy organization and to the effective operation of any business system.

To be effective, a business system must operate in two directions. Organizationally, it must follow the lines of authority which are customarily set up for the accomplishment of specific objectives, but it must also cross the lines of authority and departmental jurisdiction if it is to serve as an effective communications and coordination device. For example, a company which produces a diversified line of products may set up separate divisions for the production of each of its varied products and at the same time maintain common departments to handle procurement, finance, research, accounting, inspection, and other activities. In the ordinary course of producing a particular product, the plan for production and control is set up by the respective division so that company objectives are adhered to. The materials, machines, and labor requirements are specified, and production quotas are established for control purposes. The entire plan is a system, intended to bring a product to completion.

The several departments in the company which are not oriented to any one product but serve the needs of the company as a whole may or may not become involved in the production process of all items. For example, a research division may have no involvement with a specific product at a given time. On the other hand, the accounting department and the quality control division are usually continuously concerned with all production activity. Although these and other departments may not be directly involved in physical production, their performance is important in making efficient use of facilities, in turning out satisfactory goods, and in providing information which is helpful to management (see Figure 21-2).

A business information system should provide both an integrated and a segregated view of what is going on, as well as a means to control activity so that objectives may be achieved. Not only should the system provide an overview of the entire operation, but also it should show the individual parts and their interrelationships clearly. An effective systems will allow management to ascertain quickly the effect of cost and price changes on company profits. It will quickly pass on the most recent information from market sources so that production and finished-goods inventories may be optimized. It will keep management informed of the implications of the financial investment in plant and inventories. It will provide the data to enable management to appraise the use of the resources at its command and to suggest more effective means. Most firms have a system which does not approach this ideal: a system which has all these characteristics.

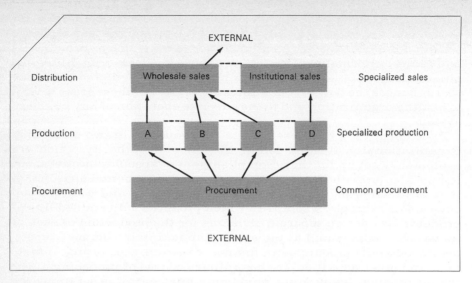

FIGURE 21-2 The system operates vertically and horizontally

The system proceeds vertically in respect to an individual product, but horizontally at each functional level to coordinate the use of total facilities and investment, and to appraise the relation of each product's effect in each functional area.

Control

Control cannot be activated until the two initial features of the system have been brought to fruition, namely, the statement of the system's objectives and the creation of an organization for achieving the objectives. Once these features have been established, it is possible to carry out the control function. We begin by setting up standards against which measured results may be compared. Correction, in keeping with the objectives, will be applied by the system. Because a system is composed of many subsystems, there are several points at which a system may bog down or errors may occur, but at the same time, there are many points at which controls may be set up.

A closed-loop system is one in which the control exercised within the system is designed to automatically introduce corrections when it is sensed that results are not as planned. An example of this is a quality control system which checks work in process and detects tendencies toward faulty output before such output actually occurs. This system predicts failures, communicates its prediction, and initiates automatic corrective action.

In contrast, an open-loop system is not an integral part of the operation. In this case, sometime after results have been recorded the performance is analyzed or interpreted. Corrective actions, if necessary, are subsequently put into effect. This is typically the form of control system used by a management which gets periodic reports of past activity sometimes days or even weeks after the event has occurred. Management looks over the reports and then institutes changes which appear desirable. This control system is tantamount to "locking the barn door after the horse has been stolen." Sometimes, however, this does not amount to too great a loss, for we should not assume that immediate or current notice of deviations and discrepancies is either essential or even possible in many areas of business activity. The real problem is to discern where to draw the line in the matter of control. In other words, how fine and how timely must the control system be? The answer to this question is often sought in the comparison of the costs involved in getting control and the value of the benefits thereby obtained.

Communication

Communication is a vital activity in the conduct of affairs, personal or public. From an individual's point of view, a person communicates with himself. This communication is self-consciousness, which enables us to raise questions about who and what we are, what we do, and particularly why we do what we do. Since this ability is one basis on which we distinguish ourselves from lower orders of life, we must agree that it is a significant mark of our distinctiveness only to the extent that we apply it.

Similarly, we recognize the potential for communication within a business enterprise (see Figure 21-3). If the system is to serve the

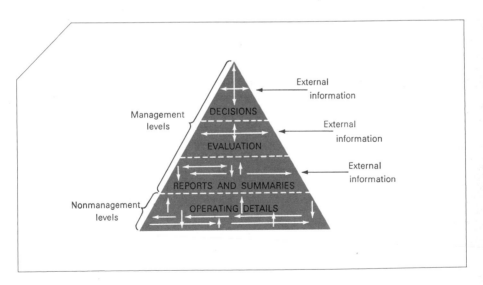

FIGURE 21-3   Information flow in the company

Arrows indicate direction of information flow.

company needs, it must do more than just record and file results of operations in the various departments. It must also provide information which makes the operators of the business aware of what they are doing and how well they are doing it. This is the basis for raising the question why things are done as they are, which should be the prelude to corrective action.

In its everyday meaning, communication refers to the transmitting of information in the form of words or signals or signs from a source to a receiver. The information may be a matter of fact or may consist of ideas, thoughts, or proposals being offered for consideration. Sometimes, of course, ideas are passed on as if they were facts, but this does not alter the nature of communication. It does suggest, however, that the communication process may be used to achieve objectives according to the wishes of the user. Implicit in the communication process are three elements: the sender, a communications device, and a receiver. All communication systems embody the requirements of capacity, accuracy, and timeliness, as well as compatibility between the sender and the receiver. The system must have the ability to handle the specific message. The information transmitted must have a common meaning for both sender and receiver.

The devices used in the communication process range from manpower to high-speed electronic computers. The accuracy of a system varies over extreme ranges depending on the components of the system. The greater the use of the individual, the greater is the opportunity for inaccuracy. The speed of a communications system varies with the manner of processing and transmitting information. People are not necessarily the delaying factor in communications, for a face-to-face communication over some vital issue may be the speediest manner of accomplishing a solution or reaching agreement.

Because of the constantly increasing burden of communications which is imposed on modern-day business operations, various approaches to the solution of the information-system problem have been applied. At one extreme the solution may be to install highly sophisticated electronic computers, and at the other it may be to employ more personnel in the information system.

Information flow

Information flow is essential to the operation of a system. The questions which have to be resolved are: What information is pertinent to the operation? To whom and when is this information pertinent?

For example, assume that the objective of a business communications system is to accumulate information on the sales volume of each product by units and by dollar value. To do this requires that detailed information be collected from the sales outlets. In a large-scale sales operation this usually means that an extremely large volume of details will originate in the ultimate sales outlets, will be summarized as it moves through the various levels of the information system, and will finally emerge as a report containing the sales information which management requires for control or other purposes. It is important to note here that a communications network designed to do such a job must be capable of assembling data on a widespread and voluminous basis and must be capable of providing information in the form and at the time required. Whether speed is an essential ingredient of the information processing depends on the particular installation.

A manufacturer of diesel locomotives has little need to determine his sales volumes quickly, since he is unlikely to be producing any locomotives that have not already been ordered, and therefore he will have contracts already on hand. At the other extreme, the manufacturer of pharmaceutical products must keep a very close check on the sales of his products. The quantity of sales and the timeliness of the information are vital factors. The manufacturer wishes neither to overstock nor to understock his supply of a particular drug which because of market conditions may meet with sudden and drastic customer acceptance or rejection. In order to be able to react quickly he needs very current, accurate, and detailed information.

BUSINESS SYSTEM—A SUMMARY

If we draw together what has been written on the preceding pages of this chapter, it is apparent that throughout the discussion of the four functions which have been labeled a system for systems design, not one of these functions may be considered apart from the others. They are completely interdependent in the development of the design of a business system. Because the firm must be considered as an organism intent on a business life, its various parts or divisions must be mutually interdependent. Each part serves its particular purpose, but all parts are integrated to the extent that the relation of one with another is governed by the relation to the total concept of the firm. The simplest restatement of this principle is found in the requirement that each department's function be consistent with the firm's overall plan for achieving its goals, which may be profits, size, or other objectives.

The communications system established for the business operation provides the lifeblood channels through which information flows and by which action or reaction is communicated and controlled. The level at which communication occurs may be intrapersonal (a person with himself), interpersonal (person to person), person to machine, or even machine to machine, depending on the technology required and available for the system.

SYSTEM AND BUSINESS PROBLEMS

Business has been defined as a collection of problems in search of solutions. This definition is apt enough if we assume a certain definition of the word "problem." For our purposes the problems of business are described by the following questions:

1 What are we doing currently? This question poses the problem of awareness of what is going on in the business and points out the need for a system which will collect and report basic details.

2 Are we doing it correctly or in the most efficient manner? This question poses the problem of planning and control and complements the first question. It points out the need for a system which reports what is being done and how well it is being done.

3 In what direction should we be heading? This question poses the problem of forecasting. Without knowledge of trends and of the internal and external influences on the conduct of business affairs, it would be impossible for the business person to guide activities into the correct channels at the opportune times.

4 How do we make certain that the information necessary to answer the above questions is made available to the right people at the right time? This question poses the need for a system, an information system, which is capable of matching data to the particular problems of the business. The basic purpose of the information system is to carry information to the decision makers.

INFORMATION

Information consists of organized data which have meaning and use within a system. "Data" is the term used to describe the usually very large volume of details which are generated by day-to-day transactions but which must be processed and organized before they can serve either to control operations or to provide information which is meaningful.

For example, a listing of employees and the hours worked by each on a particular shift is a not uncommon form of data handled by the business firm. For these data to be useful, they must be processed through several stages, finally ending up as a detailed summary of labor time and cost to be applied to a production department or products, and as entries to the individual employee payroll records which are the bases for writing the paychecks at the end of the week. It is important for the data, in their original form, to be complete, timely, and accurate; but they provide very little information until they are processed. The same circumstances hold true with the collection of large volumes of data on sales transactions to individual customers, purchases from creditors, and the requisition of materials from inventories. This vast quantity of data is the raw material from which information is generated, and the extent and form of the information are determined by the design of the system. The real meaning and use of such data lie not in the details but in the fact that by using the details we are able to determine such things as the status of the individual customer and creditor accounts and the volume of purchases and sales, or to control the availability of inventory of thousands of individual items.

The idea that data are the basic ingredients of information holds true in any area of business or science in which information is being sought. Whether data consist of business facts, the statistics collected in a population survey, the facts contained in a file full of medical case histories, or the random observations of an itinerant philosopher, information does not become available without some data processing. The data must be reviewed, the irrelevant must be sifted out, the significant must be correlated and combined, and other steps must be performed in order to assimilate a basketful of facts and figures into a thimbleful of information which has applicable meaning. This is not a particularly unique concept or task, for each of us selects that which has meaning and value for our efforts from the avalanche of data to which we are daily subjected. The business person does this on a large scale. He uses devices and techniques which allow him to accomplish his purposes more efficiently than if he had no such aids. The organization of these devices and techniques results in the "information system."

THE INFORMATION SYSTEM

The business system is in reality an information system devised to assist management in making better decisions. The information or output which is provided by the system varies from historic reporting to forecasts; that is to say, some information is merely an accumulation of details about past activities, whereas other information may be in the form of a forecast derived statistically from accumulated details.

The variety of information output

A variety of reports are required by management in the ordinary course of business operations. Some of these reports have their origins in a single department and reflect various aspects of the activity of the department. Other reports represent a consolidation of the results of related activities. In the first case, a sales analysis report may state performance details for members of the sales force by territories, by product, by customer class, by gross profit margin, or by any other basis which management considers useful. A report such as this originates at a particular level of operations, and the source of the details is confined to the sales records. Such a report requires no cross-fertilization of information between the sales unit and other departments. However, if management asks for a sales report which will allow comparison of the performance of the company sales division with the industry picture, information from external sources is required. Such a report may also involve personnel in other than the sales department, who will gather the required external information and submit it for analysis along with the internal sales details. All this is done before management sees the result of the analysis.

There are always problems to be solved and questions to be answered which involve multiple department coordination as well as information which can only come from external sources. This is particularly evident when an existing firm is looking for a new business location. Among the many factors which must be considered are raw materials sources, labor supply, transportation facilities, power supply, availability of financing, and local taxes. All these factors involve external sources of information. However, not one of these factors can be properly evaluated unless the operating requirements are first analyzed and some decisions are arrived at about what limits or constraints are imposed by the internal needs of the company. If the production process requires large quantities of water, it is not practical to consider a site which provides only a limited supply of water. Likewise, if the firm requires that many specialized services such as custom machine shops or special labor skills be readily available, an area which cannot supply these services is not eligible for consideration as a potential location.

Therefore, outputs generated by a business information system may take a variety of forms. Ordinarily, whatever the form of output, a large volume of statistics, facts, and accumulated data is usually first gathered from the basic operating levels of the firm. More is added from other internal and external sources, and output is varied according to the system plan. Generally, output may occur in any one or more of the three forms discussed below.

Reporting details   Any tabulation or straight listing of business transactions constitutes straight reporting. This form of output provides no additional information beyond the basic data, but since it may be set up in chronological, alphabetical, numerical, or some other order, it amounts to a filing system. However, we cannot overlook the significance of orderly arrangement of details, for it may be quite essential to further processing that data be in a prescribed order of flow. In addition, the collection of data is essential to all processing, and unless this collection is complete, accurate, and organized, there remains little, if any, hope for an effective operation of the information system.

If the firm handles its paperwork manually, it is easy to follow the work involved in recording and filing details and to recognize the various steps involved in the procedure. The process is physically in evidence, and the transition from the state of a large volume of assorted and unorganized business facts and statistics to an organized file of related data is easy to follow. If filing is accomplished electronically within the structure of an automatic data processing system, the customary files and ledgers of information do not exist and in their stead are reels of magnetic tape, stacks of punched cards, and other devices which make up the filing systems of modern data processing technology.

Preparing reports In order to generate reports and summaries, it is necessary for the processing system to take the accumulated details, subject them to arithmetic processes and other manipulation, and present results in the form of summaries or reports. From this processing we can visualize the preparation of financial statements, expense and payroll summaries, sales tabulations, customer and creditor account balances, inventory status reports, budget reports, and many other summarizations and evaluations of activities.

Analyses for decision-making purposes Complex analyses are drawn up for use in the solution of problems, the preparation of forecasts, and a variety of analytical techniques which management finds useful in its decision-making process. At this stage of information processing, the nature of inputs varies considerably from that described above, and the mathematical complexities involved extend far beyond the simple arithmetic procedures used in producing reports and summaries. Data entering into the decision-making process originate both from company sources and from environmental sources outside the firm. See Figure 21-4.

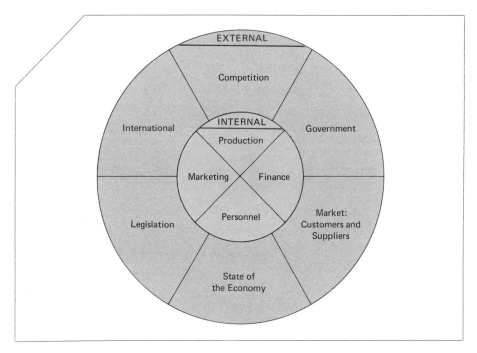

FIGURE 21-4 The internal and external environments of a business

The various areas which make up the internal environment provide data for business operational and control purposes. The external environment which is common to all enterprises is the source of data which are primarily used in long-range or strategic planning by the firm.

By way of illustration, the preparation of a sales forecast may involve the use of the historical details of past sales which had been accumulated by the internal data collection processes of the system, and also require detailed information about competition, the economy, population, and other external areas. These details are then used in a complex formula designed to provide management with information which it can apply in its forecasting decision.

Certain information-system techniques, such as operations research and simulation, are applied in the hopes of better decision making. Operations research is a scientific methodology for assessing the overall implications of various alternative courses of action. It aids in formalizing the elements of recurring decisions and also aids in establishing the relationships among these elements. It helps in the development and design of information flow to the functional areas, and in the planning, developing, and testing of alternative policies. Simulation embodies the use of a mathematical model of a set of relationships and makes it possible to pretest the effects of variation of these relationships within the model.

Each of these areas of complex analysis involves an extension of the concept of information systems far beyond the treatment accorded the topic here.

Information levels

A business information system should be designed to accept input of data from various sources and to handle their processing so that information output is generated for each of the levels of business organization according to its respective requirements. If this is done successfully, we may expect, for example, that a territory sales manager will be provided with an analysis of the performance of each of the members of this sales team, that the division sales manager will be informed of the accomplishment in each territory, and that the general sales manager will be informed of the results achieved in each division.

This illustration not only points out the successive phases of information development but also illustrates the condensation which occurs in the nature of the information as it is developed for the upper levels of business management. Some business people have issued statements which reflect the great pride they have in intimate awareness of the everyday operational details of their enterprises. Admittedly, in a small operation such awareness may be quite reasonable, but as size becomes significant, the concern of the boss with extensive details may only mean that somebody else is really watching over the business, that certain aspects of the operation are suffering by information default. A realistic portrait of the "all-knowing" boss is more likely to be that of the business leader who is able to interpret the summary reports and studies which are prepared for him and to be guided by them to initiate desirable changes in operating methods or objectives, and to make better decisions.

Volume of data and information

Where data are originated, the business person expects to process a large number of details and records. This is the level where the nature of work is basically clerical, routine, and repetitive, and is susceptible to inaccuracy and delays. Because of these very features, however, the introduction of new methods, equipment, and automatic data processing is likely to be most desirable at this level. Machines have proved themselves capable of doing such routing and voluminous tasks with accuracy and speed.

Some of the reasons why early installations of large-scale computer operations took place in the insurance industry were exactly as indicated above: the great volume of repetitive operations which are fundamental to the processing of the paperwork of organizations dealing with a very large number of accounts, and the desire for the maintenance of accuracy and timeliness of data processing in the face of the ever-increasing volume of details to be handled. These reasons, in addition to the economic justifications of the use of mechanical and electronic data processing systems, were sufficient and compelling.

Control via information

As we move up through the various levels of a business organization, we find that the demands of the managers are not so much for increased details as for information. As the performance of work moves away from the basic operational levels, as it moves into the supervisory and managerial categories, the function of the information system is to transform the details which it has gathered into information which can be applied for control or decision-making purposes. The emphasis of the information system shifts from concern with the ability to handle large volumes of repetitive data accurately and speedily to an emphasis on the ability of the system to manipulate data in a variety of ways so that upper levels of business organization are provided with the type of information which they require to do their respective jobs. To provide this information, the system must be capable of preparing data analysis, preparing complicated tabulations, solving problems, etc. At this point, techniques of operations research, simulation, and game theory may be involved.

The "exception principle"

The information system of a firm is another of the tools or devices employed in business activities, and it is expected to adhere in everyday operation to basic business management principles, particularly with respect to what is labeled the "exception principle." This principle states that only nonroutine or exceptional matters should be brought to the attention of management. Of course, the clear indication here is that the design of the system should automatically take care of the routine matters and sift out for managerial attention those which are exceptional. If the principle is applied to the operation of an information system, it should be expected that an increasingly diminished volume of output will find its way to the succeedingly higher levels of management.

However, a very real problem has come into being along with the processing capacity of modern information systems. What many business people have found is that the ability of data processing systems to provide vast quantities of output is not automatically a blessing, for in many cases this ability has resulted in nothing more than a tremendous outpouring of paperwork, the results of which have little, if any, practical application.

Timeliness of information

"Too little, too late" and "Hurry up and wait" could well be the popular titles of the extremes of information systems. Those who design and those who use such systems are vitally concerned with the speed and timeliness of a system's ability to collect and process data and to disseminate information to the users. It is important to note that the value of information is found not only in its content but in its availability at a time and place where it may be put to good use. The person who bases his stock market investment decisions on a perusal of the weekly summary of stock prices may or may not be as well informed as the individual who is in telephone contact with his or her broker. In all such situations, the information is of the same nature but operates on a vastly different basis of timeliness. The significance of the timeliness in each case cannot be condemned or extolled without an exploration of the requirements of the user. For the holder of a blue chip portfolio which he had no plan of altering, a weekly perusal of stock prices could be considered both adequate and timely. At the other extreme, for a stockholder who was operating in a volatile price circumstance and with short-term price speculation in mind, much more timely information about the market activity would be required.

The same is true of the business person and his information requirements. In some cases he wants an up-to-date availability of information pertinent to a given customer account, product sales, or item-by-item cost accumulation as a product moves through the production line. There are occasions, however, when periodic reports of customer accounts are all that are necessary, and individual item costs are neither essential nor reasonable to determine when the particular item is one of many thousands which are being mass produced.

There is a distinct need to consider timeliness and the extent to which this feature serves the information-system requirements of the firm. However, it is easy to overlook the problems which accrue within an information system when there are unwarranted pressures for speedy output; speed is held to be sacrosanct by some business people, and requests for it go unchallenged and unmolested. The effects of indiscriminate demands for quick information are felt throughout the system from the point of data collection, throughout the processing, and to the point of delivery of the output. People and machines are involved both directly and indirectly, and unless the timing of information requirements is well planned within the concept and purpose of the total information system, problems of both a human and a machine nature are certain to arise.

DATA PROCESSING SYSTEMS

Systems for handling the data that flow through any business organization range all the way from manual systems which employ clerical workforce to process facts, figures, and paperwork to sophisticated electronic computer systems which minimize the need for human or manual involvement in the processing of data. In between these two extremes we find the majority of business firms which use a combination of manual and mechanized data processing systems. Virtually all enterprises make use of some mechanical or electromechanical device such as a calculator or sorting machine to help in the everyday work of figuring out bills, updating inventory records and customer accounts, sorting records, etc. The range of equipment available for use in processing data starts with the most basic level, which is manual or manpower, and then proceeds through mechanical devices, electromechanical devices, and our most advanced systems, electronic computers.

What determines whether any one system is to be mostly a manually operated system or something much more elaborate? The answer to this question is in good part determined by the volume of data transactions to be handled; whether or not the required manpower and skills are available to do the job quickly and accurately enough to get the answers out on time and whether the cost of upgrading a data processing system to a more elaborate system, which usually means a more costly and a more complicated setup, is not so large as to offset the advantages which may come with the change in the system.

Certainly, the data processing systems which involve the greatest investment in equipment, manpower skills, and organization are the electronic systems. Such installations, in order to pay for themselves, are best applied in business situations which require the processing of large volumes of data within limited time periods and with a high level of accuracy and dependability.

These requirements seem to preclude the smaller business person from being a customer for electronic data processing systems, simply because he does not have the volume of work load needed to keep the installation busy. But the situation is quite the contrary these days, for over the years as the technology of electronic data equipment and systems has developed, different opportunities have become available to the smaller business firm so that it could avail itself of the advantages of electronic data processing. On the one hand, if one small firm is unable to support the operation of a data processing system, then maybe a combination of two or more such firms can pool their requirements and thereby be able to support the system. As a result, there has been the development of the computer utility firm which makes the services of an electronic computer available to the smaller firm at a reasonable cost. The computer utility company owns a large computer and is in business to sell time and computer-oriented services to many small operators who individually could not afford to set up and operate a computerized data processing system. Under such an arrangement as this, each of the user firms would purchase whatever time and services filled their needs. This whole idea is similar to the principle underlying the operation of other utilities from which we as consumers purchase telephone service and energy requirements.

With improving technology and reduction in the costs of producing computer components, a second opportunity is increasingly available to the smaller business in the form of minicomputers. These machines are specifically designed to be economical substitutes for manual or mechanical data systems used by smaller firms. Necessarily, they have limitations imposed on their processing and memory capacities.

Basic components of data processing

Fundamental to all data processing situations whether or not they employ electronic devices are the following components:

1 Input

2 Processing (arithmetic and logic according to instructions)

3 Memory (storage capacity)

4 Control

5 Output

It makes no difference whether the data processing application consists of the simple addition of a few numbers of whether it is an involved analysis of costs or sales data; the components of the process are identical. There must be the basic data (input); these data must be manipulated, calculated, or whatever, through a series of process steps which are correct for achieving the ultimate information objective; and this processing must occur in correct sequence (process and control). As part of any processing it is necessary to remember the process itself as well as the inputs and answers which are derived from the process (memory); and, in order to make the results available for use, there must be a final report or answer (output).

A great variety of devices are used for each of these features of data processing depending upon the nature of the data processing system employed.

Nature of the data processing system

Over the years equipment development for data processing has been prodded by technological improvement in the mechanical, electrical, and electronic areas. As a result, there is a variety of devices available which extend the ability of the individual and overcome his shortcomings in the handling of data.

The manual approach to recording and handling data which conjures up visions of the old-time bookkeeper wearing visored cap and celluloid cuffs is replaced in part by today's machine operator who with a mechanical or electrically powered machine is able to quickly and accurately handle the business facts and figures. Unlike the manual process where the man had to know the process of work, the machine operator need only know the correct procedure for making entries into the machine and then pressing the correct control buttons in some predetermined sequence to get the job done. In effect, machines have come on to the scene which are capable of being instructed as to how to carry out a process of data handling.

THE ELECTRONIC COMPUTER

The basic improvements to data processing which resulted from the introduction of the electronic computer were the vastly increased capacity of the system to handle a volume of work, the speed at which the results became available, and finally, most important, the ability of the machine to make logical decisions.

As an example of logical decision making, the electronic computer is able to determine on a yes-or-no basis the answer to a particular question and then take processing steps depending upon the specific answer it receives. For instance, in processing inventory data, as withdrawals are made from existing stock to fill customer orders, the computer may be programmed to keep constant check of the amount left in inventory and when the balance reaches or falls below some predetermined reorder quantity, to produce some output which will indicate that it is time to order more material. The computer may even be instructed to print up a purchase order and address it to some predetermined supplier. The entire process of making entries of additions or withdrawals to inventory, the continuous monitoring of the available balance, and the required issuance of a purchase order can be programmed into the computer to occur automatically. This entire process is based on some simple logic which requires the computer to check figures on a yes-or-no basis and take actions according to the answer. If the predetermined reorder point for a given item in inventory was set at 1,000 units and the last inventory balance as determined by the computer was 980 units, the next stage in the decision process would be to raise the question: Is the balance larger than the reorder point? If the answer is yes, no purchase order would be issued.

If the answer is no, as in this case, the next step in the process would be to issue the purchase order.

It is quite true that if a person were entrusted to do this job, the process would not differ, for the comparison of the two values would be necessary and any action to purchase which the individual would take would be governed by the results of the comparison. What is different with the computerized process is that a machine is programmed or instructed in the various steps of the process and thereafter the process is "untouched by human hands." To the extent this is so, the computer works faster, more accurately, and always completely consistent with the process as defined.

The logic of a computer system

The logical, although not the physical, arrangement of the components of an electronic data processing system is as shown in Figure 21-5.

In order to process any data, the details would have to be entered into the system by some means. This is the INPUT stage. All input data are stored in the MEMORY system of the computer. Whatever it is that is to be done in the nature of computation or manipulation of the data is referred to as the PROCESS which takes place in the central component of the system. All data processing results are then stored back in the MEMORY system prior to their OUTPUT in whatever form the system is capable of delivering. This could be in the form of punched cards, printed reports, magnetic tapes, or video displays.

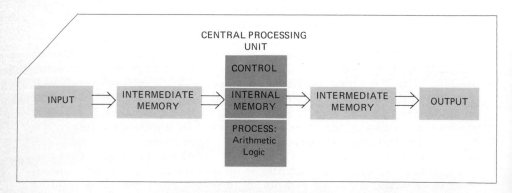

FIGURE 21-5 The components of an electronic data processing system

Data are input via intermediate memory devices into the internal memory. Manipulations and calculations are done in the process components. Results of the processing are returned to internal memory and from there via an intermediate memory to output. This entire procedure from input to output is monitored and controlled by the control unit which serves as the system's manager.

The control unit All the above activities are policed by the computer component labeled CONTROL. This unit provides the necessary supervision over the system to assure that input occurs when needed, that the proper processing sequences occur on schedule, and that output is delivered from the system when planned and in the proper form. In a manually operated data processing system, the individual provides the necessary control and sees to it that instructions are followed.

The memory unit The MEMORY or storage units of a computer consist of devices which are able to retain data in a magnetic or electrical form. These data can be recalled from the computer memory system on signal and can be used repeatedly during the course of data processing. If the process requires it, memory may also be modified. The stereo tape cartridge is a form of magnetic memory which gives up its data (music) whenever it is inserted into a tape deck. The tape can be replayed over and over again without wearing out or losing the music contents. It can be modified by recording over it. Similarly, devices are used in computer memory systems which are capable of storing vast quantities of data and keeping them readily available for use when needed in a data processing situation. Most data are held in "memories" such as tapes and disks. For processing purposes, a magnetic core memory is used because of its speed. See Figure 21-6.

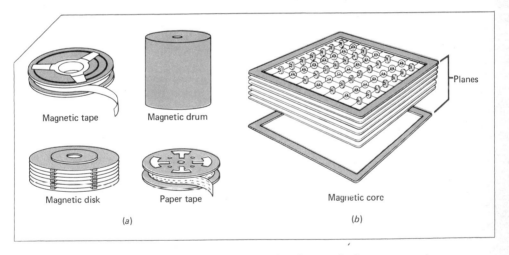

Magnetic tape   Magnetic drum

Magnetic disk   Paper tape   Magnetic core

Planes

(a)   (b)

FIGURE 21-6 Storage or memory devices in electronic data processing

(a) Secondary storage devices. These devices are intermediate memory media which hold large volumes of data available for use when needed in the data processing system. (b) Primary storage device. The core memory is the most common internal memory device and is used in the processing of data in the central processing unit. A core is molded from iron powder in the shape of a pinhead-sized doughnut. Many cores are strung together on wires to form a core plane. Several planes are stacked to form the magnetic core stack. Each core can be magnetized individually.

The types and sizes of memory systems in computers vary. One of the bases for distinguishing between what are called large-scale and small-scale computers is the data-holding capacity and the recall speed of the memory unit.

The process unit All the data processing work is done within the PROCESS unit and utilizes a memory unit such as the magnetic core. The functions performed include all arithmetic operations—addition, subtraction, multiplication, and division—and logic operations. The logic operations consist of making comparisons to determine whether items differ in size; whether the difference is positive, negative, or otherwise; and finally, whether one item is larger or smaller or equal to the other. If the computer can make this determination it is then able to take specific action depending on the results of such a comparison. Refer to the previous discussion on processing inventory data.

The input and output units These units consist of machines which can read data into and out of the system. The specific machines that are used depend on what forms of input and output the system is capable of handling. The more popular forms of input devices consist of card readers and tape readers. These machines provide the link between the computer and those who use it, for they, in effect, translate the data signals which are input into a form compatible with electronic data handling and capable of being stored in the memory system. A *card reader* is a machine which "reads" the holes punched in a Hollerith card (the familiar IBM card) and translates the pattern of holes, which represent data, into electronic signals which are then stored in memory. Similarly, a *tape reader* reads the magnetic message which is on a tape and stores it in memory where it, too, is available for processing according to instructions. Paper tape, on which data are represented by a pattern of punched holes, is similarly handled. See Figures 21-7 and 21-8.

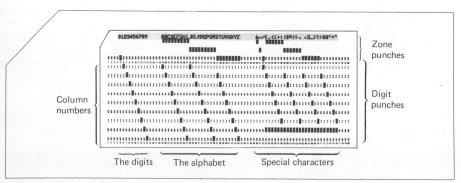

FIGURE 21-7   Hollerith code—punch card as a data storage device.

Letters, numbers, and other symbols are represented by punch patterns on the card.

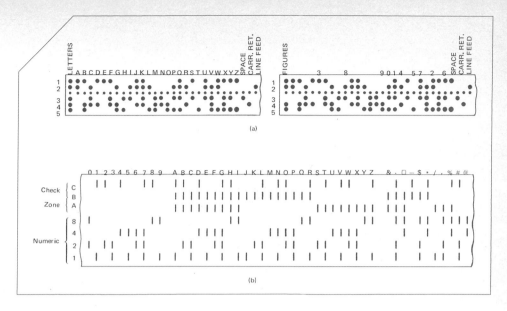

FIGURE 21-8   Paper and magnetic tapes as data storage devices

(*a*) 5-column paper tape. Each letter or number is represented by its unique pattern of holes punched in the tape. (*b*) Magnetic tape. Each mark on the tape represents a magnetized spot. Each letter, number, or symbol is represented by its unique pattern of magnetic spots on the tape.

The tape reader, called the *tape transport,* reads the data on a tape into the memory system where it is held for use in the process. The tape itself is made of plastic and its surface is coated with a material which can take a magnetic impression. The tape is prepared by "recording" the data on its surface and is read by "playing" the data into the memory.

Some computer systems are capable of input via teletypewriter or telephone hookups which allow data to be put into the system from distant locations. The reservation systems utilized by major airlines use such devices at ticket counters to access computers which may be hundreds of miles away.

Output devices used depend on the form of output desired. If an output of punched cards is desired, a card punch machine is the appropriate output device. Sometimes, the system is set up to produce magnetic tapes as output. The tape transport would be the output machine. If a printed report was desired, a printer would be used. This machine is capable of a great variety of output forms such as paychecks, letters, bills, orders, schedules, etc. It readily prints out large volumes of results in whatever form desired subject only to the physical limitation of the machine. In some cases, a particular data processing situation may call for a variety of output. Different combinations of both input and output devices may be used in the same

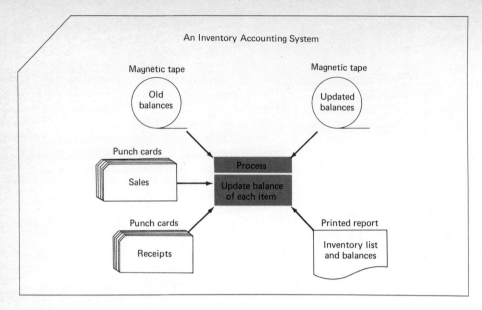

FIGURE 21-9   A system using a variety of input-output media

This process feeds old inventory balances from magnetic tape along with all the details of sales and receipts of goods which are punched on cards into the system. The process consists of subtracting the sales and adding the receipts to the old balance of each item in inventory. The result is an updated balance for each item which is printed out in a report form for management to use and is also put on a magnetic tape. This updated tape becomes the "old balance" tape the next time the process is run.

application in order to provide the results that management requires. See Figure 21-9.

YOUR LANGUAGE AND THE MACHINE'S LANGUAGE

All the data we customarily use in business communications are composed of patterns of twenty-six alphabetic symbols; ten numbers, zero through nine; and a variety of algebraic and punctuation symbols. Conversion from these symbols into symbols or patterns which an electronic computer can use is the function of the various input media (cards, tapes) and their associated machines. The letters and numbers which we can make sense out of have little meaning in magnetic or electronic circles. Therefore, before the machine system can use the data they must be reduced to a magnetic or electronic condition. This condition is the "machine language" which is binary, or two-state in nature. It is not really an unusual or new concept with most of us, for it simply refers to the fact that language symbols as we know them are represented by no more than two symbols or conditions. The Morse code does just this by assigning a pattern of two symbols, the dot and the dash, to represent our customary alpha and numeric symbols. The computer assigns two symbols similarly and these symbols may be north and south magnetic polarity or voltage and no voltage. In such fashion, conversion occurs from our language symbols to machine language symbols. Certainly, the machine language allows much faster processing of data, for reading magnetic impressions or electronic impressions can be theoretically accomplished at the speed of light. However, at the input and output stages, because mechanical devices such as card and tape readers or punches are used, the speed of processing is restricted. In the central processing system of the computer where all work is done electronically, the speed is not limited by mechanical constraints and therefore does approach the theoretical speed mentioned above.

THE INFORMATION SYSTEM AND ORGANIZATION

Putting an information system into operation involves several considerations: technical, design, and organizational. In technical respects, the present equipment available for information systems ranges from the manual methods of handling business data to the automated processes. These automated processes use electronic computers with a large capacity for storage, calculation, and speedy retrieval of information to serve a variety of company reporting, control, or analytical requirements. These processes also require the talents of specialized personnel with skills in data processing and information-system design and implementation.

The "automated" approach to data processing is forcing changes in the fundamental concepts of organization which were discussed in earlier chapters. The line organization has been very effective in firms whose state of technological development was basically mechanization. The shift to mass production called for a new approach, and the line-and-staff principle developed. The approach to organization now must be reexamined in the light of new concepts of data processing for control and decision-making purposes. Implicit in the concepts of automatic data processing (and automated production processes as well) are the information system and the information center.

Computerized data processing makes possible the development of an integrated information system. Data that are generated in every segment of the firm may flow according to plan into a central storage area where they will be carefully inventoried. Data from selected external sources will follow a similar pattern. This storeroom of information will be separate from the production, distribution, and allied functions. It will have independent status because its activity will not belong exclusively to any of these functions, and the skills required of its personnel in gathering and utilizing data will be quite unlike the skills employed in the traditional business functions.

The accumulation of sales data, production data, and the like will not be the function of these departments; rather it will be the responsibility of the information-system people. The great value of a centralized information center will be that all data can be found in a single center. Thus, when decisions must be made, all details or information to be considered will be equally available in the information center. Marketing decisions, for example, will not be made solely by marketing people on the basis of marketing needs and will not use data gathered solely by the marketing department. An integrated approach to information gathering and decision making becomes the rule.

However, the situation of having centralized information will create new relationships that are not consistent with the traditional views of organization. Each functional area of business—production, marketing, finance, etc.—will be less able to act independently. And this is as it should be, for integration of activity is vital to the success of the total enterprise. It should be pointed out that the integrated information system is a concept on its way to reality in the business world.

THE INFORMATION SYSTEM AND MANAGEMENT

Because the information system and the process of management cannot be separated, we must expect that as the system changes some impact will be felt in the area of management functions. At the intermediate management levels a significant portion of management responsibility relates to the control function. Managers have always complained that they spend too much of their time overly involved in narrow areas of work and that their job is merely to maintain the regularity of a work process. If this control activity can be relegated to the system, that is, if the elements of control can be adequately defined and programmed so that the control decisions can be made automatically, the management can be relieved of the routine burden and have more time for planning and decision making in areas which demand the use of creative talents. Management will have more time to spend in considering how their area of operations can contribute more effectively to the goals of the firm. This, in turn, will demand the development of more capable management.

At the top levels of management, the information system may be the means of extending the capabilities and creativity of those entrusted with top-level decision making and long-range planning. The new dimensions of accuracy, timeliness, and analytical capacity which are available in a computerized information system will provide management with an improved basis for analysis and decision making. The analytical techniques and data processing technology provide a strong support to creative managers who find in these devices a new and powerful tool to assist in solving economic and management problems. Because of these devices, management can be much more knowledgeable and can operate with a greater degree of awareness and certainty.

SUMMARY

Business comprises many functions which are related via the common goals of the business enterprise. In the process of achieving goals there are constant problems to be solved. Some of these problems are germane to the operations of a particular department and others cut across department lines and involve the coordination as well as cooperation of the various functional divisions in their solution. The organization of a business is the device which assigns problems to the most qualified areas.

Vital to operations is communication of information and details which are useful in decision making. Most of the activity details of the firm arise from the day-to-day operations and find their way into reports which are sent to the next higher level of management. At each successive layer of management, the extent of details becomes smaller, and reports on activity are consolidated. At the uppermost levels of management, where policy decisions are forthcoming, the information provided by the business system is based on the exception principle. The internal information is often compared with external information at this level, for top management is concerned with the influences and opportunities which may exist in the environment within which the company operates.

The information system of the firm is vital to the coordination of its various functions. If effectively planned and operated, this system is invaluable in controlling and improving operations. The output of a business system will vary according to the design of the information system and according to the devices used to implement the flow of information.

The simplest systems employ manual labor to record details and prepare reports. The most sophisticated systems employ high-speed automated electronic data processing, automated feedback and closed-loop control system, inclusion of external as well as internal information for purposes of rendering significant reports to management, and a capacity to provide service which has not yet been fully exploited.

BUSINESS ITEM

The information system at Sears, Roebuck and Co.

Sears, Roebuck and Co. has gone out of its way to guard the details of its computerized network of electronic cash registers. When it finally lifted the blackout late in 1972, it revealed a system which will help cut credit losses and inventory shortages, speed up checkout lines, assure an optimum product mix on shelves, and handle numerous accounting and personnel records once processed manually. Most important of all, the system will provide instant national sales data for the company's central buyers and a retail inventory management system to watchdog inventories for more than 40,000 merchandise departments in Sears stores throughout the country. In addition, the system will tie in more than 1,200 catalog sales offices, warehouses, and business offices, plus 1,000 of Sears' largest suppliers.

When the full system is in operation in late 1975 or early 1976, it will include 30,000 to 40,000 electronic registers, more than 600 minicomputers, and 33 larger IBM-370 main computers. Each item sold will be recorded at a register, credit transactions will be cleared, customer accounts updated, inventory balances determined, and purchase orders prepared to replenish stock if necessary. In addition, sales and tax figures will be entered into the accounting department records, and the sales clerks' commissions will be entered into the payroll records. At the central data processing center in Sears' Chicago headquarters, national unit-sale information will be compiled.

QUESTIONS

1 No one functional area of business operation stands alone. Discuss this statement from the viewpoints of company goals, internal operations, and the system concept.

2 What is a system? What is a business system?

3 Organization pervades the structure of business. Amplify this statement.

4 In what respects is a business system duodirectional? Why is this feature essential?

5 Define and illustrate closed-loop and open-loop control systems.

6 What information-system controls would you impose on the following areas of business:

a Customer accounts

b Inventory

c Company cash

d Machine output

e Labor used in production

f Expenditures for research

7 Is it possible for a business to be "self-conscious"?

8 What is communication in a business sense? What elements are implicit in the communications process?

9 What is the difference between data and information?

10 What is the fundamental purpose of the information system in business?

11 What, if any, relationship exists between the management level and functions and the nature of output from the information system?

12 What range of equipment is available for processing data? Is it all equally desirable or available to business people?

13 How does a computer-utility operate?

14 What are the basic components of data processing and how are they logically related?

15 What sort of decision-making power does an electronic computer possess?

16 What is the basic principle of computer language?

The purpose of this chapter In a free enterprise system, business operates under constant risk, for there is no certainty of profit and no certainty of success. Goods produced must be sold; debts must be collected. Natural hazards must be met and bested. The wide variety of risks and hazards encountered in business is explored in this chapter, together with methods, such as the purchase of insurance, that business people have developed for dealing with certain of these risks. Forecasting is viewed as an analytical technique used by management in predicting the business future so as to be better able to plan how to meet or circumvent the risks which appear. Forecasting is an essential preliminary to the managerial planning process. / Questions raised in this chapter include:

1 What is the nature of business risks?

2 How certain and how significant are these risks?

3 To what extent can risk be eliminated?

4 How is business forecasting related to risks?

5 How is the process of forecasting influenced by the level at which the forecasting takes place?

6 What basic economic indicators are presumed to reflect business activity, and how are they of help in forecasting this activity?

22 BUSINESS RISKS, INSUR-
ANCE, AND FORECASTING

A business risk is simply a possibility or danger of incurring a loss. In a free enterprise system, business opportunities for profit always carry with them some measure of risk—some possibility of loss. An important factor in commercial success is the business person's ability to recognize and evaluate the element of risk in a venture, and to take appropriate steps to minimize or balance out the risk. Business risk is difficult to evaluate since it may arise out of conditions beyond the control of management. In any case, an accurate estimate of the danger involved is essential whether the risk is caused by factors within the firm or outside the firm. External risks are usually more dangerous than internal risks.

The modern manager approaches the question of risk much more systematically than did his counterpart of 50 years ago. This is particularly significant, for the need for caution these days is much greater. In many industries the margin for error is very small because of the high volume of production and the intense competition. Significant losses can result from very small initial errors in judgment. Good management requires a careful calculation of risk and the exercise of good judgment about what risks shall be taken. But even with these cautions the business person still faces the element of risk in his ventures.

RISKS AND FORECASTING

The basic technique by which management can reduce risk is to increase the amount of information as well as the accuracy of the information on which decisions are based. As we noted earlier, since most business decisions concern and affect the future, information about the future must be available before reasoned judgment can take place.

Obviously, one cannot know with certainty what the future will bring, but it is possible through careful research and sound analysis to make predictions, with some accuracy, about some aspects of the future. Business forecasting attempts to foresee the changes which might affect business plans so that management can plan accordingly. Of course, business forecasting, like weather forecasting, is not at all perfect; however as we learn more about forecasting, accuracy improves.

Significant business risks

The prime risks in a business enterprise are those inherent in any competitive economy in which change and improvement provide the keys to success. In the nature of things, such risks are difficult to predict and very hard to measure precisely. We are speaking here of the really significant risks in business; the questions which business people ponder long and hard before they decide. These significant risks can be reduced to six simple, but closely related, varieties:

1 Risks involved in investment
2 Risks from price fluctuations and other economic changes
3 Risks from the effects of technological developments
4 Risks from the impact of legislative changes on business
5 Risks involving loss of markets
6 Risks involving loss of profits

The risk of investment is a general overall conception of risk which necessarily involves all the other categories of risk. The final measure of risk is, of course, the loss of business profits.

Investment in business

An essential characteristic of a capitalistic system is the need to invest in plant, facilities, materials, and labor before products become available for sale. Business income depends on previous investments such as these, and since income cannot be predicted with absolute certainty, the act of investment always carries with it an element of risk. In effect, investment is undertaken according to the business person's appraisal of risk involved in an undertaking as compared with the possible gains.

A successful investment usually proves to have been based on an accurate prediction of the cost involved and the returns to be gained. It may be important to investigate a great variety of factors before making the decision to invest. For example, successful sales depend on individual choice, and this may require producing a wide range of designs, colors, styles, and prices. Possible changes in consumer preferences or in marketing conditions must be considered. Records of past sales, if any, consumer surveys, general economic analysis, and a wide variety of management tools are available to help with the prediction, but there always remains an element of insecurity. As we have noted, errors in prediction can be costly since in modern business the margin for error is very small.

Lessening investment risks Business people are very aware of the hazards they face and they use various tools to lessen the impact of changes on their investment. It is important to ensure the flexibility of the investment program, for in a dynamic society an inflexible program is very dangerous. The less flexible any program is, the greater will be the impact of change on the program.

The business person does not always have the opportunity to maintain a flexible investment program, for there are times when he must make a specific "yes or no" decision, such as when he must commit himself to building the new plant or buying the new equipment. Such decisions must get a firm answer. On the other hand, the alternatives need not be so specific. The business person may include among his options more than just the possibility of build or purchase; he may consider the possibilities of leasing facilities. Even if this were to be done on a short-term basis it is a means of gaining flexibility in investment. Leasing minimizes investment, reduces risks, and conserves working capital, and though it may be a more costly proposition leasing may be a sound policy to pursue during periods of rapid change.

The business person can often reduce risk by controlling the rate at which his investment program proceeds. He may venture into investment very cautiously. Such a conservative approach may also contain elements of risk, for it may provide an overwhelming advantage to competitors who take a less cautious investment approach and in so doing gain the lead.

Price fluctuations and economic change

The price movements and the changes in the activity of the whole economy, which are closely related to one another, have a significant effect on the risk element in business operation. The business person is concerned with the prices he must pay for materials and labor as well as with the prices he can obtain for his product. The relationships among these prices help to determine profits. Similarly, the rate of economic activity, which is closely related to price level, helps to determine the volume of sales of any individual business, and this, too, has a significant effect on business profits.

The relationship among these factors is actually quite complex. The prices that the business person pays for materials and labor must be related to the price he expects to receive for his products when they are sold at some future date. Similarly, the amount of materials he purchases for inventory will bear a relation to the future price of materials along with the future price of his own product. On the other hand, the future price of the product depends on the general level of economic activity in the future. For example, if a manufacturer purchases a quantity of material in excess of his immediate needs, and subsequently the market price of this material rises, he stands to gain, for by his earlier excess purchase he has acquired the material at a price lower than the current price. However, if the market price declined, he would lose, for he would be using materials for which he paid a higher price than the current price.

The need to predict the future is common to nearly every business transaction, and it always involves risk. Complicating factors such as government policy, competitive price change, public opinion, foreign imports, and labor-management relations all add to the difficulty of accurate prediction and act to increase risk.

Minimizing risk from price changes In view of the complexity of the factors involved in a price change and the serious effect of price changes on profits, business people try very hard to minimize the effects of price fluctuations. Large companies may be able to exert some direct influence over prices, but this is not usually possible for smaller firms. Careful planning based on the best forecasting available can help reduce the risks due to price fluctuations. Hedging transactions, such as long-term purchasing or sales contracts, may also serve to limit the impact of serious changes in price levels.

Risk from technological change

In an age when technological changes follow one another rapidly, the risk of obsolescence is very great, particularly in manufacturing. Various means are used to minimize this risk. The business person may attempt to pay for new equipment as rapidly as possible so as to be in a position to absorb the next impact of still newer machinery on his price and profit levels. To improve the chances that the investment in equipment will provide a rapid payoff requires the business person to analyze the potential savings that a new investment may bring about. The greater this potential, the quicker is the potential payoff. The leasing of equipment may reduce the risks due to obsolescence; but it may also increase operating costs.

The best protection against the risks of technological change is an active research program. The firm that leads the way in the introduction of new equipment and methods has little to fear from obsolescence as long as it maintains its lead position. This requires a substantial program of research and development in the enterprise. The firm that lags behind in technological changes often suffers additional losses in time and assets when it is finally forced to replace obsolete equipment and methods, or retire from business activity.

Risk from changes in government policy

In many cases the fate of business depends on the legislation that deals with that particular industry. Local codes, land-use laws, labor legislation, tax legislation, legal restrictions, and licenses may become a serious burden on business operation. Today's business property may become the median strip of a double-barreled superhighway in a few months. Changes in tariff rates may price a firm completely out of a domestic market by allowing an influx of foreign goods. Social legislation may add a burden which the firm cannot bear. Federal monetary policy may aid or prevent expansion and thus affect the activity of the business firm.

In a democratic political system, changes in government policy rest with elected representatives, and everyone affected by legislation has a right to be heard. Business people may keep themselves informed of proposed changes in legislation, and may attempt to influence the passage of legislation, as may any other citizen or group of citizens. Further, a good business forecast should include a forecast of political conditions; the business person armed with a sound estimate of future legislation can plan his operations accordingly.

Risk of loss of market

The risk element that has the sharpest effect on most business people is the possibility of losing the market for their product. The reason for the loss of market may be within the control of the business person or it may be due to conditions over which he cannot exert any form of control.

Consumer demand for a product depends on a wide variety of factors, some of which are characteristic of the product, whereas others derive from general business conditions. The style, price, quantity, appropriateness, etc., of a product naturally affect its sales, but so does the amount of competition, the timing of the market effort, and the nature of the product. Fad items, for example, commonly lose their market in a very short time. Sales depend ultimately on individual consumer tastes and desires, and the prediction of these factors is extremely difficult.

Risk of loss of profits

When a risk is undertaken unsuccessfully, the most common consequence is a loss or decline of profits. This may be identified as a loss in investment, a reduction in earning power, an increase in costs, or simply an operating loss. Regardless of the indicated form of the loss, since profits are essential to continued operation in a free economy, the occurrence of losses may result in the business shutting down.

The relation of risk to profit is evident everywhere in our economic structure. The business person decides on his course of action by balancing potential profits against predicted risks. The investor—the stockholder—is guided by the same standards. The individual worker, too, is concerned with the relationship between risk and profits. For one thing, the rate of pay for work is often dependent on the risk entailed in the job, but more indirectly, the worker must balance the risk and profit when he considers taking a job with a particular firm, when he joins a labor union, or when he decides to change jobs.

Organization risks

A major risk in business, which is often overlooked in planning, is the possibility of the loss of key managers for one reason or another.

This is particularly true of small firms in which the future of the enterprise is intimately tied to the health and ability to work of a particular member of the firm, or of a small group of key men. Even in larger companies, the loss of a relatively small number of managers may cause great difficulty, especially if the firm is highly centralized in its organization. Far too often companies have tied their futures to the lives of a few key executives.

This risk may be minimized or eliminated by careful planning. A well-organized program for training replacements for key managers is desirable, though it can be costly, and training successors also creates psychological problems for those who are to eventually be replaced. Such personal considerations as these cannot be ignored. Top management and the owners have a responsiblity to themselves and to the firm to ensure that operations will not suffer if accident befalls key personnel.

Types of business risks

The business person confronts a variety of risks, many of which depend on the type of enterprise involved. There are various ways of classifying such risks depending on the purpose of the classification. For example, risks such as fire, theft, accident, and bad debts are fundamentally internal risks; price changes, technological changes, labor unrest, legislative changes, etc., are external risks which cannot be controlled by the business person.

Risks may be divided into groups according to whether they represent possible loss of earning power or possible loss of property. Risks may be either insurable or noninsurable. Each method of classification has its uses and limits and business people should take all classifications into consideration.

Insuring against risks

Some business risks can be offset by purchasing insurance. An insurance firm will assume responsibility for losses incurred from fire or theft in return for an annual payment of a premium. Actually, insurance companies will insure against the losses from any risk, but at a price. How does the insurance company determine the premium it will ask to cover the losses due to a particular risk? In much the same way that the National Safety Council predicts the number of accidents that will occur on a holiday weekend. The statistics on holiday accidents which have occurred in the past are analyzed to predict the future holiday accident rate. This process requires extensive data both on past accidents and on conditions which influence the future accident rate. The prediction of traffic accidents cannot, of course, foretell what will happen to any particular driver on the road; it can only estimate the number of accidents that will occur. In the same way, an insurance company expects that a certain number of fires will occur in a given time period, and it sets its insurance premium rates accordingly.

Desirability of insurance Most business firms insure against the possibility of catastrophe—the kind of loss which would seriously injure the business. What is a catastrophe to one firm may be a minor blow to another. The loss suffered by a small firm may be disastrous whereas the same loss would be negligible to the large firm. Smaller firms commonly insure more extensively than larger firms. The larger firm, if its risk factors are diversified, may be able to engage in self-insurance. This would save the cost of insurance premiums but would entail the firm's absorbing any losses which occur. The smaller firm does not usually have the financial means to insure itself.

The important factors to be considered are the amount of the possible loss and the impact of the loss on the business. If the loss would seriously damage the ability of the firm to do business, then insurance coverage is wise even though it may be expensive. Some of the more common examples of risk insurance available are shown in Table 22-1.

SUMMARY—INSURANCE AND RISK

The significance of the risk element in business is obviously very great. Risks exist at all times and at all levels of business activity. Some may be balanced by insurance; others may be offset by careful planning and sound research. Essentially, good management is the best provision against potential losses, and it must take into consideration the type of risk, the alternatives available, and the possibility of success with each alternative.

Some of the risks in business involve personal losses, and nearly all involve financial losses to the company concerned. Other risk penalties may be in the form of loss of intangibles such as goodwill or personal health. Risks may be due to governmental policy, technological change, price fluctuations, or general economic change. The effects of risk may be a loss of markets, loss of profits, obsolescence of plant and equipment, or the decline in the demand for a product.

In view of the extensive risks involved in doing business, it is surprising to find that the business person has usually been able to cope with these problems and still keep operating on a solvent basis. Of course, some do not. In most cases, the continued existence of a firm is really a testimony to intelligent planning by management.

FORECASTING

Perhaps the best means of minimizing the impact of risk is accurate forecasting. Forecasting means gathering data, evaluating it, and then making predictions about the future on the basis of the analysis. When business decisions are made based on forecasts developed in this systematic manner, the business person has taken a major step in the direction of sound management practices.

TABLE 22-1   Business risks and insurance protection

Risk classification	Form of protection
Loss of earning power	Business interruption insurance
	Profits insurance
	Rent insurance
	Life insurance on key personnel
Loss of property:	
Destruction or damage	Fire insurance
	Marine insurance
	Riot and insurrection insurance
	Automobile fire and collision insurance
	Aircraft insurance
	Property depreciation insurance
Theft or infidelity	Auto theft insurance
	Burglary, theft insurance
	Forgery insurance
	Fidelity bonding
Failure of others	Credit insurance
	Surety bonding
	Title insurance
Legal liability	Compensation insurance
	Employers' liability
	Public liability
	Automobile liability
	Power-plant insurance
	Elevator insurance
	Product liability
	Sports liability
	Physicians, etc., insurance
	Aircraft insurance

A wide range of insurance protection is available for meeting business risks.

Complete certainty in business forecasting, as in any other predicting, is out of the question. Business conditions change, often very rapidly, and the past is not always indicative of the future. No amount of study of the past would have permitted a person living in 1800 to predict the discovery of atomic power or the development of the Land Polaroid camera, for example. However, if most conditions were to remain the same in an economy, the past would become a useful guide to future trends.

The time span in forecasting

It is easier to forecast for the short run than for the long run, whether we are forecasting business or weather, and yet good business forecasting must be concerned with both the long and short run. Short-term predictions will be more detailed and accurate.

A typical short-run forecast may deal with future sales over a period of a few months. Such a forecast may be made within a range of more easily predictable possibilities than could a long-range forecast of sales for the next year. The long-range forecast would require consideration of general trends within the economic system, within the industry, and among competitive producers.

Levels of the forecasting problem

It is evident that there are different levels for forecasting. One level may involve analysis to determine seasonal variation patterns. At this level, the basic data required for the analysis are actual historical data of the firm or industry which are both explicit and documented in the form of month-to-month recordings. Using these data the business person may be able to answer the question: What seasonal variability is to be expected in the future? There are several other areas of forecasting by the business firm which display "internal" data features (see Table 22-2).

When the data necessary for forecasting are not available from company records and must be searched for from sources within the business environment, a different level of forecasting activity is involved. Much of this external data can be obtained from government

TABLE 22-2　Forecasting applications

Data Sources: Internal and external environments
Nature of Data: Explicit and Implicit

Forecasting applications

Internally based	Broadly based
Seasonal pattern	Technological developments
Extrapolation of sales curve	International influences
Determining manpower requirements	Political tendencies
Establishing equipment requirements	Gross national product
Cost estimation	Social trends and impacts
Budgeting	Market direction
Setting inventory levels	Competition
	Customer characteristics

The nature of the application determines the source of data and the extent to which they are explicitly available or must be implied from other data or circumstances.

or trade sources. Several of these sources are described later in this chapter under the heading "Basic Economic Indicators." On the other hand, all the data needed will not be found so neatly tabulated, and, in effect, the business person often has to resort to using implicit data—data which are implied by circumstances—and must exercise personal judgment both in interpreting such implicit data and in deciding on the validity of their inclusion in the forecasting process. Hunches, intuition, "seat-of-the-pants" bases for making decisions or evaluations are not foreign to the forecasting process. These inputs, as significant as they are to the forecasting process, are only usable when they are translated into explicit measurements. The manager who "feels" that business is going to be better cannot plan how many more units to produce or whether he needs additional production capacity or labor force until he converts his "feeling" into some specific quantity such as "10 percent improvement over last year" or "10,000 more units this year than last."

Depending on the scope of the forecasting which a business attempts, data may be drawn solely from company sources at the one extreme or may include market, social, technical, economic, and political inputs at the other extreme. The latter, most broadly based, level of forecasting is the most difficult and requires the formulation of explicit mathematical models which describe the environment and the interactions of its various features. Some examples of this type of forecasting are sales forecasting models which attempt to describe the market environment mathematically in order to depict the influences of variations in environmental factors; input-output models which are devices for mathematically structuring an economic system or part of it and demonstrating the results of variations in the interacting factors which make up the system; and demographic models which attempt to specify sociological relationships and to portray interactions among such factors as education, occupation, shifting preferences, and population characteristics.

Areas for forecasting

Any future event is fair game for forecasting. However, the business forecast is most often applied to:

Sales

Production

Financial matters

Materials (price, availability, etc.)

Personnel problems

Facilities (cost, use, requirement, etc.)

Such forecasts are of course interrelated, since the sales forecast plays an important part in the production forecast, which, in turn, affects forecasting for materials and facilities, and so forth. Although the data used for forecasting in each area are different, the general procedure is roughly the same.

CHANGES IN BUSINESS ACTIVITY

One of the tools which forecasters can use in their work is the record of historical changes in business activity. In the past, the behavior of the economic system has fluctuated widely, and many of the changes seem to follow regular patterns. There will also be some very irregular changes which cannot be either explained or patterned.

In a general way, however, the tempo of business activity consists of alternating upward and downward movements of varied length and intensity which are called *cycles*. The exact causes of these cyclic changes are not completely understood. The more closely any period of business activity is examined, the greater the number of changes and alterations we can discover.

If we examine the activity of an entire century, we find long-term growth and decline. These long-term movements are called *secular trends*. Short-term variations may be regular or seasonal movements. In addition, there are random changes in activity which reflect unusual and unaccountable events (see Figure 22-1).

Business cycles

Any chart that shows business sales, production, shipments, or prices over a period of years will usually describe the data by means of a wavy graph line. The rise and fall of business activities are not usually regular and there is seldom any long period during which no change in activity occurs. The economic system is dynamic, and it changes constantly. Each rise in rate of activity is followed by a decline, and then another rise, and so forth. The period from one peak of activity to the next peak is called a business cycle. These cycles of business activity have been studied very carefully but we are still a long way from understanding either the underlying causes of these cycles or the way to prevent declines in the cycles.

Experts have identified many different business cycles—periods when business activity increased, fell, and increased again. Most of the cycles were of short duration and the degree of rise and fall was relatively modest. But before 1929 there was a long period of rising activity, followed by a deep and sustained fall—the Great Depression of the 1930s. Various explanations of this depression and its origins have been advanced, but none is completely satisfactory. Business people and economists are still searching for an explanation of the business cycle and the means of controlling it.

We have, however, learned a great many things about the characteristics of the business cycle in recent years. If we study a period when business activity has reached a low point and is beginning to rise once again, we find that the economic system, as compared with the low period just preceding the rise, is characterized by:

1 Rising stock prices

2 Higher overall prices

3 Increases in production

4 Increases in sales
5 Increases in inventories
6 Increased credit buying
7 Higher interest rates

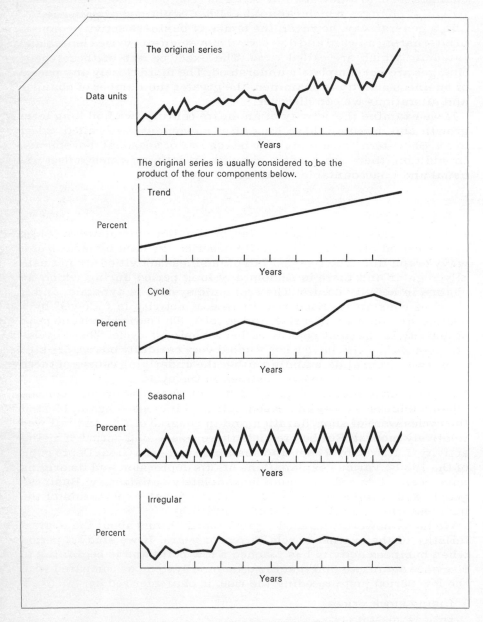

The original series

Data units

Years

The original series is usually considered to be the product of the four components below.

Trend

Percent

Years

Cycle

Percent

Years

Seasonal

Percent

Years

Irregular

Percent

Years

FIGURE 22-1 Components of a business time series

There are other evident characteristics of the change, but these seven factors are basic indicators which show the economy is reviving again. The increase continues until once again a peak is reached. How do we know when the peak is reached? Unfortunately, we become aware of the peak once the economy starts to slow down again. This is a paramount problem for forecasters. Peaks can only be determined after they have been reached and passed.

When the peak has passed and activity slows, we cannot be certain that it will continue to slow down indefinitely; it revives, sometime sooner, sometimes later, and moves on until another peak, maybe a higher one, is reached. If the slowdown does not last long it is called a recession. If the slowing down is prolonged it is called a depression.

Trends

The business cycle and long-term trends can be clearly seen only when the level of business activity is charted over a long time period. If the activity is charted for only 1 year, it is usually only the seasonal variation which will show itself clearly. Trends are a measure of long-term changes in activity. Charting the activity of a single company or an industry or an economy over a period of many years will show the trend or direction of that activity. One company's trend may differ from that of the industry of which it is a part, but usually the two are related and the comparison of a company's trend with that of its entire industry and the economy is very useful to the company management.

Lag and lead

Researchers have found that, as business activity waxes and wanes in the business cycle, certain factors tend to change before others. For example, when economic activity changes speed, the firms which produce consumer durable goods are usually affected by the change before other industries. Changes in residential building, automobile production, and the basic commodity price index usually precede changes in the overall business cycle. These indicators seem to chart the course to be followed later by other industries and other forms of economic activity. No one is certain of why these factors "lead" in the trend of economic activity and other factors "lag." The fact they do is important knowledge for forecasters.

BASIC ECONOMIC INDICATORS

The business forecaster has available a number of useful basic standards or yardsticks for measuring economic activity. These yardsticks may be related to the whole economy or to the state of particular parts of the economy. They are useful in forecasting, planning for sales, investment planning, and various other aspects of business enterprise. Some of the best-known and most useful of these indicators are the wholesale price index, the consumer price index, the industrial production index, national income, and the average workweek.

National income and product

The estimates made of national income (the total of everyone's income) and gross national product (the total of all goods and services produced) are also useful indicators of economic activity levels. If the estimates, which are prepared by a rather complex procedure, are reasonably accurate, they can tell the forecaster a great deal about the general health of the whole economy as well as the health of a particular section of the economy. When these indicators are used in conjunction with other information, they provide a means for verifying many of the assumptions that the forecaster must make about the future.

Industrial production index

The industrial production index is published monthly by the Federal Reserve Board (see Figure 22-2). It measures the actual amount of physical output from mines and factories in the economy; therefore, it is a major indicator of the production rate of the country. It shows the forecaster whether production is rising or falling. The index is presented in two categories, mining and manufacturing, with the

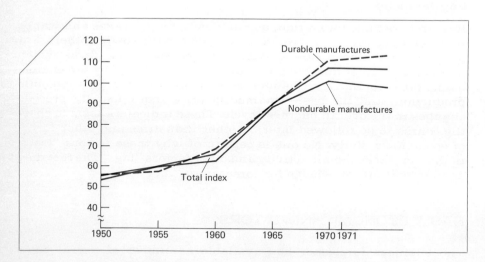

FIGURE 22-2 Industrial production index (selected years)

Source: *Federal Reserve Bulletin,* Board of Governors of the Federal Reserve System.

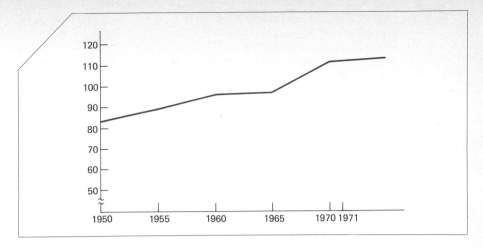

FIGURE 22-3   Wholesale price index (selected years)

Reported on a weekly and monthly basis, this prime economic indicator represents the combined relative change in the prices of commodities in primary markets. Source: U.S. Department of Labor, Bureau of Labor Statistics.

manufacturing category further detailed to show the production of durable and nondurable goods. Indexes are reported for several major mining and manufacturing groupings. This allows a particular firm to compare its own output index with the level of output of its own industry grouping.

Wholesale price index

The monthly index of wholesale prices (see Figure 22-3) is a comprehensive measure of general commodity price levels prepared by the Bureau of Labor Statistics. It is an important index because changes in price influence the economy at every level.

This index is designed to measure changes in the prices of all commodities sold in the country's prime markets. It focuses on the prices paid by the first large-volume class of buyers; therefore, it is not designed to measure prices received by wholesalers, jobbers, or distributors. Prices are collected for more than 2,000 commodities ranging from raw materials to finished goods. These commodities are representative of the important products of each industry.

Consumer price index

The Bureau of Labor Statistics also prepares an index which measures changes in the prices of goods and services purchased by urban wage earners and clerical workers. The consumer price index (see Figure 22-4) is useful as an indicator of the influence of purchasing power on the consumption of specific goods and services. Since the

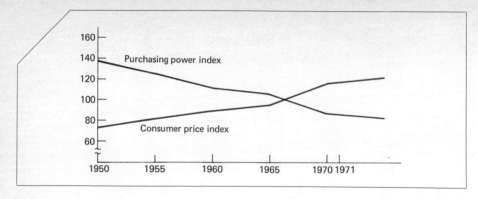

FIGURE 22-4   Consumer price index and purchasing power index (selected years)

The consumer price index presents the combined relative change in the prices that city wage earners and clerical worker families pay for rent, food, apparel, and transportation. The purchasing power index shows that a 1970 dollar is worth 86 cents compared with the 1967 dollar or that it takes $1.16 to purchase in 1970 what a dollar would purchase in 1967. Source: U.S. Department of Labor, Bureau of Labor Statistics.

consumer must first buy those things that are necessary for life, a rise in prices will reduce the demand for those goods which are not necessities.

Measures of price changes are also measures of change in the value of the dollar. The higher the price, the less a dollar is able to purchase. The inversion of a price series (1.00/price) will give a purchasing-power series (see Figure 22-4).

The purchasing power of the dollar is a useful measure that is often used as a base for automatic wage increases in industries in which union-management labor contracts provide for cost-of-living adjustments in wages.

Average workweek in manufacturing

The tempo of business activity is closely related to the length of the average workweek. When business activity is at its peak, the average length of the workweek tends to increase. When business activity drops off, the average workweek also falls off. This indicator is useful but it should be used in conjunction with other indicators, because the reason for the changes in the workweek have to be uncovered before the significance of the change can be assessed. A drop in the average workweek resulting from seasonal variations in activity would be considered a normal change which could be anticipated, whereas a drop in the workweek during a period when the seasonal activity is normally high would call for some other explanation.

Business failures

The number of business failures in a given time period is obviously a sensitive indicator of the general state of business. Since these data are available, the forecaster can obtain a careful breakdown of business failures by industry, geographic location, capitalization and size, and various other bases (see Figure 22-5).

SUMMARY—FORECASTING

Forecasting consists of gathering and analyzing business and economic data and using the analysis to help formulate predictions of future trends in economic activity. It may be done for any time period and for almost any phase of business, though forecasting is most commonly used in sales, production, finance, material control, and other major business areas.

The forecaster makes use of a number of factors in his work. He is concerned with seasonal variations in economic activity, in the overall changes in economic activity called the business cycle, and in long-range trends within the economy.

Forecasting also makes use of a number of basic economic indicators including the wholesale and consumer prices indexes, the industrial production index, gross income and gross national product figures, the average workweek, and the statistics on business failures. Each of these measures throws light on the state of the economic system and helps the forecaster prepare a prediction.

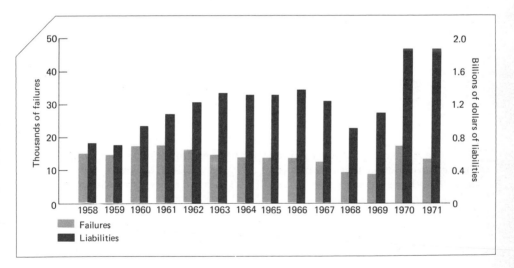

FIGURE 22-5 Failures and liabilities

Source: Dun & Bradstreet, Inc., N.Y.

The business person's forecasting know-how and expertise range from simple guesswork to the use of very sophisticated quantitative techniques of analysis and projection. The range of data which he uses in making his analyses may be as explicit as the historical data which he has recorded on his firm's books or as implicit as the interpretations he gives to certain insights or conversations which he has experienced.

BUSINESS ITEMS

Does a lower birth rate result in a better life?

There are many who foresee significant benefits to be gained as a result of the lowering birth rate in the United States. Many others feel that the anticipated benefits, as well as some negative effects, are all greatly exaggerated.

Those foreseeing benefits anticipate that as the population growth slows down and finally stabilizes in the twenty-first century, the following results will be obtained.

Productivity will increase because the average worker, being older, will be more experienced and will be working with more capital equipment at his disposal. By the year 2000 it is expected that the average age of the United States population will be 34—up from 28.1 in 1972.

The average standard of living will rise, for with smaller families, each breadwinner's paycheck will be spread over fewer consumers.

Public spending will shift away from such needs as an expanding educational system—because of decreasing school enrollments—into other, more important, local spending such as crime prevention, pollution control, and recreational facilities.

Marketing will have to change its tactics and sell to an older group of consumers. As the age composition of the population changes, so will marketing efforts.

Tanks for thoughts

Four big companies—DuPont, Scott Paper, Lever Bros., and Monsanto—are paying to get a peek at what may be in store for the 1980s. These four companies are backing a project called "Aware" to the tune of $40,000 per year per company for 3 years in an attempt to predict the long-range changes in the social, economic, and technological environments that the companies will face in the next decade.

This effort is being carried out by a small but prestigious California think tank called the Institute for the Future which utilizes a forecasting technique known as Delphi. This technique relies on a panel of experts who answer elaborate questionnaires. Their answers are summarized and the questioning repeated until consensus on future trends is reached.

Major issues with which this project is concerned are: the quality of life, the energy crisis, worker discontent, and business procedures. Some of the preliminary results forecast for the 1980s are that the quality of life is likely to decay; the energy crisis will be resolved by market forces; worker discontent will increase but productivity will increase nevertheless; and business procedures will not change until the mid-1980s.

Project Aware is not a crystal-ball venture. Its experts realize that the future is a very foggy environment. All they seek to do is highlight what may be some of the obstacles in the fog.

QUESTIONS

1 Are the risks that business people face today any more significant than those faced by their predecessors?

2 The past holds no risks for the business person. Under what conditions and why?

3 Would you agree that insurance is a means of eliminating risk?

4 Does the nature and extent of risk faced by business have any relation to the form of economic system in which the business operates? How and why?

5 Technological change implies improvement. How can any risk be involved in technological change?

6 If a machine is purchased and the purchaser knows that it is capable of doing a satisfactory job in terms of quantity, quality, and cost, then what risk is involved in such an investment? Explain.

7 What is the most common business consequence of unsuccessful risk taking?

8 What is forecasting? How certain are its results?

9 The terms "cycle," "secular trend," and "seasonal variation" are common to the forecaster. What is the meaning of each term and how are they interrelated?

10 All that a good forecaster has to be able to do is forecast the turning points of business activity. Discuss.

11 Name three basic economic indicators. In what respects may they be considered as basic?

12 When the forecaster refers to "lag" and "lead" characteristics what is he referring to and why is he interested in these features?

The purpose of this chapter American business people and consumers are unable to avoid the impact of international business activities. The business person is aware of the impact of foreign-made goods in his American marketplace, and he has already experienced the greater potential for growth and profits which exist in foreign markets and investments in business abroad. / Consumers in the United States are aware of the international sources that provide items ranging from food and clothing to automobiles and power plants. American labor particularly sees the international market as a threat to its livelihood because of the very low wage rates paid by foreign competitors. / Because of the significance of the topic of international business to producer and consumer alike, some further understanding of its involvements and potential is very desirable. / Questions raised in this chapter include:

1 Why is it important to study international business?

2 How have the characteristics of international business changed?

3 What are the forces which make business on an international basis necessary?

4 How does international trade differ from doing business abroad?

5 How do matters of law, politics, taxes, and education enter into international business dealings?

23 / INTERNATIONAL BUSI-NESS

American business people must now view business in the international sphere even though they may not be directly involved in transactions outside the United States. We are all aware that, in terms of time, the earth continues to shrink in size; and little by little we are forced to think more in global terms than national terms. The concept that we should not have trade relations with certain nations is rapidly disappearing. We currently have a variety of trade relations with the Soviet Union and probably during this decade will open significant trade relations with the People's Republic of China.

There are at least four significant reasons why all business people should study the international business scene. First, foreign business may seriously impair the demand for American-made goods in American markets. This applies to small business and large business alike. Wholesalers and retailers need larger and larger volumes of sales for growth and profit, and if sales and profit goals are more easily attained by merchandising foreign-made goods, this is the course they will follow. Discount stores especially look to foreign sources of supply because in many instances they are cheaper than domestic sources. The consequence of this action on domestic sources is of little concern to discounters. Countless American businesses have folded under the impact of foreign competition. In many instances, however, it was an unnecessary consequence; American business did nothing to counter the outside forces. The old Singer Sewing Machine Company, feeling the pressure of foreign competition, changed its role from a manufacturer of sewing machines to a merchandiser of a wide line of small appliances, largely imported. Thus Singer capitalized on foreign competition at a time when other sewing machine companies submitted to it and closed their doors.

Second, foreign markets may offer greater potential for future growth and profits than domestic markets. The proposition seems to have considerable merit. The overseas market is growing twice as fast as the domestic market, and the rate of growth is increasing. We should also consider the obvious, yet often ignored, fact that of the some 3 billion people on this earth, only a small fraction, 200 million, are in the United States.

The third reason for considering international operations is that

537

Who is dealing with the Soviet Union	
Company	*Area of cooperation*
Bechtel	Construction methods, planning
Boeing	Civil aviation, air transport technology
Brown & Root	Oil and gas development
Control Data	Computers, peripheral equipment, systems design, software
Dresser Industries	Oil and gas exploration
General Dynamics	Shipbuilding, aircraft construction, telecommunications, computers
General Electric	Power and electrical engineering, atomic power plants
Hewlett-Packard	Medical electronics, measuring equipment, minicomputers
ITT	Communications technology, electronic components
Joy Mfg.	Coal mining equipment
Litton Industries	(Not available)
Monsanto	(Not available)
Occidental Petroleum	Oil and gas drilling, refining, agricultural chemicals
Singer	Computers, electronic instruments, textile equipment
Stanford Research Institute	General science and technology
Tenneco	(Not available)
Texas Eastern Transmission	(Not available)

Source: *Business Week*, Jan. 12, 1974.

investment in business abroad may yield greater returns on capital than additional domestic investment. But getting businesses established overseas will become more and more difficult. We are not the only developed nation seeking foreign business investment; if it is a good proposition for us it may also be a good proposition for Japan, the U.S.S.R., and other nations. In addition, there is growing resentment in some countries of the invasion or take-over of business by foreign groups. It is interesting to note that as we continue to invest in foreign countries, foreign countries increase their investment in American business.

The fourth reason why we need to be concerned with international business is the increasing dependence of the United States on foreign countries for an ever-increasing list of raw materials. Petroleum and certain minerals are two very important imports that are vital to maintaining our economic growth and standard of living. At one point in time we had nearly complete control over the oil wells of the Middle East and the copper mines in South America, but those days are gone forever.

THE CHANGING NATURE OF INTERNATIONAL BUSINESS

International business is certainly not a new area of activity—remember the adventures of Marco Polo and the Boston Tea Party—but a number of new dimensions have emerged in recent years that warrant our attention. Once the province of only the very large American business, international business now involves firms of moderate size. The possibility of an employee of business being involved with some aspects of international business increases each year. Another significant change is the volume of international trade. As national boundaries and tariffs disappear, more and more goods move into international trade.

For many years, and until recently, international business was primarily foreign trade—the buying and selling of goods in foreign markets. Today, more and more firms, not necessarily very large ones, own and operate businesses in foreign countries. This increased movement of American capital and American management outside the United States is the principal change in international business during the past decade.

INTERNATIONAL TRADE

International trade as such does not constitute a significant portion of our gross national product, but it is important in certain segments of our economy. There are dozens of food items and raw materials that are not indigenous to the United States, and we depend 100 percent on foreign sources of supply to have them. In some instances, the amount of a raw material we import, petroleum, for example, may be the difference between scarcity and plenty. The dollar value and the percentage of our new supply of certain commodities are shown in Table 23-1. Notice our great dependence on outside sources for

TABLE 23-1   Importance of imports to total supply—selected commodities

Commodity	Imports, millions of dollars				Percentage of new supply			
	1960	1965	1968	1969	1960	1965	1968	1969
Coffee	1,003	1,058	1,140	894	100	100	100	100
Silk	27	20	18	14	100	100	100	100
Bauxite	80	149	147	172	80	79	86	87
Manganese ores	82	110	46	39	93	96	95	92
Textiles	136	240	242	267	NA	55	34	36
Iron ores	322	444	454	402	31	36	35	30
Sewing machines	35	67	95	109	21	37	42	44

Source: U.S. Department of Commerce, Bureau of Census.

TABLE 23-2 Japan's growing hunger for raw materials

	Imports	
	Fiscal 1967	Fiscal 1975 (est.)
Copper (thousands of tons)	483	742
Lead (thousands of tons)	86	128
Zinc (thousands of tons)	182	387
Nickel (thousands of tons)	53	110
Iron ore (millions of tons)	55	200
Coking coal (millions of tons)	24	100
Petroleum (millions of cubic meters)	121	261
Lumber and pulp (millions of cubic meters)	33	60

Data: Mitsui and Co., Japan Iron and Steel Federation.
Source: *Business Week*, Jan. 24, 1970.

bauxite, which is a basic ingredient in the production of aluminum, and manganese ore, which is a vital ingredient in the production of metals that have superior performance characteristics.

As national incomes around the globe rise and as discretionary spending—spending for nonessentials—by consumers everywhere increases, more and more raw materials must be obtained to satisfy this demand. As a nation's raw material resources become depleted, new sources must be developed, and these will often be inferior sources or sources in far-off and underdeveloped countries. It is not uncommon today for underdeveloped countries to require that some processing of raw materials take place before the materials leave the country. This, of course, is aimed at increasing the countries' rate of industrialization without capital outlays on their part.

Japan provides us with an excellent illustration of this situation. Japan is one of the world's fastest-growing nations, and yet it is a nation that has very limited raw material resources. Some indication of its growing raw material needs is shown in Table 23-2. But this is only part of the story. Within a generation, the Japanese will exhaust the few natural resources remaining beneath their island. Their sources of iron ore will run out during this decade.

Consequently, Japanese industry is investing billions of dollars in raw material sources all around the globe. Some illustrations are iron ore mines in Australia; copper mines in the Congo, Ecuador, and Canada; and metallurgical coal mines in Virginia. Coal costs Japanese industry nearly double what steel mills in the United States are paying, but to them it is worthwhile because a costly source of supply is better than no source at all.

A picture of the extent to which certain American industries and

TABLE 23-3 Domestic exports in relation to domestic output—
selected commodities

	Exports, millions of dollars				Percentage of output			
Commodity	1960	1965	1968	1969	1960	1965	1968	1969
Cotton farm products	982	487	460	281	41	20	32	23
Milled rice	148	241	347	347	52	55	62	59
Leaf tobacco	378	378	511	529	32	31	43	41
Sulphur	41	64	66	56	35	44	25	32
Cottonseed oil	55	79	40	35	13	15	17	14
Medicinals	260	168	216	246	9	36	35	37

Source: U.S. Department of Commerce, Bureau of Census.

firms may be dependent on foreign markets is presented in Tables 23-3 and 23-4. The specific commodity groups were selected for this illustration to show areas where there was the greatest and least involvement in foreign markets. For several commodity groups more than one-third of their output finds its outlet abroad.

The logic of foreign trade

Foreign trade takes place for two reasons. First, some nations want and need certain commodities that exist only in other countries. We like to have coffee, silks, and bananas, but they are not grown in this country. Since our iron ore resources are decreasing in quantity and

TABLE 23-4 Percent of earnings from foreign operations

Firm	Percent
Burroughs	41
Coca-Cola	55
Dow Chemical	48
Gillette	51
Hoover	60
IBM	54
International Flavors and Fragrances	52
Merck	44
NCR	53
Revlon	38
Sperry Rand	50
Sunbeam	38
Xerox	46

Source: Business Week, Jan. 12, 1974.

quality, we must import high-grade iron ore. We either do without certain things or engage in foreign trade.

A second reason can be explained by the theory of comparative advantage. A century ago, the United States specialized in producing agricultural goods, and exchanged them for the manufacturing output of European nations. We had an abundance of good farm land; many European nations did not, but they had the manufacturing capability that we lacked.

In theory, at least, a nation tends to specialize in the things it can do best and sell them in foreign markets. It imports the things that it needs from other nations that can produce them best. But a comparative advantage can come from several sources. When we say "can produce them best," we mean produce at least cost. A nation may be blessed with abundant natural resources such as our farm lands or the diamond mines of South Africa; it may maintain a comparative advantage through its organization and management know-how; or it may achieve low production costs by paying low wages. Labor is the prime cost of doing business all over the world, but our wage rates are the highest of all.

Our chief complaint against the free movement of goods into this country is the disparity of wage rates among nations. Rapidly rising labor costs in this country have made it possible for countries that heretofore had no comparative advantage to compete favorably in the American market. The rubber footwear industry is a case in point. Within the past 10 years dozens of American producers have closed their doors because of foreign competition.

There are at least two factors at work that may give us a comparative advantage over other nations in the years ahead. First, wage rates in many foreign countries, Japan and European nations especially, are rising more rapidly than ours. If we can maintain technological superiority over our competition we may be able to bring labor costs, per unit of production, in line with costs elsewhere.

The second factor is the devaluation of the American dollar in world money markets. In many instances it takes fewer foreign dollars to buy goods made in America than it did just a few years ago. This should stimulate foreigners to buy more from us. Turning the coin over, it takes more American dollars to buy a Toyota or a Mercedes-Benz than it did before devaluation set in. Having a comparative advantage, therefore, may be only a temporary condition.

Tariffs

Tariffs are nothing more than duties levied by the federal government against certain goods coming into this country. Tariffs cause prices to rise and, of course, discourage imports. Tariffs may be levied for a number of reasons, but their main purpose is to raise the cost of foreign-made goods to the level of domestic producers. As a result, tariffs force us to pay higher prices for many goods. The principal defense for tariffs is that they protect the American worker. This may be true in the short run for some workers, but in the long run it is costly for the American consumer. Tariffs may become a subsidy for inefficient producers. We must expect that if we restrict the flow of goods into this country through tariffs, other nations will do the same, to the detriment of the American worker. In the long run we should expect that the use of tariffs to protect domestic industry will gradually phase out. If the concept of a world market becomes a reality, there will be no place for tariffs.

INTERNATIONAL BUSINESS

Foreign trade as described above can be conducted by an American business person with little or no direct contact with the other party. Contracts are often made through middlemen, and financial matters can be handled by banks which are expert in foreign-trade matters. Hence the American business person dealing with a Japanese manufacturer does not need to know anything about Japanese management or the Japanese business environment. Operating a business in a foreign country is another matter, however, because the environment cannot be ignored. To a great extent, the study of international business is a study of international environments.

It is difficult to generalize about international business because what can be said about one country may not apply to another, even though it is adjacent. In Europe, especially, significant cultural changes can be found by moving very short distances. In land area, Great Britain, Belgium, the Netherlands, Denmark, and West Germany together are smaller than our state of Texas.

Before exploring the problems of managing business on the international scene, we need to recognize that there can be differences in the way the foreign establishment is connected to its American parent. The foreign operation can be virtually independent of the parent, with nationals providing the entire labor needs. It can be operated as a branch of the American firm with a resident manager, or several levels of management could come from the home office. As a rule, first-line supervisors and all workers will be nationals. There is such a vast difference in customs that an American-trained foreman would have great difficulty maintaining a productive workforce. In some instances the host country may prescribe the basic structure of management. However, it is very common to find a blend of American and national management in firms owned abroad.

Looking at the differences—management

Managers of business in European countries occupy business and social positions that are quite different from those of their American counterparts. They are referred to by many students of international business as a management elite, because they are capable and because they occupy positions far removed from lower levels of management. Decentralization is a distinctive feature of American organizations, and one reason that it is practiced is that it reduces the ability gap between organizational levels, and puts authority in the hands of lower-level managers, who are considered important too. European organizations are far more centralized—hence the spread between organizational levels. Some authors consider this elite concept to be just an extension of the idea of the elite in many professions in Europe. But we must not overlook the fact that Europeans have not made a concerted attempt to train managers for business; there is, by our standards, at least, a shortage of competent managers. Schools of business administration at both the undergraduate and the graduate level are few and far between outside the United States, and there is evidence that such schools are an effective way to prepare managers.

European business is much more family-centered than American business. In many instances the basic goal of business is to perpetuate the means of supporting the family—to provide employment for the family. As a consequence, there is little opportunity for outsiders to rise in the organization and establish broader goals for the firm. The management elite concept is quite apt to stay alive as long as businesses are family-centered. An American manager working with European managers can easily become frustrated because of the encumbering management philosophy.

Organizational differences

The concept of the management elite is closely tied in with some different notions that prevail about approaches to organization. European managers and managers in other nations have continued the policy of maintaining tight control and influencing activity in all segments of the organization. Even in larger organizations there is a hesitancy to delegate significant amounts of authority to lower levels.

This system exists primarily because subordinate levels do not have the required training and skill to accept additional authority. Further, no attempt is made to develop managers on the job. Foreign business still suffers from its relatively rigid class system which prevents large numbers of people from rising above the class into which they were born.

Foreign business organizations are far less democratic than their American counterparts. In many respects they resemble American business of a past generation. Highly centralized, paternalistic, and authoritarian organizations in America today are considered on the road to disaster, but these characteristics are considered necessary in many nations abroad. Why can business abroad get away with these practices? Basically because workers expect something far different from their employment than Americans.

The cultural differences mentioned above lead to yet another difference in organization. American business uses a large number of specialists as members of staff and functional divisions, in order to have sources of ideas that can assist the line management. But many foreign managers cannot see the need for such organization append-ages; they consider the line organization enough. Foreign managers take great pride in the fact that they are managers; that they are an elite; that they are the source of all ideas, authority, and everything else that it takes to make an organization run. They insist on a clear and uncluttered organization which they feel cannot be achieved with staff divisions.

However, in spite of our at least seminegative comments about European and other managers and their organization, we must admit that they have a long history of success. These managers are suc-cessful in their environment, and many foreign-trained managers have been very successful in the United States. But there is a price for their success. Foreign business remains relatively smaller and less efficient than American business, and its high degree of central-ization hinders innovation. Returns on investment are generally low by our standards, and it takes a long time to train a manager in their system. Europeans do not mind these negative aspects of their sys-tem, for they are consistent with their values. It is better, by their standards, for a person to mature as a manager by a slow and me-thodical process. Such a manager will be likely to stay with the firm until retirement—so why hurry?

This points out another feature of foreign managements and orga-nizations: there is very little movement of management personnel between firms. The attitude of Europeans toward management job-hoppers is quite negative. They feel that a person is of questionable character if he moves from firm to firm in an effort to speed up his rate of promotion. This attitude is quite the opposite of ours, and can be traced to a number of cultural differences, such as the more re-served nature of foreign business people, less concern for material progress, loyalty, and a wait-for-your-turn attitude.

Relations with governments

The relations that an American firm may expect with host govern-ments is a most important aspect of international business. Success can hinge on this single issue. Unfortunately, there are no uniform guidelines that can be applied to all foreign situations. Each country is sovereign and consequently it will prescribe rules and regulations which best serve its purposes; one nation will welcome the same type of business that another will reject. It all depends on what the host nation seeks to achieve through involvement with foreign business.

There was a time when American business people could go into a country and virtually dictate the conditions under which they would operate. This was due in part to the inexperience of foreign govern-ments in dealing with American business people and to the overwhelming power of the United States. This time has passed, and in the future American business must expect to give full value for what it gets from doing business in a foreign country.

Areas of law

We can get a better picture of the relationships that an American business abroad will have with the host nation if we examine some of the applicable areas of law. These are the same basic areas of law that concern American business operating in America, but of course the laws themselves may differ. The specific areas of concern are business law, labor law, tax law, and general law.

Business law Business law is basically contract law and related areas of law such as agency, negotiable instruments, sales, and the like. In a well-developed business society such as ours, laws in these areas have been applied for so long that they are codified, and the rights and responsibilities of parties are fairly clear. To be sure, there are new situations that must be adjudicated, but by and large, business people are quite certain of the law; they have a good idea of how it applies and how its application will affect them. This is not necessarily the case in less developed nations or in nations that lack political stability. Where highly developed legal codes exist, there may be differences in the rights and responsibilities of parties from one nation to another.

Laws of several of the oil-rich nations of the Middle East are to a great extent based upon tradition and/or religious teachings, and since many of these nations have had only a brief business history, there may be many events that are not covered by specific laws. That rights and responsibilities vary from one nation to another is well understood by business people. We have our views as to the meaning of a contract: it is a promise to do something or to refrain from doing something under specified conditions. Violations of a contract may result in penalties. In Japan, a contract may be more an "if" relationship than a "will" relationship. Contracts in Japan are not viewed as legally binding if changing conditions make their original provisions obsolete. This means that a contract may not be enforceable if enforcement would cause one party to suffer losses.

Many an American author has found that the copyright protection that he enjoys here does not exist in many foreign countries. Many an American business that has spent considerable time and money building a brand name through quality merchandise and strong promotion has found the name used indiscriminately in other countries. In some foreign countries, if a manufacturer thinks he can profit by using the name Goodyear, Magnavox, Delco, or FoMoCo, he will use it. There have been cases where items bearing false trademarks have found their way into American markets. This has been especially true in the area of automotive replacement parts.

Labor laws Foreign nations permit operation of American business primarily because it aids in the development of their economy. The types of activity that are permitted depend on the nation's stage of development and the need to complement existing business. A prime factor in the economic development of any nation is employment and the development—upgrading—of the labor force. Consequently, labor laws are very important in most foreign countries, and their impact on profitable business operation can be substantial.

Since a basic reason for permitting foreign business to operate, especially in underdeveloped countries, is to provide employment opportunities, a considerable portion of labor law is in this area. American business should expect a host nation to require that a stated minimum percentage of a firm's labor force be nationals, and the requirement may run as high as 9 out of every 10 employees. An additional requirement may be that a certain percentage of the management group also be nationals; such a law is saying, perhaps indirectly, that American business must train and educate the labor force. In many nations the only prior work experience of potential employees is on farms where only outmoded equipment is available for use.

Minimum wage laws apply in most countries, but their impact on profitable operation can be the greatest in underdeveloped countries where the bulk of the workforce is grossly unskilled, and many workers are unable to perform at a level where payment of the minimum wage is economically justified. As a result, many foreign businesses have been forced to mechanize more rapidly than planned to keep labor costs within reasonable bounds.

In many countries, once an employee has completed his probationary period of employment the law will guarantee him tenure, and he can be discharged only for gross violations which are identified in the law. When he is fired or when his employment is otherwise terminated, an employer may be required to pay indemnities to compensate the worker for the loss of his job. Since employment opportunities for unskilled workers are limited, governments want to do all that they can to prevent separations. Since these laws may apply only to workers having tenure, employers are careful who they permit to remain, and the turnover of nontenured workers runs very high. Some American business people operate abroad to take advantage of cheap labor, only to find that the idea is an illusion. It seems to be an economic fact of life that greater levels of industrialization cause higher levels of wages.

Labor unions Labor unions have existed for centuries in many foreign countries, but their power and their role in employer-employee relations can vary considerably. Basically, if little is done for workers through labor law, then there is a broader role for the union to play. In some countries matters relating to employment security, employee benefits, working conditions, and the like are so fully covered by law that they are not subject to collective bargaining. In the past, most

European strikes and work stoppages have been directed against governmental policies rather than against a particular employer. The role of a union at the plant level in Europe is generally less influential than in America. The reason for this, as indicated above, is that many issues that are the subject for collective bargaining in the United States are covered by law in other countries.

Tax laws In Chapter 6 we learned that proprietorship and partnership incomes are not subject to business tax because business profits are considered the personal income of the owners. Corporation income is taxed but at rates thay may be lower than those applying to personal income. A reverse situation is quite apt to exist in foreign countries. Also, since the existence of a corporation is legally documented, it is difficult for the corporation to avoid being a taxpayer. Since proprietorships and partnerships do not need legal documentation, there may be many businesses—taxpayers—whose identiy is unknown to the tax collector.

Another major difference in tax laws among nations is the preferential treatment afforded certain industries. With the exception of depletion allowance granted the oil industry, the United States tends to tax all businesses alike whether they be engaged in essential or nonessential activity. However, to get at the real impact of taxes, we need to look further. United States tax laws permit charging certain expenses against income which may or may not be allowed in foreign countries, such as a president's salary of $750,000 or more. Some nations may deem this excessive and place a limit on such expenses. Our laws relating to the depreciation of physical assets may be more lenient than laws of other nations. In short, the basis on which a host nation requires profit to be measured could be as important a consideration as the tax rates.

General laws As time goes by, businesses all over the globe are subject to more and more laws and regulations. By and large, a nation that has not experienced abuses by business enterprise will have fewer restrictions than a nation that is faced with pollution, price fixing, restraint of trade, monopolistic practices, and the like. A firm contemplating business in a foreign land should look beyond the laws that currently apply and try to visualize how laws might apply if it conducted its affairs according to one pattern as opposed to another.

Education

Although last on our list of differences, education is perhaps the most important consideration of all, because education bears on all aspects of life—business and otherwise. What a business can and cannot do depends on the abilities of its employees which are directly related to their level of education. Fortunately for business, it is possible to evaluate a nation's educational system by inspecting the product of the system. Thus business can know what it is getting into.

Within the firm, the educational level of workers dictates the structure of organization and the entire operating process. If there is a shortage of competent managers, as there is quite likely to be in foreign countries, the firm must be highly centralized. If employees do not have the capacity to develop, the firm will of necessity remain small. If workers are not literate, and in many nations a high percentage are not, written instructions are useless and supervision will be of the "watch and see" type. This is a time-consuming approach to supervision which severely restricts a manager's span of control.

Outside the firm there are a number of implications that bear on education. The entire recruiting program depends on reaching individuals who are interested in working and who have the necessary qualifications. American business relies on written communication extensively because it is understood by most people. Picture recruiting in a society where most people are illiterate and have no conception of what work in a factory is like. How would you find employees? Picture also the process of marketing your product, of laying out work for individuals, of obtaining a group effort, and so on.

As an aside, there is a delightful island in the Caribbean that is a wintertime mecca for tourists. Tourism supports the island. Some native youngsters go to school sometimes between 4:00 and 7:30 P.M., but they are more apt to be working in a service occupation as the rest of the family do. These natives are polite and happy, and they try to please, but by our standards, many of them are quite incompetent because they lack education. Imagination and the ability to discern are products of education. Help abounds everywhere and it is all native. In a particular cafeteria one will see, as he selects his breakfast, a fruit and juice specialist, an egg specialist, a pancake and French toast specialist, and a beverage specialist, among others. It may also be observed that no one person has the capacity to properly set a table in the dining room; again, a number of specialists are employed. Eight to ten people are employed to do what we would consider the work of two. At the end of the cafeteria line a person sits in front of a large keyboard to tally your bill. But there are no numbers on the keyboard; only pictures. Every item on the menu is pictured on the keyboard and the checker pushes the picture of every item on your tray. The keyboard is connected to an adding machine which totals the bill on a slip of paper. Employees do not have the capacity to relate price to merchandise, and three times a day the keyboards must be changed. Remember, in this discussion we are not talking about a particular people. We are showing the impact of education on business operation. In the United States you will see this same phenomenon in any place where educational attainment is low.

PREPARING FOR EMPLOYMENT IN INTERNATIONAL BUSINESS

The thought of being a part of the international business scene has a great appeal for many young people. There seems to be more interest in working abroad than working in a "foreign office" here in the

States. Before leaping headlong into such a venture, there are a number of factors that should be considered. Working abroad can be a marvelous experience or it can be hell.

A first consideration should be the country itself. The experience one would have in a developed country would be quite unlike the experience one would have in an undeveloped country. London, Paris, Rome, and Tokyo are exciting cities, but they are extremely expensive places to live especially if one attempts to maintain an American standard of living. Inflation has hit most nations much harder than it has hit us. In general these cities are more polluted and congested than most of our cities. A person going abroad would have to adjust to a lower level of amenities than he or she has been accustomed to at home. Central heat, air conditioning, and running hot water are luxuries that cannot be afforded in most living accommodations abroad.

A second consideration is the fact that there are generally fewer opportunities in foreign offices than in the home office. The overall scope of a firm's domestic activity is, as a rule, many times greater than its foreign activity. Some managerial positions abroad may not be open to Americans because of the insistence of host nations that nationals be employed wherever possible.

A third consideration relates to the specific preparation that is necessary for working abroad. Those who become a part of the foreign-operation management will probably be used at a relatively high organization level, but to be qualified for such an assignment means that something other than routine preparation is needed.

Spier suggests[1]:

The future international executive is likely to be a home-based specialist who must be capable of synthesizing environmental variables with the policies of the multi-national enterprise. He must be competent in resolving differences of foreign national executives of the company with the overall objectives of the parent company; and he must understand the implications of national economic policies with respect to the objectives of the company.

More specifically, this executive must be able to communicate effectively with his foreign-based subordinates. To do this he must be familiar with the functional areas of business and their relationships; he must have something to communicate. Production, distribution, finance, and the like are universal in business no matter where it takes place. He must have an understanding of human behavior so that he can reach those with whom he must communicate, and he must, of course, understand the objectives of the firm. But these general requirements are little different from what we expect of the American executive working in this country.

Over and above this preparation, the executive must understand

[1]Leo Spier, "The Role of International Business in University Education," paper presented at the Conference on Education for International Business, Tulane University of Louisiana, New Orleans, Nov. 30 and Dec. 1, 1967.

many things about the environment wherein the firm operates, and to gain this may require a living and working experience in that environment. All the references made previously to the differences between our society and others are merely descriptive. The true meaning comes only from direct association and involvement. The optimum training, of course, would permit the American manager to respond to people and situations in about the ways a native would, and this requires exposure and time. There are many jobs in international business that do not require this degree of preparation but they are primarily jobs of a highly specialized nature.

One of the more trying experiences for the manager of foreign business, especially if he is located abroad, is adjusting to local traditions and patterns of behavior that he does not understand. Differences in philosophies may make the ability to compromise effectively a basic management skill. That "everything stops for tea" is a fact in many foreign countries; that there is a right time and a wrong time to work is a belief held in some societies, and we must remember that not all people believe that having more money and physical possessions is good.

SUMMARY

It is undeniable that international business operations will continue to expand over the long run. Nations of the world will become more dependent on one another as native sources of raw materials become depleted and new sources must be found. That so much of the world remains underdeveloped, by our standards, guarantees that there will be "work to be done" for years to come.

Over the years our involvement in business overseas has shifted from foreign trade—buying and selling in foreign markets—to the building and operating of business abroad. Thus, American businesses actually operate in foreign countries with American managers working with native managers. Although the percentage of the workforce that is American is small, Americans occupy the key decision-making positions.

American business cannot operate abroad in the same manner as it does at home. Business, no matter where it is conducted, is a creature of its environment. Thus there are good and poor countries for a given type of activity. The manufacture of outboard motors in Belgium is good business for Johnson, but making them in next-door France or West Germany might be a poor idea.

Opportunities for employment in international business should increase for those who are qualified. As a nation, we are no longer in the position of being able to tell another country that we are coming in and will do this and that. More and more, many foreign nations realize that they have something that other nations need and this affords them the opportunity to flex their muscles. Our actions, therefore, will have to be in accord with the wishes of the host nation.

BUSINESS ITEMS

Foreign competition at home

American industry at one time could rely on government-imposed quotas to protect it from the impact of foreign imports. A few years ago the United States textile makers did persuade Washington to impose quotas to check a Japanese import invasion.

The picture has changed. The United States mills are not threatened by imports, but, instead, are confronted with competition from mills in the United States which are owned by the Japanese. At least a dozen major Japanese textile companies have plans for extensive United States expansion by purchase or construction of plants in the United States.

This move by the Japanese was not solely in response to the imposition of import quotas. Equally important is the fact that the advantage of lower wage scales in Japan and the willingness of Japanese labor to seek employment in the smelly, ill-lit mills in Osaka have disappeared with the rise in Japanese living standards. Furthermore, the United States offers both political and economic stability which are not easily found in other parts of the world.

United States textile manufacturers expect some strong competition from this new Japanese thrust but at the same time raise the question of whether the Japanese have adequately researched the volatile American fashion market. Ignorance in this respect would mean potential losses for the Japanese.

An international view of labor

South Korea has benefited from the investments of American businesses since the end of the Korean war. During recent years, Korea has been subject to a Japanese business invasion which has reestablished Japanese economic supremacy there. There are several reasons why Korea is very attractive as a base for export industries. Most significant is the fact that the wage level is one-tenth that in the United States and one-sixteenth that in Japan. The Korean government is credited with an "understanding" of the labor problems of business. This "understanding" is evidenced by the absence of minimum wages, the barring of strikes by employees of foreign companies except banks, and by the fact that under some collective bargaining agreements, the labor union has no say on wages.

QUESTIONS

1 Explain why business people today, large or small, should be interested in international business.

2 Foreign markets offer greater potential for growth and profits than domestic markets. Do you agree? Explain.

3 Explain the changes that have taken place in the nature of international business in recent years.

4 International trade contributes a very small amount to our gross national product, yet it is extremely important. Explain why.

5 Explain the "logic" of foreign trade.

6 What is our chief complaint against the free movement of goods into this country? Is it a valid complaint? Explain.

7 What is the purpose of a tariff? In the long run are they justified? Explain.

8 For what reasons are executives in some foreign countries referred to as a "managerial elite"?

9 As a generalization, are foreign businesses more or less centralized than American business? What are the reasons for this?

10 How does the European management philosophy differ from the American management philosophy?

11 We feel that Europeans pay a price for their approach to organization and management. Explain what this "price" is.

12 What differences are we apt to find in the business law of foreign countries?

13 How might labor law in foreign countries affect the operation of an American-owned business more so than labor law in this country?

14 European labor unions differ little from American labor unions. Do you agree? Explain.

15 What differences can one expect in tax laws when doing business overseas?

16 How do varying degrees of education affect the internal operation of a business?

17 Why are opportunities for employment in international business fewer than in domestic business?

18 What specific training is needed for those who manage international business?

The purpose of this section   Most readers of this text will someday be employees of business, and if asked today to describe the type of job they ultimately seek they would use such words as "responsibility, opportunity, freedom from supervision, and reward." But none of these descriptive terms is characteristic of any particular job. / Any job you hold will be conditioned by environmental factors, the firm's approach to organization, the quality of personnel working for you, the quality of management leading you, and your attitude toward the job. Good jobs depend on these factors rather than on such descriptive terms as production, marketing, finance, or vice president. / This section will show the relationship of a number of considerations previously discussed to jobs and careers, in order to emphasize what is and what is not important. / Questions raised in this section include:

1 What basic decisions should a person make at the outset when planning for a job or career?

2 Is it better to work for a large or small firm?

3 What effect do organization and management have on jobs and careers?

4 Is it a good idea to go into business and be self-employed?

5 Is there a best road to the top?

ORGANIZATION, MANAGE-MENT, AND CAREERS

This material is designed to serve two purposes. First, it will provide a review of many concepts of organization and management covered earlier in this text, and second, it will apply much of this material to a number of career decisions that you eventually will have to make. In this section no attempt will be made to describe specific positions such as accountant, sales manager, or director of purchasing; rather, we will explore some of the more basic and ultimately more meaningful considerations relating to careers. For a number of reasons, there is a danger in building a discussion of careers around specific job titles. First, job titles may be misleading; they may not describe what a job involves and what opportunities may spring from it. Second, specific jobs may vary in importance from one type of establishment to another. The job of cashier in a supermarket is not particularly highly rated and often leads nowhere, but the job of cashier in a bank is a significant post that can offer opportunities for advancement. A chief accountant in one firm may find that his main responsibility is to coordinate a number of routine tasks performed by his staff, and in another firm a person holding a job with the same title may be the chief financial officer. Third, the content of specific jobs may change significantly in a relatively short time and thereby alter their attractiveness. Finally, there is no guarantee that the job you may have in mind will exist 2 or 3 years from now when you enter the job market.

Most college graduates today will seek careers in some segment of American business. The great majority of them will be employees for all their working days rather than owners of businesses (self-employed). For most people, then, the career decision boils down to what type of work one wants to do and for what type of employer.

In general, business college graduates will develop careers that are managerial in nature, not technical, although knowledge of technical skills may be necessary. The reason for this is that a college education in business should emphasize and develop personal skills, which are managerial skills. No college has the resources or the capacity to teach all the technical skills with which its graduates should be familiar. These are best learned on the job. The selection of a major such as marketing or management serves much more as the means for channeling student interest than as the means for providing technical training. The study of accounting may be an exception to this generalization.

More and more students are seeking careers with various government agencies and not-for-profit institutions, but their ultimate goals probably differ little from those who will be employed by business. Management-type jobs are common to all situations where cooperative effort is required for the achievement of a goal.

WORK IN GENERAL

It is impossible for an outsider to determine the best career goal for anyone, although psychologists can help a great deal. Some people because of their personal makeup could do well in a variety of jobs, whereas others for the same reason will never find happiness and success. Very often the difference between good and poor employment depends on the attitude one brings to the work situation. The person who devotes his or her life to chasing the almighty dollar will lose many of the satisfactions that work can bring. Making a lot of money in American business is always possible, provided that a person is capable and willing to make the necessary sacrifices. In some ways we envy the executive who earns $50,000 to $100,000 or more per year. We envy him in part because we do not realize how much a person must give of himself to be worth such a salary. Actually there are more jobs available in the higher echelons than there are qualified takers. In general the higher a person's salary, the more he must give of himself to his employer, and consequently the less time and energy he has for other things. Depending on circumstances there is a balance that every career-minded person should seek between giving and receiving.

Work means different things to different people. To some people, work—any work—is an imposition, and the less they have to do the better. About the only way to satisfy such people is to give them more for doing less. This certainly is not consistent with the goals of American business. Work need not be undesirable, and one's attitude toward work need not be negative. Work should be and can be a rewarding experience especially for college-trained people. It can be and should be the means for satisfying a broad range of human goals and aspirations.

Work can be undesirable to a person for a number of reasons. Two that stand out are a poor matching of the person and the job, and a poor attitude toward one's work. Often the second reason is an outgrowth of the first. In many ways a person selecting a job or an employer needs to be a manager, for he should plan and organize before taking any action.

HOW MUCH WILL I EARN?

The amount of money you will earn through your job depends on a number of factors and some of these factors may be beyond your control. Our basic philosophy is that persons should be paid what they are worth but this in itself offers little explanation of how things work. Basically there are five factors that influence what workers are paid.

1 Where will you be working? An accountant in one section of the country will earn more or less than a person doing the same thing in another section of the country. At any point in time there are prosperous areas and there are depressed areas and this bears on wage rates. A person working in northern Maine, New Hampshire, or Vermont will probably receive much less pay for his efforts than a person doing the same thing in New York City. In sections of the country where service industries are the main employer, such as sections of Florida, wages tend to be lower for comparable work. We will not explore the reasons for these differentials, but the person who is free to work anywhere will probably make out much better than the person who insists on working "close to home."

2 Similarly, the industry in which you work has a bearing on earnings. In our society there are depressed industries and prosperous industries. At this writing, footwear and textiles are depressed and steel is prosperous. One could expect to be paid more by a steel producer than a textile plant for doing the same job.

3 Company attitude toward wages is also a factor. Some firms pay lower than the going rates and offset this with an improved work environment and greater degree of security.

4 The importance of the job to the firm is another factor. A particular job can have different values in different firms. The job of chief accountant in a job-order machine shop which grosses $400,000 per year can be more important than the same job in a brewery that grosses $4,000,000 per year. The brewery has a small number of routine transactions whereas the machine shop has a large number and variety of transactions.

The approach a firm uses in organizing has a bearing on the importance of jobs. Some firms prefer to break down the total task of business operation into a large number of relatively simple jobs, such as one would find in a bureaucracy. Another approach is to break down the total task into a smaller number of relatively complex jobs. As we shall see later, the amount of responsibility a person has bears on earnings.

5 A blending of the four factors discussed above results in a rate range for each job. A particular job might have a rate range of $800 to $1,000 per month. A person who meets the minimum requirements of the job will earn $800 and the person who meets the maximum requirements will earn $1,000. No matter how good a person is, he cannot be worth over $1,000 per month on this job. To be worth more to the company, one must move to another job that has a higher ceiling.

This discussion points out that there is much more involved in earning good wages than being intelligent, industrious, cooperative, and the like. Being at the right place at the right time also helps.

SOME BASIC DECISIONS

For most people the selection of a career is a multistep process that continues for many years. More often than not a person's first job after college is a compromise, and it may tell the person more about what he or she does not want for a career. It takes time to get into the right work channels. However, the road to the desired employment can be shortened if a person will sit down and provide answers to several basic questions.

1 Am I primarily interested in security? This is a very important consideration because security will vary depending both on the type of work being done and on the type of employer. There are many jobs where the work is laid out in a sequence of steps that can be easily learned. Satisfactory job performance consists of following the work plan. There are few, if any, decisions that must be made. Jobs in a bureaucratic organization have these characteristics—jobs such as a credit interviewer, bookkeeper, or inventory clerk.

In work of this nature there is little risk of doing the wrong thing provided the work plan is followed. The possibility for errors in judgment that could mean loss of the job is very low. Here it is easy for a person to develop a high degree of confidence in his ability to do the job right. This is the source of security.

Other jobs may require initiative, judgment, and consequently risk-taking. The holder of such a job must make decisions that could be good or bad and thus strengthen or weaken his hold on the job. Most management-type jobs fall into this category.

Many people prefer employment with organizations which can virtually guarantee that there will always be a job available. There are many government jobs at the local, state, and federal level where civil service protection approaches the state of guaranteed employment. Employment with public utilities such as power and telephone companies and with educational institutions has a high level of employment stability. There are many lines of business that are very volatile in terms of employment opportunity. Here both the risk and the opportunity for employment develop at a rapid pace.

Should security be emphasized in career selection? Is this a good or bad emphasis? Certainly some measure of security is essential, but the particular level of security that is best depends on the person involved. Some of us like to assume risk because often the stakes are high. Others desire a minimum of risk. Obviously people hold all types of jobs for all types of employers and with complete satisfaction. However, we should keep in mind a previous statement regarding security wherein it was implied that there is a relatively high negative correlation between security and the opportunity for individual initiative.

2 Should I work for a large or small company? A "this way" or "that way" answer to this question has very little meaning. Many large firms restrict the size of each operating unit to retain the flavor of small business. We should note, too, that growth is a characteristic of American business, and the firm that is small today may be an industrial giant in a decade.

The principal difference between employment in the large and the small firm lies in the degree of formality present in the conduct of affairs. Jobs in the small firm tend to be less well defined, and a person may not know from hour to hour or day to day what he or she will be doing—it often depends on what needs to be done at the time. Part of this stems from the fact that fewer people must carry the entire load and that planning is often shorter in range and more general in nature. Personal contact, oral agreement, temporary grants of authority, and an informal atmosphere prevail in the small firm. In large organizations more formal relations must exist because of the volume of activity that must take place and the numbers of people involved. The written memo—"Put it in writing"—takes the place of face-to-face communication, formal reports take the place of personal observation of events, and affairs tend to become more structured or systematized.

Both types of business offer excellent career opportunities, but individual effort tends to show up more quickly and more often in the smaller business unit. Many of the characteristics of the large and small firm as employers can be inferred from a review of the material in Chapter 6 concerning the proprietorship, partnership, and corporation.

3 Should I develop a specialty? This is a question of degree, for everyone below the top man in the organization is concerned with some special area of activity such as manufacturing, marketing, or finance. Business operation requires both specialists and generalists. A specialist could be a marketing cost analyst, a market researcher, a program scheduler, or a computer programmer. A generalist, such as a marketing manager or production coordinator, is concerned with broader areas of activity. As a rule, the generalist is more often found in small business and in upper levels of big business. But again this is a question of degree, for a salesperson's job is more general in nature than a payroll programmer's, and a market research manager's job is more general than an interviewer's or a statistician's.

The specialist's job requires relatively more technical skill than personal skill. There may, therefore, be a greater risk of obsolescence for the specialist. The auditor today is a far cry from his predecessor because the computer has replaced so many manual operations in the record-keeping function. However, the demand for specialized knowledge is great, and a person need not worry over obsolescence provided he is aware that change is taking place and prepares himself for it.

The decisions a person makes in these three areas—security, size, and specialization—will automatically rule out many types of employment and careers. If a person seeks the ultimate in security and desires to be a specialist, his career should perhaps be with some branch of the government. If, on the other hand, a person seeks to maximize his experience, personal development, and income, employment with certain government agencies is perhaps a poor decision.

RESPONSIBILITY AND JOBS

Every employee of a business must have some responsibility, and the principal difference between a high-rated and a low-rated job is the amount and type of responsibility the job entails. Generally, higher-rated and higher-paying jobs involve greater responsibility regardless of their type. There are certain types of responsibility that are very important to management, such as the responsibility for the work of others; and there are areas of responsibility that are considered to be less important, such as the responsibility for the money in the cash drawer. Thus the services of the foreman in the cutting room employing thirty people may be worth $300 per week, while the supermarket cashier or bank teller may be worth only half as much.

The reason for assigning different values to different types of responsibility is not difficult to see. The cutting room foreman is directly involved with the basic goals of the firm, producing goods. Through the efforts of the foreman, costs can be lowered, quality improved, and a direct contribution made to the achievement of goals. Conceivably, this foreman could double his value to the firm through better utilization of his workers. But the person who is responsible for the firm's cash receives it, counts it, and deposits it. This he or she does to perfection and is paid $140 per week. Does this person have the same opportunity to improve his or her worth to the company in this job as the foreman? Obviously not. The holder of any job must accept some responsibility, but the acceptance of certain types of responsibility offers greater opportunity for growth and advancement than others.

ORGANIZATION AND JOBS

There are several features of organization that make a significant impact on jobs and careers. No job is a good job because of its title. The difference between desirable and undesirable employment may rest with the organizational structure. If any of the features of organization enumerated on page 172 are lacking, the job, regardless of

its title, could leave much to be desired. In addition we should examine the general nature of organization in terms of the extent to which it is centralized.

Centralization

If an organization is centralized, the bulk of responsibility and authority remains at relatively high organizational levels. Subordinates, rather than acting on their own initiative, act according to policy or directives from above. It is difficult for a subordinate to make a name for himself or herself in a highly centralized organization because one is not permitted to make significant decisions. As a result, individual growth may be a slow process, and future opportunities may be an unknown. Employment in such firms is not necessarily bad or undesirable; it may be the ideal type of employment for certain people. As mentioned earlier, some people will prefer the circumstances wherein the bulk of decisions are made at higher organizational levels.

Decentralization

Decentralization disperses responsibility and authority throughout the organization. As a result, important jobs may exist at relatively low organizational levels. This situation puts greater emphasis on individual thought and action and tends to swiften the rate of individual development. The following example describes what work in a decentralized situation might be like.

Bill Thornton, a sales engineer for a large manufacturer of electrical equipment that pioneered in the decentralization concept, operates in a clearly defined territory in southern New England. His basic responsibility is to serve as a commercial ambassador for the firm and meet the sales quota which he established through consultation with upper management. Apart from the occasional sales meeting, Bill is pretty much on his own to locate and develop those customers who will enable him to achieve his sales goal. The allocation of his time, talent, and energies among customers or potential customers is largely his decision. Upper management is more concerned with the achievement of goals than with what Bill does on a day-to-day basis. Of course, if Bill fails to meet his goals, then upper management will need to observe the operation more closely. In conversation Bill related: "It is amazing how a person can work for a company whose annual sales exceed $10 billion and still feel as though he were working for himself."

Generally speaking, employment in a decentralized company tends to be more demanding of individual action and offers greater opportunity for growth and development than employment in a centralized company. But there are other important considerations.

MANAGEMENT AND JOBS

There is a tendency, perhaps, to overemphasize organization in relation to employment and careers. Important though organization is, it does not give a complete picture of what work will be like. Organizations are not charts; they are people. You will not be working for an organization but for a person. The type of people you work for can be more important, especially on a day-to-day basis, than the basic organization structure of the firm.

You will work for a manager, although you too may be a manager. If the history of the firm or the department shows that people stay at the same job for years on end, there is reason to question the quality of management. If promotion among management personnel hinges on years of service alone, there is reason to question the quality of management. If there is evidence that a manager makes certain that no subordinate will show up better than he, or if he surrounds himself with mediocre talent, there is reason to question the quality of management.

The degree of competition that management permits among employees is a good indicator of the opportunities that might exist for the exceptional employee. A manager can foster growth and development of his subordinates, or he can squelch their every effort. Certainly the quality of management will be a major consideration in the selection of an employer or the locale of a career.

LINE, STAFF, AND FUNCTIONAL JOBS

Jobs in business are classified as line, staff, or functional. The same classification applies to the military, to not-for-profit institutions, and to other types of employment. Basically the staff exists to help the line organization or some other staff unit. The staff is the source of ideas, and the line is the source of action. A sales manager's job is line, for it is basic to the firm's existence; and the head of market research or personnel has a supporting or service function to perform for line managers.

The principal difference between line and staff jobs is the relation of the activity to the basic goals of the firm. Line jobs for most firms are in the area of production and marketing. Staff jobs by their nature are quite variable and depend on the type of assistance that the line needs. Remember that before the staff part of an organization comes into being, every function and all activity fall on the shoulders of the line organization.

It is this fundamental difference in the nature of line and staff jobs that creates a difference in the work environment. The task of the line is quite clear; produce 10,000 units a month at a cost of $8.50 per unit or sell 10,000 units a month at a price of $15 per unit. Because of the

very specific nature of line activity, individual performance can be subjected to very exacting standards, and an individual's progress up the line can be based directly on merit. In the line it is relatively easy to pinpoint responsibility and to locate those who are failing to perform up to standard.

Staff jobs are of a different nature, and it may be more difficult to accurately appraise individual performance as well as the need for the job. For example, the marketing manager has a staff assistant called a market analyst. It is his job to appraise market conditions for the marketing manager. But is it possible to determine a "best" sales forecast, or is it possible to determine the "best" audit by the auditing group? Obviously it is not. The value of a staff performance may be dependent upon the manner in which the line utilizes the staff service.

We cannot say that line jobs are better than staff jobs or vice versa; much depends on the individual and his interests. There is some evidence that line jobs pay better than staff jobs, that promotional opportunity to high management levels is better in the line, and that staff jobs are more vulnerable than line jobs. This is especially true when a firm goes on a cost-cutting crusade. But these generalizations may be insignificant in the firm that is dynamic, progressive, and well managed. Functional jobs provide a compromise because they permit specialization yet allow for the exercise of authority.

SELF-EMPLOYMENT

Approximately one in twenty working people in the United States is self-employed. Many more express a desire for self-employment but for a variety of reasons—money, inertia, etc.—have not made the move. People enter business as owner-manager for a wide variety of reasons which are enumerated on page 22, but an evaluation of self-employment as a career and an evaluation of one's fitness for self-employment should involve much more than a reading of this list. The mere fact that people go into business for a variety of reasons, however, complicates the task of evaluation. It is difficult to establish standards or bases for comparison because a person's goals and objectives in self-employment may be personal in nature, and the sole criterion for making a decision may be a personal satisfaction which precludes objective measurement.

The move to self-employment therefore depends on two factors: first, personal desire and, second, the means to start the venture. It is hoped that every person contemplating self-employment will make a critical appraisal of his qualifications as an owner-manager, but in our system of business there is no way that this can be made mandatory. Some of the qualifications for and basic characteristics of self-employment are explored below.

Qualifications

One of the most demanding qualifications for self-employment is the capacity to discipline one's actions. An owner-manager is the business, and he must expect complete and continuous involvement in the affairs of the firm. The self-employed person will probably devote more hours to breadwinning than the salaried or hourly paid employee. In larger organizations there may be additional layers of management which can pick up errors or fill in during absences, but small businesses generally do not have this resource to fall back on.

Discipline must also be exercised over the use of business funds. There is a great temptation when the money starts to roll in to use it for personal wants or needs. This is a most important consideration for trading businesses—wholesale and retail—where very often less than 10 cents of each dollar of sales will be profit. The balance must be reserved to replenish stocks and pay expenses. Poor money management is a common cause of business failure among small businesses. Where sales activity fluctuates significantly from season to season, the problem of money management assumes greater importance.

The owner-manager must have the capacity to budget his time—to distinguish between those activities that should consume his time and those he should delegate to someone else. Very few owner-managers like all aspects of running a business, and the area most frequently ignored is record keeping. After all, how many people go into business because they like or are adept at record keeping? The authors have seen many small businesses wither and die because of the owner's lack of attention to relatively simple functions: the garage owner who was too busy repairing cars to send out bills, the service station owner who was more interested in getting home than counting the cash, and the retail store operator who spent his closing-up time counting Coke bottles while a part-time clerk counted the money. If a person cannot do everything, he should determine where his talents lie and should then engage, on a part-time basis if necessary, the services of competent workers to fill in the voids.

No reference has been made as yet to the matter of technical competence. Should the owner-manager be technically competent? Not necessarily. Technical skill may be vital to a firm's existence, but the owner-manager does not have to be the one who has it. A retired liquor salesman decided to invest his savings in a machine shop not because of his technical competence or interest in the field but because there was a market for machine-shop services. He hired a production man and an office worker and devoted most of his time to customer development. He and his employees together built a thriving business.

The owner-manager needs some skill, but his skill might be the capacity to organize rather than the capacity to design a machine, or the capacity to sell the services of the firm rather than the capacity to perform the technical functions. There is considerable evidence that technical incompetence on the part of owner-managers is not a significant cause of business failures.

A final comment on self-employment relates to the common illusion that self-employment and independence go together. Self-employment allows a person to work independently of superior management but not independently of bosses. No business person, self-employed or otherwise, can rid himself or herself of the ultimate boss—the customer. The impact of consumer wants is felt more immediately and more directly by management in the small firm than in the large firm. The owner-manager is more apt to have direct contact with the customer and the customer knows that the owner-manager has the authority to act. The owner-manager is more closely tied to the business, for in reality he or she is the business.

WHAT DO YOU HAVE TO SELL?

It is consistent with the American philosophy that gaining employment or advancing up the ladder is basically a "buy and sell" proposition wherein the applicant seeks to sell his abilities to an employer, the buyer. This involves many of the considerations that enter into the merchandising of any goods and services—supply, demand, product appeal, price, and so on.

The most critical question facing the person seeking employment is: What do I have to sell? This question must be answered even though it may appear on the surface that the answer is "Nothing." In most instances this will be the correct answer if one appraises one's marketability in terms of specific skills. Few college graduates have specific skills or experiences that can be transferred to business practice, but this does not mean that they have nothing to sell. It does mean that the "product" being marketed is the individual and the special features that make the product appealing to the buyer are personal characteristics.

Obviously business would like to hire people who have just the right amount of experience for the job in question, but this is not always possible. Basically business is looking for potential when it recruits college graduates—the potential to perform the immediate task and the potential to grow. Equally important, business seeks the type of person whose personal qualities are compatible with those of others. Running a successful business is a matter of teamwork. The hiring firm already has a team and seeks to add to it certain capabilities and personalities that will yield greater strength and balance.

Most college graduates have the mental capacity needed to perform the jobs that will be available to them; yet many college graduates have little or no market value. Their main weakness is apt to be a sour, negative, or neutral personality and disposition. The inability to work effectively with others, the inability or failure to communicate effectively, and the unwillingness to make the sacrifices that responsible employment demands are common causes of failure.

Good grades may help a student to get his first job, but beyond the first job, individual performance becomes the primary criterion for success. Students should accomplish at least two things during their college days: become more educated persons and develop those human qualities that make the difference between an acceptable person and an outstanding personality.

THE ROAD TO THE TOP

A person planning a career in business should give thought to his or her progress up the ladder. Somewhere there is a spot that appears to be ideal—the career goal. The goal may be just one step above the starting level or it may be to become the number one person in the organization. Now the question arises: Is there one starting point that is better than all others? Is production, marketing, finance, law, or some other function the best road to the career goal?

Over the years a number of studies have been conducted to find out how the presidents of our largest and most successful organizations got to the top. To those who expect a specific answer to this question, the results of these studies will be disappointing. Some of the general findings are:

1 Formal education through college and into graduate school now constitutes the primary qualification for advancement.

2 The special needs of the firm at the time can be a significant factor in filling the top job. If a strong marketing emphasis is needed as opposed to production and finance, a marketing man may get the nod, and so on.

3 A student of business is much better advised to develop human skills during his college days than attempt to develop a narrow specialty. Human skills have universal application and will never become obsolete; this does not apply to specialized skills.

A study, "Evidence on the Validity of Management Education," by Fred Luthans and others, says in part[1]:

If one assumes that a college education is a necessary prerequisite to management, then the next logical question becomes what kind of education? Almost every educator and practitioner has a ready answer to this question. On the one hand, there are those who advocate a broad liberal arts education as the best type of preparation for executive work. Because of this reasoning, much criticism has been leveled against the business schools for emphasizing vocationalism and high degrees of specialized training. Although the business community is generally espousing the concept of a broad liberal education through speechmaking and editorializing, they are clamoring at the placement offices for highly trained specialists in engineering, accounting, finance, marketing, personnel, and production. The relatively higher starting salaries for these

[1]*Academy of Management Journal,* December 1969, pp. 455–475.

specialized graduates is indicative of this demand. . . . When a statistical test of differences between means was calculated, it was found that there were no significant differences between any of the educational majors. . . . This conclusion implies more emphasis on individuality than on a common specialized formal education.

In other words, the specific educational background of a person is not in itself a criterion for success or failure; the manner in which a person develops is the important criterion.

SUGGESTIONS FOR FURTHER READING

PART 1 BUSINESS AND THE EXTERNAL ENVIRONMENT

Anderson, R. A. and W. A. Kumpf: *Business Law,* 9th ed., South-Western Publishing Company, Incorporated, Cincinnati, 1972, part XII.

Galbraith, J. K.: *The New Industrial State,* Houghton Mifflin Company, Boston, 1967.

Faltermayer, E. K.: "We Can Afford a Better America," *Fortune,* March 1969.

Golgart, C. W.: "Changing Times in Management," *Advanced Management Journal,* January 1970.

Farmer, R. and W. D. Hogue: *Corporate Social Responsibility,* Science Research Associates, Inc., Palo Alto, 1973.

Grunchy, A. G.: *Comparative Economic Systems: Competing Ways to Stability and Growth,* Houghton Mifflin Company, Boston, 1966.

Jennings, J. O.: "Why All the Confusion Over Profits," *Nation's Business,* September 1966.

Nader, R.: *The Consumer and Corporate Responsibility,* Harcourt Brace Jovanovich, Inc., New York, 1973.

Samuelson, P. A.: "The Businessman's Shrinking Prerogatives," *Management Review,* March 1972.

"The American Corporation Under Fire," *Newsweek,* May 24, 1971.

Thompson, D. N.: *Franchise Operations and Antitrust,* D. C. Heath and Company, Lexington, Mass., 1971.

Ways, M.: "How to Think about the Environment," *Fortune,* February 1970.

"Why Companies are Fleeing the Cities," *Time,* Apr. 26, 1971.

"Will Ecology Kill Small Business?" *Business Horizons,* April 1972.

PART 2 ORGANIZATION AND MANAGEMENT: THE INTERNAL ENVIRONMENT

Anderson, R. A. and W. A. Kumpf: *Business Law,* 9th ed., South-Western Publishing Company, Incorporated, Cincinnati, 1972, parts VIII and IX.

Brown, J. K.: "The Board of Directors and its Work Routine," *Conference Board Record,* March 1972.

Carson, I.: "How Top Men Make Up Their Mind," *International Marketing,* April 1971.

Eggers, H. C.: "The Evaluation of Human Assets," *Management Accounting,* November 1971.

Heywood, J. J.: "Getting Down to Basics: The ABCs of Managerial Success," *Supervisory Management,* May 1972.

————: "Getting Down to Basics: The Old Masters of Management," *Supervisory Management,* May 1972.

Hicks, H. G.: *The Management of Organizations,* 2d ed., McGraw-Hill Book Company, New York, 1972.

Knox, A. M.: "What Keeps a Businessman Busy?" *Business Management,* August 1971.

Leavitt, H. J., W. R. Dill, and H. B. Eyring: *The Organizational World,* Harcourt Brace and Jovanovich, Inc., New York, 1972.

Loehwing, D. A.: "Sadder but Wiser," *Barrons,* Oct. 4, 1971.

McGregor, D. M.: "The Human Side of Enterprise," *Management Review,* November 1957.

Mintzberg, H.: "A New Look at the Chief Executive's Job," *Organizational Dynamics,* vol. 1, no. 3, 1973.

Myers, M. S.: *Every Employee a Manager,* McGraw-Hill Book Company, New York, 1970.

Odiorne, G. S.: *Management by Objectives,* Pitman Publishing Company, New York, 1965.

"The Board, It's Obsolete Unless Overhauled," *Business Week,* Special Report, May 22, 1971.

Townsend, R. C.: "America, Inc.," *The New York Times Book Review,* May 30, 1972.

Walker, A. H. and J. W. Lorsch: "Organizational Choice: Product or Function?" *Harvard Business Review,* November–December 1968.

Whyte, W. F.: *Men at Work,* Richard D. Irwin, Inc., Homewood, Ill., 1959.

PART 3 THE BUSINESS FUNCTIONS AND THEIR PERFORMANCE

Ammer, D. S.: *Manufacturing Management and Control,* Appleton-Century-Crofts, New York, 1968.

————: "Materials Management as a Profit Center," *Harvard Business Review,* January–February 1969.

Backman, J.: "Is Advertising Wasteful?" *Journal of Marketing,* January 1968.

Buzzell, R. D.: "Marketing in the 1970s," *Journal of Marketing,* January 1970.

"Consumers Battle at the Grass Roots," *Business Week,* Feb. 26, 1972.

Curie, R.: *Work Study,* Pitman Publishing Company, London, 1961.

Elsaid, H. H.: "The Function of Preferred Stock in the Corporate Financial Plan," *Financial Analyst Journal,* July–August 1969.

Green, J. H.: *Production and Inventory Control Handbook,* McGraw-Hill Book Company, New York, 1970.

Lazer, W.: "Marketing's Changing Social Relationships," *Journal of Marketing,* January 1968.

Linden, F.: "The Consumer Market in 1980: An Overview," *Conference Board Record,* June 1972.

Marrah, G. L.: "To Lease or Not to Lease," *Financial Executive,* October 1968.

Searby, F. W.: "Use Your Hidden Cash Resources," *Harvard Business Review,* March–April 1968.

Stancil, J. M.: *Cash Management: The Management of Working Capital,* International Textbook Company, Scranton, Pa., 1971, pp. 269–283.

Sullivan, B.: "An Introduction to Going Public," *Journal of Accountancy,* November 1965.

Timms, H. L. and M. F. Pohlen: *The Production Function in Business,* 3d ed., Richard D. Irwin, Inc., Homewood, Ill., 1970.

"What Managers Should Know About Advertising," *Industry Week,* May 29, 1972.

"Why the Finance Man Calls the Play," *Business Week,* Apr. 8, 1972.

PART 4 SELECTED BUSINESS CONSIDERATIONS

Andrus, R. R.: "Creativity: A Function of Computers or Executives," *Journal of Marketing,* April 1968.

"Are We Seeing Japan All Wrong?" *Industry Week,* Feb. 28, 1972.

Brown, F. E. and A. R. Oxenfeldt: "Should Prices Depend on Cost?" *Michigan State University Business Topics,* Autumn 1968.

Cateora, P. D.: "The Multinational Enterprise and Nationalism," *Michigan State University Business Topics,* Spring 1971.

"Computers: Are They Magic or Menace?" *International Management,* July 1971.

Dymsza, W. A.: "Export Expansion—American Style," *Michigan Business Review,* May 1971.

"Europe's New Shopping Center," *Business Abroad,* October 1968.

Gabor, A. and C. W. J. Granger: "Price Sensitivity of the Consumer," *Journal of Advertising Research,* 1964.

Levin, R. I. and C. A. Kirkpatrick: *Quantitative Approaches to Management,* McGraw-Hill Book Company, New York, 1965.

Myers, C. A. (ed.): *The Impact of Computers on Management, The MIT Press,* Cambridge, 1967.

Stevens, R. W.: "Scanning the Multinational Firm," *Business Horizons,* June 1971.

Trotter, W. R.: "Organizing a Management Information System," *Advanced Management Journal,* April 1969.

"When Figures are Stranger than Fiction," *Business Week,* Oct. 4, 1969.

Wilcke, G.: "A 'Foreign' Steel Town in the U.S.," *The New York Times,* July 2, 1972.

GLOSSARY

Ability test A testing procedure used to measure a person's ability to perform a specific task or function.

Account executive An executive who is responsible for handling relations between an advertising agency and the agency's client.

Accounts receivable Unpaid bills due the firm from customers.

Acid-test ratio A measure of a firm's ability to pay off current liabilities with the cash which could be available from their highly liquid assets such as cash and accounts receivable.

Ad hoc committee A committee appointed for a one-time purpose.

Ad hoc policy A special policy established for a special and often unique situation.

Administration The performance of the executive duties in an organization.

Administrative agencies Units of government set up to "administer" the law of the land.

Administrative law Law aimed at regulating officials, boards, and other commissions created by law.

Advertising The process of informing others of the existence and availability of a product and of creating a demand for the product.

Affluent society A society which has an abundance of wealth.

Agency shop A provision in a union contract which requires that all employees in the bargaining unit who do not join the union pay a fixed amount monthly to the union, usually the equivalent of union dues, as a condition of employment.

Agent An individual who represents and/or acts in behalf of another person.

Analysis The process of breaking down information into smaller identifiable units.

Analytical process The procedures involved in breaking down something into smaller individual units, such as breaking down crude oil into its various by-products.

Antitrust laws Laws enacted to prevent the rise of monopolies in the business world.

Apprentice A person, usually a young person, who enters into an agreement to learn a skill trade and to achieve a journeyman status through supervised training and experience. Such agreements are common in trades such as bricklaying and plumbing.

Apprentice training A prescribed period of training to learn an art or trade usually under the supervision of a skilled worker.

Aptitude test A test to determine a person's capacity or natural ability for learning.

Arbitration In labor relations, the act of presenting the pros and cons of a grievance to a third party, the arbitrator, for purposes of obtaining a decision.

Arithmetic mean The average value of a group of numbers.

Array An arrangement of things in a definite manner. An array of numbers according to their magnitude.

Asset Any item of property that has value.

Authority The right of a person to command or order others, who are usually in a subordinate relationship to the one having authority.

Automation The use of self-regulating machines in performing tasks.

Backward integration A form of expansion in which facilities that provide parts, supplies, or raw materials are acquired.

Balance sheet An accounting statement which sets down all the assets, liabilities, and capital or equity of a firm as of a given date.

Banker's acceptance A draft drawn by the seller of goods upon the bank of the buyer. Usually accompanied by a bill of lading.

Bankruptcy A state of financial ruin which results when a business, or a person, cannot meet outstanding debts.

Bargaining agent The union which has been voted in as the exclusive representative of all employees in the bargaining unit for purposes of collective bargaining.

Bargaining unit Those individuals eligible to vote for and be represented by the bargaining agent. Generally, management personnel is excluded from the bargaining unit.

Basic stock list In retailing, a list of items carried that are little affected by style changes.

Bill of lading A shipper's receipt for goods, which serves as a contract between shipper and carrier for the transportation of the shipment.

Bill of materials A list of materials and parts to be used in the production of a particular item.

Binary language A language based on two symbols or characters.

Black list In industry, a term once used to identify workers who had taken part in union organizing activity. Some businessmen would not hire people whose names appeared on this list because they disapproved of pro-union activity. This practice, although illegal, is still used by some employers.

Board of directors The top managing body of a corporation, whose members are elected by the voting membership of the corporation (stockholders).

Bond A long-term, interest-bearing promissory note issued by a corporation. It is not a sign of ownership as is the case with a share of stock; rather, a bondholder is a creditor.

Boycott Efforts by an organized group, such as a union, to discourage the purchase, handling, or use of products of an employer with whom the group is in dispute.

Break-even analysis An arithmetic or graphic technique used to determine what level of sales (in dollars or units) is necessary to cover all costs. A higher level of sales results in profits; a lower level of sales results in losses. At break-even there is neither profit nor loss.

Break-even point The exact level of sales (in dollars or units) at which neither profits nor losses are being incurred.

Budget A plan for conducting a business over a specified period of time. It includes elements such as a sales budget, a purchasing budget, a labor budget, and a production budget.

Budget (financial) A financial plan for a business for a specified period of time.

Building-block machine tool A tool made up of units with interchangeable tools which can be assembled in a variety of ways to perform a variety of tasks.

Business An organization consisting of a person or a group of persons who produce and distribute goods and services for private profit.

Business credit Deferred payment for purchases extended to buyers of goods and services by the seller.

Business cycle The period of time from one peak of business activity to the next.

Business environment The total interrelationships between business and the community.

Buyer's market A situation in which market conditions favor the buyer of goods and services.

Callable (stocks and bonds) Stocks and bonds which can be called in (purchased) by the company at specified times or, perhaps, at any time.

Capacity The measure of the volume of output which a system is capable of producing.

Capital The assets needed to operate a business.

Capital expenditure budget A plan for spending to acquire long-term assets.

Capital goods Goods (assets) used to produce other goods. Also called producer goods.

Capital investment The amount of money necessary to establish assets (plant and equipment) required to do business.

Capital turnover The rate at which assets of a firm are converted into cash through normal business operations.

Capitalism An economic system characterized by private ownership and the profit motive.

Cash discount An outright reduction or lowering of the original sales price.

Cash dividends Corporate profits distributed to stockholders in the form of cash.

Cash-flow cycle The series of business transactions which comprise the flow of cash out from the firm (wages, materials, purchases, various expenses, etc.) and its return principally in sales of goods and services; this cycle repeats itself.

Casualty insurance Insurance to cover casualty losses such as those resulting from automobile or elevator accidents.

Centralized organization An organization in which the majority of all authority and decision-making powers are vested in the extreme top levels of management.

Centralized purchasing system A system in which one person or office is responsible for all purchases.

Charter The legal document granted by a government to a corporation, giving it the right to do business as a corporation.

Chattel mortgage A document by which the owner of goods transfers title to a mortgagee. Often used as security pending payment of an obligation to the mortgagee.

Checkoff A practice whereby the employer, by agreement, regularly withholds union dues from employees' wages and transmits them to the union.

Chief executive officer The individual who is accountable to the board of directors for the actions and performance of the firm. Usually the president or the chairman of the board.

Civil action Any noncriminal proceeding, such as a suit for nonpayment of a debt.

Civil conspiracy doctrine A nineteenth-century regulation outlawing concerted action by workmen to regulate conditions of employment.

Close corporation A corporation in which ownership is held by a few stockholders, and whose shares are not usually sold on the market. Sometimes referred to as a "private" corporation.

Closed-loop system A system which automatically introduces corrections when it senses that results are not as planned.

Closed shop An organization in which union membership is required before a person can be hired.

Collateral loan A loan secured by the pledge of title to personal property.

Collateral-trust bond A bond secured by other stocks and bonds.

Collection cycle The activity that takes place between the extension of credit and the receipt of payment.

Collective bargaining Generally, the activity involved in negotiating and administering a union contract.

Commercial credit Credit extended by companies with which a firm does business.

Commercial paper Notes, drafts, checks, and certificates of deposit as used in business.

Common carrier Any person (carrier) which holds itself out to the general public to transport property, as a railroad.

Common law Law that has its origin in custom and tradition rather than in an elected body such as a legislature.

Common stock Stock of a corporation that carries the right to vote and to share in the dividends when declared.

Commonwealth v. Hunt A court case (1842) which established the basic legality of labor combinations (unions) when utilized for proper purposes.

Communism A social system wherein the state owns all property.

Comparative advantage A term used in comparing two nations which identifies the bases on which each has an advantage in terms of natural resources, location, or other economic features over the other.

Competition A market condition where there are very large numbers of producers of a good who serve very large numbers of consumers. No producer or consumer controls price.

Complementary products Products that tend to round out a line of products, as shaving cream and blades complement razors.

Compulsory arbitration Arbitration wherein the parties are bound by the decision of the arbitrator.

Computer A device capable of automatically processing data or controlling activity under the control of a "program." May be based on mechanical, hydraulic, or electronic principles of operation.

Conditional sales contract A sales contract in which title to the goods remains with the seller until the goods are paid for in full or until some other condition is fulfilled. Such contracts are commonly used with automobile sales and permit the title holder to repossess if the contract is violated.

Conditioning process A manufacturing process in which a material, such as plastic, is shaped into a product, such as a cup. Nothing is added to the material, but its shape or character is altered.

Confirmation As used in purchasing, a statement from a supplier that he accepts the buyer's purchase order.

Conglomerate A corporate merger of heterogeneous businesses which retains autonomous operating control in its various divisions and is financially controlled at the top executive level.

Constitutional law Law dealing with the activity of state and federal governments.

Consumer credit Credit involving the ultimate consumer such as charge accounts, credit cards, or installment accounts.

Consumer goods Goods sold to and used by the ultimate consumer.

Consumer price index An index reflecting the composite level of a select group of consumer goods at a particular time as related to the level of prices which existed in a certain base period.

Continuous system A production system that operates around the clock, such as an oil refinery.

Contract An agreement between two or more parties wherein each agrees to do or refrain from doing certain specified acts.

Contribution The difference between revenue and variable costs which first is applied to cover fixed costs and any remainder is profit.

Control The process of making events conform to plan.

Convenience goods Goods that are relatively inexpensive and are purchased often.

Coordination The bringing together of a number of separate elements to form an organized and coherent unit.

Copyright The exclusive right, protected by law, to publish one's literary works, as in the copyright of a textbook.

Corporate charter A written instrument which is a grant of powers granted by a state to a corporate entity.

Corporation A form of business in which ownership is vested in shares of stock and an owner's liability is limited to his investment. Corporations are formed under state law.

Correcting unit The part of automated equipment which executes the necessary change to bring the process back into line after an error.

Correlation The degree to which two or more variables—production and employment, for example—are mutually related.

Correlation analysis The statistical technique applied to determine the extent to which a relationship exists between two sets of information.

Cost of distribution All costs involved in the process of moving goods from the manufacturer to the consumer.

Cost-plus pricing The practice of adding a percentage of the cost of an item to its cost to determine the selling price.

Cost-value analysis A technique applied to measure both the cost and the value to be derived from a particular activity in an effort to determine whether the activity would be worth pursuing.

Credit The giving of goods and services for a promise of future payment.

Credit instrument Any document that identifies a credit obligation, such as a promissory note.

Creditor The person or firm to which payment is due for goods or services purchased.

Credit terms Specification of the terms for paying credit obligation such as net/10 days, or 2/10, n/30.

Criminal action Any action between a person and the state involving the violation of duties which the person owes to the community (society); examples of violation are arson, murder, and price fixing.

Criminal conspiracy doctrine The philosophy that concerted action by employees against their employer for economic gain is a crime against the state.

Cross-over analysis A technique based on cost analysis which indicates at what volumes of activity alternative means of production should be employed.

Cross-over points A term used in cost-volume analysis which describes the point at which it is more economical to use one method of operation in preference to another.

Current assets Cash or property that can be converted into cash through normal business operations within a short period of time, such as inventory and receivables.

Current liabilities Obligations that are due or will become due in a short period of time, such as trade accounts payable.

Current ratio A comparison of current assets and current liabilities, which shows the capacity to meet current obligations.

Custom or job-order production The production of goods to customer specifications as opposed to predetermined specifications as used in mass production.

Data Unorganized details.

Debenture bond A bond issue which is unsecured. (The opposite of a collateral-trust bond.)

Decentralization of industry A form of industrial organization in which the plants of an industry are spread over a broad geographic area.

Decentralized organization The process of delegating significant amounts of authority to lower levels of management.

Decision making The activity of choosing between alternatives.

Deflation A period during which there is a decline in the general price level.

Demand The willingness and ability to purchase a good or service.

Demand curve A statement of the quantities of a good or service that are likely to be purchased at different prices.

Demurrage A charge made by railroads when freight cars are not unloaded within a prescribed time period.

Depreciation The loss in value of a piece of property, such as a machine, over a period of time.

Dexterity test A test designed to measure how well a person can use his body—fingers, hands, arms, etc.

Differential costs The difference in cost between an existing situation and a proposal.

Diminishing returns With each additional unit of input to a process the results or returns are less than from the previous unit of input.

Directing The process of supervising subordinates.

Direct labor Labor that is applied directly to the production of a good or service.

Direct material Material that becomes a part of the product, such as an automobile tire, in the manufacturing process.

Dispatching The authorization for activity to begin, such as the movement of materials to the manufacturing area.

Diversification The act of expanding by adding a variety of products to the company's line.

Dividends The portion of a firm's earnings that is distributed to the stockholders.

Division of labor The separating of tasks into easily learned segments.

Dormant (secret) partner A partner whose identity is not known to outsiders and who does not participate in the management of the partnership.

Draft A negotiable instrument ordering a specific individual (usually a bank) to pay a specified sum to bearer or a particular individual on demand or on a specified date. This type of instrument is common in the export business.

Durable goods Goods that have a relatively long life, such as automobiles, refrigerators, and machines.

Economic-lot concept A technique which attempts to select the most economical lot, costwise, based on certain cost factors. Generally relates to purchasing or production.

Economic man A term applied to that individual who applies economic reasoning prior to making his decision; it implies that this individual has both the information and methodology necessary for sound decisions.

Elastic demand The circumstances in which a change in the price of a product results in a disproportionate change in its demand.

Electromechanical devices Mechanical equipment powered by electricity.

Electronic computer A device capable of computing by means of the flow of electrons.

Electronic money This term envisages that time when money will not change hands and in its place transactions will be recorded and payments made by electronic means using computers.

Entrepreneur The individual who organizes, manages, and assumes the risks of a business. The originator of a business.

Equitability of wages Equal pay for equal work.

Equity capital The investments made in the business by the owners and belonging to them.

Exception principle The principle of management which states that normal or routine matters should be handled in an established procedure and only those matters which are abnormal or exceptional should be referred to management for disposition.

Excise tax A tax levied on the manufacture, sale, or consumption of a commodity within a country.

External data Data or information from sources outside the firm.

Fabrication The name given to the process of converting materials into parts or goods.

Fact-finding board In labor relations, a group of individuals appointed under government authority to investigate, assemble, and report the facts in a labor dispute.

Factoring The practice of selling accounts prior to their due date, generally at a discount.

Factors of production Those ingredients necessary to produce goods and services: capital, labor, materials.

Fair-trade laws State laws permitting manufacturers of branded goods to establish and enforce retail prices.

Featherbedding A union practice of forcing employers to employ unnecessary labor.

Feedback The capacity of a machine to evaluate its own performance and to correct it whenever it deviates from the plan. Output returns as input.

Fiduciary One who is involved in a relationship of confidence or trust with others, as a lawyer in his relationships with a client.

Financial budget The plan of operations translated into dollar terms.

First line of management The level of management above the workers—a foreman in a factory, for example.

Fixed assets Property items that have relatively long life, such as machines and buildings.

Fixed capital The long-term investment in resources which represent primarily the land and equipment necessary to do business.

Fixed costs Costs that remain the same in total even though the level of activity (production) may increase or decrease.

Fixed liability A liability that does not become due in the current period of operation such as a mortgage. That portion of a fixed liability that falls due in a given year is a current liability for that year.

Flow diagram A diagram of a work area showing the sequence of the operations involved in a process and the location in the area where each operation takes place.

Flow-process chart A list of the operations to be gone through, the time involved for each operation, and the distance traveled, listed in chronological order.

Foreign corporation A corporation doing business in any state other than the state of incorporation.

Forward integration Enlarging a firm's area of operation to include activity nearer the ultimate consumer—for example, a manufacturer opening retail outlets.

Franchise A privilege granted to an organization to conduct business or perform services possibly within a stated area or route. (Transportation routes are set up on such a basis.)

Freedom of enterprise The freedom to engage in the business of one's choice as long as it is not prohibited by law.

Free market Unrestricted movement of goods into and out of the market; occurs when no regulations such as tariffs hamper the flow.

Fringe benefits Those rewards or benefits received by employees in addition to their regular pay; these include vacations, insurance, pension benefits, etc.

Functionalization A plan for organizing a firm around its functions, such as production, purchasing, and distribution.

Garnishment A legal attachment of an employee's wages to pay a debt owed by the employee to someone other than the employer.

General partner A partner who is liable for the debts of the business and who shares its profit and responsibility.

General (ordinary) partnership A voluntary legal relationship between two or more persons to carry on a business as co-owners for a profit.

Generalist One who is versed in many fields. Opposite of the specialist.

General-purpose equipment Equipment which can be used on a variety of jobs or to produce a variety of products depending upon the skill of the operator using the machine.

Goodwill The value of a business over and above the fair market value of its net assets.

Grievance A complaint that has been formally presented for action.

Gross profit The income from the sale of goods less the cost of these goods to the firm.

Guaranteed annual wage A plan whereby certain employees are guaranteed that they will be paid every week of a given year.

Hedging A method used to spread the risks of incurring losses due to fluctuating prices of a good by buying and selling in future markets.

Hiring hall An office maintained by a union for referring workers to jobs or for the actual hiring operation.

Hollerith card Popularly known as an IBM card; a card on which data are recorded in the form of a pattern of punched holes.

Human relations The area of business which deals with the problems arising from the interrelationships of people at work (especially in the management-subordinate type of relationship).

Hypothesis In research, a suggested or plausible answer to a problem.

Impact of taxation The burden of a tax, which ultimately falls on a certain person or business.

Incentive wage system Methods of wage payment which relate earnings of workers to their production, individually or as a group.

Incidence of taxation Relates to the one who is initially responsible for paying a tax.

Income and expense statement A statement of the incomes and costs of operation for a period of time. Also called the profit and loss statement.

Industrial production index An index reflecting the level of industrial activity as related to the level which existed in a certain base period.

Industrial relations The area of business concerned with the relationships between management and unions (workers).

Industrial Revolution The era in history when man applied his innovative talents to the industrial (manufacturing and service) environment and developed many technological advancements.

Inelastic demand The circumstances in which change in the price of a good has little or no effect on demand.

Inflation A state of the economy in which the supply of money increases at a faster rate than the supply of goods and services, with the result that prices rise, and the dollar buys less.

Informal organization Activities and relationships that exist apart from the formal organizational relationships.

Information Organized details.

Information center The focal point in an automated system, to which all information and data are channeled.

Information retrieval The process of finding the information desired; this process requires organization of files or memory systems in such a way that information is readily located and accessible when required.

Information system A system for handling information that is entering or leaving a business, or that is generated by or circulating in a business.

Injunction A restraining or cease and desist order issued by the courts to prevent people or organizations from doing certain things. Ignoring an injunction may result in a contempt of court citation.

Intangible assets Generally "paper" assets such as stocks and bonds, or goodwill.

Integrated information system The tieing together of the many parts which comprise an information system so that each part serves the total objective of the system even while each part is also served by the system.

Intelligence test A test designed to measure the relative mental capacity of a person.

Interest test A psychological test designed to measure the degree of interest an individual has in different types of activities.

Intermittent process A process designed to produce a variety of products—a job-order machine shop, for example.

Internal data Data or information generated within the firm.

Intuitive pricing The practice of setting prices based on the intuition of the responsible party. Often used when new products are being brought on to the market.

Inventory-turnover ratio An index which depicts the rate at which goods are sold and stock replenished by calculating the number of times the average inventory is sold in a given period of time.

Investment banker An individual, or firm, that handles the sale of large volumes of stocks and/or bonds for a corporation.

Investor One who gives money to a firm by purchasing the firm's bonds or stocks. He is usually interested in the security of his funds and in the rate of return on his investment.

Invoice An itemized list of goods, sent by the seller to the buyer, stating the prices, reference numbers, quantity of goods, and credit terms.

Job analysis A detailed breakdown of a job into the following components: (a) duties and responsibilities, (b) machines and tools used, (c) physical and mental attributes required, (d) working conditions, and (e) relation of this job to other existing jobs.

Job description The segment of a job analysis which is concerned with describing the characteristics of the job (not the individual who performs the job).

Job evaluation A procedure used to determine what each job is worth in relation to all other jobs.

Job order production Production for a particular order.

Joint venture An enterprise owned and operated by two or more independent firms.

Journeyman A qualified craftsman, who has generally mastered his trade by serving an apprenticeship.

Judging system A part of an automated process which evaluates how the process is doing in relation to the guidelines set down in the memory unit.

Labor pool An established source from which prospective employees are recruited.

Labor turnover The movement of employees into and out of a company, as evidenced by the number of accessions to and separations from the payroll during a period of time.

Laissez faire "Leave it alone." A philosophy of minimum government interference with economic affairs popularized by Adam Smith in the late eighteenth century.

Layoff Involuntary separation of workers from employment for a temporary period; the possibility of recall is implied.

Leadership The basic task of management, which deals with directing and coordinating the human activities of a business.

Letter of credit A written promise by a bank to honor drafts drawn, under the conditions of the letter of credit, upon it or some other bank.

Liability That which is owed to others.

Liability insurance Insurance which protects the insured holder from claims recorded against him by other individuals.

License A legal document granting permission to an individual or business to engage in certain activities or to operate certain types of equipment.

Lien A right or claim against specific pieces of property.

Limited partnership A partnership in which certain members are liable for the debts of the partnership only up to the amount they have contributed to the business.

Line organization A form of organization in which orders and authority flow in a straight line from the chief executive to lower management levels.

Line and staff organization A form of organization that combines line executives and staff executives. The line executives make all the decisions and issue orders but use the advice of the staff members.

Line layout The arrangement of equipment used in production according to the chronological operations to be performed on the product. Also known as production-line layout.

Line of credit A prearranged amount of credit open to a customer at all times.

Linear programming A technique for determining the best or optimal product mix by taking a variety of factors into consideration at the same time.

Lobbyist A person who represents and fosters the particular interests of his clients among those in government who are in a position to help him get what he wants.

Lockout A temporary withholding of work from a group of employees by their employer during a labor dispute to compel a settlement.

Long-term costs Certain costs to which business is committed over a long time period as opposed to short-term costs which may be terminated on short notice.

Long-term credit (funds) Credit which falls due generally more than a year from date extended.

Magnetic core A device used in computer memory systems which consists of tiny ceramic donuts capable of representing data in binary form.

Magnetic disk A device, similar in appearance to a phonograph record, which is used as part of the memory system of an electronic computer; it carries data in the form of magnetic impressions on both surfaces of each disk.

Magnetic tapes A memory device in an electronic computer system which carries data on the surface of a plastic tape; this surface is coated with a material which takes magnetic impressions.

Management The direction of human behavior toward a particular goal or objective, or the control and coordination of all activities within a business so as to work toward a particular goal or objective.

Manager The title given to an individual who performs the functions of management, or, any person who is responsible for the work of others in the organization.

Manning table A list of positions, or numbers of workers, to be used in the operation of a particular machine, process, or department of a business.

Manufacturing Changing raw materials into a finished product by some chemical or mechanical process.

Manufacturing overhead All costs arising out of the manufacturing process other than the costs for direct labor and direct materials.

Marginal cost The addition to the total cost brought about by the production of one additional unit.

Market research The activity concerned with finding out what customers want and how products are accepted.

Mass production A production system that utilizes repetitive operations to produce large quantities of a standard product. Also known as standardized production.

Master budget An overall compilation of the individual budgets made by each department.

Materialism A preoccupation with material things.

Mean (arithmetic average) In statistics, a measure of central tendency obtained by totaling a series of values and dividing by the number of values.

Measures of central tendency In statistics, indexes of central location: the mean, median, and mode.

Mechanization The conversion of hand (manual) operations into mechanical operations.

Median In statistics, the value of the middle number in an array of numbers.

Mediation An attempt by a third party to help in negotiations or in settlement of a dispute between the employer and the union. The mediator cannot force a decision.

Memory unit The part of an automated machine which knows what the machine should be doing at each step of the operation.

Merchandizing The activities that pertain to selecting and buying merchandise for resale, marketing it, pricing it, and promoting its sale.

Merger The combining of two or more organizations into one.

Micromotion analysis A technique applied to the study of motions involved in doing work. Concerned with very detailed analysis of work movements which are too minute or fast to be perceived without using such devices as high speed motion pictures.

Middle management Generally considered to be the levels of management above the foreman level, but not including top management.

Mode In statistics, the most frequent value in a group of values.

Monopoly A market environment in which one party or group has exclusive power over the supply of a given commodity or service.

Morale The reaction of a group of workers to the total working conditions and relationships.

Mortgage An interest in land or other property given by the owner to his creditor as security for a debt owed to the creditor.

Mortgage loan A loan advanced to a borrower who secures the loan by giving the lender an interest in his property.

Motion study A study to determine the best possible sequence of motions for accomplishing a task.

Motivation research The study of the factors which determine people's behavior, or why they do or do not do things.

MTM Methods-time-measurement. The classification of basic human motions, and the assignment of time values to each. A technique utilized in setting time standards.

National income The total value of all earnings of people and firms in the country.

Nationals A term usually applied to the native personnel who staff the positions in the overseas offices or plants of a corporation or business.

Negative motivation The procedure of invoking penalties to make people perform in a specified manner.

Negotiable instrument A commercial paper which may be transferred from one individual to another. It is a form of exchange and may, in a sense, be used as money.

Net worth The excess of total assets over total liabilities; the value of the owner's equity in the company.

Nondurable goods Goods which have a relatively short lifetime (food, tobacco, clothing).

Nonprofit corporation A convenient way of holding property by an organization that has no owners. Property is in the hands of trustees, as in a private university.

No par stock Stock that does not have a printed value on the stock certificate.

Normal capacity A measure of the usual or typical maximum level at which operations take place. Need not be the absolute maximum output possible.

Normal curve A statistically developed distribution which when plotted gives a bell-shaped symmetrical curve that has the same number of frequencies and the same range of values on both sides of the arithmetic mean, its center and highest point.

Norms Normal or anticipated readings or measurements used as standards for comparison with actual results so that the extent to which occurrences deviate from the norms may be observed and thereby initiate control activity if necessary.

Norris-LaGuardia Act of 1932 An act that restricted the use of the injunction in labor disputes, and outlawed the "yellow-dog" contract.

Note A written promise to pay a specific sum.

Objective The aim or goal of a business.

Obsolescence The process of becoming outmoded, which occurs when a new machine or method can do the job better.

Oligopoly A market situation in which few producers control the supply of goods or services, thereby controlling demand from a large number of buyers. The automobile industry is considered an oligopoly.

100 percent inspection A quality-control technique in which every item produced is examined.

On-the-job training A method of teaching in which the trainee is placed in the actual working environment under supervision.

Open (book) account Short-term credit used in normal purchasing activity, the charge account.

Open-end mortgage A mortgage which allows for adding to the amount of debt beyond the original debt.

Open-loop system A system that generates information but does not analyze it and does not institute corrective action.

Open shop An employment condition in which union membership is not a requirement for obtaining and keeping a job.

Operating statement A summary of expenses and revenue during a particular period of time, which shows the profit or loss from operations.

Operation-process chart A graphic presentation of the steps involved in a process, using symbols to identify activities.

Operations research The study of the overall implications of alternative courses of action.

Opportunity cost That which one foregoes to get something else. For example, the opportunity to earn interest is lost if the principal is used to buy equipment.

Optimum capacity The amount of output which allows the minimum cost per unit to be incurred.

Optimum speed The best speed—not necessarily the fastest; best may be interpreted in terms of cost factors, wear and tear on equipment and personnel, etc.

Organization The process of grouping activities, delineating lines of authority and responsibility, and establishing any other relationships necessary to carry out the operations of a business efficiently.

Organization chart A visual representation of the formal relationships among the departments and officers existing in a particular organization.

Overhead A business expense which is not chargeable on a direct basis to a particular product or portion of work. This typically includes all expenses except direct labor and direct material.

Overlapping authority When more than one person has authority over a single circumstance.

Overtime Work performed in excess of the basic workday or workweek, as defined by law, collective bargaining agreement, or company policy.

Partnership A voluntary relationship between two or more individuals as co-owners in a business for profit.

Par value stock A stock with a fixed dollar value, stated on the stock certificate. The par value has no relation to market value.

Patent The exclusive right to make and sell an invention, granted to an inventor, which is good for 17 years but not renewable.

Peak capacity The total possible amount of production, working at the highest rate of speed, with no regard for efficiency. The emphasis is on output.

Perfect (pure) competition A market situation in which one individual or firm has control of the production and marketing of a product.

Permissive society A society which does not repress expression, good and bad.

Personal property As opposed to real property (land and buildings), items such as furniture and automobiles.

Personality test A test designed to measure the emotional characteristics of an individual, with the intention of estimating the chances of a person getting along in a particular environment.

Personnel transfer The moving of an individual to a new assignment or a different area either within the plant or in a different geographical area at the individual's request.

Philosophy The sum total of the individual's ideals, outlook, opinions, and attitudes on a particular issue. One's philosophy indicates what is right in one's mind.

Piece-rate plan A monetary (incentive) plan based on units of production rather than time worked. A set amount of money paid for each unit completed satisfactorily.

Pirating When used in reference to personnel activities it refers to "stealing" employees of other firms who you wish to add to your staff. This is done by any reasonable or unreasonable method—the objective being to capture the quarry.

Planning The function of management which deals with developing a course of action or pattern of directives. It determines what should be done, by whom, when, and how.

Plant-turnover ratio The relationship between the physical facilities of the firm and its income from sales. The ratio of sales dollars to physical facilities in dollars. It shows the amount of sales generated for every dollar invested in physical facilities.

Point-method rating A technique for evaluating the relative worth of an individual or a job by examining specific characteristics, rating each characteristic on a point scale, and then ranking the total sum in relation to the sums for other individuals or jobs.

Policy A general rule within which management is to make its decisions and plans. It expresses the company's feelings and attitudes toward a particular activity.

Preemptive right The right of a stockholder to purchase a portion of a new stock issue of stock equal to his current percentage holdings.

Preferred stock Stock of a corporation that has priority over common stock in respect to dividends and ownership claims.

Price The amount of money that a good demands.

Price agreement An arrangement between two or more firms to maintain prices at a certain level.

Price index A figure which represents the relative change in prices between a base year and a particular point in time.

Price leadership The situation which occurs when the competition among large producers of a given product is such as to set a uniform price level in the industry.

Primary data Information obtained directly by the user from its original source.

Principle A basic law; a fundamental truth.

Private corporation A corporation established by private interests for charitable, benevolent, or profit purposes.

Private law Law which deals with the rights and liabilities between private persons, corporations, partnerships, and other organizations.

Private property Exclusive rights and interests possessed by one or more individuals in land or other property.

Process analysis Determination of the operations necessary to produce a good, and of the proper sequence of these operations.

Process layout The grouping together of equipment according to the function it performs regardless of where this function or operation is used in the production operation. Such a setup is used in a job-shop environment.

Process production Production organized according to the process through which the product proceeds rather than according to the product itself.

Producer goods Those items used in the creation of additional goods and services.

Production The creation of value.

Production capacity The total number of units that can be produced within a specified unit of time (hour, week, year).

Production transfer The moving of an individual to a new assignment or a different area either within the plant or in a different geographical area, as decided upon by management.

Productivity The amount of output per fixed unit of input.

Professional manager An administrative or supervisory employee (not an owner of the business) whose job is to control activities and direct them toward stipulated goals.

Profit and loss statement A listing of revenues and expenses associated with doing business during a specified period of time and the net results of subtracting expenses from revenues to determine whether a profit or loss results.

Profit center A concept applied for control purposes which seeks to associate costs and revenues with a specific center, an area of activity or a product, so that profitability can be pinpointed and controlled.

Profit margin The difference between (unit) cost and (unit) selling price.

Profit-sharing plan An incentive program in which the participants are awarded a certain portion of the profits. The idea is to increase effort and efficiency so as to increase overall profits, thereby increasing the reward to each participant.

Progressive taxation A method of taxing whereby the tax rate increases as the tax base increases, such as the federal personal income tax. The opposite of regressive taxation.

Promissory note A written promise by the maker of a note to pay upon demand or at a definite time a stated sum of money to bearer or to order.

Promoters The persons who plan the formation of a corporation and who sell or promote the idea to others.

Promotion The act of elevating or raising an individual to a position of greater responsibility, authority, status, and pay.

Proportional taxation A method of taxation wherein the tax is a fixed percentage of the base, such as a 4 percent sales tax.

Proprietorship The form of business which is characterized by a single owner. It is the most common form of business organization today.

Proxy A written authorization by a stockholder giving another the right to vote for the assigning party.

Public law Law which deals with the relation of government and the individual.

Public relations The aspect of business which deals with promoting a favorable company image to customers and the public.

Punched cards Popularly known as IBM cards, used in connection with automated data processing; each card contains data represented by a pattern of holes punched on the card.

Purchasing agent The individual in a company who is assigned the authority and responsibility for buying supplies and materials.

Purchasing power The amount of goods and services that a given amount of money can buy.

Quality control The manufacturing function which ensures that designated standards are met throughout the manufacturing cycle, or that stipulated limits are not exceeded.

Quartiles Measurement of values according to position in an array of data; first quartile measures value at 1/4 of total number of items; second quartile measures midpoint value; third quartile measures value at 3/4 position.

Rand formula A plan under which a worker pays the monthly union dues but is not considered a union member—for workers who do not wish to join the union.

Real income The actual purchasing power of a dollar. The amount of goods and services a dollar will buy as of a given time.

Real property Real estate such as land and buildings.

Receivables turnover rate The number of times which the average accounts receivable are contained in the total sales of a specific period; if year's sales are $100,000 and average accounts receivable is $12,500, the receivable turnover ratio is 8.

Reciprocity The process of returning a favor. An agreement or arrangement in which each of two or more individuals, firms, countries, or nations grants the other a favor.

Recruitment (of workers) The function of management that is concerned with actively seeking or searching out prospective employees and encouraging them to become employees.

Rediscounting The practice of discounting promissory notes in one's possession. A bank may rediscount a customer's note with a Federal Reserve Bank to obtain additional funds to loan to customers.

Regressive taxation A method of taxing wherein the tax rate decreases as the tax base increases. The opposite of progressive taxation.

Repetitive operations A series of operations performed over and over to produce large quantities of uniform products. This is the common procedure used in mass production operations.

Reporting pay Minimum pay guaranteed to a worker who is scheduled to work, reports for work, and finds no work available. Also known as call-in pay.

Retailer A business person who sells to the final consumer.

Right-to-work law State legislation which prohibits any contractual requirement that a worker join a union to get or keep a job.

Risk The degree of chance or uncertainty inherent in a situation or environment.

Routing Determining the path and sequence of operations of materials through the production process.

Sales promotion The activity which deals with making the sales effort more effective.

Sample inspection determination of product quality by evaluating a small quantity of the units produced.

Scheduling Determination of when activity should be started in order to have goods ready for delivery as promised.

Seasonal variation A change in the level of activity from one time of the year to another in a consistent pattern year after year.

Secondary boycott Efforts by a union to discourage the purchase, handling, or use of products of a company involved in a labor dispute.

Secondary data Information not obtained by the user from its original source but from previously collected references.

Secular trend The long-term movement of a time series, reflecting growth, stagnation, or decline.

Secured loan A loan secured by pledging certain property as security.

Self-insurance A method of protecting a company against risk by setting up contingency funds within the company.

Seller's lien The seller's right to retain possession of particular goods until they are paid for by the buyer.

Seller's market A situation in which market conditions favor the seller of goods.

Seniority An employee's status relative to that of other employees, used in determining priority for promotion, layoff, vacation, etc. Generally based on length of service.

Sensor unit A part of automated machinery which senses what is being done.

Service industry An industry that offers some type of skill (manual or mental) or service rather than producing goods for sale.

Sherman Antitrust Act of 1890 A law regulating the creation, growth, and strength of monopolies.

Shopping goods Expensive goods which are purchased infrequently. A great deal of comparison shopping is usually done with these goods, such as clothing and furniture.

Short-term funds Funds borrowed for a length of time ranging usually from 30 days to no longer than 1 year.

Sight draft A draft (negotiable instrument) that is payable on demand.

Simplification The procedure of making a product line or production process simpler, less complex, or less difficult.

Simulation An imitation of business situations to permit evaluation of alternative courses of action.

Socialism An economic system characterized by state or government ownership of basic industries.

Span of control The number of subordinates that a supervisor can effectively manage.

Specialization The breaking down of an operation or process into several simplified individual tasks.

Special-purpose equipment Equipment designed to do limited processing.

Speculative buying Buying in the present with an eye on future prices and with the hope of profit from resale.

Staff (organization) A group of people who provide specialized services to the line managers in the company.

Standard cost A predetermined cost level, such as a standard cost for the material used in a unit of production.

Standard deviation A measure of dispersion of values about a mean or central value.

Standard of living A measure of the material level of living which a person's income can command; it depends upon not only the number of dollars earned but also the level of prices of those things consumed.

Standardization The process of establishing specific criteria levels (weight, dimensions, and grade of material).

Statement of financial condition A summary of the assets, liabilities, and net worth (owner equity) of a business as of a particular moment of time.

Statistics The methods involved in collecting, describing, and analyzing numerical data.

Statutory law Laws enacted by a legislative body.

Stock certificate A written document indicating ownership of a specific number of shares of stock.

Stock option The right assigned to an individual to purchase additional amounts of a stock under stipulated terms set down in the option.

Stock splitting The exchange of a single share of a company's stock for a larger number of shares, such as a 2 for 1 split. A 2 for 1 split would have the effect of reducing the market price of a share of stock from $150 to $75. The reasoning is that more people will buy stock at $75 per share.

Subsistence income A level of income just about high enough to keep body and soul together—and nothing more!

Sunk cost A past expenditure or outlay which, by itself, should not be used as the basis for making a decision. A cost that the firm can do nothing about.

Supplemental unemployment benefits (SUB) The payment of weekly amounts to laid-off workers in addition to their state unemployment compensation benefits. Such payments are made by the employer under terms spelled out in the union contract.

Supply The amount of goods available for sale.

Supply curve A diagrammatical chart indicating the quantity of goods a producer would be willing to offer for sale at various prices.

Synthetic process The process of putting materials or parts together to form a new product. (Making an automobile is a good example.)

System A regularly interdependent group of activities which are unified by organization to work for a common goal.

Technology The application of scientific knowledge to the solution of problems.

Time and motion study An analysis of the various motions involved in an operation, and of the length of time taken by each motion. The purpose of time and motion study is to establish a standard method for doing an operation and a standard amount of time for its completion.

Time standard The period of time an average worker should take to perform a particular operation, task, or job under normal working conditions.

Tolerance The limits within which a measurement must fall, such as 1.000 inch $\pm$ 0.005.

Trade aceptance A draft drawn by the seller against the purchaser of goods and accepted by such purchaser.

Trade creditors The people to whom a firm owes money for goods supplied and/or services rendered.

Trademark A name, device, or symbol used by a manufacturer or seller to distinguish his goods from those of others. Trademarks may be registered and copyrighted to ensure that others will not take advantage of them.

Trading goods Goods purchased for resale as in wholesale and retail trade.

Transfer cost The cost that a department must bear for goods and services supplied by another department.

Trend The growth or decline of activity over an extended period of time.

Trial and error pricing Selling a product at various prices in a number of areas and then evaluating the response to each price.

Universality of management functions The concept that managers, no matter what they manage or at what level they manage, are concerned for the same basic functions.

Value The relative worth, utility, or importance of a thing, such as an idea, a product, or a process.

Variable costs Costs which vary directly with the volume of activity (production).

Vested rights Rights which are inherent in a situation or event, and which cannot be taken away, such as the right of a stockholder to vote.

Vestibule schools Training areas which simulate the actual working environment.

Video display The presentation of data on the face of a cathode-ray tube (video or TV tube).

Vox populi A latin expression: "Voice of the people."

Wage differentials Variations in wages for the same type of work in different industries, geographic areas, and the like.

Wholesale price index A composite index representing the average price level of selected items at the wholesale level; use to indicate price movements.

Wholesaler A business that sells to, or negotiates sales with, customers who buy for resale.

Working capital Cash or assets that will be converted into cash within 1 year.

Workmen's compensation insurance Insurance, required by the state and financed by employers, which provides payment to workers or their families for injuries or illness suffered in connection with their work.

INDEX

INDEX

Durable goods, 57

Economic indicators, 529–532
Economic-lot concept, 301, 479
  and purchasing, 480
Economic purchase lots, 301
Economic system, 39
Education and business, 33, 548
Efficiency, 8, 9
Electronic computer, 505
Employee rating, 363
  chart, 365
  formal programs, 364
  point method, 364
  purposes of, 363
  systems, 364
Employment:
  and automation, 69
  in industry, 59
  in international business, 549
  in service industries, 72
Employment agencies, 345
Employment trends, 59
Environment, social, 30
Equipment:
  building-block machine tools,
    266
  general-purpose, 265
  numerically controlled, 266
  return on investment, 268
  special purpose, 265
Exception principle, 501
Expenses, 397

Factor comparison method in job
    evaluation, 357
Factoring, 386
Fair Labor Standards Act (1938),
  328
Fair trade laws, 90
  legality of, 91
Fatigue allowance in time study,
  296
Federal administrative agencies,
  38
Federal assistance agencies, 86

Federal Communications
  Commission, 84, 86
Federal control:
  of business, 79
  of monetary policy, 82
  of monopoly, 81
  of stock and financial
    operation, 82
Federal control agencies, 82
Federal court system, 37
Federal Power Commission, 85
Federal Reserve System, 82
Federal Trade Commission, 83, 86
Federal Trade Commission Act,
  81
Financial condition, statement
  of, 397
Financial planning and policies,
  378
Financial statements, 397–398
Financing, 375
  alternatives to, 390
  and the firm, 375
  functions, 376
  small business, 389
Fixed costs, 311, 401, 477
  depreciation of, 312
Flow diagram, 293
Flow-process chart, 292
Follow-up, production, 310
Forecast, sales, 235
Forecasting, 523–526
  methods, 237
Foreign trade, 541
Foreman, 256
  training of, 355
Franchise, 79
Fringe benefits, 367
  cost of, 368
  value of, 368
Functionalization, 148
  practical, 149
  pure, 148
Functions, 157
  assignment of, 157
  basic business, 55
  defined, 157